Aging as a Social Process

Second Edition

Aging as a Social Process

An Introduction to
Individual and Population Aging

Second Edition

BARRY D. McPHERSON
Wilfrid Laurier University

Butterworths
Toronto and Vancouver

Aging as a Social Process
© 1990 Butterworths Canada Ltd.

Printed and bound in Canada

The Butterworth Group of Companies

Canada	Butterworths Canada Ltd., 75 Clegg Road, MARKHAM, Ontario, L6G 1A1 and 409 Granville St., Ste. 1455, VANCOUVER, B.C., V6C 1T2
Australia	Butterworths Pty Ltd., SYDNEY, MELBOURNE, BRISBANE, ADELAIDE, PERTH, CANBERRA and HOBART
Ireland	Butterworths (Ireland) Ltd., DUBLIN
New Zealand	Butterworths of New Zealand Ltd., WELLINGTON and AUCKLAND
Puerto Rico	Equity de Puerto Rico, Inc., HATO REY
Singapore	Malayan Law Journal Pte. Ltd., SINGAPORE
United Kingdom	Butterworth & Co. (Publishers) Ltd., LONDON and EDINBURGH
United States	Butterworth Legal Publishers, AUSTIN, Texas; BOSTON, Massachusetts; CLEARWATER, Florida (D & S Publishers); ORFORD, New Hampshire (Equity Publishing); ST. PAUL, Minnesota; and SEATTLE, Washington

Grateful acknowledgment is made for permission to reprint or adapt copyrighted material from: Melvin M. Tumin, *Social Stratification: The Forms and Functions of Inequality*, © 1967, p. 27. Reprinted by permission of Prentice-Hall, Inc., Englewood Cliffs, N.J.

Canadian Cataloguing in Publication Data

McPherson, Barry D.
    Aging as a social process

2nd ed.
Includes bibliographical references.
ISBN 0-409-89335-8

1. Aging — Social aspects.   2. Aged — Social aspects.
I. Title.

HQ1061.M38 1990   305.26   C90-094248-7

Sponsoring Editor — Gloria Vitale
Editor — Julia Keeler
Cover Design — Brant Cowie
Production — Nancy Harding
Typesetting — McGraphics Desktop Publishing

To the scholars and practitioners in the Canadian gerontology "family"
who exponentially increased their output from 1983 to 1990.
Without your creativity, energy, and commitment, this second edition
would not have been possible or necessary.
Thanks to you, we now have a more complete Canadian body of knowledge
to share with the next generation of students, practitioners, and scholars.

Contents

List of Highlights

List of Tables

List of Figures

Foreword

This is the definitive textbook in Canada in the social study of aging. I therefore consider it an honor to have been asked to contribute a foreword, as I did for the first edition.

Selecting a textbook for a course in the social aspects of aging or social gerontology has become increasingly difficult because of the proliferation of texts written at widely varying levels. All too often, in recent texts, the emphasis is on simplification, brevity, and style rather than on comprehensive, and thus complex, coverage. There has been too little attention to teaching critical approaches to scholarship, or to nurturing a healthy disrespect for the written word, which is essential if the student is to become a mature scholar. This extensively revised and expanded edition of *Aging as a Social Process* is thus most welcome. The virtues of the first edition are retained. The extensive coverage of the field continues, and since the volume of scholarship has increased dramatically, this makes for a lengthier book. It would be longer if not for the book's emphasis on recent contributions, and a rigorous selection of the most valuable sources.

The number of papers and books published in some of the newly fashionable areas of aging studies, such as social support, elder abuse, health promotion, or technology and aging — all areas treated extensively for the first time in this edition — is very large. This text carefully sifts and synthesizes these literatures and appropriately cautions the student about methodological issues, theoretical or conceptual problems, and the dangers of trendiness. I have not seen another text quite so current in its coverage. For example, the treatment of the family includes a lengthy review of the very recent research on sibling relationships. Multicultural research on aging, virtually absent from Canadian gerontology at the time of the previous edition, now receives several pages of explicit treatment, while running through the analysis in several areas as qualifying material concerning general patterns. The discussion of social policy issues includes the area of intergenerational equity — not yet as important in Canada as in the United States, but something which the educated student should be able to deal with.

The book testifies to the new maturity of Canadian research in social gerontology, where its coverage is excellent. This is a necessity for the Canadian student, but a virtue for non-Canadian readers. Without sacrificing the readability needed for a textbook, Barry McPherson has provided a solid reference source to social gerontology, particularly useful to those wanting coverage of the Canadian literature as well as the significant research from the United States, Britain, and other countries. This group should include not only academics but those making and affected by public policy in the aging area (and isn't that just about everybody?).

While the social processes of aging, as described in this text, are viewed as interwoven with biological and psychological dimensions of aging, the title appropriately flags this book as a social scientist's approach to the field. The book is not just about individual aging or the elderly. It properly covers the ways in which individual and population aging affect all the social institutions of society. Sociology has the lead role, but the cast of characters includes anthropology, political science and policy studies, economics, demography, kinesiology, urban studies, criminology, family studies, and many other disciplines in the social sciences and humanities. The book explicitly invokes theory as an important tool for understanding the social processes of aging. In addition to a presentation of general theoretical controversies, which hinges on the difference between normative and interpretive sociology, there is an analysis of almost all the specific content issues in terms of middle-range theories or models. This is a gentle way to introduce the student to the importance of theory.

There is an explicit treatment of the nature of science and methodological issues, but again, the critical review of substantive studies invokes these methodological principles to help the student understand the (often limited) significance of specific studies or of the accumulated wisdom in a particular field. For example, the elder abuse literature, the text tells us, has to be understood in terms of grave problems of sampling, measurement, and conceptualization.

Students will find this edition more readable and entertaining than the first edition, because of its format, a newly added glossary, and the use of 'highlights' that emphasize and humanize key points. This is a book for serious students of social gerontology, in and out of the classroom; it is also a book to be treasured by the long-established scholars and practitioners in the field.

Victor W. Marshall
Professor of Behavioural Science
and
Director, Centre for Studies of Aging
University of Toronto

July 1990

Preface

Adults in the middle and later stages of the life cycle represent a large proportion of the population in most industrialized nations. Moreover, social, economic, and political changes are having a significant impact on the aging process and on the elderly. As a result of these societal changes and the growth of the older segment of our population, many practitioners in the public and the private sectors are addressing the special needs and interests of older adults. Among those who need to acquire a thorough understanding of the social processes of aging are health care personnel, occupational therapists, immigration personnel, psychologists, architects, dietitians, recreation and media personnel, social workers and agency administrators, kinesiologists, religious leaders, lawyers, economists, politicians, journalists, educators, financial planners, manufacturers and business administrators, sales and marketing personnel, policy planners, urban and regional planners, and engineers — to name only a few.

The first edition of this book, published in 1983, synthesized what we knew about aging and the aged as we entered the 1980s. At that time there were relatively few sources of knowledge for the student or the practitioner. However, throughout the 1980s our breadth and depth of knowledge about the aging process have grown significantly because of increased research and policy work by well-trained personnel. In Canada, this growth in both the quantity and the quality of information has resulted in the publication of ten monographs since 1986 in the ongoing Butterworths Series on Individual and Population Aging; in expanded and special issues of the *Canadian Journal on Aging*; in the revised and expanded second edition of V. Marshall's *Aging in Canada: Social Perspectives* (1987); in the publication of such topical monographs as *Old Age in the Welfare State* (1984, 1989) by J. Myles; *Aging: Retirement, Leisure and Work in Canada* (1985) by A. Roadburg; *Aging and Health Care: A Social Perspective* (1985) by N. Chappell, L. Strain and A. Blandford; in M. Baker's survey, *Aging in Canadian Society* (1988); and in three volumes in the Canadian Association on Gerontology's Collections Series. In addition, there have been numerous provincial and federal reports on emerging issues pertaining to the needs or the status of the elderly. Similarly, in the United States, we have witnessed the initiation of highly specialized research journals (see below), the revision of earlier review chapters, and the publication of books and bibliographies on special topics (such as elder abuse, drug abuse) or special groups (such as the rural elderly, women, the frail or disabled elderly).

This revised edition incorporates the new information that has been published as of early 1990. As well, the book includes new or expanded sections on salient topics that have emerged from research and policy work in the 1980s, including: the availability and types of informal and formal support mechanisms and services for the elderly; gender and aging; ethnicity and aging; the issues of elder abuse and drug abuse; rural aging; the adoption and the use of new technology by older adults; health care for an aging population; the meaning and the use of time by older adults; and social policy for an aging population. Another new feature of this edition includes the use of Highlights to supplement the material in the text. These feature case studies or vignettes about older adults, summaries of key studies, and supplementary information that will enhance your understanding of aging matters. This edition also includes a Glossary to assist readers in understanding key concepts. These concepts appear in boldface type the first time they are discussed in detail. In addition to reflecting the exponential growth in knowledge, these changes in emphasis, style, and content are based on feedback from my own students, from instructors who used the first edition, from practitioners who use the book as a reference, and from book reviews of the first edition. Let me now turn to a brief discussion of the content and the structure of the book, and how the material contained in it reflects the current body of knowledge about aging and the aged, especially as it pertains to aging Canadians.

Before social policies and programs for the elderly can be initiated, we must identify and verify that a problem or a situation exists, we must understand why and how the problem evolved, and we must derive and consider alternative solutions. Guesswork or hunches are not sufficient. Rather, valid information must be available if effective policies and programs are to be introduced. The need to provide the professions listed above with valid information has led to an increasing concern with the problems of aging and the aged, and a concomitant interest in describing and explaining the process and the product of aging from a social science perspective.

At first, studies were mainly descriptive. They sought to draw attention to a specific situation (such as the near-poverty status of many elderly women) or to provide a policy or a solution for some perceived social problem affecting the elderly. However, this approach often led to an exaggeration of the problem or to the creation and perpetuation of myths. Since the 1960s, however, sociologists, psychologists, economists, demographers, political scientists, anthropologists, and social gerontologists have initiated research to describe *and* explain phenomena associated with both the aging process and the status of being old. As a result, more reliable and valid information is available as a basis for developing policies and implementing social services. Moreover, this research has refuted many myths about the elderly, thereby changing or eliminating some of the prejudiced perceptions that we hold about the elderly.

This book is a synthesis of social science research concerning individual and population aging. The structure and the content are based on an undergraduate course on the sociology and the social psychology of aging that I have taught since 1971. Throughout, the emphasis is on identifying, describing, and explaining patterns, processes, and problems concerning individual and population aging, rather than on describing programs or providing prescriptions to assist the elderly. This approach enables students and practitioners to acquire basic knowledge essential for careers in fields related to gerontology, and to develop a better understanding of the aging process as it will influence them and their parents in the future.

Throughout the book, a variety of theoretical and methodological orientations are used to describe and explain the aging process. Although it is desirable to write a text from a single theoretical perspective, it is difficult to do so since the social science literature on aging phenomena is highly eclectic and is based on a number of theoretical perspectives from various disciplines. The quality of the research also varies greatly. Therefore, you are introduced to a variety of research methods and theoretical frameworks that represent the state of the art in social gerontology as we enter the 1990s.

In organizing the book, an attempt was made to avoid the social-problems orientation found in many other textbooks. In fact, whether aging constitutes a social problem for more than a very small segment of the older population is questionable. The material in this book is based on the premise that aging is a social process that involves the interaction of the personal system (the individual), various social systems that influence the behavior of the aging individual, and changing social, economic, and physical environments. Thus, although individual experiences may vary, there are common patterns to the aging process. Individuals born at about the same time (an age cohort) are influenced by similar historical or social events (economic depressions, a baby boom, world wars, or changes in cultural value systems). Moreover, individuals with similar ascribed (race, sex) or achieved (educational level, social class, occupation) attributes also tend to exhibit common patterns of behavior throughout the life cycle. In short, how individuals age is greatly influenced by the culture, by the social structure, and by social processes within particular social contexts.

The objectives of this text are threefold:

1. To assist you in understanding the process of aging from a sociological and a social-psychological perspective. Where possible, alternative explanations for specific aspects of the aging process are emphasized more than descriptions of the process or specific problems.

2. To provide you with basic concepts, theories, and methodologies that can be used to understand social phenomena related to individual and population aging.
3. To sensitize you to the fact that aging is not just a biological process, but is an equally complex social process. In fact, you may well be left with the impression that relatively little is known about aging as a social process. Herein lies a challenge to the curious, innovative reader who may wish to pursue a career in the field of social gerontology.

The book comprises four parts. Part One provides background information about aging as a social phenomenon; sensitizes the reader to some critical parameters that influence the aging process and the status of being old; describes aging and the status of being old in a number of cultural contexts; presents demographic information about the size, composition, and distribution of the aging population; and introduces theories and methods that are used to understand the aging process from a social science perspective. Part Two presents a micro-level analysis of the aging process. Here the focus is on aging individuals who must adapt to changes in their physical and psychological systems. In Part Three, a macro-level analysis focuses on the social structure and the environment in which we age. Part Four is concerned with aging and social participation patterns, particularly within the family and the labor force, and at leisure. In addition, a new chapter written for this edition examines the informal and formal support systems and the social policies that have emerged to meet the needs of an aging individual and an aging population.

TO THE STUDENT

Each chapter begins with a general overview and concludes with a summary of major research findings. Within each chapter key references are cited in the text or in a note. These serve a twofold purpose. First, they indicate that there is some theoretical or research support for the statement. Second, they serve as a teaching aid to help you find and use primary sources in the basic literature. These references will be particularly useful if you are required to write a term paper on a specific topic, or if you wish to acquire additional information about a particular area. In this edition, many of the references cited in the first edition have been deleted. Thus, if you are interested in references that give a historical perspective to the topic, you should consult the first edition.

Attempts were made to include material from most of the social sciences, although sociology and social psychology are the major disciplines represented. The material includes an analysis of the process of aging, as well as an analysis of the end product of that process — the status of being old in a particular society and in a particular social and physical environment. Throughout, information on the aging process is presented from both a micro (individual) and a macro (societal) perspective. Finally, unlike the first edition where most of the information was based on U.S. studies, the information in this edition reflects the rapid growth throughout the 1980s in the quantity and the quality of knowledge about aging in Canada.

As in any dynamic and rapidly growing discipline, information quickly becomes dated. Therefore, the reader who wishes to acquire the most recent information should regularly consult general reference sources such as *Current Contents, Sociological Abstracts,* and *Psychological Abstracts.* More importantly, there are numerous gerontology journals, including: *Gerontological Abstracts, Abstracts in Social Gerontology, Aging, The Gerontologist, International Journal of Aging and Human Development, Research on Aging, Experimental Aging Research, Annual Review of Gerontology and Geriatrics, Educational Gerontology, Ageing and Society, Aging and Work, The Canadian Journal on Aging, Journal of Gerontological Social Work, Journal of Aging Studies, Journal of Minority Aging, Journal of Cross-Cultural Gerontology, Clinical Gerontologist, Gerontology and Geriatrics Education, Journal of Housing for the Elderly, Journal of Religion and Aging, International Journal of Technology and Aging, Journal of Applied Gerontology, Journal of Aging and Social Policy, Journal of Women and Aging, Journal of Elder Abuse and Neglect, Psychology and Aging,* and *Journal of Aging and Health.* Of particular importance is the format change for the *Journal of Gerontology*, the major research journal in the field. Since January 1988, reflecting the growth of knowledge and specialization in the field, this journal has been published as four journals within one journal: *Journal of Gerontology: Social Sciences; Journal of Gerontology: Psychological Sciences; Journal of Gerontology: Biological Sciences;* and *Journal of Gerontology: Medical Sciences*. It is likely that this journal will become four distinct journals as more and more scholars and practitioners enter the field during the 1990s.

Further reflecting the growth of knowledge in the 1980s, some important general resource materials have been published for the gerontology student and practitioner. These include: G. Maddox et al. (1987), *The Encyclopedia of Aging*; D. Harris (1985), *The Sociology of Aging: An Annotated Bibliography and Sourcebook*; D. Harris (1988), *Dictionary of Gerontology*; the American Association of Retired Persons' *Computerized AgeLine Database* (call 800-345-4BRS for information) and *Thesaurus of Aging Terminology*; the U.S. National Institute on Aging publication, *Age Words: A Glossary on Health and Aging* (1986); the *Bulletin* of the National Clearinghouse on Technology and Aging (University of Massachusetts Medical Center, Worcester, Mass.); the Statistics Canada 1985 General Social Survey where the older population was deliberately oversampled (N = more than 4000 over 55 years of age); *An Inventory of Data Files on Aging in Ontario* (V. Marshall et al., 1989); and the Handbook on Aging Series edited by J. Birren, especially the *Handbook of Aging and the Social Sciences* (3d ed., 1990) edited by R. Binstock and L. George, and the *Handbook of the Psychology of Aging* (3d ed., 1990) edited by J. Birren and W. Schaie.

Despite the growth indicated above, research in this field, relative to other disciplines, is still in its infancy. This should lead you to question carefully and to discuss with others the research findings presented in any single study. A true understanding of the aging process will occur only when you become a critical reader who is able to decide whether conclusions are logical and valid. One published article on a particular subject does not represent the 'absolute' truth. Indeed, even many articles on a topic may not provide a complete and valid explanation of a particular process, pattern, or problem. This is especially true in the field of social gerontology, where such factors as race, gender, ethnicity, education, place and type of residence, health, income, occupation, or personality can have a profound impact on the process of aging and on the status of the aged. Many studies in social gerontology reflect only one 'slice' of a particular social system (often white, middle-class males). Other essential social, personal, or structural factors may not be considered in the analysis of the results. I encourage you to search for and consider alternative explanations and to be demanding in what you accept as fact. As a final comment, the test of how well a text serves as a learning resource is whether students find the material useful, interesting, clearly written, and comprehensive. Please provide feedback concerning this book to your instructor and to the author.

Barry D. McPherson
Wilfrid Laurier University
Waterloo, Ontario, Canada

July 1990

Acknowledgements

Writing a text can be a lonely and formidable task if carried out in social isolation. Fortunately, I received considerable formal and informal support from a number of colleagues who should not remain anonymous. The primary sources and documents required to write and update the text were retrieved by Heather Allen and Jackie MacPherson. Bill Forbes provided moral support and carried more than his fair share of the analysis and writing of the journal articles we coauthored while I was consumed by this project. As well, Leroy Stone, the Director of the Population Studies Division of Statistics Canada, provided considerable direct and indirect assistance in the location and retrieval of recent Canadian data. Six colleagues provided a thorough substantive and editorial critique of the new chapter on social support and social policy. In alphabetical order, a sincere thanks for this critical evaluation to Heather Allen, Neena Chappell, Ingrid Connidis, John Hirdes, Barbara Payne, and Carolyn Rosenthal. A special thanks is owed to Victor Marshall for his comprehensive and insightful Foreword and for his continuing leadership in the field of aging. Finally, appreciation is extended to Janet Bannister for juggling my decanal schedule to create the many blocks of time that were needed to write and edit the manuscript, and for coordinating the many other tasks that were associated with this project.

On the production side, I am indebted to the following for providing the photographs reproduced in the books: Ray Applebaum, Executive Director of the Older Adult Centres' Association of Ontario; Maurice Green, Photographer for the University of Waterloo; Jim Hertel, Photographer for Wilfrid Laurier University; Claire Posen, Communications Executive for the Seniors Secretariat, Health and Welfare Canada; and Jennifer Schipper, Director of Marketing and Community Relations, Baycrest Centre for Geriatric Care. The production of a book requires, as well, considerable effort and dedication by many employees of the publisher. I have been fortunate to have had an excellent working relationship with the following members of the Butterworths team, past and present, who supported this project and facilitated a very short production schedule. I hereby acknowledge, with thanks: Gloria Vitale for her encouragement and persistence in launching a second edition; Marie Graham, Catherine Haskell, Linda Kee and Jim Shepherd for their efficiency and their concern for quality control; Julia Keeler for her speedy but careful copyediting; and Craig Laudrum and Lisa Charters for adopting the project and filling the Butterworths 'empty nest' with a cadre of enthusiastic and energetic sales representatives.

Deserving a special paragraph of recognition is Noni Coleman, Research Grants Officer at Wilfrid Laurier University. For a year she became totally immersed in this project, sacrificing many hours of leisure and rescheduling lunch and coffee breaks to produce a carefully edited manuscript in a remarkably short period of time. Not surprisingly, during this period her normal responsibilities were performed with the usual high level of perfection and efficiency that I have observed throughout the past three years. Moreover, she voluntarily assumed the added roles of task motivator, editor, proofreader, and critic. While typing the manuscript, she carefully thought about the material and did not hesitate for a minute (from page 1 on!) to inform me if the grammar, style, or content was incorrect, not up to par, or incomprehensible. Noni, thank you for your interest, dedication, support, and competence. The next season will be more relaxing and enjoyable.

For their indirect input to this second edition, thanks are due, as well, to the many instructors, students and practitioners across Canada who took the time to inform Butterworths or me about what they liked and disliked in the first edition. Hopefully, your input has contributed to increased clarity, accuracy, and completeness in the synthesis, analysis, and interpretation of this rapidly expanding body of knowledge. Please share similar constructive criticisms following your reading of this edition.

Finally, like many others of my generation who are involved in gerontology in Canada, I did not have the opportunity to study aging phenomena as an undergraduate student. Rather, like the others, my interest and early "training" was kindled and fostered within my roots, long before "aging" and "gerontology" appeared in the curriculum, or before professional meetings were held on a regular basis. In my case, lacking the formal training that is available today, as an undergraduate student I had the opportunity to regularly visit my paternal grandfather who, well into his eighth decade of life, independently maintained his own apartment. There, while consuming beer and Hockey Night in Canada, I first learned that aging is a social process. Indeed, I was often never sure who was playing the role of kinkeeper or confidant! Generations subsequent to my grandfather's have similarly provided evidence that life after retirement is full of meaningful leisure and travel, that the generation gap is more myth than fact, and that adaptation to a 'half-empty nest' is difficult, but possible. To the McPherson clan — past, present, and future — thank you for the memories, the insights, the opportunities and the support.

Part One

AN INTRODUCTION TO INDIVIDUAL AND POPULATION AGING

Although aging has traditionally been considered a biological process, increasing research attention is being directed to the impact of sociocultural, historical, and environmental factors on the processes of individual and population aging. This increased interest has led to the development of a large body of research within the field of social gerontology.

Chapter 1 introduces the concept of aging as a social phenomenon, outlines historical and contemporary developments in the field of social gerontology, alerts the student to some conceptual and methodological concerns, and introduces environmental and sociocultural variables essential to the study of individual or population aging.

Chapter 2 describes the process and product of aging in selected societies throughout history, analyzes the changing status of the elderly in preindustrial and industrial societies, especially following the onset of modernization, and examines, primarily within the North American context, the process and product of aging within indigenous, racial, ethnic, rural, religious, and poverty subcultures.

Chapter 3 provides the reader with information about demographic processes and indicators that describe the size, composition, and distribution of the population by age. This chapter also describes the social and environmental characteristics of older cohorts within a society, from both a historical and a contemporary perspective.

Chapter 4 introduces the goals and methods of scientific inquiry, as well as some specific methodological concerns that must be considered when studying the elderly and the aging process. Most of the chapter discusses the major conceptual perspectives and social theories that have been used to stimulate, guide, and explain aging phenomena from a social science perspective. The section on social science perspectives and theories introduces the two general levels of analysis used throughout the book: the micro (or personal) level that pertains to individual aging, and the macro (or societal) level that pertains to cohort or population aging. It is essential to note that these are not separate processes; there is constant interaction across the life cycle between individual and population aging, and between the individual, the culture, and the social structure.

1
Aging as a Social Phenomenon

Courtesy of Ontario Senior Games Program, operated by the Older Adults Centres' Association of Ontario

INTRODUCTION

During the past twenty to thirty years, birth-rates have declined and life expectancy has increased in most modern industrial societies. As a result, approximately 12 percent of the population in North America now is made up of people over 65 years of age. This proportion is expected to increase to about 14 percent by the year 2000, and to about 20 percent by 2021, when most of the 'baby boom' age **cohort** has reached 65 years of age. Moreover, between now and 2010, when the first of the 'baby boom-ers' begin to turn 65, the proportion of those over 65 who are over 80 could reach 25 percent. This older segment of the elderly population will include a large percentage who are frail, dependent, and institutionalized. It is this phe-nomenon, where an increasing percentage of the population is composed of people over 60 or 65 years of age, that is known as **population aging.**

In contrast, **individual aging** refers to the structural, sensory, motor, behavioral, and cognitive changes in a given organism over time, especially with respect to how these fac-tors influence **life chances** and **lifestyle** at vari-ous stages of the life cycle. An individual's re-actions to these biological, physiological, and psychological changes and his or her behavior at different periods in the life cycle are closely related to the individual's past and present social context. The social processes and struc-ture of a particular society can greatly influence the aging process for an individual or for a specific age cohort. In short, individual and population aging are social processes that may differ within various contexts.

It will be apparent throughout this book that the study of aging and the aged is complex and involves many levels of analysis. These include physical, sensory, and motor changes within the individual; the impact of population aging on the individual and on society; the impact of social change on the status of the elderly; the patterns of aging unique to age cohorts or gen-erations; the interaction among different age cohorts within a society; the culture-based pat-terns of aging; and the interaction of social and psychological processes with biological pro-cesses, especially with respect to how the latter

influence the former at different stages in the life cycle.

The major aim of this book is to provide valid knowledge about aging as a social process. The book also illustrates the approaches and tech-niques used by social scientists and gerontolo-gists to describe and explain how individuals and cohorts adapt to personal changes, to socie-tal changes, and to a changing social, physical, and cultural environment as they pass through stages in the life cycle. Throughout, the empha-sis is on social phenomena — on identifying, describing, and explaining repeated patterns of events, behavior, and thought that occur as individuals or cohorts interact in various social and physical environments throughout their middle and later years.

AGING AS A SOCIAL PHENOMENON

For many years aging was considered to be a biological process that was inevitable, univer-sal, and irreversible. The process began at birth and was characterized by ten to twenty years of growth, followed by a plateau or decline in the size and efficiency of the organism. This decline is evident in external signs such as skin wrinkles, change in hair color, loss of hair, and, more subtly, through internal changes such as a decline in vision, hearing, lung capacity, en-ergy reserves, strength, and reaction time. However, not everyone experiences these changes at the same rate or to the same extent.

Although the average life span in earlier cen-turies was shorter than it is today,[1] some people lived long past their 'normal' life expectancy. These exceptions were studied carefully to determine a possible explanation for their lon-gevity (Kebric, 1988). Because these few ex-amples showed longer life was possible, indi-viduals searched for a magic potion or the Fountain of Youth many centuries ago.[2] Note that these early explanations for longevity were based on genetic and hereditary factors over which the individual had little or no control.

Along with this interest in understanding and extending the life span, some societies were concerned with improving the quality of care for their elderly citizens, primarily to ensure that they were adequately housed, fed, and clothed. As a result, many practices initiated in the late nineteenth century in Western Europe and in the first third of the twentieth century in North America sought to prevent or relieve the physical suffering of the elderly. The few social policies that were initiated assisted the destitute elderly as well as families who no longer could care for and cope with their elderly parents or grandparents (Forbes et al., 1987:1-15).

In the late nineteenth and early twentieth centuries, the growth of disciplines such as psychology, sociology, anthropology, economics, and political science drew attention to the fact that a biological organism, regardless of its genetic background, does not age in a vacuum but within various **social systems**. Social scientists began to focus not only on the physical and social status of elderly citizens but also on the social, cultural, economic, and psychological factors that influenced the aging process. They were motivated by the desire to understand a social phenomenon and by a realization of the need for valid and reliable scientific knowledge that could be used as the basis for professional practice and for government policies relating to the elderly.

Recognizing that aging is not only a biological process, scientists sought to understand how sociocultural and environmental factors interact to influence individual and population aging. Aging is viewed as a social process characterized by continuities in behavior and by health, economic, and social losses[3] that occur when the individual interacts within an age structure made up of numerous **age strata**. As a result of the values and social expectations in a specific culture, interaction among age cohorts can enhance or destroy the status, rights, responsibilities, and power of individuals throughout the **life cycle**. In short, life chances and lifestyle are influenced by (1) physiological, sociological, and psychological factors unique to an individual or age cohort; (2) the social structure of a given society; and (3) social, economic, and historical changes[4] that occur within a given sociocultural context.

In summary, longer life spans and a decline in birthrates and immigration have increased the actual number and the proportion of the elderly in the total population. Moreover, the elderly are becoming increasingly visible and vocal. [5] Thus, as a society's age structure changes with population aging, and as concomitant social and historical changes occur, the aging process both for individuals and cohorts may change. Aging is a dynamic rather than a static process, and its influence on specific individuals and cohorts at one stage of the life cycle is related to experiences at earlier stages. Furthermore, aging is characterized by cultural norms that guide intergenerational and intragenerational interaction. Thus, because society changes, people in different age cohorts may age in different ways (Riley, 1987; Uhlenberg, 1988).

Much of the initial research and writing in social gerontology focused on the status or the problems of being old. Because the emphasis was on the institutionalized elderly, early studies tended to emphasize the negative aspects of aging. This created a stigma about aging and about being old, which, in turn, led to a denial of aging and to the alienation of the elderly from society (Connidis, 1981). With a shift in the 1960s to studies of older adults who live in the community, research began to focus more on the process than on the problems of aging. Recently, there has been an emphasis on the need to develop a 'life span perspective' in order to understand the influence of earlier stages on later ones (Hareven and Adams, 1982; Dannefer, 1983, 1988). Beginning with the following two sections, this book will focus on the process and the product of aging as a social phenomenon.

THE AGING PROCESS

Aging is a dynamic process that involves physical, psychological, and social change[6] and adaptation throughout the life cycle. These structural and behavioral changes and adaptations that occur over the years, within and between individuals and cohorts, constitute the process of aging. While the aging process is not fully understood, there is common agreement that it is inevitable, universal, irreversible, and complex; that individuals and age cohorts experience different types and rates of aging; and that genetic, physical, psychological, environmental, and social factors are directly and indirectly involved. This section outlines various facets of the aging process and introduces concepts to facilitate an understanding of the process.

Types of Aging

Although the following facets of the aging process are introduced as distinct phenomena, interaction does exist between the various processes. For example, a decline in visual acuity[7] (a biological change) may lead to an inability to read or drive a car, thereby imposing some degree of intellectual or social constraint on a person's lifestyle. Similarly, forced retirement (a social act) may initiate psychological (depression), physical (decreased endurance), or social (absence of friends) losses that create problems for the individual and for society. Furthermore, with the exception of chronological aging, there is variation within and between individuals in the onset and degree of aging among the various systems. For example, an individual may appear physically 'old,' but his or her social or psychological behavior may be that of a younger adult.

Chronological Aging

Chronological aging (the passage of calendar time) determines rights (often via legal statutes) and influences lifestyle. For example, chronological age, especially during childhood, determines when a person can join the Scouts, what teams to play for, and who to play with at school. However, the differences between individuals mean that chronological age provides only an approximate indication of structural growth and decline, psychological or physical performance, social and emotional development, and patterns of social interaction. Chronological age can be deceiving; a 30-year-old may have the facial features of a 40-year-old, yet act and dress like a 20-year-old. Some may perceive this person to be 'old' for his or her age, while others may perceive the person as 'immature.' This example illustrates that age and aging have a social meaning that is defined within a particular social or cultural context.

Throughout the life cycle, all members of a society, particularly adults, must obey laws pertaining to their rights and obligations as citizens. In many cases these laws refer to a specific legal age (Cain, 1976; Eglit, 1985) before or at which a particular social function or right can or cannot be exercised. These include such rites of passage as beginning school, driving a car, being eligible to vote, being eligible to marry, and being required to retire. Unfortunately, many of these legal ages are established arbitrarily according to some preconceived norm as to what is the best or 'normal' chronological age for each right or obligation. In some cases legal age is based on the best available knowledge about **chronological age norms** — how most individuals behave in a given situation or perform a particular task at a specific chronological age.

Legal age may also be determined by 'functional' aging. This term refers to the relationship between chronological age and how well an individual can perform specific physical, social, or psychological tasks. In this sense, functional aging may be a more useful and meaningful construct than chronological aging. Functional aging takes into consideration individual differences and the fact that aging is a multifaceted process wherein an individual at a certain age may be 'older' or 'younger' than others. For example, with the abolishment of mandatory retirement, the right to continue working might be based on how well individuals continue to perform job responsibilities, rather than on reaching the chronological age of 60, 65, or 70. In order to make this decision, however, employers will have to develop valid predictor measures of job performance.

The use of chronological age to determine legal age fails to account for individual or cultural differences in needs or abilities. While legal age introduces social order and control to a society, it may also impose constraints on individual rights and personal freedom. For example, legislation that makes retirement at age 65 mandatory implies that people become economically useless at that age. While some persons may no longer be able to perform their tasks or may not wish to continue working, others have the capacity and desire to continue contributing to the social system. Similarly, some may be ready to drive a car at age 16; others may be ready earlier; and others much later. An illustration of intercultural variation in the interpretation of legal age is mandatory retirement. The mandatory age may be 55 to 70 in industrialized nations; it may occur whenever an individual is no longer functionally able to perform in primitive or less industrialized nations; or, in some societies, there may be no mandatory retirement age at all. (Interestingly, these same options can apply to the self-employed, since they are usually exempt from institutionally imposed social constraints on the right to work or retire.)

In summary, chronological aging provides an approximate measure of the stage of growth and the expected pattern of behavior and change within an individual. The following measures relate to functional aging and to an understanding of the type and rate of aging within individuals, between individuals within a society, and among individuals in culturally diverse societies.

Biological Aging

Biological aging refers to internal and external changes in the structure and functioning of the organism that influence behavior and longevity. One outcome of this process is senescence, wherein genetic and environmentally induced changes take place in the muscular, skeletal, reproductive, neural, and sensory systems. Many are visible changes: loss of hair, change in hair color, change in skin texture, and change in stature, gait, and posture.

The rate and incidence of the internal biological changes influence the number of years an individual is likely to survive. Many of these changes and their accompanying adaptations also influence the social and psychological processes of aging. Similarly, the lifestyle or the stress or depression in an individual can either retard or accelerate the biological process. This facet of the aging process is beyond the scope of this book. The interested reader should consult the following references for more information on this subject: Shock, 1977; Rockstein and Sussman, 1979; McGaugh and Kiesler, 1981; Finch and Schneider, 1985; Schneider and Rowe, 1990.

Psychological Aging

Psychological aging involves possible changes in personality, cognition, emotional arousal, psychomotor skills, learning, memory, motivation, or creativity (Birren and Schaie, 1985, 1990). This type of aging involves interaction between cognitive and behavioral changes within the individual and environmental factors that affect his or her psychological state. For example, declining vision, memory, and attention span may lead to an abandonment of a lifelong interest in reading. This in turn can dramatically alter the leisure lifestyle of an individual and lead to boredom, depression, and a deteriorating quality of life.

Similarly, stressful events such as losing a spouse through divorce or death, declaring bankruptcy, or losing a job may alter the behavioral and mental processes of an individual at any chronological age. The degree to which an individual adapts often depends not only on personal psychological processes and capacities, but also on the amount of support and assistance received from significant others within the family and the community.

There is also interaction between the biological and psychological systems. For example, a change in the endocrine system may lead to changes in emotional behavior or mental processes. Similarly, the loss of appetite that may accompany prolonged depression can result in a general deterioration of health. Psychological aging also involves cultural and subcultural differences in the process. These cultural factors ascribe a social meaning to age and aging that is unique to a given culture. For example, for the elderly members of some cultural groups, entering a hospital for exploratory tests can be a frightening experience. In their cultural group or country of origin, it may be believed that people go to die in a hospital, not to be tested or to get better.

Social Aging

Social aging represents regular patterns of behavior in individuals or groups as they interact with others within a specific social system. This may be a microsystem (such as the nuclear family) or a macrosystem (such as a nation or a region of the world). Aging as a social process varies considerably within and between cultures. Unlike the biological or psychological aging processes, which are relatively similar from one culture or subculture to another, social aging involves reciprocal interaction between the social system and the aging individual. An identical twin separated at birth from his or her sibling and raised in a different family, community, or country would exhibit aging patterns similar to those in his or her own social situation rather than that of the sibling.

Aging occurs within a social structure that provides a degree of order and stability. Within this structure, individuals occupy a number of status positions at socially determined and appropriate stages in the life cycle. These include the status of child, sibling, friend, student, apprentice, spouse, parent, boss, grandparent, retiree, widow or widower, and great-grandparent.

This structure of differentiated social positions forms an age-status system. Associated with each of these positions are role expectations or norms relating to how one should behave with others who occupy a specific position. Because these positions tend to be occupied at particular stages in the life cycle, much social behavior is influenced by age-related norms. Many social systems are characterized by age grading, wherein responsibilities or expectations are related to chronological age or social positions (see chapter 7).

Although learning and adopting patterns of social interaction by age is an element of the social aging process, the importance of the social structure cannot be ignored, as Linton (1936) noted many years ago. The age structure of a society is stratified like a ladder. While some societies distinguish among many strata (infancy, early childhood, preadolescence, adolescence, young adulthood, middle age, old age, very old age), others have only a few (childhood, adulthood, old age).

Regardless of the number of stages, the behavior and status of the members of each stratum are influenced by the expected rights and responsibilities assigned on the basis of age and by attitudes toward specific age groups. For example, some societies value the elderly (Japan); other societies (Canada and the United States) may devalue them and consider them less attractive, less interesting, and less worthwhile than younger people. That is, being old may mean that one has a marginal and stigmatized status in the society (Ward, 1984).

Within each culture, social timetables define the approximate chronological age when one enters or leaves various stages and occupies social positions (Fry, 1980). In fact, institutionalized rites of passage are sometimes initiated to provide continuity and to announce the transition from one position to another. Some examples include graduation, marriage, bar mitzvah ceremonies, and birthday celebrations. Special social events may signify a new status. In preindustrialized societies this might involve becoming a warrior or elder; in more developed societies, special status is accorded when individuals marry, purchase their first car or home, or receive a promotion. Within age cohorts the meaning and significance attached to similar rites of passage and to a particular age may vary by social group. For example, marriage may have more significance for lower-class women than for upper-class women, while a job promotion may have more significance for an upper-middle-class executive than for a blue-collar laborer.

The meanings attached to membership in an age stratum or to specific events are subject to change. In your parents' or grandparents' day a woman who had not married by her mid-20s was often stigmatized and labeled an 'old maid.' In contrast, a single woman in her mid-20s is today viewed as 'liberated.' She is praised for protecting her future by not rushing into marriage and for pursuing an education and a career. In fact, in many instances she may be envied by her age peers who are preoccupied with raising young children and meeting mortgage payments. It is this change in meanings that renders chronological age a poor predictor or indicator of the needs, capabilities, or interests of older adults. Increasingly, major life events are no longer clearly defined by age. To illustrate, a woman can become a mother for the first time as a teenager or in her early 40s. As a result, passage into the role of grandparent may occur as early as 30 or as late as 70 years of age.

The composition of the age structure also has

FIGURE 1.1
COHORT DIFFERENCES AND THE AGING PROCESS

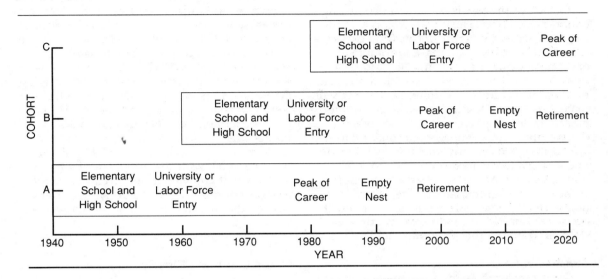

an impact on the social definition of aging. The population in any society is composed of subgroups known as age cohorts. These include all persons born during a particular five- or ten-year period, or who enter a stage in life such as university, marriage, the labor force, or the armed forces at about the same time (Ryder, 1965; Rosow, 1978). Over time, the number in any cohort at a particular stage in life may be large or small, creating unique problems for society or for members of the cohort. For example, those born between 1945 and the early 1960s composed one of the largest birth cohorts ever, and were part of the postwar 'baby boom.' The arrival of this cohort led to an urgent need for more schools during the 1950s and 1960s, and to a dramatic growth of suburban housing in the 1960s. By about 2010, this cohort will form the largest group ever of retirees, possibly creating a unique economic drain on public and private pension funds. Interestingly, but perhaps not surprisingly, the 'baby boom' was followed by a 'baby bust' generation born in the 1970s and 1980s (McDaniel, 1986). This decreased fertility rate resulted from changing values and norms concerning marriage, family size, and child rearing.

The relative size of each cohort is not the only factor to have an impact on the aging process. The unique background, the shared experiences of economic, political, and social events, and the common sequencing of life events also influence cohorts (Elder and Liker, 1982). These commonalities influence values and lifestyle and differentiate a given cohort from other younger or older cohorts who experience the same phenomena, but at different stages in life. For example, during the early 1980s, a period characterized by inflation and high unemployment, cohort A in figure 1.1 was approaching its peak career years, and was probably coping reasonably well with the prevailing social and economic conditions. In contrast, cohort B was about to enter the labor force during a period of high unemployment, and therefore many members likely experienced difficulty in obtaining employment. Finally, cohort C was just entering the life cycle and was less likely to be directly affected by the prevailing economic climate. Thus, inflation and high unemployment in the early 1980s should have a different impact on these distinct age cohorts. Some of these factors may have an influence on members of the age cohort throughout the life cycle (for example, cohort B). Figure 11.1 also illustrates the cohort effect with respect to the impact of legislation on social and economic security in the later years.

The aging process is also influenced by age cohort interaction. These intercohort relations can be described in terms of rules and expectations that have the potential to promote cooperation or conflict between generations. This potential is often related to social differentiation within a culture — different age strata will have greater or lesser status, and therefore greater or lesser power. In societies where the elderly are valued, intergenerational relations are positive and the movement of a cohort from one stratum to the next occurs without fear or regret. In contrast, in societies where youth is valued more highly than old age, intergenerational rivalry and conflict is more likely to occur, especially if the elderly resent the loss of status and power that they once held.

Conclusion

The aging process involves individual and social change from the cellular to the societal or cultural level (Kiesler et al., 1981; Pampel, 1981). While each process functions independently and at its own rate, there is also interaction between the biological, psychological, and social processes. Consider an individual who experiences a social or physical loss such as widowhood or loss of vision. One outcome of the loss may be depression, which in turn may trigger biochemical changes and may lead to additional mental or physical problems. There is a need to study aging within the social context; scientists know less about the social and cultural aspects of aging than about the biological and psychological processes. Similarly, there is a need to understand the reciprocal relationship between individual aging and social change. As society changes because of wars and economic cycles of growth and recession, individuals in various cohorts age in different ways.

THE PRODUCT OF THE AGING PROCESS: THE MIDDLE-AGED AND ELDERLY ADULT

In the previous section the focus was on the aging process. This section emphasizes the

outcome or product of that process, namely, the status of being middle-aged or elderly. Although these periods are not the end of the process (as is frequently assumed), they do represent unique stages of development for the individual and for society. Until recently, because of the increase in the number and visibility of the elderly, social gerontologists focused on the problems associated with the postretirement stage in life, rather than on the process of aging per se. As a result, many negative myths and stereotypes about aging and the elderly have been generated and perpetuated because of limited observations and the lack of research on the community-dwelling elderly. Highlight 1.1 provides you with an opportunity to assess your level of knowledge and to clarify possible misconceptions about the elderly. Note 8 at the end of the chapter provides the correct answers.

Myths about the Elderly

In the absence of scientific knowledge about the aging process, personal observations or folk myths become the basis for social, psychological, or biological beliefs about old people. Although most of these beliefs are unfounded and negative in orientation, they tend to be accepted as facts. As a result, myths may negatively influence the behavior and expectations of middle-aged and elderly individuals — the self-fulfilling prophecy. In addition, they may influence the behavior and attitudes of others toward all older people or to anyone who happens to have a supposed 'middle-aged' or 'aged' characteristic. For example, men who are prematurely bald at age 25 may be considered 'old'; if they are prematurely gray at 30, they may be viewed as 'middle-aged.'

Stereotypes based on limited observations or on untested opinions are frequently present at all stages in life. For example, a visit to a shopping center after school hours might lead one to believe that all adolescents spend their leisure time smoking and 'hanging out.' Of course, this is a myth; only a small percentage of adolescents engage in this behavior on a regular basis, if at all. Nevertheless, young people may be stereotyped as lazy because of such

---

HIGHLIGHT 1.1

SOME FACTS ABOUT AGING: TRUE OR FALSE

In order to dispel myths, to define social reality, and to sensitize individuals to the prevalence of social myths and stereotypes concerning the later years, Palmore (1977, 1980a, 1981, 1988), Miller and Dodder (1980), and Martin Matthews et al. (1984), developed versions of a true-or-false 'Facts on Aging' quiz. The items in the test are based on documented research.

T	F	1.	Older people tend to become more religious as they age.
T	F	2.	Most old people are set in their ways and unable to change.
T	F	3.	The majority of old people are seldom bored.
T	F	4.	The health and socioeconomic status of older people (compared to younger people) in the year 2000 will probably be about the same as now.
T	F	5.	Older persons have more acute (short-term) illnesses than persons under 65.
T	F	6.	The majority of old people are seldom irritated or angry.
T	F	7.	Older workers have less absenteeism than younger workers.
T	F	8.	The aged have higher rates of criminal victimization than persons under 65.
T	F	9.	The majority of the aged live alone.
T	F	10.	Older persons who reduce their activity tend to be happier than those who remain active.

It is important to stress that this quiz reflects knowledge of facts, and cannot be regarded as a direct measure of attitudes. In reality, where misconceptions are found, and they have been found in all age groups, they are often due to a lack of personal experience with older adults, to inaccurate conclusions based on personal observations of elderly people from a distance rather than through direct interaction, or to a passive acceptance of the ideas and images presented in the mass media.

SOURCE: Reprinted by permission of *The Gerontologist*, 17 (April 1977), 315-320, and 21 (April 1981), 431-437.

---

observations. Similarly, through personal observation and (to some extent) through the role of the media in presenting and perpetuating stereotypes, certain myths about the elderly have become institutionalized and thereby accepted as fact. For example, the elderly are believed to be physically infirm, inactive, poor, asexual, irritable, lonely, isolated, obsolete, irrationally afraid of aging and death, set in their ways, and in need of institutionalization. Equally bizarre is the glamorous notion that retirement represents the beginning of the carefree and 'golden' years of life.

Because of the prevalence of these myths, older people are often stigmatized. Some may attempt to counteract this discrimination by coping strategies such as the use of facial creams, hairpieces, hair tints, faddish clothes, or cosmetic surgery; or by adopting the language, values, and lifestyle of younger generations. In short, some middle-aged and elderly persons have recognized that chemical, surgical, and behavioral adaptations can be initiated to avoid conforming to a cultural definition of 'old age.'

The Social Reality of the Middle and Later Years of Life

Contrary to prevailing myths, only a minority of the elderly experience poor health, institutionalized living, poverty, loneliness, or isolation. However, the greater the longevity of an individual, the greater the likelihood that one or more of these conditions will have some impact on the individual's life. These problems are mainly experienced by the very old (those over 80). If the elderly have certain ascribed or achieved characteristics, they are more likely to experience one or more of these problems. For example, as we will see later in this chapter, such factors as being female, being a member of a lower social class, being black, being a member of a native group, and having less education than one's age peers will influence not only the process of aging but also one's social, economic, health, and psychological status. In reality, some people at all ages are faced with disadvantaged status because of these social constraints.

The aging process leads to individual differences among both the middle-aged[9] and the elderly, who must continually adjust and adapt to changes in their unique social world. How an individual thinks and behaves at one stage is partly determined by what he or she was like at an earlier stage in life. The individual who is cautious, conservative, and introspective when young is likely to exhibit these same characteristics in the middle and later years. Thus, there is both continuity and diversity in the aging process. As you will learn throughout this book, the elderly are an extremely heterogeneous group as measured by a variety of social, psychological, and physical characteristics (Maddox and Lawton, 1988; *The Gerontologist*, 29(5), 1989). We cannot speak about them as one group of people — 'the aged' or 'the elderly.' To focus on the 'average' or the 'central tendency' is misleading and results in incomplete knowledge and inappropriate policies and services.

Contrary to prevailing stereotypes or myths, old age is not characterized exclusively by economic, health, psychological, or social losses and problems. Rather, many of the apparent problems are societally induced outcomes rather than biological outcomes. Thus, not all observed deficits among adults are age-related. Rather, some age-associated losses or declines may be related to lifestyle habits (exercise, nutrition, smoking, drug and alcohol use, occupational requirements) or to psychosocial factors unrelated to the aging process (stress, gender, race, education). Although aging is frequently viewed as a social problem, many advantages accrue to both society and the individual from aging and being older. Palmore (1979) lists the following advantages of aging for the individual: less criminal victimization, fewer accidents, availability of pensions and other guaranteed income, tax benefits, payment of medical expenses, reduced rates on consumer goods and services, and freedom from child rearing and work. Some of the advantages to society cited by Palmore include lower criminal activity,

greater political participation, increasing participation in voluntary associations, and increasing quality of work abilities.

Aging Effects and Cohort Effects

It is commonly observed that people at different stages of life exhibit not only different physical traits but also different cognitive, emotional, and social behavior as they interact with others. While there are individual differences in appearance and behavior within a given age cohort, the differences are most pronounced between members of different generations. For example, those who are now in their 60s and 70s are generally considered to be more religious and more conservative than younger age cohorts. There appear to be two possible explanations to account for these generational differences.

First, differences may result from changes with age, as the individual matures and develops (aging effects). An obvious example is the external physical changes that occur from birth on, and which are reflected dramatically after about 40 years of age (such as changes in hair coloring and facial contours). Because aging is a dynamic rather than a static process, we all change and adapt to some extent as we occupy different social positions within a variety of social systems. For example, an authoritarian, autocratic individual who is promoted to a supervisory position might find that a more democratic and communicative style is more effective in motivating younger workers. Thus, behavioral changes can occur over time, and the behavior of an individual at age 50 may be different from that exhibited at age 25. This is especially so if the expectations associated with a particular social position change or if new social positions are acquired.

Changes within the individual (aging effects) may not be sufficient to account for the behavioral differences among various age cohorts. Rather, the impact of specific historical events unique to each cohort must also be considered (cohort effects). As noted earlier, a society consists of a series of successive age cohorts that pass through the life cycle as if on an upward-bound escalator (Ryder, 1965). Each cohort may experience particular events differently from the preceding or following cohorts. For example, the onset of double-digit inflation in the early 1980s had an influence on all cohorts, but it was perhaps most traumatic for the elderly who were living on a fixed income, and least traumatic for children and teenagers who were still financially dependent on parents. Similarly, a depression, a war, an energy crisis, social or political unrest, or high unemployment can have a lasting effect over the entire life cycle on the life chances and on the cognitive and behavioral processes of a specific cohort.

In summary, the outcome of the aging process for the individual and for society is dependent on changes within the individual over the life cycle, on different social experiences and historical events encountered by members of each cohort, and by the interaction of these two processes. However, it must be continually recognized that there are individual and cultural differences in the aging process, both within individuals and within cohorts. Individuals, cohorts, and societies do age differently. It is because of this interaction of individual differences and cross-cultural differences that the aging process is relatively difficult to understand.

THE FIELD OF SOCIAL GERONTOLOGY: HISTORICAL AND CONTEMPORARY PERSPECTIVES

A historical approach to a topic is often considered by students to be uninteresting, trivial, or irrelevant. However, a historical analysis enables us to better understand our current situation through an appreciation of our 'roots.' With an understanding of the past we may be in a better position to predict the future if we see similar events or patterns evolving at a later stage in history. This section presents a general overview of how and why the field of gerontology, and particularly social gerontology, has evolved.[10]

Early History

Throughout history mankind has been preoccupied with the search for two major im-

provements to the quality of life — wealth and the prolongation of life and vigor. The latter goal is evident in the earliest writings of philosophers and historians who described the status and treatment of the aged in many societies. For example, those who lived a longer-than-normal life span were often held in awe and were sometimes feared, since it was believed that they possessed some magic power.

The fact that some people lived longer than others led to the creation of myths and folk tales to explain this longevity. The earliest literature was characterized by three themes (Gruman, 1966). The 'antediluvian theme' was based on the belief that people in the past had avoided death by various means and had lived perhaps as long as 900 years. According to the 'hyperborean theme,' there are unique cultures in which people experience exceptional longevity. This was thought to occur because of such factors as social isolation, diet, genetics, high levels of physical activity, and special treatment of the aged. Examples of cultures in which individuals are thought to live at least 100 years (centenarians) are the Vilcabambans of Ecuador (Leaf, 1975), who reportedly have 1,100 centenarians per 100,000 population, and the Abkhasians of Georgia in the USSR, with a reported sixty centenarians per 100,000 population (Benet, 1974). By comparison, in many industrialized societies there may be fewer than three people per 100,000 who live to the age of 100. However, the extreme longevity among the Vilcabambans and Abkhasians has not been substantiated, since birth records are rarely available (Medvedev, 1974; Mazess and Forman, 1979). Moreover, individuals in these societies may exaggerate their age to attain high status, to escape military duty when they are young, or to pretend to be something they are not in order to gain attention from visiting scholars, journalists, or tourists — a practice that has long been of concern to social and cultural anthropologists.

The third theme, 'rejuvenation,' was symbolized by the search for the Fountain of Youth. The modern equivalent involves the use of mineral baths, special nutrients, hot tubs, exercise, health spas, cosmetic surgery, or hormones and chemicals to present a younger physical appearance and to promote a longer life span.

Social Gerontology in the Twentieth Century

Although anthropologists had previously documented the status and treatment of the elderly in a number of primitive tribes and agrarian societies, until the 1920s interest in the aged was limited to providing social welfare programs and developing social policies. This interest resulted from the increased visibility of the elderly as a group — a group that was forming a larger percentage of the population. Most early research was motivated by an attempt to ameliorate a perceived social problem rather than by the desire to understand the process of aging. This is illustrated by the publication in 1922 of a book by Abraham Epstein (*Facing Old Age*) in which he advocated income maintenance, employment, and social welfare for the elderly.

Prior to the 1920s, the literature dealt chiefly with the study of childhood and adolescence, since these were viewed as the essential developmental stages in the life cycle. However, two exceptions were *Senescence, The Second Half of Life*, published in 1922 by the psychologist G.S. Hall, and *Problems of Aging*, published in 1939 by E.V. Cowdry. This latter book presented the results of the Stanford Later Maturity Project. These influential works stimulated social scientists to examine the interrelationships between social structure, social institutions, and individual and group behavior as they are related to aging and the elderly.

It was not until the early 1940s, however, that sociologists began to study age as a possible explanatory factor in social behavior. During this period Chen (1939) discussed the social significance of old age, Landis (1940) studied the attitudes and adjustment of aged rural residents in Iowa, and Cottrell (1942) published an inventory of propositions concerning adjustment to age and sex roles. Similarly, Parsons (1942) noted the importance of age and sex in the social structure, while Linton (1942) stressed the importance of age as a social category and the need to understand the formation and function of age norms.

By the 1940s, then, the knowledge component of the field of social gerontology was beginning to evolve from three perspectives:

(1) studies concerned with programs of welfare and social policies for the aged; (2) studies by social scientists who were primarily interested in using age to gain a better understanding of social behavior in general; and (3) studies by social scientists whose main objective was to understand and explain the aging process and the status and behavior of the aged. It was this latter group that began to label themselves as social gerontologists, in addition to their identification with other disciplines such as psychology, sociology, anthropology, political science, or economics.

Highlight 1.2 presents a time line that outlines some of the key events in the development and growth of the field of social gerontology since 1940. While it is not possible or necessary to list every relevant publication, contributor, or event, the time line indicates the emergence of major publications and professional associations devoted to the study of aging and the aged as a social phenomenon.

From a more analytical perspective, Mullins (1972, 1973) suggested that scientific specialties evolve through four stages of development: normal, network, cluster, and specialty. This model can help us understand the emergence of social gerontology as an area of specialization that is now accepted as a legitimate area of scientific inquiry (Sackmary, 1974).

The first or 'normal' stage is characterized by a low degree of organization, with only a few papers being published by individuals who have a range of scholarly commitments (Mullins, 1973:21). This stage reflects the development of social gerontology prior to 1945. Until then, only a few relevant publications existed, much of the work was concerned with identifying and solving a social problem unique to old age, scholars were isolated from each other, there were no formal gerontology organizations, and few if any scholars devoted their careers exclusively to research on aging.

The second or 'network' stage is characterized by the initiation of frequent, regular communication among first-generation scholars via conferences, newsletters, and journals; by the formation of national and international associations; and by the appearance of theoretical and conceptual essays and empirical studies, often in anthologies and conference proceed-

Highlight **1.2**

A TIME LINE DEPICTING THE DEVELOPMENT OF THE FIELD OF
SOCIAL GERONTOLOGY SINCE 1940

Date	Event

The Normal Stage (up to 1945)

1940 Publication of the journal *Geriatrics*.

The Network Stage (1945-60)

1945 L. Simmons, *The Role of the Aged in Primitive Society*. A major review of the anthropological literature on the status and treatment of the elderly in primitive societies. It showed a negative relationship between status and the growth of technology in society.

1945 The Gerontological Society of America was established and held annual meetings thereafter to promote the scientific study of aging from multidisciplinary perspectives, and to stimulate communication among scientists, researchers, teachers, and professionals (see Achenbaum, 1987b).

1945 The first issue of the *Journal of Gerontology* was published.

1946 The American Psychological Association added a 'Maturity and Old Age' section.

1948 O. Pollak, *Social Adjustment in Old Age*. A significant study that shifted the focus from the problems to the process of aging. It also identified the University of Chicago as a leading research center in social gerontology.

1948 The International Association of Gerontology was founded in Liège, Belgium.

1952 The Gerontological Society organized a 'Psychology and Social Sciences' section. This reflected the growing interest in and acceptance of this perspective for the study of aging phenomena.

1953 R. Havighurst and R. Albrecht, *Older People*.

1959 L. Cain (ed.), 'The Sociology of Aging: A Trend Report and Bibliography,' *Current Sociology*.

1959-60 a) J. Birren (ed.), *Handbook of Aging and the Individual: Psychological and Biological Aspects*.
b) C. Tibbitts (ed.), *Handbook of Social Gerontology: Societal Aspects of Aging*.
c) E. Burgess (ed.), *Aging in Western Societies*.
These handbooks summarized the state of knowledge in gerontology in the late 1950s.

The Cluster Stage (1961-75)

1961 *The Gerontologist:* a second journal published by the Gerontological Society to focus on the more applied and professional interests of those working with and for the aged.

1961 E. Cumming and W. Henry, *Growing Old: The Process of Disengagement*. The first attempt to develop a social gerontological theory to explain satisfaction or adjustment in the later years.

1961 First White House Conference on Aging. These conferences are held every ten years in the United States to draw scientists and professional workers together to make recommendations for consideration by Congress.

1965 A. Rose and W. Peterson (eds.), *Older People and Their Social World*.

1967 E. Youmans, *Older Rural Americans*. One of the few studies to consider aging in a rural context.

1968 M. Riley and A. Foner (eds.), *Aging and Society. Volume One: An Inventory of Research Findings*. This landmark volume presented and interpreted the empirical findings of social science research to this date.

1968 E. Shanas et al., *Old People in Three Industrial Societies*. A cross-national comparative study of the social situation of older people in Denmark, Great Britain, and the United States.

1968 B. Neugarten (ed.), *Middle Age and Aging: A Reader in Social Psychology*. The first collection of readings on the social psychology of aging.

1969 R. Havighurst et al., *Adjustment to Retirement: A Cross-National Study*.

1969 M. Riley et al. (eds.), *Aging and Society. Volume Two: Aging and the Professions*. A statement of the concerns and involvement of a number of professions in the care of the aging and aged.

HIGHLIGHT 1.2 (continued)

Date	Event
1970	E. Palmore, *Normal Aging: Reports from the Duke Longitudinal Studies, 1955-69*. The first interdisciplinary longitudinal study.
1972	M. Riley et al., *Aging and Society. Volume Three: A Sociology of Age Stratification*. Presents a model of aging that stresses the interaction between history and the social structure as it affects various age cohorts.
1972	D. Cowgill and L. Holmes (eds.), *Aging and Modernization*.
1972	R. Atchley, *The Social Forces in Later Life: An Introduction to Social Gerontology*. The first textbook written for students enrolled in an undergraduate course on social gerontology.
1972	Canadian Association on Gerontology founded.
1974	National Institute on Aging established in the United States to promote research on all facets of gerontology.

The Specialty Stage (1975-)

Date	Event
1975	R. Rapaport and R. Rapaport (eds.), *Leisure and the Family Life Cycle*. The first examination of leisure within the family context across the life cycle.
1975	Association for Gerontology in Higher Education formed to facilitate leadership development for training programs which were being established in universities and colleges in the United States.
1976	J. Schulz, *The Economics of Aging*. A comprehensive economic analysis of the aging process.
1976-77	Three new handbooks were published which represented the state of knowledge up to the mid-1970s. These were revised in 1985 and 1990.
	a) R. Binstock and E. Shanas (eds.) *Handbook of Aging and the Social Sciences* (1976).
	b) J. Birren and W. Schaie (eds.), *Handbook of the Psychology of Aging* (1977).
	c) C. Finch and L. Hayflick (eds.), *Handbook of the Biology of Aging* (1977).
1979	*Research on Aging: A Quarterly Journal of Social Gerontology* was first published.
1980	V. Marshall, *Aging in Canada: Social Perspectives*. This was the first reader presenting a collection of articles pertaining to aging and the aged in Canada. A second edition was published in 1987.
1982	*Canadian Journal on Aging* was first published.
1983	*Aging as a Social Process*. The first textbook on aging published in Canada.
1986	N. Chappell, L. Strain, and A. Blandford, *Aging and Health Care: A Social Perspective*.
1986	S. McDaniel, *Canada's Aging Population*. This monograph launched the Butterworths Series, Perspectives on Individual and Population Aging.
1987	G. Maddox et al. (eds.), *The Encyclopedia of Aging*.
1987	*Journal of Aging Studies* was first published.
1988	D. Harris (ed.), *Dictionary of Gerontology*.
1988	G. Fennell et al., *The Sociology of Old Age*. A critical analysis of aging in Great Britain.
1989	*Journal of Women and Aging* was first published.
1990	The third editions in the *Handbook of Aging* series were published; and *Abstracts in Social Gerontology* was first published.

ings. This stage in social gerontology ran from the mid-1940s to about 1960, and was characterized not only by increasing scholarly interest in the field, but also by 'missionary' work to convince others that the area was a necessary and legitimate field of inquiry.

In the 'cluster' stage, which ran from about 1961 to 1975, a second generation of researchers were trained by first-generation gerontologists.

Much of this training occurred at centers designed to focus on one or more aspects of gerontology. Thus, whereas the first generation were trained in isolation in a department of sociology, anthropology, social work, or psychology (that permitted them to study aging as one aspect of a doctoral program), many in the second generation were educated at the Ph.D. level within a gerontology program. This created a 'cluster' of scholars — faculty and students — who reinforced and stimulated one another's interests and thinking (Mullins, 1973:22-23). This stage was also characterized by increasingly sophisticated theoretical and empirical work, by the appearance of edited books of readings, and by the publication of the first textbooks.

The final or 'specialty' stage is attained when a field becomes recognized as a legitimate area of inquiry and when scientists identify themselves as specialists in the area. Since 1975, social gerontology has been increasingly accepted by policymakers, the public, and research agencies as a necessary and legitimate field of inquiry.[11] Students at both the undergraduate and graduate levels (the third generation) are electing to specialize in one aspect of the field or in social gerontology in general. There is now available a 'critical mass' of mature and productive scholars from the second and third generations, both within the disciplines of psychology and sociology and within the more general field of social gerontology. This critical mass not only increases the opportunities for graduate work by aspiring fourth-generation gerontologists, but also serves as a catalyst for increasing the quality of knowledge about social phenomena associated with aging and the aged. This stage is characterized by the initiation of highly specialized research journals (see Preface).

In summary, the development of social gerontology as a field of study has evolved primarily since 1945. In the early years the emphasis was on a description and treatment of the problems and status of the elderly. However, in recent years there has been increased interest in understanding the social dynamics of the aging process and the status of the aged from the perspectives of disciplines such as psychology, sociology, political science, economics, family studies, leisure studies, and health studies. In addition, phenomena associated with aging can be studied by professions such as nursing, social work, architecture, urban and regional planning, recreation, and physical education, and from the perspective of the humanities, music, literature (Lyell, 1980; Kebric, 1983; Wyatt-Brown, 1989), and art (McKee and Kauppinen, 1987).

This complex mix of disciplines, professions, and the arts constitutes the field known as social gerontology. It has two main components — the disciplines of scientific inquiry that seek to describe and explain the process of aging, and the professions that seek to solve the practical problems associated with aging. Generally, gerontology can be defined as the interdisciplinary discovery of knowledge by those affiliated with the biological sciences, clinical medicine, and the behavioral and social sciences[12] and the application of this knowledge by social planners and practitioners in the field of human services. However, since all fields of study are dynamic rather than static, perhaps the best way to identify and define a field is to examine the subject matter presented at conferences and to read articles published in the major journals.[13]

FACTORS INFLUENCING THE PROCESS AND PRODUCT OF AGING

In the preceding sections, overviews of the process of aging and of the historical development of social gerontology have been provided. The following sections describe and explain a variety of social facts and processes related to aging. However, before beginning this more finite analysis, a number of caveats must be introduced in order to prevent later misinterpretations. The patterns and processes of aging vary among individuals and groups depending on social, environmental, biological, and psychological factors. In addition, a number of methodological and conceptual matters must be considered in the interpretation of research findings. This section provides a checklist of a number of methodological, theoretical, and conceptual factors that you must consider when interpreting or applying findings from the literature in social gerontology.

Aging: A Multidimensional Process

Aging does not occur in a vacuum. Rather, aging involves an interaction of biological, psychological, social, and cultural factors, any or all of which may proceed at different rates for a specific individual or cohort. Such factors as rate of biological aging, changes in physical or mental health, changes in environment, past and current economic status, and availability of informal and formal support, can influence the aging process and the state of being old.

Conceptual and Methodological Concerns

Levels of Analysis

The aging process functions on three levels. At the 'individual' level an investigator identifies and explains internal or external changes in the process, over time, within or between individuals. This approach is common in biology and psychology, where investigators try to account for individual changes or differences in such domains as physiological functioning, the physical structure of the organism, learning abilities, personality, memory retention, and life satisfaction.

Aging can also be studied from the perspective of the 'social system.' Here the focus is on understanding the influence of the structure of society on the individual or cohort aging process. This level of analysis is also concerned with the outcome of interaction between the individual and other individuals, groups, or social institutions. The social-system approach identifies and explains common patterns of social behavior that are influenced by age (age norms) and by interaction between a succession of age cohorts in a particular society (Elder, 1975). This approach is concerned with understanding social processes such as age grading, age stratification, socialization, discrimination, and integration.

The third level of analysis, the 'comparative' approach, concentrates on the search for cultural or subcultural differences in the process of aging (Gutmann, 1977; Keith, 1980, 1990; Palmore, 1980b, Cowgill, 1981, 1986; Holmes, 1983; Foner, 1984; Kertzer and Keith, 1984; Krout, 1986; Driedger and Chappell, 1987). If the emphasis is on comparing entire societies, the approach is referred to as cross-cultural or cross-national research. However, comparative analysis can also be employed within a society in which subcultural differences are identified and

explained. For example, many studies have compared the differences between whites, blacks, Hispanics, or native people with respect to the status of the elderly and the process of aging. Similarly, a comparison between religious, economic, or regional groups is a comparative subcultural analysis of aging. In short, the process of aging and the status of the aged may vary by subgroups because of cultural differences within or between societies.

Cross-Sectional, Longitudinal, and Cohort Analysis

In chapter 4, research methods will be discussed in detail and the reader will be alerted to some of the limitations associated with the most common research designs used to study aging phenomena. This section reinforces the earlier point that we must learn to distinguish between age changes (aging effects) and age differences (cohort effects).

In the cross-sectional method of research, subjects of various ages are tested once and tables or graphs are derived that show a relationship between age and a particular social parameter. However, cross-sectional research designs can only indicate *differences* between age groups; they cannot be used to conclude that *changes* have occurred because of aging.

Longitudinal research designs involve repeated testing of the same subjects over a longer time, often ten years or more. A major difficulty with this method is that subjects move, die, or drop out of the study, and a considerably smaller sample may be left at the end of the testing period. Moreover, bias may be introduced because subjects are often volunteers, or because those who drop out of the study may differ in intelligence, social class, or health status from those who remain in the study. Nevertheless, this method enables researchers to examine age changes over time.

A third method, which has some advantages over cross-sectional and longitudinal research designs, is known as cohort analysis. This method involves collecting the same information at different times, with different individuals in the same age cohort being studied each time. For example, some national surveys are repeated at regular intervals, with approximately the same number of respondents in each cohort. While the respondents in each survey are usually different, they are representative of the same age cohort, and changes with age as well as differences between age cohorts may be inferred.

In summary, it is important, as you read research articles and newspaper accounts of studies completed on aging phenomena, that you understand the method used and the limitations of possible interpretations or conclusions that can be drawn. Differences related to age can be drawn from cross-sectional studies, whereas changes related to the aging process may best be inferred from longitudinal studies or cohort analyses.

The Influence of the Environment

In addition to personal factors, a number of external factors in the physical and social environment interact with age to influence the status and behavior of individuals at specific stages in the life cycle. In general, we must be concerned with three factors about the environment in which older adults live: the *location* (rural/urban, climate, regional factors), the *quality* (of housing, air, water, composition of the neighborhood), and the *quantity* (amount of public and private space in homes, apartments, or institutions). The remainder of this chapter includes an overview of the major social, cultural, and physical environmental factors that influence the behavior and status of the aging individual or cohort. In the following subsection the physical context in which people live and age is examined. Here, as Lawton (1980:16-17) notes, we must consider not only the conditions in the objective physical environment but also the meaning of the subjective environment as perceived and interpreted by an individual.

Geographical Region
The geographical environment includes climate, altitude, terrain, and the natural distribution of plant and animal life. While very little is known about the relationship between geographical factors and the aging process, environmentalists are giving increasing attention to the impact of various ecological factors (such as air and water pollution) in specific regions, on both short- and long-term physical and mental health and for the quality of life in general. For example, in North America, living in a highly industrialized city fosters a different lifestyle from living on a farm or in a small nonmetropolitan community. Similarly, aging in the highly industrialized and densely populated cities of Manchester, England, or Frankfurt, West Germany, represents a different environmental experience from that encountered by those living on the Seychelle Islands in the Indian Ocean.

For many elderly people who are economically independent, climate and terrain seem to have a special subjective meaning. For example, in the United States some people over 65 have migrated from the heavily populated and colder northeast and midwest regions to the more temperate southeast and southwest regions. For some, this is a seasonal migration; for others, it represents a permanent move. In Canada, some people move permanently to Victoria, British Columbia, or to the Niagara region of Ontario (Northcott, 1988), while large numbers of 'snowbirds' winter in Florida and other southern states (Northcott, 1988; Tucker et al., 1988). The increasing density of the elderly population in an area has both a direct and an indirect influence on the process of aging for individuals, on the age structure of the region, and on the delivery of social services (Longino and Biggar, 1982; Monahan and Greene, 1982). For example, a high concentration of older people restricts most social interaction to those who are 60 to 80 years of age and stimulates the provision of consumer goods and services that meet the specific needs of an older population.

Type and Quality of Housing
The individual who lives in an apartment in the core of a city experiences a different lifestyle from the suburban home owner or the farmer. Similarly, in the later years, home owners, age-integrated apartment dwellers, retirement-community residents, senior-citizen (age-segregated) apartment dwellers, and residents of partially or totally institutionalized dwellings will have different lifestyles, and will experience different problems and processes related

to aging. The type of housing in which an older adult lives can greatly influence the frequency, type, and quality of social interaction and the amount of mobility within the community (see highlight 1.3).

Rural/Urban Environments

Since the time of the Industrial Revolution there has been a population shift from rural to urban and suburban areas, although the trend has been reversed somewhat in recent years. One outcome of this migration pattern has been the disruption of the relatively stable and predictable social and cultural patterns that characterized rural lifestyles. Not surprisingly, most studies concerned with this demographic shift have focused on the impact of this migration pattern on the urban milieu (Fischer, 1972, 1975) rather than on the rural milieu (Coward and Lee, 1985; Krout, 1983, 1986; Ryan, 1985; Keating, forthcoming).

Urban sociologists and ecologists have sought to describe the structure, processes, and problems of urban social life. They have been particularly interested in the size, density, and heterogeneity of the urban population; the nature of social interaction and social relations; the similarities and differences within and between urban and suburban areas; and the demographic composition of residential neighborhoods (racial, ethnic, and class differences). They have also examined the impact of a particular social structure on social relations and on crime; and the influence of the physical structure (residential, commercial, and industrial sectors) of the community on interpersonal relations and lifestyles.

On a micro level of analysis, the more tangible characteristics of a neighborhood are also important factors in lifestyle and life satisfaction (Lawton, 1980:37-50). As Lawton (1980:38) notes, 'the neighborhood may be a source of aesthetic enjoyment, physical security, sensory variety, basic resources, help in emergencies, social interaction, interesting things to do, the feeling of territorial pride and many other satisfiers of human needs.' In short, the neighborhood has the potential to provide stability, familiarity, and identification, and, like the place of employment, serves as a central focus for daily social interaction.

Most research studies on the elderly and most social services for the elderly have been concerned with urban residents.[14] As a result, much less attention has been paid to those elderly persons who live on a farm, in a village, in a small town, in a small city, or in the outlying sections of large urban centers. Yet there are a number of special circumstances of living in a nonmetropolitan area that need to be understood, especially given the fact that between 20 and 33 percent of elderly North Americans live in nonmetropolitan centers. Of these, less than 3 percent in Canada actually live on a farm. However, in some villages and towns, as many as 25 to 30 percent of the residents may be over 65 years of age. These environments, negatively referred to as 'geriatric dormitories' (Cape, 1987:85), often include a particularly large proportion of elderly, widowed women.

Given the diversity and size of the elderly rural population, it is important that we acquire a thorough understanding and appreciation of this unique subgroup within the elderly cohort. In general, some elderly residents of rural communities have a disadvantaged status compared to their urban counterparts. Some of these disadvantages include: a lower annual and lifetime income; a lower level of education; less access , if any, to public transportation; less adequate housing in terms of quality, quantity, and options; fewer policies and social services for older adults, and the services, where available, often less accessible because of distance or a lack of transportation; and less awareness or knowledge of available services in nearby larger communities. In addition, although many of the rural elderly report the presence of a strong, informal support network of friends and neighbors, frequently the rural elderly do not have much in-person contact with their children who have moved to urban centers (Krout, 1988). Thus, some rural elderly persons find it difficult to remain independent because formal assistance programs for health and housing needs are seldom available, and these types of needs are seldom met on a long-term basis through an informal network composed of friends and neighbors. This is especially true where the friends and neighbors are also elderly and facing many of the same needs.

One outcome is that elderly persons may

have to be removed from their 'roots' to a larger community when formal services are inadequate or unavailable, or when informal support networks fail to insure continued independence. While interdependency with others is an ideal goal in contrast with total dependency, a situation where the elderly care for the elderly may ultimately not be satisfactory. Quite obviously, there is a need to design specific policies that will provide more complete and accessible services and assistance for the elderly living in various types of rural environments.

In summary, behavior at various stages in the life cycle is a function of the interaction between aging individuals and the social and physical environment. Therefore, you must be alert to differences and similarities in the aging process because of varying physical environments (see chapter 8). Specifically, geographical region, type and quality of housing, and size, density, and composition of the community and neighborhood must be assessed to determine whether these factors have an impact on a particular process or problem associated with aging.

The Influence of Social and Cultural Differentiation

Throughout history, the status and the power of individuals in most societies have been evaluated on the basis of biological or social characteristics such as age, gender, religion, wealth, race, marital status, ethnic background, national origin, education, or occupation. These attributes, which may be either ascribed (such as race) or achieved (such as education), are assigned different values within each culture. They influence the process by which individuals aspire to or are allocated to different social positions within that society. For example, in contemporary North America one is generally evaluated more positively if one is white rather than black, male rather than female, rich rather than poor, young rather than old, and educated rather than uneducated (Tumin, 1967:27).

Once these evaluations of social worth become institutionalized, they lead to the ranking of individuals and to systems of stratification.

The outcome of this process of social differentiation is that some individuals have greater status and receive greater rewards than others. This in turn can lead to inequalities that influence life chances and lifestyle, or to competition and conflict among occupants of the various social strata (O'Rand, 1990).

It would be considerably easier for the scholar to study stratification systems and the aging process if each dimension were a separate entity. However, the social world is more complex than this, and many of these dimensions interact with each other. Thus, although age is the social dimension of major interest in this text, a number of other social variables interact with age to determine who has access to social positions and the accompanying power, prestige, and wealth (Tumin, 1967:39-42). These interactions are especially relevant for our later discussion of social integration, social interaction, social support, and the quality of life in the later years.

The following subsections introduce you to the major stratification systems and illustrate how a number of social categories interact with age to influence both the process of aging and the state of being old. All of these categories are discussed in more detail throughout the book. However, it is important for you to be aware of these interacting factors as you begin to study aging as a social process.

Finally, as noted earlier, there is an age stratification system (an age structure) in which social and chronological age serve as criteria for acquiring or giving up particular positions within social institutions. This age structure influences the pattern of social interaction that evolves within a variety of social systems at different stages in the life cycle. Thus, the reader must recognize that each age cohort comprises a heterogeneous mix of individuals, who vary in economic, racial, ethnic, gender, religious, educational, health, and marital-status dimensions.

Social and Economic Stratification

A society is divided, like a ladder, into a number of distinct social classes or social strata. The number of strata can range from a simple trichotomous division (professionals, white-collar workers, blue-collar workers) to a scale that involves at least six strata (upper class, upper middle class, middle class, lower middle class, upper lower class, and lower class). There appear to be common values, attitudes, behaviors, and a general lifestyle associated with each stratum within the social structure, and these characteristics are often passed from generation to generation.

The system of social stratification, although it does not act independently of the others, tends to have a greater influence than other stratification systems (for example, gender or racial) on life chances and lifestyles at all stages of the life cycle. This occurs primarily because there is inequality among social groups in terms of wealth, prestige, and education.

Although there are often significant differences between age cohorts with respect to values and behavior, differences also exist within each age cohort. Each cohort is a heterogeneous group that includes members with different class, ethnic, racial, and religious backgrounds. As a result of these within-cohort variations in social characteristics, subgroups within each cohort experience different life chances and lifestyles with respect to how they think and behave at various stages in the life cycle (see highlight 1.3).

These differences also influence the chronological age at which major life events occur. Children from an upper-class family who attend a prestigious university or professional school often enter the labor force at a later age, but with greater income and prestige, than the children of a blue-collar worker who may leave high school at age 16 and immediately enter the labor force. Of course, the reverse scenario may also occur, wherein the child of an upper-class family drops out of high school while the child

---

HIGHLIGHT 1.3

CLASS BACKGROUND MATTERS: DIVERSITY IN WIDOWHOOD

The transition to widowhood, itself a traumatic experience, can lead to unforeseen lifestyles because of variations in social class. Mrs. A and Mrs. B are 70 years of age, live in the same city, and have both been widowed for five years. Here the similarities end, partly due to class differences and the concomitant life experiences and opportunities.

Mrs. A is among the invisible poor in society, since, when her husband died, his meager pension benefits were lost. A housewife most of her life, she lacks her own pension, has few savings left, and is totally dependent for her survival on old-age security payments and the guaranteed income supplement. Unable to find employment, she has recently moved from her rented home to a sparsely furnished rooming house. In her small room she cooks, eats, and sleeps, sharing a bathroom with other lodgers. Faced with declining strength and mobility, she finds that the climb to the third floor is becoming more difficult, as is shopping for food and other necessities. Living in a deteriorating neighborhood with a high crime rate, she never ventures out at night. She has become a 'prisoner in her own room' because her children and friends live too far away to provide support and transportation. For Mrs. A the 'golden years' have not materialized. The next transition likely involves a move to a publicly funded, institutionalized setting where, in fact, her quality of life may improve.

In contrast, Mrs. B, having raised her family, entered university at age 50, and then, upon graduation, began a career as a journalist. Now, at age 70, she is constantly seeking new challenges and new adventures. She has written a successful novel and still contributes a weekly column to a number of newspapers. Living in a downtown condominium, she consults her stockbroker weekly, takes tennis lessons three times a week, has a wide circle of female friends, and dates regularly. Her volunteer work at a local elementary school one day a week keeps her in touch with the younger generation, so she is ready for the annual visit of her grandchildren, who live in the West. While she has considered 'wintering' in the South, she prefers to take three or four trips a year to more exotic destinations in Europe or the Far East. She is currently debating whether to trade in her 1987 hatchback for a sportier, faster European or Japanese model. For Mrs. B, widowhood did not represent a loss of economic or social resources. If anything, the transition to singlehood may have given her more freedom and incentive to reap the benefits of the 'golden years.'

from a lower-class family proceeds through university to a successful career in business or a profession. Throughout the adult years the processes associated with aging for these subgroups will vary. Although both groups belong to the same age cohort, the aging process may differ dramatically with respect to life expectancy, incidence of illness, place of residence, adaptation to retirement, economic status, family and friendship interaction, volunteer activity, residential mobility, use of leisure time, and life satisfaction. It is because of this class-based diversity within age cohorts that we need to use more representative samples in gerontology research studies.

Although old age is often characterized by physical, psychological, and social losses, not all individuals suffer these declines or experience them at the same rate. For example, it is commonly believed that one of the major problems of old age is the likelihood of being poor. However, as Henretta and Campbell (1976) noted, the factors that determine retirement income are the same as those that determine income before retirement, namely, education, occupation and marital status. Similarly, Dowd (1980) argues that the lives of the elderly are largely dependent on the relative power resources they retain. While everyone may experience some reduction in salary and some loss of power (status, privilege, prestige) after retirement and thus be disadvantaged compared to younger age cohorts, not all members of a cohort will find themselves in an impoverished state, either immediately or in the long term.

In summary, the process of social stratification influences an individual's access to status, power, and wealth, and hence influences life chances and lifestyle. Although it is frequently noted that the elderly have less status than those in younger age cohorts, if sufficient income is available during retirement, status among age peers will likely be retained.

Racial and Ethnic Stratification

In multicultural societies such as the United States, Canada, South Africa, or Australia, the social structure is also stratified by racial or ethnic background. The division of society into racial or ethnic groups is based on social perceptions or definitions of the relative superiority or status of certain groups. These subcultures are often labeled as **minority groups**, and because of prejudice, stereotyping, and ethnocentrism on the part of the majority group, their members often experience institutionalized discrimination. However, the mere possession of ethnic or racial characteristics does not necessarily imply discrimination. Rather, it is the relative ranking within a society that determines whether a particular group will be viewed as a 'minority' group and thereby experience discrimination.

This discrimination is more likely to come from persons in the groups immediately above them in the ranking structure. This occurs because the lower group may be perceived as a threat to the higher group's relative position in the social structure. Unfortunately, members of many minority groups have fewer opportunities and privileges within a society, because of prejudiced attitudes or overt or subtle discrimination by members of the dominant group.

This process of social ranking by ethnic or racial background can be further complicated by the inevitable relationship between class and racial or ethnic status. Not all members of a minority group have the same levels of education, income, or ability. Gordon (1964) devised the concept of 'ethclass' to refer to a group having a specific ethnic background and class position. For example, in North America, recently arrived upper-class Vietnamese physicians or scientists may have greater social status and opportunities than lower-middle-class blacks. This element of social reality exists despite the fact that blacks in general have a relatively higher ranking than recent Vietnamese immigrants.

Where individuals are located in the ethnic and racial stratification system, both in the past and at present, can have a profound influence on the process of aging and the status of the aged (Manuel, 1982; Murguia et al., 1983; Driedger and Chappell, 1987; Markides and Mindel, 1987; Ujimoto, 1987). In 1981, of the 2.2 million seniors in Canada, about 600,000 reported an ethnic origin other than British or French (Statistics Canada, 1981 census). Unless total structural and cultural **assimilation** occurs, ethnicity remains as an important ascribed factor across the life cycle. For example, it is estimated that about 24 percent of all persons who do not speak English or French are elderly, and that, among seniors, twice as many women as men do not speak French or English (Secretary of State, 1988:22). This means that one's ethnic and racial traditions (such as language, values, beliefs, customs) can influence lifestyles and life chances, especially where ethnic identity is strongly or totally preserved. However, we still know relatively little about the impact of ethnic and racial factors on aging and the aged because most research studies have focused on white Anglo-Saxons. We do know that ethnicity and race can have an influence, along with social class (ethclass), on educational attainment, on where one lives, on housing conditions, on health and disability, on social patterns, on access to and use of social-support services, on economic dependency, and on the informal support provided by members of the extended family. We also know that minority women are at the greatest risk in terms of poverty, dependency, and health problems. This is especially true for women of the first generation in some ethnic and racial groups that immigrated to North America early in the present century.

One outcome of subcultural differences in life chances and lifestyle is that the status of the aged can vary greatly by race, ethnicity, and religion. This is reflected in how the aged view their own position within the minority group and within mainstream society; in how they are treated by their own subgroup; and in how their situation compares to the aged in the dominant group and in other minority groups. Thus, the status of the elderly Jew or Mennonite may be relatively higher than that of the elderly Protestant, while the relative status of the elderly black within his or her own social group may be superior to that of the elderly white because of apparent closer family ties among blacks. Similarly, the status of the elderly person living in Japan is generally superior to that experienced by his or her Japanese age peer living in North America. This occurs because acculturation has led to changes in the values of Japanese living in North America and their perceived obligations to elderly members of the family.

There is considerable interethnic variation or heterogeneity among ethnic groups with respect to aging and the status of aged. This occurs for a variety of reasons, including: the specific year(s) in which members of the group arrived in the new country and what economic and political conditions and opportunities they encountered; the age at which they emigrated and whether they were educated in the host society; the region and the community where they settled — the size, rural or urban, degree of visibility; the willingness or ability to be assimilated into the host society, especially with respect to learning and using the English language by the first and second generation; the degree to which they have experienced discrimination at different stages in the life cycle; and the level of educational attainment pursued by subsequent generations — whether offspring acquired the value systems, beliefs, and customs of the host society, including loss of respect or the sense of obligation to aging parents. Taking into account some of these factors, Driedger and Chappell (1987) identified four 'eth-elder' types found in Canada: Traditional Aboriginal Elderly; Urban Jewish Elderly; European Prairie Farm Elders; and French Charter Minority Elderly (highlight 1.4).

Unfortunately, many social policies and social services are designed for members of the dominant or majority group in a society. For example, studies have shown that elderly persons in some racial or ethnic groups under-utilize social services available in the community (Ujimoto, 1987). This may occur because of lack of knowledge about the availability of services and programs, or because of differences in language, customs, or beliefs that make it difficult for them to use or accept the service, especially within long-term care institutions for the elderly. This suggests that culturally relevant and appropriate policies and services must be developed for a multicultural society, and that members of various ethnic groups must be integrated as employees and volunteers within social and health care settings (highlight 1.5).

In addition to interethnic variations in the status and needs of the elderly, there are also significant intraethnic group variations within some racial and ethnic groups. These differ-

HIGHLIGHT **1.4**

A TYPOLOGY OF ETH-ELDERS

The four eth-elder types vary in place and type of residence, in educational attainment, in type of occupation, in socioeconomic status, in degree of ethnic identity and assimilation, in degree of modernization, in use of mother tongue, and in religion. All seem to retain high status and receive a high degree of social support from members of the family.The traditional aboriginal elderly group is made up of native Indians and Inuit who live in the Far North and remain a primitive, food-gathering society. They have maintained their identity, language, and way of life, and represent the smallest proportion of the elderly in Canada. The urban Jewish elderly constitute the largest proportion of the elderly in Canada. They are highly educated and have been employed in high-status occupations, primarily in Toronto, Montreal, and Winnipeg. They have maintained their ethnic identity around a distinct religion and have not been assimilated into mainstream society to the same extent as European groups. In fact, of all ethnic groups, the Jewish community is known for strongly supporting its elderly members through the provision of community services, homes for the aged, and long-term care facilities.

Between the two extreme types described above, Driedger and Chappell identified two other common types of ethnic-group elders in Canada. The European prairie farm elders emigrated from Britain, Germany, France, the Ukraine, the Netherlands, and Scandinavia. They settled in the West around small villages and towns that became unique and distinct cultural islands (for example, the Hutterite settlements). Now, as elders, many have left the farm to live in a nearby village or town where they are less isolated and have more access to needed services. Many of their children continue to farm nearby and, hence, family ties are strong and informal family support is available. The final type, the elderly of the French Charter minority, primarily live in Quebec, where they have fought to retain their identity. Yet they are living in a francophone society that is experiencing rapid modernization. Many of these elderly persons have moved during their life from a peasant farm to a modernized rural village or to a larger urban center. The following typology illustrates how socioeconomic status, degree of urbanization, and type of eth-elder are interrelated. These factors can have a profound impact on the later-life needs, support, and quality of life of adults from varying ethnic groups.

ETH-ELDER TYPES BY SOCIOECONOMIC STATUS AND DEGREE OF URBANIZATION*

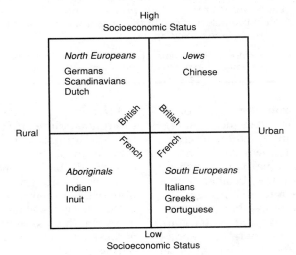

SOURCE: *Reprinted with permission from Driedger and Chappell (1987:95).

HIGHLIGHT 1.5

MULTICULTURAL DIVERSITY IN HEALTH CARE NEEDS

During 1988, members of the Ontario Advisory Council on Senior Citizens travelled throughout Ontario, meeting with over 400 groups and individuals to explore the concerns of seniors from the various ethnic communities. From the findings, an in-depth report entitled *Aging Together: an exploration of attitudes toward aging in multicultural Ontario* was produced. When meeting with these seniors, we learned the important role culture plays in shaping their desires and perceptions about health and health care, and it was evident that a number of very real concerns exist.

Everywhere we visited, seniors told us of the barriers which are created by the lack of awareness and understanding of their needs among members of the health professions. An Italian woman, for example, told us that seniors from their community need "doctors who understand the family situation", adding that most physicians do not understand "the special needs of Italian seniors". Another individual told us that doctors "don't understand how people of different cultures experience pain". A South Asian senior said doctors "don't understand illness with a tropical background". The discomfort felt by Chinese seniors when asked to disrobe in a physician's office was also explained to us.

Because physicians are frequently unaware of cultural preferences and norms which contradict western medical practices, many multicultural seniors are reluctant to go to a North American-trained physician. We are aware that many do not understand Ontario's health-care system and the role physicians play in it. Also many do not fully understand the nature of physician-patient relationships in Ontario, but whose fault is this? Should we not assure that they be given a full explanation *in a language they understand?*

Multicultural seniors typically place a great deal of trust in their physicians, whether or not they understand them. One individual said that many Italian seniors "just say 'yes' to an English-speaking doctor because they don't understand". A health-care professional reported "a tendency to take a medical professional's word at face value". Hence, many multicultural seniors may not receive the care they need.

When visiting physicians ethnic seniors have difficulty in obtaining both language and cultural interpreters. Family interpreters are often seen to be inappropriate, simply because of the personal nature of medical visits. This is especially true when seniors require psychogeriatric services.

One health-care professional told us, "We can't expect (ethnocultural seniors) to accept (North American-trained health-care professionals) until they feel we value their ideas, views and traditions and will listen to them". These words present a blue-print for action. Only by listening and communicating can we fulfil the implied promise made to individuals from diverse ethnocultural backgrounds when we welcomed them as part of the Canadian mosaic.

SOURCE: Written by Mrs. I. St. Lawrence as a guest editorial for the Ontario Gerontology Association *Bulletin/ Newsletter* (September 1989), and reprinted with permission.

---

ences primarily derive from the degree of assimilation experienced by subsequent generations. As members of subsequent generations become more acculturated within the mainstream society, the traditional values, beliefs, and customs of the group may be abandoned. For example, there are four distinct generational groups among Japanese-North Americans: the Issei (first or immigrant generation); the Nisei (second generation, born in Canada); the Sansei (third generation); and the Yonsei (fourth generation). Each generation has been socialized at a different period in history and in

a different social environment with respect to discrimination against the Japanese and in terms of social opportunities (Ujimoto, 1987). Perhaps the most obvious change has been the loss of the traditional Japanese value of **filial piety**, whereby children have a filial duty or obligation to honor their parents and to care for them in the later years of life. Ujimoto (1987:116-117) notes that this loss of filial piety may also occur because of such social structural changes as multigenerational families, in which it becomes difficult for elderly offspring to support very old parents, and because of the availability of a social-welfare system which provides more formal support to the frail elderly. However, many long-term care institutions are not designed to serve members of an ethnic group who have specific language, food, cultural, and health care needs.

Among recent immigrants, a large number (more than 6,000 per year, or 4 to 6 percent of all immigration) are elderly parents who arrive in Canada to be reunited with their adult children. These elderly persons are often widowed, and are more likely to be women than men, although the male-female ratio varies by country (Secretary of State, 1988:44). Many leave lifelong roots in a familiar neighborhood or village for a foreign culture, a different value system, and, frequently, entrance into a family lifestyle that is foreign to their way of thinking. They are too old to learn English and because of language difficulties they may not be able to communicate with their grandchildren. They may become housebound and totally dependent on their offspring for survival and mobility in the community. Many are unable to understand their children's busy 'western' way of life, they feel isolated and abandoned in their adult child's home, and the older men, especially, feel they lack the traditional power and status held by a family patriarch in the home country. The older women in this group are often lonely and emotionally starved. If their child lives in the heart of an ethnic community, they may find companionship by walking to a nearby ethnic club; but if the adult child lives in the suburbs, they are much more likely to be isolated, housebound, and lonely. Not surprisingly, a number often decide, with the willing agreement of their 'foreign' children, to return to their homeland after a few years of exile in their child's adopted homeland.

In summary, the process of ethnic and racial stratification in multicultural or pluralistic societies influences the process of aging and the status of the aged. This variation occurs because of the relative ranking of the minority group and the extent to which a particular group or generation adheres to subcultural values. As you study social gerontology, be aware that the stratification process may vary by racial and ethnic groups within and between societies.

Gender Stratification

As our population is aging, women constitute an increasingly larger percentage, especially among the elderly. Figure 1.2 illustrates the widening numerical imbalance between men and women. Recent demographic evidence documents that women live longer than men and that at the older ages women have a greater likelihood of surviving (McDaniel, 1986; Gee and Kimball, 1987). Indeed, today, women over 85 outnumber men by 2:1, a ratio that is predicted to rise slightly until it levels off early in the twenty-first century. This demographic shift in the sex structure of modern societies is partly the result of migration (more females have migrated to North America in recent years), but is mainly the result of a substantially greater life expectancy for females. This gender advantage in life expectancy has increased from about two years in 1931 to the current difference of seven years (73 for men, 80 for women). In addition, because women tend to marry older men and because divorce rates are increasing, approximately 85 percent of elderly women will experience being single and old at some point in the later years (Olson, 1988). This status is often reached (for example, at widowhood) at a time when they are most likely to become more dependent on others.

Given these statistics, aging is clearly a women's issue. This conclusion becomes even more compelling when we discuss such age- and gender-related issues as widowhood, poverty, health status, elder abuse, housing needs, institutionalization, crime, drug use, sexuality, the empty nest, caregiving via informal and formal support, and myths and stereotypes about aging and the aged. While it is relatively easy to describe and analyze **sex** differences in males and females as they age, it is much more difficult to analyze **gender** differences that derive from the socially determined attributes linked to the social roles of men and women. Gender represents a social definition according to which, traditionally but not legally, males have been ranked as superior.[15] This societal definition has resulted in gender inequality whereby females are often, if not always, excluded from full participation (LaFontaine, 1978). As a result, women are perceived

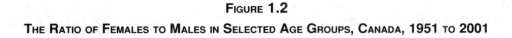

FIGURE **1.2**

THE RATIO OF FEMALES TO MALES IN SELECTED AGE GROUPS, CANADA, 1951 TO 2001

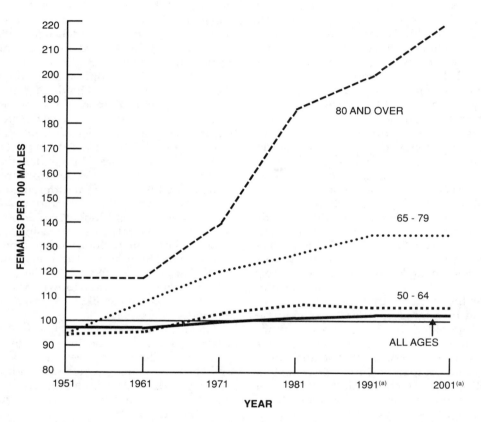

ª The "high-growth" scenario here, in fact, is based on a growth rate just above replacement level. This is a much lower rate
  of growth than occured in Canada during the Depression years.

SOURCE: Reprinted with permission from McDaniel (1986:109).
ORIGINAL SOURCE: Canada. 1983. *Fact Book on Aging in Canada*. Ottawa: Minister of Supply and Services Canada. p.21.
          Reproduced with the permission of the Minister of Supply and Services Canada, 1990.

to lack social, economic, and political power, and thereby occupy a secondary status in a group, institution, or society.

The status of older women is often even lower because they experience 'double jeopardy' — they are old and they are female. This discriminatory situation can be magnified where sexist attitudes are present (for example, older women are asexual) or where policies favor males (for example, some private pension plans do not include survivor benefits, so that a widow loses the pension benefits accruing to her spouse when he dies). Is it any wonder that some very elderly women are dependent and poor? Furthermore, how women adapt in the later years is often related to their gender-role socialization experiences and to the extent that they have experienced institutionalized discrimination. Problems related to health, housing, income, or social support that are encountered early in life may become exaggerated as women age (Olson, 1988). This in turn may place an added burden on the daughters or daughters-in-law who, perhaps burdened themselves, must provide care for an aging woman of the previous generation. This situation is especially pronounced among black females in the United States, where poverty and single-parenting are more likely to be present.

Although a definitive explanation for the existence and continuation of gender stratification is lacking, some insight can be gained by examining the following models and by considering the process of gender-role identification and socialization. Eichler (1973) suggested that three models can assist in understanding the phenomenon of gender stratification. The first suggests that women comprise a social caste. As a result, they are denied mobility because of an ascribed attribute (being female). The basic assumption of this model is that women are less valued in the labor market. However, Eichler argues that there are many exceptions to the caste rules with respect to the female role. For example, women do not socially avoid outsiders (males); they can be socially mobile when they marry outside their own class; and there are differences in social ranking among women that are as great as those between men and women. Furthermore, some women have higher status and higher skill levels than some men. Because there are many exceptions to this model, gender stratification should not be viewed as a caste system.

A second model considers women to be members of a minority group that experiences economic and psychological disadvantages emanating from a power struggle between the sexes. Eichler suggests that this model also fails to fit social reality, since these conditions should lead to the formation of 'gender consciousness,' which in turn should lead to social conflict and social change. Certainly, the feminist movement of the 1970s and 1980s has raised the consciousness of many women, young and old. Whether there has been significant and permanent social change remains to be seen. However, given that the feminist movement has begun to address some of the concerns of this

age group, significant change may be expected in the years ahead (Cohen, 1984; Lesnoff-Caravaglia, 1984; Bell, 1986; Dulude, 1987).

The third model suggests that women constitute a unique class based on their ability to compete in the labor market. In fact, early in the twentieth century sex status became the basis for a classlike struggle for equal rights that continues today. Eichler criticizes this view, however, because it does not distinguish between employed and unemployed women. She further argues that this model is not adequate to explain gender differences: there is a double standard of evaluation by which women as a group are divided into two categories — those who are economically independent (the employed), and those who are not (the unemployed or the housewife).

The system of gender stratification and its consequent inequality are perpetuated through the gender-role socialization process. Gender identification usually begins at birth, since a child's significant others compulsively attempt to 'make a girl a girl and a boy a boy.' Each society has definite ideas about what constitutes appropriate male and female behavior. These ideas can even vary significantly within a society by social class, ethnicity, or region.

Throughout this book reference will be made to research that substantiates the existence of gender differences in the process of aging or in the status of the aged. However, it should be noted that while there has been a considerable increase in our knowledge about women and aging,[16] myths and stereotypes still abound. This is not surprising, since women have seldom been the subject of study in most scientific disciplines. Moreover, much of our knowledge is still based on generalizations or inferences drawn from studies of males. That is, male behavior and experiences are considered the norm, and women are inferred to be different (Burwell, 1984).

In connection with aging, the following situations merit special research and policy attention with respect to women: (1) because women have generally been excluded from full participation in society, they are dependent on men and may therefore lack the power to change this status; (2) a woman's social status has traditionally been derived from her father and later her husband; (3) aging in women is often characterized by role losses — the children leave home, the woman retires, she loses her physical attractiveness and is stigmatized (Posner, 1980), and her spouse and friends die; (4) aging women experience discrimination because of a double standard (Sontag, 1975); and (5) there are class, racial, and ethnic variations among women in their adaptation to the aging process. Unfortunately, the aging woman is sometimes depicted in the media as asexual, physically obsolete, a widow, uneducated, and poor. Yet, not all older women live in poverty and isolation, as any travel agent will verify! Moreover, most elderly women cope reasonably well, perhaps because of strong family and friendship ties (Gee and Kimball, 1987; Connidis, 1989).

Finally, like the total population of older adults, older women are not a homogeneous group. Rather, the population of older women at present, and perhaps even more so in the future, comprises and will comprise subgroups that vary by age, education, income, ethnicity, social status, and marital status. For example, there may be significant differences in the social situation of women who are 60 to 75, 75 to 84, or 85 and older (Chappell and Havens, 1980). While older females clearly constitute an ever-increasing majority of the elderly population, not all women experience the dual stigmatization of being both old *and* female — the 'double-jeopardy' phenomenon. However, some may experience triple jeopardy (being old, female, and poor) or multiple jeopardy (being old, female, poor, and a member of a disadvantaged minority group). In short, as with most other aspects of aging, a description of ideal, generalized patterns of aging by gender should be avoided. In this way stereotypes concerning the process of aging in women are less likely to be perpetuated.

Education, Religion, and Marital Status

These elements do not constitute a stratification system per se either alone or in combination. However, they do represent three additional social factors that must be considered in the study of the aging process and of the status of the middle-aged and elderly person. The av-

erage amount of formal education attained by each successive birth cohort is increasing, especially for women and members of minority groups. The current middle-aged and elderly segments of the population have attained higher levels of formal education than previous generations, but less than later generations will attain. Since education influences both income and lifestyle, changes in the level of educational attainment for an individual or cohort can have a subsequent influence on the style and quality of life in the later years. Specifically, levels of educational attainment have been found to be positively correlated with such factors as type of occupation, income, health, values, attitudes, a positive self-concept, life satisfaction, longevity, and adjustment to retirement. Education does not cause any of these events or characteristics, but it does provide an opportunity set by which a particular lifestyle is more likely to be adopted. For example, persons with college degrees are more likely to spend their leisure time reading, studying, joining clubs, doing volunteer work, attending concerts, and playing or watching sports. Thus, the educational background of subjects used in gerontology studies should be carefully considered; the university-educated retiree will probably adapt to retirement differently from the retiree who left school at age 16 and remained a blue-collar worker.

Religious affiliation and degree of religious involvement or commitment also influence to some extent the process and the product of aging. Much of this influence derives from the tenets and philosophy of a particular religion and the effects these have on an individual's lifestyle. Religion also influences attitudes toward and the status of the aged. For example, religious groups such as the Jews, Mennonites, Hutterites, and Amish in North America adhere to the belief that high-quality care for the elderly is a right. It is interesting to note that the latter three groups live in unique rural subcultures outside mainstream society.

Marital status is another influential factor in the aging process. Whether one is never-married, married, separated, divorced, remarried, or widowed influences daily life throughout the life cycle (Connidis, 1989). One's economic status, interaction with family and friends, degree of social isolation, mobility, availability of health care, and leisure activities are all affected to some extent by marital status. In most instances the lifestyle of the married 30-year-old is different from that of the single 30-year-old, just as the economic status of the still-married 65-year-old female is generally better than that of her widowed age peer. When one analyzes the aging process and compares individuals of a particular age cohort, variations in marital status should be considered as a possible factor in explaining life chances and lifestyles.

In summary, the elderly population represents a heterogeneous group of individuals with a variety of personal characteristics, social attributes, and lifelong experiences. It is important that you remember this diversity as you study the aging process, as you work directly with older adults, or as you design and implement policies or programs for those in the later years of life.

SUMMARY AND CONCLUSIONS

In this introductory chapter you have been introduced to the concept of aging as a social process influenced by the social and age structures of society, by a variety of social processes, and by social, political, and economic change within a given culture or subculture. These factors have an influence on both individual and population aging, and they interact with other factors that are more closely related to biological and psychological aging.

You have been alerted, as well, to the prevalence of myths concerning aging and the aged; to the difference between aging, cohort, and historical effects; to a number of methodological and theoretical matters that must be considered in the interpretation of research findings; and to cross-cultural and subcultural variations in the aging process, particularly with respect to the treatment and status of the elderly. In addition, this chapter has discussed briefly a number of demographic, sociocultural, and environmental factors, and some major stratification systems that influence the aging process. All of these parameters are discussed in more detail throughout this book. Finally, the chapter provides a brief descriptive and analytical discussion of the historical development of the field of social gerontology.

Based on the information presented in this chapter, it can be concluded that:

1. Chronological aging represents only an approximate measure of the normative development or changes within an individual or age cohort. There is great variation in physical, emotional, social, and psychological development within and between individuals. The chronological aging of an individual interacts with a societal history, with a personal history, and with a number of sociodemographic factors (such as class, gender, ethnicity, education, place of residence).

2. Functional aging is a more accurate measure of aging, since individual differences by age are considered. Functional aging reflects the relationship between biological maturation or deterioration and how well, if at all, an individual can adapt and perform specific physical, social, or cognitive tasks.

3. Psychological aging involves the reaction to biological, cognitive, sensory, motor, emotional, and behavioral changes within an individual, as well as the reaction to external environmental factors that influence behavior and lifestyle.

4. Social aging involves patterns of interaction between the aging individual and the social structure. Many social positions are related to chronological age, and individuals are expected to conform to the age-based norms associated with these positions. Social aging is also influenced by the size and composition of the social structure as it changes over time, by change within a society, and by cultural and subcultural variations in attitudes toward aging and the aged.

5. A number of unsubstantiated beliefs about aging and the aged are accepted as fact. These myths may influence the

behavior and expectations of aging individuals, as well as the attitudes of younger people toward older people, especially those outside the kinship system.

6. Aging as a social process can be studied on three levels of analysis: the 'individual' level (the micro level), which is concerned with age changes within individuals and age differences between groups of individuals; the 'social system' level (the macro level), which is concerned with the influence of the social structure on the aging individual and the influence of various social processes on aging individuals or age cohorts; and the 'comparative' level, which attempts to explain aging by searching for cultural or subcultural variations or similarities within or between societies.

7. Age differences between individuals or cohorts can be inferred from cross-sectional research studies, whereas changes with age may be inferred from a longitudinal study. Cohort analysis may be used to infer age changes and age differences.

8. The aging process is influenced by elements in the physical environment such as geographical region, the type and quality of housing and neighborhood, and rural or urban residence.

9. Ascribed or achieved attributes of an individual (gender, race, religion, education, income, class, marital status, ethnicity) influence life chances and lifestyle, and are important factors in the analysis of aging as a social process. These attributes acquire different social meanings or values within different cultures and at different points in the life cycle.

10. The evaluation of these attributes by means of social differentiation creates class, racial, ethnic, and gender stratification systems in many societies. These systems interact with age to influence both the process of aging and the status of being old. Individuals located near the least-valued end of these various stratification systems may be disadvantaged (blacks, females) throughout life, and may experience increased discrimination, segregation, or isolation as they age.

NOTES

1. For example, the average life span in early Greek and Roman societies was 20 to 40 years (Goldscheider, 1971).

2. Ironically, Ponce de León, while searching for the Fountain of Youth in the year 1513, discovered the coast of Florida. This state has one of the highest percentages of elderly residents and has become a popular retirement haven. While neither a potion nor a fountain has ever been discovered, contemporary North Americans still pursue their cosmetic and physiological dreams of eternal youth through the use of wrinkle creams, hair coloring, health spas, cosmetic surgery, and a variety of nutrient products.

3. These involve a loss at retirement of social status, identity, and power; and the loss of friends and spouse through retirement, separation, divorce, or death.

4. Some unique social, economic, and historical events that have had an impact on the aging process and the status of the elderly include the Depression of the 1930s, World Wars I and II, urbanization, the immigration and migration of young people, the 'baby boom' of the late 1940s and early 1950s, a declining birthrate, and greater life expectancy. Some present and future factors include double-digit inflation, high rates of unemployment among those under 25, the need to retain the older worker in the labor force, the advent of automation in industry, computer-induced unemployment, the birth-control pill, the abolishment of mandatory retirement, and the feminist movement.

5. Conflict between age groups has led to the increasing use of the label 'gray power' as more and more senior citizens and preretirement adults seek to improve their position by lobbying for changes in laws and social policies.

6. The changes, although usually thought to involve losses, can be positive. For example, gray hair may be seen as a sign of distinction; retirement, which is often feared as a period of economic hardship, can be a rewarding experience that provides the opportunity to acquire new knowledge, skills, and friends. While changes are inevitable, whether they are viewed

as positive or negative depends on the perception of the individual and the reaction of others in society.

7. Chapter 5 discusses the relationship between changes in the physical system and how the individual adapts to changing social and physical environments.

8. The correct responses are 1-F; 2-F; 3-T; 4-F; 5-F; 6-T; 7-T; 8-F; 9-F; 10-F.

9. There is, in fact, a real paucity of information about the middle years, other than that which pertains to such phenomena as the 'midlife crisis' (which may be a myth), the change of careers in midlife, the reaction of women to the 'empty nest' after their children leave home, the reentry of women into the labor force, and the onset of a decline in physical and mental energy (Borland, 1978; Tamir, 1982).

10. The student who is intrigued with the historical development of this field should read the following works as well as the classical studies and books that are cited in this overview: Adler, 1958; Birren, 1959; Gruman, 1966; Streib and Orbach, 1967; Shanas, 1971; Birren and Clayton, 1975; Binstock and Shanas, 1976:4-34; Riegel, 1977; Freeman, 1979; Oliver and Eckerman, 1979; Achenbaum, 1987a, b; Achenbaum and Levin, 1989; Morris, 1989; and Streib and Binstock, 1990.

11. However, gerontology programs and research are still highly dependent on the traditional disciplines of biology, psychology, and sociology. Thus, a totally separate and discrete professional identity may never develop.

12. Four sections are included within the Gerontological Society of America. The *biological sciences* section is for scientists interested in the aging of animals and plants, the senescence of isolate cells in culture, the evolutionary aspects of life-span limitation, and in the biochemical, structural, and functional aspects of aging biological systems. The *clinical medicine* section is for professionals (physicians, dentists, nurses) engaged in clinical research, education, or treatment relating to aging patients. The *behavioral and social sciences* section is for research scientists, educators, and practitioners in such fields as psychology, sociology, anthropology, ecology, economics, and political science. The *social research, planning, and practice section* is for researchers, educators, and practitioners in the human-service field. Members include social workers, social planners, directors of facilities and service programs, public administrators, policymakers, and environmental designers and planners. The Canadian Association on Gerontology includes the following sections: biological sciences, health sciences, social sciences, psychological sciences, and social welfare and practice.

13. See *The Gerontologist*, no. 5, each year for the program of the annual meeting of the Gerontological Society of America, as well as the annual index in the numerous journals listed in the Preface of this book. In Canada, the Fall *Newsletter* of the Canadian Association on Gerontology includes the program and abstracts for the annual scientific and educational meeting. Areco's *Quarterly Index to Periodical Literature on Aging* is also a useful resource, as is *Abstracts in Social Gerontology* (March, 1990-).

14. The student who is interested in the structure and processes of social life in rural environments should consult the journal *Rural Sociology*. However, even here there are few studies pertaining to aging or the aged. Similarly, while many introductory sociology textbooks include a chapter on urban or rural sociology, aging in a rural setting is seldom discussed.

15. One explanation for this devalued female status is that the female role, as traditionally viewed, does not reflect the highly valued (by males!) attributes of achievement, aggressiveness, competitiveness, independence, and productivity.

16. See Barnett and Baruch, 1978; Dulude, 1978, 1981; Matthews, 1979; Seltzer, 1979; Abu-Laban and Abu-Laban, 1980; Block et al., 1980; Fuller and Martin, 1980; Holahan, 1981; Troll, 1981; Markson, 1983; Rossi, 1984, 1986; Gee, 1986; Sinnott, 1986; Cape, 1987; Gee and Kimball, 1987; Olson, 1988; Connidis, 1989; Grambs, 1989; McDaniel, 1989; Seniors Secretariat, 1989; Huyck, 1990.

REFERENCES

Abu-Laban, S. and B. Abu-Laban. (1980). 'Women and the Aged as Minority Groups: A Critique,' pp. 63-79 in V. Marshall (ed.). *Aging in Canada: Social Perspectives*. Don Mills, Ont.: Fitzhenry and Whiteside.

Achenbaum, A. (1987a). 'Can Gerontology be a Science?' *Journal of Aging Studies*, 1(1), 3-18.

Achenbaum, A. (1987b). 'Reconstructing GSA's History,' *The Gerontologist*, 27(1), 21-29.

Achenbaum, A. and J. Levin. (1989). 'What Does Gerontology Mean?' *The Gerontolgist*, 29(3), 393-400.

Adler, M. (1958). 'History of the Gerontological Society,' *Journal of Gerontology*, 13(2), 94-100.

Atchley, R. (1972). *The Social Forces in Later Life*. 1st ed. Belmont, Calif.: Wadsworth Publishing Co.

Barnett, R. and G. Baruch. (1978). 'Women in the

Middle Years: A Critique of Research and Theory,' *Psychology of Women Quarterly*, 3(2), 187-97.

Bell, M. (1986). *Women as Elders: Images, Visions, and Issues*. New York: Haworth Press.

Benet, S. (1974). *Abkhasia: The Long-Living People of the Caucasus*. New York: Holt, Rinehart & Winston.

Binstock, R. and E. Shanas (eds.). (1976). *Handbook of Aging and the Social Sciences*. New York: Van Nostrand Reinhold.

Binstock, R. and E. Shanas (eds.). (1985). *Handbook of Aging and the Social Sciences*. 2d ed. New York: Van Nostrand Reinhold.

Birren, J. (ed.). (1959). *Handbook of Aging and the Individual:Psychological and Biological Aspects*. Chicago: University of Chicago Press.

Birren, J. and V. Clayton. (1975). 'History of Gerontology,' pp. 15 - 27 in D. Woodruff and J. Birren (eds.). *Aging: Scientific Perspectives and Social Issues*. New York: Van Nostrand Reinhold.

Birren, J. and W. Schaie (eds.). (1977). *Handbook of the Psychology of Aging*. New York: Van Nostrand Reinhold.

Birren, J. and W. Schaie (eds.). (1985). *Handbook of the Psychology of Aging*. 2d ed. New York: Van Nostrand Reinhold.

Birren, J. and W. Schaie (eds.). (1990). *Handbook of the Psychology of Aging*. 3d ed. San Diego, Calif.: Academic Press.

Block, M. et al. (1980). *Women over Forty: Visions and Realities*. New York: Springer Publishing Co.

Borland, D. (1978). 'Research on Middle Age: An Assessment,' *The Gerontologist*, 18(4), 379-86.

Burgess, E. (ed.). (1960). *Aging in Western Societies*. Chicago: University of Chicago Press.

Burwell, E. (1984). 'Sexism in Social Science Research on Aging,' pp. 185-205 in J. Vickers (ed.). *Taking Sex into Account: The Policy Consequences of Sexist Research*. Ottawa: Carleton University Press.

Cain, L. (ed.). (1959). 'The Sociology of Aging: A Trend Report and Bibliography,' *Current Sociology*, 8(2), 57-133.

Cain, L. (1976). 'Aging and the Law,' pp. 342-68 in R. Binstock and E.Shanas (eds.). *Handbook of Aging and the Social Sciences*. New York: Van Nostrand Reinhold.

Cape, E. (1987). 'Aging Women in Rural Settings,' pp. 84-99 in V. Marshall (ed.). *Aging in Canada: Social Perspectives*. Markham, Ont.: Fitzhenry and Whiteside.

Chappell, N. and B. Havens. (1980). 'Old and Female: Testing the Double Jeopardy Hypothesis,' *The Sociological Quarterly*, 21(2), 157-71.

Chappell, N. et al. (1986). *Aging and Health Care: A Social Perspective*. Toronto: Holt, Rinehart & Winston.

Chen, A. (1939). 'Social Significance of Old Age,' *Sociology and Social Research*, 23(July-August), 519-27.

Cohen, L. (1984). *Small Expectations: Society's Betrayal of Older Women*. Toronto: McClelland and Stewart.

Connidis, I. (1981). 'The Stigmatizing Effects of a Problem Orientation to Aging Research,' *Canadian Journal of Social Work Education*, 7(2), 9-19.

Connidis, I. (1989). *Family Ties and Aging*. Toronto: Butterworths.

Cottrell, L. (1942). 'The Adjustment of the Individual to His Age and Sex Roles,' *American Sociological Review*, 7(5), 617-20.

Coward, R.T. and G.R. Lee (eds.). (1985). *The Elderly in Rural Society: Every Fourth Elder*. New York: Springer Publishing Co.

Cowdry, E. (ed.). (1939). *Problems of Aging*. Baltimore: William and Wilkins.

Cowgill, D. (1981). 'Aging in Comparative Cultural Perspective,' *Mid-American Review of Sociology*, 7(2), 1-28.

Cowgill, D. (1986). *Aging around the World*. Belmont, Calif.: Wadsworth Publishing Co.

Cowgill, D. and L. Holmes (eds.). (1972). *Aging and Modernization*. New York: Appleton-Century-Crofts.

Cumming, E. and W. Henry. (1961). *Growing Old: The Process of Disengagement*. New York: Basic Books.

Dannefer, D. (1983). 'Sociology of the Life Course,' in R. Turner (ed.). *Annual Review of Sociology*. vol. 9. Palo Alto, Calif.: Annual Reviews, Inc.

Dannefer, D. (1988). 'Differential Gerontology and the Stratified Life Course: Conceptual and Methodological Issues,' pp. 3-36 in G. Maddox and P. Lawton (eds.). *Annual Review of Gerontology and Geriatrics*. vol. 8. New York: Springer Publishing Co.

Dowd, J. (1980). *Stratification among the Aged*. Monterey: Brooks/Cole Publishing Co.

Driedger, L. and N. Chappell. (1987). *Aging and Ethnicity: Toward an Interface*. Toronto: Butterworths.

Dulude, L. (1978). *Women and Aging: A Report on the Rest of Our Lives*. Ottawa: Canadian Advisory Council on the Status of Women.

Dulude, L. (1981). *Pension Reform with Women in Mind*. Ottawa: Canadian Advisory Council on the Status of Women.

Dulude, L. (1987). 'Getting Old: Men in Couples and Women Alone,' pp. 323-39 in G. Hofmann Neimiroff (ed.). *Women and Men: Interdisciplinary Readings on Gender*. Toronto: Fitzhenry and Whiteside.

Eglit, H. (1985). 'Age and the Law,' pp. 528-53 in R. Binstock and E. Shanas (eds.). *Handbook of Aging and the Social Sciences*. 2d ed. New York: Van Nostrand Reinhold.

Eichler, M. (1973). 'Women as Personal Dependents,' pp. 36-55 in M. Stephenson (ed.). *Women in Canada*. Toronto: New Press.

Elder, G. (1975). 'Age Differentiation and the Life Course,' pp. 165-90 in A. Inkeles et al. (eds.). *Annual Review of Sociology*. vol. 1. Palo Alto, Calif.: Annual Reviews, Inc.

Elder, G. and J. Liker. (1982). 'Hard Times in Women's Lives: Historical Influences across Forty Years,' *American Journal of Sociology*, 88(2), 241-69.

Epstein, A. (1922). *Facing Old Age: A Study of Old Age Dependency in the United States and Old Age Pensions*. New York: Alfred A. Knopf.

Fennell, G. et al. (1988). *The Sociology of Old Age*. Philadelphia: Open University Press.

Finch, C. and L. Hayflick (eds.). (1977). *Handbook of the Biology of Aging*. New York: Van Nostrand Reinhold.

Finch, C. and E. Schneider (eds.). (1985). *Handbook of the Biology of Aging*. 2d ed. New York: Van Nostrand Reinhold.

Fischer, C. (1972). 'Urbanism as a Way of Life: A Review and an Agenda,' *Sociological Methods and Research*, 1(2), 187-242.

Fischer, C. (1975). 'The Study of Urban Community and Personality,' pp. 67-90 in A. Inkeles et al. (eds.). *Annual Review of Sociology*. vol. 1. Palo Alto, Calif.: Annual Reviews, Inc.

Foner, N. (1984). *Ages in Conflict: A Cross-Cultural Perspective on Inequality between Old and Young*. Irvington, N.Y.: Columbia University Press.

Forbes, W. et al. (1987). *Institutionalization of the Elderly in Canada*. Toronto: Butterworths.

Freeman, J. (1979). *Aging: Its History and Literature*. New York: Human Sciences Press.

Fry, C. (1980). 'Cultural Dimensions of Age: A Multidimensional Scaling Analysis,' pp. 42-64 in C. Fry (ed.). *Aging in Culture and Society: Comparative Viewpoints and Strategies*. New York: Praeger Publishers.

Fuller, M. and C. Martin (eds.). (1980). *The Older Woman: Lavender Rose or Gray Panther*. Springfield, Ill.: Charles C. Thomas.

Gee, E. (1986). 'The Life Course of Canadian Women: An Historical and Demographic Analysis,' *Social Indicators Research*, 18, 263-83.

Gee, E. and M. Kimball. (1987). *Women and Aging*. Toronto: Butterworths.

Goldscheider, C. (1971). *Population, Modernization and Social Structure*. Boston: Little Brown & Co.

Gordon, M. (1964). *Assimilation in American Life*. New York: Oxford University Press.

Grambs, J. (ed.). (1989) *Women over Forty: Visions and Realities*. New York: Springer Publishing Co.

Gruman, G. (1966). *A History of Ideas about the Prolongation of Life: The Evolution of Prolongevity Hypothesis to 1800*. Philadelphia: American Philosophical Society.

Gutmann, D. (1977). 'The Cross-Cultural Perspective: Notes toward a Comparative Psychology of Aging,' pp. 302-26 in J. Birren and W. Schaie (eds.). *Handbook of the Psychology of Aging*. New York: Van Nostrand Reinhold.

Hall, G.S. (1922). *Senescence, the Second Half of Life*. New York: Appleton.

Hareven, T. and K. Adams. (1982). *Aging and Life Course Transitions: An Interdisciplinary Perspective*. New York: Guilford Press.

Harris, D. (ed.). (1988). *Dictionary of Gerontology*. New York: Greenwood Press.

Havighurst, R. and R. Albrecht. (1953). *Older People*. New York: Longmans, Green.

Havighurst, R. et al. (1969). *Adjustment to Retirement: A Cross-National Study*. Assen, the Netherlands: Van Gorcum.

Henretta, J. and R. Campbell. (1976). 'Status Attainment and Status Maintenance: A Study of Stratification in Old Age,' *American Sociological Review*, 41(6), 981-92.

Holahan, C. (1981). 'Lifetime Achievement Patterns, Retirement and Life Satisfaction of Gifted Aged Women,' *Journal of Gerontology*, 36(6), 741-49.

Holmes, L. (1983). *Other Cultures, Elder Years: An Introduction to Cultural Anthropology*. Minneapolis, Minn.: Burgess Publishing Company.

Huyck, M. (1990). 'Gender Differences in Aging,' pp. 124-33 in J. Birren and W. Schaie (eds.). *Handbook of the Psychology of Aging*. 3d ed. San Diego, Calif.: Academic Press.

Keating, N. (forthcoming). *Aging in Rural Canada*. Markham, Ont.: Butterworths.

Kebric, R. (1983). 'Aging in Pliny's Letters: A View from the Second Century A.D.,' *The Gerontologist*, 23(5), 538-45.

Kebric, R. (1988). 'Old Age, the Ancient Military, and Alexander's Army: Positive Examples for a Graying America,' *The Gerontologist*, 28(3), 298-302.

Keith, J. (1980). 'The Best is Yet to Be: Toward an Anthropology of Age,' *Annual Review of Anthropology*, 9, 339-64.

Keith, J. (1990). 'Age in Social and Cultural Context,' pp. 91-111 in R. Binstock and L. George (eds.). *Handbook of Aging and the Social Sciences*. 3d ed. San Diego, Calif.: Academic Press.

Kertzer, D. and J. Keith (eds.). (1984). *Age and Anthropological Theory*. Ithaca, N.Y.: Cornell University Press.

Kiesler, S. et al. (eds.). (1981). *Aging: Social Change*. New York: Academic Press.

Krout, J. (1983). *The Rural Elderly: An Annotated Bibliography of Social Science Research.* Westport, Conn.: Greenwood Press.

Krout, J. (1986). *The Aged in Rural America.* New York: Greenwood Press.

Krout, J. (1988). 'Rural vs. Urban Differences in Elderly Parents' Contact with Their Children,' *The Gerontologist*, 28(2), 198-203.

LaFontaine, J.S. (ed.). (1978). *Sex and Age as Principles of Social Differentiation.* New York: Academic Press.

Landis, J. (1940) 'Attitudes and Adjustment of Aged Rural People in Iowa,' Ph.D. thesis, Louisiana State University.

Lawton, M.P. (1980). *Environment and Aging.* Monterey: Brooks/Cole Publishing Co.

Leaf, A. (1975). *Youth in Old Age.* New York: McGraw-Hill.

Lesnoff-Caravaglia, G. (ed.). (1984). *The World of the Older Woman: Conflicts and Resolutions.* vol. 3, Frontiers in Aging Series, New York: Human Sciences Press.

Linton, R. (1936). *The Study of Man.* New York: Appleton-Century-Crofts.

Linton, R. (1942). 'Age and Sex Categories,' *American Sociological Review*, 7(5), 589-603.

Longino, C. and J. Biggar. (1982). 'The Impact of Population Redistribution on Service Delivery,' *The Gerontologist*, 22(2), 153-59.

Lyell, R. (ed.). (1980). *Middle Age, Old Age: Short Stories, Poems, Plays and Essays on Aging.* New York: Harcourt Brace Jovanovich.

Maddox G. and M.P. Lawton. (1988). *Annual Review of Gerontology and Geriatrics.* vol. 8. New York: Springer Publishing Co.

Maddox, G. et al (eds.) (1987). *The Encyclopedia of Aging.* New York: Springer Publishing Co.

Manuel, R. (ed.). (1982). *Minority Aging: Sociological and Social Psychological Issues.* Westport, Conn.: Greenwood Press.

Markides, K. and C. Mindel. (1987). *Aging and Ethnicity.* Beverley Hills, Calif.: Sage Publications.

Markson, E. (ed.). (1983). *Older Women: Issues and Prospects.* Lexington, Mass.: Lexington Books.

Marshall, V. (ed.). (1980). *Aging in Canada: Social Perspectives.* Don Mills, Ont.: Fitzhenry and Whiteside.

Martin Matthews, M. et al. (1984) 'The Facts on Aging Quiz: A Canadian Validation and Cross-Cultural Comparison,' *Canadian Journal on Aging*, 3(4), 165-74.

Matthews, S. (1979). *The Social World of Old Women: Management of Self-Identity.* Beverly Hills, Calif.: Sage Publications.

Mazess, R. and S. Forman. (1979). 'Longevity and Age Exaggeration in Vilcabamba, Ecuador,' *Journal of Gerontology*, 34(1), 94-98.

McDaniel, S. (1986). *Canada's Aging Population.* Toronto: Butterworths.

McDaniel, S. (1989). 'Women and Aging: A Sociological Perspective,' *Journal of Women and Aging*, 1(1), 47-67.

McGaugh, J. and S. Kiesler (eds.). (1981). *Aging: Biology and Behavior.* New York: Academic Press.

McKee, P. and H. Kauppinen. (1987). *The Art of Aging: A Celebration of Old Age in Western Art.* New York: Human Sciences Press.

Medvedev, Z. (1974). 'Caucasus and Altay Longevity: A Biological or Social Problem?' *The Gerontologist*, 14(5), 381-87.

Miller, R. and R. Dodder. (1980). 'A Revision of Palmore's Facts on Aging Quiz,' *The Gerontologist*, 20(6), 673-79.

Monahan, D. and V. Greene. (1982). 'The Impact of Seasonal Population Fluctuations on Service Delivery,' *The Gerontologist*, 22(2), 160-63.

Morris, R. (1989) 'Challenges of Aging in Tomorrow's World: Will Gerontology Grow, Stagnate, or Change?' *The Gerontologist*, 29(4), 494-501.

Mullins, N. (1972). 'The Development of a Scientific Specialty: The Phage Group and the Origins of Molecular Biology,' *Minerva*, 10(1), 51-82.

Mullins, N. (1973). *Theories and Theory Groups in Contemporary American Sociology.* New York: Harper & Row.

Murguia, E. et al. (1983). *Ethnicity and Aging: A Bibliography.* San Antonio, Tex.: Trinity University Press.

Neugarten, B. (ed.). (1968). *Middle Age and Aging: A Reader in Social Psychology.* Chicago: University of Chicago Press.

Northcott, H. (1988). *Changing Residence: The Geographic Mobility of Elderly Canadians.* Toronto: Butterworths.

Oliver, D. and J. Eckerman. (1979). 'Tracing the Historical Growth of Gerontology as a Discipline,' presented at the 32d Annual Meeting of the American Gerontological Society, Washington, D.C.

Olson, L. (1988). 'Aging Is a Woman's Problem: Issues Faced by the Female Elderly Population,' *Journal of Aging Studies*, 2(2), 97-108.

O'Rand, A. (1990). 'Stratification and the Life Course,' pp. 130-50 in R. Binstock and L. George (eds.). *Handbook of Aging and the Social Sciences.* 3d ed. San Diego, Calif.: Academic Press.

Palmore, E. (ed.). (1970). *Normal Aging: Reports from the Duke Longitudinal Studies, 1955-1969.* Durham, N.C.: Duke University Press.

Palmore, E. (1977). 'Facts on Aging: A Short Quiz,'

The Gerontologist, 17(4), 315-20.

Palmore, E. (1979). 'Advantages of Aging,' *The Gerontologist*, 19(2), 220-23.

Palmore, E. (1980a). 'The Facts on Aging Quiz: A Review of Findings,' *The Gerontologist*, 20(6), 669-72.

Palmore, E. (ed.). (1980b). *International Handbook on Aging: Contemporary Developments and Research*. Westport, Conn.: Greenwood Press.

Palmore, E. (1981). 'The Facts on Aging Quiz: Part Two,' *The Gerontologist*, 21(4), 431-37.

Palmore, E. (1988). *The Facts on Aging Quiz: A Handbook of Uses and Results*. New York: Springer Publishing Co.

Pampel, F. (1981). *Social Change and the Aged*. Lexington, Mass.: D.C. Heath Co.

Parsons, T. (1942). 'Age and Sex in the Social Structure of the United States,' *American Sociological Review*, 7(5), 604-20.

Pollak, O. (1948). *Social Adjustment in Old Age: A Research Planning Report*. Bulletin 59. New York: Social Science Research Council.

Posner, J. (1980). 'Old and Female: The Double Whammy,' pp. 80-94 in V. Marshall (ed.). *Aging in Canada: Social Perspectives*. Don Mills, Ont.: Fitzhenry and Whiteside.

Rapaport, R. and R. Rapaport (eds.). (1975). *Leisure and the Family Life Cycle*. London: Routledge and Kegan Paul.

Riegel, K. (1977). 'History of Psychological Gerontology,' in J. Birren and W. Schaie (eds.). *Handbook of the Psychology of Aging*. New York: Van Nostrand Reinhold.

Riley, M. (1987). 'On The Significance of Age in Sociology,' *American Sociological Review*, 52(1), 1-14.

Riley, M. and A. Foner (eds.). (1968). *Aging and Society. Volume One: An Inventory of Research Findings*. New York: Russell Sage Foundation.

Riley, M. et al. (1969). *Aging and Society. Volume Two: Aging and the Professions*. New York: Russell Sage Foundation.

Riley, M. et al. (1972). *Aging and Society. Volume Three: A Sociology of Age Stratification*. New York: Russell Sage Foundation.

Rockstein, M. and M. Sussman. (1979). *Biology of Aging*. Belmont, Calif.: Wadsworth Publishing Co.

Rose, A. and W. Peterson (eds.). (1965). *Older People and Their Social World*. Philadelphia: F.A. Davis Co.

Rosow, I. (1978). 'What Is a Cohort and Why?' *Human Development*, 21(2), 65-75.

Rossi, A. (ed.). (1984). *Gender and the Life Course*. New York: Aldine.

Rossi, A. (1986). 'Sex and Gender in an Aging Society,' *Daedalus*, 115, 141-69.

Ryan, N. (1985). *Rural Aging in Canada: An Annotated Bibliography*. Guelph, Ont.: University of Guelph Gerontology Research Centre.

Ryder, N. (1965). 'The Cohort as a Concept in the Study of Social Change,' *American Sociological Review*, 30(6), 843-61.

Sackmary, B. (1974). 'The Sociology of Science: The Emergence and Development of a Sociological Specialty,' Ph.D. dissertation, Department of Sociology, University of Massachusetts.

Schneider, E. and J. Rowe (eds.). (1990). *Handbook of the Biology of Aging*. 3d ed. San Diego, Calif.: Academic Press.

Schulz, J. (1976). *The Economics of Aging*. Belmont, Calif.: Wadsworth Publishing Co.

Secretary of State (1988). *Aging in a Multicultural Canada: A Graphic Overview*. Ottawa: Secretary of State, Policy, Analysis and Research Directorate (Multiculturalism).

Seltzer, M. (1979). 'The Older Woman: Facts, Fantasies and Fiction,' *Research on Aging*, 1(2), 139-54.

Seniors Secretariat. (1989). *Women in an Aging Society*. Ottawa: Minister of Supply and Services Canada.

Shanas, E. (1971). 'The Sociology of Aging and the Aged,' *The Sociological Quarterly*, 12(2), 159-76.

Shanas, E. et al. (1968). *Old People in Three Industrial Societies*. New York: Atherton.

Shock, N. (1977). 'Biological Theories of Aging,' pp. 103-15 in J. Birren and W. Schaie (eds.). *Handbook of the Psychology of Aging*. New York: Van Nostrand Reinhold.

Simmons, L. (1945). *The Role of the Aged in Primitive Society*. New Haven, Conn.: Yale University Press.

Sinnott, J. (1986). *Sex Roles and Aging: Theory and Research from a Systems Perspective*. Basel: Karger.

Sontag, S. (1975). 'The Double Standard of Aging,' pp. 32-33 in *No Longer Young: The Older Woman in America*. Occasional Papers in Gerontology, no. 11. Detroit: Institute of Gerontology, University of Michigan-Wayne State University.

Streib, G. and R. Binstock. (1990). 'Aging and the Social Sciences: Changes in the Field,' pp.1-17 in R. Binstock and L. George (eds.) *Handbook of Aging and the Social Sciences*. 3d ed. San Diego. Calif.: Academic Press.

Streib, G. and H. Orbach. (1967). 'The Development of Social Gerontology and the Sociology of Aging,' pp. 612-40 in P. Lazarsfeld, W. Sewell, and H. Wilensky (eds.). *The Uses of Sociology*. New York: Basic Books.

Tamir, L. (1982). *Men in Their Forties*. New York: Springer Publishing Co.

Tibbitts, C. (ed.). (1960). *Handbook of Social Gerontology: Societal Aspects of Aging.* Chicago: University of Chicago Press.

Troll, L. (1981). 'Age Changes in Sex Roles amid Changing Sex Roles: The Double Shift,' pp. 118-43 in C. Eisdorfer (ed.). *Annual Review of Gerontology and Geriatrics.* vol. 2. New York: Springer Publishing Co.

Tucker, R. et al. (1988). 'Older Anglophone Canadians in Florida: A Descriptive Profile,' *Canadian Journal on Aging*, 7(3), 218-32.

Tumin, M. (1967). *Social Stratification.* Englewood Cliffs, N.J.: Prentice-Hall.

Uhlenberg, P. (1988). 'Aging and the Societal Significance of Cohorts,' pp. 405-25 in J. Birren and V. Bengtson (eds.). *Emergent Theories of Aging.* New York: Springer Publishing Co.

Ujimoto, V. (1987). 'The Ethnic Dimension of Aging in Canada,' pp. 111-37 in V. Marshall (ed.). *Aging in Canada: Social Perspectives.* Markham, Ont.: Fitzhenry and Whiteside.

Ward, R. (1984). 'The Marginality and Salience of Being Old: When Is Age Relevant?' *The Gerontologist*, 24(3), 227-32.

Wyatt-Brown, A. (1989). 'The Narrative Imperative: Fiction and the Aging Writer,' *Journal of Aging Studies*, 3(1), 55-65.

Youmans, E. (1967). *Older Rural Americans.* Lexington: University of Kentucky Press.

2
Aging from a Historical and Comparative Perspective: Cultural and Subcultural Diversity

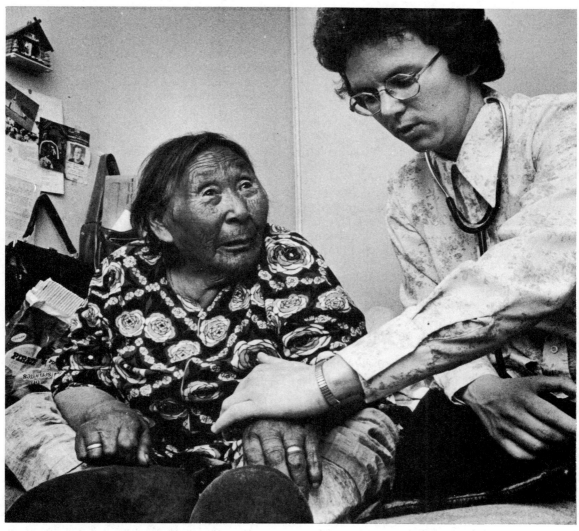

Health and Welfare Canada, Information Directorate

INTRODUCTION

The experiences and meaning of aging and the **status** of the elderly vary within and between cultures. Cultural factors that affect the status of the elderly (such as respect for the aged) are influenced by structural or social system factors (industrialization, a changing family structure). This interaction between the cultural and structural levels of analysis must be considered when searching for explanations of aging phenomena, and when designing and implementing policies for an aging population. The first part of this chapter illustrates the diversity in status and treatment of the elderly from a historical and comparative perspective. The second part considers subcultural variations in the status of the elderly, primarily within the North American context.

THE MEANING OF CULTURE

The **culture** of a society or of a subgroup within a society develops when a group shares a way of life at the same time and place.[1] The culture provides a symbolic order and a set of shared meanings to social life, and is composed of nonmaterial and material elements. The nonmaterial elements include norms, customs, values, beliefs, knowledge, and sanctions. These are symbolically represented through material elements or artifacts such as laws, language, art, dress, folklore, technology, literature, music, art, ceremonies, and games. Those products that are highly valued are transmitted from one generation to the next through the process of socialization.

Of particular importance in understanding the social life and processes of a society are its values and norms. **Values** are the internalized criteria by which members select and judge their own and others' goals and behaviors in society. Values tend to be trans-situational in that they are reflected in all institutions within a society. They include principles such as democracy, equality of opportunity, freedom, achievement, competition, goal orientation, and respect for the elderly. **Norms** are derived from and closely interrelated to basic values. Norms serve as guidelines to acceptable behavior in specific social situations. For example, many norms concerning how we dress, how we spend our leisure time, or when we work are related to age or to the social positions we occupy.

In most societies there is a high degree of cultural integration or consensus about how people think and behave. This is reflected in the phenomenon known as **ethnocentrism**, wherein members regard their mainstream culture as superior to all others. This ethnocentric tendency influences how we behave toward persons from other cultural backgrounds, including members of **subcultures** in our own society.

Some behavioral patterns, values, and social institutions are similar from one culture to another, although they may be expressed in different forms. For example, all societies have some form of political, social, and economic organization, a common language, and a way of socializing members.

THE HISTORICAL AND COMPARATIVE APPROACH TO UNDERSTANDING THE AGING PROCESS

Just as the biologist seeks to describe and explain similarities in structure and function between different species in order to arrive at generalizations or laws, scholars in the social sciences and humanities seek to understand the process of aging and the status of the aged in a variety of cultural contexts. This approach to the study of aging phenomena was initiated with the publication in 1945 of Simmons's classic study of the role of the aged in a number of primitive societies. For many years thereafter, scholars sought to describe the status of the elderly in a variety of primitive, premodern, and postmodern societies. These studies indicated that age is an important factor in the stratification system of many societies, and that the status of the elderly varies both across societies and within a society at different historical periods.

Much of this information was based on the literature or the cultural artifacts (such as paintings) of a particular society or era (McKee and Kauppinen, 1986), on personal observations or interviews by anthropologists or gerontologists, and on the use of data such as birth, marriage and death records, or census material. Through this information we acquired ideas, images, and stereotypes about what it was like to be old at a given period in history or in a specific society.

However, much of this work was descriptive and is not sufficient to increase our depth of knowledge about the variety of cultural differences in aging. As a result, since the late 1970s, three new subspecialties within gerontology have emerged to add to our body of knowledge about cultural variations in the aging process. First, historians and sociologists interested in social change studied the definition of aging and the aged, variations in the aging process, and the meaning and significance of individual and societal perceptions of aging at different historical periods.[2] For example, historical studies of aging indicate that the status of the aged has not always been as low as it is at present. Thus, historians and sociologists strive to identify patterns of thought and behavior that are repeated in a variety of contexts (cultural universals), as well as those unique to a specific culture or historical period (cultural variations).

A second development has been a growth in the study of age and aging from an anthropological perspective.[3] Whereas most of the early work described the role of the elderly in a particular society, anthropologists have become more interested in understanding the patterns of aging in various cultural or subcultural contexts. Using cultural factors, they explain variations along a continuum of possible patterns of aging. Specifically, those scientists with an interest in the anthropology of aging have studied the status and treatment of the elderly in a society, and the consequences of social change for their involvement in the political, social, and economic life of the society; the consequences of social change by social class and gender; the roles and functions of adults at different stages of the life course; the rituals and symbols associated with age and aging in different cultural contexts; how age grading is a factor in the social organization of the society and the extent to which the elderly are considered central or marginal in the society; and how culture influences social behavior.

Since there are over 3,000 societies in the world (Fry, 1985), there is considerable variation in both the process of aging and the status of the aged. Moreover, these age-related factors may vary as societies change and as history evolves. Nevertheless, societies can be categorized into three general types according to the extent to which they have experienced industrialization and modernization. Throughout this chapter, you are introduced to aging in primitive, preliterate hunting and gathering societies; to aging in premodern or preindustrialized societies; and to aging in postmodern or postindustrialized societies. Many of these studies describe variations within a specific society. There have been few cross-cultural studies that compare aging phenomena in two or more cultures.[4] Moreover, until the 1970s there were few studies that considered the cultural heterogeneity of the aging process within a society at a given point in time.

This recognition and acceptance of the premise that the social structures of modern societies are heterogeneous led to the emergence of the third subspecialty concerned with cultural variation in the aging process. Most of this interest occurred in the multicultural societies of Canada and the United States, where such factors as race, ethnic background, and national origin were identified as important factors in the experiences and opportunities of aging adults.[5] In addition, aging and the status of the aged were found to vary within unique subcultures. These latter studies examined the processes and consequences of race, ethnicity, religion, or national origin on individual and population aging, both separately and collectively. Topics of particular interest concerning those with a unique racial, ethnic, religious, or national background include: images and attitudes about aging and the aged; lifestyles and opportunities of the elderly; unique aging problems (such as housing, health, income); access to informal support networks; and the need for, access to, and use of formal programs and services. Finally, there are significant gender and social-class variations within ethnic or racial groups that must be considered by scholars and practitioners. Scholars have also concluded that there is a need for unique policies, programs, and services to enhance the quality of life of the minority aged and to reduce later life inequities between members of the dominant group and the various minority groups.

THE MODERNIZATION HYPOTHESIS AND THE CHANGING STATUS OF THE AGED

Our knowledge of early societies is based chiefly on archeological evidence and on the few documents produced by philosophers or historians of the time (Laslett, 1985). Clearly, longevity was greatly influenced by climate, availability and type of food, natural disasters, disease, medical knowledge, and relations with other tribes or groups. Until about the middle of the seventeenth century, the average life expectancy seldom exceeded 40 years (although those with higher status generally lived longer). Because there were few elderly citizens, those who survived were often held in esteem and awe, and received preferential treatment.

Prior to the Industrial Revolution, two major types of societies existed. In the primitive hunting-and-gathering societies the oldest member was considered a source of knowledge about rituals and survival skills. In a society where social differentiation was based largely on age, authority was linked to age and elders held influential positions in the social, political, and religious spheres of life (Goody, 1976). For example, based on an analysis of seventy-one primitive societies, Simmons (1945, 1952) found that status and treatment of the aged was governed by tradition and rituals unique to each culture. The elderly were expected to contribute as much as possible by assisting with economic and household chores; by teaching the young people games, customs, songs, and dances; by serving as the repository of rites and traditions; by counseling the young about hunting, growing crops, and warfare; and by serving as chiefs or elders of the community. Press and McKool (1972) noted that there were four prestige-generating components for the aged in the Mesoamerican era: the 'advisory' component, or the degree to which the advice and opinions of the aged were heeded; the 'contributory' component, or the degree to which the aged participated in and controlled ritual and economic activities; the 'control' component, or the degree of direct authority of the aged over people and institutions; and the 'residual' component, or the degree to which the aged retained prestige because of their earlier contributions to society.

The second major type of preindustrialized society was the agrarian-peasant model. According to this model, the elderly owned or controlled the land and were considered the heads of extended families made up of at least three generations. In these societies, the elderly had experience and knowledge of survival skills, husbandry, history, ritual, and law. When the elderly were no longer able to contribute, they 'retired' and transferred control of the family resources, usually to the oldest son. They were then cared for by the family and the community because of past contributions (the residual component of prestige), and because they were the major source of knowledge about the culture.

As Laslett (1985) concluded, the status of the aged probably varied between and within societies, depending on locale and period. For example, there were a few instances (such as in some Inuit societies) where the old were forced to die, by their own hand or by the hands of relatives, once they were deemed a burden to society. From an exchange perspective, when costs exceeded contributions, the old were forced to leave the community so others would have a better chance to survive.

With the onset of the Industrial Revolution, first in Great Britain and Western Europe and then in North America, societies experienced dramatic social changes as they moved from rural, agricultural societies to urban, technological societies. As a result, new social structures, cultural values, political and social systems, and social processes evolved, and these had a profound impact on the lifestyle of all cohorts, but particularly on the aged. For the individual, industrialization generally resulted in a higher level of educational attainment; improvements in health care and living conditions, which increased longevity; independence from parents after late adolescence or early adulthood; greater personal wealth; and an increase in leisure time because of shorter working hours.

At the societal level, the Industrial Revolution led to major changes in the social and economic system (Burgess, 1960; Cowgill,

1974a). First, there was a shift from home to factory production with the result that the family was no longer the center of economic production. This meant a separation of work and home and a dramatic increase in the number of people dependent on nonfamily employers for their economic security. Accompanying this shift in place of employment was a trend to increased migration to cities, especially by younger age cohorts. This urbanization resulted in greater social differentiation, the development of multiple social groups (family, work, neighborhood), exposure to new values and norms, and the establishment of public schools.

A third trend was the breakup of the extended family and the emergence of the nuclear, conjugal family, often living in a different community from that of the parents. A fourth trend was the rise of large organizations and the creation of new occupations requiring skills that the young could acquire through apprenticeship or formal schooling. Many of the skills possessed by the elderly became obsolete, mandatory retirement was invoked, and a certain level of formal education was increasingly demanded as a prerequisite to employment. Because new knowledge was being generated so rapidly, the knowledge acquired by the elderly through experience was no longer worth as much. Finally, industrialization brought new technology to the medical field. The quality of medical care improved, thereby reducing infant and childhood mortality rates and prolonging adult life. The result was an increased life expectancy, a larger population, and a larger proportion of old people within the population.

Prior to industrialization, the structures of preliterate and preindustrial societies were relatively static. It is generally agreed that during these periods of history the elderly were accorded high status, power, and prestige within the community and the family because of their wisdom and experience and because they controlled the scarce resources (such as property, land, money). This period was viewed by many early gerontologists as the 'Golden Age' of aging (Achenbaum, 1978; Fischer, 1977). This period in history has been sharply contrasted with the period after the significant social changes induced by the Industrial Revolution,

the French Revolution, and the American Revolution. The process by which society moved from the preindustrial 'Golden Age' to the industrial world is known as **modernization**.

Cowgill and Holmes (1972) argued that with the onset of modernization and the significant accompanying social, political, and economic changes, the status of the elderly declined. As a result the aged lost power, security, and status because they no longer had functionally essential social roles and were no longer looked to for knowledge and information. Also, because adult children no longer lived in the family home, many did not believe they had a moral, social, or legal obligation to support their aging parents.

To test the assumption that the status of the aged declined with the onset of modernization, Cowgill and Holmes (1972) reviewed the work of Simmons (1945) concerning the relationship between cultural traits and the status of the aged in preindustrial societies. They had anthropologists describe aging and the status of the aged in fifteen different cultures and subcultures. These ranged from preliterate societies, such as the Sidamo of southwest Ethiopia, to semi-industrialized societies, such as Thailand in the 1960s, to highly modernized societies, such as the United States.

Based on their analysis of these societies, they concluded that increasing modernization of societies accounts for the declining status of the aged. They found that the status of the aged is high in societies where they perform useful, valued functions. However, there were some cases that did not agree with the theory. For example, the elderly have an apparent continuing high status in Japan, Ireland, and Russia, all of which are modernized to various degrees. These exceptions were attributed to unique factors related to the stage of historical development within the society, or to rigid adherence to earlier cultural values, particularly those pertaining to older members of the family (Palmore, 1975b; Holmes, 1976).

For many years this 'before and after modernization' explanation of the changing status of the elderly went unchallenged. However, with the introduction of a historical and anthropological perspective to the study of gerontology, the modernization theory was reexamined by a number of scholars.[6] First, through careful historical research, serious doubts were cast on the assumption that the status of all elderly people decreased dramatically after modernization in Western societies. For example, Quadagno (1982) presented evidence from nineteenth-century England indicating that the onset of industrialization differed considerably by region and by industry. Thus, in some industries, or in some regions, the position of older people actually improved with greater mechanization. To illustrate, she noted that the invention of the sewing machine increased the output of seamstresses who did piecework at home. Because economic conditions did not favor the construction of factories in London, England, the work requested from these older women actually increased in the postindustrial era.

A second criticism of modernization theory noted that the social status of the aged in preindustrialized societies is not always as high as is assumed (Cowgill, 1974b). Harlan (1964), basing his conclusion on a study of three traditional villages in India, argued that generalizations concerning the status of the aged must be based on a representative sampling of all socioeconomic levels. Greater care should be taken to distinguish between hypothetical ideal norms of family life with regard to the authority and prestige of the aged, and the actual relationships and behavior that occur.

Laslett (1985) and Hendricks and Hendricks (1977-78), on the basis of evidence from historical demography, found that in spite of continuing stereotypes, the emotional, physical, and economic needs of the aged were not better met prior to industrialization. The status of the elderly in modernized societies is no lower and may actually be higher than it was prior to industrialization. Many positive examples from postindustrial societies can be given of how the aged are supported by their children, of how their economic status has improved because of income security plans, of how programs of social support have enhanced rather than diminished their position, and of how mandatory retirement can relieve the aged of the burden of work and reward them with freedom and leisure time. In short, the assumption of a difference in treatment of the aged before and after modernization is misleading, and is not supported by Laslett's (1985) analysis of early demographic evidence.

Laslett (1985) concludes that the transition in the status of the elderly occurred as much as a century or more *after* the onset of industrialization. This change was related to a changing social structure and changing social values that coincided with a demographic transition (see chapter 3) whereby postmodernized societies were characterized by low fertility rates and lowered mortality rates.

There is also evidence that the status of the elderly in some preindustrialized societies was never as high as we have been led to believe. For example, Stearns (1976) suggests that in preindustrial France the elderly were held in disdain. This callous, pessimistic image of old age was held by all age groups in France, including the elderly themselves. These attitudes resulted from the cultural belief that old age is an unpleasant time, and that old people are nuisances. These views were held much longer in France than in the United States, despite the onset of modernization at about the same time in both countries.

A number of authors have felt that the before-and-after-modernization explanation may not be as simple as suggested. This view is based on the observation that the processes of modernization proceeded at different rates and by different stages within various societies. Moreover, the elderly are a heterogeneous group and not all members of the older cohorts may experience a change in status (Dowd, 1981). Modernization can affect societies in different ways, since a particular event may not have an impact until as long as five decades after its occurrence (Achenbaum and Stearns, 1978).[7] Indeed, Achenbaum (1985) has concluded that the elderly may be among the last age groups to be affected by the modernization process.

The process of modernization may have varying degrees of influence on different age cohorts and subcultural groups within a society because of their experience with and adherence to different value systems. An evaluation of the meaning of old age and the status of the aged may depend on the social environment and the value structures of various age cohorts. For example, because of a particular religious doctrine that rejects modern influences, elderly Amish and Old Order Mennonites in North America have retained leadership roles in the church, community, and family. Similarly, in a comparative examination of European nations and the United States, Burgess (1960) found a number of societal differences that may have consequences for the way the aged are treated. For example, he reported that the aged are less concentrated and less visible in North America; that there is a more decentralized government in North America, which enables three levels (city, state, federal) of authority to be concerned about the aged; that there is greater cultural and regional diversity in values and lifestyle in North America; and that there are stronger historical and cultural ties between generations in Europe.

From a more empirical perspective, Palmore and Manton (1974) found that the relationship between the degree of modernization and the status of the aged in thirty-one countries could be represented by a bowl-shaped curve (curvilinear). Immediately after the onset of modernization, the status of the aged may decline. However, the long-term effect of social change is that the difference in status between the aged and non-aged decreases and the relative status of the aged rises. They suggested that in the more modernized nations the status of the aged is improving, although it may or may not rise to the level attained prior to modernization.

In the United States, the change in intergenerational relations occurred just after the American Revolution and before the onset of industrialization. Fischer (1977), for example, presents a historical analysis of the period from 1770 to 1820 when age equality became one of the bases for building a new society. Following the American Revolution, priority seating by age at town meetings was replaced with priority seating by wealth; a single style of dress was permitted for men of all ages (before the Revolution, the elderly dressed in a different style); and a new vocabulary to express contempt for old people evolved (incorporating terms such as 'old fogy'). Once initiated, this devaluation of the elderly continued through the late 1800s and early 1900s, particularly after the Civil War (1861-65).

According to Achenbaum (1974, 1978, 1985), the image of the elderly as obsolete was fostered by a number of interdependent events. First, medical research suggested that the longer people lived, the more likely they were to suffer from incurable pathological disorders. Second, with the rise of bureaucracies, the work experience of the elderly was not valued as highly as the possession of newer job skills. A third factor was the acceptance of the view that the energy and strength of youth needed to be developed and exploited. Thus, the onset of technological change, the increase in bureaucratization, and changes in social values contributed to a loss of self-esteem, self-worth, and self-respect on the part of the elderly.

In summary, there is conflicting evidence concerning the status of the aged in preindustrial societies compared to modern, urban societies. Just as some earlier societies held the elderly in high esteem while others abandoned them, similar patterns can be found in contemporary societies. For example, just as the elderly were abandoned by some nomadic tribes, today they are often abandoned in institutions for the aged, where, because of advanced technology, they can be kept alive beyond the point where it may not be worth living.

As we will see, there are some universal patterns in the process of aging and the status of the aged, but numerous cultural variations between and within societies do occur. While a definitive explanation for such variations is lacking, the rate and degree of social change (from a traditional, agricultural society to an industrialized urban society) does have some influence on the observed differences. But cultural traditions, changes in family kinship structure, the pressure from youth for age equality, and adherence to a particular religious doctrine can also lead to cross-cultural differences.

The next two sections present brief descriptions of aging in various preindustrial and industrial societies. These societies, which are representative of many, provide only a general overview of the modal pattern. The descriptions are based on various accounts from each society at a given point in history. Thus, we see only a 'snapshot' of a specific period in a society's development, rather than a historical 'movie' of the society over a period of many years. The presentations also tend to overlook variations within the society among a variety of cultural subgroups.

Most importantly, we must recognize, as we do with many areas of research, that there may be a significant gap between the stated values or attitudes of respondents and their actual behavior. Thus, even where people tell an investigator that they 'respect their elders and look after them,' careful observation in a number of settings may or may not support this ideal view (Fry, 1985).

AGING AND THE AGED IN PREINDUSTRIAL SOCIETIES

Preliterate Societies

Preliterate societies have no written languages, therefore knowledge, beliefs, and survival skills are found in the memories of those with the greatest experience, the elders. The economic system is based on production and consumption within domestic kinship groups, and the dependency of children on their parents is linked to a degree of obligation toward the old in the family unit (Goody, 1976). Generally, preliterate societies were of two types. The least developed were nomadic hunting and gathering societies as exemplified by some Inuit tribes. The more stable preliterate societies were subsistence agrarian communities, such as the Anasazi Indians who, from 550 to 750 A.D., inhabited the Mesa Verde area in what is now southwestern Colorado.

In societies where there is a surplus of food, where the oldest members control property, and where knowledge of survival, rituals, and customs is stored by the elderly, their status is high and they are protected. In societies where food is scarce, where property is nonexistent, or where leadership is based on perceived ability rather than on longevity or familial ties, the elderly may be abandoned or put to death (gerontocide), with or without ceremony. In both types of preliterate societies, older men commanded greater respect than older women. Highlight 2.1 compares the status of the elderly in a variety of preliterate societies.

Literate Preindustrial Societies

In literate preindustrial Eastern and Western cultures, the status of the aged seemed to vary according to prevailing living conditions, religious beliefs, and cultural values. For example, the elderly appeared to have high status and power in the early years of the Hebrew, Greek, Roman, and American societies. They lost status as wars, migration, and changing values accorded higher status to youth and to those who acquired wealth and made functional contributions to the society, regardless of age. In highlight 2.2 brief descriptions of the status of the aged in early literate and preindustrialized societies are presented for different regions and cultures.

AGING AND THE AGED IN INDUSTRIALIZED SOCIETIES: THE IMPACT OF MODERNIZATION

With the onset of the Industrial Revolution, first in Great Britain and later in other societies, great economic, political, and social changes occurred. Generally, these changes are referred to as modernization (or, for non-Western nations, as Westernization). Modernization has the potential to change the relative status and roles of all age cohorts within a society. The following sections outline the process of aging and the status of the aged in various modernizing or modern societies. Again, only a broad 'snapshot' is presented here.

Samoa

The traditional authority of Samoan elders changed with the introduction of Western cultural values and a Western economic system based on the exchange of goods (Maxwell, 1970; Holmes, 1972; Watson and Maxwell, 1977:46-58; Rhoads, 1984). The traditional culture was a subsistence society involving a number of extended families who lived in a seaside village headed by an elected chief. In each village there was sharing within and between families, and the aged were respected and cared for by the extended family.

THE STATUS OF THE ELDERLY IN PRELITERATE SOCIETIES

In nomadic tribes, abandonment of the aged was relatively common. Holmberg (1969:224-25) reported that the Sirino tribe in Bolivia abandoned their elderly when they became ill or infirm. The Yakuts of Siberia forced their elderly to become beggars and slaves. The Chukchee of Siberia ceremoniously killed the aged in front of the members of the tribe (de Beauvoir, 1972). However, within the Chukchee tribe, behavior differed, depending on whether the tribe lived in settled villages along the coast, or whether they lived a nomadic life herding reindeer. In the herding tribe, older people had knowledge about breeding and survival of the herds, and were therefore less expendable. In nomadic societies, the aged were devalued if they became a burden and had no specialized knowledge or skills, if cultural values dictated that they were no longer worthy of life (for example, because of declining physical strength), or if children sought revenge on their parents.

In societies where the majority of the population was illiterate, face-to-face interaction was the primary means of teaching and ruling. Information and skills were acquired and retained through years of experience. The elderly were information banks for the society. Since survival and the passing on of the culture to the young depended on this information, the aged were held in high esteem. For example, Maxwell and Silverman (1970) examined twenty-six societies to determine the extent to which the aged were involved in the following six types of information processing: (1) as hosts of feasts, games, or visiting groups; (2) as consultants on survival skills or ritual; (3) as decision makers for groups; (4) as entertainers; (5) as arbitrators of disputes; and (6) as teachers of the young. They found a strong relationship between the amount of useful information held by the aged as expressed by their participation in information-processing activities, and the esteem accorded to them by other members of the society.

Other factors leading to a higher status for the aged in preliterate societies were stability of residence, a viable system of food production, the availability of low-skill functional roles, a nuclear family, and a system of religion in which the elderly were thought to be able to communicate with the gods. Simmons (1960), Rosow (1965), de Beauvoir (1972), and Goody (1976) described such practices as old chiefs conducting political or religious meetings; old Incas still making a contribution by serving as scarecrows; elders educating the children in the evenings; old Omaha Indians advising the young to leave the choice morsels in the kettle for them, lest 'your arrow twist when you shoot'; and old Aztecs having access to stimulants prohibited to others because it would 'warm their blood.'

In the early 1800s Christianity was introduced to the islands. Contact with Westerners increased when the United States took control of Eastern Samoa after 1900. During and after World War II transportation facilities were expanded; the literacy rate increased, and old people were no longer seen as important repositories of information; industries were established and provided employment and money; Western material goods (such as canned foods) were imported, and food sharing decreased; tourism was encouraged and this led to even more contact with Westerners. As a result of these influences, the power and authority of the elders in the community decreased. However, the elderly were still treated with respect within the family, and children contributed to the economic support of the elders in their extended family.

The Anicinabe of Georgian Bay

The Anicinabe, a term meaning 'original people,' inhabited the islands and mainland of Georgian Bay in Ontario (Vanderburgh, 1987). In the prereserve and premissionary era, an elder played a traditional role as the repository of native knowledge and culture. The elders, if no longer able to be involved in subsistence work, were responsible for transmitting knowledge and culture to the children of the tribe.

THE STATUS OF THE ELDERLY IN LITERATE PREINDUSTRIAL SOCIETIES

The Ancient Hebrews

This is one of the earliest societies for which there exist written records and well-preserved artifacts. It is also one of the first societies in which long life was viewed as a blessing rather than a burden. In the years between 1300 B.C. and 100 A.D., the Hebrews were a nomadic desert tribe essentially made up of a large extended family. This family consisted of wives, concubines, children, sons and their wives and children, slaves, servants, and any others who attached themselves to the domestic group for protection. They were ruled by the eldest man, the patriarch of the family, who was the religious leader, judge, and teacher. He controlled all aspects of political, religious, economic, and social life and was identified by his long gray beard — a sign of wisdom, experience, and authority. In this relatively stable yet nomadic culture, aging, at least for men, represented increasing wisdom, respect, and power.

The City-States of Ancient Greece and Rome

According to ancient Greek literature, there was a dread and hatred of old age. The Greek gods were depicted as eternally youthful and beautiful, and much of the literature commented on the declining physical and mental strength of the aged. In ancient Greece, power was more likely to be associated with wealth than with age, and if an older man attained respect and power, it accrued to him because of his wealth.

Like the Greeks, elderly Romans lost power and influence as they aged, unless they were wealthy. This is not surprising, since evidence from burial remains indicates that life expectancy may have been only 20 to 30 years. The citizen-soldier was a dominant figure; death, even by suicide, was sometimes seen as preferable to suffering the indignities of physical, mental, and social deterioration. For most of the elderly, aging was hated and feared. This was especially true in the declining years of the Greek and Roman civilizations, when barbarism placed a premium on youth and strength. Survival of the fittest prevailed, and those who could not contribute to the society were abandoned or put to death.

Japan

Plath (1972) notes that there is no evidence in over a thousand years of recorded history that the Japanese abandoned their aged as a matter of custom. Japanese citizens followed the Confucian precepts that demanded honor for all elders and for parents in particular. However, he also notes the high rate of suicide among Japanese elders, particularly among women, and wonders whether this is a pattern reflecting the earlier custom of self-sacrifice (a cultural norm dating back to early Samurai practices). Plath also draws attention to the recurring Obasute theme in Japanese folklore, whereby old people in a village are required to make a pilgrimage to Oak Mountain with a young kinsman during their seventieth year. Here, they are expected to wait for death or be pushed off the cliff.

England

After the decline of the Roman civilization, the Roman church prevailed as the ruling authority throughout feudal England and Western Europe. Although one might expect the status of the aged to improve with the rise of Christianity, this was not the case. The Church was more interested in recruiting new members than in performing social work. However, by the sixteenth and early seventeenth centuries, longevity increased and such precepts as charity, hospitality, and care for one's fellow man began to be practiced as basic tenets of parish life. As a result, there was a growing concern for the treatment of the aged, especially if they were poor. For example, almshouses provided a form of institutionalized care. However, since manpower was scarce, all were expected to work as long as they were able, including the elderly. The state became involved in supporting the aged with the passage of the Elizabethan Poor Laws in 1603. As a result, prior to the onset of the Industrial Revolution, the elderly who did not have families to care for them were looked after by the parish, with some limited financial assistance from the state. These poorhouses were by no means seen as the ideal form of care for the elderly.

Colonial America

The rigors of colonial life placed a premium on strong, healthy adults, and the colonies were initially a young male-dominated society, with a median age of about 20 years. In fact, less than 2 percent of the residents were over 65. Being highly religious, the Puritans took their cue from the Bible and honored their elders by letting them occupy leadership positions and permitting them to sit in the most prestigious seats at town meetings. This status was not solely based on religious beliefs; it was also related to wealth, in that the elderly owned the land and resources and hence could command respect from their families. Because wealth played a role in acquiring status, those who were poor or destitute were scorned or driven from the town so they would cease to be an economic burden. As in many other societies, older women did not receive the same respect as older men.

As the settlement of the West began in the 1800s, emphasis was still placed on the strength, vigor, and vitality of young men. In many cases, the pioneers were sons of eastern colonials who decided to break from the family to seek their own fortune and lifestyle in their 'little house on the prairie.' According to Fischer (1977), the declining status of the aged in North America began not with industrialization, urbanization, and greater literacy, but with the change in cultural values after the American Revolution. This led to an emphasis on equality based on performance and income, and a westward migration away from the influence and control of one's parents. One outcome was that many of the elderly were left in the eastern colonies to fend for themselves and ended their lives alone, often in poverty.

Specifically, they taught mythic and local history, native language, healing methods and beliefs, and native rituals. With the arrival of Christian missions and the creation of schools on the reservations, missionaries and teachers controlled the knowledge and culture that were transmitted to the youngest generation. This information involved the skills that were needed for survival in the 'modern' world — English, mathematics, science, and so forth. As a result, by the 1960s the role of elder had disappeared, and the older members of the tribe had lost prestige and their autonomy. As modern ways infiltrated the tribe, elderly natives were neglected by their families and the tribe, and were forced to enter non-native long-term care institutions. Today however, the native elderly are regaining some degree of importance due to a policy of the federal government that created Native Cultural/Educational Centers across Canada. Vanderburgh (1987) describes how the native elders of the Anicinabe were recruited by the staff of a Center established in 1974 on Manitoulin Island. In order to record and transmit elements of the traditional culture, the oldest surviving elders have become volunteer 'elders' in the traditional sense. In this role they pass on their knowledge, as told to them by their grandparents, concerning rituals, crafts, language, and anecdotal narratives about the life and history of the Anicinabe. As a result of this volunteer work, the elders have recaptured, at least to some extent, the traditional role of elder, along with a small measure of status within the tribe.

The Union of Soviet Socialist Republics

Although many societal resources are directed toward youth, the treatment and the status of the aged in the Soviet Union reflect the traditional values of peasant societies. McKain (1972) reports that the status of the elderly is conferred not by age, but by attaining a new status such as retiring or becoming a grandparent (the grandmother, or *babushka*, is a respected Russian figure). Respect for the aged in modern Soviet society is derived from the role they play in teaching the young, from the grandparents helping to raise grandchildren in the home, from social conventions that require the aged to receive special assistance or preferred treatment in public, and from grandparents living with children and actively participating in daily decisions. Similarly, many political leaders are elderly men who represent experience and long-standing loyalty to Soviet policies.

Perhaps the key factor in the continued high status of the elderly is the shortage of housing and labor, and the fact that both the husband and wife are usually employed. The grandparents, particularly the *babushka*, help raise the children and perform domestic chores. Although Soviet senior citizens receive pensions, they are expected to contribute to society in some productive way by helping the family, working on the farm, or doing part-time work for the state. In return, they are provided with leisure opportunities and free medical care.

Japan

In order to understand the present status of the aged in Asian cultures (Martin, 1988), some basic Oriental philosophical and religious principles need to be introduced. While the countries vary in many respects, there are some commonalities (Piovesana, 1979). First, there is a belief that age represents an accumulation of wisdom. Second, filial piety or respect for parents is a Confucian concept that is reinforced by the principle of ancestor worship. This practice maintains a link with the past, and ensures respect for parents who will be the next ancestors to be worshiped. Finally, within Asian societies, the unity of the family and the crucial role of the elderly are cultural norms that have persisted to the present. Thus, as Palmore (1975b) notes, a vertical system of relationships exists whereby seniority and age are essential in determining the nature of interpersonal interaction in all social situations.

Modernization began in Japan in the Meiji era (1868-1912), and the process was greatly intensified after World War II, when most of Japan was rebuilt. A detailed analysis of the status of the aged in industrialized Japan has been completed by Palmore (1975a, 1975b, 1975c). He found that the pension system is inadequate, and that less money is spent per person on older people than in any other industrial society; only a minority of the elderly Japanese are self-supporting. Today, about 10 million Japanese are 65 and older, but this number will increase to about 16 million by 2000 and to 21 million by 2025. At the present time, about 70 percent live with their children; this figure is expected to decrease to 50 percent by the year 2000. While the tradition of filial piety and the remnants of a vertical social structure contribute to the integration of the aged into society, and to the continuing respect received from younger age cohorts, this can be expected to change in the future.

Palmore (1975c) presents evidence that the status of the aged has not declined much since the onset of industrialization. As examples, he cites a number of factors, including the national holiday on September 15 called 'Respect for the Elders Day,' the special meaning and celebration attached to one's 60th birthday (Kanrecki), and the norm of giving up one's seat to an old person on a bus or train. However, perhaps in recognition that the status of the elderly was declining, the National Law for the Welfare of the Elders was passed in 1963 to perpetuate the traditional respect granted to the elderly. This law requires that the elderly be given respect, that they be given the opportunity to work, and that they be given the right to participate in social activities.

Although Palmore (1975b) argues that there has only been minimal loss of status by Japanese elders since industrialization, some evidence suggests otherwise. Sparks (1975) and Plath (1972) found that although children may care for their parents, an increasing number do so reluctantly. Indeed, some abandon their parents or pass them from one sibling to another, thereby meeting the minimal norm of filial duty. Plath cites the continuing high rates of suicide among the elderly as evidence of their dissatisfaction with life. He also observes that even where elderly parents reside with the children, their quality of life may be low since they may not be included in family conversations and activity.

In effect, the elderly are sometimes reduced to the level of domestic laborers or servants. Similarly, Maeda (1975) states that the elderly often live in a small room without privacy, that there is frequent intergenerational conflict between the mother and the daughter-in-law, and that the elderly are economically dependent on their children (Kamo, 1988). As a result of these conditions, there has been a rapid development of old people's clubs and federations, which give the elderly a center in which to engage in social activities independent of their children.

China and Hong Kong

The social structure and ideology of China is considerably different from that of Westernized societies. China was traditionally an agricultural state ruled by a series of emperors. At the local level, the organization of the community was based upon the kinship group where filial piety prevailed. Women of all ages, as well as young people, had low status. In short, the older generation had power, prestige, and authority in family and community life, both of which were highly related (Treas, 1979; Yin and Lai, 1983; Davis-Friedmann, 1983; Ikels, 1983; Streib, 1987).

In the late nineteenth century, contact with the West led to an influx of industrial technology, the beginning of foreign trade, and the urbanization of youth. As a result, the young in urban areas demanded more formal education. Once this was acquired, they began to question traditional values such as the lower status of women and automatic leadership by the elderly. At the same time, rural peasants were distressed by the economic situation and sought to overthrow the political system. Modernization, along with internal political unrest, combined to bring the Communists to power in 1949 after the Socialist Revolution (Cherry and Magnuson-Martinson, 1981). As a result, through political ideology, equalization of age relationships was advocated, with a resulting loss of status by the aged and an increase in status by other age groups.

Although there is now generational independence, filial piety still exists, since the old are housed with the young, but only in exchange for domestic and child care assistance. As Treas (1979) notes, traditional intergenerational assistance and respect prevail to a greater extent in rural areas, where the regime has imposed less age equalization in the hope of not alienating the broad base of political support. In the urban areas, mandatory retirement and pensions are being introduced, and many of the elderly, particularly women, engage in voluntary work to maintain the respect of the community.

China and Hong Kong represent societies that reflect intracultural variation in the status of the aged. There are at least three distinct social, economic, cultural, and political structures: traditional Chinese rural villages; traditional Chinese urban communities; and the urban, non-Communist, industrialized society of Hong Kong. In the traditional rural villages; the status of the elderly remains high and they are cared for by the family (or by the community if their children have migrated from the village). In the modernizing cities of mainland China, there are few elderly people, since many return to their native village when they grow old. However, those who remain have lost status, especially if they do not have the skills and education to continue performing functional tasks. If they do not have these skills, they are 'encouraged' to retire as early as age 50. With the onset of the socialist revolution and economic reform, the status of the aged has declined in terms of prestige, parental authority, and ritual roles (Chen, 1989).

In Hong Kong, the potential for generational conflict is high. The elderly who experience the most difficulty are those who do not have relatives, or whose relatives are themselves economically deprived. In this situation, old people may be cared for by other elders or by neighbors in the community (Chow, 1983; Gallin, 1986).

In summary, the Republic of China cannot, as yet, be classified as a modern nation. However, the onset of modernization, combined with political turmoil and the introduction of socialism, has led to a cultural and political revolution. Although the status of the aged has declined, especially in the larger urban areas, the elderly have experienced a rise in their standard of living. Modernization cannot totally account for the increased status of youth and women. Political questioning of the need for age equality was also a significant factor, as it was in the United States prior to the onset of modernization (Fischer, 1977). However, a major difference between the United States and China is the active role played by the Chinese government in promoting an age-equalization policy. In short, age-stratification systems and the relative status of age groups do not exist in a political or cultural vacuum. In China, the privileged position of the elderly may be eroded further if the government policy of restricting family size to one child succeeds. In this demographic scenario, thirty years from now a middle-aged couple with one teenager will have to support four elderly parents, most of whom will not have a pension.

Israel

Israel represents another example of how the process of aging and the status of the aged varies in an emerging society (Talmon, 1961; Weihl, 1970, 1972, 1983). The State of Israel was formed in 1948, although the first kibbutz was established by Jewish immigrants in 1909. Israel is largely composed of immigrants who are classified as 'veterans' or 'non-veterans' (Weihl, 1970). The veterans emigrated early in life and developed the society; the non-veterans arrived later in life and had to adapt to existing institutions and norms. Generally, these immigrants came either from eastern European countries or from the Middle East and the Orient. The non-European aged, in general, have had more difficulty in adjusting because of their higher illiteracy rates and because Israeli pension payments are based on length of residency and employment in the country (Weihl, 1970). Thus, because of economic necessity and cultural tradition, a large percentage of non-Europeans live with their children.

A unique feature of Israeli society is the kibbutz. A kibbutz is a group of 50 to 1,000 people who live in a self-sustaining economic and household community (Feder, 1972; Wershow, 1973). For the most part kibbutzes are agricultural cooperatives (although some industries have been established) that emphasize common ownership of property and equality in production and consumption. All members of the kibbutz must work hard to produce sufficient food and goods for themselves. The oldest men and women in the kibbutz are called *vatikim*. In addition to receiving the same benefits as regular members, they are usually given better-quality housing. They also benefit from close family bonding, since three generations usually live within the kibbutz.

This bonding has been a source of support in the past. However, there is increasing intergenerational conflict between young members, who wish to see the farming become more mechanized, and the *vatikim*, who adhere to the philosophy of manual labor to produce goods. Although the elderly oppose retirement because it reflects a life without purpose or meaning, they nevertheless engage in a process of gradual retirement that involves lighter tasks and reduced hours of work. In this way they become more dependent on communal institutions, and as their numbers increase because of longevity, they become a greater economic burden (Shomaker, 1984). As a result, some *kibbutzim* have established industries where the elderly can be assigned to work at easy but tedious tasks, thereby enabling them to continue in some functional capacity. However, for the old women in particular, this creates a problem; they cannot adapt to the repetitive factory chores to which they are assigned.

In summary, although the system is not without social strain, the Israeli kibbutz represents a model in which many of the basic problems of aging (economic security, family and community relations, health care, and retirement) have been addressed and partially solved. This situation has evolved because of a religious and social commitment to equality, regardless of age.

Canada and the United States

Canada and the United States represent unique multicultural societies. For this reason, it is extremely difficult to describe a modal pattern of aging in each country (Jackson, 1985; Driedger and Chappell, 1987). Nevertheless, some features of these societies make the status of the aged different from the societies described previously.

Although aging and the aged in Canada and the United States are relatively similar, there are some important differences. First, Canada is more socialistic, perhaps because of its historical ties to Great Britain. As a result, the aged tend to receive larger (but still inadequate) government pensions. They also receive greater health care benefits through subsidized medical plans operated by the public and private sectors. Second, although the historical and social development of the two countries has followed a similar pattern, Canada has generally been slower in adopting new ideas, values, and norms (for example, the 'gray power' movement and senior citizen activist groups appeared much earlier in the U.S.). Third, the climate in Canada is less conducive to retirement villages, and many Canadian retirees, or 'snowbirds,' winter in the southern United States. Finally, most Canadian cities and towns have fewer native, ethnic, and racial minorities, and except for the native Inuit and Indian groups, those that do exist may be less disadvantaged and more acculturated than blacks or Hispanics in the United States. However, Canada does have a large French-Canadian (francophone) population (22 percent) with different social, religious, and political values from those of the dominant anglophone population (Driedger and Chappell, 1987). These Canadian and American differences are noted throughout the book, particularly with respect to public-sector support, the adoption of new ideas, and the status of the elderly in minority groups.

AGING AND THE AGED IN SUBCULTURES

The Concept of Subcultures

Within multicultural societies such as Canada and the United States, there exist various unique subcultures. These may be natural groups based on race or ethnicity, or they may be created when members of a subgroup acquire and adhere to a set of norms, values, customs, behaviors, and attitudes that are different from those accepted and used within the larger society. In some instances the group may use a different language, and may be physically and/or socially separated from mainstream society in such homogeneous environments as a reservation, ghetto, barrio[8] or retirement community.

A subculture may form when values and norms differ in content and importance from those of mainstream society, when they cease to be a fad and become stable over time, and when they begin to regulate the behavior of individuals in the group. Once these values and norms are adopted by a number of individuals, who may or may not interact with each other, they begin to influence the existing occupational and leisure lifestyles, or they lead to the creation of new lifestyles. This sharing of norms, values, attitudes, language, behavior, and dress gives the subgroup a distinct social identity, regardless of existing or previous social or physical commonalities. Social categories such as age, race, ethnicity, religion, and occupation often serve as the initial catalysts in the formation of a subculture.[9]

Subcultural traits can develop either from the members being physically isolated from mainstream society (on a reservation), or from their self-imposed isolation because of different behavior, beliefs, or economic opportunities (in ghettos or barrios). Through this process of isolation, and the growth of in-group solidarity via language, dress, or behavior, the degree of communication and social interaction with outsiders in mainstream society varies greatly (Lee, 1987).

The most common, intact subcultures are those based on race or ethnicity. In North America, many of these subcultures are also labeled as **minority groups** (Kent, 1971; Jackson, 1980, 1985; Manuel, 1982; Gibson, 1988). However, it is important to note that not all racial or ethnic groups are minority groups. Rather, ethnic and other minority groups experience discrimination in varying degrees, leading to different opportunity structures, rewards, and privileges within mainstream society. These can vary across time as subsequent generations of the same ethnic or racial group experience less or little discrimination, and increased opportunities for social mobility.

The various ethnic and racial groups are also stratified within mainstream society. As a result, members of some groups may have varying lifestyles and life chances compared to individuals in other racial or ethnic groups. For example, ethnicity may be a more powerful factor than age or social class on such lifestyle factors as educational attainment, the timing of role exits, health, self-concept, morale, and economic dependency. Minority-group women generally experience discrimination to a greater extent than other women, while Mexican-Americans experience discrimination to a greater extent than blacks or whites. It is important that the common characteristics of all minority ethnic or racial groups, and the unique characteristics of specific subcultures, be examined with respect to the aging process, both at a given point in time and at different historical periods.

Moore (1971) outlined five characteristics of minority subcultures. First, each subculture has a unique history, and the cultural origins and the life history of the group within the dominant society must be considered. Second, this history is often marked by discrimination, stereotypes, and repression, by restrictions on where members can live in a community or nation, and by persistence in retaining the native language. Third, there is great variation within subcultures, between individual groups (different Indian tribes) and within a specific group (blacks living in New York City versus blacks living in the rural South).

A fourth characteristic of minority subcultures is that they often develop their own coping organizations (church, clubs, family) in order to survive independently of mainstream society. Finally, many subcultures experience social change within the group that can influence their lifestyle in different ways. For example, older blacks may adhere to a philosophy of 'Uncle Tomism' in which they accept discrimination and second-class status. In contrast, younger blacks may be more likely to adhere to 'black power' values and ideals in which they seek equality in society, sometimes by the use of force or by legislation (Affirmative Action).

Although there is a need to understand the process of aging within the various subcultures, a number of problems are associated with obtaining this information (Ujimoto, 1981; Gibson, 1988). First, like cross-cultural studies, analyses of subcultures have been primarily descriptive, qualitative studies of one specific social milieu. Structural characteristics and meanings may be described that do not apply across all strata within a particular subculture.

Another problem is that of distinguishing subcultural boundaries from each other (the black subculture, the Hispanic subculture, and the subculture of poverty), and from the dominant culture itself.

A third problem is identifying the extent to which the individual is influenced by or committed to the norms and values of the subculture; for example, the extent to which the lifestyles of elderly blacks are influenced by the black subculture. Another problem is the extent to which scientists who are not members of the group are able to obtain valid evidence from members of subcultural groups. If the scientists and the members of the group are unable to speak the same language, or if the scientists are unable to understand the in-group values, customs, beliefs or jargon, the data may be misinterpreted. Similarly, members of the subgroup may be suspicious of researchers and may mislead them or present the 'ideal' response rather than describe the real situation. Finally, research of this type often depends on a convenience sample. Hence, the lower- and lower-middle-class segments or elderly respondents may be eliminated from the sample because of language difficulties or because they are reluctant to participate.

In order that the subcultural diversities in life chances (a social structural factor) and lifestyle (a cultural factor) can be appreciated, the process of aging and the status of the aged are described below for indigenous (native), racial, ethnic, rural, religious, and poverty subcultures. Unfortunately, most of this information is based on a summary of the findings from a variety of studies, rather than on in-depth analyses of a specific type of subculture in a variety of settings.

Indigenous Subcultures

Indigenous people are those whose ancestors were the original inhabitants of a region or country. In most situations, these people have either been assimilated to varying degrees because of social, political, or technological change, or have retained their original identity by remaining isolated from mainstream society. The following subsection describes aging among two groups, one indigenous to North America, and one that is unique to the Soviet Union.

North American Indians

Indians are today among the least visible and most deprived of the minority groups in North America. At present, between 30 and 50 percent of Indians live on reservations in rural areas in Canada and the United States. However, for those over 65 years of age, about 75 percent live on reservations, often in substandard housing. Although there is great cultural diversity among tribes, generally their lifestyle and life chances lead to economic deprivation, an average life expectancy in Canada of 47 for women and 46 for men, hunger and malnutrition, little educational opportunity, substandard housing, and difficulty in obtaining regular employment.

In short, members of this subculture are often alienated from traditional lifestyles, resentful and suspicious of mainstream society, and relatively powerless to change their social and economic conditions. Rogers and Gallion (1978), in their study of elderly Pueblo Indians, suggested that there are some characteristics common to most Indian tribes that make them different from mainstream society. These include a deep-rooted loyalty to and identification with the family and tribe, rather than loyalty to the self; a great respect for the elderly and their traditional values and lifestyle; a feeling of stress as a result of **acculturation** and contact with mainstream society; and a population that is increasing rapidly and in which the elderly make up a smaller and smaller percentage of the total Indian population.

Given the harsh living conditions of most Indians, it is easy to imagine that the plight of the elderly Indian is generally worse than that of the elderly person in mainstream society.[10] However, even though 75 percent of the Indian population over 65 years of age live on reservations, relatively little information is available on the aging process in this unique subculture.[11]

For many elderly Indians, total annual income is generally below the poverty line, which is the minimum amount needed for bare subsistence. In addition, many elderly Indians support unemployed children and their families on this limited income (Williams, 1980). The status of the aged Indian is lowered further by a lifetime of poor health compounded by a lack of access to health care facilities (Bienvenue and Havens, 1986). Most reservations have no nursing care facilities, and elderly Indians who need regular health care must enter a nursing home away from the familiar lifestyle of the reservation. There, they seldom have access to their native food, they see family and friends infrequently, and they often experience cultural shock.

Indians who migrate to urban settings learn that marketable skills are necessary for survival. Those who are educated in the public school system and who adopt Christianity and the values of mainstream society generally show less respect for the aged. These young, educated Indians are increasingly occupying leadership roles, which in the past were held only by the elders. This shift in power and prestige can result in intergenerational conflict (Williams, 1980).

In summary, the elderly on reservations experience poverty, malnutrition, loss of respect, and poor general health. Despite the intervention of federal health and financial assistance programs, the aged still suffer higher unemployment, more substandard living conditions, and greater poverty than any other minority group in North America. While other ethnic and racial groups have been assimilated into the dominant culture to some degree, the Indian, like the Eskimo, has remained both culturally and physically isolated. Fortunately, because many share a household on a reservation with other members of the family, an informal support network is available (Bienvenue and Havens, 1986). Because statistics indicate that Indians have a shorter life expectancy than whites, it has been argued that the eligible age for federal assistance should be lowered from 60 to 45 years of age. In this way, a larger number would then be eligible to collect assistance earlier in life.

The Abkhasians of the Georgian Republic

This society of collective farms in and around rural villages is located in the Caucasus Mountains in the southern USSR. It has become identified as a unique subculture because of the vitality and apparent longevity of its citizens. However, recent evidence suggests that within this society only 0.3 percent of the population is over 90 years of age, compared to 0.2 percent throughout the rest of the Soviet Union (Palmore, 1984; Bennett and Garson, 1986). In this society the elderly are highly valued, and their prestige seems to increase with age. This is one reason birth records, if they exist at all, may be altered: people wish to appear older than they actually are and thereby acquire greater status. Hence, in the absence of accurate birth records, age exaggeration may begin at about the age of 70 in order to enhance one's status and worth in the society (Fry, 1985).

The Abkhasians work at their own pace from childhood to death, and are never fully retired. Throughout, there is stability in lifestyle, with an emphasis on the attitude that work is essential for everyone regardless of age. These people appear physically younger than their years, and they have the culturally induced expectation and the hope that they will live long lives.

Although an explanation for this longevity is lacking, heredity, combined with various sociocultural factors, seems to account for the extended life. Longevity in this subculture may be influenced by many factors: a system of folk medicine; a low-calorie, low-cholesterol diet of vegetables and milk; lack of competition among workers; and a strong bond with a large extended family, including nonrelatives who have the same surname. All of these combine to provide a serene, secure, and healthy lifestyle. However, as Benet (1974) notes, the younger generation is consuming more calories per day than earlier generations, and the Soviet government has introduced worker competition into the collective system. It will be interesting to observe whether these and other factors change the longevity and status of the elderly in the next century.

Racial and Ethnic Subcultures

Racial subcultures are those in which such ascribed physical features as skin color, eyelid fold, or physical stature predominate to make the members appear different from those in mainstream society. However, it is not the physical characteristics that set them apart socially, politically, or economically. Rather, it is the social meanings assigned to these features by the dominant group, which views itself as superior. Adherence to subcultural values and attitudes by members of the minority group will also set them apart. It must be stressed, however, that there is great variation within subcultures, just as there is within mainstream society. For example, although a majority of blacks are located in the lower socioeconomic stratum, they are also found in the middle and upper levels. Thus, not everyone in the subculture ages or experiences the later years in a similar way (Jackson, 1980, 1985; Jackson et al., 1990).

Ethnic subcultures are those in which cultural characteristics such as language, religion, or national origin influence lifestyle and life chances. In the United States and Canada, many ethnic groups have immigrated at specific historical periods and been subsequently acculturated to varying degrees. Some common examples are the Irish in Boston, the Poles in Chicago, the Ukranians in Western Canada, the Scots in Nova Scotia, and the Italians in Toronto and Boston. In addition, large ethnic groups such as the French Canadians in Quebec have formed a distinct major culture with their own institutions within the larger society. These ethnic groups provide a framework of common values, identity, and history as well as a social network providing assistance and friendship. In short, ethnicity, like race, can influence how specific individuals adapt to the aging process (Gelfand and Kutzik, 1979; Gelfand, 1981, 1982; Holzberg, 1981; Jackson, 1985; Driedger and Chappell, 1987; Markides and Mindel, 1987; Ujimoto, 1987).

Although they form two distinct subcultural groups, both the Chinese and Japanese in Canada and the United States have relatively similar cultural backgrounds. The first generation, who were foreign-born, were socialized to the traditional values of individual dependence on the family, the importance of the family for social support, and the necessity of obedience to and respect for the eldest members of the family and community. This first-generation group has had great difficulty in adjusting to growing old in a foreign culture (Kalish and Moriwaki, 1973; Ujimoto, 1981, 1987; Chan, 1983; Sugiman and Nishio, 1983; Wong and Reker, 1985). While the problem is less severe for each succeeding generation born in North America, the problems of being part of a subculture remain. For example, each generation has experienced a degree of discrimination, although less so than Indians and blacks. The Chinese and Japanese in North America appear to adapt more easily to the postretirement years than do blacks, Indians, or Hispanic Americans. As with most subcultures, there are variations in economic, educational, and health status within each group. This is particularly so among the more recent generations that have experienced considerable social mobility. Thus, when examining the current status of the elderly Asian North American, it is important to distinguish between those who are foreign-born and those who are native-born.

It is also important to distinguish between elderly Chinese North Americans (Cheng, 1978) and elderly Japanese North Americans (Ishizuka, 1978). Although there are many similarities in the cultures and patterns of historical entry into North America, there are also significant differences. For example, among the Chinese, there are still a large number of elderly single males whose families or brides were never permitted to emigrate. Older Japanese women are well represented, because they live longer and because Japanese brides were permitted to emigrate. Thus, the early-generation Chinese elder is often a man with no family, while the elderly Japanese is more likely to be a woman with a family. In addition, the Japanese are generally more integrated within a community, while the Chinese are more likely to live in segregated Chinatowns within large urban centers — a pattern that has inhibited assimilation into the dominant culture. Highlights 2.3 and 2.4 illustrate the unique process of aging within Chinese and Japanese subcultures in North America.

Rural and Religious Subcultures

Rural Subcultures

We know far less about aging in a rural environment than we do about aging in an urban environment. However, our level of knowledge is increasing annually as more and more scholars and practitioners are recognizing that aging in a rural community represents a unique process.[12] In a rural environment, lifestyles are influenced by such factors as an agricultural economic base; low population density; geographical isolation; fewer social, health, and recreational services than in urban areas; an out-migration of young people to urban centers; a social life revolving around the family and community; later retirement; and limited public transportation facilities.[13] Rural life is often further influenced by homogeneous religious or ethnic traditions and values. As a result, a folk society may exist wherein the belief and value systems emphasize traditions, one's roots, kinship ties, helping others in the community, independence, and rigid adherence to religious, ethnic, and community values (Youmans, 1967, 1977; Ansello and Cipolla, 1980; Hodge and Quadeer, 1983; Krout, 1986; Cape, 1987; Coward and Lee, 1985; Keating, forthcoming).

Just as there are unique methodological problems associated with the study of racial and ethnic subcultures, there are also some special concerns that must be addressed with respect to the study of rural aging (Martin Matthews and Vanden Heuvel, 1986; Krout, 1986; Keating, forthcoming). First, there are definitional problems as to what constitutes 'rural.' To date, rural settings in various research studies have included: any non-metropolitan area; a farm; a village; a town; a small city; a rural county; or the outlying area of large cities. Thus, the definitions are often inconsistent from study to study, so that it becomes impossible to compare the findings. A second and related problem is the tendency to ignore the heterogeneity of rural environments: some are isolated and truly rural, some are within commuting distance of metropolitan areas and represent modern 'bedroom' communities in a rural setting rather than traditional and typical rural subcultures; some are impoverished and some are wealthy; and some are composed of lifelong elderly residents, while others include recently arrived retirees and young and middle-aged adults who commute to urban areas to pursue

AGING IN A CHINESE SUBCULTURE

The Chinese immigrated to North America in two major waves (Wu, 1975). The first to arrive were young, illiterate, unskilled male laborers who came during the 1850s to work as 'coolies' on the railways and in the gold mines. They came from Canton province, and most intended to make their fortune, buy land in China, and return to live on that land in their old age. However, this group stayed in North America, despite experiencing discrimination and hostility. As a result, many withdrew into the relative security of urban Chinatowns, or lived in small towns where they opened laundries or restaurants to serve mainstream society. The second wave of Chinese immigrants, the Mandarins, arrived after 1948 when the Communists occupied mainland China. Most of these immigrants were older, and because of their age, few learned English. This remains a problem, since only about 1 percent of elderly Chinese speak or read English (Fujii, 1980). As a result, they often lack knowledge about services available to them within mainstream society.

Throughout their lives both groups were employed in low-paying jobs, most of which did not include eligibility for private or government pension plans. For the first generation in each immigrant cohort, life was characterized by poverty, illiteracy, adherence to traditional cultural values, and generally poor health because of inadequate access to medical care (Carp and Kataoka, 1976). With each subsequent generation, the importance of an education has been emphasized, especially for boys. Consequently, many Chinese North American professionals and businessmen now serve both the Chinese and dominant cultures. Moreover, each succeeding generation has sought and generally achieved social mobility within larger society.

The situation of the elderly Chinese North American is closely related to whether childhood socialization took place in China or North America. Those who were socialized in China are more likely to adhere to traditional Chinese values, which are often different from those of their children. The older Cantonese in North America are more likely to be men with no families who are in poor health, who lack access to recreational facilities, who use drugs frequently, and who have a high suicide rate. Kalish and Moriwaki (1973) refer to these individuals as 'geriatric orphans.' For both groups, even where a family exists, the value of filial piety is seldom adhered to by subsequent generations. Because they are ineligible for many forms of government financial and social assistance, elderly Chinese people survive on a limited income, often by living with others in a single room, usually within Chinatown.

A major problem of the elderly Chinese has been their inability to afford adequate medical care and their inability to communicate their personal health problems to English-speaking medical personnel. This problem increases when they are institutionalized in nursing homes where they are often unable to communicate with English-speaking staff or fellow residents, and where they usually do not receive their ordinary diet. They become even more isolated in this environment than they were in the larger society.

With the increasing level of education and income acquired by each succeeding generation, the status of elderly Chinese North Americans is improving, and will increasingly parallel the status of aging white Americans and Canadians. While elements of the subculture may always have some impact on the individual, this will be less traumatic as acculturation occurs among future generations. In fact, there is some evidence that cultural roots can be of special significance in enhancing the status of minority elders compared to the status of many elderly persons in mainstream society. This occurs when special institutions and services are established by and for members of the subculture, with or without government assistance (Wu, 1975).

a career. In short, there are a variety of 'rural' subcultures that introduce both quantitative and qualitative differences in the process and the product of aging. At the individual level, rural residents may be lifelong farmers, 'hobby' farmers, farm owners, farm laborers, business-

AGING IN A JAPANESE SUBCULTURE

Japanese North Americans appear to be a racial group that is more socially and economically advantaged, at all ages, than other minority groups. However, this was not always the case. Like the Cantonese immigrants, Japanese immigrants arrived in North America after the 1880s to seek their fortune and then return to Japan. Like the Chinese, the first wave (the Issei) were primarily unskilled laborers, many of whom were second or later-born sons who migrated because their older brothers had inherited the family land and wealth. Unlike the Chinese, however, they were permitted to bring their wives and families or to send for Japanese brides.

The Japanese stressed the importance of learning English and attaining an education so that their children could obtain better jobs. Despite being imprisoned as possible traitors and being forced to sell their property during World War II, the first- and second-generation Japanese in North America have attained a higher socioeconomic status than most other minority groups. This is remarkable, because they did not have easy access to higher education, to jobs, or to the vote.

Most elderly Japanese North Americans are widows, are in good health, and live as independently as possible, since housing is not generally a problem (Montero, 1980a, 1980b). Elderly Japanese of the first(Issei) generation know little English; the third (Sansei) and fourth (Yonsei) generations know little, if any, Japanese. While this creates intergenerational communication problems for some elderly people, it also reveals that the Japanese in North America are less tied to their cultural roots, although there is still respect and support for the family and elders.

Despite the social mobility and cultural assimilation experienced by second- and third-generation Japanese Americans, the quality of relationships with elderly parents has not declined. Osako (1979) notes that the old receive assistance from their children and adjust to a state of dependency and reduced authority without losing self-esteem. This occurs because both generations adhere to the tradition of group goal-orientation, rather than to an individualistic ethic emphasizing self-improvement.

Although relatively little is known about this racial subculture, there appear to be fewer unique problems associated with aging, perhaps because the Japanese North Americans have sought assimilation into the dominant culture. In fact, in recent years there has been a trend toward increased interracial marriage and greater suburbanization. These processes hasten assimilation and further weaken traditional values and the solidarity of the group (Keifer, 1974; Osako, 1979). As a result, the meaning and experience of old age become similar to those of the dominant culture.

men, professionals (lawyers, physicians, dentists, teachers), industrial laborers, local workers, or commuters.

A third methodological concern is whether 'rural' as a concept should be considered as part of a dichotomous variable (rural or urban) or as a continuum (from those who live in an urban megalopolis to those who have always worked on a small, isolated farm). How 'rural' is viewed will determine whether factors related to rural aging are interpreted in comparison with other rural elements, or with factors in nonrural environments. Again, studies have been inconsistent in how information from rural settings is interpreted. Notwithstanding these methodological caveats, we have acquired considerable knowledge about aging and the aged in a rural

subculture, including changes that have occurred as a result of modernization.

In the early twentieth century, living in a rural environment in old age often meant a struggle to survive, especially before universal pension plans were introduced. During this time a father held on to his land as long as he was able to work. When his health declined, control was passed either to the oldest son, or to all sons who stayed on the farm out of a sense of responsibility for the parents. Synge (1980) notes that in rural Ontario the father maintained control, but that sons built their own homes on the family property and contributed to the welfare of the extended family. Farmers who experienced the most difficulty in the later years were often those who were childless. They were almost totally dependent on neighbors or hired laborers for assistance. Thus, old age in the early twentieth century was not a time of retirement and leisure for most farm couples.

With the onset of rural modernization, however, and the out-migration of youth, the elderly in many rural areas have been caught between traditional and modern cultures. In many rural areas the incidence of poverty, substandard housing, and poor health is higher than in urban areas. Moreover, where there is a widely dispersed population, it is difficult to deliver social or health services, particularly in-home health care. In addition, if formal support systems are available, they may be underutilized because the elderly are not aware of the services, because the elderly wish to remain totally independent, or because the lack of public transportation renders the services inaccessible.

When their children migrate to cities or other regions of the country, the rural elderly are often isolated. They become highly dependent on other aging neighbors and on social services that are often inadequate. They are, in many cases, the victims of triple jeopardy — they are old, poor, and isolated. The end result is a restricted social life that often involves 'retirement to the porch' (Lozier and Althouse, 1975). This restricted lifestyle may not be conducive to their mental or physical health. Moreover, this pattern of infrequent intergenerational contact is foreign to their value system and to their past experiences.

In reality, less than 3 percent of Canada's rural elderly residents live on farms. However, between 25 and 33 percent of those living in rural villages or towns are over 65 years of age, and a large percentage of these elderly residents are women. Those who have lived their entire life in a rural setting are part of a unique subculture that has been, and is, characterized by such values and beliefs as : a strong will and sense of independence; a willingness to assist, and accept assistance from, neighbors and kin; a lack of political power due to a small population density; and a greater acceptance of the status quo whereby declining or inadequate housing, income, health or transportation is not perceived or reported as problematic in the later years. This willingness to depend on informal care and assistance may become problem-atic in those aged subcultures where the care-givers (neighbors) are themselves elderly. In this situation, when personal needs exceed the ability of the informal caregivers and the availability of formal services, individuals may have to be moved from the rural community to a facility in a larger urban centre. As with members of ethnic or racial groups, a move to a 'foreign' environment can be traumatic. It is for this reason that more policies and programs for elderly rural residents need to be designed and implemented so that the elderly will be able to age within the familiar and comfortable rural subculture.

Religious Subcultures

Although new religious subcultures (or cults) have arisen within urban centers in recent years, many religious groups selected a rural, pastoral lifestyle many years ago. The Amish, the Mennonites (Bond et al., 1987; Quadagno and Janzen, 1987), and the Hutterites are a few of the unique religious subcultures that survive in rural areas throughout North America. In urban areas, Jews represent the epitome of a religious group that places a high value on the study of gerontology and on the care of their elderly (Gelfand and Olsen, 1979; Cottle, 1980; Driedger and Chappell, 1987). In other societies, individuals and groups are formally or informally stratified by religion (for example, India, Sikh versus Hindu; Ireland, Catholic versus Protestant). This stratification system can have a profound impact both on the process of aging and on the rights, privileges, and status of the elderly, especially older males. Highlight 2.5 illustrates the impact of a religious subculture on the status and lifestyle of elderly Druze males.

A Poverty Subculture

Within almost every large city, there is a unique subculture made up of homeless people who live in single-room dwellings or who sleep in parks, subways, missions, or alleys on or near skid row. These individuals, primarily men, make up a transient, impoverished subculture (Eckert, 1980). In order to explain the existence of skid rows from a social-psychological perspective, Bogue (1963) theorized that men arrive on skid row for the following reasons, ranked in order of importance: economic difficulties, poor mental health combined with alcoholism, poor social adjustment, or physical handicaps. He also suggested that a skid row exists to provide a milieu in which homeless persons can be rehabilitated.

Tindale (1980) interviewed 60- to 75-year-old indigents who were 16 to 20 years of age during the Depression of the 1930s. He found that these men had a lifestyle of poverty before, during, and after the Depression and that they were never able to establish a regular pattern of employment. They often experienced marriage failure, drank heavily, and suffered from poor health. While the Depression made it difficult for them to get established, it was not the Depression per se that led them to a skid-row existence. As Tindale (1980:94) notes, they are 'both the product and the producers of their history.' Now that these old men no longer work, they have little if any contact with their family. They survive and cope with the aging process (except for the physical problems) because life after 65 is not very different from that before 65. The skid-row subculture provides a certain kind of security where residents are respected and unthreatened by their fellow indigents, with whom they share money and goods in order to survive (Rooney, 1976).

In order to survive 'on the streets,' men and women living in single-room occupancy (SRO) hotels develop informal networks to help them fulfill their daily needs. Much of this social support system is composed of the staff and residents of the hotel. Many indigents live in the same hotel for years and find the residence to be a secure support system. This system is not easily replaced if the hotel is demolished in the wave of urban renewal (Cohen et al., 1988). Indeed, Cohen et al. (1988) report that in New York City more than 100,000 low rent SRO apartments have disappeared since 1971.

Some of these indigent people may move to single-room occupancy hotels in other parts of a city as skid-row areas are redeveloped. However, as Cohen and Sokolovsky (1980) report, many skid-row occupants, because of their previous history, have lower monthly incomes than the usual SRO dwellers and may be unable to pay the weekly rent. Thus, they truly become homeless. Also, by being unable to live in an SRO hotel they lose the benefit of assistance from hotel staff as their health deteriorates (Erikson and Eckert, 1977). Clearly, the members of this vulnerable aging and poverty subculture pose an interesting challenge for the social welfare system. Their lifelong nomadic and poverty lifestyle makes it particularly difficult for them to adjust to traditional long-term care institutions when they lose their independence.

In summary, as Bahr and Caplow (1973) concluded, many of the characteristics of skid-row life result from the interaction of poverty, personality problems, and aging (Stephens, 1976). Skid row is often the net that catches single men and an increasing number of women (Lally et al., 1979, Cohen et al., 1988), and locks them into what is essentially an institutionalized way of coping with poverty as they move across the life cycle.

Summary: Aging and Subcultures

In pluralistic societies such as Canada and the United States, there is a need to understand the culture and lifestyle of the various racial, ethnic, and other groups that make up the heterogeneous population. Subcultural groups often have a number of common social characteristics, such as poor education, high rates of unemployment, low incomes, inadequate health care, lack of facility in the English language, and substandard housing. However, there are also many differences between groups, differences that reflect unique cultural backgrounds and specific histories in North America. These differences influence the aging process for members of a particular subculture. This influence often depends on the extent to which the group is isolated from the dominant culture through discrimination or self-segregation. Similarly, the influence of the subculture on individual members depends on the extent to which cultural roots are rejected, and on the degree to which the person is assimilated into the structure and value system of the dominant culture.

For those who are now old, the indigenous,

AGING IN A RELIGIOUS SUBCULTURE

In the Middle East, the Druze are a minority religious sect (Gutmann, 1976). They live in highland villages in Syria and Israel, and follow a traditional way of life in an agricultural economy. In order to coexist with the dominant Muslim world from which they are separated, they raise their sons to be policemen and soldiers for the majority government. For the Druze, religion is central to their identity and way of life, particularly for men. The basic tenets of the religion are kept secret from the outside world, from all Druze women, and from young Druze males who are labeled *jahil*, or 'the unknowing ones.'

As a man enters late middle age, he is invited to become an *agil* and receive a copy of the secret religious text. If he accepts this invitation he gives up alcohol and tobacco and devotes a great deal of time to prayer. As men age, their lives become almost completely ruled by religious duties. Admittance to the religious sect gives men increasing power as they age, because they are thought to serve as a passive interface between Allah and the community. As Gutmann (1976:107) notes, the older Druze 'switches his allegiance from the norms that govern the productive and secular life to those that govern the traditional and moral life.' Religion enables men to continue being active in the community, but on a different level and for a different purpose from when they were younger.

---

racial, or ethnic subculture appears to have a significant influence on lifestyle. These elderly people have historically had less access to the life chances that were available to many of their age peers. Their disadvantaged situation does not improve, and indeed may worsen. Moreover, they are likely to adhere to their basic cultural values, customs, and beliefs, and are often unable to function in a rapidly changing world. Even their children become strangers as they become acculturated and adopt the values and lifestyles of the host society.

In short, to understand the aging process within subcultures, such factors as subcultural values, inadequate incomes, the culture gap between generations, possible lower life expectancy, and linguistic differences must be considered. These elements can create handicaps that influence life chances and lifestyles. They can be particularly influential when isolation, racial or ethnic discrimination, and age discrimination combine to influence the economic and health status of the aged.

SUMMARY AND CONCLUSIONS

This chapter has defined the concepts of culture and subculture, and indicated how the status of the aged and the process of aging

varies across cultures and subcultures. The aging process and the status of the aged was described for preliterate and literate preindustrialized societies, and modernized societies. Particular emphasis was given to the impact of the process and rate of modernization on the function and status of the elderly. The status of the aged was described within a variety of indigenous, racial, ethnic, rural, and religious subcultures, primarily in a North American context.

Based on the information presented in this chapter, it can be concluded that:

1. The meaning of aging, the status of the aged, and the process of aging varies across cultures and subcultures, and at different historical periods.
2. While some universal patterns in the aging process and the status of the aged are observed, cultural and subcultural variations are numerous.
3. In hunting-and-gathering societies where there was a surplus of food, the older members (at least until they became infirm) generally held influential positions in the social, political, and religious spheres of tribal life. They were considered to be a source of knowledge of rituals and survival

skills.

4. In rural, agrarian, and peasant societies where the elderly own or control the land, power and status are retained until land is transferred to a son.

5. It is frequently assumed that the elderly lose power and status when a society becomes industrialized and modernized. To date, the evidence is conflicting. In some societies the status of the elderly declined following modernization; in some, their status declined before modernization, often after an industrial revolution; in some, their status remained at the pre-modernized level; in some, their status declined even without the onset of modernization; and in some, their status declined initially following modernization, but eventually increased after social and technological changes had taken place.

6. Even where support of aging parents is a cultural or subcultural norm, it may not be the preferred pattern. As a result, the quality of the relationship may be low and the physical, emotional, or psychological needs of aging parents may not be met.

7. The subcultures of some racial, ethnic, and religious groups influence the process of aging, particularly the status and treatment of the elderly. Subcultural factors can influence the life chances and lifestyles of the elderly, especially if there is a significant intergenerational cultural gap between aging parents and their children or grandchildren.

NOTES

1. Generally, two levels of culture have been identified. High culture, which in Western society includes classical music, ballet, theater, poetry, and the fine arts, has traditionally been considered the domain of the upper class or the well-educated social elite. Mass or popular culture is made up of those cultural elements that are transmitted by means of the press, the electronic media, or other forms of mass communication. How-

ever, Gans (1974) has also derived five 'taste' cultures wherein age and social class strongly influence who identifies with each level. These include high culture, upper-middle culture, lower-middle culture, low culture, and quasi-folk culture.

2. See Achenbaum, 1974,1978,1985; Hendricks and Hendricks,1981:29-80;Laslett, 1985; Rosenmayr, 1985.

3. See Fry, 1980a, 1980b, 1985; Keith, 1980, 1982, 1985, 1990; Quadagno, 1982; Stearns, 1982; Haber, 1983; Holmes, 1983; Sokolovsky, 1983, 1989; Foner, 1984; Kertzer and Keith, 1984; Rosenmayr, 1985; Cowgill, 1986.

4. Some exceptions include: Simmons, 1945; Shanas et al., 1968; Havighurst et al., 1969; Cowgill and Holmes, 1972; Fry, 1980b; Keith, 1982; Shin and Lee, 1989.

   In 1986 the *Journal of Cross-Cultural Gerontology* began publishing articles concerning non-Western societies, Western societies (comparing subcultural groupings or ethnic minorities), and comparative studies of aging.

   As well, readers interested in this topic should consult the special issue of *Research on Aging*, 5(4), 1983.

5. See Manuel, 1982; Markides et al., 1984, 1990; Jackson, 1985; Dobrof, 1987; Driedger and Chappell, 1987; Markides and Mindel, 1987; Ujimoto, 1987; Canadian Public Health Association, 1988; Gibson, 1988; Rathbone-McCuan and Havens, 1988; Secretary of State, 1988; the *Journals of Gerontology*, 44(1), 1989; Ontario Advisory Council on Senior Citizens, 1989; Jackson et al., 1990.

6. See Cowgill, 1974b; Fischer, 1977; Achenbaum, 1978, 1985; Amoss and Harrell, 1981; Quadagno, 1982; Stearns, 1982; Haber, 1983; Dowd, 1984; Foner, 1984; Fry, 1985, 1988; Cowgill, 1986.

7. Achenbaum and Stearns (1978) suggest that the concept of modernization may be more appropriate for tracing the development of the changing status of the aged in Britain, France, Germany, and North America, and that it may *not* be appropriate for Japan, Russia, Turkey, and Latin American nations.

8. A barrio is a Mexican-American residential community within a large city in the southwestern United States. Here, Spanish is spoken almost exclusively, and a strong cultural identity is maintained.

9. Theories to explain the process of subcultural emergence and development have been proposed by Arnold (1970), Cohen (1955), Shibutani (1955), and Pearson (1979).

10. See Levy, 1967; Doherty, 1971; Goldstine and Gutmann, 1972; Jeffries, 1972; Cowgill, 1974b;

Murdock and Schwartz, 1978; Rogers and Gallion, 1978; Bienvenue and Havens, 1986.

11. Little information is available because of the inaccessibility of many reservations, language problems, a general mistrust of outsiders, and a determination to keep Indian culture, lifestyle, social stucture, and problems private.

12. See Ryan (1985) for an annotated bibliography of rural aging in Canada, and Keating (forthcoming) for a thorough discussion of rural aging.

13. An excellent visual image of aging in a rural environment can be found in a narrated videotape by Dr. Anne Martin Matthews. This forty-minute tape examines independence, loss of transportation, and loneliness among the elders of a rural county in Ontario. The tape is available from the Office of Educational Practice at the University of Guelph.

REFERENCES

Achenbaum, W. (1974). 'The Obsolescence of Old Age in America, 1865-1914,' *Journal of Social History*, 8(Fall), 48-62.

Achenbaum, W. (1978). *Old Age in the New Land: The American Experience since 1790*. Baltimore: Johns Hopkins University Press.

Achenbaum, W. (1985). 'Societal Perceptions of the Aging and the Aged,' pp. 129-48 in R. Binstock and E. Shanas (eds.). *Handbook of Aging and the Social Sciences*. 2d ed. New York: Van Nostrand Reinhold.

Achenbaum, W. and P. Stearns. (1978). 'Essay: Old Age and Modernization,' *The Gerontologist*, 18(3), 307-12.

Amoss, P. and S. Harrell (eds.) (1981). *Other Ways of Growing Old: Anthropological Perspectives*. Stanford, Calif.: Stanford University Press.

Ansello, E. and C. Cipolla (eds.). (1980). 'Rural Aging and Education: Issues, Methods and Models,' *Educational Gerontology*, 5(4), 343-447.

Arnold, D. (ed.). (1970). *The Sociology of Subcultures*. Berkeley, Calif.: The Glendessary Press.

Bahr, H. and T. Caplow. (1973). *Old Men Drunk and Sober*. New York: New York University Press.

Benet, S. (1974). *Abkhasians: The Long-Living People of the Caucasus*. New York: Holt, Rinehart & Winston.

Bennett, N. and L. Garson. (1986). 'Extraordinary Longevity in the Soviet Union: Fact or Artifact,' *The Gerontologist*, 26(4), 358-61.

Bienvenue, R. and B. Havens. (1986). 'Structural Inequalities, Informal Networks: A Comparison of Native and Non-Native Elderly,' *Canadian Journal on Aging*, 5(4), 241-48.

Bogue, D. (1963). *Skid Row in American Cities*. Chicago: Community and Family Study Center.

Bond, J. et al. (1987). 'Familial Support of the Elderly in a Rural Mennonite Community,' *Canadian Journal on Aging*, 6(1), 7-17.

Burgess, E. (ed.). (1960). *Aging in Western Societies*. Chicago: University of Chicago Press.

Canadian Public Health Association. (1988). *Ethnicity and Aging*. Ottawa: Canadian Public Health Association.

Cape, E. (1987). 'Aging Women in Rural Settings,' pp. 84-99 in V. Marshall (ed.). *Aging in Canada: Social Perspectives*. Markham, Ont.: Fitzhenry and Whiteside.

Carp, F. and E. Kataoka. (1976). 'Health Problems of the Elderly of San Francisco's Chinatown,' *The Gerontologist*, 16(1), 30-38.

Chan, K. (1983). 'Coping with Aging and Managing Self-Identity: The Social World of the Elderly Chinese Women,' *Canadian Ethnic Studies*, 15(3), 36-50.

Chen, M. (1989). 'Status of the Elderly in Urban China,' paper presented at the 18th annual meeting of the Canadian Association on Gerontology, Ottawa, October 26-29.

Cheng, E. (1978). *The Elderly Chinese*. San Diego, Calif.: Campanile Press, San Diego State University.

Cherry, R. and S. Magnuson-Martinson. (1981). 'Modernization and the Status of the Aged in China: Decline or Equalization? ' *Sociological Quarterly*, 22(2), 253-62.

Chow, N. (1983). 'The Chinese Family and Support of the Elderly in Hong Kong,' *The Gerontologist*, 23(6), 584-88.

Cohen, A. (1955). *Delinquent Boys*. New York: Free Press.

Cohen, C. and J. Sokolovsky. (1980). 'Homeless Older Men in the Inner-City: Skid Row and SRO,' presented at the 33rd annual meeting of the Gerontological Society of America, San Diego.

Cohen, C. et al. (1988). 'Gender, Networks, and Adaptation among an Inner-City Population,' *Journal of Aging Studies*, 2(1), 45-56.

Cottle, T. (1980). *Hidden Survivors: Portraits of Poor Jews in America*. Englewood Cliffs, N.J.: Prentice-Hall.

Coward, R. and G. Lee (eds.). (1985). *The Elderly in Rural Society*. New York: Springer Publishing Co.

Cowgill, D. (1974a). ' The Aging of Populations and Societies,' *The Annals*, 415(September), 1-18.

Cowgill, D. (1974b). 'Aging and Modernization: A Revision of the Theory,' in J. Gubrium (ed.). *Later Life: Communities and Environmental Policy*. Springfield, Ill.: Charles C. Thomas.

Cowgill, D. (1986). *Aging around the World*. Belmont,

Calif.: Wadsworth Publishing Co.

Cowgill, D. and L. Holmes. (1972). *Aging and Modernization*. New York: Appleton-Century-Crofts.

Davis-Friedmann, D. (1983). *Long Lives: Chinese Elderly and the Communist Revolution*. Cambridge, Mass.: Harvard University Press.

de Beauvoir, S. (1972). *The Coming of Age*. Warner Paperback Library.

Dobrof, R. (ed.). (1987). *Ethnicity and Gerontological Social Work*. New York: Haworth Press.

Doherty, E. (ed.). (1971). 'Growing Old in Indian Country,' in *Employment Prospects of Aged Blacks, Chicanos and Indians*. Washington, D.C.: National Council on the Aging.

Dowd, J. (1981). 'Industrialization and the Decline of the Aged,' *Sociological Focus*, 14(4), 255-69.

Dowd, J. (1984). 'Beneficence and the Aged,' *Journal of Gerontology*, 39(1), 102-8.

Driedger, L. and N. Chappell. (1987). *Aging and Ethnicity: Toward an Interface*. Toronto: Butterworths.

Eckert, K. (1980). *The Unseen Elderly: A Study of Marginally Subsistent Hotel Dwellers*. San Diego, Calif.: Campanile Press.

Erikson, R. and K. Eckert. (1977). 'The Elderly Poor in Downtown San Diego Hotels,' *The Gerontologist*, 17(5), 440-46.

Feder, S. (1972). 'Aging in the Kibbutz in Israel,' pp. 211-26 in D. Cowgill and L. Holmes (eds.). *Aging and Modernization*. New York: Appleton-Century-Crofts.

Fischer, D. (1977). *Growing Old in America*. London: Oxford University Press.

Foner, N. (1984). *Ages in Conflict: A Cross-Cultural Perspective on Inequality between Old and Young*. New York: Columbia University Press.

Fry, C. (1980a). 'Towards an Anthropology of Aging,' pp. 1-20 in C. Fry (ed.). *Aging in Culture and Society: Comparative Viewpoints and Strategies*. New York: Praeger Publishers.

Fry, C. (ed.). (1980b). *Aging in Culture and Society: Comparative Viewpoints and Strategies*. New York: Praeger Publishers.

Fry, C. (1985). 'Culture, Behavior, and Aging in the Comparative Perspective,' pp. 216-44 in J. Birren and W. Schaie (eds.). *Handbook of the Psychology of Aging*. 2d ed. New York: Van Nostrand Reinhold.

Fry, C. (1988). 'Theories of Age and Culture,' pp. 447-81 in J. Birren and V. Bengtson (eds.). *Emergent Theories of Aging*. New York: Springer Publishing Co.

Fujii, S. (1980). 'Minority Group Elderly: Demographic Characteristics and Implications for Public Policy,' pp. 261-84 in C. Eisdorfer (ed.). *Annual Review of Gerontology and Geriatrics*. vol. 1. New York: Springer Publishing Co.

Gallin, R. (1986). 'Mothers-in-law and Daughters-in-law: Intergenerational Relations within the Chinese Family in Taiwan,' *Journal of Cross-Cultural Gerontology*, 1(1), 31-49.

Gans, H. (1974). *Popular Culture and High Culture: An Analysis and Evaluation of Taste*. New York: Basic Books.

Gelfand, D. (1981). 'Ethnicity and Aging,' pp. 91-117 in C. Eisdorfer (ed.). *Annual Review of Gerontology and Geriatrics*. vol. 2. New York: Springer Publishing Co.

Gelfand, D. (1982). *Aging: The Ethnic Factor*. Cambridge, Mass.: Winthrop Publishers, Inc.

Gelfand, D. and A. Kutzik (eds.). (1979). *Ethnicity and Aging: Theory, Research and Policy*. New York: Springer Publishing Co.

Gelfand, D. and J. Olsen. (1979). 'Aging in the Jewish Family and the Mormon Family,' pp. 206-21 in D. Gelfand and A. Kutzik (eds.). *Ethnicity and Aging: Theory, Research and Policy*. New York: Springer Publishing Co.

Gibson, R. (1988). 'Minority Aging Research: Opportunity and Challenge,' *The Gerontologist*, 28(4), 559-60.

Goldstine, T. and D. Gutmann. (1972). 'A TAT Study of Navajo Aging,' *Psychiatry*, 35(4), 373-84.

Goody, J. (1976). 'Aging in Nonindustrial Societies,' pp. 117-29 in R. Binstock and E. Shanas (eds.). *Handbook of Aging and the Social Sciences*. New York: Van Nostrand Reinhold.

Gutmann, D. (1976). 'Alternatives to Disengagement: The Old Men of the Highland Druze,' pp. 88-108 in J. Gubrium (ed.). *Time, Roles and Self in Old Age*. New York: Human Sciences Press.

Haber, C. (1983). *Beyond Sixty-Five: The Dilemma of Old Age in America's Past*. New York: Cambridge University Press.

Harlan, W. (1964). 'Social Status of the Aged in Three Indian Villages,' *Vita Humana*, 7, 239-52.

Havighurst, R. et al (eds.). (1969). *Adjustment to Retirement: A Cross-National Study*. Assen, the Netherlands: Van Gorcum.

Hendricks, J. and C. Hendricks. (1977-78). 'The Age Old Question of Old Age: Was It Really So Much Better Back When?' *International Journal of Aging and Human Development*, 8(2), 139-54.

Hendricks, J. and C. Hendricks. (1981). *Aging in Mass Society: Myths and Realities*. 2d ed. Cambridge, Mass.: Winthrop Publishers.

Hodge, G. and M. Quadeer. (1983). *Towns and Villages in Canada*. Toronto: Butterworths.

Holmberg, A. (1969). *Nomads of the Long Bow*. Garden City, N.Y.: Natural History Press.

Holmes, L. (1972). 'The Role and Status of the Aged in a Changing Samoa,' pp. 73-89 in D. Cowgill and L. Holmes (eds.). *Aging and Modernization*. New York: Appleton-Century-Crofts.

Holmes, L. (1976). 'Trends in Anthropological Gerontology: From Simmons to the Seventies,' *International Journal of Aging and Human Development*, 7(3), 211-20.

Holmes, L. (1983). *Other Cultures, Elder Years: An Introduction to Cultural Gerontology*. Minneapolis, Minn.: Burgess Publishing Co.

Holzberg, C. (1981). 'Cultural Gerontology: Towards an Understanding of Ethnicity and Aging,' *Culture*, 1(1), 110-22.

Ikels, C. (1983). *Aging and Adaptation: Chinese in Hong Kong and the United States*. Hamden, Conn.: Archon Books, Shoe String Press.

Ishizuka, K. (1978). *The Elderly Japanese*. San Diego, Calif.: Campanile Press, San Diego University.

Jackson, J. (1980). *Minorities and Aging*. Belmont, Calif.: Wadsworth Publishing Co.

Jackson, J. (1985). 'Race, National Origin, Ethnicity, and Aging,' pp. 264-303 in R. Binstock and E. Shanas (eds.). *Handbook of Aging and the Social Sciences*. 2d ed. New York: Van Nostrand Reinhold.

Jackson, J. et al. (1990). 'Cultural, Racial, and Ethnic Minority Influences on Aging,' pp. 103-23 in J. Birren and W. Schaie (eds.). *Handbook of the Psychology of Aging*. 3d ed. San Diego, Calif.: Academic Press.

Jefferies, W. (1972). 'Our Aged Indians,' pp. 7-10 in *Triple Jeopardy — Myth or Reality*. Washington, D.C.: National Council on Aging.

Kalish, R. and S. Moriwaki. (1973). 'The World of the Elderly Asian American,' *Journal of Social Issues*, 29(2), 187-209.

Kamo, Y. (1988). 'A Note on Elderly Living Arrangements in Japan and the United States,' *Research on Aging*, 10(2), 297-305.

Keating, N. (forthcoming). *Aging in Rural Canada*. Toronto: Butterworths.

Keifer, C. (1974). *Changing Cultures, Changing Lives*. San Francisco: Jossey-Bass.

Keith, J. (1980). 'The Best Is Yet to Be: Toward an Anthropology of Age,' pp. 339-64 in B. Siegel et al. (eds.). *Annual Review of Anthropology*. vol. 9. Palo Alto, Calif.: Annual Reviews, Inc.

Keith, J. (1982). *Old People as People: Social and Cultural Influences on Aging and Old Age*. Cambridge, Mass.: Winthrop Publishers.

Keith, J. (1985). 'Age in Anthropological Research,' pp. 231-63 in R. Binstock and E. Shanas (eds.). *Handbook of Aging and the Social Sciences*. 2d ed. New York: Van Nostrand Reinhold.

Keith, J. (1990). 'Age in Social and Cultural Contexts: Anthropological Perspectives,' pp. 91-111 in R. Binstock and L. George (eds.). *Handbook of Aging and the Social Sciences*. 3d ed. San Diego, Calif.: Academic Press.

Kent, D. (ed.). (1971). 'The Elderly in Minority Groups,' *The Gerontologist*, 11(1), 26-98.

Kertzer, D. and J. Keith (eds.). (1984). *Age and Anthropological Theory*. Ithaca, N.Y.: Cornell University Press.

Krout, J. (1986). *The Aged in Rural America*. Westport, Conn.: Greenwood Press.

Lally, M. et al. (1979). 'Older Women in Single Room Occupant (SRO) Hotels: A Seattle Profile,' *The Gerontologist*, 19(1), 67-73.

Laslett, P. (1985). 'Societal Development and Aging,' pp. 199-230 in R. Binstock and E. Shanas (eds.). *Handbook of Aging and the Social Sciences*. 2d ed. New York: Van Nostrand Reinhold.

Lee, J. (1987). 'The Invisible Lives of Canada's Gray Gays,' pp. 138-55 in V. Marshall (ed.). *Aging in Canada: Social Perspectives*. Don Mills, Ont.: Fitzhenry and Whiteside.

Levy, J. (1967). ' The Older American Indian,' in E. Youmans (ed.). *Older Rural Americans: A Sociological Perspective*. Lexington: University of Kentucky.

Lozier, J. and R. Althouse. (1975). 'Retirement to the Porch in Rural Appalachia,' *International Journal of Aging and Human Development*, 6(1), 7-15.

Maeda, D. (1975). 'Growth of Old People's Clubs in Japan,' *The Gerontologist*, 15(3), 254-56.

Manuel, R.C. (ed.). (1982). *Minority Aging: Sociological and Social Psychological Issues*. Westport, Conn.: Greenwood Press.

Markides, K. and C. Mindel. (1987). *Aging and Ethnicity*. Beverley Hills, Calif.: Sage Publications.

Markides, K. et al. (1984). *Ethnicity and Aging: A Bibliography*. San Antonio, Tex.: Trinity University Press.

Markides, K. et al. (1990). 'Race, Ethnicity and Aging: Conceptual and Methodological Issues,' pp. 112-28 in R. Binstock and L. George (eds.). *Handbook of Aging and the Social Sciences*. 3d ed. San Diego, Calif.: Academic Press.

Martin, L. (1988). 'The Aging of Asia,' *Journal of Gerontology: Social Sciences*, 43(4), S99-113.

Martin Matthews, A. and A. Vanden Heuvel. (1986). 'Conceptual and Methodological Issues in Research on Aging in Rural versus Urban Environments,' *Canadian Journal on Aging*, 5(1), 49-60.

Maxwell, R. (1970). 'The Changing Status of Elders in a Polynesian Society,' *Aging and Human Development*, 1(2), 137-46.

Maxwell, R. and P. Silverman. (1970). 'Information and Esteem: Cultural Consideration in the Treatment of the Aged,' *Aging and Human Development*, 1(4), 361-92.

McKain, W. (1972). 'The Aged in the USSR,' pp. 151-65 in D. Cowgill and L. Holmes (eds.). *Aging and Modernization*. New York: Appleton-Century-Crofts.

McKee, P. and H. Kauppinen. (1986). *The Art of Aging: A Celebration of Old Age in Western Art*. New York: Human Sciences Press.

Montero, D. (1980a). 'The Elderly Japanese-Americans: Aging among the First Generation Immigrants,' *Genetic Psychology Monographs*, 101(1), 99-118.

Montero, D. (1980b). *Japanese-Americans: Changing Patterns of Ethnic Affiliation over Three Generations*. Boulder, Colo.: Westview Press.

Moore, J. (1971). 'Situational Factors Affecting Minority Aging,' *The Gerontologist*, 11(1), 83-93.

Murdock, S. and D. Schwartz. (1978). 'Family Structure and the Use of Agency Services: An Examination of Patterns among Elderly Native Americans,' *The Gerontologist*, 18(5), 475-81.

Ontario Advisory Council on Senior Citizens. (1989). *Aging Together: An Exploration of Attitudes towards Aging in Multicultural Ontario*. Toronto: Ontario Advisory Council on Senior Citizens.

Osako, M. (1979). 'Aging and Family among Japanese Americans: The Role of Ethnic Tradition in the Adjustment of Old Age,' *The Gerontologist*, 19(5), 448-55.

Palmore, E. (1975a). 'The Status and Integration of the Aged in Japanese Society,' *Journal of Gerontology*, 30(2), 199-208.

Palmore, E. (1975b). *The Honorable Elders: A Cross-Cultural Analysis*. Durham, N.C.: Duke University Press.

Palmore, E. (1975c). 'What Can the USA Learn from Japan about Aging?' *The Gerontologist*, 15(1), 64-67.

Palmore, E. (1984). 'Longevity in Abkhazia: A Reevaluation,' *The Gerontologist*, 24(1), 95-96.

Palmore, E. and K. Manton. (1974). 'Modernization and Status of the Aged: International Correlations,' *Journal of Gerontology*, 29(2), 205-10.

Pearson, K. (1979). *Surfing Subcultures of Australia and New Zealand*. St. Lucia: University of Queensland Press.

Piovesana, G. (1979). 'The Aged in Chinese and Japanese Cultures,' pp. 13-20 in J. Hendricks and C. Hendricks (eds.). *Dimensions of Aging: Readings*. Cambridge, Mass.: Winthrop Publishers.

Plath, D. (1972). 'Japan: The After Years,' pp. 133-50 in D. Cowgill and L. Holmes (eds.). *Aging and Modernization*. New York: Appleton-Century-Crofts.

Press, I. and M. McKool. (1972). 'Social Structure and Status of the Aged: Toward Some Valid Cross-Cultural Generalizations,' *Aging and Human Development*, 3(4), 297-306.

Quadagno, J. (1982). *Aging in Early Industrial Society: Work, Family and Social Policy in Nineteenth Century England*. New York: Academic Press.

Quadagno, J. and J. Janzen. (1987). 'Old Age Security and the Family Life Course: A Case Study of Nineteenth-Century Mennonite Immigrants to Kansas,' *Journal of Aging Studies*, 1(1), 33-49.

Rathbone-McCuan, E. and B. Havens (eds.). (1988). *North American Elders: US and Canadian Perspectives*. Westport, Conn.: Greenwood Press.

Rhoads, E. (1984). 'Reevaluation of the Aging and Modernization Theory: The Samoan Evidence,' *The Gerontologist*, 24(3), 243-50.

Rogers, J. and T. Gallion. (1978). 'Characteristics of Elderly Pueblo Indians in New Mexico,' *The Gerontologist*, 18(5), 482-87.

Rooney, J. (1976). 'Friendship and Disaffiliation among the Skid Row Population,' *Journal of Gerontology*, 31(1), 82-88.

Rosenmayr, L. (1985). 'Changing Values and Positions of Aging in Western Culture,' pp. 190-215 in J. Birren and W. Schaie (eds.). *Handbook of the Psychology of Aging*. 2d ed. New York: Van Nostrand Reinhold.

Rosow, I. (1965). 'And Then We Were Old,' *Trans-Action*, 2(2), 20-26.

Ryan, N. (1985). *Rural Aging in Canada: An Annotated Bibliography*. Guelph, Ont.: Gerontology Research Centre, University of Guelph.

Secretary of State. (1988). *Aging in a Multicultural Canada: A Graphic Overview*. Ottawa: Policy, Analysis and Research Directorate, Multiculturalism.

Shanas, E. et al. (1968). *Old People in Three Industrial Societies*. New York: Atherton Press.

Shibutani, T. (1955). 'Reference Groups as Perspectives,' *American Journal of Sociology*, 60(6), 562-69.

Shin, E. and J. Lee (1989). 'Convergence and Divergence in the Status of the Aged: An Analysis of Cross-National and Longitudinal Variations in 32 Selected Countries,' *Journal of Aging Studies*, 3(3), 263-78.

Shomaker, D. (1984). 'Economic Pressures Resulting from Aging of Kibbutz Society,' *The Gerontologist*, 24(2), 313-17.

Simmons, L. (1945). *The Role of the Aged in Primitive Society*. New Haven: Yale University Press.

Simmons, L. (1952). 'Social Participation of the Aged in Different Cultures,' *The Annals of the American Academy of Political and Social Science*, 279 (Jan.), 43-51.

Simmons, L. (1960). 'Aging in Preindustrial Societies,' in C. Tibbitts (ed.). *Handbook of Social Gerontology*. Chicago: University of Chicago Press.

Sokolovsky, J. (1983). *Growing Old In Different Societies: Cross-Cultural Perspectives*. Belmont, Calif.: Wadsworth Publishing Co.

Sokolovsky, J. (ed.). (1989). *The Cultural Context of Aging: World-Wide Perspectives*. Westport, Conn.: Greenwood Press.

Sparks, D. (1975). 'The Still Rebirth: Retirement and Role Discontinuity,' in D. Plath and E. Brill (eds.). *Adult Episodes in Japan*. Leiden, the Netherlands: Brill.

Stearns, P. (1976). *Old Age in European Society: The Case of France*. New York: Holmes & Meier.

Stearns, P. (ed) (1982). *Old Age in Preindustrial Society*. New York: Holmes & Meier.

Stephens, J. (1976). *Loners, Losers and Lovers*. Seattle: University of Washington Press.

Streib, G. (1987). 'Old Age in Sociocultural Context: China and the United States,' *Journal of Aging Studies*, 1(2), 95-112.

Sugiman, P. and H. Nishio. (1983). 'Socialization and Cultural Duality among Aging Japanese Canadians,' *Canadian Ethnic Studies*, 15(3), 17-35.

Synge, J. (1980). 'Work and Family Support Patterns of the Aged in the Early Twentieth Century,' pp. 135-44 in V. Marshall (ed.). *Aging in Canada: Social Perspectives*. Don Mills, Ont.: Fitzhenry and Whiteside.

Talmon, Y. (1961). 'Aging In Israel — A Planned Society,' *American Journal of Sociology*, 67(3), 284-95.

Tindale, J. (1980). 'Identity Maintenance Processes of Old Poor Men,' pp. 88-94 in V. Marshall (ed.). *Aging in Canada: Social Perspectives*. Don Mills, Ont.: Fitzhenry and Whiteside.

Treas, J. (1979). 'Socialist Organization and Economic Development in China: Latent Consequences for the Aged,' *The Gerontologist*, 19(1), 34-43.

Ujimoto, V. (1981). 'Theoretical and Methodological Issues in the Study of Aged Ethnic Minorities,' presented at the 9th biennial conference, Canadian Ethnic Studies Conference, Edmonton, Alta, Oct. 1981.

Ujimoto, V. (1987). 'The Ethnic Dimension of Aging in Canada,' pp. 111-37 in V. Marshall (ed.). *Aging in Canada: Social Perspectives*. Markham, Ont.:

Fitzhenry and Whiteside.

Vanderburgh, R. (1987). 'Modernization and Aging in the Anicinabe Context,' pp. 100-110 in V. Marshall (ed.). *Aging in Canada: Social Perspectives*. 2d ed. Markham, Ont.: Fitzhenry and Whiteside.

Watson, W. and R. Maxwell. (1977). *Human Aging and Dying: A Study in Sociocultural Gerontology*. New York: St. Martin's Press.

Weihl, H. (1970). 'Aging in Israel,' pp. 107-17 in E. Shanas (ed.). *Aging in Contemporary Society*. Beverley Hills, Calif.: Sage Publications.

Weihl, H. (1972). 'Selected Aspects of Aging in Israel, 1969,' pp. 197-209 in D. A. Cowgill and L. Holmes (eds.). *Aging and Modernization*. New York: Appleton-Century-Crofts.

Weihl, H. (1983). 'Three Issues from the Israeli Scene,' *The Gerontologist*, 23(6), 576-78.

Wershow, H. (1973). 'Aging in the Israeli Kibbutz: Some Further Investigations,' *International Journal of Aging and Human Development*, 4(3), 211-27.

Williams, G. (1980). 'Warriors No More: A Study of the American Indian Elderly,' pp. 101-11 in C. Fry (ed.). *Aging in Culture and Society: Comparative Viewpoints and Strategies*. New York: Praeger Publishers.

Wong, P. and G. Reker. (1985). 'Stress, Coping, and Well-Being in Anglo and Chinese Elderly,' *Canadian Journal on Aging*, 4(1), 29-37.

Wu, F. (1975). 'Mandarin-Speaking Aged Chinese in the Los Angeles Area,' *The Gerontologist*, 15(3), 271-75.

Yin P. and K. Lai. (1983). 'A Reconceptualization of Age Stratification in China,' *Journal of Gerontology*, 38(5), 608-13.

Youmans, E. (ed.). (1967). *Older Rural Americans*. Lexington: University of Kentucky Press.

Youmans, E. (1977). 'The Rural Aged,' *The Annals of the American Academy of Political and Social Science*, 429(Jan.), 81-90.

3
Population Aging:
A Demographic Perspective

Health and Welfare Canada, Information Directorate

INTRODUCTION

With the transition from predominantly agrarian rural societies to more industrialized, urban societies, there have been dramatic changes in the size, composition, and distribution of the world's population. This chapter provides an overview of population aging from a demographic perspective.

According to Hauser (1976), changes in the structure and size of societies have been characterized by four interrelated demographic elements. Many of these changes have subsequently influenced the aging process and the status of the aged. The first is a **population explosion**, first in the more developed regions of the world and, after World War II, in the developing nations in Asia, Africa, and Latin America. The world's population increased from about 1 billion inhabitants in 1800 to about 4 billion in 1970 (Hauser, 1976:61) to about 4.9 billion in 1986 (United Nations, 1988). United Nations projections indicate that if fertility rates remain relatively constant, by the year 2020 the world population will total about 7.8 billion, with 1.4 billion people residing in the more developed countries and 6.4 billion residing in the less developed countries.

This explosion has been explained by the **demographic transition** theory, which argues that the age structure of a society changes in four distinct stages. In the preindustrial stage there is little population growth; high birth rates are accompanied by high death rates resulting from famine, epidemics, and wars. The second (or transition) stage is characterized by a continuation of high birth rates, but with mortality rates decreasing significantly, especially among infants and children. These decreases result from technology-related improvements to living conditions such as sanitary water, preventive medicine, consistent food supplies, and better and more accessible medical care. As a result, this stage is characterized by rapid population growth (this stage did not occur in the developing countries until after World War II). The third stage occurs when a nation becomes a modern industrialized society, and is characterized by low birth and death rates. The fourth stage occurs when nations become highly industrialized. At this stage birth

and death rates remain low and balanced, and many countries approach zero population growth (ZPG). The major factor in the last two transitional stages is the decline in fertility rates. It is this decline in birth rate that initiates the process of population aging (Northcott, 1984; McDaniel, 1986). As McDaniel (1986:51) notes, 'individual decisions about the utility or desirability of children, taken collectively, do have unintended population consequences many years hence.'

The second demographic element in the transition to an industrial society is known as the **population implosion**. The population becomes concentrated in a relatively small area, primarily through urbanization. This trend can have different effects on elderly people, both in developed and in developing nations. For example, the quality of urban life does not rise to the same extent in developing countries as it does in developed countries. This is partly because there is usually a higher population density in a smaller area, which can lead to crowded living conditions and competition for scarce resources such as jobs, housing, food and water.

Population displosion is the third demographic element in the transition from folk to modern societies. This process involves the appearance of greater heterogeneity in the population within a geographical location. This heterogeneity increases the likelihood of conflict between various social groups, which may occur when a subgroup seeks to attain social, economic, and political equality with other visible groups. This increasing heterogeneity also requires the introduction of policies and programs that will meet the needs of a diverse elderly population.

The final element is a **technoplosion**. Technological development proceeds rapidly and leads to dramatic changes in the work and leisure lifestyles of people of all ages, although the elderly often have difficulty in accepting and adapting to technological change. When a technoplosion occurs, such as increasing computerization in the workplace and at home, it is often the elderly who are the last to adjust to the change, if indeed they ever do. Yet, technological devices such as microwave ovens, remote control TVs and stereos, cellular telephones, or electronic monitoring devices can assist the elderly person to remain independent and thereby enhance the quality of life in the later years.

Scientists have tried to determine the causes of population changes and what effect these changes have on different age cohorts in a population. Before you can understand the social processes associated with aging, it is necessary to understand the age structure within which these processes operate. The purpose of this chapter is to paint a broad picture of the age composition and distribution of the population throughout the world and in particular countries. This information also provides essential facts for those concerned with developing policies and programs for an aging population (Siegel and Taeuber, 1982: McDaniel, 1986, 1987; Binstock and George, 1990: 350-454). Specifically, knowledge of demographic facts and changing demographic patterns enables policymakers to respond to changing patterns and needs before a crisis occurs (such as a bankrupt pension or health care system).

Demographic information must be considered and interpreted along with valid information about relevant social, political, and economic values, and about the existence of any underlying tensions that may influence future policies (for example, language, federal-provincial responsibilities, youth versus elderly priorities, or perceived rights). Thus, demographic information can provide a starting point for initiating or revising policies in response to the challenges created by an aging population in such areas of public life as the economy, the health care system, the social security and social welfare system, housing, transportation, recreation, and education. For example, a specific policy question facing many community governments is whether to build a school, a senior citizen center, or a chronic care facility. This decision involves the building of a facility that must meet the needs of a specific segment of the population for the next thirty to fifty years. Since current and projected demographic information confirms that aging is a particularly important issue for women, highlight 3.1 discusses some of the particular problems facing older women in an aging society.

The chapter begins with a brief nontechnical introduction to the field of **demography**. The remainder of the chapter presents a discussion of selected demographic patterns relevant to the aging process. Throughout, a few tables and figures are used to illustrate trends and patterns. It is important that you pay attention to the 'numbers' in these graphics, since they can provide you with valuable information not only about the past but also about your own future. For example, write down the year you were born, and add 25. You will probably be a full-time member of the labor force by that year. Add 40 to your year of birth; by this time you will probably be a parent and established in a career. Add 65 and 70, respectively, to your birth year; this will give you the years when most of your birth cohort will retire. You now have an estimate of the demographic profile of your life for some major life stages.

More important than the actual year at which these events will occur for you are: (1) the demographic and social characteristics of your birth cohort in relation to those who were born before and after you; (2) a demographic profile of the social, economic, and political conditions that prevail when you and others reach a particular stage in the life cycle; and (3) the impact of particular social and historical events on your cohort and on others at a given point in history. These are the general concerns of demographers who search for patterns of change over many decades and then, based on varying assumptions, provide projections for the future.

Some textbooks include many pages of demographic statistics or facts. However, even as this book was being written, 'current' published statistical profiles were becoming dated. For example, there is almost always a two-year lag from when the information is collected from individuals through the census or a survey until it is published as aggregated population statistics.[1] Moreover, statistical summaries can be as confusing as they are illuminating because there is often variation in the sources and years of the data, in how the data are categorized in tables or figures, in how a cohort is defined, in how many age categories are used, or in how indices are computed.[2] For example some tables present data for one-, five-, or ten-year cohorts. Similarly, some studies place all

DEMOGRAPHIC AGING: THE ROLE AND OUTCOME FOR WOMEN

The fertility rate of a nation is the most important variable in population aging. Yet, it is the most difficult to explain and predict. It is also a variable that is largely influenced by women's thoughts and values. Therefore, decisions and practices during the childbearing years of earlier cohorts of women can have profound effects on earlier and later age cohorts. It is the long-term decline in birthrates that has led to the growing proportion of elderly people in most modernized nations. This seems to have occurred because of a value shift wherein couples, but particularly women of childbearing age, consciously decide to have smaller families – if they decide to have a family at all! In fact, it has been projected that as many as 16 percent of women in Canada may forego maternity and remain voluntarily childless, often to pursue a career (Statistics Canada, 1984b:33).

In addition to having a profound influence on fertility rates and, hence, on the size of the elderly population, women constitute a large proportion of the elderly population, especially among the very oldest cohorts. Because of the greater life expectancy of women, an unbalanced sex ratio that begins in mid-life becomes exaggerated in late life. For example, in 1981 there were 124 women aged 65 to 79 for every 100 men of the same age. For those 80 and over, this ratio was 184 women to 100 men. This trend is expected to continue so that by the year 2000 the ratio is projected to be 134 and 218 women per 100 men in these two age groupings. This sex imbalance in the later years is further compounded by the pattern whereby women marry men approximately two years older than themselves and, hence, are even more likely to outlive their spouse. Thus, an elderly woman may live ten or more years as a widow. Finally, such other recent lifestyle and demographic patterns as more younger women entering the labor force earlier in life, higher divorce rates, delayed marriages, or never marrying, likely reduce, delay, or curtail childbearing even further.

These demographic and lifestyle patterns change the age-sex structure of a society over a period of time. As a result, individual life chances change, particularly for women. To illustrate, the elderly women of today who were born before 1925 spent much of their life devoted to home and child care. Now, in the later years, they usually lack a pension, and, if widowed, may have lost the economic security of the spouse's pension if it did not include survivor benefits. They also have few savings, having spent little or no time in the labor force. If they do have a pension, either their own or that of their deceased spouse, they may be penalized in the amount of monthly allocation they receive because women live longer. That is, in order that the total value of the pension or annuity be sufficient to provide a stipend for 'life,' it must be 'stretched' over a longer time period. Therefore, because women are expected to live longer, the average monthly payment is lower than that allocated to a male. In many cases, this reduced payment may not be sufficient to maintain an adequate or expected standard of living.

In contrast to the above generation, those women born after the late 1940s may be entering the labor force earlier in life, or reentering in mid-life, and may remain as primary wage earners in the labor force for most or all of their adult life. Thus, they are more likely to arrive at the later years with a full pension, savings, and investments, assuming that they have engaged in full-time work for most of the years. Moreover, because society is experiencing smaller birth cohorts, the promotion and political opportunities for women within a smaller labor force may be greater than those available to their peers in earlier age cohorts. Of course, we must not overlook the fact that women may receive lower pay, and that women may work in jobs lower than their educational status merits.

Clearly, as will be evident throughout your lifetime, the trends and effects of demographic aging are intimately related to female beliefs, decisions, and actions taken, or not taken, at earlier or present stages in history. Thus, while women increasingly constitute a numerical majority of the elderly population, their status during these years is closely linked to their demographic past and to their lifetime opportunities in the labor and marriage markets.

persons over 65 in one category; others use over 60; others use five-year (61-65, 66-70, 71-75, 76-80, 81-85) or ten-year intervals (60-69, 70-79, 80-89). These variations in the reporting of data make it difficult to compare information from a variety of studies, especially within or across countries. These variations also suggest that we must be careful in how the information is interpreted and used, especially when comparing statistics over a period of time.

Clearly, those aged 60 to 65 are different (in health and past experiences) from those who are over 85. Data involving the elderly should be divided into a number of categories in order to obtain a more accurate picture of age cohorts. To illustrate, three cohorts of elderly persons might include the following age groups: 65-74; 75-84; 85+. Another way to conceptualize the diversity within the population over 65 years of age might be to classify individuals not on a quantitative (e.g., chronological age) measure, but on a qualitative measure that relates to functional age: independent, partially dependent, fully dependent.

This chapter focuses more on general trends and patterns of demographic changes in the population than on statistics for a specific country or region of that country. Actual statistics are presented to illustrate important ideas or patterns, particularly if comparative information is available over time or among regions or countries. You should examine and interpret the trends, patterns, and implications revealed by the numbers, rather than simply memorize the numbers. Appendix 1, which provides a general discussion of how to read a table or figure, should be consulted before beginning the next section of the chapter.

You should also visit the government publications section of your library to examine the most recent statistics and trends for your country, region, town, and neighborhood.[3] These trends should then be interpreted to determine their implications for you, your parents, and the older citizens in your geographic locale with respect to the social, political, economic, legal, labor force, and leisure domains. For example, you should be interested not just in those who are over 65 at present, but rather in the characteristics of age cohorts that will turn 65 in the next twenty to thirty years.

The study of aging does not only involve two dichotomous groups — those under 65 and those over 65. Rather, the interrelationships among age cohorts within the age structure must be considered. For example, in periods of high unemployment, if a large proportion of the population between 16 and 25 is unemployed, and if a large proportion over 50 is also unemployed, it might be useful to look for elements of conflict between these two cohorts as they compete for a scarce resource, namely, a job that provides income.

In contrast, when there is consensus among age cohorts, social integration and cooperation should prevail. An increase in the number or proportion of one age group, such as the elderly, can result in a number of population-induced social changes that must be addressed. These might include: (1) in the economic domain, a need for higher pensions, or the onset of high rates of inflation that force more elderly people to seek work after retirement; (2) in the political domain, a redistribution of votes in a region, the development of senior-citizen advocacy groups, and the election of elderly candidates; (3) in the educational domain, the need for adult education, the closing of elementary schools, and an increase in the use of educational television; (4) in the legal domain, an increase in the number of crimes committed by old people (such as stealing to obtain necessities), an increase in crimes against the elderly in urban areas, and a need for legal assistance by the elderly; and (5) more generally, the creation and provision of services to an older client group by leisure, health care, and social workers in each community (Longino, 1982).

AN INTRODUCTION TO THE DEMOGRAPHY OF AGING

The situation of a specific age cohort at a particular period in history cannot be fully understood without an awareness of the antecedent experiences in their life history and the size and composition of other age cohorts in society. This information is provided by demographers, who study three basic processes related to population dynamics: fertility, mortality, and migration. At the macro level of analysis, aging is a demographic process that involves changes in the size, composition, and territorial distribution of the population. The first interest in population aging occurred in France at the end of the nineteenth century when it was observed that the proportion of citizens over 65 years of age exceeded 5 percent (Laslett, 1985; Myers, 1985). This percentage, high for the 1800s, raised concerns in France about the survival of the nation, including its ability to defend itself.

In order to describe the population and to identify the patterns and impacts of change, demographers usually report statistics by using a mean, median, or percentage. Based on patterns from the past, on current statistics, and on assumptions about the future, they make 'projections' of what might happen, rather than 'predictions' of what will happen. In order ultimately to arrive at plausible and realistic projections,[4] demographers must understand and consider a variety of social, psychological, economic, political and environmental factors in the selection of their assumptions. These assumptions should be based on knowledge about: the biological development of humans (is the maximum life span or the life expectancy likely to increase or decrease?); the quality of the environment at work and at home; the availability of, access to, and use of the health care system; the belief systems and behavioral patterns of people (changes in lifestyle factors such as diet, smoking, exercise, alcohol and drug consumption); changing values and norms and diversity by class and gender regarding family size, birth control, marriage, and higher labor-force participation rates by women of all ages. In addition, demographers need to incorporate a range of assumptions that permit them to make a low, medium, or high projection with respect to future fertility rates, population size, the sex ratio, and so forth.

As assumptions or facts change, demographers revise their projections. For example, early projections for the baby-boom cohort born from the mid 1940s to the late 1960s indicated that members of this cohort would experience greater competition for jobs than any other cohort to date. Yet, when the first projections were made, demographers did not include as assumptions the impacts of an energy crisis and double-digit inflation on the economy. As a result, they vastly underestimated the degree of unemployment or underemployment that faced this large cohort in the late 1970s and early 1980s. Needless to say, their projections have been revised accordingly.

Employing census information[5] and vital-statistics registrations,[6] demographers use birth, death, and migration rates to determine the size and shape of the age structure. They collect and analyze statistics such as labor-force participation and unemployment rates, crime rates relating to specific age groups, internal migration rates, and family size. They are also interested in the distribution of the population by geographical region, age, sex, income, occupation, race, religion, and ethnic background. However, they are not merely content with describing changes in the age structure. Rather, they search for possible explanatory factors (social, political, economic, or historical events) that may lead to changes in fertility, mortality, or migration rates, and examine the consequences of these changes in birth, death, and migration rates. Some of these consequences include significant political, social, or economic changes for the society at large, and significant lifestyle changes for individual members.

In addition to these obvious descriptive variables through which they observe trends and make projections, demographers have also devised a number of demographic indicators. These are useful in analyzing patterns of change in population size, composition, and distribution. Some of the common indices that pertain to aging are introduced in the following subsections. Remember that demographic statistics represent generalizations at the macro societal or population level, and that in reality there is often variation in the composition and distribution of the elderly population within and between countries. To illustrate, in 1986 the population 65 years and over in Canadian towns with fewer than 10,000 residents was 14 percent (Stone and Frenken, 1988: table 3). However, there was considerable variation above and below this average by province, as follows: Saskatchewan (20 percent), Manitoba (19 percent), P.E.I. and Nova Scotia (16 percent), On-

HIGHLIGHT 3.2

AGE EXAGGERATION AND INFLATED LIFE SPANS

In chapter 2 we learned that, contrary to earlier reports by gerontologists, objective evidence now refutes the hypothesized pattern of an excessively long life among the Abkasians. There are also errors in age data collected in contemporary North America due to ignorance of correct age, to inflation of actual age later in life, to carelessness in reporting or recording ages, or to a tendency to round off age to a year ending in 0 or 5. Thus, objective documentation from a variety of sources must be obtained to validate the true chronological age of our oldest surviving citizens. Kraus (1987:20) illustrates this point by describing how the truth emerged following the 1986 death of a man who had received considerable attention as the oldest living resident of Canada. Notices of his death indicated that he was 118 years of age. This age was derived from his own reported age when he accepted a Centennial Award in 1967. At that time, he claimed that he was 99 years of age. Following his funeral, one of his sons admitted that his father had inflated his actual age by 11 years at the time of the Centennial Award. This admission was subsequently substantiated by an examination of the father's marriage certificate and of the family Bible that recorded his birthdate, and by a report of his father's own admission of his true age in response to a question from a great-grandson a week before he died.

---

tario (15 percent), Quebec (13 percent), British Columbia (12 percent), Alberta (11 percent), Newfoundland (9 percent), and New Brunswick (4 percent). Furthermore, not all of the regional variation may be revealed by a particular table or graph, because of the way in which the index was constructed; because a significant social, political, or economic fact was unknown or ignored; because the social or economic situation has changed dramatically since the figures were calculated; because information was not available; or because not all of the available information was included in the table or figure.

Life Span

The **life span** is the theoretical maximum number of years an individual can live, usually because of biological limits. Much of our evidence for determining the current life span for humans, which is about 100 to 110 years (Fries, 1980), is based on individual cases.[7] A major weakness of this measure is that it is based on evidence supplied by long-living individuals, and some of these people may exaggerate their advanced age to obtain publicity or status (highlight 3.2).

Another weakness is that the life-span measure represents extreme cases, and these may represent genetic, lifestyle, or environmental anomalies that might never occur again. Thus, Kraus (1987) and others propose a measure that records the 'usual' life span rather than the 'maximum' life span. This is the age to which 1 percent of a particular birth cohort survives. Using data from the United States and Canada since 1960, Kraus found that the usual life span in North America had increased at least two years. Not surprisingly, this increase was greater for females (about 4 percent) and less for males (1 to 2 percent). Moreover, the percentage of the population over age 90 more than doubled in both countries over this twenty-year period. This certainly casts further doubt on the controversial hypothesis (Fries, 1980; Fries and Crapo, 1981) that the maximum life span has become essentially fixed, and that there is a 'rectangularization' of the survival curve (Fries, 1980). In reality, most North Americans die before reaching 100 years of age, although an increasing number are attaining centenarian (100 years of age) status. For example, whereas only about 4,000 U.S. residents were centenarians in 1970, by 1980 the number had risen to 26,000. It is projected that by the end of this century there will be over 100,000, and 1.4 million by 2040, largely because of advancements in medical science and technology (Jorgensen, 1989:89).

Life Expectancy

Life expectancy is the average number of years of life remaining for an individual at a given age. It is determined by recording the death rates for each age at a particular time. Then, 'life tables' are constructed, which make it possible to project the average number of years of life remaining for a person. The two most frequently cited statistics are life expectancy at birth and life expectancy at retirement (or age 65). [8]

Obviously, this measure is related to death rates; a low death rate for a certain age group means a correspondingly high life expectancy. Therefore, it is not surprising to find that as infant mortality has decreased over time, as the standard of living has increased, and as medical care has improved, the average life expectancy at birth for a particular cohort has also increased. These mortality assumptions have recently become more important in population projections. Of particular note are the reduced death rates because of the improved treatment of chronic diseases in the later years (Crimmins, 1984; Kraus, 1988) and because of healthier lifestyles. In early Roman times, life expectancy at birth was 20 years; by 1900 in North America, it was 45 to 50; in the late 1980s, it had increased to about 77 years in Western industrialized nations, to 55 to 65 years in developing nations such as India and China, and to 45 to 55 in the less developed nations in Africa and East Asia (Myers, 1985; United Nations, 1988). Much of this positive increase in life expectancy in developing countries and for less affluent segments of a population, particularly for females, is due to increased public spending on health care (Williamson, 1988). It is projected (Myers, 1985) that by the year 2000 life expectancy at birth in the less developed regions will increase to 62.4 years, with the greatest gains being made in African and Asian countries. [9]

Regional variations in life expectancy in a country may reflect differences in standards of living, climate, or migration patterns of particular groups. For example, the average life expectancy in different sectors of a metropolitan area may vary by as much as four years above or below the area average. This variation results from differences in the quality of life among different social classes. Similarly, although there has been an increase in life expectancy at age 65, the increase has been considerably less than that at birth. Since 1900 in North America the average life expectancy at age 65 has increased only from about 12 years to 17 years.

The pattern of life expectancy throughout the world at any given historical point is influenced by the social and physical conditions that have an impact on an age cohort. Events such as famines, epidemics, wars, and depressions can have a profound impact on a specific age cohort in a specific country. At the same time, the event may have little or no influence on the life expectancy of another age cohort in that society, or on a similar age cohort in another country. For example, a lengthy war could have a significant influence on the life expectancy of those under 25, but considerably less impact on those over 40.

In North America, whites have a higher life expectancy at birth than nonwhites; female rates are higher than those for males (Nathanson, 1984); those living in the North have a higher life expectancy than those living in the South; those in urban areas have higher rates than those in rural areas; and those with higher levels of education and higher incomes have higher rates than those who are less educated and those who have lower incomes. For example, the life expectancy at birth in the United States (based on 1986 statistics) is 74.8 years for the total population, 71.2 for all males, 78.2 for all females, 75.4 for whites, and 69.4 for blacks (U.S. Department of Commerce, 1987). The basic causes for the decreased life expectancy for blacks seem to be linked to such interrelated factors as nutrition, poverty, crime, and access to health care. One interesting pattern that has been noted by demographers is the 'crossover' effect: after about age 80, the life expectancy of nonwhites in North America is greater than that for whites. This suggests that if nonwhites survive to age 80, they are likely to live longer than whites. For example, at age 80 life expectancy in the United States is 6.9 for white males versus 7.1 for black males, and 8.8 for white females versus 9.0 for black females (U.S. Department of Commerce, 1987).

As a cohort ages, life expectancy at later stages in the life cycle is strongly influenced by such related lifestyle factors as marital status, education, occupation, and income. Studies show that those men and women who have achieved distinction in a particular occupation live longer, on the average, than men or women in the general population. To illustrate, the mortality rate of those listed in *Who's Who in America* was approximately 30 percent below that of their age peers in the general population (*Statistical Bulletin*, 1968:2-5; 1979:3-9). However, even within this group of elites, there are occupational differences. For example, women who were community service workers, government officials, librarians, curators, or scientists experienced the lowest mortality rates. Those who were physicians, surgeons, performers, or entertainers had higher mortality rates. For them, such factors as risk, stress, and atypical working hours may account for a lowered life expectancy.

Another important way to measure life expectancy is to consider the qualitative aspects of the concept, rather than merely the quantitative aspect. Thus, measures of disability-free or active life expectancy have been used to focus on the quality of life and to consider such issues as access to life support mechanisms, the economic costs of continuing a life, and the right to die. As proposed by Wilkins and Adams (1983), the measure of disability-free life expectancy subtracts the expected years of long-term institutionalization and disability from expectation of life. This index allows for comparisons to be made between different social groups. For example, Wilkins and Adams (1983:1078) report that whereas a male with a high income can expect to enter old age at 60 and have ten years of disability-free life, a man with a low income can expect to have ten years of disability-free life beginning at 49 years of age. For women, the beginning of disability-free old age is projected to be 60 if she is poor and 65 if well-to-do.

In summary, life expectancy is closely related to such factors as sex, standard of living, and lifestyle, with women living longer in most countries. However, it must be remembered that life expectancy figures are averages, and are based on the assumption that age-specific mortality rates will be the same in the future as they are at present (Marshall, 1980). Thus, individuals within each birth cohort may die earlier or live longer depending on their own unique biological, psychological, and social aging processes. Similarly, there may be cohort differences because of period effects; a particular cohort may be more susceptible to higher (war or epidemic) or lower (discovery of a wonder drug) mortality rates. Finally, it must be noted that there is variation by country in the definitions of 'elderly' or 'old.' For example, where life expectancy at birth is 45, a person becomes 'old' sooner than in a country where life expectancy is 70 years. Similarly, there are different ages for mandatory retirement; these ages range from about 55 years to 70 years. However, despite these variations, the United Nations, and most countries, normally use age 60 or 65 as the benchmark to determine who should or should not be included in the aged population. In the following sections, references to the aged population will usually mean those 65 and older. Again, it must be recognized that the aged are a heterogeneous group wherein there is variation within a specific cohort (65 to 70) and between chronological age groups (65 to 74 versus 75 to 84 versus 85+).

Crude Birth and Death Rates

Crude birth and death rates record the number of births and deaths per one thousand people during a one-year period. They provide a relative measure by which frequencies of births and deaths can be compared over time. Generally, in Western, industrialized nations, both rates have fallen since the early 1900s, with the exception of the baby-boom years from the mid-1940s to the early 1960s (see highlight 3.3).

Throughout the world, the projected average crude birth and death rates are 25.0 and 9.3 respectively for the 1990 to 1995 period. For the period 2000 to 2005 they are projected to fall to 22.3 and 8.5 respectively (U.S. Department of Commerce, 1987). In North America, the current crude birth rates are 14.8 in Canada and

HIGHLIGHT **3.3**

FROM BABY BOOM TO BABY BUST IN NORTH AMERICA

Fertility rates began to decline gradually throughout North America in the early 1900s, reaching a low point in the Depression years of the 1930s. This decrease continued through World War II. However, following the end of the war, marriages interrupted by the war were resumed, and postponed marriages occurred. As a result, birthrates began to rise dramatically in the late 1940s, resulting in a peak in the number of live births during 1958 in Canada and during 1964 in the United States. This sudden bulge created what is known as the 'baby boom' generation, which is generally considered to include those born between 1946 and the mid-1960s. This unique cohort was followed by a period characterized as a 'baby bust.' This era lasted into the early 1980s. This ten- to fifteen-year age cohort, labeled the 'baby bust' or 'shrunken' generation (McDaniel, 1986), occurred as social values changed concerning marriage, divorce, and the ideal family size; and as the women's movement encouraged and facilitated greater opportunities for women in the labor force. This demographic phenomenon of boom and bust is clearly illustrated in the following population pyramid[a] in which the 'baby boom' generation (depicted by the shaded bulge), is followed in history by a very large indentation for those under 15 years of age. Similarly, this phenomenon can be illustrated by the decrease, in Canada, from a fertility rate of 3.5 children per female of childbearing age in 1946 to a rate of 1.6 in 1986.

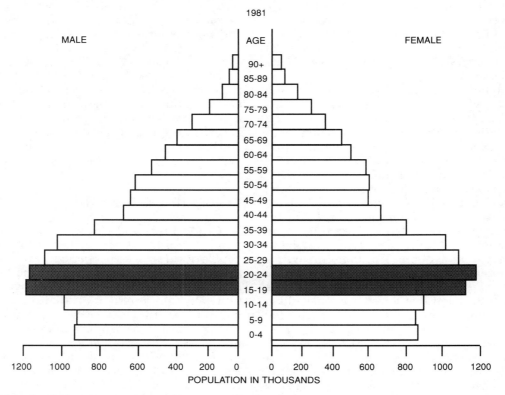

[a]SOURCE: Reprinted by permission from McDaniel, 1986:95.
ORIGINAL SOURCE: Statistics Canada. (1985). *Population Projections for Canada, Provinces and Territories, 1984-2006*. Catalogue No. 91-520. Ottawa: Minister of Supply and Services. Reproduced with the permission of the Minister of Supply and Services Canada, 1990.

These dramatic demographic shifts in the age structure have had, and will continue to have, a dramatic impact on the life chances and lifestyles of those within these two unique generations, as well as for those in other generations. Because of its size, the baby boom generation has been stressed and competitive. Individuals have experienced large and crowded classrooms throughout their school years, the job and housing markets have been scarce and therefore highly competitive, highways have become crowded, baby boomers have actively pursued a leisure lifestyle, and they have experienced high divorce rates. Now in middle age, they will start to retire in 2010, and by 2025 almost all of the baby boomers will be retired, assuming 65 remains the normal retirement age.

This generation has been socialized to expect government social assistance, and they have been highly consumer oriented. Less likely to have built savings for retirement, and given their large numbers, they may expect and demand a public and private pension system to be indexed to inflation so as to maintain their standard of living. Moreover, beyond 2035, a large number will likely place increasing demands on the health care system. The increased longevity, both of their generation and the previous generations, combined with a shrinking labor force because of the following baby bust generation, may exert considerable pressure on the baby-bust generation to support this unique large cohort of elderly persons. These pressures may affect the quality of life for everyone, retirees and workers alike.

But this may not be an easy task, since members of the baby bust generation have been disadvantaged in terms of life chances, especially in the labor force. Because they followed a large generation, those born in the smallest generation have had to compete in an overstocked labor market, which could be compounded by a poor economy at any point in their adult years. The early members of this generation may also be blocked in terms of promotion opportunities, especially if mandatory retirement is eliminated and members of the baby-boom generation remain in supervisory, managerial, and leadership positions into their 70s.

Clearly, the time at which one is born at any point in history, and the subsequent characteristics of the age structure of the society, may have a considerably greater influence on life chances than personal ability, motivation, or even family social status. It will be interesting to observe the fertility patterns that emerge as the baby-bust generation moves through the child-rearing years in the next decades. Will the present pattern persist, will there be a further decrease, or as some demographers predict, will there be another boom? If the present depressed fertility rates continue, we may need to greatly increase immigration rates to maintain population growth and to meet labor-force needs.

15.5 in the United States; the comparable crude death rates are 7.2 and 8.7 respectively. In contrast, some countries in Asia and Africa have a crude birth rate as high as 49 per 1000 people, and crude death rates may reach as high as 20 to 25 in some African countries (United Nations, 1988).

Crude birth rates fluctuate between and within countries, depending on religious beliefs, birth-control availability and use, and social norms concerning marriage and family size. Similarly, crude death rates vary because of such factors as availability of preventive medicine, quality of sanitary services, quality of health care, and the incidence of degenerative diseases, wars, or natural disasters. For example, the eradication of cardiovascular diseases, cancer, and other lifestyle-related diseases in industrialized countries could decrease crude death rates and increase life expectancies

by about five years. This is similar to what happened when tuberculosis and influenza were virtually eliminated as causes of death.

The Sex Ratio

The **sex ratio** is the number of males per one hundred females in a given population. A ratio of 1.0 indicates an equal number, and a ratio of less than 1.0 indicates that there are fewer males than females in that particular age group. Figure 3.1 illustrates two patterns that are found in most modernized nations. Although males outnumber females at birth (about 106 male births per 100 female births), females outlive males as chronological age increases (the dotted line). This changing sex ratio results from a higher incidence of mortality among men, primarily because of accidents prior to early adult-

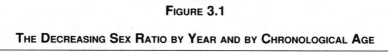

FIGURE 3.1

THE DECREASING SEX RATIO BY YEAR AND BY CHRONOLOGICAL AGE

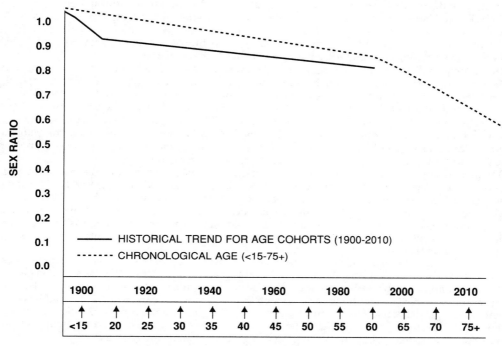

SOURCE: Adapted from reports by Statistics Canada and the United States Bureau of the Census.

hood, degenerative diseases in the middle and later years, and historical events. For example, the sex ratio for all ages in the USSR was 89 males per 100 females in 1985, partly because of the large number of male fatalities during World War II (United Nations, 1988). Similarly, in countries where female death rates are higher (for example, at childbirth), the ratio may be much higher than 100 men per 100 women (for example, in India or Pakistan). As illustrated by the solid line in figure 3.1, the sex ratio has decreased throughout history, as well as across the life cycle for a given cohort.

In North America men outnumbered women in the early 1900s because of higher immigration rates for men. However, the trend, especially since World War II, has been toward a steady decrease in the number of men to women at all ages, but particularly after age 65. This trend can be accounted for by a number of related factors. First, a shift in immigration patterns occurred: although there was a decrease in the actual number of immigrants to North America, more females than males immigrated in the 1930s and 1940s. Many of these people are now older widows. Second, although there have been significant medical advances in this century, the longevity of men has not increased significantly, since they experience a higher incidence of cardiovascular disease than women. Third, men of all ages tend to have higher accidental-death rates.

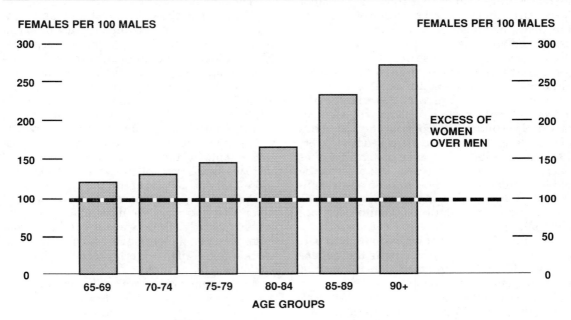

FIGURE 3.2

THE RATIO OF FEMALES TO MALES AMONG OLDER AGE GROUPS, CANADA, 1986

SOURCE: Reprinted with permission from Stone and Fletcher (1986: chart 2.6.1)

ORIGINAL SOURCE: Statistics Canada (1985). *Population Projections for Canada, Provinces and Territories, 1984-2006*. Catalogue No. 89-515E. Ottawa: Minister of Supply and Services. Reproduced with the permission of the Minister of Supply and Services Canada, 1990.

As aging has become increasingly viewed as a women's issue, statistics depicting the sex ratio have been reversed to indicate the ratio of females to males, especially in the later years. For the population 65 years of age and older, the sex ratio in the late 1980s was 138 and 148 women for every 100 men in Canada and the United States respectively. The higher rate in the United States may be partially accounted for by greater involvement in foreign wars and a higher rate of violent crimes. More importantly, as figure 3.2 illustrates, women constitute a higher proportion of the older population as age increases. As noted earlier, this ratio is even higher in rural areas, where elderly women tend to live out their life on the family farm, or in nearby towns and villages. Although this ratio of females to males in the older age groups has increased dramatically since the early 1970s,

the pattern seems to have leveled off in recent years as the gap between male and female mortality rates narrows in the later years. Moreover, as future cohorts of older women enter later life with years of labor-force participation behind them, the ratio may decline further should female mortality rates increase somewhat (for example, due to job stress, automobile accidents while commuting, industrial accidents, etc.).

The Dependency Ratio

With the onset of population aging, social policy analysts and political alarmists warned that the elderly were becoming (or would become) a prohibitive social burden for modern society. Indeed, some policymakers and journalists have spoken of an emerging crisis in which pension and health care systems become bankrupt. They argue that this is likely to occur when the number of dependent elderly persons increases to the point that those in the labor force can no longer bear the burden of financing the pension, housing, and health care costs associated with the later years. This is likely to occur, they argue, because of a shrinking labor force due to zero population growth. However, although there will be an increase in social security and health care costs, there may also be a decrease in the costs associated with elementary and secondary school education. A series of studies led Denton and his colleagues (1986, 1987) to conclude that even if fertility rates decrease, future increases in the size of the older population will not 'impose an unmanageable burden on the economy or on the working-age population' (Denton et al., 1987:37).

A crude measure that has been used to partially support these arguments is the **dependency ratio,** which indicates the number of nonworkers who must be supported directly or indirectly by those in the labor force. Clark et al. (1978) divided the population into three categories that represent general estimates of the relative number of people who are workers and dependents. These categories are workers, young dependents, and old dependents The total dependency ratio is an approximate measure of the economic support that must be provided by those who are in the labor force to those who are unemployed, or 'dependent.' The higher the ratio, the greater the number of dependent people in the population who must be supported by those in the labor force, and by health and economic assistance programs in the private and public sector. The dependency ratio is determined by identifying all those who are under 19 and over 65 years of age (the young and old dependents), and dividing this number by those who are 'eligible' to be in the labor force, namely, all those between 20 and 64 years of age.

In North America the dependency ratio has increased over time. This increase has occurred because the proportion of those over 65 years of age has increased, while the fertility rate has decreased, thereby lowering the number of eli-gible workers under 64 years of age. If mandatory retirement was delayed or eliminated and more older people remained in the labor force, the ratio would decrease.

The dependency ratio for the total population can be subdivided into 'young' and 'old-age' ratios. The **old-age dependency ratio** can be determined by dividing the number of people 65 and older by the number of those 18 to 64 years of age. At present, the old-age dependency ratio is about 20 percent in Canada, and about 19 percent in the United States (that is, 20 adults over 65 in Canada, and 19 adults over 65 in the United States, are supported by 100 younger people of labor-force age). It is projected that, by the year 2031, this ratio will increase to 52 percent in Canada (McDaniel, 1986: 113) and 39 percent in the United States (Siegel and Taeuber, 1986:83). This is the period when you and your younger siblings will be retired. Clearly, these statistics indicate that there may be an increased burden on those of working age — if the elderly are really 'dependent,' as the index implies.

Dependency ratios are crude measures, for a variety of reasons. First, dependency ratios may be constructed according to different criteria (Gibson, 1989). Some include 15- to 64-year-olds in the labor force, while others include 18- to 64-year olds or 20- to 64-year olds. Second, the ratios are usually based on the assumption that all persons of labor-force age are actually employed. More recently, therefore, some measures eliminate those 15- to 64-year-olds who are not in the labor-force (such as students or prisoners), and include those over 65 who are still employed and who are therefore not 'dependent.' Similarly, late entrants to the labor force (college graduates) are seldom excluded, and adjustments are seldom made to account for unusually high periods of unemployment. Moreover, most measures do not account for different or varying rates of female labor-force involvement, at a given point in time or across history. Finally, such factors as varying immigration rates, delays in retirement, changes in mandatory retirement legislation, changes in economic productivity and real income, or the amount of volunteer (unpaid) work are seldom considered (Crown, 1985; Chen, 1987; Gibson, 1989). Thus, although dependency ratios are frequently used to provide an index of the economic burden placed on a society by its dependent members, they are crude estimates only. They can be used to provide a historical picture or to make projections within a society if the measures at each point in time have employed the same factors and the same assumptions. Increasingly, this is less likely to be the case, and therefore the degree of burden depicted or projected may present a distorted view of the real social and economic world at the time. In fact, dependency ratios have been conveniently used by politicians or journalists to introduce pessimism and fatalism into our view of the future (Gibson, 1989).

Recognizing the importance of informal social support that is available within the family, Siegel (1981) constructed a ratio of adult children (45 to 49 years of age) to elderly parents. This ratio provides an index of the amount of support for the elderly that is available within families (the family dependency ratio). Using 1975 data, he found that the child-to-parent ratio in the more developed regions of the world was 92 children (who were 45 to 49 years of age) per 100 parents (who were 65 to 74 years of age). In the less developed regions, this ratio was 163 adult children per 100 parents. Siegel projects that by 2000 these ratios will decrease to 86 and 149 respectively. These family dependency ratios are higher in the less developed countries because of higher birth rates and death rates. The ratio suggests that the few surviving elderly in less developed countries have more children to support them in the later years.

The Number and Proportion of Elderly People: Population Age

Like its individual members, the population of a nation may be viewed as 'young,' 'youthful,' 'mature,' or 'aged.' Although the absolute number of elderly persons in the nation might indicate the age of the population, this index is not sufficient. Decreased fertility rates and lower immigration rates will increase the proportion of the aged within the total population, whereas an increase in fertility and immigration rates will decrease the proportion

of the aged population. Unlike the individual, who can only grow older, the age of a nation can increase or decrease over time.

In order to monitor change in the age of a given population, the United Nations classifies nations as 'aged' if 10 percent of the population are over 60 or 65; as 'mature' if between 7 and 9 percent are over 60 or 65; as 'youthful' if between 4 and 6 percent are over 60 or 65; and as 'young' if fewer than 4 percent are over 60 or 65 years of age. Table 3.1 illustrates the age of selected nations at four specific time periods. In this table, 60 years is the determinant of population age.

Generally, 'aged' nations are highly industrialized and have low birth and death rates and long life expectancies. 'Mature' nations are partially industrialized and have low death rates. 'Mature' nations still have high birthrates, and are characterized by increasing longevity, largely because of decreased infant mortality and better medical and health practices. A 'young' or 'youthful' nation is one wherein there is little, if any, industrialization, and where there are high birth and death rates and short life expectancies.

Since 1970, there has been a large increase in the number of nations that have moved from the 'young' to the 'mature' category. Not surprisingly, most of the 'aged' nations are the more developed nations in Europe and North America; 'youthful' and 'young' countries are found in Africa, Central and South America, and South Asia. Over the next three decades, some of the 'mature,' 'youthful,' and 'young' nations are projected to become 'aged' nations. This profound change in age structure (for example, in China, Chile, Kuwait) may pose considerable problems for these rapidly changing societies — problems more severe perhaps than those experienced by 'aged' nations where the percentage of elderly persons is higher.

The increase in the proportion of the elderly in the modernized nations will result from further declines in birth rates and from the aging of large birth cohorts born earlier, such as the baby-boom cohort, which will reach 65 after 2010. Furthermore, some countries already have attained or are approaching zero population growth. In the less developed countries,[10] a projected high fertility rate combined with

TABLE 3.1

ACTUAL AND PROJECTED POPULATION AGE: PERCENTAGE OF THE POPULATION OVER 60 YEARS OF AGE

United Nations Category	Actual		Projected	
	1970[a]	1980	2000	2020
WORLD		8.3	9.7	12.6
More developed regions		15.2	18.3	22.4
Less developed regions		6.0	7.5	10.6
AGED (10% over 60)				
Sweden		21.9	22.5	28.4
German Democratic Republic	15.6	19.6	21.4	25.4
France	13.4	17.0	19.6	24.6
United States	9.9	15.7	15.7	22.0
Canada	8.1	12.8	15.8	23.0
Soviet Union	7.7	13.1	17.5	19.4
Japan	7.1	12.9	20.9	26.5
Israel	6.8	11.5	11.5	15.6
Hong Kong	3.9	10.0	13.2	21.7
Cuba	5.9	10.4	13.0	17.4
MATURE (7-9% over 60)				
China		7.3	10.1	16.4
Chile		8.1	9.8	14.6
Jamaica		8.5	7.6	11.4
Albania		7.0	8.9	12.9
YOUTHFUL (4-6% over 60)				
Egypt		6.8	7.0	9.5
Mexico	3.7	5.2	6.3	10.0
Union of South Africa	4.1	6.3	6.2	7.6
Peru	3.1	5.5	6.6	10.0
Venezuela		4.5	5.7	9.2
Zambia	2.2	4.3	4.2	4.6
Saudi Arabia		4.4	4.6	7.4
Turkey		6.4	8.0	10.7
YOUNG (4% or less over 60)				
Kuwait		2.3	5.4	10.3
Nicaragua		3.9	4.7	6.9
Kenya		3.0	3.0	3.7
Botswana		3.3	3.5	4.2

[a] The percentages reported for 1970 were included in table 3.1 (p. 84) of the first edition of *Aging as a Social Process*. These figures indicate the change in percentage and category for some nations.

SOURCE: Adapted from United Nations, *Periodical on Aging*, 1(1), 1984: tables 3, 10, 17, 24, 31, 38. United Nations Office at Vienna, Centre for Social Development and Humanitarian Affairs (UNOV/CSDHA).

reduced infant and child mortality will produce only moderate increases in the proportion of the elderly. However, if fertility rates decline dramatically in developing nations, as some demographers assume, then the proportion of elderly in the total population will increase more rapidly.

In terms of the absolute number of persons in the world 60 years of age and over, the total in 1980 was 371 million; of these, approximately 173 million lived in developed countries and about 198 million lived in the less developed countries. This figure of 371 million represents about 8 percent of the total world population. By the year 2000 the projections are for a population of 596 million persons over 60, with 234 million in the more developed countries and 362 million in the less developed countries (United Nations, 1984).

The speed of population aging increased 2

percent in Canada during the decade from 1976 to 1986, when nearly 10.7 percent of Canadians were 65 years of age and over. In contrast, it took thirty years (1946 to 1976) for the percentage of Canadians aged 65 and over to increase by 1.6 percent (Stone and Frenken, 1988:9). In 1986 in North America, about 2.7 million Canadians and 28.5 million Americans were 65 years of age or more. By the year 2000, these numbers will increase to an estimated 4 million Canadians and 35 million Americans. By 2012, the first cohorts of the baby-boom generation will be 65 years of age. It is projected that for a seven-year period in the early 2020s, over 1.4 million per year will enter the elderly population in the United States (Myers, 1985).

During the next fifteen years (1990-2005) there will be dramatic increases in the number of elderly persons in the 75-and-over and 85-and-over age groups, and there will be a further rapid expansion after 2030, when the baby-boom cohort reaches 85. This rapid aging of the older population itself is a recent phenomenon that can be linked to a variety of physical, genetic, social, environmental, and psychological factors that contribute to longevity. Highlight 3.4 describes some of the characteristics and lifestyle situations of the oldest cohort of North Americans.

COMPOSITION OF THE AGING POPULATION

This section presents information concerning the composition of the aged population

---

HIGHLIGHT **3.4**

THE OLDEST COHORT OF NORTH AMERICANS

In Canada, those 80 and over represented 2.1 percent (537,000 persons) of the total population recorded in the 1986 census (Stone and Frenken, 1988). More importantly, for this group, which tends to be the heaviest user of human support services, there is a projected growth rate of 4 percent or more per annum in the remaining years of this century (Stone and Frenken, 1988:35). It is projected that, by 2001, the group 80 years and older will represent almost 25 percent of the older population in Canada (McDaniel, 1986:43). Most of this growth is attibutable to the greater longevity of women. For example, the sex ratio in the 65 to 69 age group is 120 women for every 100 men, whereas it is 229 women for every 100 men among those 85 and over.

Despite such rapid current and expected future growth, this segment of the population has received relatively little research attention, often because the 80-and-over group is hidden in statistical analyses that report data for those 65 and over.[11] Although not all of this oldest age cohort are institutionalized (25 percent of the men and 40 percent of the women over 85 are institutionalized in Canada), many of these individuals cannot function independently. If they lack strong family ties, they are more likely to be institutionalized. This oldest cohort are those in the elderly population who are most at risk, and they are those most likely to need formal support services, especially since more than 70 percent are women, and over 80 percent of the women are widowed. Many therefore live alone, but are frail and often have a physical condition that prohibits the use of public or private transportation. Hence, they are housebound, and only leave to obtain medical assistance. Not surprisingly, this oldest age group is the heaviest user of the health care system, particularly with respect to acute hospital stays and the care and treatment of chronic illnesses and disabilities. Born in the earliest years of this century, many of these survivors have not had much formal education beyond elementary school, and many are living on minimal incomes received from government old-age security payments.

Although some may view this group as an unnecessary burden to society, the cohort will grow in size until well into the twenty-first century. As a result, specific policies and programs need to be designed to meet their unique needs. It is quite likely that this group will be better educated, more affluent, and healthier. As a result, they will increasingly seek to remain independent as long as they possibly can, and will demand adequate home-support services and alternative housing options. Herein lies a challenge for readers involved in program or policymaking positions where community-dwelling clientele are or will be over 85 years of age.

---

according to a number of demographic and social characteristics. This information enables us to understand better the lifestyles, status, and problems experienced by present and future cohorts of elderly persons. Although the focus here is on the elderly of North America, the reader must remember that some (but not necessarily all) of these factors will apply to the elderly in every country. Some factors may not necessarily apply to all future elderly cohorts in North America. Whether a factor influences the aging population is very much dependent on historical events, cultural traditions, geography, population distribution, degree of modernization, and type of political system.

Educational Status

In the early part of this century, effort and ability were more important prerequisites than educational attainment in obtaining and advancing in a job. However, academic achievement has become increasingly essential to success. Today, the level of educational attainment influences our attitudes, values, behavior, friendships, job opportunities, and income throughout the life cycle, particularly in modernized nations.

It was not until after World War II that educational opportunities increased, as did the value placed on attaining high-school diplomas and college degrees. The present cohort of older people has generally completed less formal education than younger cohorts. At present only 5 percent of elderly Canadians and 10 percent of elderly Americans report that they have earned a university degree. At the same time, the proportion of elderly Canadians and Americans reporting fewer than nine years of education is over 50 and 35 percent respectively. These percentages are averages and do not account for gender, ethnic, class, or racial differences. For example, in the United States, a lower percentage of blacks than whites complete a high-school or college education; and in both Canada and the United States, whereas a higher percentage of women than men complete high school, a lower percentage of women complete college.

Statistics on educational attainment include many people who were foreign born and who immigrated to North America when they were beyond high-school age. Many of those in the present cohort of older people were not formally educated in North America. Therefore, with the recent decrease in immigration rates, a larger percentage of each age cohort in the future will have completed at least some high school because of statutes requiring attendance until the age of 15 or 16.

As noted above, the level of educational attainment of the over-65 population is lower than that of younger age cohorts. Moreover, there is considerable variation in educational attainment by age within the elderly cohort. To illustrate, in Canada, the proportion of the elderly reporting fewer than nine years of education decreases from 61 percent in the 85-and-over age group, to 58 percent in the 75 to 84 age group, to 48 percent in the 65 to 74 age group, to about 20 percent for those in the 25 to 64 age group (Statistics Canada, 1984a:chart 5). A corresponding trend of increasing percentages is found for the higher educational categories. Thus, future cohorts of elderly persons will have achieved considerably higher levels of educational attainment. Although the level of educational attainment of the elderly will increase, it is still expected to lag behind the under-65 population, at least until the relatively well-educated baby-boom cohort reaches age 65 after about 2010. However, the age-cohort gap in educational attainment could narrow faster because of the increasing trend for adults to enroll in college and university credit and noncredit courses. It also remains to be seen how educational television will influence the formal and informal educational pursuits of adults at all ages.

Marital Status

Quite simply, most older men are married and most older women are widowed. This discrepancy increases further with advancing age. The importance of this characteristic is that whether one is married or not can greatly influence living arrangements, economic status, and the size and quality of the informal support system for older adults (Connidis, 1989). To illustrate, between 75 and 80 percent of men over 65 in Canada and the United States are married, whereas only 40 percent of women over 65 are married. At present, less than five percent of those over 65 become divorced. In the future, however, with higher proportions of divorced or separated persons in younger cohorts, there will be more single persons in future cohorts of elderly persons. There may also be higher proportions of never-married and recently divorced persons in future elderly cohorts. Thus, women who are widowed or divorced at 65 to 70 years of age may live alone for ten to fifteen years. This pattern of an uneven ratio between widows and widowers has resulted from a number of factors, including higher death rates for men, the social norm of men marrying younger women, a higher remarriage rate for widowers, an informal social norm that discourages elderly widows from remarrying, and the unavailability of older men should older women wish to remarry. The social consequence of this pattern is a large number of older women who live alone, often in poverty (Gee and Kimball, 1987: 54-63).

Regardless of gender, those who are married have a higher life expectancy than their single counterparts. It is suggested that this pattern occurs primarily because married couples have a different lifestyle from that of unattached persons: they live in better housing, they eat better, they take better care of themselves; in addition, a spouse is likely to make sure that prompt medical attention is received when illness occurs.

Labor-Force Participation

Because fewer people are self-employed, especially in urban areas, and because of the introduction of mandatory retirement, the proportion of those over 65 in the labor force has declined steadily throughout this century, particularly in the past three decades. In 1900, about two of every three elderly males were employed; by 1981 only one in four was in the labor force. In 1981, only about one-tenth of the women aged 65 to 69 were still in the labor force. These rates drop dramatically to one in seven men and one in twenty women for the 70

to 74 age group. Thus, a large proportion of the elderly population will be unemployed for the remainder of this century, despite a large number who want to work or need to work for economic survival. Moreover, for some, retirement is occurring earlier than age 65, and an increasing number are becoming unemployed during the middle (45 to 64) years.

The average duration of unemployment increases with age. For the middle-aged and elderly, the earlier the unemployment, whether temporary or permanent, the greater the loss in income and the greater the number of years spent without sufficient income. This has a profound effect on the psychological adjustment of many, and on the quality and style of life for most. Recently, it has been argued that forced retirement at age 65 is discriminatory. As a result, the mandatory retirement age has been increased to 70 years for most occupational groups in the United States. In Canada, mandatory retirement has been abolished in some provinces. However, in other provinces, mandatory retirement is being challenged in the courts, and at the federal level it is being challenged as a violation of the Charter of Rights.

Labor-force participation by both men and women declines in the later years, although an increasing number of women have been entering the labor force when their families leave home or because of economic necessity if they are divorced or widowed. Many of these women remain employed until age 65 or later, often in part-time or low-paying occupations.

In summary, most elderly people are retired. For some this status is voluntary. However, a growing number retire only because they cannot obtain or retain a job. Among those who are employed after 65, between 50 and 66 percent are only employed in part-time positions. Again, in some cases this is by choice. For others, part-time work represents the only type of employment they can obtain, or the maximum amount of time they can devote to earning an income without becoming ineligible for government pension benefits. In short, older employees who wish to work are generally found in low-paying occupations. For those who need to work, even obtaining a job does not guarantee that their economic needs can be met.

Economic Status

This subsection briefly describes the economic status of the elderly individual. (Chapter 11 presents a more extensive analysis of the economic impact of retirement.) The discussion begins with some caveats. First, with respect to this topic, perhaps more so than any other area, statistics become obsolete very quickly. Therefore, the most recent and accurate statistics should be obtained from the government documents section of your library. Second, statistics that are reported in the media may be manipulated or misinterpreted in order to depict a particular view—for example, the impoverished elderly.

Furthermore, as we shall see, sufficient information is seldom available. This is either because complete information was not collected from individuals, or because the statistics are aggregated and treat the aged as one homogeneous group. Aggregate data for those over 65 years of age may include such diverse situations as the very wealthy who report little job-related income but who have large investments and equity; those who are employed full- or part-time; those retirees who receive social security and pension payments; and those retirees who receive minimal social security payments and no private pension payments. Thus, in order not to distort reality, statistics on the economic status of the elderly need to be presented (1) for the retired, the partially retired, and the full-time worker; (2) for the young-old and the very old; (3) for married couples, the separated and divorced, the widowed, and the never-married; (4) for racial and class groups; (5) for males and females; (6) for total assets, not just current income; and (7) for single versus dual pensioners (where both spouses receive private pension payments).

Finally, since education affects lifelong earnings and influences the various sources of income for the elderly, this factor must be considered in any discussion of the economic status of older adults. To illustrate, the 1981 Canadian census found that the income for elderly men ranged from $8,400 for those with less than grade 9 to $25,900 for those with a university degree. For women, the difference was $5,700 to $14,000 (Statistics Canada, 1984a:table 9).

Moreover, the source of income after age 65 is also largely influenced by level of educational attainment, especially for men. Elderly men with a university degree received the largest percentage of their total income from employment income (31 percent), whereas the largest contributor to the income of elderly men with less than grade 9 education was government transfer payments (51 percent). Elderly women with less than grade 9 education were even more dependent on government transfer payments, receiving 72 percent of their total income from this source (Statistics Canada, 1984a:table 10).

Researchers should also be aware that individuals may intentionally misrepresent the information they report about their assets, income, and expenditures. They do so because they view these topics, like sex, to be confidential matters. Or they may unintentionally provide incomplete or inaccurate information because they do not really know their economic situation apart from income from pension plans or employment. For these reasons, Henretta (1979) argued that the economic status of the elderly should be measured by net worth or wealth, rather than by annual income.

Finally, there does not appear to be common agreement concerning the meaning of 'poverty,' 'inadequate income,' or 'inadequate standard of living' (Hogg et al., 1981; Schulz, 1988:44-48; Gee and Kimball, 1987:53-54), or the point at which social problems arise related to each of these categories. For example, the 'poverty index' in the United States is calculated as three times the annual amount of money income (before taxes) that is needed to purchase food to maintain a minimum adequate diet. A multiple of three is used because it is assumed that a family spends about one-third of its income on food. Yet family size is not considered as a factor (although marital status is). Moreover, the 'hidden poor,' who live with and are supported almost totally by relatives, are usually not included among those living below the poverty line. In Canada, a person lives below the poverty line if more than 58.5 percent of income is required to provide the basic economic necessities of food, shelter, and clothing. The percentage figure varies according to region. In 1981, for a family of two, the

Statistics Canada poverty line was $8,595 on average, with a value of $6,877 for rural areas and $9,451 for urban areas having a population greater than 500,000 (Gee and Kimball, 1987:54). In March 1989 the poverty level for a family of four was $24,370 in Canada.

The economic status of the elderly appears to be improving because of the increased size and availability of public and private pension plans, because salaries and savings have increased, because of tax concessions and increased subsidies for the elderly (in-kind income such as subsidized housing, transportation, medical care, and food), and because families are more likely to provide income than services to aging parents. However, since the aged are not a homogeneous group, there are variations from this average. For example, in the United States, only about 11 percent of elderly whites live below the poverty line, compared to about 32 percent of elderly blacks and 21 percent of elderly Hispanics (American Association of Retired Persons, 1985). Similarly, marital status can significantly influence annual incomes in the later years. To illustrate, the average reported income in 1981 for Canadians over 65 years of age was $18,200 for married couples, $11,000 for unattached men, and $9,000 for unattached women (Health and Welfare Canada, 1983:44). Moreover, as Gee and Kimball (1987:54) reported, 'it is a virtual certainty that more than one-third of Canada's elderly women are poor.' Indeed, they reported that over 60 percent of unattached elderly women existed at or below the poverty line in 1982, and in 1983 an additional 18 percent had incomes less than $9,999, which put them perilously close to the poverty line.

The poverty index is based solely on before-tax money income. Therefore, if in-kind income (such as health plans, food stamps, subsidized housing), transfer payments (government pensions or social security), tax benefits (income tax deductions or property tax relief), within-family transfers (cash from children), and an adjustment for underreporting of income are taken into consideration, an individual's actual financial status will often be higher than that reported.

Speaking about the situation in the United States, Schulz (1988:61) concluded that 'poverty among the aged, as measured by the government's poverty index, is now much lower than in past years; when in-kind income is considered, poverty practically disappears using this measure. Large numbers of the elderly, however, remain clustered just above the poverty level, and many still experience a large drop in their standard of living when they retire.' Because the poverty index distorts the economic status of the elderly, some attention has been directed toward introducing a more subjective component in assessing the standard of living or quality of life experienced by the elderly person.

Unlike the purely objective measurements based on minimal survival needs, subjective approaches take into account a range of needs and wants related to the real standard of living of older persons. One such measure is the United States Bureau of Labor Statistics' Retired Couples' Budget. This index provides three different levels of modest but adequate standards of living. The budget pertains to urban families only and is adjusted annually in response to changes in the Consumer Price Index. Although the Retired Couples' Budget is not widely used, it does acknowledge that after retirement the standard of living can vary greatly because of three main factors: assets, expenditure patterns of disposable income, and the impact of inflation, especially on rental costs and fixed or decreasing incomes.

Although it is difficult to obtain complete and accurate information about assets held by the elderly, generally they have nonliquid equity in a home and some liquid assets such as cash, bank deposits, stocks, or bonds, which yield varying rates of interest. However, the longer one lives, the more likely it is that these liquid assets will be converted to cash to maintain a minimal standard of living. Ultimately, nonliquid assets (such as a home) may have to be sold in order to pay for institutionalization or health care. As with other sources of financial support, whites, men, and the married generally have more assets during retirement.

Despite the persistence of the idea that the elderly have fewer economic needs than younger age groups, they still have a need for food, shelter, and health care. Moreover, the need for these specific items remains constant or increases with age, yet they are highly susceptible to inflation. According to most studies, most elderly people spend a higher proportion of their budgets on food, shelter, and health care than other age groups. The average annual income of those over 65 may decrease by about 50 percent, but their consumption patterns do not decrease at the same rate. It is usually impossible to save money after retirement, and preretirement assets must often be used to maintain a comparable standard of living. This dependency on preretirement assets becomes particularly pronounced the longer one lives.

The expenditure pattern after retirement is further complicated by inflation, which causes the purchasing power of those with relatively fixed incomes to erode even further and at a faster rate. Moreover, the 'real' dollar value of savings, investments, and private pensions has declined so that $1.00 earned twenty years ago is worth less than 50 cents when it is spent today. Although government pension plans are indexed to inflation, many private plans are not. Moreover, even where a government plan is pegged to inflation, the increase, like salaries for the employed, usually lags at least a year behind the real rate of inflation.

In summary, although the economic status of the elderly has improved in the past two decades relative to earlier retiree cohorts, their status relative to younger age groups has not changed significantly. Clearly, there is a curvilinear relationship between age and income that varies from near zero (a small 'allowance' from one's parents) in early childhood, to a maximum in the years before age 64 (if steadily employed), to a level that likely falls below or approaches that of the starting salary received by an individual upon entrance into the labor force as a full-time employee.

For most of the current elderly cohort the major source of income is government transfer payments such as Old Age Security. For example, in Canada these payments constitute the major source of income for 74 percent of elderly women and for 59 percent of elderly men. At present and in the future, a larger percentage of each new cohort of retirees will have access to private pension plans. The elderly are gaining increasing tax relief and public health assistance, as well as discounts on goods and services, that compensate somewhat, but not entirely, for inflation. Thus, although only a small percentage of the elderly live in 'poverty' conditions, many experience a decline in their standard of living, either when they avoid using their savings or when they begin to draw on their savings. This erosion of savings has a particularly harsh effect on widows, who usually outlive their husbands by many years.

Ethnic Status

Although less important than fertility and mortality rates in determining the size and composition of the age structure, immigration rates have contributed to the diversity of our aging population in North America. Across history, because of these different waves, and the different home countries represented in these waves, Canada and the United States have become diverse cultural nations. Since most immigrants are young adults who bring or later have children, their arrival originally decreases the proportion of people over 65 in a country. However, as they grow older, they eventually increase the size of the oldest age cohorts.

At present, members of the elderly population are quite likely to use a language other than English or French. This reflects the high immigration rates from European countries in the early 1900s. Many of these immigrants continue to employ their native language at home, and to adhere more to elements of their ethnic culture than do members of later generations. Some of these ethnic groups, as measured by the proportion of elderly persons, are much older than others (Driedger and Chappell, 1987:7; Jackson, 1985:272). For example, table 3.2 presents Canadian statistics that reflect the history of migration for different ethnic groups (such as Russians), and the presence of low fertility rates among others (such as Jews). These variations also suggest that the special needs of the aged may be quite diverse, and that they may vary by ethnic group at different periods in history. For example, almost 50 percent of foreign-born Russians are elderly at present, whereas only about 4 percent of the Portuguese ethnic community is elderly, because the Portu-

TABLE 3.2

ETHNIC COMPOSITION OF THE ELDERLY POPULATION IN CANADA, 1981

Ethnicity	% 65+
Russian	47.8
British	11.1
French	7.8
Jewish	16.5
Polish	14.5
Ukrainian	13.7
German	10.3
Chinese	6.7
Italian	6.7
Portuguese	4.3
Native peoples	3.5

SOURCE: Adapted from Driedger and Chappell, 1987:7-11.

guese arrived in North America more recently. Thus, as we enter the 1990s, there is a need for policies and programs that will serve the large number of elderly persons of Jewish or European origin. In the next century, the elderly will consist of a higher proportion of elderly Italians, Portuguese, East Indians, and East Asians, who may present different needs and challenges to social and health care policymakers.

DISTRIBUTION OF THE AGING POPULATION

Variation by Geographical Region

The United Nations has subdivided the world into eight regions. According to the 1980 estimate, as well as projections for the year 2000, the population of persons 60 and over makes up a higher percentage of the population in the more developed regions, particularly in Europe, North America, the Soviet Union, and Oceania. However, it is projected that there will be about a threefold increase between 1980 and 2020 in the elderly population in the less developed regions as mortality and fertility rates decrease, and as the availability and quality of health care increases (see table 3.3).

Although we have relatively little choice about which country of the world we can reside in, there is considerably greater freedom, at least after about age 15, to choose a region within a country, a rural or urban environment, a neighborhood, and a type of housing within that neighborhood. All of these factors provide clues about the needs of people, their lifestyles, and the belief and normative systems that guide their thinking and behavior. Like other age groups, most of the elderly in North America live in those states (New York, California, Pennsylvania, Illinois, Michigan, Texas, Ohio, and Florida) and provinces (Quebec, Ontario, and British Columbia) with the greatest population density.

Although the number of elderly people located in a particular region is important from a policy perspective, the proportion of elderly people may be more important, since social support services must be provided where the proportion is high. Thus, the geographical distribution of the elderly, in proportion to the total population, reveals a different residential pattern. In Canada, Prince Edward Island (with 12.7 percent), Saskatchewan (12.7 percent), Manitoba (12.6 percent), and British Columbia (12.1 percent) have the highest proportions of elderly citizens. With the exception of British Columbia, which has a high rate of in-migra-

TABLE 3.3

THE GLOBAL DISTRIBUTION OF PERSONS 60 AND OVER (IN THOUSANDS)

Region	Estimated (1980) and Projected (2000, 2020) Number of Persons 60 and Over)		
	1980	2000	2020
World	370,850	595,301	987,233
More developed regions	172,734	233,682	308,308
Less developed regions	198,116	361,619	678,925
Africa	23,237	41,822	81,041
Latin America	23,312	41,768	80,504
Northern America	38,941	48,864	74,916
East Asia	91,843	162,122	283,899
South Asia	74,478	142,036	266,679
Europe	81,684	101,705	124,717
Oceania	2,644	3,836	6,181
USSR	34,711	55,148	69,296

SOURCE: Adapted from United Nations, *Periodical on Aging*, 1(1), 1984:table 1. United Nations Office at Vienna, Centre for Social Development and Humanitarian Affairs (UNOV/CSDHA).

tion by retirees, the other provinces are characterized by low incomes, high out-migration of the young, and high old-age dependency ratios. At the other end of the scale, less than 4 percent of those in the Yukon and Northwest Territories are 65 and over; and the percentages for Alberta and Newfoundland are 8.1 and 8.8 percent respectively.

In the United States, after Florida (17.6 percent), South Dakota, Missouri, Arkansas, Kansas, Iowa, Nebraska, Oklahoma, and Rhode Island all report that more than 13 percent of their populations are 65 years of age and over. Like British Columbia, Florida has a high incidence of in-migration by retirees, while the midwest states reflect out-migration by the young from farms to urban areas. This variation in the distribution of the elderly must be considered when establishing policies and providing services to meet the needs of specific age groups (Longino, 1982).

There are also some significant variations at the county level that can have an impact on the need for financial resources and social services. As an illustration, let us consider the geographical distribution by county for southern Ontario, a province where the population 65 and over,

and 80 and over, grew 14.3 and 18.9 percent respectively from 1981 to 1986 (Moore et al., 1989). In absolute numbers, more than 25 percent of those 65 and older in Ontario lived within and on the fringe of Metropolitan Toronto; yet these census divisions represent the smallest proportions of the total population over 65 years of age. This occurs because of a large in-migration of younger adults from other provinces and from other countries.

As figures 3.3a and 3.3b graphically illustrate, the highest concentrations of adults over 65 years of age, and over 80 years of age, are in the rural and small town census divisions, particularly those in the Haliburton, Georgian Bay, and Lake Huron districts. This pattern has emerged because of the out-migration of the young to urban areas, the aging in place of longtime residents, and the increasing in-migration of early retirees to these recreational areas.

Figures 3.4a and 3.4b illustrate the absolute increase in the population (65 and over and 80 and over) from 1981 to 1986. Here it is important to note that several of the counties where the percent of the population over 65 or over 80 was small in 1981 and 1986 are the counties

FIGURE 3.3a

PERCENT OF THE POPULATION AGED 65 AND OVER, 1986
by Census Division, Southern Ontario

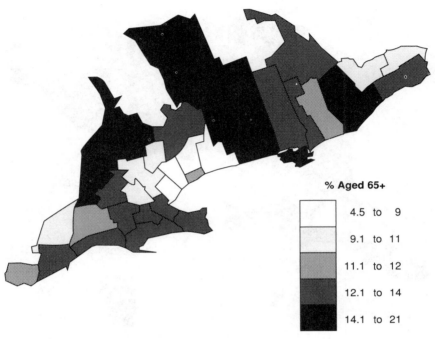

% Aged 65+

	4.5 to 9
	9.1 to 11
	11.1 to 12
	12.1 to 14
	14.1 to 21

SOURCE: Reprinted with permission from Moore et al. (1989: figure 5).
ORIGINAL SOURCE: Census of Canada, 1986.

where the older population is growing most quickly. That is, longtime residents are now reaching 65 and beyond as they age in place. This is particularly true in the suburban areas surrounding Metropolitan Toronto. Moore et al. (1989) project that the most rapid growth in the elderly population by 1996 and 2006 will occur in the regional municipalities surrounding Metropolitan Toronto as the suburbanites of the 1960s, 1970s, and 1980s age in place. This assumes, of course, that there is not a large out-migration to recreational regions within and outside the province. If this projection is accurate, policy and program planning should begin soon to meet the needs of this demographic shift in the age of the population in Metropoli-

tan Toronto.

On a worldwide basis, rural areas have tended to have higher proportions of older persons than urban areas, particularly in the less developed countries of Asia and Africa (Myers, 1985, 1990). The same pattern holds in North America, where there is a large out-migration of younger people to urban areas, so that the older population is left behind to age in place.

Rural-Urban Distribution

In both Canada and the United States, more than 75 percent of those 65 years of age and over

FIGURE 3.3b

PERCENT OF THE POPULATION AGED 80 AND OVER, 1986
by Census Division, Southern Ontario

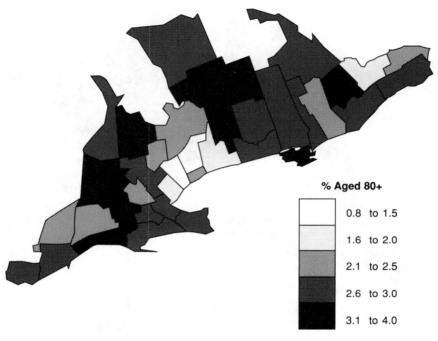

% Aged 80+

	0.8 to 1.5
	1.6 to 2.0
	2.1 to 2.5
	2.6 to 3.0
	3.1 to 4.0

SOURCE: Reprinted with permission from Moore et al. (1989: figure 13).
ORIGINAL SOURCE: Census of Canada, 1986.

live in urban areas; the remaining 25 percent live in rural areas, often on farms or in villages. Of those who live in urban areas, about 60 percent live in large cities; 40 percent live in communities with fewer than 25,000 inhabitants. In small towns with a population of 1,000 to 2,499 people, 14.7 percent of the residents were aged 65 or more (Stone and Frenken, 1988:table 3).

The elderly person who lives in the central city experiences a different social and physical environment from one who lives in a suburban area, a small town, or on a farm. Residents of the central core may have poorer housing, may be more dependent on public transportation, may have higher living costs, and may be more susceptible to crime.

The current cohort of elderly persons is overrepresented in the central cities and in small rural towns with a total population of fewer than 2,500 inhabitants. In the metropolitan areas, the elderly living in the central core usually own their homes. However, because of a lack of income, because of the lower value of homes compared to those in the suburbs, and because of strong attachments to the neighborhood, they tend to remain in the central area. This aging-in-place phenomenon occurs even when the racial composition of the neighborhood changes, or when a home begins to need major repairs, some of which may not be affordable. In the small rural towns, the overrepresentation of the elderly is primarily a function of the out-migration of the young to larger

FIGURE 3.4a

PERCENT CHANGE IN THE POPULATION AGED 65 AND OVER, 1981-1986
by Census Division, Southern Ontario

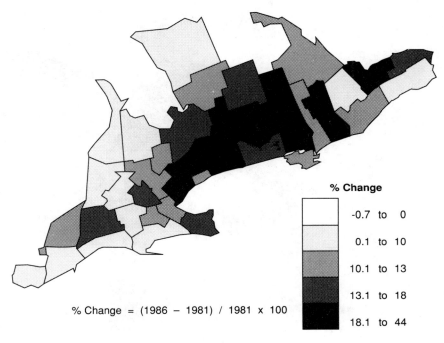

% Change

	-0.7 to 0
	0.1 to 10
	10.1 to 13
	13.1 to 18
	18.1 to 44

% Change = (1986 − 1981) / 1981 x 100

SOURCE: Reprinted with permission from Moore et al. (1989: figure 9).
ORIGINAL SOURCE: Census of Canada, 1981 and 1986.

centers and the in-migration of retired farmers.

This pattern of age segregation in specific sections of the larger cities reflects to some extent the age of a neighborhood. That is, the elderly are situated in the central core because this is where housing was located when they first purchased a home. Similarly, recent immigrant groups have tended to settle in core areas because housing is less expensive, because public transportation is available, and because the labor market is usually nearby.

The suburban fringe areas around cities expanded greatly after the 1950s. In the early years of a suburban development, the age of the occupants is generally under 40. With time, the population in the suburbs ages, since most individuals tend to remain in the same house throughout adulthood, with only a small percentage making a move after retirement. Thus, the suburbs that were constructed in the 1950s are increasingly likely to have a large proportion of elderly people as children leave and the aging parents remain in the family home. It is often not until the original owners grow too old to look after a home or until a spouse dies that the property is resold, often to a younger couple, thereby initiating a new cycle in the age structure of the neighborhood.

Within the next twenty years suburban areas will include an increasingly larger proportion of older individuals. Whether the suburbs become age-segregated neighborhoods will depend on migration patterns between communities. For example, the onset of the energy

FIGURE 3.4b

PERCENT CHANGE IN THE POPULATION AGED 80 AND OVER, 1981-1986
by Census Division, Southern Ontario

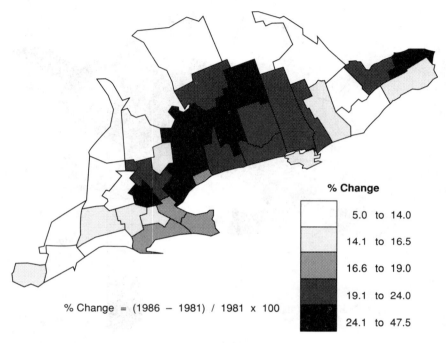

% Change

	5.0 to 14.0
	14.1 to 16.5
	16.6 to 19.0
	19.1 to 24.0
	24.1 to 47.5

% Change = (1986 − 1981) / 1981 x 100

SOURCE: Reprinted with permission from Moore et al. (1989: figure 15).
ORIGINAL SOURCE: Census of Canada, 1981 and 1986.

crisis, combined with inflationary housing prices and the changing lifestyles of young adults, has led some younger couples to move into the central city for economic and social reasons. This pattern decreases the proportion of the elderly in the central core and hastens the aging of the suburbs. Similarly, with decreases in immigration rates, fewer immigrants are moving into the central core. The proportion of the elderly in the inner core may not change much in the future, since the loss of immigrants may be offset by in-migration to the central core by younger, working couples. Finally, the higher proportion of younger inhabitants in the suburbs may not change if minority groups and second- and third-generation immigrants continue to migrate, first to the older suburbs and then to the newer suburbs as their economic situation improves.

In summary, while most elderly people tend to remain in the central core of large cities or in small rural towns, most neighborhoods are age-integrated. However, because neighborhoods are developed at different times, between-neighborhood variation in the average age of occupants is a common pattern. This internal community migration must be monitored by the public and private sectors in order to meet age-specific needs as demographic changes occur. If the proportion of the elderly increases in a suburban neighborhood, resources may need to be shifted from the youth sector to the senior sector within that neighborhood. For example, community recreation departments may need to expend an increasing proportion of their human, physical, and financial resources to provide facilities and programs for middle-aged and elderly adults. Similarly, owners of business establishments may need to change the types of merchandise or services they offer.

Geographical Mobility

In the previous section it was noted that the proportion of elderly people in a given region or community is influenced primarily by the elderly aging in place, and by the out-migration of younger people. However, an increasing factor in the distribution of the elderly population is the residential movement patterns of the elderly (Warnes, 1982; Northcott, 1988; Rosenberg et al., 1988). Much of the early movement accompanies retirement, and reflects a need or desire for a temporary (for example, seasonal) or permanent change in lifestyle. Later, moves are often initiated in response to declining economic or health status, which necessitates a change to a smaller or more institutionalized residential setting. Any change in the distribution within a given geographical unit is a function of cohort survival, plus net migration in and out of the area.

In a detailed examination of the geographic mobility of older Canadians from 1971-1981, Northcott (1988) found that over 10 percent of the elderly change their place of residence each year. However, these moves are more likely to be of short rather than long distance; that is, there are 20 intraprovincial moves for every interprovincial move. Moreover, since over 50 percent of the elderly have lived in their current residence for more than ten years, some of this movement reflects multiple moves by some elderly people. The majority of moves are local and do not involve a change of city, town, village, or municipality. Interprovincial migration rates tend to peak at ages 60 to 69 for males and 60 to 64 for elderly females. Some of these interprovincial moves reflect a return to the province of origin. Older movers are more likely to be recently retired; to be separated, divorced, or widowed rather than married; and to be female. Those with higher income and education are more likely to move to another prov-

ince, and anglophones are more likely to move than francophones (Northcott, 1988:64).

The direction of moves tends to be westward if it is a permanent move, and southward (for example, to the U.S.) if it is a seasonal move. Those areas experiencing net losses of older residents include Quebec, the Prairies, and many of the larger cities; net gains have been experienced by British Columbia, southern Ontario, and cities such as Victoria, B.C., and those in the St. Catharines and Niagara Falls region of Ontario. Since larger segments of the elderly cohort are becoming healthier and wealthier, we can expect higher rates of mobility and migration among this sector of the population in the near future.

Housing and Living Arrangements

Despite the prevailing myth that the elderly are institutionalized, only about 9 percent of those over 65 in Canada (Schwenger and Gross, 1980) and just over 5 percent of those over 65 in the United States live in institutions.[12] Most of those who are institutionalized are over 75, female (widows), and Caucasian. Thus, it appears that at least 90 percent of the elderly are still living in the community, although they are not randomly distributed by country, by region, by place of residence, by neighborhood, or by type of housing.

The vast majority of the elderly live in private households, and most elderly people own their own homes. Even among the 85-and-over age group, 71 percent of the men and 59 percent of the women live in private households (Statistics Canada, 1984a). For the elderly, the home represents a major financial asset. In the United States, about 50 percent of the homes owned by those over 65 were constructed before 1940, and are currently subject to high maintenance costs. Thus, while a home is an asset, it can also become a financial liability in the later years, especially if maintenance costs cannot be met, resulting in structural deterioration and declining value.

In the past, many elderly people lived with an adult child or another relative. Today, the trend is for both generations to seek autonomy and independence. More than 70 percent of men over 65 are married and living with a spouse. However, because of greater longevity and a tendency not to remarry, only 30 to 35 percent of all women over 65 live with a spouse. Thus, excluding those who live with someone in the extended family and those who live with a spouse, about 13 percent of elderly men and 32 percent of elderly women 65 and over live alone. For those who are 85 and over, the percentages who live alone are 18 percent for men and 28 percent for women (Stone and Frenken, 1988:45). Living alone, especially if one is poor, ill, and without friends, can lead to social isolation, loneliness, and a further decline in physical or mental health.

Finally, whereas only 3 to 9 percent of the younger (under 75) segment of the elderly population in North America are institutionalized, this percentage increases to about 30 percent for men and 40 percent for women after the age of 85 (Stone and Frenken, 1988:49-50). The level of institutionalization varies dramatically by province, perhaps because of the varying strength or availability of family support, the type and availability of community support, and the availability of long-term care institutions (Forbes et al., 1987; Stone and Frenken, 1988:53-54). Specifically, of Canadian widows 85 and over, 41 percent were living in institutions in 1986. However, on a provincial basis this ranged from a low of 30 percent in Nova Scotia to a high of 51 percent in Alberta (Stone and Frenken, 1988:table 7).

THE FUTURE OF DEMOGRAPHIC AGING

As observed throughout this chapter, population aging is a demographic process that is here to stay, at least for the duration of your life span. A succinct view of our future is revealed by summarizing McDaniel's (1986:93-114) insightful analysis of future Canadian trends:

- The trend toward low fertility rates is unlikely to be reversed.
- Mortality rates are low, and are not likely to become much lower, although some gains in life expectancy can be expected if, because of advances in medi-

cine and lifestyles (for example, a reduction in cardiovascular disease due to healthier lifestyles; early identification and higher remission rates for cancer), there are reductions in deaths attributable to diseases in the later years.
- The maximum potential life span is not likely to increase.
- Immigration rates are not likely to increase dramatically, although shifts in the number of immigrants per annum will continue to fluctuate depending on policy decisions emanating from economic needs and goals.
- Primarily due to continued low fertility rates (a projected low of 1.4 by 1996), the median age of the population will rise from 30 years in 1983 to 41 years in 2006, and to 48 years in 2031.
- Depending on fertility rates, the percentage of the population 65 years and over in 2031 is projected to be 18.9 percent (if there are 1.4 children per woman by 1996) or 26.6 percent (if there are 2.2 children per woman by 1996). Since the low-growth scenario is more likely, within 40 years approximately 25 percent of the population will be composed of people over the age of 65.
- The ratio of females to males among the very old (80+) will continue to increase.
- There are no dramatic changes projected for the total dependency ratio; however, the old-age dependency ratio is projected to increase from about 21.6 in 1991 to 51.6 in 2031.

The net effect of these projections is that creative and realistic social, health, and economic planning is required in advance of these demographic shifts. To be successful in this planning, we need to continually revise the assumptions inherent in demographic projections. Then, we need to use the resulting demographic information to arrive at rational and flexible policies and programs that will meet the needs of diverse groups within the heterogeneous elderly population of the future.

SUMMARY AND CONCLUSIONS

In this chapter, the emphasis has been on population aging rather than on individual aging. The reader has been introduced to demographic indices and patterns that indicate the size, composition, and distribution of the age structure throughout the world, along with projections for the future.

There has been about a twenty-year increase in the average human life span during the past century. Moreover, the absolute numbers of elderly people and the proportion of those over 65 have grown significantly. This 'graying' trend has resulted because of increasing longevity owing to better health care, decreasing birth and infant mortality rates, higher standards of living, and a decreasing immigration rate. Women have a higher life expectancy than men, and the ratio of men to women decreases over the life cycle. This pattern of increasing longevity and proportional growth of persons over 65 is most pronounced among whites and females, especially in more developed nations.

Although the elderly are still a numerical minority, they comprise an increasingly larger proportion of the population in all countries because of declining fertility and greater longevity. This trend is likely to continue, so that by the beginning of the next century 16 percent of the population in North America will be 60 years of age and over. Similar trends are likely to occur in other countries. However, the greatest increase will likely occur in the older, more developed nations, and in the developing nations as fertility controls are introduced and adopted. Thus, there is cross-national variation in the number and proportion of the aged compared to the total population.

Within a country the elderly are not a homogeneous group, but vary greatly, especially with respect to health, ethnicity, economic status, sex, and class. These variations are likely to continue in the future, particularly where the society itself is experiencing population aging and considerable social change. In North America, if immigration rates decrease, the elderly population will become more homogeneous in cultural orientation and past life experiences. This is not to say that each cohort that passes 65 will be a homogeneous group: rather, they will be more comparable in terms of language, customs, values, and life experiences than the present older age cohorts, many of which include members who were not born in North America.

In conclusion, this demographic analysis of population aging has indicated that:

1. Population aging is a reflection of three basic demographic processes: fertility rates, mortality rates, and migration rates.

2. The life span represents the theoretical and biological limits to the maximum number of years an individual can live. At present, the life span for humans is about 100 years, although most will die before this age.

3. Life expectancy is the average number of years of life remaining for an individual at a given age. At present, the life expectancy at birth is about 77 years in the more developed nations, and about 45 to 55 years in the less developed nations.

4. Higher life expectancies are predicted for Caucasians, females, urban dwellers, the married, and those with higher levels of educational attainment and income.

5. There is a 'crossover' effect in life expectancy for nonwhite males: after about age 80, their life expectancy exceeds that of white males.

6. Although males outnumber females at birth, the sex ratio (males per 100 females) declines with age. At present, the sex ratio for the population over 65 years of age is 138 and 148 females per one hundred males in Canada and the United States, respectively.

7. The old-age dependency ratio represents the number of nonworkers over 65 years of age who are supported by those in the labor force who are 18 to 64 years of age. At present, each person over 65 in North America is supported by approximately five people in the labor force. The ratio in the less developed nations is about half that in the more developed nations.

8. The population of a nation may be labeled as 'young,' 'youthful,' 'mature,' or 'old,' depending on the proportion of people in the total population who are over 60 or 65 years of age. A majority of the aged nations are the most developed nations; the young and youthful countries are found in Africa, Central and South America, and South Asia.

9. With declining birth rates and increased longevity, populations are increasingly moving from the 'young' or 'youthful' classification to the 'mature' to the 'aged' classification.

10. At present, the elderly constitute a higher percentage of the total population in the more developed nations and regions of the world than the less developed nations and regions.

11. Although it is increasing with each birth cohort, the level of educational attainment of the population 65 and over is lower than that of younger age cohorts.

12. Most older men are married, and most older women are widowed. This discrepancy widens for those over about 70 years of age.

13. The proportion of those over 65 in the labor force has declined steadily throughout this century in industrialized societies.

14. Of those who are employed after the age of 65, many (especially women) are employed in low-paying part-time positions.

15. The economic status of the elderly has improved in recent decades, but their relative economic status compared to younger cohorts has not changed significantly.

16. Only a small percentage of the elderly live in 'poverty' conditions, but many (especially older widows) experience a decline in their standard of living after retirement.

17. Those most likely to fall below the poverty line are elderly nonwhites and families headed by women.

18. Of those over 65 years of age, approximately 9 percent in Canada and 5 percent in the United States are institutionalized. Most of those who are institutionalized are Caucasian, female (widows), and over 75 years of age.

19. Within North America, the elderly generally live in those states and provinces with the greatest population density.

20. In North America, about 75 percent of those over 65 live in urbanized areas.

21. The racial composition of those living within the inner city varies. Only about 30 percent of elderly whites live in the central core, compared with over 50 percent of elderly blacks and Hispanics, who often live in racially homogeneous ghettos in the United States.

22. The suburbs that were built in the 1950s are likely to have a large proportion of elderly people in the next few decades.

23. The majority of moves after 65 years of age are local. The direction of longer moves tends to be westward or southward.

24. In North America, most of the elderly own their homes, especially in smaller urban areas and in rural areas.

25. About 13 percent of elderly men and 32 percent of elderly women between 65 and 74 years of age live alone. This percentage increases to about 18 and 28 percent respectively after the age of 85.

26. Although the elderly are still a numerical minority, they constitute an increasingly large proportion of the population in each nation, especially where fertility rates have decreased and where longevity has increased. In the future, large increases in the proportion of elderly citizens can be expected in developing nations if fertility controls are introduced and adopted.

NOTES

1. For example, preliminary results from the 1991 Canada census may not appear until late 1992 or early 1993.
2. For example, the old-age dependency ratio mentioned later has been variously compiled using the following ages in the denominator: 15 to 64, 18 to 64, and 20 to 64. Thus, the specific ratios for a given year may differ according to the source consulted. The trend over a number of years is most meaningful if the same denominator is employed from one study to another, and from one country to another.
3. Some useful statistical sources that are available in the periodicals or government publications sections of most libraries include: publications from the United Nations Social Development Division, such as the annual *Demographic Yearbook* (New York), the semiannual *Bulletin on Aging* (Vienna); reports of the United States Bureau of the Census (Washington); reports of Statistics Canada (Ottawa); the *Canada Yearbook*; reports of the World Health Organization (Geneva); reports of the International Labor Organization (Geneva); reports from the United Nations Educational, Scientific and Cultural Organization (Paris); reports from the National Council on the Aging (Washington); reports from city, state, or provincial social agencies; *Info-Age*, published periodically (1988-) by the National Advisory Council on Aging (Ottawa); journals such as *Demography, Social Indicators, Population Studies*, and the numerous gerontology journals; the monthly *Social Security Bulletin* (Washington, D.C.: U.S. Government Printing Office); the quarterly *Statistical Bulletin* (New York: Metropolitan Life Insurance Co.); microdata sets from censuses and surveys (for example, *U.S. Current Population Survey*; Statistics Canada microdata files); and demography sourcebooks that concentrate on individual and population aging (Stone and Fletcher, 1980, 1981, 1986; Gutman, 1982; Health and Welfare Canada, 1983; Statistics Canada, 1984b; Cowgill, 1986; McDaniel, 1986; Zopf, 1986; Ministry of State (Seniors), 1988; Ontario Gerontology Association, 1988; Stone and Frenken, 1988; Myers, 1990).
4. Population projections are made by taking the existing population in a given year and then making assumptions about future fertility rates, mortality rates, and migration rates. These assumptions make it possible to project, but not to predict, the size and proportion of the population in total and for age, sex, and race categories. Because they are projections rather than predic-tions, demographers often include low, medium, and high projections based on possible variations in the fertility, mortality, and migration rates. In this chapter, the medium projection rates are reported.
5. Most countries now have a census every ten years, in which there is an attempt to count every citizen. For example, in the United States, a census is conducted in years ending in 0; in Canada, a census is conducted in years ending in 1. In addition, there is often a minicensus taken halfway between the complete censuses (for example, in 1986 and 1996 in Canada). Unfortunately, every census undercounts the population because of inaccuracies in reporting, and because some people are not available to be interviewed or counted (such as illegal aliens, those who cannot speak English or French, or those who are traveling). For example, the 1970 U.S. census reported an underestimate of approximately 5 million people, many of whom lived in the slums and core areas of large cities.
6. Registrations are required for such events as birth, immigration, death, marriage, obtaining a driver's license, buying a house, and paying income and property taxes.
7. It is difficult to determine the life span of earlier civilizations and generations, because registrations of births and deaths were not recorded, or were inaccurate or incomplete until about the mid-nineteenth century (Laslett, 1985).
8. To determine your own life expectancy, enter the row in a specific life table for your sex, race, country, and year of birth. Move across to the column that matches your current chronological age. This figure indicates the average number of remaining years you can expect to live. Generally, if you were born in North America between 1970 and 1980 you can expect to live, on the average, about 73 years if you are a male and about 80 years if you are a female. For individuals who survive to age 65, a woman can expect to live 19 more years and a man 15 more years (Ministry of State [Seniors], 1988).
9. You must be careful not to misinterpret an increase in life expectancy to indicate an increased life span. In reality, an increased life expectancy at birth is largely due to increased survival in early life, and perhaps decreased mortality rates in later life, rather than an elongation of the life span (Yin and Shine, 1985).
10. Siegel (1981) defines the 'most developed countries' as Canada, the United States, those in temperate South America, those in Europe, the Soviet Union, Japan, Australia, and New Zealand; the 'less developed countries' are those in all

other areas of the world. For more detailed projections by country in each region of the world, see the tables in the United Nations' *Bulletin on Aging* and *Periodical on Aging*.

11. Some exceptions include: Lehr, 1982; Streib, 1983; Suzman and Riley, 1985; Manton, 1986; Longino, 1988; Serow and Sly, 1988.

12. According to Schwenger and Gross (1980), the higher rate in Canada is the result of a cultural norm to institutionalize 'deviant' citizens, and a harsh climate that necessitates support during the winter months. However, the major reason may be the socialized health-insurance scheme, which makes it financially easy for the sick and dying elderly to enter hospitals and homes for the aged. The lower percentage in the United States can be accounted for by the higher personal cost of health care and fewer available beds in institutions, at least until recent years.

REFERENCES

American Association of Retired Persons. (1985). *A Profile of Older Americans*. Washington, D.C.: American Association of Retired Persons.

Binstock, R. and L. George (eds.). (1990). *Handbook of Aging and the Social Sciences*. 3d ed. San Diego, Calif.: Academic Press.

Canada Yearbook. (1988). 120th Anniversary. Ottawa: Ministry of Supply and Services.

Chen, Y.P. (1987). 'Making Assets Out of Tomorrow's Elderly,' *The Gerontologist*, 27(4), 410-16.

Clark, R. et al. (1978). 'Economics of Aging: A Survey,' *Journal of Economic Literature*, 16, 919-62.

Connidis, I. (1989). *Family Ties and Aging*. Toronto: Butterworths.

Cowgill, D. (1986). *Aging around the World*. Belmont, Calif.: Wadsworth Publishing Co.

Crimmins, E. (1984). 'Life Expectancy and the Older Population,' *Research on Aging*, 6(4), 490-514.

Crown, W. (1985). 'Some Thoughts on Reformulating the Dependency Ratio,' *The Gerontologist*, 25(2), 166-71.

Denton, F. et al. (1986). 'Prospective Aging of the Population and Its Implications for the Labour Force and Government Expenditures,' *Canadian Journal on Aging*, 5(2), 75-98.

Denton, F., et al. (1987). 'The Canadian Population and Labour Force: Retrospect and Prospect,' pp. 11-38 in V. Marshall (ed.). *Aging in Canada: Social Perspectives*. Markham, Ont.: Fitzhenry and Whiteside.

Driedger, L. and N. Chappell. (1987). *Aging and Ethnicity: Toward an Interface*. Toronto: Butterworths.

Forbes, W. et al. (1987). *Institutionalization of the Elderly in Canada*. Toronto: Butterworths.

Fries, J. (1980). 'Aging, Natural Death, and the Compression of Morbidity,' *New England Journal of Medicine*, 303, 130-35.

Fries, J. and L. Crapo. (1981). *Vitality and Aging: Implications of the Rectangular Curve*. San Francisco: Freeman.

Gee, E. and M. Kimball. (1987). *Women and Aging*. Toronto: Butterworths.

Gibson, D. (1989). 'Advancing the Dependency Ratio Concept and Avoiding the Malthusian Trap,' *Research on Aging*, 11(2), 147-57.

Gutman, G. (ed.). (1982). *Canada's Changing Age Structure: Implications for the Future*. Burnaby, B.C.: Simon Fraser University Publications.

Hauser, P. (1976). 'Aging and World-Wide Population Change,' pp. 59-86 in R. Binstock and E. Shanas (eds.). *Handbook of Aging and the Social Sciences*. New York: Van Nostrand Reinhold.

Health and Welfare Canada. (1983). *Fact Book on Aging in Canada*. Ottawa: Ministry of Supply and Services.

Henretta, J. (1979). 'Using Survey Data in the Study of Social Stratification in Late Life,' *The Gerontologist*, 19(2), 197-202.

Hogg, S. et al. (1981). 'Concerning the Definition of Poverty in the Elderly,' pp. 165-84 in J. Crawford (ed.). *Canadian Gerontological Collection III*. Winnipeg, Man.: Canadian Association on Gerontology.

Jackson, J. (1985). 'Race, National Origin, Ethnicity, and Aging,' pp. 264-303 in R. Binstock and E. Shanas (eds.). *Handbook of Aging and the Social Sciences*. 2d ed. New York: Van Nostrand Reinhold.

Jorgensen, B. (1989). 'Current Big Boom in Centenarians Poses New Challenge for 21st Century,' *The Globe and Mail*, October 11, 1989:B9.

Kraus, A. (1987). 'The Increase in the Usual Life Span in North America,' *Canadian Journal on Aging*, 6(1), 19-31.

Kraus, A. (1988). 'Is a Compression of Morbidity in Late Life Occurring?: Examination of Death Certificate Evidence,' *Canadian Journal on Aging*, 7(1), 58-70.

Laslett, P. (1985). 'Societal Development and Aging,' pp. 199-230 in R. Binstock and E. Shanas (eds.). *Handbook of Aging and the Social Sciences*. 2d ed. New York: Van Nostrand Reinhold.

Lehr, U. (1982). 'Social-Psychological Correlates of Longevity,' pp. 102-47 in E. Eisdorfer et al. (eds.). *Annual Review of Gerontology and Geriatrics*. vol. 3. New York: Springer Publishing Co.

Longino, C. (ed.). (1982). 'Symposium: Population Research for Planning and Practice,' *The Gerontologist*, 22(2), 142-69.

Longino, C. (1988). 'Who Are the Oldest Americans?'

The Gerontologist, 28(4), 515-23.

Manton, K. (1986). 'Past and Future Life Expectancy Increases at Later Ages: Their Implications for the Linkage of Chronic Morbidity, Disability, and Mortality,' *Journal of Gerontology,* 41(5), 672-81.

Marshall, V. (1980). *Last Chapters: A Sociology of Aging and Dying.* Monterey, Calif.: Brooks/Cole Publishing Co.

McDaniel, S. (1986). *Canada's Aging Population.* Toronto: Butterworths.

McDaniel, S. (1987). 'Demographic Aging as a Guiding Paradigm in Canada's Welfare State,' *Canadian Public Policy,* 13(3), 330-36.

Ministry of State (Seniors). (1988). *Canada's Seniors: A Dynamic Force.* Ottawa: Ministry of Supply and Services.

Moore, E. et al. (1989). *An Atlas of the Elderly Population of Ontario.* Kingston, Ont.: Queen's University, Department of Geography.

Myers, G. (1985). 'Aging and Worldwide Population Change,' pp. 173-98 in R. Binstock and E. Shanas (eds.). *Handbook of Aging and the Social Sciences.* 2d ed. New York: Van Nostrand Reinhold.

Myers, G. (1990). 'Demography of Aging,' pp. 19-44 in R. Binstock and L. George (eds.). *Handbook of Aging and the Social Sciences.* 3d ed. San Diego, Calif.: Academic Press.

Nathanson, C. (1984). 'Sex Differences in Mortality,' *Annual Review of Sociology,* 10, 191-213.

Northcott, H. (1984). 'The Aging of Canada's Population: An Update from the 1981 Census,' *Canadian Studies in Population,* 11(1), 29-46.

Northcott, H. (1988). *Changing Residence: The Geographic Mobility of Elderly Canadians.* Toronto: Butterworths.

Ontario Gerontology Association. (1988). *Fact Book on Aging in Ontario.* Toronto: Ontario Gerontology Association.

Rosenberg, M. et al. (1988). *Components of Change in the Spatial Distribution of the Elderly Population in Ontario, 1976-1986.* Kingston, Ont.: Queen's University, Department of Geography.

Schulz, J. (1988). *The Economics of Aging.* 4th ed. Dover, Mass.: Auburn House Publishing Co.

Schwenger, C. and M. Gross. (1980). 'Institutional Care and Institutionalization of the Elderly in Canada,' pp. 248-56 in V. Marshall (ed.). *Aging In Canada: Social Perspectives.* Don Mills, Ont.: Fitzhenry and Whiteside.

Serow, W. and D. Sly. (1988). 'Trends in the Characteristics of the Oldest-Old: 1940-2020,' *Journal of Aging Studies,* 2(2), 145-56.

Siegel, J. (1981). 'Demographic Background for International Gerontological Studies,' *Journal of Gerontology,* 36(1), 93-102.

Siegel, J. and C. Taeuber. (1982). 'The 1980 Census and the Elderly: New Data Available to Planners and Practitioners,'*The Gerontologist,* 22(2), 144-50.

Siegel, J. and C. Taeuber. (1986). 'Demographic Perspectives on the Long-Lived Society,' *Daedalus,* 115, 77-117.

Statistical Bulletin. (1968). 49(1), 2-5 ('Longevity of Prominent Women').

Statistical Bulletin. (1979). 60(1), 3-9 ('Longevity of Prominent Men').

Statistics Canada. (1984a). *The Elderly in Canada.* Ottawa: Minister of Supply and Services.

Statistics Canada. (1984b). *Current Demographic Analysis, Fertility in Canada: From Baby Boom to Baby Bust.* Ottawa: Minister of Supply and Services.

Stone, L. and S. Fletcher. (1980). *A Profile of Canada's Older Population.* Montreal: Institute for Research on Public Policy.

Stone, L. and S. Fletcher. (1981). *Aspects of Population Aging in Canada: A Chartbook.* Ottawa: Ministry of Supply and Services.

Stone, L. and S. Fletcher. (1986). *The Seniors Boom: Dramatic Increases in Longevity and Prospects for Better Health.* Ottawa: Ministry of Supply and Services.

Stone, L. and H. Frenken. (1988). *Canada's Seniors.* Ottawa: Ministry of Supply and Services.

Streib, G. (1983). 'The Frail Elderly: Research Dilemmas and Research Opportunities,' *The Gerontologist,* 23(1), 40-44.

Suzman, R. and M. Riley (eds.). (1985). 'The Oldest Old' (Special Issue). *Milbank Memorial Fund Quarterly,* 63(2), 177-451.

United Nations. (1984). *Periodical on Aging, 1984.* New York: United Nations, Department of International Economic and Social Affairs.

United Nations. (1988). *1986 Demographic Yearbook.* 38th issue. New York: Department of International Economic and Social Affairs, Statistical Office.

U.S. Department of Commerce. (1987). *Statistical Abstract of the U.S.* Washington: Bureau of the Census.

Warnes, A. (ed.). (1982). *Geographical Perspectives on the Elderly.* London: John Wiley & Sons.

Wilkins, R. and O. Adams. (1983). *Healthfulness of Life.* Montreal, P.Q.: The Institute for Research on Public Policy.

Williamson, J. (1988). 'Welfare State Development and Life Expectancy among the Aged: A Cross-National Analysis,' *Journal of Aging Studies,* 2(1), 13-24.

Yin, P. and M. Shine. (1985). 'Misinterpretations of Increases in Life Expectancy in Gerontology Textbooks,' *The Gerontologist,* 25(1), 78-82.

Zopf, P. (1986). *America's Older Population.* Houston, Tex.: Cap & Gown Press.

4
Understanding Aging: The Use of Scientific Perspectives, Theories, and Methods

Health and Welfare Canada, Information Directorate

INTRODUCTION

This chapter initiates a shift in emphasis from description to explanation. In order to provide you with the necessary conceptual tools and methodologies to study and understand aging phenomena, the threefold purpose of this chapter is (1) to describe the goals and methods of scientific inquiry; (2) to indicate the methodological approaches and concerns to be addressed when studying the process of aging; and (3) to illustrate the major theories and conceptual frameworks[1] that have been used to explain social phenomena associated with aging and the aged.

As will become readily apparent later in the chapter, there is not at present, nor is there likely to be in the future, a single theory that explains how individuals or populations age. A number of competing yet sometimes complementary perspectives have been proposed to provide understanding of social or physical phenomena related to the aging process.

Scientists are constantly striving to develop more complete and parsimonious explanations for social or physical phenomena. Although additional perspectives and theories will be developed in the future, a complete explanation for aging phenomena is unlikely to emerge, because of the complexity of the social world.

As you read this chapter, learn the concepts, theories, and theoretical perspectives so that they can assist you in understanding the process of aging. Accept them as the best available information at this time, recognizing that as you read this book new explanations or models for aging phenomena are likely being developed and tested in a number of disciplines. In short, the theories and methods presented in this chapter represent the 'state of the art' in social gerontology. Because this state is likely to change over the next ten years, you must begin reading the major journals in order to remain current with respect to theory, methods, and substantive information.

The Purpose and Goals of Science: The Search for Knowledge

In order to help you to discover, describe, and understand social phenomena pertaining to the aging process, this and the following sections discuss the purpose and process of the scientific approach to acquiring knowledge. By the end of this chapter you should understand, and be prepared to play, the 'science game' (Agnew and Pyke, 1987), regardless of whether you study aging or some other social or physical phenomenon. The scientific approach involves formulating a relationship or hypothesis, obtaining reliable observations or facts to support or refute the relationship, explaining the observations, arriving at conclusions that separate fact from myth, and searching for order and patterns in events.

The ultimate goal of all scholarly inquiry is to offer possible and plausible insights, interpretations, and explanations about our social world. As scholars, we are motivated by simple curiosity (why and how does some social pattern or problem occur? why do people, individually or collectively, behave in a specific way?), by the urge to question taken-for-granted myths or assumptions (the elderly are impoverished; elder abuse is a common outcome of caregiving), by a desire to draw attention to and resolve inequities in the social world (the poverty of elderly widows; the inadequate health care and housing of elderly ethnic males and females), and by a need for reliable and valid information in order to develop viable policies and programs. In this search for understanding and truth, scholars in the social sciences seldom, if ever, arrive at the absolute truth, mainly because of the complexity inherent in the interaction between aging individuals and an ever-changing social world. Thus, in order to gain as complete an understanding as possible of a given social fact or pattern, scientists pursue three main goals: description, discovery, and explanation.

The scientist observes and describes objects or events to obtain facts rather than opinions. In the field of sociology, scientists are interested in the structure and composition of social systems (which range in size and complexity from a married couple to the entire world), and in the interactions and changes that take place within and between social systems. The psychologist is interested in describing phenomena occurring within and between individuals, while the social psychologist studies the individual within a small social system or group.

Although the acquisition of facts is an important step in the scientific process, by itself it is not sufficient to advance knowledge. The scientist must then proceed to discover and test patterns of general relationships. This involves searching for and observing the regular and coincidental occurrence of events such as retirement and loss of status, or widowhood and changing patterns of support and friendship. The sociologist searches for repetitive patterns and relationships between properties of social systems, while the psychologist searches for relationships between characteristics of the individual (such as age and personality traits), or between individual characteristics and environmental stimuli (such as level of morale and quality of housing).

The final and most crucial goal of science is to account for observed relationships or patterns through scientific explanation. This not only enables us to understand why the relationship occurs, but also sometimes enables us to predict when and under what circumstances it will reoccur. However, because there are many scholars within a discipline who approach a given problem with different theories, assumptions, and methods, we often have alternative interpretations or explanations of the same phenomena. Although competing interpretations or explanations may be confusing to the student or the layman, the presence of alternative views serves as a stimulus for further research to arrive at a more complete explanation. Unfortunately, seldom in the social sciences do we ever arrive at the explanation, which, if supported by research evidence, is expressed as a law.

Nonscientists also pursue the three goals of description, discovery, and explanation as they attempt to understand and guide behavior in everyday life. The major difference between the scientific and nonscientific approaches is the use by scientists of relatively standardized methods to discover and test relationships, and the degree to which they search for alternative or more complete explanations. The scientist is an intellectual craftsman (Mills, 1959; Nisbet, 1976) who has acquired the tools of a particular discipline, who employs these tools to gain insight into social or physical phenomena, and who is motivated to discover a more complete or a better explanation of the phenomenon under investigation. The nonscientist, in contrast, is usually satisfied with the simplest and most obvious explanation for a particular event.

In summary, the goal of science is to describe, discover, and explain repetitive phenomena. While scientists from different disciplines might ask different questions and employ different approaches to arrive at an understanding of a specific phenomenon, they all generally adhere to the following principles and practices inherent in the scientific method of inquiry:

1. Science is a logical process which demands that explanations make sense. Both deductive (from the general to the specific) and inductive (from the specific to the general) logic are used to arrive at explanations.
2. For scientists, there must be a rational (logical) explanation for every event, since it is assumed that behavior does not occur by chance.
3. The scientist is interested in explaining general patterns, regardless of time and place (for example, why and how do individuals acquire and lose status as they age?).
4. Science is characterized by adherence to objectivity and by the need to verify facts and observations. A given fact, relationship, or theory should be tested and verified by a number of scientists who, although working in isolation, follow the same general procedures. In short, findings must be replicated and reproduced before they can be accepted as explanations.
5. Scientific evidence is always subject to revision and change. In fact, the history of any science generally shows that sooner or later what has previously been accepted as 'the' explanation is often revised or rejected because of new evidence. Science proceeds by the elimination of unsupported hypotheses. For example, at one time many gerontologists accepted

the theory that all older people 'disengage' as they grow older; today, evidence suggests that this is not a universal or inevitable process. Similarly, it was once believed that the elderly could not and should not have sexual relations; but recent biological, psychological, and sociological evidence suggests that they not only can, but that many want to — and do.

Concepts, Propositions, and Theories

To provide descriptions of social or physical phenomena, it is necessary to use concepts, definitions, and classification schemes. A **concept** is an abstract, generalized idea about an object or phenomenon. For example, 'aging' is a concept that expresses a dynamic change in the appearance and behavior of individuals. It represents a theoretical view of a social, biological, or psychological process. As such, it provides a common means of communication among scientists interested in a similar phenomenon. A concept is only a theoretical frame of reference. In order for it to be useful in generating knowledge, it must be measurable, either directly or indirectly. Each concept has associated with it one or more variables that can be used to measure the concept and to relate it to other concepts. For example, chronological age is a variable that represents the aging of an individual in years from birth. However, the concept of 'age' can be expressed by using other variables, such as 'functional age' or 'legal age,' which explain various facets of the aging process. In short, a **variable** is a symbol to which numbers may be assigned. Generally, these variables are related to each other either as an **independent variable** (a presumed cause, an antecedent event) or as a **dependent variable** (a predicted or presumed outcome, a consequence of an earlier event).

Scientists and students need to be precise and consistent about the meaning of the concepts and variables they use. Therefore, two types of definitions are necessary — theoretical and operational. The **theoretical definition** (or nominal definition, as it is sometimes called) gives the standard, general meaning of the concept. The **operational definition** specifies the procedures that are necessary to measure the variable. To illustrate, a theoretical definition of functional age might be 'an indicator of age that is based on level of performance in a variety of daily self-maintenance or job-related tasks'; an operational definition of this concept might be 'the level of performance in such tasks as adding speed, writing speed, perceptual motor speed and accuracy, reaction time and decision making.' All concepts must have both a theoretical and an operational definition; in this way, scientists can understand each other when they communicate, and they can use and measure the concepts in similar ways as they seek to explain phenomena.

Taken together, a number of concepts can be linked into typologies, taxonomies, or schemas that facilitate the analysis of individual or group phenomena. For example, figure 8.2 (page 278) illustrates a classification scheme for studying the relationship between degree of independence and type of housing; highlight 1.4 (page 25) presents a typology of older adults with ethnic roots.

To this point we have discussed concepts, definitions, variables, and classification schemes. However, these pertain only to the first goal of science, description. In order to explain or predict social phenomena (that is, to discover relationships), a theoretical statement is needed that suggests a hypothesized relationship between two or more concepts or their variables. For example, we have moved from the descriptive level to the explanatory level when we generate and test statements such as the following:

1. As age increases, the level of health decreases.
2. The greater the age of an individual (at least until mandatory retirement), the higher the earned income.
3. There is an inverse relationship between the distance from the center of a metropolitan area and the age of the residents.
4. As the degree of modernization increases, the status of the elderly in a society declines.

The discoveries that result from scientific inquiry are stated as **propositions**. These can have varying degrees of explanatory power and empirical (research) support. Those that have some explanatory power and little empirical support are known as **hypotheses**; those with high explanatory power and strong empirical support are known as **laws**. However, as noted earlier, the social sciences in general, and social gerontology in particular, have few if any laws. In short, the goal of discovery involves a constant search to obtain support for relationships between independent and dependent variables. It is important to recognize that variables per se are not tested; rather, it is the relationship between variables that must be supported by research evidence.

It is not sufficient, however, to describe concepts, or to discover and test relationships between concepts. The ultimate goal of the science game is to account for the discovered relationships through scientific explanation. In short, this final step involves constructing a new theory or using an existing one to explain the aging process.

Although there is no universally accepted definition of a **theory**, it is generally defined as a set of interrelated propositions (made up of defined concepts or variables) that present a logical, systematic, and reasonably complete view of a phenomenon. This view is constructed by specifying the relationships among variables in order to explain and predict the phenomenon. In short, a theory is the product of scientific inquiry as well as a tool for scientific inquiry. As a tool, a theory serves as a conceptual scheme: (1) to provide assumptions and definitions; (2) to summarize and synthesize existing knowledge; (3) to translate facts into empirical generalizations; (4) to guide and stimulate thinking by raising questions and indicating gaps between theory and research; and (5) to serve as a stimulus to search for more complete or alternative explanations.

As a product of science, a theory provides a summary of existing or anticipated findings. It also identifies propositions that need to be tested, and it helps to provide explanations for unexpected findings. A theory represents a simpler model of how the complex social or physical world operates; it guides the development and implementation of policy; it provides a conceptual system to accept or reject, and therefore further stimulates the development and accumulation of knowledge; and it enables us to make predictions, and thereby introduce some element of control in our lives. Thus, we rely to a greater extent on theories or models as we move from description to discovery to explanation.

There are many types of theories and many theoretical perspectives, even within a given discipline. For example, in sociology we find the competing theoretical perspectives of conflict theorists, functional theorists, system theorists, social exchange theorists, symbolic interaction theorists, and phenomenological theorists. This variety enables sociologists to select theories and theoretical perspectives appropriate to the specific question or problem they wish to study. In short, as Ritzer (1975) has noted, sociology is a multiple-paradigm[2] science and 'no aspect of social reality can be adequately explained without drawing on insights from all of the paradigms.' Just as different research methods are needed, so too are different theoretical perspectives and paradigms[3] necessary, since each is based on different assumptions and utilizes different concepts. However, ultimately one perspective usually proves to be superior to another in providing a more complete or valid explanation of a specific phenomenon.

This variety in theoretical approaches to a phenomenon may be initially confusing; however, the presence of competing theoretical perspectives is necessary for a discipline, as long as the competing theoretical perspectives introduce alternative views of the world, and thereby advance understanding of the phenomenon. Unfortunately, sometimes the presence of competing perspectives can inhibit or prevent an ideal examination of a specific phenomenon. For example, most theories represent either a micro (individual) or macro (societal) view of the world. In reality, some aging phenomena, if they are to be completely understood, require both a micro and a macro level of analysis (for example, the issue of mandatory retirement).

Research Settings and Methods

Introduction

In the previous subsection the more creative and intellectual aspects of the research process were described. Having developed concepts, propositions, and perhaps even a theory, the researcher now begins to make and record observations. This stage permits testing of the explanatory value and power of a proposition, or of a series of interrelated propositions — a theory.

This section briefly describes three settings (library, field, and laboratory) where research can occur, and four general techniques (survey research, secondary analysis, participant observation, controlled experiments) that are commonly used to answer questions about a specific phenomenon.[4] While these settings and techniques are used in all of the social sciences, including social gerontology, some are more applicable to specific disciplines or specific research questions. For example, survey research in the field is a common tool in sociology, while controlled laboratory experiments are more prevalent in psychology.

Since social gerontology tends to be a hybrid field made up of anthropologists, sociologists, psychologists, social psychologists, economists, and political scientists, all of the following settings and techniques have been used to answer questions about the aging process, or about age differences among individuals at specific stages in the life cycle. However, because of the nature of the process, social gerontology has a number of unique methodological concerns that create problems not only in the design of studies, but also in the interpretation of findings. These issues are addressed later in this chapter.

Just as the prescribing of medicine by a physician is guided by the patient's apparent symptoms, the choice of research setting and method is guided by the theoretical question that needs to be answered. That is, the research process involving observation and interpretation is not initiated randomly. This decision to examine the relationship between certain variables derives from a review of the existing literature, along with the creative insight of the scientist. Thus, if a scientist is interested in accounting for the level of life satisfaction among widows, he or she is unlikely to include such variables as eye color, maiden name, or zodiac sign. Rather, the existing literature and the logical process of deduction are used to construct a theory that includes such variables as

income, education, ethnicity, perceived health, number of friends, or degree of participation in the labor force.

In short, the research process seeks to answer questions with more precision and understanding than would result were we to rely on common sense or chance. This is not to suggest that significant research findings have not occurred serendipitously, but it is certainly true that the chance of finding a significant and complete explanation, and finding it sooner, is greater if a scientific approach is used.

Library Settings

Both qualitative and quantitative data useful in answering some research questions may already be available and stored in public or private archives such as libraries, museums, and data banks. The research technique that uses this material is called secondary analysis. The most common type of secondary analysis involves the use of existing data sets collected for some other purpose (Patrick and Borgatta, 1981). Thus, the use of existing opinion polls, census, or registration data represents a form of secondary analysis. For example, an analysis of the relationship between age and the leisure patterns of Canadians (McPherson and Kozlik, 1987) was based on a previous survey conducted to examine the frequency and type of leisure activities engaged in by the total adult population of Canada. The responses had not previously been analyzed to determine whether differences existed between the types of leisure activities selected by different age cohorts. A major weakness of secondary analysis is that the data set may lack essential independent or control variables that are needed to provide a complete explanation for any age differences that may be found.

Another type of secondary analysis is known as content analysis (highlight 4.1). In this more qualitative analysis, the research scientist searches for patterns and characteristics included in textual material (Holsti, 1969). For example, studies using content analysis have determined the type and prominence of roles played by elderly people; their personality, dress, and actions; and the beliefs and actions of other age cohorts toward the elderly as described in children's books, school textbooks,

HIGHLIGHT **4.1**

A CONTENT ANALYSIS OF LETTERS EXCHANGED
WITHIN A MENNONITE IMMIGRANT FAMILY, 1877-1912

Using a life-course perspective of aging and family relationships, Quadagno and Janzen (1987) analyzed the role of religious and ethnic traditions in preserving family stability, in providing support and security in old age, and in shaping the life course of descendents. Using a series of letters between the eldest son and the parents, which were written from 1877 until 1912 when the father died, the authors reconstructed the life cycle for two generations of a Mennonite family who migrated from Russia to the Kansas plains in 1874. The letters, stored in a Mennonite Library in North Newton, Kansas, recorded family events and crises, community events, and beliefs and values. Any gaps in the correspondence, and as much verification of events as possible, were compiled by examining land transaction records, birth and death records, and census records.

Using these methods, the authors found that, because of a strong belief in family support and a traditional Mennonite pattern of inheritance, accumulated property or wealth was fairly transferred to each of their offspring. In return, the children provided considerable social support to their parents. Thus, by using a content analysis of letters stored in a library, we learn how traditional values and practices brought from Russia were transplanted from one generation to the next. Yet, at the same time, we learn that, as social, political, and economic situations changed over a thirty-four-year period in the Midwest, some of the traditional patterns of inheritance and family support were altered because of the mobility and needs of the offspring. Had only quantitative data been available (for example, place of residence of each son and daughter, marital and occupational status of the children), the actual amount of reciprocal family support, and the expressed feelings toward parents and offspring, would not have been known. However, a qualitative analysis — an examination of the content of the family letters in detail — captured the strength and meaning of family support as it evolved over three decades.

SOURCE: Adapted from Quadagno and Janzen (1987).

---

fiction, plays, the movies, and in television commercials and serials. Often these interpretive studies of the literature focus on negative portrayals or stereotypes of aging (Hendricks and Leedham, 1987).

Field Settings

A great deal of social research tends to be conducted in real-life settings rather than in artificial laboratory environments. These research situations can involve many people, such as a national sample of senior citizens, or they can involve only a few people, such as an interview with all physicians over 80 years of age who still practice medicine. Survey research is the most common method used in the field. This technique generally involves either the use of face-to-face or telephone interviews, or a questionnaire that is mailed or given to the respondent. The information collected can be used to describe a phenomenon (for example, the number of widows over 70 years of age who

live below the poverty line), to test the relationship between variables (whether those of a specific age are more likely to vote in local or national elections), or to determine attitudes, beliefs, or behavior before and after specific events (a questionnaire or interview with elderly individuals when they enter a nursing home might be repeated one year later to determine whether attitudinal or behavioral changes have occurred). An increasingly popular method for analyzing the meaning of aging is the use of life-history analyses. This time-consuming method involves detailed interviews with elderly respondents to reconstruct their life course and to analyze and interpret their meanings of the events (such as immigrating to North America) that shaped their own life course. Often this method is combined with analyses of diaries, family photo albums, letters to and from friends and relatives (Manheimer, 1989; Wacks, 1989).

The major advantage of survey research is

that it permits observations to be made for samples representing much larger populations. Unfortunately, this method can be very expensive and time-consuming. Also, when a questionnaire is used, much information may be lost because the investigator cannot probe the respondent to obtain a more detailed interpretation of what is meant by a particular response. Nor can it be determined whether the respondent correctly understood the question. There are also a number of disadvantages or limitations to using surveys with older respondents. For example, elderly people appear to be more prone to agree with statements regardless of the content; to use a smaller proportion of response categories on a given scale; to use the extreme response categories (high or low); and to give the same response to all questions in a set of questions that have similar response categories. These factors do not appear to be related to level of education, but they may be related to fatigue (long questionnaires or interviews), to declining health, or to lack of experience with multiple-response instruments.

A second major type of field research is participant observation or ethnography. In this technique, investigators are involved as observers of, or participants with, the respondents as they engage in social interaction in one or more social settings over a period of time (Fry and Keith, 1986; Keith, 1988; Reinharz and Rowles, 1988). In some cases the role of the researcher is unknown to the subjects in the study. This sometimes helps to prevent the intentional distortion or misrepresentation of information or behavior by the subjects. At other times, the purpose of the investigator's involvement is known, and he or she participates either as a regular member of the group or purely as a passive observer. The advantages of this method are that the researcher can obtain information about specific cultural or subcultural environments; can understand the quality of relationships; can study topics where direct questions or measurements are not possible; and can study phenomena where informants or respondents may be unwilling or unable to report accurately about their behaviors.

The major limitations of this method are that it often lacks the use of standardized instruments (such as a questionnaire), which makes it difficult to replicate the study exactly; it can be very time-consuming; and it requires special observational and conversational skills on the part of the participant observer. The use of this method also raises ethical concerns if informed consent to be studied is not obtained, thereby representing a possible invasion of the right to privacy (Kimmel and Moody, 1990).

A third type of research method employed in the field is the field experiment. In this approach, one or more independent variables are manipulated by the experimenter under controlled conditions (Schaie, 1977). Although a major weakness of this approach is the inability to control all possible confounding factors, this is compensated for in part by the realism attached to the results, compared to the results from a laboratory experiment. An example of a field experiment in social gerontology involved a comparison of tenants living in high-rise apartment buildings who did, or did not, have access to an on-site public health nursing program (Flett et al., 1980). It was found that those in buildings with access to on-site nursing had better health and lower rates of hospital admission than the control group who did not have access to on-site nursing.

Field research also involves validation or feedback research to determine the effectiveness of some program, policy, or intervention (Smyer and Gatz, 1986; Wan, 1986). The research may be initiated at various stages to determine: (1) whether some progress has been made toward achieving a specific goal (such as greater independence); (2) at the conclusion of a program to measure whether the objectives have been attained, whether a policy has been effective, or whether an intervention has been used and is of some benefit; (3) prior to the initiation of a policy or program to complete a needs assessment; (4) at any stage after the initiation of a program or policy to measure cost-effectiveness; (5) prior to the initiation of a new policy or service to identify any opposition to the new policy or program; and (6) at any time to identify gaps or inequities in existing policies or programs. This type of applied field research may involve mailed or telephone surveys, face-to-face interviews, field observations, or secondary analyses (for example, of policies or legislation, budgets, usage statistics). The

HIGHLIGHT **4.2**

AN EVALUATION OF
AN IN-SERVICE TRAINING PROGRAM

Nursing home aides are the primary caregivers for elderly persons residing within institutions. Yet, these essential personnel in the health-care field receive little formal training. In order to evaluate the effectiveness of an in-service training program offered by a community college, Skinkle and Grant (1988) surveyed 140 nursing homes in Saskatchewan to identify which homes had or had not provided their staff with this in-service program. They identified 92 nursing homes where the program was offered. Then, they classified the nursing homes as rural or urban, and randomly selected four homes from each of the following types: urban, aides trained; urban, aides not trained; rural, aides trained; and rural, aides not trained. Forty-one graduates of the in-service program and forty-five aides who had not been offered the program completed an evaluation questionnaire designed to measure knowledge about nursing skills, about the aging process, and about the philosophy of long-term care. In addition, an assessment was made of the perceived effectiveness of the health-care team in which the aides worked, and of their attitudes toward the elderly.

This comparative evaluation showed that graduates of the in-service training program (there were no rural-urban differences) had significantly more knowledge about nursing skills, the aging process, and the philosophy of long-term care than those who were not exposed to the program. The program attendees were also more likely to indicate that their health-care team was functioning effectively. The authors concluded that the in-service program was successful in meeting its goals of enhancing knowledge and fostering a cooperative and effective team approach to caring for the elderly.

Moreover, interviews with three chief administrators who had implemented the program, but whose nursing aides were not included in this study, indicated that their aides actually applied the knowledge gained from the program. On the basis of this evaluation, the authors concluded that this type of in-service training program is a worthwhile investment, and recommended that it should be implemented in all nursing homes.

SOURCE: Adapted from Skinkle and Grant (1988).

---

more frequently high-quality evaluation research, intervention research, or policy analysis is completed, the more sensitive policy-makers and practitioners are to assessing the needs of elderly clients in the public or private sector. Moreover, this type of research can also sensitize us to social change and to the needs of different age cohorts. For example, a policy and subsequent program designed to meet the transportation needs of the urban elderly in 1980 may be totally inadequate to meet the needs of the elderly in 1990 or 2000. Highlight 4.2 describes the methodology for a study designed to evaluate the effectiveness of an in-service training program for nursing home aides.

Laboratory Settings

In psychology and in most of the physical and natural sciences, controlled experiments are completed in laboratories so as to eliminate extraneous factors that might influence the relationship being studied. Subjects are randomly assigned to groups, conditions of the experiment are randomized, variables are precisely manipulated, and accurate, reliable, and valid instruments are used to measure the effects of the experiment (Mangen and Peterson, 1982; Birren and Cunningham, 1985; Nesselroade and Labouvie, 1985).

For example, Bowles and Poon (1982), testing for age differences in recognition memory processing, had young and elderly subjects respond to a study list of 120 words. The words were displayed on a screen for two seconds. The subjects were then presented with 120 pairs of words and were asked to indicate which word in the pair had been on the original list. While no significant difference in accuracy was observed between the two age groups, it was found that those older adults who performed at a higher level had better verbal ability as measured by a standard vocabulary test. Thus, within the controlled laboratory experiment, verbal ability was introduced as a control variable.

Summary

There are many research settings and techniques available to scientists who wish to study social phenomena. Although these have been presented as separate approaches, in reality a social scientist may use more than one of these methods within the same study. In fact, there are strong arguments in favor of integrating qualitative and quantitative methods in the study of aging topics (Connidis, 1983; Reinharz and Rowles, 1988). The use of participant observation, archival data, and survey research within a study can provide unexpected information, as well as more complete data. The advantage of a multi-method study (Marshall, 1981) can be illustrated by a study of the degree of social isolation among residents of a nursing home. The degree of isolation can be examined by observing the frequency of visits to public places in the home, by interviews with the residents and staff, and by a secondary analysis of daily staff reports that include anecdotal comments about the behavior of residents.

There are some unique methodological problems to be considered when studying the aging process. Some of these problems are outlined later in this chapter. The next subsection emphasizes the need to link theory and research so that the research process produces valid, complete, and reliable knowledge. If the information derived from the research process does not meet these criteria, then application of the knowledge in policy or practice is not valid.

The Link between Theory and Research

As with the age-old question 'Which came first, the chicken or the egg?' scientists and philosophers of science have debated whether theory or research, as interrelated facets of the science game, should be initiated first (Merton, 1957; Lastrucci, 1967; Snizek, 1975). To date, agreement has not been reached on this question, and may not ever be reached, since the priority of one over the other is very much related to the style, experience, and ability of the individual scientist.

Scientists do agree that both theory and research are necessary and that there is a strong relationship between the theoretical orientation and the preferred method of inquiry. For example, Snizek (1975) found that sociologists who focus on the individual tend to stress deduction and to use empirical, quantitative techniques and procedures in their research. In contrast, those who focus on group characteristics tend to rely more upon induction, and to use an interpretive or intuitive analytical approach. That is, the research design is guided by the research question and the theoretical perspective. For example, symbolic interactionists tend to use participant observation as their major research technique, and to rely on qualitative rather than quantitative data.

The interaction of theory and research seems to operate much like the problem of the chicken and the egg. Theory suggests ideas for research and helps to explain the research findings; the research process tests theories and stimulates the revision of existing theories. Research also facilitates the construction of new theories to fit the existing evidence. To put this idea in more scientific terms, the theoretical products of scientific inquiry are concepts, propositions (hypotheses), and theories. The methodological processes include the logical processes of induction and deduction, and empirical processes such as sampling, operationalization of the variables, instrumentation, observation, measurement, data analysis, and interpretation.

The process of developing a scientific body of knowledge can begin with observations, from which propositions and theories are derived (the first-research-then-theory approach). It can also begin with the construction of hypothetical propositions and theories that are later tested to determine whether the relationships are supported or refuted (the first-theory-then-research approach). Regardless of the starting point, the ultimate goal is to use research evidence to support or refute a hypothesis or theory. If the evidence fails to provide support, the hypothesis or theory needs to be revised, or more valid supporting evidence needs to be obtained.

In actuality, a composite approach is usually

employed. That is, observations are not made without some preliminary theoretical work, and theory development does not proceed too far without testing at least some of the propositions in the postulated theory. At the present stage of development in social gerontology, the amount of research completed far exceeds the amount of theoretical work. Thus, a greater emphasis has been given to making observations, to collecting evidence to describe phenomena, and to testing relationships between variables. One reason for this approach has been the atheoretical basis of much research wherein it has been assumed, falsely, that old age is a problem. As a result, the development of hypotheses or theories that more adequately and completely explain aging as a social process has been neglected. This is a normal stage of development for any new field. However, if the scientific process continues as it has in other disciplines, we can expect that the knowledge derived in the next decade will be increasingly cumulative rather than representing random, unrelated facts (Forscher, 1963). Moreover, the quantity and quality of theoretical development should increase as new scholars are better prepared to play this facet of the science game. However, whether gerontology per se ever becomes a science is unlikely, since gerontology as a field of inquiry involves many sciences and many theoretical perspectives (Achenbaum, 1987).

METHODOLOGICAL CONCERNS IN SOCIAL GERONTOLOGY

Introduction

With the increasing emphasis on deriving more complete knowledge about the aging process rather than on dealing with aging primarily as a social problem, more attention is being directed to methodological issues.[5] This emphasis is necessary in order to design better studies and to interpret more accurately data patterns and observations. In this section some of the more important methodological concerns are discussed so that, as you read journal and newspaper articles, you will be better pre-

pared to consider the reliability and validity of both the findings and the interpretations of the observations.

Research Designs and the Interpretation of Data

The production of valid knowledge involves not only asking the 'right' questions, but also answering the questions with the appropriate procedures. Not only must the study be designed correctly, but the interpretation of the findings must be accurate and must not be inflated beyond the information provided by the observations.

To date, most social gerontology research has either examined differences between age groups on a number of variables, or examined changes that occur within age groups or individuals as they pass through various stages in the life cycle. Both of these questions can be influenced by historical events and cultural differences. Thus, social scientists, and you as readers of their work, must be careful to distinguish among the effects of aging, cohort differences, and historical and environmental influences when studying the process of aging and the behavior of the elderly (Maddox and Campbell, 1985; Dannefer, 1988a, 1988b).

As we have seen, aging involves diversity within and among individuals, between cohorts, and across and within cultures. Thus, it is important that we capture this diversity by separating universal processes of aging from culture-specific processes, and that we understand how cultural factors influence aging (Palmore, 1983; Gibson, 1988; Dannefer, 1988a, 1988b). Moreover, we must control for variations within an ethnic or racial group by class, gender, income, or education; we must use the life-course perspective to consider cohort effects (Hagestad, 1990); and we must avoid using general labels whereby intergroup variability is lost (for example, all elderly people with Cuban, Puerto Rican or Mexican-American roots should not be classified as Hispanics, which implies that they have had the same cultural and lifelong experiences). Furthermore, we need to pay special attention to conceptual and methodological issues (such as definitions of rural; duration of rural residency; research by scholars with an urban background) in research conducted within rural environments (Martin Matthews and Vanden Heuvel, 1986; Keating, forthcoming).

To explain whether differences noted at a particular age have always been present, or whether the extent and the nature of diversity within a population change with age, we need longitudinal data on large, representative samples. That is, we need to learn whether the diversity develops gradually over the life course, whether it develops suddenly because of some age-specific event, or whether the within-cohort diversity fluctuates from decade to decade within the life of a cohort. Dannefer (1988a, 1988b) states that cohort heterogeneity may vary in amount and rate of development across the life course of an age cohort, and that there may be five possible trajectories for this diversity across the life course: (1) the radial fan or increasing-divergence pattern, wherein people become more diverse as they age; (2) a U-shaped curve, with much diversity early and late in life and considerable similarity in the middle; (3) a constant pattern of diversity that remains from birth across the life course; (4) a sudden increase in diversity at some age due to a trigger event (such as retirement at age 65); and (5) a convergence from considerable diversity in early life to considerable homogeneity in later life. In order to answer research questions, social scientists have generally collected data using either a cross-sectional or a longitudinal design. In the following subsections, the issues raised by the use of each method are discussed, and an alternative design is introduced.

Cross-Sectional Designs

Because the cross-sectional design is the least costly in terms of time and money, it has been widely used by social scientists. This design involves recording observations or responses by individuals of different ages and then reporting the results according to age group. For example, in a study of the relationship between age and attendance at movies in 1990, the results might be as reported in table 4.1.[6]

While it appears that movie attendance declines with age, we cannot conclude that differences between age groups are due to growing old (an aging effect). Rather, we can only conclude that at one point in history (such as 1990) there were age differences in the frequency of movie attendance. The data indicate that younger age cohorts are more likely to attend movies three or more times per year. Furthermore, there are often variations within specific age groups in specific variables. These differences may be greater than those between age groups. For example, it appears (table 4.1) that males of all ages attend more movies than females. Thus, the low frequency of attendance by those over 55 might be a reflection of the fact that there are more females than males in that age group.

The differences between age groups might also suggest that there are generational or cohort differences in lifestyle that are revealed by sampling movie attendance at a particular point

---

TABLE 4.1

THE POSSIBLE RELATIONSHIP BETWEEN AGE AND MOVIE ATTENDANCE: A CROSS-SECTIONAL DESIGN

Age	Percentage attending three times or more per year in 1990		
	Males and Females	Males	Females
14-19	58	65	52
20-24	54	62	50
25-34	45	52	39
35-44	33	41	25
45-54	20	31	14
55-64	15	20	10
65-74	11	19	9
75 and over	8	12	6

in history. For example, it is quite likely that those over 65 never attended movies to any great extent at any time in their lives. This pattern may have evolved either because movies were relatively unavailable in their early years, or because they were unable to afford the cost of attending movies when they were young. In either situation, this cohort, unlike later generations, probably never adopted movies as a salient part of their leisure lifestyle. Similarly, in later life they may not wish to spend part of their limited and relatively fixed income on the ever-increasing price of admission to movies.

This design identifies differences between age groups, but does not permit us to adequately explain why the differences vary by age. That is, the data pattern may reflect generational or cultural differences in lifestyle (immigrants may be less inclined to attend movies, and the over-65 group is made up of many who immigrated to this country in early adulthood), changes with age, or the unique impact of specific historical events (such as a depression or an energy crisis) on a particular age group at some point in their life cycle. Therefore, alternative designs must be considered to arrive at more complete and valid explanations of phenomena related to changes with age.

In summary, the cross-sectional design enables us to make observations and describe characteristics of various age strata in society at a certain time. However, it can rarely provide explanations about the process of aging experienced by a given cohort. While this design alerts us to patterns of behavior that may vary by age, we must be careful not to misinterpret the results of studies using a cross-sectional design.

Longitudinal Designs: The Search for Changes with Age

Longitudinal designs can give a more accurate and complete explanation of the aging process, because they follow the same individuals or groups for a number of years (a panel study). However, very few studies of this nature have been completed, because this type of research is expensive and time-consuming. Also, original subjects are often lost through death, relocation, or refusal to continue[7] (Schul-

singer et al., 1981; Shock, 1985; Campbell, 1988; Rogosa, 1988; Deeg, 1989; Forbes et al., 1989).

With this design it is possible to observe direct evidence of changes in individuals and groups as they age, either in prospective studies (where subjects are retested at regular intervals) or, although less desirable, in retrospective studies (where individuals respond to similar questions as they pertain to specific earlier stages in their life cycle). This method, which is based on a life span or life course perspective, can be used, as well, to examine the rate at which events occur or that change occurs with respect to time. This technique, known as event history analysis (Campbell and O'Rand, 1988), enables us to study how much time passes before a consequent event occurs (for example, childbirth following marriage, retirement following disability, the end of mourning following widowhood, remarriage following divorce). Using this longitudinal technique, researchers can compare variations by gender, social class, education, place of residence, or ethnicity for various aging-related events.

Table 4.2 presents hypothetical data for a longitudinal study completed in the year 2005. These data indicate the frequency of movie attendance across the life cycle for 1910 and 1940 birth cohorts. As can be seen, few of the 1910 cohort attended movies prior to 1945. Yet, with soldiers returning from World War II, and with a more stable economy and increased marriage rates, a large percentage of this generation might have begun to attend movies in their leisure time. This effect on a particular age cohort at a particular point in their life cycle is known as a 'period effect.' It represents a change in behavior because of environmental events, rather than because of reaching a specific chronological age (age 45 in this case).

This table also illustrates the need to avoid 'cohort-centrism'; that is, making generalizations about the aging process and the status or behavior of the elderly on the basis of only one cohort. Since the life experiences of each birth cohort can vary, it is important that longitudinal studies include at least two age cohorts to control for possible differences in life experiences (period effects and socialization differences). For example, the results shown in table

TABLE 4.2

THE POSSIBLE RELATIONSHIP BETWEEN AGE AND MOVIE ATTENDANCE: A LONGITUDINAL DESIGN

Year	Age	Percentage of 1910 birth cohort attending three times or more per year	Year	Age	Percentage of 1940 birth cohort attending three times or more per year
1925	(15)	10	1955	(15)	58
1935	(25)	15	1965	(25)	62
1945	(35)	42	1975	(35)	60
1955	(45)	40	1985	(45)	57
1965	(55)	30	1995	(55)	52
1975	(65)	22	2005	(65)	40

4.2 indicate that the 1940 birth cohort exhibits a higher frequency of movie attendance at all ages than the 1910 cohort. Furthermore, this cohort has a relatively stable pattern of movie attendance across the life cycle, with only a slight decline in attendance occurring in the later years.

Although longitudinal designs have some advantages over cross-sectional designs, there are some inherent limitations to their explanatory power. For example, unless the study is of sufficient duration, period effects at a particular stage may be missed. Similarly, unless more than one age cohort is included, possible between-cohort differences may be missed. Thus, generalizations on the basis of one cohort can be misleading (see highlight 4.3).

Finally, as in cross-sectional designs, intra-cohort variations by sex, social class, marital status, ethnicity, educational attainment, or other relevant variables must be considered and reported. Unfortunately, these controls are often neglected in longitudinal studies, since more emphasis is placed on changes or differences at subsequent times. That is, variation within a cohort may increase of decrease because of maturation or specific period effects. For example, frequency of movie attendance at age 35 may decrease significantly from that at age 25 for the large segment of each cohort who become parents, and therefore have less time or money for leisure (a maturation effect). Or, attendance may decrease at a certain point for all adult cohorts, regardless of chronological age, because the movie industry over a period of five years produces movies that primarily

appeal to a teenage market (a period effect). Similarly, another shift in the themes of movies (about subjects such as single parenting or remarriage) at a particular point might result in an increase in movie attendance by adults in two or three adjacent cohorts who are separated or divorced. That is, they might be attracted back to movie theatres as part of the dating process, as well as by movies that depict themes related to their current situation.

Cohort Analysis: A General Model for Isolating Age Changes and Age Differences

In response to the limitations in the use of cross-sectional and longitudinal designs for studying the aging process, cohort analysis has been developed (Schaie, 1965, 1967; Glenn, 1977; Hastings and Berry, 1979; Glenn, 1981; Campbell and Hudson, 1985; Kosloski, 1986; Schaie, 1988). This sequential design accounts for maturational change, cohort differences, and environmental (period and cultural) effects, thereby reducing the confusion of age changes with age differences. In order to isolate possible explanatory factors, Schaie (1965) derived a general developmental model that obtains similar information about individuals who were born at different times and who are measured at different times.

While ideally this approach should involve a longitudinal, prospective study over three or more generations, many cohort analyses involve a retrospective, cross-sectional analysis of information stored in archives. For example, national surveys (opinion polls, government census) often ask the same questions at regular

TABLE **4.3**

THE POSSIBLE RELATIONSHIP BETWEEN AGE AND MOVIE ATTENDANCE: A COHORT ANALYSIS

Birth cohort	Year of measurement Percentage attending movies three times or more per year (age in years)							
	1945 (1)	1955 (2)	1965 (3)	1975 (4)	1985 (5)	1995 (6)	2005 (7)	2015 (8)
(a) 1930	10	12	33	30	21	11	4	—
(Your grandparents)	(15)	(25)	(35)	(45)	(55)	(65)	(75)	
(b) 1950	—	—	58	62	60	41	52	40
(Your parents)			(15)	(25)	(35)	(45)	(55)	(65)
(c) 1970	—	—	—	—	72	60	69	61
(Your generation)					(15)	(25)	(35)	(45)

intervals. However, at each interval different people represent the specific birth cohort. This eliminates the need for a longitudinal study where the same individuals must be followed for many years. To illustrate this design, imagine we are in the year 2015 and have constructed a table based on one item (movie attendance) that has been included in a national survey every ten years since 1945. Table 4.3 illustrates hypothetical patterns of movie attendance across the life cycle for three birth cohorts — those born in 1930, who represent your grandparents' generation, those born in 1950, who represent your parents' generation, and those born in 1970, who represent your generation.

In this type of analysis[8] it is possible to observe cross-sectional age differences (read down column 5 for the year 1985); to study age changes within a cohort over time (read across rows a, b or c); to compare patterns of movie attendance by cohorts of the same chronological age (at 35 years) at different points in history (compare cells 3a, 5b, and 7c); and to note whether patterns of attendance change across the life cycle from one cohort to another (compare rows a, b and c). For example, the hypothetical data in table 4.3 suggest that, except for the 1930 cohort, which was socialized to movies relatively late in life (compare cells 1a and 2a versus cell 3a), there seems to be increasing frequency of movie attendance by the later cohorts, both initially (cell 1a versus cell 3b versus cell 5c) and later in life (cell 4a versus cell 6b versus cell 8c).

Moreover, despite increasing attendance by the younger cohorts, there is a decreased involvement among all cohorts after age 35 (cells 3a to 7a, cells 5b to 8b, cells 7c to 8c). For the two most recent cohorts this trend begins sooner in that the peak is reached at about age 25 and age 15 respectively (compare cells 4b and 5b, and cells 5c and 6c).

Through cohort analysis it is possible to compare the impact of period effects on each cohort. For example, to determine whether excessive inflation and high unemployment were significant factors in movie attendance around 1995, an investigator might note that there was a sharp decrease in attendance by the 1930 cohort. But this might be expected because of retirement, and the decrease might be similar to results for all cohorts when they reach 65 years of age. However, an examination of cells 5b, 6b, and 7b and cells 5c, 6c and 7c suggests that both of these cohorts reported a decreased frequency of attendance in 1995, before rising slightly and then continuing the overall pattern of declining attendance by age.

Finally, in order to clearly demonstrate the necessity to control for the historical experiences encountered by a given cohort as they age, consider the following example of how changes in a social institution, or a change in social structure, can alter the behavior and status of the aged from one cohort to another. Cain (1981:91) reports that most of those who were 60 to 80 years of age in 1945 had rural or immigrant backgrounds, had only completed

HIGHLIGHT 4.3

THE DANGER OF INTERPRETING DATA FROM A LIMITED SAMPLE

Dr. Cope Schwenger (1983), in a critique of the conclusions reported in a report entitled *Suicide among the Aged in Canada*, identified the misinterpretations that can occur when data are examined for only one year. This reanalysis of the data in the original report stresses, as well, the importance of using the most recent data. As he illustrates, when the analysis is expanded to include the period from 1976 to 1981, rather than just 1977 as was used in the report, different conclusions emerge (table 4.4). Had the year before or the year after been used, a different picture would have emerged.

TABLE 4.4

SUICIDE RATES PER 1,000 POPULATION, BY SEX AND AGE (CANADA, 1976-1981)

	65-69	70-74	75-79	80-84	65+
Male					
1976	0.19	0.24	0.25	0.20	0.22
1977	0.29	0.28	0.24	0.21	0.27
1978	0.26	0.29	0.29	0.38	0.29
1979	0.27	0.26	0.24	0.18	0.24
1980	0.29	0.25	0.39	0.37	0.31
1981	0.25	0.36	0.29	0.46	0.30
Female					
1976	0.09	0.09	0.06	0.07	0.07
1977	0.11	0.08	0.06	0.06	0.08
1978	0.11	0.09	0.05	0.09	0.09
1979	0.11	0.08	0.08	0.07	0.08
1980	0.10	0.10	0.08	0.05	0.08
1981	0.11	0.09	0.06	0.09	0.09

SOURCE: Adapted from *Causes of Death, Statistics Canada* (84-203) 1976, 1977, 1978, 1979, 1980, 1981, as cited in Schwenger (1983). With permission from the Centre for Studies of Aging, University of Toronto.

In the original report (Department of National Health and Welfare, March 1982:24), it was concluded that 'suicide rates (in the elderly) for both sexes decline with age and that in the 65 to 69 group the rates for both sexes exceed those for the overall elderly.' An examination of table 4.4 indicates that the pattern quoted in the report is correct for women 65 and over, but not for men. Only in the years 1977 and 1979 did the rates decline by age for men. More importantly, in 1978, 1980 and 1981, the rates for men 75 to 79 and 80 to 84 are considerably higher than the rates for men 65 to 69. That is, rates do *not* appear to decline with age among elderly men. Moreover, an examination of the 65+ column for males indicates that, with the exception of 1979, suicide rates have risen annually from 22 per 1,000 (1976) to 30 per 1,000 (1981). Thus, in order that the validity of the conclusions and the utility of any practical applications of the findings be enhanced, more than one year should be sampled. For example, if policymakers had acted quickly, counseling programs for depressed, lonely seniors might have been canceled prematurely on the basis of the data provided for 1977.

elementary school, were employed in blue-collar jobs, and had relatively poor nutrition and medical care throughout their life. In contrast, those 60 to 80 years of age in 1970 were more likely to be native-born, urban dwellers, white-collar workers, and to have had the advantage of full access to medical care, adequate nutrition, a variety of leisure opportunities, and higher income than their parents. Similarly, Glenn (1981) stresses that all 'side' information representing possible period effects must be considered before age effects are inferred from cohort analyses. Specifically, in an examination of patterns of alcohol consumption by age, Glenn (1981) stressed that before it can be concluded that consumption declines with age, an historical analysis of societal norms and laws concerning alcohol consumption must be completed.

Problems Associated with Selecting the Sample

In all research studies a representative sample of the population is required to insure the validity of the results (Sinnott et al., 1983: 49-69; Maddox and Campbell, 1985). Unfortunately, when a given population has special characteristics, it is often difficult to derive randomly selected and representative probability samples. In many studies involving the elderly, it is difficult to obtain a sampling frame, because there is usually not a readily available list of individuals 65 years of age and over. As a result, investigators either draw a sample from those who are visible in church or senior-citizen groups, or they depend on volunteers, especially for longitudinal studies. Yet we know that volunteers may be better educated, healthier, more mobile and social, and more liberal in attitudes, beliefs, and lifestyles. Some of these characteristics could bias the results of a specific study.

Moreover, even when a random sample is selected, it is often drawn from a large, readily available group. Therefore, the sample may not really be representative of the total elderly population in the region or country. To date, many gerontology studies have used white, middle-class urban males as subjects. Yet, as we have seen, the elderly, like other age groups, are heterogeneous. The end result of this tendency to study white middle-class subjects, some of whom are volunteers rather than being randomly selected, is that the generalizability of the results can be questioned (Nesselroade, 1988).

Similarly, because white middle-class males tend to be overstudied (as are college freshmen and sophomores by psychologists), women who are married or in the labor force, elderly women, members of certain racial and ethnic groups, and those at the lower end of the socioeconomic strata have been highly underrepresented in gerontology studies. While there has been an increased emphasis in recent years on the study of blacks, women in the labor force, and blue-collar workers, the full range of the social spectrum has yet to be adequately studied because of inadequate sampling procedures. Furthermore, most studies have used samples unique to a particular setting, community, region, or country, with few national or cross-national samples being included. This use of limited, biased samples can also occur in secondary analyses, where incorrect conclusions can be drawn if data from only one year are used in a study (highlight 4.3).

To offset some of these problems, gerontologists are striving to include people of different racial, ethnic, and social backgrounds when selecting their sample. For example, a two-stage sampling design seeks, in the first stage, to identify and describe elderly residents residing within a large probability sample of households in a region or country. The second stage involves drawing a representative sample to account for intracultural variations, especially with respect to those variables that could be important in the interpretation of the findings (such as gender, class, place of residence, health status). For example, in a study of the leisure lifestyle of elderly men, employment, marital, and family status can dramatically influence lifestyles. Contrary to common assumptions, all men over 65 are not retired, married grandfathers. Rather, the following characteristics might be found within a group of 65- to 69-year-old males who live within the same neighborhood:

- never married and presently unemployed

- married and presently employed full-time
- widowed and retired
- widowed, remarried, and presently employed
- married and employed, with the youngest child still living at home and attending university
- divorced, retired, remarried to a younger woman who is employed full-time. He may have a child from this marriage in high school, plus be a grandfather as a result of the first marriage.

Problems Associated with Collecting Data from the Elderly

Obtaining information from the elderly is somewhat similar to collecting information from very young children. It requires special skills, techniques, and instruments (Mangen and Peterson, 1982) that are not normally needed for other age groups (Rodgers and Herzog, 1987; Herzog and Rodgers, 1988). For example, it is especially important to establish rapport, since older people may be skeptical of research and unsure of scientists or their staff, perhaps suspecting they may be some kind of government 'spies.' A second concern is that many of the current cohort of elderly people were not 'raised' on questionnaires or multiple-choice questions, and may therefore have difficulty in completing them. In fact, Marshall (1987a) states that while response rates for older respondents may be in the 60 to 65 percent range, completion rates drop to 40 to 50 percent. This occurs because of such factors as language difficulties, health problems, outright refusals to start or continue an interview, lack of motivation because the topic is of no interest, or interference from protective relatives, who prevent or interrupt an interview. The elderly may also be more likely, as are children, to respond in socially approved directions, to respond with a 'no opinion' or 'don't know,' or to be unwilling to admit the true state of their everyday moods or of their economic or health status.

Furthermore, in an interview situation, the reliability of the information collected may be lessened because of an inability to recall items, because of hearing or visual deficiencies, or because of fatigue or a short attention span. This is most likely to occur with the very old, many of whom may be institutionalized. Once rapport is established, it may be difficult to restrict the conversation to the items in the interview, and to remain within the desired time limit. If an interview with a retiree is conducted in the household, the spouse may interject opinions or influence the responses of the interviewee (Gibson and Aitkenhead, 1983).

As a final concern, there is a need to devote more attention to the process of aging and to the status of the aged among special and minority groups. If this is to occur, then questionnaires or interviews should be conducted in the language of the group, and members of the minority group should play a major role in the research process (in designing the study, as interviewers, as participant observers). This involvement will establish rapport and credibility with the respondents. It will also ensure that cultural factors unique to the minority group are considered in the design of the study and in the interpretation of the evidence.

It is also important to study the frail elderly, especially those living in the community (Streib, 1983). Since they are difficult to locate and interview, they are often excluded from research studies. Yet they constitute an important segment of the elderly population, especially when matters such as independence, elder abuse, social support, and caregiving are being studied. Both qualitative and quantitative methods should be used to study this special group, such ethical issues as informed consent and privacy must be addressed, and the cooperation and assistance of caregivers must be obtained.

SOCIAL SCIENCE PERSPECTIVES AND THEORIES

Introduction

In this section of the text, a number of conceptual perspectives and theories for studying the aging process and the aged are introduced.

While students often react negatively to the word 'theory,' it is important to recognize the use and value of theory before rejecting this way of thinking about social phenomena (Montgomery and Borgatta, 1986). Thus, theories should be regarded as 'tools of the trade' that will help you to become better employees — whether your goal is to become a practical, applied problem solver (social worker, policy-maker or administrator) or a knowledge generator (a social or physical scientist), or whether you are mainly interested in a better understanding of yourself and others. Since no one conceptual perspective or theory is totally adequate to account for any social process or social problem, a number are described in this chapter. Those that are introduced represent the approaches that have been most frequently used to date. [9]

In their efforts to advance understanding, social scientists often strive for the simplest possible view of the world. As a result, theoretical and methodological approaches are often dichotomous or bipolar in nature. For example, scientists tend to use micro or macro theoretical approaches to understanding a phenomenon; basic or applied research; qualitative or quantitative approaches to recording observations; dichotomous analyses of findings (male/female, worker/retired, old/young); or a conflict-or-consensus perspective. Thus, there are many subcultures within science, as there are in society, and each subculture has unique or favorite methods, theories, assumptions, and views of the world (Dannefer, 1988a). Moreover, these subcultures often create new theories that are often mirror images of existing theories.[10] In fact, much of the progress of science proceeds somewhat similarly to a basic law of physics; namely, for every action there is an equal and opposite reaction. Regardless of whether the reaction may be less than, equal to, or greater than the original theory in terms of explanatory power, the new theory or model serves as a useful conceptual device to stimulate thinking and to advance knowledge about the phenomenon.

In order to facilitate your understanding of the various approaches to aging, this chapter uses a dichotomous approach. However, it must be remembered that a social phenomenon is seldom black or white. Rather, there are gray areas where there is usually either convergence, overlap, or interaction between dichotomous categories or processes. Although social gerontologists have studied the 'aged' as opposed to the 'young,' understanding the process of aging requires an analysis of all stages of the life cycle, and of how the various stages interact with each other. The focus of study in social gerontology should be both on the dynamic process of aging and on the state of being old.

To achieve this objective, social scientists working in the field of social gerontology use perspectives, theories, concepts, and methods from their basic discipline, and from those recently developed by social gerontologists. They approach the study of aging on one of two basic levels of analysis — the micro or macro level (Marshall, 1986, 1987b; Birren and Bengtson, 1988; Passuth and Bengtson, 1988).

At the micro level of analysis the concern is with changes in either the biological/physical system or the psychological/personal system, as well as with the interaction between these micro systems. In comparison, the macro-level approach is concerned with the impact of social structure, processes and problems as they relate to the aging population or individual. At the macro level we are also interested in individuals as they function within and as part of the various social systems, whether the system be a married couple, an extended family, an organization, a community, a society, or the world. For each level, different conceptual perspectives have evolved within the basic social sciences and social gerontology. Similarly, theories have been developed that are most applicable at either the micro level or the macro level of analysis.

In the following subsections, conceptual perspectives and theories from the social sciences that help us to understand aging phenomena are described and discussed, first for the micro level of analysis and then for the macro level. It is important to recognize that the micro level of analysis has primarily involved a concern with the adjustment of the aging individual to society. This concern with the individual is reflected in a social psychological orientation to the study of aging. In contrast, the macro level of analysis focuses on stability and change in the age structure of an organization or society, and how this structure influences the aging individual. As a result, a historical and sociological orientation to the study of aging is utilized. As the astute reader will note, the major emphasis, at least until recently, has been on explaining phenomena associated with the elderly themselves, rather than with the process of aging. Moreover, more emphasis has been placed on individual aging than on population aging. In reality, however, personal troubles are connected to public issues. Thus, there is a need to connect everyday aging experiences (the micro level) with the historical, political, economic, social, and demographic context (the macro level) in which aging occurs.

Two General Sociological Perspectives

The sociologist Dawe (1970) identified two contrasting perspectives that have guided both general sociological research and gerontological research. The **normative perspective** suggests that established rules (norms) and status hierarchies are present in society in order to provide social control or social order. This order is deemed necessary for the survival of the society. According to this perspective, it is assumed that individuals learn roles by internalizing shared norms and values through socialization. These roles are generally adhered to without question by the majority (conformity prevails). Where rules are broken (deviation from the norms), varying types of sanctions are imposed by significant others or by the formal agents of social control (in western democracies, the legislatures). This perspective argues that social order is maintained by adherence to the norms of social institutions external to the individual. That is, we are like puppets who follow societally imposed rules; thus we have little, if any, control over our lives. This view of the social world is reflected in the life-span or life-course perspective that prevails at both the micro and macro levels, and in the structural-functionalist and age-stratification perspectives that will be described later.

In contrast, the 'second sociology,' or the **interpretive perspective,** views individuals as social actors who, through processes of negotiation, define, interpret, and control their institutionalized roles. In this way, individual actors create the social order. As a result, institutions and structures can be changed when people engage in interaction. According to this perspective, individuals seek to give meaning to their lives by imposing their own definition of a situation. They control their destiny, and that of others, by introducing changes in societal institutions as they are perceived to be needed. That is, individuals create and then use norms through conflict, negotiation, and compromise with others during interaction, and thereby socially construct reality. As Marshall and Tindale (1978-79) suggest in their plea for a radical scholarship in gerontology, there is a greater need to consider the historical context in which individuals grow old. They argue that we need to study aging phenomena from the perspectives and realities of the elderly, rather than from that of scholars under 65 years of age. This 'interpretive' view is exemplified by symbolic interactionism, phenomenology, ethnomethodology, critical theory, neo-Marxism, and social exchange theory.

Micro-level Perspectives

The Life-span Developmental Perspective

Social scientists interested in human development have historically directed most of their attention to infancy, childhood, and adolescence. This emphasis evolved because most social, emotional, behavioral, and cognitive changes occur during these early stages of life. For years, the adult stages of the life cycle were ignored or, if studied, were considered as stages isolated from the earlier stages of life.

Although there is no general theory that accounts for social behavior at all stages in the life course,[11] social scientists have increasingly recognized that human development is a lifelong dynamic process wherein the events, experiences, and roles of one stage in life are influenced by earlier stages (Honzik, 1984; Kastenbaum, 1984; Hagestad and Neugarten,

1985; Passuth and Bengtson, 1988). There appears to be a cyclical pattern to the process whereby individuals acquire prestige, power (social and physical), and independence as they age, at least up to a certain stage. Thereafter, at some later stage, prestige and power begin to decline and the individual may become, once more, a dependent being.

In order to provide some structure to the life-span perspective, the life cycle is divided into stages, and each stage, although interconnected with others, is studied as a separate entity. For example, one common breakdown is that proposed by the psychologist Erikson (1950). He identified eight stages of psychosocial development: early infancy, later infancy, early childhood, middle childhood, adolescence, early adulthood, middle adulthood, and late adulthood. Many other schemes have been proposed, including some that attach a chronological age span to each stage or period of development (Riley, 1979).

It must be recognized, however, that there are individual differences within a given stage or age range, and that development may begin late in one stage and overlap into the next. Moreover, some individuals may experience asynchronization of role or maturational development (Hogan, 1981). For example, those who are grandparents in their thirties, those women who have a child in their forties, those who retire in their forties, and those who initiate a second career in their forties or fifties all deviate from what are considered 'normal' ages at which these events should occur in the life course. As a result of individual differences and asynchronization, it is difficult to delineate precisely the temporal period at which stages begin and end. This same process may also occur at the cohort level of analysis. That is, because of an event such as a war or a baby boom, disordered cohort flow may result in undersized or oversized cohorts respectively. The appearance of these atypical cohorts may, in turn, induce unexpected or atypical changes in age-graded institutions such as schools or universities (for example, overcrowded classrooms) and may increase or decrease the life chances of a particular age cohort.

One approach for studying the aging process from a developmental perspective is to reconstruct the life script of individuals. In this way, retrospective interviews or questionnaires seek to identify crucial events and turning points at each stage of the life cycle, thereby providing a biography for a given individual. For example, significant sociocultural events (such as a war or a depression) may interact with significant personal events (the first job, the birth of a child). In this situation, the occurrence of a significant personal event at the time of a major sociohistorical event makes the event significant and salient to an individual, and thereby vividly remembered. You might wish to interview a grandparent or an elderly neighbor in order to gain insight into personal and societal factors influencing their life history.

To date, the life-span perspective has primarily been used by psychologists interested in the 'personal' or micro-level system, particularly as it pertains to early socialization and adaptation in infancy, childhood, and adolescence. As a result, until recent years, relatively little attention has been given to adult development, especially in the later years of life. This lack of interest is surprising, because a more complete understanding of the total developmental process would result if the processes and characteristics of the later developmental stages were understood. Similarly, little attention has been paid to the impact of an aging population on the aging individual. However, the life-span perspective can link the micro (developmental psychology) and macro (age-stratification theory) approaches to the study of aging.

This perspective involves an analysis of the interaction of earlier psychological, biological, and social processes and how these processes may have lasting, cumulative, or delayed effects at a later stage in life. Not all early events have a later impact; there are unique events that can occur only at a specific stage, and which can have an impact only at that stage. Therefore, the major goals of this perspective are to determine how and why earlier and later events in the life cycle are interrelated; how these processes and characteristics change or remain stable over the life cycle; and how specific events (such as an economic depression) at a specific stage of the life cycle have an impact on different age cohorts within different cultures.

The major assumptions underlying this perspective are:

1. That adults pass sequentially through all stages.
2. That individuals have certain goals or tasks to be accomplished within each stage, and most adults succeed in doing so.
3. That development is cumulative, orderly, and hierarchical, so that in most cases one stage must be completed before the next stage can begin.
4. That aging is a lifelong process which, if it is to be explained, involves understanding antecedent and consequent events.
5. That the process of aging involves the interaction of psychological, biological, and social processes.
6. That historical events and social and environmental change must be considered when studying the life course of an individual or cohort (Riley, 1979:4-5).

While these assumptions may apply to cognitive, motor, and maturational development, they may not be valid for all behavior and role sequences in adulthood. For example, mid-life career changes, divorce, childlessness, single parenting, and delayed marriage are life events that vary from the 'normal' stages and sequences of the 'normative' life-cycle model. Thus, because of individual differences, there may be several 'normal' life-cycle patterns, especially during periods of rapid social change. The onset of these individual events or social changes can have varying degrees of influence on an individual depending on what stage he or she is at in the life cycle when the event occurs. Therefore, attempts to understand phenomena in later life using the life-span perspective must consider historical and personal events earlier in the life cycle, as well as demographic changes in the structure of an aging society.

The Symbolic Interactionist Perspective

Whereas the life-span perspective was a subset of the normative perspective, **symbolic interactionism** is a subset of the interpretive perspective. The individual is considered to be an active participant in a specific social situation or setting. Through this process the individual defines and interprets a specific setting, in personal terms, as a result of interacting with significant others verbally or symbolically (through dress, gestures, language, mannerisms). In this way, social meaning is attributed to the symbols and behavior, and shared meanings of the situation are derived according to the meaning the situation has for each individual. Our interaction with others involves interpreting the meanings of their actions, and behaving in a way that reflects our own intended meaning.

Symbolic interactionists have identified three processes that lead to specific meanings and hence to cognitive or behavioral acts. First, an individual defines the social situation in terms of how it operates and what it means to him or her (Thomas, 1931).[12] Second, individuals observe and interact with others in order to examine and arrive at a definition of the 'self' (Cooley, 1902). In this process we as individuals consider how others see us and how others evaluate what they see in us. As a result of this evaluation and interpretation, which operates continuously, we arrive at a view of ourselves and a situation and behave accordingly.

The third process involves what Goffman (1959) refers to as 'the presentation of self.' Individuals define the situation and then decide how they will present themselves to others in terms of dress, manner and content of verbal interaction, and general and specific behaviors. For example, as university students you may present yourself differently to others depending on whether you are at an 8:30 a.m. class, at an interview for a job, at a bar late in the evening, at a dormitory with age-peers, or at home for a visit with your parents. Different dress, speech, and behavior patterns are selected in order to present a self appropriate to the specific situation.

In short, symbolic interactionism represents an analysis[13] of a specific social process or situation that occurs in everyday life. The focus, then, is on social interaction as a process, and on the various meanings and interpretations each participant brings to that interaction. This perspective does not normally take into account the larger social system in which the specific setting is found, nor does it normally take into account past experiences or the impact of historical events. Rather, it is concerned with how each individual interprets and assigns meaning to a specific event, behavior, or situation. This approach has been used with older people to examine the meaning and lifestyle of living in nursing homes (Gubrium, 1975), in retirement villages (Jacobs, 1975; Marshall, 1975, 1978-79), in age-segregated apartments (Hochschild, 1973) and in single rooms on or near skid row (Tindale, 1980). This approach has also been used to study the process of labeling and stigma management among older women (Matthews, 1979); widowhood (Martin Matthews, 1987); intergenerational relations (Rosenthal, 1987); and has been used to understand the process of aging and dying (Marshall, 1980).

The Phenomenological Perspective

While it is similar to symbolic interactionism, this perspective focuses on the use of language and knowledge as elements of daily behavior, rather than on the symbols and overt behavior. Thus, this perspective seeks to examine the meanings of social life for the participants as expressed in the language of those who are experiencing everyday situations. For example, to understand the aging experience, researchers study how 'the meaning of age is presented and negotiated from moment to moment as people participate in sometimes elusive but serious conversation' (Gubrium and Buckholdt, 1977:viii). Through this micro-level analysis of the discussions of the elderly and their caregivers, we gain an understanding both of how the elderly come to view themselves, and how they are viewed by others, including family, policymakers, and other age cohorts.

The Social Exchange Perspective

At both the individual (personal) and collective (society) level, social interaction can be viewed as a process wherein all who are involved seek to maximize the rewards (gains) and reduce the costs (losses), whether they be material (money, goods, or services) or nonmaterial (friendship or assistance). Social interaction involves reciprocity (give and take); each actor in the relationship strives to balance the costs and rewards. Unfortunately, this perspective tends to ignore the quality of exchange relations. According to this view of the world (Emerson, 1976), interaction will be initiated and continued as long as it is rewarding to both parties, even though the rewards are unlikely to be equal. When one actor gains more than the other, and the interaction continues, power accrues to one side in the exchange relationship. That is, the actor for whom the cost is greater is 'in debt' to the other and is therefore subject to compliance in future interaction between the two actors.

In reality, most social relationships do not operate as if they were 'balanced' budgets. Rather, they include some degree of imbalance wherein one side cannot reciprocate equally. That side becomes dependent and is obligated to try to redress the balance in the future. In most exchange relationships participants strive to maximize their power, yet maintain a fair outcome. Not surprisingly, status characteristics can influence exchange rates. For example, since status factors can influence our perceptions, possessing such valued characteristics as being white, male, highly educated, wealthy, and young can strengthen one's position in the negotiation process. Thus, to be black, female, illiterate, poor, or old can place one at a disadvantage in social interaction. To have two or three less highly valued status characteristics is to experience double or triple jeopardy in social exchange relationships. Later in this chapter we will see how aging is conceptualized as a process of social exchange wherein the elderly have few resources to exchange and are subject to compliance and lowered status in social relationships.

Micro-level Theories

Introduction

In the following subsections, we will look first at theories from the social sciences that have been used to explain aging phenomena at the individual level of analysis; these are followed by more specific theories that have been developed by social gerontologists to explain the aging process, or the status of being old, from the perspective of the individual. At the outset it must be recognized that none of these theories provides a complete explanation of aging. Some theories apply to growing old (the process), while others pertain to being old (the end product); some apply only to the individual, others to both the individual and to cohorts.

Role Theory

The two basic concepts associated with role theory are **status** and **role.** Social status refers to a socially defined position within a given social structure that is separate from, but related to, other positions. Status can be achieved by an individual through personal choice, or by competition and use of training and abilities. Examples of acquired or achieved status positions include lawyer, father, employer, or spouse. Status positions may also be ascribed at birth (male or female, black or white), or they may be acquired at some later stage in life (widow or retiree).

Associated with each status position is a social role. This represents a social definition of the behavioral patterns, rights, and responsibilities expected from those occupying a specific status position. The definition results in a set of role expectations derived from what the individual expects while occupying that status, and, more important, what others expect of the individual in a given situation. These normative expectations serve as guidelines for behavior in specific situations. However, as interactionist theorists suggest, there is a wide range of permissible behavior for any given role, especially with respect to informal roles (such as that of college roommates) that are found outside the normative social structure. Inadequate role performance can be explained by deviant behavior (the individual ignores normative behavioral expectations), by an inadequate or incomplete socialization process, or by conflicting role expectations.

Although some scholars have assumed that status and role are inevitably linked, Rosow (1985) suggests that an individual may hold a status without a defined role. He also indicates that a role may be performed that is not intrinsic to a specific social status. He lists three major types of roles:

1. An 'institutional' role (role and status are both present) such as occupation, family, class, race, age, sex, or ethnicity.
2. A 'tenuous' role (status present, role absent) such as honorary position (professor emeritus, an honorary chairman of the board), nominal position (the executive who is 'put out to pasture' by being given a title with no functional responsibilities), or amorphous position (the aged who are excluded from social participation, such as widows and the chronically unemployed).
3. An 'informal' role (formal role and status are both absent) not linked to an institutionalized status (confidants; opinion, symbolic, or charismatic leaders; heroes and villains; deviant social types, such as blackmailers, pool hustlers, and prostitutes).

To role theorists, social behavior can be explained by examining the various processes that result when roles are acquired, performed, and lost (Biddle and Thomas, 1966; Sarbin and Allen, 1968; Biddle, 1979). This dynamic process involves role learning, role change, and role transition.

Role learning often involves the acquisition of a new status and takes place through the process of socialization; role change involves a change in role expectations associated with the same status. For example, the status of 'child' remains intact as long as one's parents are alive, but the role expectations change as the individual moves through the life cycle.

The process of role transition results when an individual gains or loses a status position, and must thereby acquire or give up specific role behaviors (George, 1980). For example, the change of status from student to employee, or from being single to being a spouse, requires the acquisition of a new repertoire of behavioral standards, rights, and responsibilities, along with the loss of some rights and duties associated with the previous status (Rosow, 1985).

These processes of role learning, role change, and role transition can sometimes create role conflict for individuals. This occurs either because they are unsure about how they should behave in a given situation, or because two or more reference groups or significant others (parents and age peers) have contradictory expectations regarding role performance. For example, the recent widow may be unsure whether she should remain socially isolated and endure a long period of mourning, or whether, after a brief period of mourning, she should become socially active. This conflict may arise because her significant reference groups (children, the church, age peers) hold different beliefs concerning the behavior expected of a widow.

Inevitably, role changes have an impact on the individual's identity, self-image, and social behavior. In most cases, the impact is greatly influenced by the reaction of significant others and salient reference groups. Role changes pose a challenge to the individual and often require behavioral and cognitive adjustments and adaptation. Since many role changes are linked to chronological age or to reaching particular stages in the life cycle, it is not surprising that social scientists and social gerontologists have used role theory in an attempt to understand aging phenomena, particularly the status of being old.

The first use of this theory in gerontology was based on the premise that movement through the life cycle, especially in the later years, is characterized by a loss of or reduction in major social roles (worker, parent, or spouse). It was also based on the assumption that the process of aging involves major role transitions or role exits such as widowhood, retirement, the death of friends, and loss of independence (Marshall, 1980:82). As a result of the prevalence of these role changes, old age was seen as a time of physiological, psychological, and social loss; as a period when new social relationships and roles typical of later life are adopted; and as a period involving the acquisition of a devalued status with few meaningful roles, or, to use Burgess's (1960) concept, a 'roleless' role.

Because role loss was thought to be an almost inevitable process, early social gerontologists sought to explain the loss of meaningful institutionalized roles in later life; the devalued status of the aged and the occupancy of tenuous roles; the lack of an adequate socialization process for later-life roles (widow or retiree); and the impact of these processes on identity, self-concept, self-esteem, and social interaction.

This role-loss perspective dominated the thinking within social gerontology for many years; more recently aging has been viewed as less problematic. That is, aging is increasingly viewed as a process of role transition and change wherein most individuals transfer successfully, and adjust effectively, to new role sets (George, 1980). Moreover, aging throughout the life cycle is viewed as a process that involves both gains and losses in a variety of interrelated roles. For some elderly people the transition may be stressful, and coping may be difficult; for others it will be uneventful and successful. It has been found that in most cases a change or loss of social roles is not usually sufficient to threaten one's identity or lower one's self-esteem (Larson, 1978).

Reference-Group Theory

According to reference-group theory (Hyman and Singer, 1968), individuals identify with groups or significant others, and use them as a frame of reference for their own behavior, attitudes, values, beliefs, and feelings. Individuals normally adopt the standards of a group they perceive as positive, and reject those of a group perceived as negative.

Kemper (1968) suggests that there are three general types of reference groups that influence the socialization process and role learning. The 'normative reference group,' such as the family, provides guidelines for conforming behavior by establishing norms and espousing particular values. The 'comparison reference group' enables individuals to evaluate themselves or their situations in comparison with others, and thereby make decisions that shape attitudes and behavior in a particular role. The 'audience reference group' normally does not interact directly with the individual; rather, the individual attributes certain values and attitudes to the audience group, and attempts to behave in accordance with those values.[14]

At any given time, the reference groups for an individual can be past, present, or future (anticipatory socialization) groups; the individual does not have to be a member of the group in order for it to be salient. As we age, we selectively utilize a variety of reference groups that guide our behavior.

The amount of influence a reference group has on the attitude formation, attitude change, or social behavior of an individual is closely related to the degree of identification with the reference group. To illustrate, an individual's pre-retirement orientation and degree of adjustment to retirement may be related to reference-group identification with family, friends, and peer cliques at work. All of these groups are significant to work and retirement decisions, and to personal adaptation.

Socialization and Social Learning Theory[15]

Socialization is a lifelong process that enables an individual to participate in a society by learning appropriate symbols for communication, and by learning particular roles that will assist in developing a self-image or identity. Socialization is both a process and an end product. As a process, socialization involves learning skills, traits, knowledges, attitudes, language, beliefs, norms, values, and shared behavioral expectations associated with present or future social roles. The process may vary because of such factors as gender, socioeconomic status, community or ethnic differences, cultural differences, and individual differences in the lifestyle and values of socializing agents.

The product (successful socialization) involves the demonstration of adequate and acceptable performance in specific social positions and the development of an identity, a self-image, and a sense of self-esteem associated with a position in a particular social group. This implies that socialization is a two-way process that involves the individual defining the self and acquiring new knowledge and skills through interaction with and feedback from others. These significant others, in turn, may be socialized by the process of interaction.

Most socialization occurs during childhood and adolescence, and socialization research has generally focused on those stages.[16] However, since the 1960s there has been an increasing recognition that socialization is a lifelong process, and that we cannot possibly be socialized in childhood for all the social positions we may occupy in later life. As we age, the socialization process tends to be concerned with learning more specific roles and behaviors, and tends to be more voluntary and interactive in nature than in the earlier years. Furthermore, there are three basic differences between socialization processes in earlier and later life. These include (1) a shift in emphasis from values and motives to a concern with overt behavior; (2) a synthesis or revision of old knowledge rather than the acquisition of new material; and (3) an emphasis on learning specific role skills (such as those associated with being a parent) rather than on learning general behavioral traits (honesty, diligence, obedience).

Regardless of the stage in the life cycle, three factors influence the process of learning the requirements of full adult participation in society: (1) the social structure; (2) the stages and techniques of socialization; and (3) the socializing agents or significant others.

The social structure can lead to different socialization outcomes. For example, an elderly widow who is forced to give up her home will be socialized quite differently for her future roles depending on whether she moves in with a child, enters a senior-citizen apartment, or becomes totally institutionalized in a home for the aged. Because the individual and the social structure are interrelated, there are interrelated variables that influence the extent to which individuals are socialized. From society's perspective, these include the capacity of social organizations to establish clear goals and expectations, to provide facilities and resources for role performance, and to control performances through positive and negative sanctions. From the perspective of the individual, socialization involves the ability to learn the required norms, behaviors, and values; to perform as required or expected; and to be motivated to perform.

The techniques used at various stages in the life cycle must also be considered in any analysis of the process of socialization. During infancy and childhood, the individual is greatly influenced by the family and school. The individual may be a passive actor who learns directly and indirectly the values, skills, and behaviors that are more formally taught. By late childhood and early adolescence, however, the individual becomes a more active participant in the process. Because of the influence of the media and the peer subculture, a view other than that of the family is presented, and the individual must make decisions as to what values and behaviors are to be internalized.

Throughout the adult years, with the possible exception of learning occupational roles, the process becomes more informal, voluntary, and specific, and may also involve less passive role taking (the structuralist view) and more active role making, negotiation, and accommodation (the interactionist view). The individual is more likely to shape the norms to which he or she will adhere through a continuous process of negotiation and accommodation with others in specific social situations (Marshall, 1980:78). Adult socialization involves a continuous process of acquiring new values and behavior appropriate to adult status positions and group memberships. In order to better understand this process of adult socialization, three specific concepts need to be introduced: anticipatory socialization, desocialization, and resocialization.

Anticipatory socialization occurs when an individual accepts the beliefs, values, and norms of a status position to which he or she wishes to belong, or will belong, but to which he or she does not yet belong. In this way the individual is prepared for the new status. For example, to prepare for the large amount of leisure time available during retirement, an individual may begin to take longer vacations, or may work shorter weeks or fewer hours for a few years prior to retirement. Similarly, some individuals learn to cope with the inevitability of death through an indirect process of anticipatory socialization wherein they 'bury their peers' (Marshall, 1975).

Desocialization occurs when the individual experiences role loss or 'role emptying'[17] rather than the acquisition of new roles. Associated with this process is the frequent inability to give up the prestige or power associated with the role. Desocialization often leads to a devalued social position characterized by ambiguous norms, role discontinuity, and status loss. If this is the case, it is not surprising that some individuals deny aging or fight the process of desocialization in order to maintain their roles and status.

Resocialization involves a basic and often rapid change in lifestyle when an individual enters a new social status, such as widow or retiree, or a new social situation, such as a home for the aged. The individual must often informally learn the new expectations, values, and behaviors associated with the new status. There is at present little, if any, socialization to the status of being old, largely because there are few role models and few norms. Throughout the adult years, 'retroactive' socialization may also occur, wherein members of older age cohorts are socialized by younger age cohorts with respect to new social norms or modes of lifestyle.

The elderly sometimes are labeled as eccentric or deviant, perhaps because of an inadequate or incomplete socialization or resocialization process. Thus, new residents of a home for the aged might adapt more successfully and quickly if a structured 'resocialization' program were available to assist their transition to the institutionalized setting. After all, freshmen are 'oriented' to college life, informally and formally, and formal orientation programs are used to integrate prisoners into penal institutions.

In addition to the social structure, and the stages and techniques of socialization, the third major element in the socialization process is the socializing agent. Socializing agents include parents and siblings within the family, distant relatives, neighbors in the community, teachers and peers within the school, leaders in voluntary associations, sport and entertainment stars, and peers in the workplace. While some of these socializing agents are more influential at one stage in the life cycle than at another, peers, voluntary association leaders, neighbors, and media stars tend to be influential at all stages. In particular, the media have become significant socializing agents that teach or reinforce values and attitudes, and serve as a source of norms and values.

Having briefly examined the process of socialization, let us turn now to an overview of one major socialization theory that can account for role change and role transition as we age — social imitation theory. While many theories have been proposed to account for social learning, including the classical stimulus-response-reinforcement models, social imitation theories argue that most social behavior is learned through observation, imitation, interaction, and emotional identification with significant others. No direct reinforcement is required for the learning to occur.

Since this process continues throughout the life cycle, there is a shift from a reliance on compulsory and exemplary role models (parents or teachers) during childhood and early adolescence, to a greater reliance on symbolic models (media figures) and specific role models (those occupying status positions into which an individual aspires or is required to move). These models are voluntarily selected by the individual from a wide variety of possible models in his or her social world. This theory is illustrated by 'widow-to-widow' programs wherein a recently bereaved woman is encouraged to interact with another widow who assists her in becoming socialized to her new status. It is likely that both retirees and widows engage in some anticipatory socialization prior to moving into their new roles by observing and imitating the attitudes and behavior of those who have already successfully or unsuccessfully completed the passage.

Social Exchange Theory

The social exchange perspective is useful in explaining continuing patterns of interaction among individuals, in accounting for the allocation by age of roles and resources in social groups, and in explaining the acquisition of power and independence by some individuals. A basic assumption of this theory is that individuals search for social situations in which valued outcomes are possible, and in which their social, emotional, and psychological needs can be met. Since this goal may involve acquiescence and compliance by an individual or group, a fair exchange may not be readily apparent in every social relationship. Thus, knowledge of past experiences and of present personal needs, values, and options is required by social scientists prior to determining the equity of an observed social exchange. This is especially the case when this theory is used to explain the situation of the elderly. Although no one theory can explain all aging phenomena, social exchange theory is more useful than

some, since it can apply to both the individual and cohort levels of analysis. As a result, this theory has gained increasing acceptance as a viable explanatory mechanism for many facets of the aging process, including informal social support in the later years (see chapter 10).

The strongest proponent of this theory within gerontology has been Dowd (1975, 1978, 1980), who explains aging behavior as a process of social exchange. He suggests that the decreased interaction noted in the later years is the result not of an inevitable process of disengagement, but of a series of exchange relationships across the life cycle. As a result of these exchange relationships, relative social power diminishes as one ages. This forces compliance and an unbalanced relationship wherein the elderly experience greater costs and fewer rewards.

As one ages, few resources, other than experience, are available for exchange. This leads to conforming behavior and fewer interactions. For example, as the occupational skills of the older worker become outmoded or obsolete, he or she is forced to accept mandatory retirement in return for modest pension benefits (social assistance), and, in most cases, a reduced standard of living. Similarly, when individuals are perceived to be no longer able to care for themselves, they are institutionalized and cared for as a repayment for past debts. As Dowd (1978:353) observes, 'old people, after decades of accumulated investment in society in the form of commitment to work and family, are frequently forced to reap such rewards as loneliness, prestige loss, and social and economic discrimination.' He notes that not all elderly persons experience these losses, that many do not see these losses as unjust, and that many are not even aware that the balance can be redressed. However, some elderly persons do actively seek to restore a more equitable distribution of resources. They perceive that the injustice is a source of lowered life satisfaction, and that a greater age consciousness is needed to restore equity (Dowd, 1978).

The relationship in modernized societies between older and younger age cohorts involves the aged experiencing varying degrees of increasing dependence, and a concomitant loss of power in relationships. Unless an attempt is initiated to restore some degree of balance, the relationship becomes institutionalized and the elderly are viewed as being dependent upon others (Dowd, 1975). According to Dowd, the aging process can be shown as a curvilinear relationship between chronological age and the amount of power. In general, there is increasing power, prestige, and privilege between about 20 and 60 years of age, with a decrease in these attributes thereafter. However, the slope and shape of the curve can vary by such personal factors as class, gender, race, level of education, and ethnicity.

The slope and shape of the curve can also vary by such structural factors as modernization, age-homogeneity of a social system, and by the initiation of social change wherein the elderly attempt to restore the balance of power by reducing the costs of interacting with younger age cohorts (Dowd, 1980). For example, Emerson (1962) suggests that a relationship can be balanced by four possible operations: (1) disengaging or withdrawing, thereby eliminating the relationship; (2) extending the power network by developing new roles, such as the Gray Panther activist who campaigns for social change; (3) reacquiring high status when obsolete skills are suddenly needed, or when there is a shortage of labor that creates a demand for the older worker; and (4) forming a political coalition with other less powerful groups (such as unemployed youth), thereby gaining power against the middle-aged power bloc.

Labeling Theory

Throughout life we are evaluated and 'labeled' by others as we interact within various social systems. In some instances the labels are formally attached (such as nicknames); in others they are unspoken but informally recognized by a variety of significant others with whom one interacts (a person is perceived to be intelligent, aggressive, decisive, inefficient, or dishonest). Labels can be positive or negative, although they often tend to be negative, especially with respect to aging and being old.[18]

According to this theory, primary labeling occurs when significant others perceive an individual's behavior to differ in quality or type from normative standards. As a result of this perception, an individual is labeled as 'delinquent,' 'unstable,' 'eccentric,' 'senile,' or 'charismatic.' That is, the labeling is a social judgment and represents an interpretation of the meaning of repeated patterns of behavior. The label is not an inherent property of the behavioral pattern. Rather, it reflects the meaning attributed by others to behavioral acts and is a product of a particular social system. For example, D'Arcy (1980) noted that there was an increase in the number of persons over 70 years of age who were labeled mentally ill after the introduction of a policy of free hospitalization for mental illness in Saskatchewan. However, after the early 1960s, policy and legislative changes concerning the delivery of health care and the care of the aged broadened the alternatives for the care of the elderly. As a result, there was a dramatic decrease in the number of persons over 70 who were labeled as mentally ill. That is, changes in the structure and processes for delivering psychiatric care in the province resulted in changes in the nature and frequency of labeling older persons.

If the process of labeling is repeated, it is often internalized within the individual's self-concept. People become dependent upon socially induced labels to understand and demonstrate who they are. As a result, secondary labeling occurs; the individual accepts the label and is indirectly socialized into playing the role of 'delinquent,' 'mental patient,' 'dependent person,' or 'charismatic leader.' In this way the cycle of socially induced behavior is reinforced. Obviously, not all individuals are labeled. For unknown reasons, labeling is more likely to occur for some individuals than for others, and occurs more in some situations than in others.

Within the field of social gerontology, Kuypers and Bengtson (1973) were the first to suggest that this theory might assist in understanding the behavior of the elderly. They presented a 'social breakdown' model wherein the elderly are labeled as deficient, incompetent, or obsolete because they experience role loss, vague normative standards and few reference groups as they grow older. They turn to societal sources for a definition of the self. However, society propagates stereotypical views of the elderly and they are labeled as useless, dependent, or incompetent. Elderly people, in turn, may accept these negative labels. They are then socialized to particular roles, and may behave according to how they are expected to act. In recent years, especially since the arrival of the women's movement, many older women now fight back against the social forces that label them as useless or socially irrelevant (Matthews, 1979).

In response to this process of 'social breakdown,' Kuypers and Bengtson (1973) proposed a 'social reconstruction' model wherein the individual, with the assistance of significant others within various social systems, can increase the level of competence. This process involves eliminating the image that to be dependent (a nonworker) is to be incompetent; providing social services to improve adaptive capacity and coping skills; and giving the elderly greater control and power over their own social lives. Bengtson and Kuypers (1986) argue that this model can be applied to the process whereby family caregivers must adapt to the sudden onset of dependence by an elderly member of the family.

The social breakdown model implied that the process applies to most older persons, and that the phenomenon occurs because of the interaction between the society and the individual. However, George (1980:43) argues that 'negative self-evaluation in later life is the exception rather than the rule.' Most older people have the personal resources and coping skills to maintain a positive self-image, and thereby adjust to role transitions as they age. It is also likely that this process of social breakdown via labeling would be less likely to occur in an age-homogeneous environment (such as a retirement community or senior citizen apartment complex), where a subculture of the elderly can foster positive rather than negative labels.

Activity (Substitution) Theory

Activity theory was the first theory in North America to attempt to provide a description of, and a prescription for, successful or ideal aging in the later years of life. The idea of slowing down but keeping active in order to adjust successfully to aging was first suggested by Havighurst and Albrecht (1953). Later, Burgess (1960) suggested that old age should not be viewed as a 'roleless role,' but that individuals should replace lost roles or social activities with new ones. This theory argued that individual

adaptation involved continuing an active lifestyle of social interaction in order to maintain the self-concept and hence a sense of well-being or life satisfaction. The maintenance of this active lifestyle involved replacing lost roles, by either re-engaging in earlier roles or engaging in new roles.

The basic assumptions of this theory are (1) that the middle-aged and the aged have identical psychosocial needs; (2) that individuals will resist giving up roles in order to stay active; (3) that successful aging involves a substitution of lost roles (spouse, friend, or worker) or lost activities (work, childrearing, or sport) with new roles or activities in order to maintain the self-identity; and (4) that suitable roles or activities are available and that the individual has the capability to become involved in these new domains. Thus, the basic hypotheses of the theory are that high activity and maintenance of roles is positively related to a favorable self-concept, and that a favorable self-concept is positively related to life satisfaction (or adjustment, successful aging, well-being, morale). In short, a high degree of social activity and role involvement is positively related to life satisfaction in the later years of life.

For a number of years this theory was accepted without question and, in fact, was the basis for much of the social programming and services provided to the elderly — that is, keep them busy by providing a range of activities and social roles, and they will age 'successfully.' However, with the appearance of disengagement theory in 1960 (Cumming et al., 1960), scientists and practitioners began to question the validity of the activity theory of aging. The appearance of a second theory within social gerontology stimulated questions and led to research studies that sought to support or refute either theory. As a result, a number of studies were initiated, with a variety of samples, to seek support for the proposition that life satisfaction among the elderly is positively related to high levels of role and activity involvement. While some studies have supported the proposition, and others have failed to find support, few have refuted the theory by finding support for the opposing hypothesis — namely, that high activity is related to low levels of satisfaction.

However, the evidence to support the theory has not been overwhelming and, hence, a number of criticisms and reservations about the theory have been raised. For example, in a classic study by Lemon et al. (1972), which was the first formal statement and test of activity theory, the relationship between five types of social activity[19] and life satisfaction was examined for those who had recently purchased homes in a California retirement community. They found that only informal social activity with friends was related to life satisfaction, and hence little if any support for the theory was provided. More recently, Longino and Kart (1982) replicated the work of Lemon et al. (1972) and concluded that there was strong support for the theory. To provide for greater variation in the background characteristics of the subjects, they drew probability samples from three distinct types of retirement communities. Specifically, they found that informal activity (such as that found in primary relationships) was positively associated with life satisfaction, whereas formal activity was negatively associated with life satisfaction. They concluded that activity theory has some merit as an explanatory model, but that it needs to be tested in a variety of theoretical or environmental contexts to enhance the relevance of the theory.

Opponents of activity theory have suggested that activity levels can decrease without a loss of morale; that some individuals have never been socially active in their lives, yet exhibit satisfaction; and that not all individuals have the economic or interpersonal resources to replace lost roles. Moreover, there has been virtually no consideration of the quality or meaning of the activity that serves as the substitute. To keep busy at mundane, repetitive, socially sanctioned tasks may not result in a high sense of morale or life satisfaction if the activities or roles have little intrinsic meaning to the individual. Another criticism is that the theory is not a theory at all. Rather, it represents a set of assumptions that may apply only to some individuals as they age. It has also been noted that activity theory might illustrate the chicken-and-egg dilemma. Are older people satisfied because they are active, or are people who are satisfied more likely to be involved in social roles and activities?

In summary, activity theory may explain the situation of some older people, especially those who have adhered to a lifelong pattern of high interaction. In reality, as will be seen in the next subsection, aging is an individual process that involves selective replacement of and selective disengagement from some roles and activities. More important, as suggested by Longino and Kart (1982), self-conception may be an important intervening variable between social activity and life satisfaction, especially for those who prefer to interact with age peers. In short, the pattern that constitutes 'successful' aging for a given individual is likely to be closely related to his or her personality, self-concept, health, economic resources, and previous lifestyle, and to whether he or she lives in an age-homogeneous or age-heterogeneous environment. The greater opportunity provided by an age-homogeneous environment may facilitate an adaptation process wherein high activity is necessary for high levels of satisfaction.

Disengagement Theory

The appearance of disengagement theory in the early 1960s (Cumming et al., 1960; Cumming and Henry, 1961) represented a landmark in social gerontology. There was now an alternative to activity theory as an explanation for social aging. Although the development of disengagement theory was supposedly not motivated by a specific attempt to refute activity theory, it is often seen as the antithesis of activity theory.

Disengagement theory derives from both the developmental and the functionalist perspectives. Old age is viewed as different from middle age, and change and adaptation in the later years are seen as functionally necessary, both for the individual and for society. Because of the inevitability of death, because of the probable decrement in ability as one ages, because of the value placed on youth, and because of the need to ensure that tasks are efficiently completed and roles filled, both individuals and society demand disengagement. A mechanism must be available whereby youth can enter and advance in the labor force, whereby roles can be filled by those who are generally more competent, and whereby the death of an individual is not disruptive to the functioning of the social system. Faced with these necessities, normal aging is viewed as a functional and voluntary process that involves the inevitable withdrawal or disengagement of the individual from society and of the society from the individual. In reality, however, many forms of disengagement are not voluntary, for example, widowhood or mandatory retirement.

Disengagement results in decreased interaction between an individual and others in society, and is hypothesized to be a universal process that is satisfying to both the individual and society. Disengagement is believed to be satisfying to the individual because it provides release from normative constraints; the individual is released from pressures to behave as expected (for example, expectations of high performance on the job are reduced), and is given more freedom to deviate from societal expectations without negative sanctions being invoked. What is ordinarily viewed as 'eccentric' behavior is considered socially acceptable among the elderly.

From the perspective of society, disengagement permits younger members to enter functional roles, thereby facilitating turnover without intergenerational conflict. It also ensures that equilibrium and stability will be maintained, since members are replaced in the functional roles of society before their death. For example, without mandatory retirement most leaders and workers would die while still employed, and the social system could lose equilibrium until they were replaced. In short, disengagement is seen as a process wherein individuals, supported by societal norms and customs, voluntarily and gradually withdraw from social roles and decrease their social interaction. As a result, the individual is thought to experience a high level of satisfaction, well-being, or morale in the later years of life.

The construction of disengagement theory, like activity theory, resulted in many studies that sought to support or refute this explanation of social aging, including some revisions and clarifications of the theory by the original authors (Cumming, 1963; Henry, 1964). The major criticisms were directed at the idea that the process was universal and that everyone withdraws from his or her previously established role set. Clearly, a comparison of preindustrialized societies (with no retirement and with high status of the aged) with modern industrialized societies (with mandatory retirement and a lower status of the aged) suggests that the process is not universal.

Similarly, a number of empirical studies within the same society have indicated that withdrawal is not a typical pattern. Moreover, there may be different types of disengagement, and people in different social situations may disengage to varying degrees. For example, an individual may be socially engaged in a work role but psychologically disengaged[20] from it (the role no longer has interest, meaning, or value for the individual). Similarly, an individual may be disengaged organizationally (he or she may no longer attend religious services) but engaged nonorganizationally (he or she may engage in private prayer or may listen to religious services on radio or television). Moreover, individual differences in health or economic status, and the loss of friends through death or migration, may account for disengagement, rather than age per se.

Disengagement might also occur at early stages in the life cycle, which often happens for those who live on skid row. Or, because of personality differences, it may occur at different periods in the life cycle, or take different forms. For example, Cumming (1963) suggested that there were two styles of adapting to the environment — 'impingers' and 'selectors' — and each would react differently to disengagement. For example, the impinger continues to seek and initiate interaction; the selector is reluctant to initiate interaction and might appear withdrawn and apathetic. In fact, some individuals are socially or psychologically 'disengaged' throughout the life cycle, while others are fully engaged[21] in social interaction until death, although the nature of the activities may change as they adjust to the aging process.

Another criticism of the theory is directed at the cause-and-effect relationship: is the process initiated by the individual or by society? The individual may be socialized to disengage, to see this as an expected pattern of behavior in the later years, and to conform voluntarily by behaving as expected. In contrast, it may be that the society withdraws from the individual; because youth is more highly valued (at least in many modernized societies), the elderly may be forced to withdraw because there is a lack of access to social roles, to power, or to interaction.

Other criticisms of disengagement theory have commented on the logical weakness of the theory and on the methodology used to test the theory (Maddox, 1970; Hochschild, 1975, 1976; Markson, 1975; Passuth and Bengtson, 1988: 336-37). Most of the studies have been cross-sectional, and no attempt has been made to control for age versus cohort effects; the theory has been tested mainly from the perspective of the individual rather than from that of the society,[22] and chronological age has been used as the major independent variable when, in fact, decreased health status, perceived imminence of death, or economic hardship may lead to disengagement.

Another concern is that the definition of disengagement has been variously interpreted to imply isolation, loneliness, or passivity, and that disengagement has been interpreted as the antithesis of activity when in fact an individual can be disengaged but still active in a number of smaller roles. Finally, disengagement theory, as originally postulated, did not examine the importance of psychological commitment to or the meaning of involvement in social interaction. The conscious thoughts and feelings of individuals concerning their own conceptions of aging have seldom been considered as factors in the occurrence of disengagement.

In summary, there is little empirical support that decreased role involvement and social interaction is universal and inevitable, or that this decreased interaction or disengagement is related to life satisfaction or morale. While some individuals disengage, others remain highly active. Whether, why, and to what extent these two patterns lead to more or less life satisfaction is not clear. In all likelihood, the way in which an individual behaves in the later years may be related to maintaining role flexibility. That is, some roles are continued, some are discontinued, some are intensified, some are reduced, and some are played for the first time. In order to achieve this role flexibility a combination of structural disengagement (from work, family, or organizations) and continued interaction with age peers, in age-appropriate activities, may enhance life satisfaction.

Finally, although it is yet to be tested, Hochschild (1975) proposed an alternative theory which hypothesized that disengagement varies according to type of society (preindustrial, industrial, or postindustrial). Focusing on internal variations in engagement in an industrial society, she suggests that social class and sex roles account for variation in engagement. Hochschild (1975:565-67) argues that, for men, orientation and access to work during the middle years is class-related. This orientation, in turn, influences engagement in other social spheres (such as the family and leisure).[23]

Furthermore, engagement is seen to be of two types: 'social' engagement, which refers to interaction with others at work, in the family, and in leisure pursuits, and 'normative' engagement, which refers to the emotional importance and meaning attached to interaction. The social and normative engagement patterns adopted during middle age generally remain part of one's lifestyle in the later years.

Whether, and in what manner, an individual disengages in later life might be predicted and explained by knowledge of his or her social and normative engagement pattern, which in turn is related to class. Hochschild (1975:566) hypothesizes that older men who have access to work (those in the highest social class) and a history of valuing work highly (normative engagement) will demonstrate a higher level of social and normative engagement in their work than in their family or leisure. Alternatively, those who are prevented from working (mandatory retirement), but who enjoyed their work would be socially disengaged but normatively engaged in work; socially rather than normatively engaged in the family; and socially and normatively engaged in a leisure pursuit that resembles an occupation (such as making and selling crafts). In short, engagement in work strongly influences engagement in the family and leisure domains during the middle and later years.

Continuity Theory

Through the early-life socialization process, the individual learns and internalizes habits, commitments, preferences, and dispositions that become part of the personality and lifestyle. These tend to persist as an individual grows older, and to remain prominent factors in social interaction unless there is a reason for change. Continuity theory argues that as individuals age, they strive to maintain continuity in their lifestyle. Indeed, there are pressures within society to seek and maintain continuity in lifestyles, role relationships, and activities. According to this theory (Atchley, 1971, 1989), individuals adapt most successfully to aging if they maintain a lifestyle similar to that developed in the early and middle years. Thus, it is unreasonable to predict that an individual who has always preferred to live alone will adjust to retirement by joining voluntary associations or by traveling with a group. Similarly, an individual who has adhered to a very expressive and instrumental lifestyle, in which he or she is highly engaged in people and activities, will not likely disengage unless there is a radical reason for a change (such as failing health).

In short, continuity theory suggests that the pattern of adjustment to aging, and whether it is successful or not for the individual, is highly related to maintaining consistency in the established lifestyle. As a result, planning for the later years should involve knowledge of and adherence to a lifestyle established by the middle years. This is especially important with respect to establishing a variety of meaningful and satisfying leisure activities in the middle years that can be pursued in the later years.

While this theory has generally been supported by research evidence, two critiques have raised doubts about the validity and completeness of the theory. First, Covey (1981) notes that whereas most conceptualizations of continuity theory focus on the individual level of analysis, continuity in lifestyle can only occur where there is compatible interaction between individual characteristics and the social structure. For example, a social structural factor such as mandatory retirement leads to discontinuity in the occupational role. Covey concludes that structural constraints can be overcome and continuity can be maintained when the individual has a high level of personal resources (wealth, power, health) that can be used to prevent or delay the impact of social structural forces that require role exit.

Another critique (Fox, 1981-82) indicates a number of conceptual and measurement prob-

lems associated with the theory, and concludes that there is little evidence that continuity is an adaptive form of behavior in the later years. In fact, it is suggested that continuity in lifestyle can be maladaptive if an individual adheres to outmoded values and behaviors. However, whereas continuity theorists initially ignored the impact of such factors as social change in cultural values, modernization, and the possibility of **acculturation** (for example, by immigrants), more recent use of the theory assumes that some evolution and change occurs across the life cycle (Atchley, 1989). Thus, maintaining continuity involves adapting to both internal and external changes, and coping with discontinuity because of illness, disability, role loss, or loss of skill.

Macro-level Perspectives

Introduction

In chapter 2 we learned that, through the work of anthropologists, cultural theories of aging and such concepts as 'age grading,' 'old age' and 'elders' have been derived to explain intra- and intercultural variation in the process of aging and in the status of the aged (Kertzer and Keith, 1984; Keith, 1985, 1990; Fry, 1988). This section introduces perspectives and theories that focus on the systems and structures of society and on population aging. These views do not imply that the individual is neglected or unimportant; rather, they suggest that behavior across the life cycle is influenced by the social environment, and specifically by the social structure — that is, the relatively stable and enduring system of norms, values, and social relationships that occur in social groups and social institutions. The following subsections describe macro perspectives and theories and provide some additional conceptual tools to enable you to better understand how the social system, whether small (a married couple) or large (a nation), influences behavior as we age.

The Structural-Functionalist Perspective

The structural-functionalist perspective, a product of North American sociology from the 1950s and 1960s, focuses on the relationships between social structures and social institutions and the resulting influence on the individual. For example, a functionalist might ask what function the family, as a social institution, serves in society; what influence does it have on individual behavior in each society? Clearly, not only the function but the structure of the family varies cross-culturally, particularly when primitive tribes and highly modernized societies are compared.

This view of the world argues that there is a commonly accepted, agreed-upon order (a structure) to society, that most efforts are directed toward maintaining the existing forms and functions of social institutions (the family, the political system, or the economic system), and that each element of the structure (such as the family) can be analytically viewed as having a manifest (intended, purposeful) or latent (unintended) function. Social action by an individual is determined and regulated by a formal yet abstract set of rules derived from the structure of the society. Thus, the key concepts of functionalism include **norms, roles,** and **socialization.**

From this perspective, aging is seen as a process whereby the individual adjusts to role changes (such as retirement or widowhood). A major concern is with how the individual fulfills his or her functions in given social institutions. This perspective argues that an individual's failure to adapt represents an inability to fit into the existing social structure, not that the structure is ineffective or inappropriate for that period in history.

It must also be recognized that not all social relationships are functional. Some are dysfunctional and detract from the stable functioning of society; others are afunctional and do not contribute directly to the maintenance of the social order, nor do they threaten the existence of a system (Marshall, 1986:16). For example, with the proportion of the population over 60 years of age increasing, mandatory retirement may become dysfunctional. That is, an ever-growing segment of the population may become economically dependent on an ever-shrinking labor force that must contribute an increasing percentage of its income to support the older generations. At the same time, the policy of mandatory retirement might also be dysfunctional for a society in that it eliminates

from the labor force individuals who have a great deal of experience and knowledge.

To summarize, this perspective assumes that all components of the social structure are necessary, are interrelated, and have some useful function in maintaining consensus and conformity within the social system. Thus, societal norms structure the roles available to different age groups. For example, the societally imposed (institutionalized) act of mandatory retirement deprives the older individual of a major social role in order to realize a specific societal function, namely, to permit younger people to enter the labor force. As a result, the older worker is required to accept and adapt to this role loss. In order to facilitate this adaptation, society legitimates the nonwork role of retiree, and in many societies provides an economic reward (a pension). The individual is expected to comply with this process and 'fit in' to the existing, stable order without opposition.

The Conflict Perspective

Whereas functionalism perceives the social world to be normative and static, the conflict perspective views society as dynamic and changing. According to this perspective, conflict is inevitable. Society is composed of competing groups who either presently control the resources (such as authority, power, money, goods, or services), or who believe that they are deprived, exploited, or manipulated. The latter group believes that change must be initiated in order for them to obtain an equal share of the resources. Those who adhere to the conflict perspective believe that social interaction involves negotiation and compromise to resolve conflict. Only in extreme cases does conflict lead to a civil war or revolution.

Conflict theorists search for and identify power groups, and attempt to explain how they manipulate or control other social groups (Tindale and Marshall, 1980). For example, it has been argued that modern, industrialized societies are controlled by middle-aged males. This has led to conflict between youth, who have yet to gain power, and the middle-aged; and more recently, to conflict between the elderly, who have lost power and authority, and the middle-aged. In fact, it has been suggested that a voting coalition of the young and the elderly may form in the years ahead if the economic status of these two disadvantaged groups does not improve. That is, age-strata conflict may evolve because of perceived inequities in power and inadequate access to valued resources.

The System Perspective

This perspective is adapted from engineering and the biological sciences, and is closely related to functionalism. The system approach to understanding social phenomena focuses on a description and analysis of the structure and composition of social systems (their boundaries, elements, and environments); the functions (integration, socialization), processes (stratification, social change, or social control), and problems (conflict or discrimination) of social systems; and the interrelationships between a variety of social systems (large versus small, simple versus complex, groups, organizations, institutions). An older couple, a family, a nursing home, a retirement community, or a society can be analyzed as distinct social systems, or as social systems that interact with other social systems.

A **social system** is made up of a group of individuals who interact with each other according to a shared set of beliefs, values, and norms. More specifically, a social system consists of three subsystems: a normative subsystem, a structural subsystem, and a behavioral subsystem (Loy, 1972). The normative subsystem, or culture, includes beliefs, folkways, laws, norms, sanctions, and values. The values represent the goals of the system; the norms indicate the preferred pattern or method to achieve the goals; and the sanctions represent the rewards or punishments for conforming or deviating from the norms. The structural subsystem (or social structure) consists of regular, patterned interaction among a set of social positions. For each social position (such as father) there is a social role, status, and rank. The behavioral subsystem involves the social (age, sex, or race), physical (height, weight, or motor ability), and psychological (personality or attitudes) characteristics of the members of a social system that influence whether and how they play specific roles.

In social gerontology, systems analysis can be used to study the social structure within which individuals age, and to study the way in which individuals or groups adapt. It can also be used to study how the possession of particular social, physical, and psychological attributes can influence goals, behavior, and cognitions at specific stages in the life cycle. Obviously, this analysis can involve the study of a simple dyad (the retired couple), a specific group (the members of a senior-citizen center), a particular institution (the extended family), or a specific society (Canada or the United States). Moreover, each of these systems can be studied as separate entities, or as they relate to other social systems within that community or nation, or, perhaps, even with systems in other societies (cross-cultural research).

The Marxist Perspective

Based on Marx's theory of capitalist development, this critical perspective emphasizes that the constraints imposed on individuals result from the unequal distribution of power and resources that is embedded within the capitalist form of production. In the capitalist economic system, a few are favored (the elite); the majority (the masses) are excluded from full access to social and economic opportunities. The elite seek to maintain these advantages, thereby creating tensions and strains between competing factions. In the field of gerontology, this perspective has spawned interest in a political-economy perspective on aging, and in a feminist perspective on aging.

The Feminist Perspective

This perspective argues that, because of gender stratification, women are oppressed by males, who hold the power in gender relations. Basically, men are seen to have access to the power derived from participation in the public sphere of social life; women are restricted to the private world of the home. Feminist scholars emphasize that the male view of the world should not be the norm, and that the situation of women can best be understood through an examination of female social experiences by female researchers. They argue that equality will only be attained through analysis, theory development, and political action based on a unique understanding of the female world by females.

Despite the increasing use of this perspective in the social sciences during the 1980s (Burwell, 1984; Cohen, 1984; Stacey and Thorne, 1985), relatively few studies in social gerontology have employed this perspective (Rossi, 1986; Gee and Kimball, 1987; McDaniel, 1989). This is surprising, since aging is so often a women's issue, especially in the latter years of the life cycle. Since the feminist perspective involves a commitment to social issues and to social change, a focus on the situation of women as they age, and on the everyday experiences of older women, can lead to new ways of looking at problems heretofore examined from a male perspective. For example, it has been argued from the feminist perspective that the factors influencing the onset of poverty in later life are different for women than for men (McDaniel, 1989). First, many elderly women, because of irregular work histories, have few if any pension benefits. Second, many older women are not eligible for survivor's benefits when their spouse dies. Third, they live longer and thereby are more likely to exhaust their financial resources. Fourth, when they become ill they seldom have a spouse to care for them, as they cared for their spouse. In short, poverty, as seen in this light, is less an aging problem and more a women's problem. That is, older women are devalued and powerless in a male-dominated society that oppresses all women, and this situation can be magnified for elderly widows who live a long life. In reality, the impoverishment of older women is socially constructed and imposed, and, hence, the feminist perspective allows us to view the experiences of aging through the eyes of women, rather than by focusing on sex as a variable wherein the experiences of men are often considered normative and ideal.

Macro-level Theories of Aging

Age Stratification

Most of the micro-level theories in social gerontology focus on how the individual adjusts to being old; the age stratification theory is concerned with aging relative to all stages in the life cycle. Thus, the elderly are studied, not in isolation, but in relation to other age strata. This theory focuses on how the structure of society affects the aging individual, and on differences between age strata rather than on conflict between them.

As described and explained by Riley and her colleagues (Riley, 1971, 1985; Riley et al., 1972), this model of aging is based on the premise that chronological age determines behavior in two general ways. First, it controls to a certain extent the maturation or development rate for physical, mental, and psychosocial capacities. Second, society allocates the opportunity to play specific social roles (and their accompanying rights, privileges, status, and power) on the basis of age. Therefore, society is said to be divided into age strata[24] (as it is into class strata). Each stratum is made up of individuals who have some similar characteristics because they are at the same stage in the life cycle (the life-course dimension). Each stratum consists of those who have had similar experiences[25] because they have shared a common history (the historical dimension).

In the conceptual development of this model, Riley (1971) introduced a structural analogy between class strata and age strata, and a process analogy between social mobility and aging. She proposed four commonalities pertaining to class or age stratification systems. First, relatively similar behavior and attitudes can be expected from those at a specific position in the age or class structure because they have had a common history and lifestyle. Second, whereas movement through the class structure is possible, but not inevitable, movement through the age structure is inevitable and occurs in one direction only. Third, in both the age and class structures, interaction can occur among individuals within and between strata (intergenerational relations, class dominance or conflict). This interaction is governed by social norms, and may be influenced by the development of stratum consciousness, which in turn may lead to class- or age-related consensus or conflict. Finally, the type and frequency of interaction within and between strata in both age and class structures is related to the degree of social, political, or economic change in a given society. Change may be initiated by, or may specifically affect, members of one stratum more than members of another. For example, as the structure of society changes because of modernization, the status of the aged may change.

Riley et al. (1972) developed a two-dimensional model (at the societal and personal levels) to account for behavior at different stages in the life cycle. At the societal level of analysis the theory of age stratification argues that the population is divided into age strata because of cohort flow. That is, fertility, migration, and mortality determine the size and composition of each stratum.[26] Through the process of role allocation or age grading, individuals gain access to social roles and to their accompanying rewards on the basis of chronological, legal, or social age. Age is the criterion for entry into, and exit from, institutions within a given society. Moreover, age norms control the number who can play a given role at a specific point in history. For example, the legal school-leaving age can be raised or lowered, as can the age of mandatory retirement, in order to achieve equilibrium in the size of the labor force. From the societal perspective, social systems are made up of age-related roles whereby those of a particular stratum have certain role expectations and are accorded certain rights, privileges, and status. An age-related status system evolves, and inequality between the strata may be inevitable.

On the personal level, the theory of age stratification proposes that chronological aging involves first an increase and later a decrease in social, physical, and cognitive capacities, and in the development of psychosocial skills deemed essential to a specific society. As individuals age they have the capacity and opportunity to acquire new roles, to relinquish old roles, and to interact with role players within their stratum and other strata. This interaction is facilitated by age-related norms. It is assumed that individuals have relatively little input into the system, that they must passively adhere to societally induced norms, and that they must accept the allocated social roles and implied social inequality.

This theory, which first appeared in the early 1970s, was widely accepted as a viable explanation of changing behavior and status across the life cycle, despite the fact that few research studies explicitly tested the theory. Nevertheless, the theory has been criticized, especially by those who adhere to an exchange or a symbolic interactionist perspective of social phenomena. Generally, the criticisms have involved two related concerns: whether and to what degree there is conflict between strata, and the failure of the theory to account for the interaction between age and other social categories such as race, gender, ethnicity, and social class.

Interaction between members of different social or age strata can be characterized by cooperation (either voluntary or through compliance and conformity) or conflict, with varying degrees of perceived and actual inequality being observed (Henretta, 1988). In many societies throughout history, some degree of class conflict has been inevitable. This conflict is either controlled for the assumed benefit of society (a functionalist perspective), or it becomes overtly manifested in varying forms of conflict in order to bring about change for the betterment of the individual and the society (the conflict perspective). Age conflicts also appear to be present in some societies. These occur because structural inequalities produce different views of how rewards should be allocated. Age conflict is enhanced when members of subsequent birth cohorts have unique attitudes, opportunities (such as better education), and beliefs, based on their particular social and historical experiences. Each stratum becomes cohort-centric; it interprets events in the social world through its own unique experiences. This cohort-centrism makes it difficult to see and accept the view of other cohorts and, hence, to resolve differences. Cohort-centrism also creates the possibility that some level of age-stratum consciousness may be developed. However, as Foner (1979:235-36) suggests, except in college students in the 1960s, age-stratum consciousness has yet to be developed to the stage where it fosters open and serious age-strata conflict. Moreover, because there are laws against age discrimination, age-based conflict may become increasingly irrelevant for social behavior (Dowd, 1987).

Implicit in the discussion of age-related inequality is the view that some of this inequality is also class-related. Within each stratum there is also a system of social stratification similar to that which operates across the entire society. Tindale and Marshall (1980) suggest that conflict between generations occurs because those with a specific class background experience significant social-historical events differently from others in the age cohort. As a result, they develop a combined age- and class-related consciousness that may induce conflict. For example, in North America, the radical youth movement of the 1960s primarily involved a middle- or upper-middle-class college-age cohort. This cohort, or generational unit, rebelled against the power it perceived to be held by the middle-aged and the elderly in society. Thus, age strata per se do not denote social inequality, as do social strata, and cannot account for social inequality (Streib and Bourg, 1984).

This interaction of perceived age and class inequality has also been studied by Dowd (1980, 1987). He noted that the elderly at the bottom of the class structure experience more problems than the elderly in other social strata. Using an exchange and symbolic interactionist perspective, Dowd views aging as a process of negotiation or exchange among individuals. Conflict occurs when there is a perceived or actual unequal distribution of resources. As a result, one group seeks to redistribute resources to restore equity and balance to the system. Dowd argues that as we age we lose control over our lives because we lose access to sources of power, and with advancing age we are unable to negotiate a fair exchange. The elderly acquire low status and lose power, unless they are members of the upper classes and have residual sources of power. Most of the elderly seem to accept this devalued status and subordinate position in the age stratification system. Dowd suggests that rather than passively accepting this situation, the elderly must reject the status quo as the best solution for society or for themselves. That is, they must strive to remain engaged in meaningful social positions in order to improve their negotiating position relative to those in other age strata. Although it is unlikely that the class position of an elderly individual can be improved, by cooperation and the development of an age-stratum consciousness the overall position of all elderly people might improve.

The Subculture of Aging

A **subculture** is a distinct social subsystem that arises within a larger social system. It is characterized by a unique set of beliefs, attitudes, values, norms, customs, and language. Once these characteristics become accepted by a number of individuals, who may or may not engage in face-to-face interaction, they begin to influence the lifestyles of those who identify with the subculture.

Adapting this framework to the process of aging, Rose (1962, 1965) argued that the social identity and self-concept of the older person was maintained or enhanced by membership within an age-based subculture. That is, individuals interacted more frequently with others of the same age rather than with other age cohorts in the society. In this way, age-related roles were established and a subculture evolved. He noted that the likelihood of an aged subculture forming, and thereby facilitating individual adjustment, is quite high, since elderly people have similar backgrounds, experiences, and needs, and are therefore attracted to each other for support and interaction. In addition, the elderly are often excluded from interaction with other age cohorts in mainstream society.

The outcome of creating an aged subculture may have both positive and negative effects on the individual and on society. On the positive side, for the individual it may lead to the development of an age-group consciousness that results in social action to improve opportunities and lifestyles. On the negative side, this action may create intergenerational conflict as various age cohorts compete for scarce resources. This age-consciousness may also reinforce the individual's self-concept of being old and devalued, thereby leading to dissatisfaction with life. Yet, a subculture formed within a retirement community may lead to higher levels of social integration. This in turn can help to develop a positive self-image because identity is primarily based on age-related status elements, such as high levels of mobility and health (Longino et al., 1980).

As with all theories, a number of criticisms have been raised concerning the subcultural view of aging. First, it has been argued that the theory is not really a theory but rather a concept that facilitates a description of the behavior of some elderly people, and that serves as a guide for social action. Second, it was assumed by Rose (1965) that there was a general subculture of the aged to which all elderly people belonged. However, there is great variation within the elderly population, not only in terms of their personal characteristics, but also in terms of their reference groups and social environments. For example, elderly derelicts and elderly millionaires do not interact with each other, and each type is differentially integrated into mainstream society (Streib, 1985).

The type of environment in which elderly people live also influences their normative system. For example, an age-segregated versus an age-integrated environment would have a different impact on the interaction pattern of an elderly person. Similarly, being a member of a religious or ethnic group that places a high value on the status of the aged represents a different social environment from that encountered by the elderly living on or near skid row. Moreover, as Longino et al. (1980) noted, the meaning of living in a particular type of retirement community must be considered when analyzing the impact of a subculture on the individual. They found that, contrary to the prevailing myth, residents of some retirement communities were not seeking a socially active lifestyle; they had moved to the community in order to obtain services or to enjoy the environment, not to seek the company of other old people. Thus, the impact of a specific subculture on the behavior of an elderly person can vary according to the type of community, the motivation for living in that community, the saliency of other subcultures in which the individual interacts, the availability of organizations to facilitate social interaction among the elderly, and the extent to which a given aged subculture is integrated with or segregated from other age cohorts.

In summary, all age cohorts are made up of individuals with heterogeneous characteristics and with varying patterns of social interaction and feelings of age-consciousness. To date, there is little, if any, evidence to suggest that there is a subculture of the aged to which all individuals beyond a particular chronological age belong.

The Aged as a Minority Group

As we learned in chapter 2, the process of aging varies among members of minority groups. It has also been suggested that the aged are themselves a deprived group in society (Barron, 1953): the elderly become victims of differential and unequal treatment compared to other age cohorts because they are labeled as 'old,' 'obsolete,' or 'dysfunctional.' As a result, they are devalued and perceived to be a **minority group** that exists on the periphery of society, like blacks and women.

As a result of Barron's (1953) view that the aged constitute a minority group, a number of authors sought either to support the view that they are a minority group and therefore the object of discrimination, or to establish that they do not meet the criteria for minority group status.[27] Abu-Laban and Abu-Laban (1980) suggest that the application of the minority-group concept to the aged, and especially to women, has created controversy because it has been used for ideological reasons to draw attention to social problems. For example, while older women may possess minority-group status because they experience discrimination, they may not formally or informally be members of a minority group. This concept has also been used to make comparisons in social experiences between groups, even though women and the aged could not create their own unique society (as could an ethnic group if it so desired). Abu-Laban and Abu-Laban (1980) suggest that some of the conceptual problems with the minority-group concept can be alleviated if it is recognized that there are similarities and differences between disadvantaged groups in both their historical experiences and in where they fit into the social structure. These variations in meaning and structure need to be considered before a group is labeled as a minority group. They argue that there is little, if any, evidence to support the view that the aged, in general, constitute a minority group. At best, it may be that an aged minority group is made up of those elderly people who experience double or triple jeopardy because of their ascribed or achieved membership in an economic, racial, gender, or ethnic minority group.

Modernization Theory

Modernization theory seeks to explain aging phenomena from a structural perspective rather than from the perspective of the individual. This theory is based on a comparative analysis of societies, and an emphasis is placed on historical and cultural factors. The theory was first described in detail by Cowgill and Holmes (1972) in a cross-cultural study that analyzed the status of the aged in fourteen different societies. These societies ranged in degree of modernization from a gerontocratic tribe in Ethiopia to the highly industrialized United States. The major hypothesis of this theory was that the role and status of the aged varies inversely according to the degree of **modernization** in a society. As social change occurs and societies become more modernized, older people lose functional roles, become devalued, and subsequently lose status and security. Cowgill and Holmes (1972) based their argument on three premises concerning primitive societies:

1. There are only a few social roles and little role differentiation; hence, the elderly remain socially integrated and functional, at least as long as they are physically and mentally able to contribute to the society.
2. Social stability is the rule and social change the exception; hence, the experience and wisdom accumulated by the elderly is needed and valued.
3. Because little, if any, technology exists, human resources are highly valued; the elderly are seen to possess these needed resources.

In addition to the qualitative comparative evidence presented by Cowgill and Holmes (1972), and Cowgill (1986), recent cross-cultural and intracultural empirical studies have also supported the theory. For example, Palmore and his associates (1971, 1974) developed an Equality Index to measure the relative socioeconomic status of the aged (over 65) compared to the non-aged (25 to 64). Their findings, based on comparisons within thirty-one countries that varied in level of economic development, found that the status of the aged declines from approximate equality in non-Western societies to about one-half equality in more modernized countries (Palmore and Whittington, 1971). However, in a later paper (Palmore and Manton, 1974) it was found that there was considerable variation between employment status, occupational status, and educational attainment within the more modernized societies.[28] While employment status declines steadily with modernization, the occupational and educational status of the aged experience the greatest decline in the early stages of modernization. However, after a country has been modernized to a certain level, the rate of change levels off. Then, the differences between the aged and non-aged narrow as the status of the elderly in the occupational and educational domains begins to rise. The position of the elderly in industrial societies is also enhanced by the initiation of social support policies and programs designed to help the elderly survive in a changing world (Dowd, 1984).

As with many of the other theories described above, criticisms were raised as to the validity of this explanatory model. First, the authors were criticized for failing to precisely define 'modernization.' In particular, their use of the concept applied only to the societal level of analysis. In an effort to clarify the meaning of the relationship between increasing modernization and a declining status of the aged, Bengtson et al. (1975) stressed that there must be a clear distinction between 'modernization' (a societal or macro-level process) and 'modernity' (an individual or micro-level process whereby individuals in developing nations are exposed to technology, urbanization, and industrial experience).

Bengtson and his associates argued that 'modernity' and 'modernization' may not result in negative perceptions of the aged and in a devaluation of status, as is commonly asserted. They suggested that perceptions of the aged may also vary within a society. Using a sample of 5,450 males in six 'developing' nations, who were employed within three different occupational groups, they found that negative perceptions of aging are related to increasing societal 'modernization.' In contrast, individual 'modernity' is not related to negative perceptions of the aged, or to negative attitudes toward one's own aging. In short, negative views and declining status of the aged do not seem to accompany 'modernity.' Thus, when discussing the impact of social change on the status of a particular group, both 'societal' (modernization) and 'individual' (modernity) levels of analysis need to be considered.

A second, but related, criticism was that the authors made little attempt to explain the intervening process between the onset of modernization and the loss of status by the aged. Cowgill (1974), in a revision of the theory, identified four salient aspects of modernization and indicated how they result in a lower status for the aged:

1. The introduction of modern health technology increased longevity and led to intergenerational competition and retirement.
2. The development of modern economic technology made the jobs of the aged obsolete and led to new occupations in urban environments.
3. The onset of urbanization led to migration, and to social segregation by age and socioeconomic status.
4. The increased level of educational attainment with each subsequent generation enabled children to be better educated than their parents and grandparents.

In addition, Cowgill stressed that these technological and social changes led to an increase in the status of youth and young adults, and to an increase in the emphasis and value placed on work.

Other scholars suggested that the changing status of the elderly was not due to modernization per se, but rather to the technological and social changes that were introduced at various rates into specific societies. For example, Press and McKool (1980) argued that with increasing economic, social, and technological development, greater heterogeneity in status evolves within the society, and the elderly become less positively evaluated than younger age groups. Similarly, Maxwell and Silverman (1980) suggested that the elderly lose control of information with modernization, and that this loss of control subsequently results in a loss of au-

thority and power within the society.

Dowd (1980) argued, from an exchange perspective, that the possession of prestige and power resources (land or information) places the individual in a favorable exchange situation regardless of age. In agrarian economies the elderly controlled the ownership of land and thereby enjoyed a favorable exchange rate. In contrast, in modern societies the elderly are excluded from labor force participation and lack a favorable exchange rate; they have less esteem, prestige, and status than the elderly in more primitive societies.

A third criticism of the theory was that the explanation implied a universal, linear relationship which applied to all elderly people, and that modernization affected all cohorts of people at the same rate (Achenbaum and Stearns, 1978; Quadagno, 1980). For example, Cowgill (1974) and Palmore and Manton (1974) suggest that declining status of the elderly may be more rapid during the early stages of modernization when there is rapid social change, but may 'bottom out' in the more advanced stages. That is, in the later stages of modernization the status of the aged may rise again, although never to the same level as in the more primitive stage of development. In short, the relationship may be curvilinear over time rather than linear. For example, Cohn (1982) examined the age-specific occupational distributions in thirty countries and concluded that these distribution patterns may be a temporary phenomenon that results from the dynamic relationship between the level and rate of economic development and the changing age structure of the population. He noted that the decline in status of the elderly early in the modernization process results from a rapid increase in the number of professional and technical occupations and the subsequent occupancy of these positions by recently trained younger workers.

Despite the evidence of Bengtson et al. (1975), the impact of modernization may affect various social groups in different ways. For example, Myles (1980) noted that the status of the aged is also related to the structure of inequality in a society, which in turn is based on gender, race, and class variations within and between age cohorts. Thus, within 'postmodernized' or 'rapidly modernizing' societies, the status of the elderly is related to the degree of structured equality within that society.

A fourth criticism, mainly from historians, suggests that the onset of declining status for the elderly, if it occurs at all, may have occurred prior to or after industrialization. For example, the social historian Fischer (1977) has argued that in the United States the social values of libertarianism and equalitarianism, introduced during the French and American Revolutions, resulted in changes in attitudes and behavior toward the elderly between 1770 and 1820. The declining status of the aged and the increased power of the younger age cohorts preceded rather than followed industrialization. Similarly, the historian Laslett (1976) suggested that it is a myth that the aged have experienced a significant decline in status in modern societies. He concluded that the treatment of the aged in preindustrialized societies was not superior to the treatment they presently receive. Stearns (1981, 1982) argued that negative attitudes toward the elderly in France persisted long after modernization was initiated, and that modernization per se was not responsible for a change in the status of the aged in France.

Some authors have recently proposed that there are limits to the generalizability of modernization theory. For example, Hendricks (1982) noted that societal development does not occur at the same time or at the same rate across societies or within a single society. In fact, societal development occurs first, and perhaps exclusively, in a core area of a country, or in core countries throughout the world. Beyond this regional or international core is a peripheral region that fails to modernize at the same rate, or perhaps at all. In short, there are variations within and between societies in the onset and rate of modernization. For example, Gilleard and Gurkon (1987) found that elderly men in rural villages in Turkey retain high levels of status, compared to urban elderly males, because they continue to work. Thus, the onset or rate of modernization may vary in different regions of a country.

As an alternative explanation for the all-or-none view of modernization, Hendricks (1982) proposed an 'internal colonialism' or 'dualistic developmental' model. According to this model, power and control over resources resides in the metropolitan regions of a nation, and these regions control the development, if any, of the hinterland. As a result, the degree of declining status for the elderly within a nation varies by residential location. Those living closer to the core metropolitan area are the first to lose status, especially if they are members of an already devalued group.

Another view of the process of modernization has been suggested by Hendricks (1982) and by Tigges and Cowgill (1981). According to this macro view of development, a decline in the status of the aged as societies modernize may not occur if the least-developed or peripheral societies (Third World countries) have their development controlled by the most developed nations (the core countries). These authors argue that within the world economic system, the relation of the elderly to the means of production, and the position of the family in the production process, will vary. This results in varying degrees of status for the elderly, depending on whether they are found in a peripheral, semi-peripheral, or core nation. In the peripheral nations, or in the hinterlands of a nation, the elderly may be still involved in the production of goods within the extended family. Consequently, the elderly retain status or lose it at a different rate from those who live in more urbanized, nuclear-family-oriented environments.

The Political Economy of Aging

In order to understand the status of the elderly within a modern welfare state, political theorists and economists have become interested in the social institutions and processes that influence the meaning and experiences of aging (Estes et al., 1984; Minkler and Estes, 1984; Myles, 1989). This critical approach argues that the onset of dependency and a diminished social status and self-esteem in the later years is due to social, political, and economic matters that define and label the elderly, and that create public policies such as mandatory retirement and government-funded pensions. That is, dependency in old age is not due to biological deterioration as much as it is to political and economic forces that are socially constructed.

HIGHLIGHT 4.4

RETIREMENT IN CANADA: A POLITICAL ECONOMY PERSPECTIVE

The individualized conception of retirement, wherein individuals are viewed as being responsible for their retirement and for their economic status in later life, has been challenged by proponents of the political economy of aging perspective. According to this perspective, the onset of retirement is a crucial intervening factor between location in the social structure and status and resources in later life. That is, if forced to retire by society and to accept a pension as a reward, some older adults may begin to occupy a marginal and dependent position in society. The political economy perspective argues that individuals are not responsible for inflation that erodes their pension savings, for retirement policies that force them to leave the labor force, or for inequities in the labor market that divide workers into those employed in either a core (such as manufacturing, construction) or peripheral (such as agriculture, retail sales, self-employed, lower-level professionals) sector — the dual economy.

The division of the labor force into two sectors results in a disparity in wages, in varying patterns of employment, and in unequal fringe and pension benefits. Quite simply, as McDonald and Wanner (1987, 1990) found, men who were employed in the core sector prior to retirement have better career opportunities for promotion and salary increases, higher wages, are more likely to retire early, and are more likely to receive a private pension upon retirement. They are also less likely to need or to be eligible for a Guaranteed Income Supplement (GIS) payment. These results also held for women employed in the core sector, although more females who had been employed in this core sector received government transfer payments (GIS). In addition, more women than men in the core sector were likely to continue working past 65 years of age. In short, McDonald and Wanner (1987, 1990) illustrate that the dual structure of Canada's economy can influence when, and with what resources, an individual will retire. The macro political economy perspective, with its emphasis on structural, socioeconomic, and political processes, adds an additional dimension to the more traditional micro individualistic level of explanation for retirement patterns (see chapter 11).

SOURCE: Adapted from McDonald and Wanner (1987, 1990).

To date, this approach to aging has been concerned with such aging issues as public expenditure on the elderly (for example, health, pensions, housing, formal support); the social, political, economic, and legal rights of the elderly; how population aging changes the process of distributing public funds, sometimes creating a heavy public debt for later generations; the issue of voluntary versus mandatory retirement; the differentiation of the industrial sector of a nation into a core and a peripheral sector, so that there are different conditions for employers and workers that influence the experience of older workers and the patterns of retirement (highlight 4.4); pension accessibility; and age-restrictive policies that exclude older workers from the labor force. This perspective is based on the assumption that the elderly, as an age group, are impoverished and lack power. Yet, as many studies have indicated, this view conflicts with the experiences and feelings reported by elderly individuals. Thus, like many other perspectives, this macro-level approach to the study of aging phenomena must be integrated with micro-level approaches to account for the variety of both old-age environments and aging experiences within modern, industrialized societies (Passuth and Bengtson, 1988:344).

SUMMARY AND CONCLUSIONS

In this chapter the reader has been introduced to the purpose and process of scientific inquiry, particularly with respect to research settings, research methods, conceptual perspectives, and theoretical frameworks that are used in the study of individual or population aging as social phenomena. [29] The major focus of the chapter was on describing and critiquing research methods, perspectives, and theories that seek to explain the aging process and the status of the elderly, from either the individual or societal level of analysis.

In conclusion, it is noted that:

1. At present, no single theoretical, conceptual, or methodological perspective is prevalent within social gerontology. Rather, the field is still characterized, as are most new fields, by eclecticism in theory and methods.
2. The structural-functionalist perspective dominated the early work in social gerontology, but the symbolic interactionist and exchange perspectives are now widely used.
3. Social theories developed in the early stages of social gerontology were primarily concerned with how the aging individual adjusted to society (the micro or individual level of analysis). More recently, macro-level (societal) theories (age-stratification theory and variants of modernization theory) have stressed the impact of a changing age structure throughout history and across cultures on the aging individual.
4. Compared with many other disciplines, as well as other areas within gerontology, the quality and quantity of conceptualization, theoretical development, and methodological rigor in social gerontology need to be increased in order for the level of knowledge to advance beyond the descriptive and speculative stage.
5. The continued development of knowledge in social gerontology will depend on the initiation of theory and research directed at interaction between the individual and societal levels of analysis, as well as between the normative and interpretive perspectives.

NOTES

1. In the literature, terms such as 'theory,' 'model,' 'perspective,' and 'framework' are often used interchangeably. Generally, 'theories' or 'mod-els' are considered to be similar; they are sets of hypotheses or propositions that express relationships between variables. 'Perspectives' and 'frameworks' often represent more general, and sometimes untested, views of a phenomenon. In this text 'theory' or 'model' refers to a formal, specific explanation of some facet of the social world; 'perspective' or 'framework' is used as a more global term to refer to groups of theories or models that can be categorized according to a more general concept. These perspectives are sometimes labeled as schools of thought (functionalism, symbolic interactionism) that represent competing orientations for the study of how social behavior or societies function. They provide a general orientation for raising research questions and interpreting findings.
2. Ritzer (1975:7) defines a paradigm as 'a functional image of the subject matter within a science. It serves to define what should be studied, what questions should be asked, how they should be asked, and what rules should be followed in interpreting the answers obtained.' According to Ritzer, a paradigm has four components: (1) an exemplar, or a piece of work that stands as a model; (2) an image of the subject matter; (3) theories; and (4) methods and instruments.
3. 'Perspectives' and 'paradigms' are virtually synonymous. It must be noted that theories are *not* paradigms in themselves, but rather components of broader paradigms, perspectives, or schools of thought.
4. For more detailed information about research settings and research methods in the social sciences in general, see Babbie (1989); for information about quantitative and qualitative research methods in gerontology see Sinnott et al., 1983; Fry and Keith, 1986; Reinharz and Rowles, 1988; Schaie et al., 1988; Lawton and Herzog, 1989.
5. See Sinnott et al., 1983; Borgatta and Hertzog, 1985; McAuley, 1987; Dannefer, 1988a; Reinharz and Rowles, 1988; Schaie et al., 1988; Béland, 1989; Lawton and Herzog, 1989.
6. The data reported in tables 4.1, 4.2, and 4.3 are fictitious. These hypothetical results are presented only to illustrate research designs and interpretation of the data.
7. Because of the loss of subjects, the question can always be raised whether the final sample is similar to the original sample. For example, in a longitudinal study of movie attendance, those who no longer wish to be in the study may be those who no longer attend because of such factors as low income, declining vision, or loss of mobility.
8. Ideally, this type of analysis must be completed

for males and females and for other relevant variables (race, income, education, or religion) pertaining to the phenomenon. However, so that the explanation of cohort analysis can be simplified, only patterns for the total population are included in table 4.3.

9. Additional perspectives or theories are introduced throughout the text to assist in explaining specific aging phenomena.

10. For example, as noted later in this chapter, activity theory is the conceptual antithesis of disengagement theory.

11. The terms 'life span,' 'life course,' and 'life cycle' are often used interchangeably in the literature (see Hagestad, 1990).

12. A closely related perspective is phenomenology, which seeks to analyze how individuals perceive their social world (see Passuth and Bengston, 1988:345-46). We perceive and interpret our world selectively, and different people react in different ways to the same event or setting. Our current perceptions are often influenced by our past socialization experiences. Individuals can be expected to vary their perceptions, and thereby behave differently, with respect to such events as retirement, entrance to a nursing home, the presence of an economic depression, or the loss of a spouse. These perceptions may be influenced by such factors as past experiences, class background, amount of anticipatory socialization, degree of social support from family and friends, and physical and mental health.

13. This perspective makes extensive use of participant observation and in-depth, face-to-face interviews in order to provide an 'ethnography' of a specific social setting.

14. For example, an after-dinner speaker might write a different speech depending on whether he or she was addressing a church group, a college fraternity group, an all-male group, an all-female group, a group of businessmen and politicians, or a group of unemployed laborers.

15. There are many socialization theories (Goslin, 1969). This subsection introduces the concept of socialization, presents a general model of the process, and briefly discusses the social learning theory of socialization.

16. See Zigler and Child (1969:451-68) for an excellent overview of the various theoretical approaches to early-life socialization. They discuss the following theoretical approaches: social anthropology, psychoanalysis, a combination of social anthropology and psychoanalysis, normative-maturational, developmental-cognitive, genetic and constitutional, and learning.

17. Rosow (1985:70) describes role emptying as a process 'wherein responsibilities and normative expectations within a position simply dwindle away.' This results in few normative expectations for the elderly, and hence there is a wide range of possible interpretations about how one ought to behave in the later years. This lack of normative guidelines may foster eccentricity and even deviant behavior.

18. Interestingly, negative labels seem to arise more from societally induced evaluations by others; positive labels are more likely to be initiated by the individuals themselves.

19. The five types of activities, which involved different role relationships, were informal activity with friends, relatives, or neighbors; formal activity in voluntary associations; and solitary activity (single leisure pursuits, household-maintenance tasks).

20. 'Psychological disengagement' refers to an increasing concern with the self and a tendency to be more passive. This form of disengagement usually occurs prior to social disengagement, and is often a symptom of impending decreased social interaction.

21. The fact that there are some individuals who are still socially and psychologically engaged late in life has been variously explained by advocates of disengagement theory. They argue that these engaged individuals are unsuccessful disengagers, that they are out of sequence in their timing of disengagement, that they are biological or psychological exceptions to the norm, or that they have had an exceptionally favorable opportunity structure.

22. Although the discussion of disengagement theory might be considered as both a micro and a macro theory, it has been included in this section dealing with the micro level, since most discussion and empirical tests of the theory have been initiated on that level.

23. Those in the higher social classes generally attach more meaning and importance to their work than to the family or leisure. As a result, they gain more satisfaction from their work and are more likely to want to continue working in the later years. Additionally, they generally have access to work in old age, either because they have the skills to continue working independently, or because they control the labor market.

24. The size, proportion, and composition of the population within a given stratum may change over time within and between societies. For example, as noted in chapter 3, the proportion of those over 65 years of age has increased dramatically in recent years. Similarly, because of higher mortality rates for men and members of minority

groups, the older age strata generally include more women than men, and more whites than nonwhites.

25. Although all members of a particular stratum may have encountered a specific event (a depression or a war) at the same stage in their personal life cycles, they may have experienced the event in different ways. For example, the Vietnam War had a differential impact on men between 18 and 25 years of age depending on whether, how, and where they served in the U.S. armed forces. Some resisted the draft and never served; others fought and were wounded or killed. This not only had profound effects on the individual, but also on the sex ratio in this stratum.

26. The size of the cohort influences life chances in that a small cohort may lead to low unemployment, while a large cohort (such as the baby-boom cohort) may lead to high unemployment and severe competition for limited positions, especially during periods of economic recession.

27. Arguments for and against minority-group status for the aged are summarized in table 2 in Abu-Laban and Abu-Laban (1980:70).

28. 'Employment status' means employed or not employed; 'occupational status' refers to the prestige of the current or former occupation.

29. Environmental theories, which are discussed in chapter 8, stress that the interaction between the individual and the environment must be considered in attempts to understand the aging process and the status of the elderly. They stress that individual differences in experiences and perceptions must be examined when decisions are being made about which environment is most effective for a specific individual or for specific age cohorts.

REFERENCES

Abu-Laban, S. and B. Abu-Laban. (1980). 'Women and the Aged as Minority Groups: A Critique,' pp. 63-79 in V. Marshall (ed.). *Aging in Canada: Social Perspectives*. Don Mills, Ont.: Fitzhenry and Whiteside.

Achenbaum, W.A. (1987). 'Can Gerontology Be a Science?' *Journal of Aging Studies*, 1(1), 3-18.

Achenbaum, A. and P. Stearns. (1978). 'Old Age and Modernization,' *The Gerontologist*, 18(3), 307-12.

Agnew, N. and S. Pyke. (1987). *The Science Game*. 4th ed. Englewood Cliffs, N.J.: Prentice-Hall.

Atchley, R. (1971). *The Social Forces in Later Life*. 1st ed. Belmont, Calif.: Wadsworth Publishing Co.

Atchley, R. (1989). 'A Continuity Theory of Normal Aging,' *The Gerontologist*, 29(2), 183-90.

Babbie, E. (1989). *The Practice of Social Research*. 5th ed. Belmont, Calif.: Wadsworth Publishing Co.

Barron, M. (1953). 'Minority Group Characteristics of the Aged in American Society,' *Journal of Gerontology*, 8(3), 477-82.

Béland, F. (1989). 'Research in Social Gerontology in Quebec: An Obscure Originality or a Deserved Obscurity?' *Canadian Journal on Aging*, 7(4), 293-310.

Bengtson, V. and J. Kuypers. (1986). 'The Family Support Cycle: Psychosocial Issues in the Aging Family,' pp. 61-77 in J. Munnichs et al. (eds.). *Life Span and Change in a Gerontological Perspective*. New York: Academic Press.

Bengtson, V. et al. (1975). 'Modernization, Modernity and Perceptions of Aging: A Cross-Cultural Study,' *Journal of Gerontology*, 30(6), 688-95.

Biddle, B. (1979). *Role Theory: Expectations, Identities, and Behaviors*. New York: Academic Press.

Biddle, B. and E. Thomas. (eds.). (1966) *Role Theory: Concepts and Research*. New York: John Wiley & Sons.

Birren, J. and V. Bengtson. (eds.). (1988). *Emergent Theories of Aging*. New York: Springer Publishing Co.

Birren, J. and W. Cunningham. (1985). 'Research on the Psychology of Aging: Principles, Concepts and Theory,' pp. 3-34 in J. Birren and W. Schaie (eds.). *Handbook of the Psychology of Aging*. 2d. ed. New York: Van Nostrand Reinhold.

Borgatta, E. and C. Hertzog. (eds.). (1985). 'Methodology and Aging Research,' *Research on Aging*, 7(1), 3-152.

Bowles, N. and L. Poon. (1982). 'An Analysis of the Effect of Aging on Recognition Memory,' *Journal of Gerontology*, 37(2), 212-19.

Burgess, W. (1960). *Aging in Western Societies*. Chicago: University of Chicago Press.

Burwell, E. (1984). 'Sexism in Social Science Research on Aging,' pp. 185-208 in J. Vickers (ed.). *Taking Sex Into Account*. Ottawa: Carleton University Press.

Cain, L. (1981). Book review of *In Search of the New Old: Redefining Old Age in America, 1945-1970* by R. Calhoun (1978), in *Contemporary Sociology*, 19(1), 91-92.

Campbell, R. (1988). 'Integrating Conceptualization, Design, and Analysis in Panel Studies of the Life Course,' pp. 43-69 in W. Schaie (ed.). *Methodological Issues in Aging Research*. New York: Springer Publishing Co.

Campbell, R. and C. Hudson. (1985). 'Synthetic Cohorts from Panel Surveys: An Approach to Studying Rare Events,' *Research on Aging*, 7(1), 81-95.

Campbell, R. and A. O'Rand. (1988). 'Settings and Sequences: The Heuristics of Aging Research,' pp. 58-79 in J. Birren and V. Bengtson (eds.). *Emergent Theories of Aging.* New York: Springer Publishing Co.

Cohen, L. (1984). *Small Expectations: Society's Betrayal of Older Women.* Toronto: McClelland and Stewart.

Cohn, R. (1982). 'Economic Development and Status Change of the Aged,' *American Journal of Sociology,* 87(5), 1150-61.

Connidis, I. (1983). 'Integrating Qualitative and Quantitative Methods in Survey Research on Aging: An Assessment,' *Qualitative Sociology,* 6(4), 334-52.

Cooley, C. (1902). *Human Nature and the Social Order.* New York: Scribner's.

Covey, H. (1981). 'A Reconceptualization of Continuity Theory: Some Preliminary Thoughts,' *The Gerontologist,* 21(6), 628-33.

Cowgill, D. (1974). 'Aging and Modernization: A Revision of the Theory,' pp. 123-46 in J. Gubrium (ed.). *Late Life: Communities and Environmental Policy.* Springfield, Ill.: Charles C. Thomas.

Cowgill, D. (1986). *Aging around the World.* Belmont, Calif.: Wadsworth Publishing Co.

Cowgill, D. and L. Holmes (eds.). (1972). *Aging and Modernization.* New York: Appleton-Century-Crofts.

Cumming, E. (1963). 'Further Thoughts on the Theory of Disengagement,' *International Social Science Journal,* 15(3), 377-93.

Cumming, E. and W. Henry. (1961). *Growing Old: The Process of Disengagement.* New York: Basic Books.

Cumming, E. et al. (1960). 'Disengagement: A Tentative Theory of Aging,' *Sociometry,* 23(1), 23-35.

Dannefer, D. (1988a). 'Differential Gerontology and the Stratified Life Course: Conceptual and Methodological Issues,' pp. 3-36 in G. Maddox and P. Lawton (eds.). *Annual Review of Gerontology and Geriatrics.* vol. 8. New York: Springer Publishing Co.

Dannefer, D. (1988b). 'What's in a Name? An Account of the Neglect of Variability in the Study of Aging,' pp. 356-84 in J. Birren and V. Bengtson (eds.). *Emergent Theories of Aging.* New York: Springer Publishing Co.

D'Arcy, C. (1980). 'The Manufacture and Obsolescence of Madness: Age, Social Policy and Psychiatric Morbidity in a Prairie Province,' pp. 159-76 in V. Marshall (ed.). *Aging In Canada: Social Perspectives.* Don Mills, Ont.: Fitzhenry and Whiteside.

Dawe, A. (1970). 'The Two Sociologies,' *British Journal of Sociology,* 21(2), 207-18.

Deeg, L. (1989). *Experiences from Longitudinal Studies of Aging: Conceptualization, Organization and Output.* Nijmegen, the Netherlands: Netherlands Institute of Gerontology.

Department of National Health and Welfare. (1982). *Suicide among the Aged in Canada.* Ottawa: Policy, Planning and Information Branch.

Dowd, J. (1975). 'Aging as Exchange: A Preface to Theory,' *Journal of Gerontology,* 30(5), 584-94.

Dowd, J. (1978). 'Aging as Exchange: A Test of the Distributive Justice Proposition,' *Pacific Sociological Review,* 21(3), 351-75.

Dowd, J. (1980). *Stratification among the Aged.* Montery, Calif.: Brooks/Cole Publishing Co.

Dowd, J. (1984). 'Beneficence and the Aged,' *Journal of Gerontology,* 39(1), 102-08.

Dowd, J. (1987). 'The Reification of Age: Age Stratification Theory and the Passing of the Autonomous Subject,' *Journal of Aging Studies,* 1(4), 317-35.

Emerson, R. (1962). 'Power-Dependence Relations,' *American Sociological Review,* 27(1), 31-41.

Emerson, R. (1976). 'Social Exchange Theory,' pp. 335-62 in A. Inkeles (ed.). *Annual Review of Sociology.* vol. 2. Palo Alto, Calif.: Annual Reviews, Inc.

Erikson, E. (1950). *Childhood and Society.* New York: W.W. Norton.

Estes, C. et al. (1984). *Political Economy, Health and Aging.* Boston: Little, Brown & Co.

Fischer, D. (1977). *Growing Old in America.* London: Oxford University Press.

Flett, D. et al. (1980). 'Evaluation of the Public Health Nurse as Primary Health-care Provider for Elderly People,' pp. 177-88 in V. Marshall (ed.). *Aging in Canada: Social Perspectives.* Don Mills, Ont.: Fitzhenry and Whiteside.

Foner, A. (1979). 'Ascribed and Achieved Bases of Stratification,' pp. 219-42 in A. Inkeles et al. (eds.). *Annual Review of Sociology.* vol. 5. Palo Alto, Calif.: Annual Reviews, Inc.

Forbes, W. et al. (1989). 'The Validation of Longitudinal Studies: The Case of the Ontario Longitudinal Study of Aging,' *Canadian Journal on Aging,* 8(1), 51-67.

Forscher, B. (1963). 'Chaos in the Brickyard,' *Science,* 142, 3590.

Fox J. (1981-82). 'Perspectives on the Continuity Perspective,' *International Journal of Aging and Human Development,* 14(2), 97-115.

Fry, C. (1988). 'Theories of Age and Culture,' pp. 447-81 in J. Birren and V. Bengtson (eds.). *Emergent Theories of Aging.* New York: Springer Publishing Co.

Fry, C. and J. Keith. (eds.). (1986). *New Methods for Old Age Research: Anthropological Alternatives.* South Hadley, Mass.: Bergin and Garvey.

Gee, E. and M. Kimball. (1987). *Women and Aging.* Toronto: Butterworths.

George, L. (1980). *Role Transitions in Later Life.* Monterey, Calif.: Brooks/Cole Publishing Co.

Gibson, D. and W. Aitkenhead. (1983). 'The Elderly Respondent,' *Research on Aging*, 5(2), 283-96.

Gibson, R. (1988). 'Minority Aging Research: Opportunity and Challenge,' *The Gerontologist*, 28(4), 559-60.

Gilleard, C. and A. Gurkon. (1987). 'Socioeconomic Development and the Status of Elderly Men in Turkey: A Test of Modernization Theory,' *Journal of Gerontology*, 42(4), 353-57.

Glenn, N. (1977). *Cohort Analysis*. Beverly Hills, Calif.: Sage Publications.

Glenn, N. (1981). 'Age, Birth Cohorts, and Drinking: An Illustration of the Hazards of Inferring Effects from Cohort Data,' *Journal of Gerontology*, 36(3), 362-69.

Goffman, E. (1959). *The Presentation of Self in Everyday Life*. New York: Doubleday & Co.

Goslin, D. (ed.). (1969). *Handbook of Socialization Theory and Research*. Chicago: Rand McNally.

Gubrium, J. (1975). *Living and Dying at Murray Manor*. New York: St. Martin's Press.

Gubrium, J. and D. Buckholdt. (1977). *Toward Maturity: The Social Processing of Human Development*. San Francisco, Calif.: Jossey Bass.

Hagestad, G. (1990). 'Social Perspectives on the Life Course,' pp. 151-68 in R. Binstock and L. George (eds.). *Handbook of Aging and the Social Sciences*. 3d ed. San Diego, Calif.: Academic Press.

Hagestad, G. and B. Neugarten. (1985). 'Age and the Life Course,' pp. 35-61 in R. Binstock and E. Shanas (eds.). *Handbook of Aging and the Social Sciences*. 2d ed. New York: Van Nostrand Reinhold.

Hastings, D. and L. Berry (eds.). (1979). *Cohort Analysis: A Collection of Interdisciplinary Readings*. Oxford, Ohio: Scripps Foundation.

Havighurst, R. and R. Albrecht. (1953). *Older People*. New York: Longmans, Green.

Hendricks, J. (1982). 'The Elderly in Society: Beyond Modernization,' *Social Science History*, 6(3), 321-45.

Hendricks, J. and C. Leedham. (1987). 'Making Sense of Literary Aging: Relevance of Recent Gerontological Theory,' *Journal of Aging Studies*, 1(2), 187-208.

Henretta, J. (1988). 'Conflict and Cooperation Among Age Strata,' pp. 385-404 in J. Birren and V. Bengtson (eds.). *Emergent Theories of Aging*. New York: Springer Publishing Co.

Henry, W. (1964). 'The Theory of Intrinsic Disengagement,' pp. 415-18 in P. Hansen (ed.). *Age with a Future*. Philadelphia: F. A. Davis Co.

Herzog, R. and W. Rodgers. (1988). 'Age and Response Rates to Interview Sample Surveys,' *Journal of Gerontology: Social Sciences*, 43(6), S200-205.

Hochschild, A. (1973). *The Unexpected Community*. Englewood Cliffs, N.J.: Prentice-Hall.

Hochschild, A. (1975). 'Disengagement Theory: A Logical, Empirical, and Phenomenological Critique,' pp. 53-87 in J. Gubrium (ed.). *Time, Roles and Self in Old Age*. New York: Human Sciences Press.

Hochschild, A. (1976). 'Disengagement Theory: A Critique and Proposal,' *American Sociological Review*, 40(5), 553-69.

Hogan, D. (1981). *Transitions and Social Change: The Early Lives of American Men*. New York: Academic Press.

Holsti, O. (1969). *Content Analysis and the Social Sciences and the Humanities*. Reading, Mass.: Addison-Wesley.

Honzik, M. (1984). 'Life-Span Development,' *Annual Review of Psychology*, 35, 309-32.

Hyman, H. and E. Singer. (1968). *Readings in Reference Group Theory and Research*. New York: Free Press.

Jacobs, J. (1975). *Older Persons and Retirement Communities: Case Studies in Social Gerontology*. Springfield, Ill.: Charles C. Thomas.

Kastenbaum, R. (1984). 'When Aging Begins: A Life-span Developmental Approach,' *Research on Aging*, 6(1), 105-17.

Keating, N. (forthcoming). *Rural Aging in Canada*. Markham, Ont.: Butterworths.

Keith, J. (1985). 'Age in Anthropological Research,' pp. 231-63 in R. Binstock and E. Shanas (eds.). *Handbook of Aging and the Social Sciences*. 2d. ed. New York: Van Nostrand Reinhold.

Keith, J. (1988). 'Participant Observation,' pp. 211-30 in W. Schaie (ed.). *Methodological Issues in Aging Research*. New York: Springer Publishing Co.

Keith, J. (1990). 'Age in Social and Cultural Context: Anthropological Perspectives,' pp. 91-111 in R. Binstock and L. George (eds.). *Handbook of Aging and the Social Sciences*. 3d ed. San Diego, Calif.: Academic Press.

Kemper, T. (1968). 'Reference Groups, Socialization and Achievement,' *American Sociological Review*, 33(1), 31-45.

Kertzer, D. and J. Keith (eds.). (1984). *Age and Anthropological Theory*. Ithaca, N.Y.: Cornell University Press.

Kimmel, D. and H. Moody. (1990). 'Ethical Issues in Gerontological Research and Services,' pp. 489-502 in J. Birren and W. Schaie (eds.). *Handbook of the Psychology of Aging*. 3d ed. San Diego, Calif.: Academic Press.

Kosloski, K. (1986). 'Isolating Age, Period, and Cohort Effects in Developmental Research: A Critical Review,' *Research on Aging*, 8(4), 460-79.

Kuypers, J. and V. Bengtson. (1973). 'Social Breakdown and Competence: A Model of Normal

Aging,' *Human Development*, 16(3), 181-201.

Larson, R. (1978). 'Thirty Years of Research on the Subjective Well-Being of Older Americans,' *Journal of Gerontology*, 33(1), 109-25.

Laslett, P. (1976). 'Societal Development and Aging,' pp. 87-116 in R. Binstock and E. Shanas (eds.). *Handbook of Aging and the Social Sciences*. New York: Van Nostrand Reinhold.

Lastrucci, C. (1967). *The Scientific Approach*. Cambridge, Mass.: Schenkman.

Lawton, P. and R. Herzog (eds.). (1989). *Special Research Methods for Gerontology*. Amityville, N.Y.: Baywood Publishing Co.

Lemon, B. et al. (1972). 'An Exploration of the Activity Theory of Aging: Activity Types and Life Satisfaction among In-Movers to a Retirement Community,' *Journal of Gerontology*, 27(4), 511-23.

Longino, C. and C. Kart. (1982). 'Explicating Activity Theory: A Formal Replication,' *Journal of Gerontology*, 37(6), 713-22.

Longino, C. et. al. (1980). 'The Aged Subculture Hypothesis: Social Integration, Gerontophilia and Self-Conception,' *Journal of Gerontology*, 35(5), 758-67.

Loy, J. (1972). 'Sociology and Physical Education,' pp. 168-236 in R. Singer et al. (eds.). *Physical Education: An Interdisciplinary Approach*. New York: MacMillan.

Maddox, G. (1970). 'Fact and Artifact: Evidence Bearing on Disengagement Theory,' pp.318-28 in E. Palmore (ed.). *Normal Aging*. Durham, N.C.: Duke University Press.

Maddox, G. and R. Campbell. (1985). 'Scope, Concepts, and Methods in the Study of Aging,' pp. 3-31 in R. Binstock and E. Shanas (eds.). *Handbook of Aging and the Social Sciences*. 2d ed. New York: Van Nostrand Reinhold.

Mangen, D. and W. Peterson (eds.). (1982). *Research Instruments in Social Gerontology*. vols. 1,2,3. Minneapolis: University of Minnesota Press.

Manheimer, R. (1989). 'The Narrative Quest in Qualitative Gerontology,' *Journal of Aging Studies*, 3(3), 231-52.

Markson, E. (ed.). (1975). 'Disengagement Theory Revisited,' *International Journal of Aging and Human Development*, 6(3), 183-228.

Marshall, V. (1975). 'Socialization for Impending Death in a Retirement Village,' *American Journal of Sociology*, 80(5), 1124-44.

Marshall, V. (1978-79). 'No Exit: A Symbolic Interactionist Perspective on Aging,' *International Journal of Aging and Human Development*, 9(4), 345-58.

Marshall, V. (1980). *Last Chapters: A Sociology of Aging and Dying*. Monterey, Calif.: Brooks/Cole Publishing Co.

Marshall, V. (1981). 'Participant Observation in a Multiple-Methods Study of a Retirement Community: A Research Narrative,' *Mid-American Review of Sociology*, 6(2), 29-44.

Marshall, V. (1986). *Later Life: The Social Psychology of Aging*. Beverly Hills, Calif.: Sage Publications.

Marshall, V. (1987a). 'Factors Affecting Response and Completion Rates in Some Canadian Studies,' *Canadian Journal on Aging*, 6(3), 217-27.

Marshall, V. (1987b). 'Social Perspectives on Aging: Theoretical Notes,' pp. 39-59 in V. Marshall (ed.). *Aging in Canada: Social Perspectives*. Markham, Ont.: Fitzhenry and Whiteside.

Marshall, V. and J. Tindale. (1978-79). 'Notes for a Radical Gerontology,' *International Journal of Aging and Human Development*, 9(2), 163-75.

Martin Matthews, A. (1987). 'Widowhood as an Expectable Life Event,' pp. 343-66 in V. Marshall (ed.). *Aging in Canada: Social Perspectives*. 2d ed. Markham, Ont.: Fitzhenry and Whiteside.

Martin Matthews, A. and A. Vanden Heuvel. (1986). 'Conceptual and Methodological Issues in Research on Aging in Rural Versus Urban Environments,' *Canadian Journal on Aging*, 5(1), 49-60.

Matthews, S. (1979). *The Social World of Old Women: Management of Self-Identity*. Beverly Hills, Calif.: Sage Publications.

Maxwell, R. and P. Silverman. (1980). 'Information and Esteem: Cultural Considerations in the Treatment of the Aged,' pp. 3-34 in J. Hendricks (ed.). *In the Country of the Old*. Farmingdale, N.Y.: Baywood Publishing Co., Inc.

McAuley, W.J. (1987). *Applied Research in Gerontology*. New York: Van Nostrand Reinhold.

McDaniel, S. (1989). 'Women and Aging: A Sociological Perspective,' *Journal of Women and Aging*, 1(1-3), 47-67.

McDonald, L. and R. Wanner. (1987). 'Retirement in a Dual Economy: The Canadian Case,' pp. 245-61 in V. Marshall (ed.). *Aging in Canada: Social Perspectives*. 2d ed. Markham, Ont.: Fitzhenry and Whiteside.

McDonald, L. and R. Wanner. (1990). *Retirement in Canada*. Markham, Ont.: Butterworths.

McPherson, B. and C. Kozlik. (1987). 'Age Patterns in Leisure Participation: The Canadian Case,' pp. 211-27 in V. Marshall (ed.) *Aging in Canada: Social Perspectives*. 2d ed. Markham, Ont.: Fitzhenry and Whiteside.

Merton, R. (1957). *Social Theory and Social Structure*. Glencoe, Ill.: Free Press.

Mills, C.W. (1959). *The Sociological Imagination*. New York: Oxford University Press.

Minkler, M. and C. Estes (eds.). (1984). *Readings in the Political Economy of Aging*. Farmingdale, N.Y.: Baywood Publishing Co.

Montgomery, R. and E. Borgatta. (1986). 'Plausible Theories and the Development of Scientific Theory: The Case of Aging Research,' *Research on Aging,* 8(4), 586-608.

Myles, J. (1980). 'The Aged, the State and the Structure of Inequality,' pp. 317-42 in J. Harp and J. Hofley (eds.). *Structural Inequality in Canada.* Toronto: Prentice-Hall.

Myles, J. (1989). *Old Age in the Welfare State: The Political Economy of Public Pensions.* 2d ed. Lawrence, Kans.: University of Kansas Press.

Nesselroade, J. (1988). 'Sampling and Generalizability,' pp. 13-42 in W. Schaie (ed.). *Methodological Issues in Aging Research.* New York: Springer Publishing Co.

Nesselroade, J. and E. Labouvie. (1985). 'Experimental Designs in Research on Aging,' pp. 35-60 in J. Birren and W. Schaie (eds.). *Handbook of the Psychology of Aging.* 2d. ed. New York: Van Nostrand Reinhold.

Nisbet, R. (1976). *Sociology as an Art Form.* New York: Oxford University Press.

Palmore, E. (1983). 'Cross-Cultural Research,' *Research on Aging,* 5(1), 45-57.

Palmore, E. and K. Manton. (1974). 'Modernization and Status of the Aged: International Correlation,' *Journal of Gerontology,* 29(2), 205-10.

Palmore, E. and F. Whittington. (1971). 'Trends in the Relative Status of the Aged,' *Social Forces,* 50(1), 84-91.

Passuth, P. and V. Bengtson. (1988). 'Sociological Theories of Aging: Current Perspectives and Future Directions,' pp. 333-55 in J. Birren and V. Bengtson (eds.). *Emergent Theories of Aging.* New York: Springer Publishing Co.

Patrick, C. and E. Borgatta (eds.). (1981). 'Available Data Bases for Aging Research,' *Research on Aging,* 3(4), 371-501.

Press, I. and M. McKool. (1980). 'Social Structure and Status of the Aged: Toward Some Valid Cross-Cultural Generalizations,' pp. 47-56 in J. Hendricks (ed.). *In the Country of the Old.* Farmingdale, N.Y.: Baywood Publishing Co.

Quadagno, J. (1980). 'The Modernization Controversy: A Socio-Historical Analysis of Retirement in Nineteenth Century England,' paper presented at the annual meeting of the American Sociological Association, New York.

Quadagno, J. and J. Janzen. (1987). 'Old Age Security and the Family Life Course: A Case Study of Nineteenth-Century Mennonite Immigrants to Kansas,' *Journal of Aging Studies,* 1(1), 33-50.

Reinharz, S. and G. Rowles (eds.). (1988). *Qualitative Gerontology.* New York: Springer Publishing Co.

Riley, M. (1971). 'Social Gerontology and the Age Stratification of Society,' *The Gerontologist,* 11(1), 79-87.

Riley, M. (1979). 'Introduction: Life Course Perspectives,' pp. 3-13 in M. Riley (ed.). *Aging from Birth to Death: Interdisciplinary Perspectives.* Boulder, Colo.: Westview Press.

Riley, M. (1985). 'Age Strata in Social Systems,' pp. 369-411 in R. Binstock and E. Shanas (eds.). *Handbook of Aging and the Social Sciences.* 2d ed. New York: Van Nostrand Reinhold.

Riley, M. et al. (1972). 'Elements in a Model of Age Stratification,' pp. 3-26 in M. Riley, M. Johnson and A. Foner (eds.). *Aging and Society. Volume 3: A Sociology of Age Stratification.* New York: Russell Sage Foundation.

Ritzer, G. (1975). 'Sociology — A Multiple Paradigm Science,' *The American Sociologist,* 10(August), 156-67.

Ritzer, G. (1975). *Sociology: A Multiple Paradigm Science.* Boston: Allyn and Bacon.

Rodgers, W. and R. Herzog. (1987). 'Interviewing Older Adults: The Accuracy of Factual Information,' *Journal of Gerontology,* 42(4), 387-94.

Rogosa, D. (1988). 'Myths about Longitudinal Research,' pp. 171-209 in W. Schaie (ed.). *Methodological Issues in Aging Research.* New York: Springer Publishing Co.

Rose, A. (1962). 'The Subculture of the Aging: A Topic for Sociological Research,' *The Gerontologist,* 2(3), 123-27.

Rose, A. (1965). 'The Subculture of the Aging: A Framework for Research in Social Gerontology,' pp. 3-16 in A. Rose and W. Peterson (eds.). *Older People and Their Social World.* Philadelphia: F.A. Davis Co.

Rosenthal, C. (1987). 'Aging and Intergenerational Relations in Canada,' pp. 311-42 in V. Marshall (ed.). *Aging in Canada: Social Perspectives.* 2d. ed. Markham, Ont.: Fitzhenry and Whiteside.

Rosow, I. (1985). 'Status and Role Change Through the Life Cycle,' pp. 62-93 in R. Binstock and E. Shanas (eds.). *Handbook of Aging and the Social Sciences.* 2d ed. New York: Van Nostrand Reinhold.

Rossi, A. (1986). 'Sex and Gender in an Aging Society,' *Daedalus,* 115, 141-69.

Sarbin, T. and V. Allen. (1968). 'Role Theory,' pp. 488-567 in G. Lindzey and E. Aronson (eds.). *Handbook of Social Psychology.* Reading, Mass.: Addison-Wesley.

Schaie, W. (1965). 'A General Model for the Study of Developmental Problems,' *Psychological Bulletin,* 64(2), 92-107.

Schaie, W. (1967). 'Age Changes and Age Differences,' *The Gerontologist,* 7(2), 128-32.

Schaie, W. (1977). 'Quasi-Experimental Research Designs in the Psychology of Aging,' pp. 39-58 in

J. Birren and W. Schaie (eds.). *Handbook of the Psychology of Aging*. New York: Van Nostrand Reinhold.

Schaie, W. (1988). 'The Impact of Research Methodology on Theory Building in the Developmental Sciences,' pp. 41-57 in J. Birren and V. Bengtson (eds.). *Emergent Theories of Aging*. New York: Springer Publishing Co.

Schaie, W. et al. (1988). *Methodological Issues in Aging Research*. New York: Springer Publishing Co.

Schulsinger, F. et al. (1981). *Longitudinal Research: Methods and Uses in Behavioral Sciences*. vol. 1. Hingham, Mass.: Kluwer-Nijhoff Publishing.

Schwenger, C. (1983). 'Commentary: Suicide among the Aged in Canada: Drawing Conclusions from Demographic Data,' *Focus on Aging* (University of Toronto Programme in Gerontology), 4(2), 2-3.

Shock, N. (1985). 'Longitudinal Studies of Aging in Humans,' pp. 721-43 in C. Finch and E. Schneider (eds.). *Handbook of the Biology of Aging*. 2d ed. New York: Van Nostrand Reinhold.

Sinnott, J. et al. (1983). *Applied Research in Aging: A Guide to Methods and Resources*. Boston: Little, Brown & Co.

Skinkle, R. and P. Grant. (1988). 'An Outcome Evaluation of an In-Service Training Program for Nursing Home Aides,' *Canadian Journal on Aging*, 7(1), 48-57.

Smyer, M. and M. Gatz. (1986). 'Intervention Research Approaches,' *Research on Aging*, 8(4), 536-58.

Snizek, W. (1975). 'The Relationship Between Theory and Research: A Study in the Sociology of Sociology,' *The Sociological Quarterly*, 16(3), 415-28.

Stacey, J. and B. Thorne. (1985). 'The Missing Feminist Revolution in Sociology,' *Social Problems*, 32(3), 301-16.

Stearns, P. (1981). 'The Modernization of Old Age in France: Approaches through History,' *International Journal of Aging and Human Development*, 13(4), 297-315.

Stearns, P. (1982). *Old Age in Preindustrial Society*. New York: Holmes & Meier.

Streib, G. (1983). 'The Frail Elderly: Research Dilemmas and Research Opportunities,' *The Gerontologist*, 23(1), 40-44.

Streib, G. (1985). 'Social Stratification and Aging,' pp. 339-68 in R. Binstock and E. Shanas (eds.). *Handbook of Aging and the Social Sciences*. 2d ed. New York: Van Nostrand Reinhold.

Streib, G. and C. Bourg. (1984). 'Age Stratification Theory, Inequality, and Social Change,' *Comparative Social Research*, 7(1), 63-77.

Thomas, W. (1931). 'The Definition of the Situation,' pp. 41-50 in W. Thomas (ed.). *The Unadjusted Girl*. Boston: Little, Brown & Co.

Tigges, L. and D. Cowgill. (1981). 'Aging from the World Systems Perspective: An Alternative to Modernization Theory?' paper presented at the annual meeting of the Gerontological Society of America, Toronto.

Tindale, J. (1980) 'Identity Maintenance Processes of Old, Poor Men,' pp. 88-94 in V. Marshall (ed.). *Aging in Canada: Social Perspectives*. Don Mills, Ont.: Fitzhenry and Whiteside.

Tindale, J. and V. Marshall. (1980). 'A Generational Conflict Perspective for Gerontology,' pp. 43-59 in V. Marshall (ed.). *Aging in Canada: Social Perspectives*. Don Mills. Ont.: Fitzhenry and Whiteside.

Wacks, V. (1989) 'Guided Autobiography with the Elderly,' *Journal of Applied Gerontology*, 8(4), 512-523.

Wan, T. (1986). 'Evaluation Research in Long-Term Care,' *Research on Aging*, 8(4), 559-85.

Zigler, E. and I. Child. (1969). 'Socialization,' pp. 450-589 in G. Lindzey and E. Aronson (eds.). *The Handbook of Social Psychology*. vol. 3. Reading, Mass.: Addison-Wesley.

Part Two

A MICROANALYSIS OF AGING AS A SOCIAL PROCESS: THE AGING INDIVIDUAL

Part Two includes a brief non-technical description of changes that occur in our physical and psychological systems in the middle and later years. This serves as the basis for a more detailed discussion of how these changes may influence the behavioral and cognitive processes of the older individual as he or she interacts with a changing social and physical environment.

Chapter 5 presents information about the way in which changes in the physical structure and in the physiological, sensory, and motor systems influence social, emotional, and cognitive behavior in the later stages of life. The chapter also illustrates patterns of involvement in physical activity and exercise at various stages in the life cycle, and briefly examines changes in health status and the use of the health care delivery system. In chapter 6, the focus is on changes in the sensory, perceptual, cognitive, and personality systems that occur within the aging individual, and on how these changes influence social and cognitive behavior.

5
The Aging Process:
Adaptation to Physical Changes

Ross Davidson-Pilon, Guelph, Ontario

INTRODUCTION

It is commonly believed that the process of aging involves degenerative changes in our physical and psychological systems. These in turn are presumed to lead to inevitable physical, emotional, and intellectual losses. As a result, myths and stereotypes often portray aging and the aged in negative terms. Hence, it is commonly believed that the elderly are slower; have less strength, endurance, and energy; are chronic complainers about their acute or chronic illnesses; are uninterested in or incapable of sexual activity; and are handicapped at work and in social interaction by deterioration in vision and hearing.

Until recent years these deficiencies were attributed almost exclusively to the inevitable, genetically based biological decline of the organism. The possible influence of historical events or social experiences on the aging process was neglected. A model of inevitable biological decline for everyone was accepted, with little concern for individual differences resulting from social or environmental factors. As Charness (1981:22), a psychologist, noted: 'Aging research should become more concerned with an individual difference approach. In fact, one of the few unchallenged assertions in gerontology is that individual differences increase with age (Carroll and Maxwell, 1979).'

As noted earlier, there has been a tendency to confuse age differences with age changes. This has resulted from a reliance on cross-sectional research designs that compare members of different age cohorts on various physical or psychological variables. In this type of study older people are generally found to be inferior to younger people, especially in the accomplishment of intellectual and physical tasks. However, the observed differences between the young and the old in cross-sectional studies might also reflect differences in educational attainment, in lifestyle opportunities, in attitudes toward testing situations, in experience as subjects in experiments, in motivation to perform, or in meaningfulness of the test material.

In order to separate myth from fact, this chapter summarizes recent research evidence concerning the physical capabilities and performance potential of the older person. (In chapter 6 the psychological components of the organism are examined in a similar manner.) This chapter describes changes observed in the physical structure, physiological systems, and sensory and motor processes of older people. In addition, there is a brief discussion of changes in physical and mental health in the later years, and of the need for and utilization of health care. Throughout chapters 5 and 6 the information is presented from a social science perspective: special attention is directed to the influence of physical or psychological changes on social and intellectual behavior.

In summary, all individuals can expect some decline in health and some gradual loss of physical, motor, or mental efficiency and ability as they age. These losses, which are a result of biological changes, occur at different rates in different individuals. Most people, at least until very late in life, do not experience functional losses that seriously change or affect their social or cognitive behavior.[1] Most of us will not spend the later years as dependent persons. Rather, we will likely experience varying degrees of physical, perceptual, or cognitive losses that will require some degree of adaptation. This process of adaptation will be influenced by a variety of past and present social and environmental factors, such as previous lifestyle; personality structure and coping style; support from significant others; socioeconomic status; race; gender; and marital status. The process of adaptation to changes in the physical and psychological systems will also be influenced by historical events and social changes (wars, depressions), and by unique personal events or transitions (divorce, involuntary retirement, or widowhood) that have occurred throughout the life cycle of a given individual or cohort.

AGING, PHYSICAL STRUCTURE, AND THE PHYSIOLOGICAL SYSTEMS

Introduction

As biologists and physiologists have frequently noted, the structure and function of the human organism attains full maturity and its greatest strength and energy sometime before twenty years of age. From early adulthood on, there is a gradual and progressive decline in the structure and function of the body's various components and a resulting decrease in the general activity level of the organism.

While some of these changes are external and highly visible (such as the elasticity and texture of the skin), most are internal, and may or may not influence social behavior or work performance. Moreover, there are differences in the rate of decline for each organ or system. For example, an individual who has reached a chronological age of 65 years may have the strength and energy of a 40-year-old, and the external physical appearance of a 50-year-old. Yet the same individual may have hearing or visual problems more commonly experienced by an 80-year-old. Furthermore, this interaction of physical and physiological aging has a unique impact on the behavior, attitudes, and performance of an individual. This is reflected in the dynamic interplay between the personality or personal coping style of the individual; the attitudes, perceptions, and interaction of others; and the individual's subsequent 'presentation of self' and type and frequency of social participation.

In summary, external physical and internal physiological changes occurring with age may have varying degrees of influence on the attitudes, social participation, and performance of specific individuals. The impact of these changes may be closely related to the severity of the change, the degree to which other changes occur at the same time or rate, and the extent to which the changes are perceived by the individual as threatening or limiting. Their impact is also influenced by the coping style of the individual, by the extent to which exercise is an integral facet of the individual's lifestyle, and by the reaction of significant others toward the individual (for example, social support, discouragement, lack of interest, decreased interaction).

The following sections illustrate some of the more common age-related changes in the physical structure and physiological functioning of the human organism, as well as the possible reactions to these changes. The influence of exercise and physical activity on the aging process is also examined. Throughout, it must be remembered that modal patterns are presented, and that there are differences within and between individuals. These differences are related to such genetic and environmental factors as sex, socioeconomic status, diet, race, ethnicity, occupation, geographic location, marital status, body type, and age cohort. Unfortunately, these factors are seldom controlled in experimental situations.

Changes in the Structure and Composition of the Organism

External Changes

As we age, visible changes occur in the skin, the hair, and in the shape and height of the body. For example, during middle age the skin becomes dry and wrinkled as it becomes thinner and loses elasticity and subcutaneous fat. Similarly, hair may become thinner and lose its original color. Because of the negative connotations frequently associated with wrinkles and gray hair, some individuals actively fight a 'cosmetic battle' to change their physical appearance and thereby try to appear younger than their chronological age. Not surprisingly, a profitable cosmetics industry has evolved to meet this social need, as has a new specialty in the medical profession, the 'cosmetic surgeon.' In addition to changing one's appearance, the loss of hair and subcutaneous fat in the middle and later years leads to greater heat loss and to increased susceptibility to 'feeling cold.' This in turn may initiate a shift from outdoor to indoor activities, and perhaps even a move to a warmer climate if this is economically feasible.

For many adults, especially women, body weight increases up to about 50 years of age, although there is often a decline thereafter because of a change in body metabolism. This increase in weight is due to an accumulation of fat and a reduction in muscle tissue which appears most frequently in the abdominal area for men, and in the limbs and abdominal area for women. As a result, body shape may change from a lean and youthful appearance to a more portly, rotund, or mature appearance.

Aging adults are faced with a cultural ideal wherein a youthful body and an active and independent lifestyle are revered. To cope with observed changes in one's appearance and with felt inner changes (for example, less efficiency, decreased energy, aches and pains), older adults adopt various cognitive strategies. Hennessy (1989), in a study of body culture and aging, identified two types of adapters. The 'active copers' continued or had begun a program of physical activity, and were conscious of how they dressed and appeared. The 'reactive copers' reported that they knew they 'should' or 'ought' to be active and to pay more attention to appearance, but for various reasons did not invest time in physical activity. The visible change in body shape may result in a social labeling process whereby the individual is perceived by others to be older than his or her actual or desired chronological age. Attempts may be initiated to mask these physical changes with a particular style of dress. In fact, the fashion industry has capitalized on this recent concern with looking young by designing clothes that make one look slimmer. In reality, a combination of regular exercise and appropriate diet is a healthier behavioral adaptation to these changes in body composition. However, many individuals are unwilling to invest time and energy in these healthy adaptive behaviors.

Another visible sign of aging is the shortening of stature that begins in late middle age. This is related to changes in the structure and composition of the spine: vertebrae may collapse or intervertebral discs may become compressed. These changes are visibly reflected in an increased 'bowing' of the spine and the loss of a few inches in height.

In summary, external visible changes with age can influence how an individual perceives the self, and how others perceive and interact with the individual. For those who are secure and who live in a supportive social environment, these physical changes are seldom traumatic. However, for those whose identity and social interaction are closely related to their physical appearance, attempts to alter the presentation of the physical self may become a time-consuming battle, particularly if they are separated or divorced and anxious to attract another mate.

Internal Changes

Internal physical changes tend to have more of an impact on the performance of physical tasks than on social perceptions, attitudes, or behavior. These changes include a decrease in muscle mass and elasticity; a decrease in water content and an increase in fat cells relative to muscle cells; a decrease in bone mass and minerals so that bones are more brittle, which increases the likelihood of fractures; and a deterioration in the range, flexibility, and composition of the articulating surfaces and joints, which can enhance the likelihood of fractures or arthritis, particularly among those who live past the normal life expectancy. Many of these changes lead to decreased mobility, to changing leisure patterns, and to an inability to perform household tasks in the later years. They may also increase the incidence of accidents or falls among older adults (Ochs et al., 1985; Sterns et al., 1985; Forbes et al., 1987:69-74; Evans, 1988; Charness and Bosman, 1990), particularly where a deteriorating or dangerous environment is present (for example, steep stairs, insufficient lighting, slippery floors, a bathroom without grab-bars). Even a fear of falling may restrict mobility and decrease one's independence.

Changes in the Physiological Functioning of the Organism

Over time, most physiological systems become less efficient and less capable of functioning to the maximum capacity of the earlier years of life. Decremental functional performance is usually experienced during strenuous or stressful work or leisure activities. However, as noted in a later subsection of this chapter, it is possible to maintain a fitness or training program as we age. This training process can retard the impact of physiological age-related changes, and can enhance performance in the later years. For example, with increased levels of physical fitness, reaction times and movement times are faster (Charness, 1985; Ostrow, 1989; Spirduso and MacRae, 1990). If physiological systems function efficiently, especially under physical or mental stress, the self-image of the individual may be enhanced. As a result, physical tasks that are often thought to be beyond the capacity of the older individual may be performed (such as skiing or participating in a marathon), and an active social life in the community may be sustained well into the later years.

The Central Nervous System

The central nervous system begins to slow down with age, as evidenced by a longer response or reaction time, by the earlier onset of fatigue, by the appearance of hand tremors, and by a general slowing of the autonomic nervous system (Cerella, 1990). Changes in the autonomic nervous system may lead to changes in metabolism, in the structure and function of a number of organs, and in the activities of nervous receptors, processors, and reactors. Some of these changes may be reflected in the slower execution of a task (although, contrary to popular myth, the quality of performance seldom decreases). More will be said about the impact of aging on the sensory processes in the next major section of this chapter. In the meantime, it is important to recognize that changes in the autonomic nervous system can significantly influence emotions and behavioral reactions.

The Muscular System

Age-related changes in the muscular system result in a decrease in strength and endurance, although the rate and degree of loss seem to be related to the frequency and intensity of physical activity pursued by the individual (Shephard, 1987; Bouchard et al., 1990). In addition, the time it takes for a muscle to relax or contract, and the time required before it can be restimulated, increase in later life. This is partly because of changes in the contractile tissue in the muscle, and partly because of neurological changes. These changes can reduce the ability to engage in endurance tasks or in tasks requiring repeated actions of the same muscle group (such as digging in the garden or washing windows). A decline in muscular endurance can also reduce the efficiency of other body systems, such as the respiratory system. Furthermore, a decrement in the

muscular-skeletal systems can lead to a greater likelihood of falls: there may be reduced leg lift when walking, which increases the chance of tripping, or there may be greater difficulty in regaining balance after stumbling. However, as will be noted later, the efficiency of the muscular system can be enhanced in the later years by regular exercise and physical activity; it is possible to delay the onset of muscular changes with age, and thus improve performance in daily tasks.

The Cardiovascular System

Among the many physiological changes that occur with age, the most visible (and the most significant for behavior) are those within the cardiovascular system: there is a decrease in the maximum heart rate attainable, a decrease in the maximum cardiac output and stroke volume, and an increase in blood pressure. All of these factors combine to lower the efficiency of the system and to hasten the onset of fatigue during various levels of physical activity. These outcomes, in turn, may limit the duration and type of work and leisure activities that can be pursued with enjoyment. However, these cardiovascular changes are not inevitable; it is possible, with a regular and sufficiently intense exercise program, to lower the resting heart rate, to increase the maximum heart rate during work, and to increase the cardiac output.

It is more difficult, however, to retard the onset of arteriosclerosis and atherosclerosis. Arteriosclerosis (or 'hardening of the arteries') is a loss of elasticity in the arterial walls, which restricts the flow of blood to the muscles and organs, thereby lessening endurance in work or play. Atherosclerosis is characterized by a hardening and narrowing of the arterial walls, resulting from the accumulation of fatty deposits that partially or completely block the flow of blood. These cardiovascular diseases, which are especially prevalent among men, are difficult to prevent or treat because their pathology is still not fully understood. However, adherence to low-cholesterol diets and maintenance of a regular exercise program throughout life seem to be related to a lower incidence of these diseases.

The Respiratory System

The efficiency of the respiratory system decreases with age because of a combination of factors. These include decreases in elasticity of the lungs; in vital capacity (the amount of air that can be forcibly exhaled after a full inspiration); in diffusion and absorption capacities; and in maximum voluntary ventilation and oxygen intake. These changes reduce the efficiency of intake and the transportation of oxygen to organs and muscles.

The coordination and efficiency of both the respiratory and the cardiovascular systems are highly interrelated in determining the physical fitness capacity of a given individual. Unless individuals engage in regular endurance exercise throughout the adult years, by 60 to 75 years of age there may be as much as a 50 percent decrease in physical work capacity from the maximum value attained in early adulthood (Shephard and Sidney, 1979; Smith and Serfass, 1981; Shephard, 1987; Faulkner and White, 1990; Saltin, 1990).

In the absence of training, the cardio-respiratory systems normally function close to their maximum capacity. Hence, the less fit individual has few reserves for emergencies, and during stressful situations fatigue begins earlier and the recovery period is longer. Obviously, these physiological deficiencies can limit the type, intensity, and frequency of some forms of social behavior (sports, physical play with children or grandchildren, walking or hiking, gardening, or shoveling snow).

Summary

Increasing age brings changes in the composition and structure of the body, and there are losses in functional capacity and efficiency at the cellular, organ, and system levels. Some of these changes can be delayed or offset by regular exercise programs. Deficiencies become most apparent under stress, as in physical work, exercise, or reaction to disease or accidents. As with other changes with age, there are differences within and between individuals with respect to the onset and degree of loss in the various systems. Moreover, the impact on behavior of changes in the physiological systems is most profound when deterioration occurs in more than one system at the same time. That is, interacting changes within the central nervous system and the sensory-motor processes are likely more significant for the individual than changes experienced in only one of these systems.

Involvement in Physical Activity by Age

Introduction

Exercise and **physical activity** provide a number of beneficial outcomes for the aging adult. For example, many studies have found a positive relationship between the amount of participation in physical activity at work or play and the level of physical and mental health.[2] Similarly, it has often been demonstrated that there is an inverse relationship between level of physical activity at work or play and mortality rates. Yet, as many studies have indicated, involvement in physical activity declines with age, especially among women and among those with lower levels of formal education. This pattern appears to be virtually universal, although it varies somewhat from nation to nation and from cohort to cohort.

In the following two subsections the pattern of involvement by age in physical activity is described, and some possible explanations for this universal pattern are discussed. (Later, in chapter 12, it will be seen that a similar pattern exists for most nonphysical leisure activities). Once again, it must be remembered that most of the evidence is based on cross-sectional rather than longitudinal or cohort analysis research. Hence, it cannot be definitely determined whether the pattern reflects changes with increasing chronological age, cohort differences, or period effects for particular cohorts.

Patterns of Physical Activity across the Life Cycle

A large number of children in most modernized nations are involved to some degree in institutionalized or informal sport or exercise programs at school or in the community. However, some never become fully socialized into this type of leisure behavior, either because their parents do not place a high value on physical activity, or because they do not have an opportunity to become involved at an early age. In addition, of those who were fully social-ized to incorporate sport or physical activity into their lifestyle at an early age, many are no longer participating by the age of 15 or 16. This withdrawal during adolescence occurs because they no longer enjoy physical recreation, be-cause they develop more salient interests, or because they have been involuntarily removed by adult coaches (who have decided they lack the skill to continue competing at a specific level).

This almost universal pattern of declining involvement in physical recreation begins rela-tively early in life. In fact, in North America it often occurs before individuals have even had an opportunity to adopt physical activity as an integral facet of their leisure lifestyle. Many children have withdrawn from involvement in physical activity because of unpleasant experi-ences in sport programs, because there is no alternative to elite sport for those who are less skilled, because they have experienced failure or loss of identity, because there is an overem-phasis on performance rather than participa-

tion, or because facilities or programs are not available. For those who remain involved past childhood, physical activity may have a lower priority as adolescents search for personal iden-tity, assimilate into the youth culture, and rebel against adult values, including those that advo-cate physical activity or sport as part of a leisure lifestyle.

This pattern of less involvement by succes-sively older cohorts seems to be more pro-nounced among the less educated, among those who have lower incomes, among those who live in rural areas and small towns, among those who are engaged in manual occupations, and among females (especially if they are married and have pre-school-age children). Table 5.1 indicates age differences in the re-ported participation rates of Canadian adults in a variety of forms of physical activity. For most activities, there is a decrease in reported in-volvement after age 64. However, it must be re-membered that those in the 65+ category also include the very old (those over 80). It is inter-esting to note that a higher percentage of older

TABLE 5.1

PARTICIPATION IN THE FIVE MOST POPULARᵃ PHYSICAL RECREATION ACTIVITIES, CANADA, 1988

	Population (000's)	Walking %	Gardening %	Swimming %	Bicycling %	Dancing %
Total	21,709	69	58	46	45	37
Males, All Ages	10,690	62	61	45	46	32
10-14	892	57	34	77	90	25
15-19	1,072	51	40	58	74	38
20-24	1,038	53	34	51	50	40
25-44	4,058	62	66	44	46	31
45-64	2,481	66	77	37	28	32
65+	1,149	77	77	20	20	22
Females, All Ages	11,019	77	55	48	43	42
10-14	823	62	26	87	86	46
15-19	1,006	75	30	70	67	59
20-24	1,062	78	36	63	54	63
25-44	4,103	78	62	50	46	43
45-64	2,473	80	70	30	27	37
65+	1,552	81	57	20	15	15

ᵃ Based on 12-month participation rates.
SOURCE: Campbells' Survey on Well-Being: Canadian Fitness and Lifestyle Research Institute.

adults report being actively involved in walking. In general, a higher percentage of older adults, regardless of activity, report being physically active compared to the percentage reporting for similar surveys conducted in 1976 and 1981.

In summary, active participation in physical activity is inversely proportional to age after adolescence. However, this decline is less prevalent among males, among the better educated, among those with higher incomes, among those who live in medium-sized cities, among those in non-manual occupations, and among those who live in countries where physical activity is highly valued (as in Sweden). Although this pattern of decreasing involvement with age may be slightly less dramatic with each successive cohort that passes age 20, the pattern is of serious social concern to those in the leisure and health care professions. An increasing percentage of the aging population is made up of sedentary adults who, although retired for a longer period of time, may lack the physical capacity to participate in a variety of social and physical activities that should be possible in the later years.

Explanations for Varying Degrees of Involvement by Age Cohorts

Clearly, there are cohort differences in the type and frequency of participation in physical activity. While some of these differences might be accounted for by declining energy reserves, there are also a number of possible sociological and psychological explanations.

First, individual attitudes toward physical activity may be a factor in low participation rates. Because of unpleasant experiences early in life, adults may have a negative attitude toward exercise. This attitude may be reinforced by a belief in stereotypes or myths, namely: that the need for exercise decreases with age; that the elderly do not have, or have lost, the skill to perform most physical activities; that physical activity is dangerous to one's health; and that older adults should 'take it easy' as they age. Even among adults who do exercise, many perceive their current amount of exercise to be beneficial when, in fact, it is often insufficient to develop or maintain adequate fitness levels.

In addition to attitudes, an individual's commitment to a particular form of leisure behavior may influence his or her degree of involvement in exercise or sport programs. If a limited amount of leisure time is available, physical activity may have a low priority relative to more highly valued and established role commitments (the job, a hobby, or the family). Moreover, there are individual differences in the type of role commitments at different stages in the life cycle, particularly with respect to differences by gender, race, age, socioeconomic status, stage in the family life cycle, and nationality. That is, there may be a lack of commitment to physical activity compared to other social roles or leisure activities. In short, the degree of commitment indicates the time, energy, and economic resources that adults are willing to invest in physical activity. If this commitment is a by-product of socialization in the early years, and physical recreation is an integral facet of the lifestyle, then negotiation of role alternatives with respect to physical activity is less likely to occur in later life. Where there is a commitment to physical activity, work, the family, and other leisure roles enter the negotiation process with respect to how time, energy, and economic resources are to be expended.

From the perspective of society, the myth that the older adult is beyond help often discourages the initiation of physical activity programs for the elderly segment of the population. Because of age grading and the creation of normative age criteria, facilities and programs are seldom provided to enable adults to be physically active on a regular basis. 'Acting your age' as an adult, at least for many cohorts, implies that participation in sport or physical activity is not considered to be socially acceptable behavior. These age norms interact with gender-related norms to create greater social barriers for women. However, as Ostrow et al. (1981) noted, age is perceived to be a more potent norm than gender with respect to imposing social barriers to participation in physical activity. This age-based social norm may also lead to a self-fulfilling prophecy or stereotype which implies that the middle years and beyond are sedentary stages of life.

This process of age grading, or ageism, is

facilitated further when physically active role models are not available (McPherson, 1986; Ostrow, 1989). However, the increasing presence in recent years of physically active adults of all ages has resulted in a weakening of the restrictive age norms concerning involvement in physical activity in the middle and later years, for both men and women. Moreover, there is increasing scientific evidence that physical fitness is possible at all ages, and, more important, is beneficial to the physical and mental health of the individual. As a result, 'Master,' 'Veteran' or 'Senior' competitions by age group are now available for a number of sports and physical activities,[3] including competition in the marathon (twenty-six miles). Highlight 5.1 illustrates the type of physical activity and the degree of involvement by a number of older adults.

Another possible explanation for lower levels of participation among current cohorts of older adults is that they have been differentially socialized compared to more recent age cohorts. For any given age cohort (for example, ages 25 to 34), the values, opportunity set, and childhood and adolescent experiences in sport and leisure may have been considerably different from those of another age cohort (for example, ages 55 to 64). For most of those who were 65 years of age and over in the 1980s, the early socialization period featured an average work week of approximately fifty hours, a high value on work and a lower value on play and leisure, few vacations, little education beyond elementary school, and few opportunities to engage in any form of leisure in the late adolescent or early adult years. Moreover, many occupations demanded high levels of physical

---

HIGHLIGHT 5.1

PHYSICALLY ACTIVE OLDER ADULTS AT PLAY

The mass media, given the increased interest in physical activity and sport by the general population, periodically report the accomplishments or unusual athletic feats of aging adults. These individuals, although still exceptions to the norm, serve as exemplars of what can be accomplished in later life, and provide role models for their age peers.

- A 61-year-old potato farmer won the 875 kilometer Sydney to Melbourne (Australia) marathon.
- A 66-year-old, who holds twenty-eight age-group track records, runs 20 miles every other day.
- A 71-year-old cycled 919 miles in 10 consecutive days, including the 12,095 foot Independence Pass to Aspen, Colorado.
- A 72-year-old sophomore on a college tennis team hits 130 practice serves daily, and competes in slalom and giant slalom skiing events in the winter.
- A 77-year-old minister plays 'old-timers' hockey once a week from 11:00 p.m. to 2:00 a.m.
- A 70-year-old ran from Vancouver to Halifax in 134 days, 16 days faster than when he ran the same course at the age of 62.
- In 1983, 16 males (62 to 77 years of age) and 6 females (49 to 70 years of age) bicycled 7,700 kilometers from Victoria, British Columbia, to St. John's, Newfoundland, in 100 days at an average of approximately 90 kilometers per seven-hour day (Mittleman et al., 1989).
- Never physically active before age 65, a 75-year-old woman jogs 9 miles four or five nights a week and conducts aerobics classes three mornings a week for women aged 25 to 45.
- A 60-year-old pole vaulted 10 feet 10 inches at the World Veteran's Games in Eugene, Oregon, in 1989; a 72-year-old won five gold medals, setting two age-group records, in the 1 500, 5 000, and 10 000 meter track events, the 10 kilometer road race, and the cross-country event.
- In July 1989, 3,452 men and women from 55 to 91 years of age competed in the U.S. National Senior Olympics. Three sisters (aged 67, 73 and 77) won three gold, four silver, and five bronze medals.
- Wearing a T-shirt that read The Flying Nun, a 75-year-old nun finished sixth in a 1 500 meter race walk, thereby achieving her goal of winning a ribbon for placing in the top six.

---

strength and endurance, thereby precluding the need for physical activity in the limited leisure time available.

For many in this age cohort, leisure was a time to restore the energy needed for work. Thus, most members of the cohort, especially women, never placed a high value on, or acquired experience with, physical activity during their leisure time. It is easy to understand why, at age 65 and beyond, they report little involvement in physical activity compared to younger cohorts. If longitudinal data were available, it is quite likely that this cohort would have reported low levels of involvement in physical activity at all stages of the life cycle.

Projecting ahead, it might be hypothesized that, except where declining physical ailments inhibit involvement in an activity, adult cohorts will report high levels of involvement in physical activity throughout the adult years, including during retirement. This marked change to a more active lifestyle has occurred for a number of interacting reasons that reflect, in general, a new definition of health, increased knowledge about the benefits of lifelong exercise and active lifestyles, new definitions of aging lifestyles, changing values and norms regarding leisure, and increased opportunities and societal encouragement for adults to play. These changes were initiated by the emergence of six related social movements of the 1970s and 1980s: the 'me' generation and the sexual revolution, which stressed physical appearance; a new perspective on health promotion to ameliorate lifestyle diseases (such as stress, alcohol and drug abuse, obesity); the emergence of the exercise sciences that debunked the myths about the necessity to be inactive or sedentary in middle and later life; the fitness movement; the women's movement; and in the 1980s, the wellness movement (McPherson, 1988). Thus, when we discuss socialization and the patterns of involvement in physical activity over the life cycle, we must recognize that the saliency of physical activity varies by age cohort.

In addition to between-cohort differences, there are also individual differences within a given cohort that are based on gender, class, and education. However, since socialization is a lifelong process, resocialization into a pattern of regular physical activity, while difficult, may

be possible. Physical activity is increasingly becoming a more socially acceptable and desirable leisure activity for adults of all ages, and resocialization in the middle or later years may counteract the tendency toward declining involvement by age.

In summary, the frequency and type of involvement in physical activity begins to decline in late adolescence and continues thereafter. This pattern is more likely to be found among women, the less educated, lower income groups, and rural residents. This trend (with minor variations) is found cross-culturally, although the pattern appears to be more pronounced in North America than in other industrialized societies. While a number of alternative explanations for this pattern of declining involvement by age have been proposed, a definitive explanation is lacking. Nevertheless, it appears that the salient factors involve some combination of inadequate early life socialization and, during the adult years, a lack of opportunity, a lack of commitment for a variety of reasons, a lack of role models, and, because of ageism, the presence of cultural norms that devalue physical activity in adult lifestyles.

Outcomes of Exercise by Age

Physiological and Health Outcomes

Research evidence suggests not only that exercise is beneficial to physical and mental health at all ages, but also that a lack of regular, vigorous exercise may hasten the onset of physiological aging processes.[4] Exercise has the potential to slow or reverse some components of physiological aging, thereby enabling the aging individual to engage in leisure and work activities with greater efficiency, energy, and enjoyment. However, despite this research evidence, a pattern of increasing sedentary lifestyles with age prevails, and few adults are advised by their physicians to engage in exercise.

From the perspective of the individual, an improvement in physical fitness not only increases the likelihood of good health, but it may also lead to a longer period of independence, to a higher quality of life, to a faster and more complete recovery from some diseases, and to increased longevity. More specifically, Paffen-barger et al. (1990:43) report that three hours of weekly exercise may result in 507 days of life gained if this frequency of exercise begins at 40 years of age. Beginning at age 50, 60, or 70, the days gained amount 438, 339, or 161 respectively. Similarly, Shephard (1986) concluded that vigorous physical activity can improve the functional age of the average senior citizen by the equivalent of at least eight years. Thus, not only the quantity of life but also the quality of life can be enhanced by increased levels of physical activity. Shephard (1986:123) suggests that such an enhancement could possibly reduce the number of individuals unable to care for themselves from 30 to 10 percent.

From the societal perspective, a physically active adult population has a higher fitness level. This, in turn, may indirectly lower the cost of health care, because the number of visits to a physician decreases, as well as the number of hospital days per person and per population. Shephard (1986) has argued that the potential reduction in the costs of geriatric institutional care resulting from an increase in physical activity among the elderly could represent a saving of $1.3 billion per annum, or about $792 per citizen over the age of 65. Other societal benefits include decreased absenteeism; increased morale, productivity, and satisfaction on the job; and an enhanced lifestyle, since related behaviors (diet, alcohol, smoking, drugs) are also improved in an active, health-oriented population. Thus, from both an individual and a societal perspective, there appear to be both immediate and long-term benefits to increasing the proportion of adults who are regularly involved in physical activity.

To date, there is considerable evidence concerning the degree of improvement in physical fitness among middle-aged men who participate in graduated and regular endurance exercise programs. While little information is available about adult women, the evidence is accumulating that training outcomes similar to those in the earlier years can be realized. Moreover, adults over 60 can be trained to high levels of fitness and performance by graduated programs of walking, jogging, running, and swimming. Highlight 5.2 identifies some of the possible physiological and health benefits that can be derived from participation in physical activity programs of sufficient intensity.

All of the outcomes listed in highlight 5.2 may be developed or changed, regardless of the degree of physical activity in the earlier years.

HIGHLIGHT 5.2

EXERCISE AND HEALTHY PHYSIOLOGICAL OUTCOMES

- increased blood flow through the capillaries
- increased muscular endurance
- decreased percentage of body fat and a lower body weight
- increased flexibility
- increased cardiovascular endurance
- decreased systemic blood pressure
- less loss of strength with age
- increased and more efficient blood flow from the extremities to the heart
- increased maximal oxygen intake and physical work capacity
- lowered resting and exercising heart rate
- more rapid heart-rate recovery following strenuous exercise
- more rapid oxygen debt repayment following strenuous exercise
- increased utilization of anaerobic energy reserves
- increased neural regulatory control, including faster reaction time

Through adherence to a regular, graduated exercise program, adults in the later years of life can improve their level of physical fitness, thereby slowing the physiological aging process and enhancing their potential for a higher quality of life. It is also possible to train older adults to compete in athletic events, including marathons and distance events in swimming. While Olympic times will not result, the physical benefits of training for the individual may be relatively greater than for the younger Olympic athlete. At a minimum, even regular low-intensity activity can have major positive health consequences for the elderly (Haskell et al., 1985; Mason and Powell, 1985; Hagberg, 1989).

Psychological and Social Outcomes

Many claims have been made concerning the impact of exercise on mental health. However, compared to the physiological area there is much less evidence concerning the psychological and social outcomes of exercise programs and their impact on the mental health of adults (Taylor et al., 1985; Morgan and Goldston, 1987; Berger, 1989; Brown, 1990). While a large number of studies have examined the relationship between personality traits and involvement in sport or exercise programs, relatively few have analyzed the specific psychological or social benefits of participation in an exercise program. Those studies that have attempted to determine the psychological or social changes that accompany exercise have reported that there is an increased sense of well-being, a relief of tension, a decline in anxiety, enhanced cognitive performance, greater self-confidence, greater emotional stability, less depression, an improved self-concept, and an improved body-image.

While a number of studies have found a moderate relationship between involvement in physical activity and mental health, a satisfactory explanation for these outcomes is lacking partly because of methodological issues. For example, there are few longitudinal studies, which are needed to distinguish temporary mood changes from more permanent outcomes. Secondly, there are few well-designed experimental investigations with good external and internal validly (Brown, 1990:609). As a result, the underlying causal mechanisms in the observed relationships between exercise, physical fitness, and mental health in the population at large are not fully understood. Finally, psychological changes may be dependent on a high degree of motivation and favorable attitudes by the individual toward exercise and physical activity. For this reason it is important to develop an early commitment to physical activity so that it is incorporated into the adult lifestyle, rather than being a forced remedy reluctantly adopted to retard the aging process as the level of physical or mental health deteriorates.

AGING AND THE MOTOR AND SENSORY SYSTEMS

Introduction

In the previous section it was briefly noted that changes in the central nervous system occur with increasing chronological age. The most noticeable of these changes is a general slowing of motor, cognitive, and sensory processes. A number of alternative explanations for this observable phenomenon of 'slowing' have been proposed, including loss of neurons, which are not replaced; decrease in size and weight of the brain; diseases such as manic-depressive psychosis, coronary heart disease, strokes, or depression; changes in neural impulse transmission; hormonal changes; oxygen deficiency resulting from cardiovascular disease or changes in fitness; changes in some or all of the sequential stages in information processing; or loss of motivation or concentration.

Regardless of the cause or causes, there does appear to be a general decline in behavioral speed that is readily observed in psychomotor performance, in cognitive tasks, and in sensory and perceptual processes. This pattern is compounded when the required behavior becomes more complex. This occurs in abstract reasoning or when making rapid decisions while performing a motor task, such as in sport events, industrial jobs, or driving a car. This observable slowing can have a direct impact on a number of specific social behaviors and can lead to some characteristic behavioral reactions, many of which become generalized as stereotypes of the aged. For example, with advancing age there may be a slowing of speed, especially in complex tasks or movements, and a sacrifice of speed for accuracy. This **cautiousness**, a generalized tendency to respond slowly or not at all because of the possible consequences of a mistake, occurs in many decision-making situations.

For many years it was suggested that this pattern of cautiousness was the result of older people being more rigid and conservative, or becoming more so with advancing age; but recent evidence suggests that they become more cautious in order to avoid mistakes. That is, cautiousness is a learned behavior in reaction to a neurobiological slowness. Regardless of the underlying mechanism, this behavioral slowing can offset the chances of survival when fast reaction is required (as in a traffic situation). It may also limit complex thinking, because the mediating processes slow to the point where some of the elements, or even the goal of the task, may be forgotten. The following subsections describe some of the motor and sensory changes that occur with age, and examine their impact on individual behavior, attitudes, social interaction, and interaction with the environment.

Motor Performance

Motor performance in a multitude of daily tasks (on the job, at home, while driving, or at leisure) depends on a complex process that involves perceiving and evaluating information from the sensory organs, storing and processing this information, and responding through the voluntary muscles.[5] The most significant changes in motor performance with age are a loss of speed in decision making and a concomitant increase in reaction time. These changes are most evident when a complex decision is required and when the individual must respond rapidly. This loss is compounded if the situation is stressful (such as driving under dangerous conditions, or writing a test with implications for present or future employment).

Reaction time, which is the period from perception of a stimulus to reaction, is a com-

plex phenomenon and not easily understood. A decreased reaction time has been explained as a physical problem resulting from a number of possible physiological processes. These include an inevitable decline in signal strength as neurons and nerve cells die; an increase in reflex time for skeletal muscles; a loss of efficiency in central processing mechanisms wherein more time is required to monitor incoming signals; and a general deterioration in the sensorimotor mechanisms. Cerella et al. (1980:332) state that more complex information-processing tasks result in even greater performance decrements as one grows older. They suggest that this decrement involves two levels – a slight slowing of reaction time on sensorimotor tasks and a more severe slowing on tasks that involve mental processing. However, there are individual differences and this physical decline may not be inevitable. Moreover, an improvement in aerobic fitness may enhance the performance of daily activities, including cognitive functions (Bashore, 1990).

A loss of reaction time can be offset by changes in the strategy of performance, by practice, and by a high motivation to achieve at the required task. The most apparent change in strategy involves spending more time monitoring the input stimuli before a response is made. For example, the elderly may become more cautious and demonstrate a desire for accuracy rather than speed in performance. This suggests that learning and practice of a task may offset the effects of slower reaction times, although the evidence that practice reduces reaction time is equivocal. However, not all situations permit unlimited reaction time and errors may result if sufficient time is not available. As Welford (1958:491) notes, the increase in traffic violations and in road and industrial accidents with age is attributed more to a slowing of the decision-making processes than to sensory or motor impairment. With unlimited time to perform a task, older people will perform about as well as they did when they were younger. In fact, with unlimited time to monitor stimuli, the older person may demonstrate greater accuracy than a younger person.

Given that this slowing appears to be a universal and to some extent an inevitable phenomenon, how does it influence social behavior? If a job demands speed in decision making and in performance, then the older worker may be somewhat handicapped, more so than if the job requires merely physical strength. Although speed and accuracy in work may level off or decline slightly with age, experience can compensate for the onset of slowness. Of those who cannot continue to perform, many voluntarily or involuntarily leave the job. This may create problems of unemployability, a loss of prestige, and a lower level of income because of a loss of seniority or a shift to a lower occupational level.

In the social domain, a slowing of reaction time and decision making, especially if accompanied by some of the sensory changes noted in the next section, may reduce the frequency, quality, and type of interaction with others and with the environment. That is, perception of the social world may change, and individuals may be perceived by others to be slow, old, or incompetent. This may lead to less social interaction and further sensory deprivation, resulting in emotional and behavioral problems such as loneliness, isolation, depression, and decreased mobility. In short, in situations where a fast reaction time is essential, most older people do not perform as well as they did when younger. This slowing, in turn, may directly or indirectly influence the frequency and quality of social interaction.

Sensory Processes

Introduction

In order to interact with the physical environment and with other people, an individual must be able to send and receive information. This ability depends largely on sensory receptors, which have a minimum threshold that permits information to be received and transmitted to the brain. As one ages, this threshold increases and greater stimulation is needed in order to send information to the brain (Corso, 1981, 1987; Abramson and Lovas, 1988; MacRae, 1989).

This subsection examines the impact on the individual of changes with age in the threshold and function of the major sensory receptors and processors. These changes in efficiency may reduce the quality and quantity of information available to the organism. If the impairment is not severe, the organism may be able to compensate for the loss by a variety of means. Some of these mechanisms include using a different sense modality to a greater extent (lip reading to compensate for hearing impairment), intensifying (with a hearing aid) or correcting (with eyeglasses) the stimulus, and using experience to predict or identify the stimulus (knowing the shape of a stop sign). If two senses decline simultaneously, as vision and hearing often do late in life, the individual may be seriously limited in job performance, mobility, or general social interaction.

While many of the ramifications of sensory losses may appear obvious, the impact of these changes on the individual must be recognized by others if we are to assist older individuals to continue a lifelong pattern of meaningful social relationships. There are individual differences in the age of onset, and in the severity of and reaction to these losses. By recognizing these differences, we are less likely to apply myths and stereotypes to all elderly persons.

Vision

After middle age, gradual structural and functional changes in the eye may have an impact on social behavior (Kline and Schieber, 1985; Kosnik et al., 1988; Fozard, 1990). These changes include a thickening of the lens and a decrease in the diameter of the pupil, both of which limit the amount of light reaching the retina; less flexibility in the lens (**presbyopia**), which decreases the ability to focus on objects at varying distances; a decrease in threshold adaptation to darkness, glare, and rapidly changing light levels; and a yellowing of the lens that filters out green, blue, and violet at the shorter wave-length end of the spectrum. In addition, loss or impairment of vision may be experienced by persons suffering from glaucoma (less than 5 percent of the population) or from some degree of cataract development (as much as 60 percent of the aged population).

As a result of these changes, an individual may require greater light intensity for reading and working, and may experience difficulty in adapting to changes in illumination when driving at dusk or moving from well-lit to darkened areas, and may be unable to thread a needle except directly under a bright light. Some may also have difficulty reading road signs because of the glare in bright daylight or snow, or they may have difficulty reading a menu in a dimly lit restaurant. Others may be unable to perceive blue, green, and violet tones in the spectrum, and therefore they may have difficulty coordinating clothing colors or appreciating art or color television. While none of these changes are totally disabling, they can create problems and annoyances in daily living. For example, loss of color perception may influence aesthetic enjoyment of life; decreased visual acuity may prevent driving at night, or at all, thereby limiting mobility and increasing dependence on others.

Although visual losses (except in the extreme case of blindness) interfere less with social interaction than do hearing losses, conditions should be improved as much as possible in order to increase efficiency on the job, and to create a safer and more enjoyable environment elsewhere. In addition, living environments need to be redesigned (for example, with increased illumination, reduced glare, larger lettering on signs and in books). In this way, the environment will be safer for older adults, they will be more efficient in processing information at home and at work, and they will maintain a greater interest in themselves and others.

Audition

Along with vision, the auditory system is a major mode of receiving information from the environment. However, unlike visual problems that can be observed and more easily corrected, auditory impairment is less noticeable to oneself and to others. The older person may be unaware of an auditory deficit, and this may result in communication problems. A major hearing problem is the progressive inability to hear higher frequency sounds in music and speech (**presbycusis**). This impairment, caused by the loss of fine hair cells in the inner ear, appears after about the age of 50 and is experienced more frequently by men, especially those who have had long exposure to industrial noise (Corso, 1981, 1987; Olsho et al., 1985; Fozard, 1990). As a result of this impairment the individual may have difficulty hearing certain consonants during conversation, especially when

background noise is present (such as a radio, a television, at parties, in crowds). The speaker may have to repeat the conversation or shout, thereby making the listener self-conscious and less likely to seek out or enjoy social interaction.

A hearing impairment may affect performance on the job, and the ability to interact safely and efficiently with the environment (for example, if one is unable to hear doorbells, telephones, or car horns). Presbycusis can create stress in social situations, inhibit communication, decrease the quality of social interaction, decrease the enjoyment of life (for example, if one misses the punchline in jokes), cause fear and embarrassment, and lead to depression. In some situations, the elderly person may avoid social events. Thus, what began as a natural hearing loss may lead to social isolation. While hearing aids may provide partial compensation for hearing losses, the individual must resort to other means such as facing the speaker, lip reading, interpreting nonverbal communication (facial and hand gestures), and overcoming the fear and embarrassment of asking for information to be repeated. If these compensating mechanisms are not used, hearing-impaired individuals run the risk of being labeled as antisocial if they do not respond to the spoken word. They may also misinterpret instructions or statements, and if their subsequent behavior is different from that expected, they may be labeled as senile or stubborn or as unable or unwilling to learn.

Taste, Smell, Pain, and Touch

By about the age of 60, there is a higher taste threshold (Weiffenbach et al., 1982; Spitzer, 1988; Bartoshuk and Weiffenbach, 1990) for all four taste sensations; salt, sweet, bitter, and sour. In addition, there is a decreased saliva flow and a decrease in the number of taste buds (Engen, 1977). These changes may be compounded by smoking and by wearing dentures. Furthermore, a decline in absolute sensitivity to olfactory stimulation (ability to detect or identify odors) occurs with age (Schiffman, 1979; Corso, 1981; Van Toller et al., 1985). Therefore, when changes in taste and smell decline concurrently, there may be a decrease in food intake, a decline in nutrition, and a loss of enjoyment in eating. For example, although

Moore et al. (1982) found a minimal loss of sensitivity with age in sucrose taste thresholds, the thresholds were highly variable among the elderly. They suggested that those who experience a decline in sucrose threshold either might lose interest in certain foods or might compensate for the loss in sensitivity by greatly increasing their level of sucrose intake by eating foods with a high sugar content. Either of these adaptations may lead to dietary or medical problems.

In severe losses of taste and smell the individual may be unable to taste spoiled foods or to smell dangerous odors (natural gas, propane, smoke). Moreover, some elderly persons not only have both a poor sense of smell and taste, but also have weaker cognitive tools to identify odors. In short, changes in taste and smell may result in mealtime no longer being an enjoyable social or culinary experience. In addition, a person who is widowed and living alone may be less inclined to prepare food, especially if it no longer provides pleasure. This may lead to an improper or deficient diet, and to the onset of medical problems.

There appears to be a loss of sensitivity in touch and to vibration in some, but not all, parts of the body with advancing age (Kenshalo, 1977; Corso, 1981). Indeed, some older persons have singed their fingers on a hot stove and not noticed the damage. Although complaints about pain seem to increase with age, the research evidence is unclear about whether pain thresholds remain constant or decrease with age (Kenshalo, 1977; Harkins and Warner, 1980). Part of this confusion stems from a failure to separate the physiological variable of the pain threshold from the social and psychological elements of pain. It is not known whether observed age differences in pain perception are related to the processing capacity of the central nervous system, to changes in the peripheral receptors, to the source of the pain, to the personality and motivation of the person experiencing the pain, to changes in the cognitive processes interpreting the source and nature of the pain, or to a combination of some or all of these factors.

While pain thresholds may or may not increase with age, it appears that pain tolerance is at least partially related to motivational and cognitive factors; hence, no valid conclusions

can be drawn concerning changes in pain threshold or pain tolerance with age. Some older persons may experience pain and may frequently report the presence of pain; others may experience pain but stoically live with it and not report its presence; others will not experience pain to any greater extent than younger people. For some, the social situation, the source of the pain, and the motivational and cognitive processes may influence whether pain is perceived or reported. Some individuals may complain even about minimal levels of pain in order to receive attention from others, particularly from their adult children. Others will never complain in fear that they will be seen as unable to care for themselves.

Summary

Physiological changes with age in the sensory processes can have behavioral manifestations for the older person (Corso, 1981:201-19). A reduction in the efficiency of the sense modalities reduces the quantity and quality of information available. This in turn may reduce the ability and willingness of the individual to interact with the environment and with other people. In most cases the impairments experienced by the elderly are not severe, and the individual is able to compensate for the deficit through various forms of behavioral modification or rehabilitation (Corso, 1981:219-25).

AGING AND PHYSICAL AND MENTAL HEALTH

Introduction

For many years interest in **health** and aging was based on a 'medical model,' wherein the focus was primarily on the incidence, cause, treatment, and medical response to illness or disease among the elderly. More recently, however, a 'functional model' to study health and aging has been used.[6] This new approach has sought to describe and explain how people prevent or cope with age-related chronic disabilities, how acute and chronic illnesses influence social behavior, and how the older person functions socially and psychologically when faced with increasing dependency because of physical or mental illness. This interest has resulted in a focus on the psychological and social limitations and capacities related to the objective state of health; on the economic and social aspects of health care; on the impact of the perceived and the objective state of health on participation in such domains as the family, work, and leisure; and on the demand for and the utilization of health care in later life.

One outcome of this research has been the debunking of the myth that the elderly are frail and sickly, and that they are incapable of performing tasks or participating in social life. Most are not sick. They are healthy, active, and mentally alert. This does not imply, however, that health is not a central concern for the elderly and a major factor in their quality of life. Rather, despite increasing longevity, changing social norms, and improved and more readily accessible health care, the physical, mental, and social well-being of the aging adult is intimately related to his or her personal reaction to the onset of acute and chronic disease and to the onset of varying degrees of disability. The sections that follow discuss the relationship between social participation and such health-related factors as acute illness, chronic illness, long-term disabilities, perceived state of health, utilization of the health care system, nutrition, sexuality, drug abuse, stress, and mental disorders.

It must be reiterated that the elderly are not a homogeneous group with respect to physical or mental health. Rather, there is a wide range of individual differences in the onset and severity of acute and chronic conditions, in the availability of and access to health care, and in the physical, social, emotional, and cognitive reactions to varying degrees of declining health. Some of these differences reflect former and current lifestyles, as well as environmental factors (for example, rural versus urban residence; pollution; amount of exercise or use of alcohol, tobacco, or drugs; or nutrition). Others are more directly related to age cohort, to heredity, and to achieved or ascribed characteristics such as race, ethnicity, gender, level of educational attainment, socioeconomic status, marital status, and income. For example, there are gender differences in both reported and

diagnosed health. As Gee and Kimball (1987:31) note, 'Women get sick but men die.' Women are more likely to report a greater number of health problems than men. Moreover, women are more frequent users of health care services, drugs, and institutions. Specifically, women have more days of restricted activity, more days of bed confinement, and more visits to physicians (Chappell et al., 1986:44-45; Gee and Kimball, 1987:29-33).

Health is not just a biological or medical concern, but also a significant personal and social concern. For example, with declining health, individuals may lose their independence, lose social roles, become isolated, experience economic hardship, be labeled or stigmatized (as 'frail,' 'sick,' 'disabled,' or 'obsolete'), change their self-perception, and be institutionalized. From the perspective of society, declining health leads to absenteeism, loss of productivity, and loss of experienced workers when disability forces an early retirement. In addition, poor health among the elderly increases the dependency ratio, and the accompanying economic burden must be absorbed by those in the labor force. This is turn increases the cost of health care in the nation. An age-related decline in health has an impact on both the individual and the society. Social scientists must be aware of the relationships between health, behavior, and aging, and must include personal health status as an independent and intervening variable when studying the social process of aging.

Physical Health, Aging, and Behavior

Acute and Chronic Conditions[7]

The health of the elderly population is improving in most industrialized societies. This improvement has occurred because of advancements in lifelong nutrition, environmental and housing conditions, health standards, and health care. Although many elderly persons report experiencing symptoms of one or more chronic illnesses, only about 20 percent of the elderly population experience major activity limitations that require assistance with activities of daily living (Chappell et al., 1986:37). However, activity restriction does increase with age, and women are more likely to be restricted in the performance of activities (Wilkins and Adams, 1983). When acute conditions occur among the elderly, they may require a longer period of recovery, and when combined with a chronic illness, may sap the physical or mental reserves of the elderly individual. The onset of an apparently minor acute illness can, subsequently, have major consequences for the general health and adaptation of the older person.

In rank order, the most prevalent chronic conditions that affect the physical health of older persons are arthritis, hypertension, limb and joint disorders, heart disease, and hearing disorders (Simmons-Tropea and Osborn, 1987). Of these, arthritis, limb and joint disorders, and hearing disorders do not cause death, but they can decrease the quality of life. The major causes of death are coronary heart disease, cancer, and strokes. The poor, the nonwhite, and those with lower levels of education are more susceptible to poor health, particularly as they age. These subcultural differences seem to be related to nutritional problems, to lifestyle, to a lack of knowledge about health care, to inferior environmental conditions at work and in the home, and to a lack of access to medical care. While some of these subcultural conditions may be present for some of the elderly population, they have the greatest impact on those for whom these conditions have been present throughout the life cycle.

The impact on the individual of acute and chronic diseases or illnesses varies greatly, depending on the severity and duration of the illness, combined with the coping reaction of the individual. Most acute illnesses involve only temporary restrictions or changes in lifestyle. However, chronic conditions, which can range from minor aches and pains to long-term physical or mental disability, can severely restrict social interaction, mobility, job performance, the ability to care for oneself, and the fulfilling of family responsibilities. In addition, when activity restriction becomes severe, a loss of independence may increase the stress on caregivers (see chapter 10).

A discouraging medical prognosis can dramatically alter lifestyles in the later years. A person's reaction to such a prognosis is a social and psychological process. This reaction may be positive, and involve preventing the chronic condition from changing a lifestyle to any appreciable degree; or it may be negative, and lead to 'giving up the fight to live,' because of an inability to tolerate pain, to be patient during the recovery period, to accept the changing self-image, to become dependent on others, or to cope with the physical and mental stress associated with the ailment. Thus, the social reaction can range from little or no change in lifestyle, to some minor restrictions, to some degree of disability, to loss of independence, and, ultimately, to institutionalization.

In summary, despite a greater probability of chronic health problems with age, most older people function reasonably well in their daily activities. However, the onset of chronic and acute conditions does in some cases lead to a change in patterns of social participation. Some people may become increasingly or totally dependent on others, thereby severely curtailing their independence and mobility. Whether these changes occur, and to what degree, depends to a great extent on past and current personal styles of adapting and coping with physical stress, and on the level of social support and assistance from significant others in the family and community.

Perception of Health and Social Behavior

Despite the presence of chronic ailments, over 60 percent of the elderly subjectively report that their health is good or excellent. These self-perceptions correlate highly with objective physiological and medical evaluations. The self-ratings are more likely to be favorable for those with higher levels of income and educational attainment, and for men.

There appears to be a relationship between a positive view of one's health and higher levels of social involvement. For example, Graney and Zimmerman (1980) found that favorable self-reports of health were positively related to a higher degree of involvement in general activity, sexual activity, hobbies, clubs, and voluntary organizations. In short, adaptive behavior to changing health is influenced by self-perception. Just as age is socially defined, so too may health status be socially defined by the individual. If the personal and social meanings of the symptoms portray a composite picture of 'functional adequacy' (Hickey, 1980:52), then perceived health status will be reported as good or excellent. This perception is influenced by the level of health expectation for persons of a particular chronological age.

Perceived health status is also influenced by the reaction of significant others, particularly by those in the medical profession. At present, health care systems, although used more by the elderly than the young, are primarily designed to treat acute rather than chronic or degenerative diseases. In addition, few medical personnel at any level are trained for, or specialize in, the care of older patients. Moreover, some health care personnel have negative attitudes about working with elderly patients. If this negative attitude is perceived by elderly patients (for example, if medical personnel appear to avoid them or to show little interest in their condition), they may come to view their situation as hopeless.

Finally, quality and availability of medical care for the elderly varies greatly from nation to nation and from community to community. For example, rural areas or the central cores of large cities may lack physicians and facilities to adequately serve the predominant clientele in the area, namely, the elderly. In short, it appears that medical and sociocultural factors interact to influence both actual and perceived health. A positive perception of health may be a significant factor in the social and psychological adjustment of chronically or acutely ill individuals.

Availability, Demand for, and Utilization of Formal Health Care Services

Varying levels of access to physicians, hospitals, or home care are available to the elderly. The degree of availability varies by social policies, by economic constraints, by geographical location, and by social philosophy. For example, in highly or totally socialized nations, universal access to health care is often an underlying philosophy. In this situation (for example, in Canada), the elderly have free access to most types of health care (Schwenger, 1987). However, in reality, not all communities have the same range or quality of health care facilities or personnel. In remote communities, the demand

for health care services may not be met because a hospital, a particular machine, or a specialist is not available.

While it is a commonly held belief that aging dramatically increases the consumption of all types of health care, this is not supported by usage statistics. Roos et al. (1984), using data from the Manitoba Longitudinal Study on Aging, found that less than 25 percent of the elderly population were hospitalized in any given year; that, over a five-year period, 42 percent were never admitted to a hospital; and that 5 percent of those hospitalized consumed 59 percent of the hospital days in a one-year period. In terms of physician visits, those 65 years of age and over reported only 0.9 percent and 1.7 percent more visits per year than those 45 to 64 years of age and those 25 to 44 years of age respectively. Thus, the use of physicians by the elderly was only slightly higher than that reported by other age groups.

A variety of predisposing (age, gender, beliefs, attitudes, ethnicity), enabling (lack of spouse or family, rural residence, availability of health care personnel or facilities), and need (subjective perceptions and objective diagnoses) factors can influence the rate of health care utilization by the elderly (Anderson and Newman, 1973). Most studies indicate that need factors (decreased level of functioning) are most important in determining whether physicians or hospital services will be used by the elderly (Chappell et al., 1986; Chappell and Blandford, 1987). However, as we learned earlier, some members of some ethnic groups may not seek medical help because of differing cultural beliefs about health care, because of lack of knowledge about the availability of services, or because of language barriers when they do seek assistance (MacLean et al., 1988). Similarly, the elderly living in remote communities may also not seek medical care, because to do so may necessitate extensive travel to another community. Moreover, hospital admission rates are higher for rural residents (Shapiro and Roos, 1984). Thus, even though universal access prevails in principle, some of those most in need may not be served adequately or fully by the health care system.

Wellness and Health Promotion

Wellness, a new concept for healthy living, emerged as a cultural product in the 1980s. This concept proposes that individuals make personal decisions to promote and adhere to an active and healthy lifestyle. Some of the components of wellness include: changing societal norms about leisure lifestyles (for example, reduce drug and alcohol use, increase physical fitness); accepting self-responsibility for personal health; wise and judicious use of the medical care system; nutritional awareness and adherence to balanced, low-cholesterol diets; and an ability to recognize, manage, and reduce stress and boredom (Ardell, 1986). The onset of the wellness movement has coincided with an increased emphasis on health promotion, including programs by and for seniors (Fedorak and Griffin, 1986).

Since it is never too late to initiate lifestyle changes in terms of diet, smoking cessation, drug or alcohol use, physical fitness, or stress management, the wellness approach is being adopted by middle-aged and elderly adults. This has been fostered by popular periodicals featuring articles on how to adjust one's lifestyle in later life to enhance the quality of life. Consequently, gerontology practitioners need to be better prepared to meet the needs of future and current cohorts of older adults who are more active, more health-conscious, and more knowledgeable and discriminating in the use of health care modalities (such as drugs, diet).

Nutrition

Although many life-long dietary habits prevail, changes in diet may occur in the later years for physiological reasons, such as denture problems, diminished senses of taste and smell, and problems in digesting certain foods. In addition, a number of situational factors (such as retirement, widowhood, or lack of income) may also intervene to change the diet of an elderly person, thereby leading to potential health or social problems.[8]

Although the individual nutritional needs of older persons can vary greatly according to their biochemical processes and energy expenditure patterns, a balanced diet is essential. Yet older people may dislike preparing meals and eating alone; they may lack knowledge about

food preparation and planning balanced meals (e.g., widowers), they may have insufficient income to pay for essential foods, especially during times of inflation; they may be less mobile and therefore unable to shop; and they may be susceptible to fad diets that are advertised as nutritious and efficient.

On the positive side, an increased awareness of health (the wellness concept) can lead to the adoption of nutritious, healthful eating habits. This approach can be enhanced by paying attention to marketing and media tips about what foods to consume (for example, fish, vegetables, yogurt) for healthful living, and by increased discussion with others about food selection and preparation (quantity, variety, quality). Finally, adherence to long-term nutritional habits (for example, consuming water, milk and dairy products) may minimize age-related loss of tissue function and thereby delay or limit the onset of chronic ailments such as osteoporosis. Changes in eating habits may result in lower energy reserves or greater susceptibility to illness. It is for this reason that many community service agencies now make an effort to monitor the nutritional status of elderly people, especially the very old who live alone. One of the most successful programs is 'meals-on-wheels,' where at least one nutritious hot meal per day is delivered to the home by a volunteer. In addition, the volunteer usually visits with the recipient while the meal is eaten. In this way the mealtime provides a setting for social interaction.

Drug Use, Misuse, and Abuse

Although the use of drugs to maintain or enhance the health, comfort, and activity levels of elderly adults has become more prevalent, accurate statistics on the use of both prescription drugs and over-the-counter drugs are difficult to obtain.[9] Tuominen (1988) reports that the elderly consume 20 to 30 percent of prescribed drugs; Vestal and Dawson (1985) estimate that in the United States, those over 65 spend over $3 billion per year on prescription and nonprescription drugs, which is approximately 20 to 25 percent of the total national expenditure for drugs. Moreover, both the number and the type of medications used increase with age, and multiple use is high. For example, the 1981 Canada Health Survey found that 13 percent of men and 25 percent of women over 65 years of age take three *different* drugs at the same time (Canada Health Survey, 1981). Finally, in general, women consume more drugs than men, partly because they consult doctors more frequently. As a result of this increasing usage, the misuse or abuse of drugs among the elderly is increasingly being reported by relatives, health care workers, and social workers. In extreme cases, abuse or misuse is highlighted by the media when the outcome leads to sudden hospitalization or death.

As we age, the physiological and anatomical changes we experience alter the rate and type of drug movement within the body. As a result, we become more sensitive to some drugs, and the dosage of some drugs needs to be reduced. Since this is known and accounted for in prescribing practices, such increased sensitivity is not the cause of most adverse drug reactions in later life. Rather, the misuse and abuse is caused by a variety of personal and societal factors. These include: more chronic illness and more reported perceived health problems for which a known drug can be used as treatment; the prescribing practices of a physician to parallel the availability of new drugs; increased availability of over-the-counter drugs at more drugstores; an increasing number of drug plans that reduce or eliminate the cost of drugs; and, to make the elderly more aware of drug alternatives, the advertising of wonder drugs in magazines.

The misuse or abuse of drugs may be deliberate or unintentional, depending on the personality and the situation of a given elderly person. Some frequently reported examples of under- or overcompliance include: hoarding drugs and using drugs beyond the expiry date; purchasing an extra supply of drugs after receiving a prescription from more than one physician; using a mixture of prescribed and over-the-counter drugs without consulting a physician or a pharmacist; exchanging drugs with, and using drugs prescribed for, another person; misinterpreting the instructions on a label; not using prescribed drugs, because of an inability to open the container or to understand instructions; and failing to consume drugs on schedule or with appropriate liquids or foods.

Other elderly persons may engage in willful non-compliance either by not having a prescription filled, or by consciously deciding not to consume one or more drugs. This latter situation may arise when such adverse drug reactions as memory loss, sleepiness, agitation, confusion, or new pains occur.

The problem of drug misuse is often attributed to the behavior of the elderly person; however, physicians, pharmacists, and relatives must bear some of the responsibility. Physicians need to examine their prescribing practices carefully, especially when a patient makes repeated visits. They also need to carefully consider the possible side or interaction effects when multiple drug usage occurs, and to check that the patient is using the appropriate prescription in the appropriate way. Pharmacists need to provide labels with the drug name and instructions in large type, and to make sure that the elderly person can open the container. More importantly, they should try to monitor the use of over-the-counter drugs with prescription drugs by counseling and educating the elderly customer about possible adverse side effects of single or multiple drug use. Finally, relatives who live with an older person should provide assistance and monitoring in the use and scheduling of medication routines.

Sexuality

Although myths still persist that sexual interaction between elderly persons is harmful and unacceptable, current evidence suggests that many men and women are physiologically capable of engaging in sex beyond 80 years of age. In fact, psychological or social problems (fear of failure, fear of sexual inadequacy, anxiety about dating) and lack of opportunity (especially for older women or for those living in nursing homes) rather than biological problems are the more common reasons for not engaging in sexual activity in later life (Starr, 1985). As an illustration of one reaction to the assumed inevitability of impotence among older men, one of the older female respondents in the Starr and Weiner (1981) survey of 800 older adults in the United States responded that 'her husband was so responsive to sexual stimuli that the mere mention of the word "impotence" could give him an erection' (Starr, 1985:102).

Because sex among the elderly was often considered a taboo subject, it was difficult to obtain sufficient respondents for surveys, or to obtain valid and reliable information from the few respondents who did participate. Thus, it is not surprising that low levels of sexual activity were reported prior to the 1970s.

With the onset of the sexual revolution in the late 1960s, the study of the sexual interests, needs, and behavior of older adults increased dramatically.[10] As a result of these studies, a picture now emerges of considerable sexual behavior in the later years. This likely reflects a cohort effect (healthier adults, more open attitudes toward sex) and an increased honesty and openness in response to questions about sexuality. More frank responses have also been generated by moving away from a focus on the frequency of sexual activity to a more qualitative focus on the meaning and the type of sexual feelings experienced in later life. For example, a 69-year-old woman in the Starr and Weiner (1981:16) study stated that 'sex is much more enjoyable and satisfying now. It used to be more frequent, but each time lasts longer and has much greater sensory impact during climax for both of us.' As Thomas (1982) stressed, there is a need to ask and listen to what sexuality means to the elderly person, rather than assume that it is like an essential 'vitamin, for which there is a daily or weekly minimum requirement!'

It is still difficult to determine accurately how many older adults engage in heterosexual or homosexual behavior, with what meaning, and how frequently, because many refuse to discuss the topic. Nevertheless, cultural norms and attitudes are changing, with a concomitant increase in the number of older adults who report that they are sexually active. However, because of social, cultural, or psychological factors, there are wide individual differences in the meaning, type, and frequency of sexual behavior. Those most likely to be active are those in good physical health, those who have a high sense of esteem or self-identity, those who are happily married, those who have continued a high level of sexual activity throughout adulthood, and those who live independently in a noninstitutionalized setting. In fact, a current dilemma faced by nursing-home personnel is whether and how to provide for the sexual needs of older residents.

In summary, the image of the asexual older adult is no longer valid. Older people, given current societal attitudes toward sex, given a reasonable level of health, and given the opportunity, are more open and experimenting, and find sex to be an enjoyable and acceptable activity. However, where fear of sexual inadequacy prevails, such as for men when the erectile response slows, or for widowed women who are anxious about dating again, any social contact with members of the opposite sex may be avoided, thereby eliminating the opportunity for heterosexual activity. As you will see in highlight 9.4, some older adults actively seek social companions. Others actively seek information about dating and relationship problems not unlike that sought by teenagers awakening to their own sexuality. This reawakening for some older adults generates questions on talk shows and at senior citizen centers. For example, Starr (1985:122) reports that the following questions have been asked by seniors (the age of the questioner is in parentheses):

- How do you say no to a man who just keeps coming on? (71)
- All these men want is to check right into a motel. How do you handle that? (68)
- My wife doesn't like sex any more. She thinks I'm crazy because I want sex three times a week. What do you advise? (73)
- Do you think it's okay to bring a man into my house on the first date? (67)

In order to provide valid empirical knowledge as well as practical advice to the sexually active senior, more research on this topic is urgently needed in the years ahead.

Mental Health, Aging, and Behavior

Contrary to the prevailing myth, the majority of old people do not experience chronic brain damage,[11] nor are they mentally ill. In fact, it has been estimated that only about 15 percent[12] of the North American population over 65 experience any form of diagnosed **mental illness**, with less than 5 percent of these being institutionalized. Nevertheless, this time of life can represent one of the most difficult periods of mental and emotional adjustment in the life cycle (Birren and Sloane, 1980; Chappell et al, 1986: 37-39; D'Arcy, 1987). This period is more difficult than others because it is compounded by existing lifelong physical and mental concerns that may become more pronounced or salient in old age; because individuals experience a number of potential crises to which they must react (retirement, widowhood, chronic illness or disability, or institutionalization); because it is seen as a time of physical, social, psychological, and emotional loss; and because they may no longer have the support and assistance of personal friends and loved ones during crisis events.

This area of research has been guided by such questions as: Does aging affect mental health? Are the elderly more prone to mental illness than younger age groups? Do the elderly demonstrate more psychological impairment than younger age groups (D'Arcy, 1987)? However, it is difficult to obtain consistent and accurate statistics about mental illness at any age because of inherent weaknesses in the size and representativeness of samples; because of weaknesses in the instruments used to diagnose particular types of illness; and because there are few longitudinal studies that assess the mental health of individuals over a number of years. Furthermore, it is difficult to separate the diagnosis of depression from dementia, since a common symptom is memory impairment. Yet, this is an important distinction to make, in order to prevent inappropriate labeling and treatment. For example, dementia is a product of organic brain disease that is likely to become more prevalent with advancing age. This can lead to severe cognitive impairment for which there is no known treatment (e.g., Alzheimer's disease). Depression, on the other hand, is an affective disorder, associated with stress, which can be treated. However, if untreated or inappropriately treated, a small degree of depression can lead to severe depression and perhaps to suicide (Blazer, 1990).

Some of the risk factors or precipitants of mental illness, which can operate alone or in combination, include: genetic factors, personality, social environment, nutrition, organic deterioration, stressful life events and lack of personal coping strategies or support networks (D'Arcy, 1987). The onset of any of these precipitants, and the inability to cope with any of them, can lead to anxiety or depressive disorders, to psychiatric hospitalization, or to suicide. Since the early 1970s, admission rates for older adults to psychiatric hospitals has declined, and this decline is likely a reflection of better and more available community outpatient services and more services available in nursing homes (D'Arcy, 1987:435). Among older adults, the more common psychiatric diagnoses among men are schizophrenia and personality disorders; women are more likely to experience affective (mood) or neurotic disorders (D'Arcy, 1987:437). In addition, although the elderly experience depression to varying degrees, the incidence does not appear to increase during old age (Chappell et al., 1986:37-39). However, there are gender differences in both the incidence of, and reaction to, depression. Gee and Kimball (1987:42) report that approximately two times as many women as men report being depressed. Whether this reflects the actual rate of depression or the greater propensity of women to seek help or to report feelings remains unclear. It is clear that elderly men have the highest rate of suicide. Statistics Canada reported that, whereas the overall rate in 1986 was 22.8 suicides per 100,000 men, the rate for men over 70 was 34.9 per 100,000. Increasingly, with greater longevity, suicide is becoming a serious problem, especially among the elderly over 80 years of age (Osgood, 1985; Manton et al., 1987).

There are three general categories of **mental health** that pertain to the elderly, and each represents a serious problem for the individual and for society. First, there are temporary, periodic, emotional reactions such as depression, anxiety, fear, and frustration that may result from personal feelings about adjusting to old age. These include a noticeable decline in vision, hearing, or energy that leads to changes in leisure patterns and social interaction. They may also occur in reaction to specific life events such as retirement, the death of a spouse, or the departure of the children from the home. The effect of these events on the individual appears to be exaggerated by poverty, declining physical health or serious illness, and social isolation.

In addition to individual crises, collective crisis events in the community may be more stressful for the elderly than for other age groups (Chiriboga, 1982). For example, widespread poverty or unemployment, or the occurrence of a natural disaster, events that have an impact on the mental health of the total community, may be more traumatic for the elderly, and may lead to temporary or permanent mental health problems. In short, individual or collective crisis events can initiate emotional or mental stress that can lead to anxiety states, depression, and fear.

A second category of mental health problems encountered by the elderly are those labeled as functional disorders, such as schizophrenia, affective psychoses (manic-depressive reactions, or melancholia), psychotic depressive reactions, or paranoid states (irrational fears). These disorders result from a combination of many factors, such as irrational or excessive reactions to crisis events, social isolation after the death of a spouse, or personal reaction to a chronic physical illness. These conditions are also likely to be triggered by an inappropriate emotional reaction to stress related to personal experiences, by long-standing emotional or personality problems, or, by inappropriate individual coping or adapting strategies. These disorders do not involve an impairment of brain function, but they do require treatment and sometimes hospitalization when they lead to inappropriate social or cognitive behavior.

The third category of mental illnesses are organic disorders wherein brain damage occurs, either because of a hardening of the arteries in the brain or because the brain cells atrophy or become diseased (senile dementia). For example, Alzheimer's disease is responsible for about 75 percent of the symptoms characterized by declining memory, judgment, and learning ability. It is also often accompanied by severe personality changes. To date, there is no known cure for this progressive, fatal disease that is thought to result from cell damage in the hippocampus area of the brain cortex. While the progression of some of these organic disorders may be slowed through drug treatment,

ultimately most individuals are no longer able to care for themselves or to interact socially. Hence, institutionalization becomes necessary.

Mental health is greatly influenced by stress (Renner and Birren, 1980). Some individuals seem to be 'stress-prone,' and to be highly susceptible to stress at any age. Moreover, earlier stressors seem to be predictive of later stressors (Chiriboga and Thurnher, 1981). The social or physical environment may also induce stress. Chiriboga and Thurnher (1981) suggest that there are three levels of stressors: the micro, the mini, and the macro. The micro-stressors involve daily occurrences (for example, lost keys, a bottle or can that will not open, running out of shampoo in the shower); the mini-stressors are perceived problems within life events (stress at work) and transitions between events (children leaving home, retirement, loss of job, or widowhood); while the macro-stressors are characterized by major societal events that impinge on the individual, partly as a result of collective stress on the social system (an economic depression, a war, a mass murder, or an earthquake).

It is the ability or lack of ability to cope with stressful events at all three levels that significantly influences mental health in the later years (Chiriboga and Cutler, 1980; Horowitz and Wilner, 1980; McCrae, 1982). In general, it appears that adult women across all age categories are more stressed than men, and are generally less able to cope with the stress. For elderly women, the major sources of stress appear to be the social isolation following widowhood and an inability to adjust to retirement. McCrae (1982) suggests that differences in coping with life events can be examined by the type of stress encountered rather than by age per se. However, he did find that older persons are less likely to employ hostile reactions or escapist fantasies in coping with the stress of life events.

While some individuals strive to avoid stress, others seek stress. In fact, behavioral problems in later life for those with a high need for stimulation may result from boredom and a lack of intellectual or physical stimulation. Unfortunately, very little is known about why changes in life events induce short-term or long-term stressful reactions among some older persons. From what little is known, it appears that women, the less educated, those with lower incomes and socioeconomic status, and members of some minority groups may be more susceptible to stress. Regardless of these subcultural differences (Gutmann, 1980), the mental health needs of the elderly appear to warrant greater attention, since the incidence of elder abuse, and of suicides, alcoholism, and drug abuse among the elderly appears to be increasing in North America.

In summary, the mental and emotional health of the elderly needs to be understood more completely by scientists and better serviced by the health care system. It appears that most mental health problems evolve from the interaction of both environmental and personal factors, which can be compounded by long-lasting personality or physical characteristics that create difficulties in adapting to stressful events later in life. Among the factors that may precipitate an emotional problem are living alone; loss of physical health, which restricts activity and mobility; loss of self-esteem following a heart attack; forced retirement; loss of income; death of a spouse or close friend; marital unhappiness; sickness of a spouse; and a forced change in the place of residence. While any one of these factors may be sufficient to cause an emotional problem, in combination they can be traumatic and lead to functional disorders. For those who are poor, socially isolated, less educated, or in poor health, when a potentially stressful event occurs, the severity of mental illness can be quite pronounced and can lead to clinical depression. As D'Arcy (1987:446) concludes, 'a substantial majority of the aged appear to be mentally healthy and manifest few mental health problems.' However, for those who do manifest symptoms, adequate counseling and treatment are needed to stem the incidence of functional disorders, suicides, alcoholism, and drug abuse among the elderly population.

SUMMARY AND CONCLUSIONS

This chapter has examined the impact on social, emotional, and cognitive behavior of changes with age in physical structure; in physiological, sensory, and motor processes; and in perceived and objective physical and mental health. These changes in the physical systems of the organism affect not only the individual but also how others interact with him or her, and how society reacts to those who lose their independence and mobility. This chapter has discussed, as well, some of the physical, social, and psychological outcomes of regular exercise, adequate nutrition, and stress in the middle and later years of life. Based on the research evidence presented in this chapter, it can be concluded that:

1. After early adulthood, the physical and psychological systems of the human organism become less efficient in perceiving, processing, and reacting to stimuli in the physical and social environment. This loss of efficiency can influence social, emotional, and cognitive behavior in the later years. Moreover, a loss of efficiency can be compounded by declining physical or mental health.

2. There is a variation within and between older individuals in the rate and degree of change in the physical and psychological systems. In effect, most individuals, at least until very late in life, do not experience functional losses that seriously change or influence their social, physical, or cognitive behavior.

3. External visible changes with age may influence how an older individual perceives himself or herself, as well as how others perceive and interact with the individual.

4. After adolescence, the frequency and type of involvement in physical activity during leisure declines with age, especially among women and among those with lower levels of educational attainment.

5. Exercise is beneficial to physical and mental health for persons of all ages. A lack of regular, vigorous exercise may hasten the onset of physiological aging processes.

6. From the perspective of the aging individual, an increase in the level of physical fitness improves physical and

mental health. It may also lead to a faster and more complete recovery from some diseases, to increased longevity, to a longer period of independence, and to a higher quality of life.

7. From the perspective of society, a more physically active adult population may increase productivity and lower the health care costs of a nation.

8. For adults over 60 years of age, high levels of fitness and performance can be achieved through graduated and supervised programs of walking, running, and swimming.

9. With advancing age there is a general slowing of motor, cognitive, and sensory processes. This is normally reflected in a loss of speed in decision making and a concomitant increase in reaction time.

10. Given sufficient motivation, practice, and time to perform a task, older people generally perform about as well as they did when they were younger.

11. Structural and functional changes in vision and audition, especially if they occur at about the same time, may lower the quality of interpersonal interaction, may reduce the quantity and quality of information available to the individual, may lower job performance, and may reduce the ability to interact safely and efficiently with the physical environment.

12. Although most older people function reasonably well in their daily activities, the onset of chronic or long-term acute health conditions may lead to a change in interpersonal interaction and in patterns of participation in various social institutions.

13. The adaptive reaction to a changing health status is influenced by the individual's self-perception of health status, and by the reaction of significant others (if the individual is labeled or perceived as sick, infirm, dependent, or incompetent).

14. Contrary to common belief, the majority of old people are not mentally ill. However, some older people experience a decline in mental health, and may be classified in one of three general categories. First, they may be subject to periodic emotional reactions such as depression, anxiety, or fear. Second, they may experience functional disorders such as schizophrenia, affective psychoses, or psychotic depressive reactions. Third, and most seriously, they may be susceptible to organic disorders wherein brain damage occurs (senile dementia or Alzheimer's disease). While the prognosis for the first two categories is favorable if treatment begins early, the prognosis for organic disorders is poor, and ultimately the individual may need to be institutionalized.

NOTES

1. This does not imply that gross behavior changes do not occur because of organic deterioration or the reaction to physically or mentally stressful events. Rather, it suggests that, contrary to the prevailing myth, most elderly people do not encounter such problems. In fact, you will recall that less than 10 percent of the elderly are ever institutionalized, and when they are, it is most often very late in life.

2. See Ostrow, 1984; Buskirk, 1985, 1990; Piscopo, 1985; McPherson, 1986; Shephard, 1987; Blair et al., 1989; Bouchard et al., 1990; Goldberg and Hagberg, 1990.

3. For example, the National Senior Sports Association (1990 M St., N.W., Washington, D.C.) was created in 1980 for men and women over 50 years of age. This organization facilitates group travel to participate in organized recreational or competitive sports, or to attend spectator events with age peers. Similarly, in the United States there are now regional, state, and national 'Senior Olympic' competitions for men and women in five-year age categories (55 to 59, 60 to 64, 65 to 69, 70 to 74, 75 to 79, etc.). These competitions include 'skill' events (archery, badminton, free-throw basketball, bowling, casting, horseshoes, etc.) and 'Olympic' events (handball, racquetball, squash, tennis, walking, bicycle races, swimming, track and field events, etc.).

4. See Smith and Serfass, 1981; Shephard, 1984, 1986, 1987, 1990; Buskirk, 1985, 1990; Stacey et al., 1985; McPherson, 1988; Spirduso and Eckert,

1989; Bashore, 1990; Bouchard et al., 1990; Brown, 1990; Paffenbarger et al., 1990.

5. See Welford, 1958, 1977, 1980; Charness, 1985; Ostrow, 1989; Stelmach and Goggin, 1989; Cerella, 1990; Spirduso and MacRae, 1990.

6. See Coburn et al., 1981; Wantz and Gay, 1981; Wilkins and Adams, 1983; Haug et al., 1985; Shanas and Maddox, 1985; Siegler and Costa, 1985; Chappell et al., 1986; Marr Burdman, 1986; Canadian Medical Association, 1987; Herzog et al., 1989; Elias et al., 1990; Krause, 1990; Manton, 1990; and *Journal of Aging and Health* (1989-).

7. 'Acute' conditions are of a limited duration (such as flu or colds). 'Chronic' conditions persist over time and may be treated to reduce symptoms, pain, or trauma, but are less likely to be cured (heart disease, cancer, diabetes, or arthritis).

8. See Kart and Metress, 1984; Schlenker, 1984; Guigoz and Munro, 1985; Calasanti and Hendricks, 1986; Niewind et al., 1988; Smiciklas-Wright, 1988; Ausman and Russell, 1990.

9. See Gottheil et al., 1985; Maddox et al., 1985; Vestal and Dawson, 1985; Whittington and Maddox, 1986; McKim and Mishara, 1987.

10. Biologists, psychologists, sociologists, social workers, and medical personnel have studied such topics as sexuality and aging; sexual identity in the later years; the physiology of sex and age; sexual liberation; sex and the institutionalized elderly; love in later life; male and female differences among the elderly in sexual needs, interests, and activity; and sexual problems unique to the elderly. See Comfort, 1980; Corby and Solnick, 1980; Starr and Weiner, 1981; Thomas, 1982; Weg, 1983; Starr, 1985; Lee, 1987, 1989.

11. Senile dementia refers to chronic brain damage that is caused by circulatory problems such as hardening of the cerebrovascular arteries, or to disease states in the brain (Alzheimer's disease). When the brain cells do not receive sufficient oxygen and nutrients, they atrophy and die. Senile dementia should not be confused with forgetfulness or with functional disorders such as depression, anxiety, or paranoid reactions.

12. This percentage is only an estimate. It is probably slightly higher, since diagnostic services and counseling for the elderly are generally inadequate. Moreover, many of the elderly are unable or unwilling to seek professional help.

REFERENCES

Abramson, M. and P. Lovas (eds.). (1988). *Aging and Sensory Change: An Annotated Bibliography.* Washington, D.C.: The Gerontological Society of America.

Anderson, R. and J. Newman. (1973). 'Societal and Individual Determinants of Medical Care Utilization in the United States,' *Millbank Memorial Fund Quarterly*, 51(1), 95-124.

Ardell, D. (1986). *High Level Wellness.* Berkeley, Calif.: Ten Speed Press.

Ausman, L. and R. Russell. (1990). 'Nutrition and Aging,' in E. Schneider and J. Rowe (eds.). *Handbook of the Biology of Aging.* 3d ed. San Diego, Calif.: Academic Press.

Bartoshuk, L. and J. Weiffenbach. (1990). 'Chemical Senses and Aging,' in E. Schneider and J. Rowe (eds.). *Handbook of the Biology of Aging.* 3d ed. San Diego, Calif.: Academic Press.

Bashore, T. (1990). 'Age, Physical Fitness, and Mental Processing Speed,' pp. 120-44 in P. Lawton (ed.). *Annual Review of Gerontology and Geriatrics.* vol. 9. New York: Springer Publishing Co.

Berger, B. (1989). 'The Role of Physical Activity in the Life Quality of Older Adults,' pp. 42-58 in W. Spirduso and H. Eckert (eds.). *Physical Activity and Aging.* Champaign, Ill.: Human Kinetics Publishers.

Birren, J. and B. Sloane (eds.). (1980). *Handbook of Aging and Mental Health.* Englewood Cliffs, N.J.: Prentice-Hall.

Blair, S. et al. (1989). 'Physical Activity Patterns in Older Individuals,' pp. 120-39 in W. Spirduso and H. Eckert (eds.). *Physical Activity and Aging.* Champaign, Ill.: Human Kinetics Publishers.

Blazer, D. (1990). 'Depression in Late Life: An Update,' pp. 197-215 in P. Lawton (ed.). *Annual Review of Gerontology and Geriatrics.* vol. 9. New York: Springer Publishing Company.

Bouchard, C. et al. (1990). *Exercise, Fitness and Health: A Consensus of Current Knowledge.* Champaign, Ill.: Human Kinetics Publishers.

Brown, D. (1990). 'Exercise, Fitness, and Mental Health,' pp. 607-26 in C. Bouchard et al. (eds.). *Exercise, Fitness and Health: A Consensus of Current Knowledge.* Champaign, Ill.: Human Kinetics Publishers.

Buskirk, E. (1985). 'Health Maintenance and Longevity: Exercise,' pp. 894-931 in C. Finch and E. Schneider (eds.). *Handbook of the Biology of Aging.* New York: Van Nostrand Reinhold.

Buskirk, E. (1990). 'Exercise, Fitness and Aging,' pp. 687-98 in C. Bouchard et al. (eds.). *Exercise, Fitness and Health: A Consensus of Current Knowledge.* Champaign, Ill.: Human Kinetics Publishers.

Calasanti, T. and J. Hendricks. (1986). 'A Sociological

Perspective on Nutrition Research among the Elderly,' *The Gerontologist*, 26(3), 232-38.

Canada Health Survey. (1981). *The Health of Canadians*. Report of the Canada Health Survey. Ottawa: Ministry of Supply and Services.

Canadian Medical Association. (1987). *Health Care for the Elderly: Today's Challenges, Tomorrow's Options*. Ottawa: Department of Communications and Government Relations, Canadian Medical Association.

Carroll, J. and S. Maxwell. (1979). 'Individual Differences in Cognitive Abilities,' pp. 603-40 in M. Rosenweig and L. Park (eds.). *Annual Review of Psychology*. vol. 30. Palo Alto, Calif.: Annual Reviews, Inc.

Cerella, J. (1990). 'Aging and Information-Processing Rate,' pp. 201-21 in J. Birren and W. Schaie (eds.). *Handbook of the Psychology of Aging*. 3d ed. San Diego, Calif.: Academic Press.

Cerella, J. et al. (1980). 'Age and the Complexity Hypothesis,' pp. 332-40 in L. Poon (ed.). *Aging in the 1980s: Psychological Issues*. Washington, D.C.: American Psychological Association.

Chappell, N. and A. Blandford. (1987). 'Health Service Utilization by Elderly Persons,' *Canadian Journal of Sociology*, 12(3), 195-215.

Chappell, N. et al. (1986). *Aging and Health Care: A Social Perspective*. Toronto: Holt, Rinehart & Winston.

Charness, N. (1981). 'Aging and Skilled Problem Solving,' *Journal of Experimental Psychology: General*, 110(1), 21-38.

Charness, N. (ed.). (1985). *Aging and Human Performance*. New York: John Wiley & Sons.

Charness, N. and E. Bosman. (1990). 'Human Factors and Design for Older Adults,' pp. 446-63 in J. Birren and W. Schaie (eds.). *Handbook of the Psychology of Aging*. 3d ed. San Diego, Calif.: Academic Press.

Chiriboga, D. (1982). 'An Examination of Life Events as Possible Antecedents to Change,' *Journal of Gerontology*, 37(5), 595-601.

Chiriboga, D. and L. Cutler. (1980). 'Stress and Adaptation: Life Span Perspectives,' pp. 347-62 in L. Poon (ed.). *Aging in the 1980s: Psychological Issues*. Washington, D.C.: American Psychological Association.

Chiriboga, D. and M. Thurnher. (1981). 'Antecedents of Change in Adulthood,' paper presented at the annual meeting of the Gerontology Society of America, Toronto.

Coburn, D. et al. (1981). *Health and Canadian Society: Sociological Perspectives*. Toronto: Fitzhenry and Whiteside.

Comfort, A. (1980). 'Sexuality in Later Life,' pp. 885-92 in J. Birren and R. Sloane (eds.). *Handbook of Mental Health and Aging*. Englewood Cliffs, N.J.: Prentice-Hall.

Corby, N. and R. Solnick. (1980). 'Psychosocial and Physiological Influences on Sexuality in the Older Adult,' pp. 893-921 in J. Birren and R. Sloane (eds.). *Handbook of Mental Health and Aging*. Englewood Cliffs, N.J.: Prentice-Hall.

Corso, J. (1981). *Aging Sensory Systems and Perception*. New York: Praeger Publishers.

Corso, J. (1987). 'Sensory-Perceptual Processes and Aging,' pp. 29-55 in W. Schaie (ed.). *Annual Review of Gerontology and Geriatrics*. vol. 7. New York: Springer Publishing Co.

D'Arcy, C. (1987). 'Aging and Mental Health,' pp. 424-50 in V. Marshall (ed.). *Aging in Canada: Social Perspectives*. 2d ed. Markham, Ont.: Fitzhenry and Whiteside.

Elias, M. et al. (1990). 'Biological and Health Influences on Behavior,' pp. 80-102 in J. Birren and W. Schaie (eds.). *Handbook of the Psychology of Aging*. 3d ed. San Diego, Calif.: Academic Press,

Engen, T. (1977). 'Taste and Smell,' pp. 554-61 in J. Birren and W. Schaie (eds.). *Handbook of the Psychology of Aging*. New York: Van Nostrand Reinhold.

Evans, L. (1988). 'Older Driver Involvement in Fatal and Severe Traffic Crashes,' *Journal of Gerontology: Social Sciences*, 43(6), S186-93.

Faulkner, J. and T. White. (1990). 'Adaptations of Skeletal Muscle to Physical Activity,' pp. 265-80 in C. Bouchard et al. (eds.). *Exercise, Fitness, and Health: A Consensus of Current Knowledge*. Champaign, Ill.: Human Kinetics Publishers.

Fedorak, S. and C. Griffin. (1986). 'Developing a Self-advocacy Program for Seniors: The Essential Component of Health Promotion,' *Canadian Journal on Aging*, 5(4), 269-78.

Forbes, W. et al. (1987). *Institutionalization of the Elderly in Canada*. Toronto: Butterworths.

Fozard, J. (1990). 'Vision and Hearing,' pp. 150-71 in J. Birren and W. Schaie (eds.). *Handbook of the Psychology of Aging*. 3d ed. San Diego, Calif.: Academic Press.

Gee, E. and M. Kimball. (1987). *Women and Aging*. Toronto: Butterworths.

Goldberg, A. and J. Hagberg. (1990). 'Physical Exercise in the Elderly,' in E. Schneider and J. Rowe (eds.). *Handbook of the Biology of Aging*. 3d ed. San Diego, Calif.: Academic Press.

Gottheil, E. et al. (eds.). (1985). *Alcoholism, Drug Addiction and Aging*. Springfield, Ill.: Charles C. Thomas.

Graney, M. and R. Zimmerman. (1980). 'Health Self-Report Correlates among Older People in National Random Sample Data,' *Mid-American Review of Sociology*, 5(2), 47-59.

Guigoz, Y. and H. Munro. (1985). 'Nutrition and Aging,' pp. 878-93 in C. Finch and E. Schneider (eds.). *Handbook of the Biology of Aging*. 2d ed. New York: Van Nostrand Reinhold.

Gutmann, D. (1980). 'Observations on Culture and Mental Health in Later Life,' pp. 429-46 in J. Birren and B. Sloane (eds.). *Handbook of Mental Health and Aging*. Englewood Cliffs, N.J.: Prentice-Hall.

Hagberg, J. (1989). 'Effect of Exercise and Training on Older Men and Women with Essential Hypertension,' pp. 186-93 in W. Spirduso and H. Eckert (eds.). *Physical Activity and Aging*. Champaign, Ill.: Human Kinetics Publishers.

Harkins, S. and M. Warner. (1980). 'Age and Pain,' pp. 121-31 in C. Eisdorfer (ed.). *Annual Review of Gerontology and Geriatrics*. vol. 1. New York: Springer Publishing Co.

Haskell, W. et al. (1985). 'Physical Activity and Exercise to Achieve Health-Related Physical Fitness Components,' *Public Health Reports*, 100, 202-12.

Haug, M. et al. (eds.). (1985). *The Physical and Mental Health of Aged Women*. New York: Springer Publishing Co.

Hennessy, C. (1989). 'Culture in the Use, Care and Control of the Aging Body,' *Journal of Aging Studies*, 3(1), 39-54.

Herzog, R. et al. (eds.) (1989). *Health and Economic Status of Older Women*. Amityville, N.Y.: Baywood Publishing Co.

Hickey, T. (1980). *Health and Aging*. Monterey, Calif.: Brooks/Cole Publishing Co.

Horowitz, M. and N. Wilner. (1980). 'Life Events, Stress and Coping,' pp. 363-74 in L. Poon (ed.). *Aging in the 1980s: Psychological Issues*. Washington, D.C.: American Psychological Association.

Kart, C. and S. Metress. (1984). *Nutrition, the Aged, and Society*. Englewood Cliffs, N.J.: Prentice-Hall.

Kenshalo, D. (1977). 'Age Changes in Touch, Vibration, Temperature, Kinesthesis, and Pain Sensitivity,' pp. 562-79 in J. Birren and W. Schaie (eds.). *Handbook of the Psychology of Aging*. New York: Van Nostrand Reinhold.

Kline, D. and F. Schieber. (1985). 'Vision and Aging,' pp. 296-331 in J. Birren and W. Schaie (eds.). *Handbook of the Psychology of Aging*. 2d ed. New York: Van Nostrand Reinhold.

Kosnik, W. et al. (1988). 'Visual Changes in Daily Life throughout Adulthood,' *Journal of Gerontology: Psychological Sciences*, 43(3), P63-70.

Krause, N. (1990). 'Illness Behavior in Later Life,' pp. 228-44 in R. Binstock and L. George (eds.). *Handbook of Aging and the Social Sciences*. 3d ed. San Diego, Calif.: Academic Press.

Lee, J. (1987). 'The Invisible Lives of Canada's Gray Gays,' pp. 138-55 in V. Marshall (ed.). *Aging in Canada: Social Perspectives*. 2d ed. Markham, Ont.: Fitzhenry and Whiteside.

Lee, J. (1989). 'Invisible Men: Canada's Aging Homosexuals,' *Canadian Journal on Aging*, 8(1), 79-87.

MacLean, M. et al. (1988). 'Access to Community Health Services by Ethnic Elderly People,' *Environments*, 19(3), 61-75.

MacRae, P. (1989) 'Physical Activity and Central Nervous System Integrity,' pp. 69-77 in W. Spirduso and H. Eckert (eds.). *Physical Activity and Aging*. Champaign, Ill.: Human Kinetics Publishers.

Maddox, G. et al. (eds.). (1985). *Nature and Extent of Alcohol Problems among the Elderly*. New York: Springer Publishing Co.

Manton, K. (1990). 'Mortality and Morbidity,' pp. 64-90 in R. Binstock and L. George (eds.). *Handbook of Aging and the Social Sciences*. 3d ed. San Diego, Calif.: Academic Press.

Manton, K. et al. (1987). 'Suicide in Middle Age and Later Life: Sex and Race Specific Life Tables and Cohort Analyses,' *Journal of Gerontology*, 42(2), 219-27.

Marr Burdman, G. (1986). *Healthful Aging*. Englewood Cliffs, N.J.: Prentice-Hall.

Mason, J. and K. Powell. (1985). 'Physical Activity, Behavioral Epidemiology, and Public Health,' *Public Health Reports*, 100, 113-15.

McCrae, R. (1982). 'Age Differences in the Use of Coping Mechanisms,' *Journal of Gerontology*, 37(4), 454-60.

McKim, W. and B. Mishara. (1987). *Drugs and Aging*. Toronto: Butterworths.

McPherson, B. (ed.). (1986). *Sport and Aging*. Champaign, Ill.: Human Kinetics Publishers.

McPherson, B. (1988). 'Aging With Excellence: The Contribution of Physical Activity to Health and Wellness,' pp. 91-124 in L. McDonald and N. Keating (eds.). *Aging with Excellence*. Winnipeg, Man.: Canadian Association on Gerontology.

McPherson, B. and C. Kozlik. (1980). 'Canadian Leisure Patterns by Age: Disengagement, Continuity or Ageism?' pp. 113-22 in V. Marshall (ed.). *Aging in Canada: Social Perspectives*. Don Mills, Ont.: Fitzhenry and Whiteside.

Mittleman, K. et al. (1989). 'The Older Cyclist: Anthropometric, Physiological and Psychosocial Changes Observed during a Trans-Canada Cycle Tour,' *Canadian Journal on Aging*, 8(2), 144-56.

Moore, L. et al. (1982). 'Sucrose Taste Thresholds: Age-Related Differences,' *Journal of Gerontology*, 37(1), 64-69.

Morgan, W. and S. Goldston (eds.). (1987). *Exercise and Mental Health*. Washington, D.C.: Hemisphere Publishing.

Niewind, A. et al. (1988). 'Relative Impact of Selected

Factors on Food Choices of Elderly Individuals,' *Canadian Journal on Aging*, 7(1), 32-47.

Ochs, A. et al. (1985). 'Neural and Vestibular Aging Associated with Falls,' pp. 378-99 in J. Birren and W. Schaie (eds.). *Handbook of the Psychology of Aging*. 2d ed. New York: Van Nostrand Reinhold.

Olsho, L. et al. (1985). 'Aging and the Auditory System,' pp. 332-77 in J. Birren and W. Schaie (eds.). *Handbook of the Psychology of Aging*. 2d ed. New York: Van Nostrand Reinhold.

Osgood, N. (1985). *Suicide in the Elderly*. Rockville, Md.: Aspen Publishing.

Ostrow, A. (1984). *Physical Activity and the Older Adult: Psychological Perspectives*. Princeton, N.J.: Princeton Book Company, Publishers.

Ostrow, A. (ed.). (1989). *Aging and Motor Behavior*. Indianapolis, Ind.: Benchmark Press.

Ostrow, A. et al. (1981). 'Age Role Expectations and Sex Role Expectations for Selected Sport Activities,' *Research Quarterly*, 52(2), 216-27.

Paffenbarger, R. et al. (1990). 'Physical Activity and Physical Fitness as Determinants of Health and Longevity,' pp. 33-48 in C. Bouchard et al. (eds.). *Exercise, Fitness and Health: A Consensus of Current Knowledge*. Champaign, Ill.: Human Kinetics Publishers.

Piscopo, J. (1985). *Fitness and Aging*. New York: Macmillan.

Renner, V. and J. Birren. (1980). 'Stress: Physiological and Psychological Mechanisms,' pp. 310-36 in J. Birren and R. Sloane (eds.). *Handbook of Mental Health and Aging*. Englewood Cliffs, N.J.: Prentice-Hall.

Roos, N. et al. (1984). 'Aging and the Demand for Health Services: Which Aged and Whose Demand?' *The Gerontologist*, 24(1), 31-34.

Saltin, B. (1990). 'Cardiovascular and Pulmonary Adaptation to Physical Activity,' pp. 187-204 in C. Bouchard et al. (eds.). *Exercise, Fitness and Health: A Consensus of Current Knowledge*. Champaign, Ill.: Human Kinetics Publishers.

Schiffman, S. (1979). 'Changes in Taste and Smell with Age: Psychophysical Aspects,' pp. 227-46 in J. Ordy and K. Brizzee (eds.). *Sensory Systems and Communication in the Elderly*. New York: Raven Press.

Schlenker, E. (1984). *Nutrition in Aging*. St. Louis, Mo.: C.V. Mosby Co.

Schwenger, C. (1987). 'Formal Health Care for the Elderly in Canada,' pp. 505-19 in V. Marshall (ed.). *Aging in Canada: Social Perspectives*. 2d ed. Markham, Ont.: Fitzhenry and Whiteside.

Shanas, E. and G. Maddox. (1985). 'Health, Health Resources, and the Utilization of Care,' pp. 697-726 in R. Binstock and E. Shanas (eds.). *Handbook of Aging and the Social Sciences*. 2d ed. New York: Van Nostrand Reinhold.

Shapiro, E. and L. Roos. (1984). 'Using Health Care: Rural/Urban Differences among the Manitoba Elderly,' *The Gerontologist*, 24(3), 270-74.

Shephard, R. (1984). 'Critical Issues in the Health of the Elderly: The Role of Physical Activity,' *Canadian Journal on Aging*, 3(4), 199-208.

Shephard, R. (1986). *The Economics of Enhanced Endurance Fitness*. Champaign, Ill.: Human Kinetics Publishers.

Shephard, R. (1987). *Physical Activity and Aging*. 2d ed. London: Croom Helm.

Shephard, R. (1990). 'Costs and Benefits of an Exercising Versus a Nonexercising Society,' pp. 49-60 in C. Bouchard et al. (eds.). *Exercise, Fitness and Health: A Consensus of Current Knowledge*. Champaign, Ill.: Human Kinetics Publishers.

Shephard, R. and K. Sidney. (1979). 'Exercise and Aging,' pp. 1-57 in R. Hutton (ed.). *Exercise and Sport Sciences Reviews*. vol. 6. Philadelphia: Franklin Institute Press.

Siegler, I. and P. Costa. (1985). 'Health Behavior Relationships,' pp. 144-66 in J. Birren and W. Schaie (eds.). *Handbook of the Psychology of Aging*. 2d ed. New York: Van Nostrand Reinhold.

Simmons-Tropea, D. and R. Osborn. (1987). 'Disease, Survival and Death: The Health Status of Canada's Elderly,' pp. 399-423 in V. Marshall (ed.). *Aging in Canada: Social Perspectives*. 2d ed. Markham, Ont.: Fitzhenry and Whiteside.

Smiciklas-Wright, H. (1988). 'Nutrition and Aging,' pp. 125-53 in L. McDonald and N. Keating (eds.). *Aging with Excellence*. Winnipeg, Man.: Canadian Association on Gerontology.

Smith, E. and R. Serfass (eds.). (1981). *Exercise and Aging: The Scientific Process*. Hillside, N.J.: Enslow Publishers.

Spirduso, W. and H. Eckert, (eds.). (1989). *Physical Activity and Aging*. Champaign, Ill.: Human Kinetics Publishers.

Spirduso, W. and P. MacRae. (1990). 'Motor Performance and Aging,' pp. 184-200 in J. Birren and W. Schaie (eds.). *Handbook of the Psychology of Aging*. 3d ed. San Diego, Calif.: Academic Press.

Spitzer, M. (1988). 'Taste Acuity in Institutionalized and Non-Institutionalized Elderly Men,' *Journal of Gerontology: Psychological Sciences*, 43(3), P71-74.

Stacey, C. et al. (1985). 'Simple Cognitive and Behavioral Changes Resulting from Improved Physical Fitness in Persons over 50 Years of Age,' *Canadian Journal on Aging*, 4(2), 67-74.

Starr, B. (1985). 'Sexuality and Aging,' pp. 97-126 in

C. Eisdorfer et al. (eds.). *Annual Review of Gerontology and Geriatrics.* vol. 5. New York: Springer Publishing Co.

Starr, B. and M. Weiner. (1981). *The Starr-Weiner Report on Sex and Sexuality in the Mature Years.* New York: McGraw-Hill.

Stelmach, G. and N. Goggin. (1989). 'Psychomotor Decline With Age,' pp. 6-18 in W. Spirduso and H. Eckert (eds.). *Physical Activity and Aging.* Champaign, Ill.: Human Kinetics Publishers.

Sterns, H. et al. (1985). 'Accidents and the Aging Individual,' pp. 703-24 in J. Birren and W. Schaie (eds.). *Handbook of the Psychology of Aging.* 2d ed. New York: Van Nostrand Reinhold.

Taylor, C. et al. (1985). 'The Relation of Physical Activity and Exercise to Mental Health,' *Public Health Reports,* 100, 195-202.

Thomas, L. (1982). 'Sexuality and Aging: Essential Vitamin or Popcorn?' *The Gerontologist,* 22(3), 240-43.

Tuominen, J. (1988). 'Prescription Drugs and the Elderly in B.C.,' *Canadian Journal on Aging,* 7(3), 174-82.

Van Toller, C. et al. (1985). *Aging and the Sense of Smell.* Springfield, Ill.: Charles C. Thomas.

Vestal, R. and G. Dawson. (1985). 'Pharmacology and Aging,' pp. 744-819 in C. Finch and E. Schneider (eds.). *Handbook of the Biology of Aging.* 2d ed. New York: Van Nostrand Reinhold.

Wantz, M. and J. Gay. (1981). *The Aging Process: A Health Perspective.* Cambridge, Mass.: Winthrop Publishers.

Weg, R. (ed.). (1983). *Sexuality in the Later Years: Roles and Behavior.* New York: Academic Press.

Weiffenbach, J. et al. (1982). 'Taste Thresholds: Quality Specific Variation with Human Aging,' *Journal of Gerontology,* 37(3), 372-77.

Welford, A. (1958). *Aging and Human Skill.* London: Oxford University Press.

Welford, A. (1977). 'Motor Performance,' pp.450-96 in J. Birren and W. Schaie (eds.). *Handbook of the Psychology of Aging.* New York: Van Nostrand Reinhold.

Welford, A. (1980). 'Sensory, Perceptual and Motor Processes in Older Adults,' pp. 192-213 in J. Birren and R. Sloane (eds.). *Handbook of Mental Health and Aging.* Englewood Cliffs, N.J.: Prentice-Hall.

Whittington, F. and G. Maddox. (1986). 'A View from Sociology,' *The Gerontologist,* 26(6), 618-21.

Wilkins, R. and O. Adams. (1983). *Healthfulness of Life.* Montreal: The Institute for Research on Public Policy.

6
The Aging Process: Adaptation to Psychological Changes

Maurice Green, Waterloo, Ontario

INTRODUCTION

Just as the aging individual must adapt to changes in the physical organism (chapter 5) and to changes in various social systems (chapters 7 to 12), so too must he or she respond to changes in the various components of the psychological system (Birren and Schaie, 1977, 1985, 1990). From a life-span developmental perspective (Hultsch and Deutsch, 1981), an understanding of changes in the cognitive, learning, and personality processes involves observing and explaining behavior within the same individual over time (aging effects), or between individuals at a specific time (individual differences).

These changes, which may be incremental or decremental, and which may or may not be observed in given individuals, occur at different rates and at different stages in the life cycle. From a systems perspective, the various elements within the larger psychological system interact in their influence on the individual. More significantly, changes within the psychological system are related to changes in the physical organism and in the physical and social environments.

The following sections examine some common myths and stereotypes and briefly outline the influence of biological aging on cognition, learning, memory, and personality. The way in which adults may adapt to these psychological changes when and if they occur is also presented. As a result of the empirical evidence given here, readers should increase their awareness of possible behavioral and cognitive adaptations within themselves and others as they age. In this way, aging is viewed as a process requiring not only adaptation to the social structure and processes, but also to possible changes in the psychological processes within the individual.

In summary, aging involves adaptation to changes that may occur in the physical and psychological systems. However, these changes, which occur at different rates and times, are more than mere facts. They interact with changes in the physical and social environments to influence behavior and adaptation at different stages in the life cycle. Thus, aging should not be viewed as a process of inevitable physical, biological, and psychological deterioration. Instead, aging is a process of adaptation to specific changes, which occur at different rates and to varying degrees.

COGNITIVE PROCESSES AND AGING

Conventional wisdom suggests that as people age they experience a general and inevitable decline in mental capacities and function. As a result, it is often thought that older people become less intelligent, are incapable of thinking, lack creativity, are forgetful, and are unable to solve problems or to learn new information or skills. Yet, case studies and empirical evidence suggest that the decline in cognitive processes may be less rapid and less severe than changes in sensorimotor or physical abilities. This section presents information concerning the rate and type of change with age in intelligence, learning, memory, forgetting, and creativity (Craik and Trehub, 1981; Pratt and Norris, forthcoming).

Throughout, the reader must remember that there are individual differences within a particular age cohort and within a particular individual for each cognitive component. Moreover, most of the evidence is based on cross-sectional studies, which suggest that there are age differences between cohorts rather than that changes occur over time. These inferences based on cross-sectional data can be misleading. This is especially true if the test items or instruments are based on abilities that are more salient in the earlier years, such as nonverbal psychomotor elements that emphasize speed. Furthermore, disease, educational attainment, class background, motivation, and past and present lifestyle can influence abilities and performance in the later years. Thus, cohort differences are almost inevitable, since each successive cohort will generally have received more and better education. As a final caveat, it should be remembered that the following subsections concern individuals who are 'normal' and who do not suffer from a chronic disease such as senility.

Intelligence

Intelligence is a multidimensional construct that consists of a number of primary abilities such as verbal comprehension, reasoning, abstracting, perceptual speed, numerical facility, problem solving, and word fluency (Willis and Baltes, 1980; Schaie, 1989, 1990). However, psychologists have been unable to agree on the number, meaning,[1] or measurement of the many possible primary abilities.[2] Moreover, as Scheidt and Schaie (1978) noted, it is important to distinguish between **competence** and intelligence: intelligence refers to underlying abilities that can be applied across many general categories of situations, and competence refers to adaptive behavior unique to a specific situation or class of situations. Similarly, Clayton (1982) distinguished between intelligence, which focuses on questions of how to accomplish tasks, and **wisdom**, which involves considering whether a particular course of action should be pursued.

As a result of this conceptual and methodological uncertainty, the terms 'fluid intelligence' and 'crystallized intelligence' have been used frequently in discussing adult intelligence (Horn, 1982; Labouvie-Vief, 1985; Schaie, 1989, 1990; Woodruff-Pak, 1989). **Fluid intelligence** is influenced by physiological and neurological capacity, and represents incidental learning that is not based on culture. Fluid intelligence represents the ability to adjust one's thinking to the demands of a specific situation and to organize information to solve problems. It is measured by performance tests (novel problem solving, such as filling in a space with pieces from a puzzle, inductive reasoning, spatial location, or matching symbols to numbers) that are scored according to accuracy and speed.

Crystallized intelligence is the product of education, experience, and acculturation wherein individuals acquire specific knowledge and skills unique to their culture or subculture. Because crystallized intelligence is based on learning and experience, there may be individual differences that vary by level of educational attainment, socioeconomic status, and gender. This component is measured by verbal comprehension tests that stress vocabulary and the continual addition or restructuring of information within the cognitive system (defining the meaning of words or expressing mechanical knowledge).

Results from a number of studies and reviews[3], using both cross-sectional and longitudinal methodology, have confirmed that fluid intelligence, after reaching a peak during adolescence, declines with age. In contrast, crystallized intelligence increases with age, but once the late 70s are reached, crystallized abilities decline faster (Schaie, 1989). Schaie (1989) also notes that women may experience an earlier decline of fluid abilities, whereas men experience an earlier decline of crystallized abilities. The loss in fluid intellectual abilities may range from three to seven IQ units per decade between 30 and 60 years of age (Horn et al., 1981). This decrease in fluid intelligence may be related to a deterioration in cerebral blood flow, to neurological losses, to slower performance with age on speed tests, or to less daily use of problem-solving functions as one ages (intellectual demands may not be placed on the aging individual, and experience is used more than creative problem solving). In addition, a decrease in fluid intelligence may be related to deficits in the ability to organize information, ignore irrelevant information, concentrate, and recognize and use new information.

Increases in crystallized intelligence result from a continuing process of socialization (via formal education or experience) wherein new information is acquired. At the same time, existing verbal information is constantly being used and reinforced, especially by those who are highly verbal and reflective in their daily living.

In general, the 'classic aging pattern' with respect to intelligence indicates that, although there are individual differences, there is little significant decline until the 60s, with a more rapid decline beginning sometime after 60, especially in fluid intelligence. Where good health is maintained, verbal scores are consistently higher than perceptual-motor performance scores (speed) on all tests. This pattern holds whether the subjects are male or female, black or white, institutionalized or noninstitutionalized, or from upper or lower socioeconomic backgrounds. Moreover, studies suggest that continuity in performance is likely, although the performance levels of earlier years are not generally good predictors of the onset, direction, or degree of change in intelligence in later years. In effect, some of the decline is a function of disuse, and is reversible for many (Willis, 1985, 1987; Schaie, 1989, 1990; Schooler, 1990). Thus, older individuals can and do benefit from training designed to improve intelligence.

Given that intelligence appears to decline less rapidly and frequently than previously assumed, what are some of the possible explanations of the individual differences in measured intelligence during the middle and later years of adulthood? Recently it has been generally concluded that it is not chronological age per se (at least up to the early 70s) that leads to a decline in performance. Rather, there is a complex interaction of biological decrements (such as general physiological and neurological decline, loss of physical health, reduced blood flow to the brain), sensory losses such as hearing, and environmental factors. In fact, increasing emphasis has recently been placed on the role of environmental factors. For example, Baltes and his colleagues (Baltes, 1979; Willis and Baltes, 1980) have suggested that there are three sets of environmental elements that interact with the individual to produce developmental differences: (1) age-graded influences, such as specific socialization practices and events unique to each cohort; (2) historical influences, such as economic depressions or wars that force early school-leaving; and (3) personal life events that create crises for an individual (death of a spouse, unemployment, divorce, or a traumatic medical event).

Similarly, Labouvie-Vief and Chandler (1978) developed a theoretical framework wherein both sociocultural and situational factors were hypothesized to have considerable impact on cognitive functioning. They argue that decrements appear most frequently after retirement and may be due to the policy of mandatory retirement and to the consequent loss of social function. They suggest that the decline may also be related to physical, structural, or personality factors within the testing situation (for example, fatigue, cautiousness, lack of reinforcement and practice, low motivation, unfamiliar or meaningless test items, and test anxi-

ety), or to cultural and subcultural differences that influence ability or performance (such as socioeconomic status, race, English as the second language, birth order, or availability of reading material). Highlight 6.1 illustrates some of the factors that may have a positive or negative influence in the later years on intelligence test performance and, hence, on results.

In summary, the elderly demonstrate a range of intellectual abilities (Cunningham, 1987). There are individual differences in intelligence from birth onward, and a decline in cognitive functioning is not inevitable for everyone. While some individuals experience little or no decline throughout adulthood, others experience severe intellectual loss. Moreover, while some elderly persons perform at a slower rate on some intellectual tasks, or encounter difficulty with novel tasks or situations (such as the use of computer banking), the normal aging process does not significantly diminish the ability to solve problems. In fact, the elderly are usually able to use their accumulated knowledge and experience to offset any loss of speed in intellectual tasks.

Finally, assuming normal health, apparent differences in intelligence may be more closely related to educational and cohort differences than to chronological age. The greater intelligence demonstrated by younger cohorts is a reflection of more and better education, of more experience in test situations, of higher-quality health care during infancy and childhood, and of a greater likelihood of having acquired learned skills or familiarity with material that appears on intelligence tests. Given a stimulating and supportive environment, gains rather than losses in intelligence might be the more typical pattern, at least until the last few years of life when nearness to death is often revealed by a decline in intellectual functioning.

Learning and Memory

Introduction

Learning and memory are complementary processes that illustrate the classic 'chicken-and-egg' dilemma. Learning involves the acquisition of information or behavior, while memory involves the storage and retention of

---

HIGHLIGHT 6.1

FACTORS INFLUENCING INTELLIGENCE TEST PERFORMANCE IN LATER LIFE

In the absence of physiological or medical trauma, much of the observed difference in intellectual performance can be accounted for by a variety of past and current social and environmental factors. Some of these factors that may either increase (+) or decrease (-) test performance include:

1. The amount of experience, motivation, and training concerning the material in the tests (lack of ecological validity) (+).
2. The level of education completed[4] and the number of years since leaving school (+).
3. The absence of stress and fatigue in test situations (+).
4. The use of appropriate and meaningful test items (+).
5. The use of feedback, instruction, and practice in taking tests (+).
6. The presence of stereotypes that define the elderly as incompetent, thereby leading to a low level of test motivation (-).
7. The presence of an environment in the adult years that is conducive to intellectual stimulation (+).
8. A decreased emphasis on speed of performance (+).
9. The lifestyle during the adult years[5] (+ or -).
10. The onset of and adaptation to personal crises, including dramatic changes in job, marital, or health status (-).

These environmental explanations for the apparent decline in intelligence with age have led to the initiation of remedial programs, and to attempts to change elements of the environment in order to modify both crystallized and fluid intelligence (Willis, 1985, 1987).

---

the learned behavior. In order for material to be acquired and stored in memory it must be learned. Similarly, in order to demonstrate that material has been learned, it must be recalled from memory before the material can be used in response to a test. This illustrates the importance of distinguishing between learning and performance. When it is not possible to perform what was supposedly learned earlier, it is difficult to determine whether the material has not been learned; whether the material has been learned but not remembered; or whether the material has been learned and stored in memory, but cannot be retrieved for performance. In addition, lack of ecological validity[6] (where tasks and material are not meaningful or relevant to the individual), high anxiety in a test situation, temporary physiological or psychological states (fatigue, lack of motivation, or depression), and the requirement to perform or demonstrate learning in a short period of time can all influence performance rather than learning or retrieving per se.

Learning

The belief that 'you can't teach an old dog new tricks' is still widely held. However, empirical evidence suggests that while there are individual differences within and between age cohorts in learning ability, the elderly can learn if adequate personal and situational conditions are present (Hultsch and Dixon, 1990; McDowd and Birren, 1990). As we saw in chapter 5, there is a general slowing of the central nervous system with age. This influences the learning process as well. Older persons have the capacity to learn but it seems to take them longer to search for, code, recall, and produce the required response. Under conditions of self-pacing, where individuals can set their own rates of speed, learning is more likely to occur.[7]

Learning potential may also be restricted because of a decreased ability to distinguish relevant from irrelevant information (Hoyer and Plude, 1980; McDowd and Birren, 1990). This problem may be especially acute for women, since it has been found that they are more likely than men to attend to irrelevant stimuli (Laszlo et al., 1980). This age-related change in attentional selectivity also affects other cognitive processes, such as problem solving. Therefore, it is important to eliminate distractions in the environment for the older learner, and to enhance the learning environment with supportive instructions and guidance to enable the learner to focus only on relevant stimuli.

In addition to cognitive factors, a number of noncognitive factors also influence the ability to learn at all ages. First, there must be a willingness to use one's physical and mental capacities. The level of motivation is most likely to be high for meaningful and relevant tasks. However, overinvolvement or overarousal, resulting in an excessive drive state, may detract from performance among the elderly more than among the young. Second, the learner must not only have a sufficient level of intelligence to acquire the information, but must also have experience in learning situations; learning capacity involves acquiring and using the habits and skills of learning. Thus, older adults who have been involved in learning, education, or retraining throughout the adult years are more likely not only to want to learn but to be able to do so more efficiently. A third personal factor is health. Generally, individuals who are in good physical and mental health (especially those without cerebrovascular disease or severe uncorrected visual or auditory problems) are able to acquire new information with greater ease.

In summary, the existing evidence suggests that there are individual differences at all ages in learning performance. However, most elderly people appear to be at a disadvantage if the time to learn and respond is short. Given sufficient motivation, time, and good health, and continued and recent experience in learning situations, the performance of a 70-year-old can be relatively similar to that of younger adults. Indeed, elderly persons have demonstrated that they can master new and emerging technologies (such as electronic devices, computers) in both the home and the workplace. Moreover, most of the learning studies have been based on cross-sectional rather than longitudinal or cohort-sequential studies. Thus,

the observed age differences may reflect generational differences in years of schooling and in the desire or opportunity to use learning capacities during the adult years.

Memory

Memory is a complex process that is involved in almost all stages of information processing. One view of how memory works is illustrated by the three-stage model proposed by Murdock (1967). The first stage involves receiving information and temporarily storing this information in 'sensory stores.' For example, auditory information (such as the sound of a siren) is stored in the 'echoic memory,' while visual information (the facial features of someone you have just met) is stored in 'iconic memory.' If this information is considered important, and it is not interrupted by competing stimuli, it is transferred in the second stage, by the 'attention' process, to 'short-term memory.' From here, the information is transferred by additional rehearsal of the stimuli to a more permanent 'long-term memory.' Information can be lost in the first stage (sensory storage) by decay or replacement, at the second stage (short-term memory) by forgetting if the information is not repeatedly rehearsed, and in the third stage (long-term memory) through a failure of the retrieval system to find what has been stored. For example, there appears to be a decline with age in both recall and recognition[8] tasks, thereby suggesting that both acquisition and storage processes may change with age (Hultsch, 1985; Poon, 1985; Perlmutter et al., 1987; Hultsch and Dixon, 1990).

Some theories suggest that there are specific types of memory. For example, Tulving (1972) describes 'episodic' memory as that which operates for specific events unique to the individual (a specific trip, the first love, or a meaningful event in the life course), while 'semantic memory' represents common knowledge, vocabulary, or concepts that are shared by most people (stop signs are red, 'caution' signs mean be careful, or a round object rolls). Another dichotomy (Winograd, 1975) distinguishes between 'declarative knowledge' (memory for general knowledge) and 'procedural knowledge' (memory for how to behave or perform in specific situations).

With respect to aging and memory, the evidence suggests that a progressive decline in memory performance is not inevitable, nor is it irreversible when it does occur (Craik, 1977; Hines and Fozard, 1980; Schonfield, 1980; Poon, 1985; Perlmutter et al., 1987; Hultsch and Dixon, 1990). The older person seems to be able to remember and recall distant events (episodic memory) better than recent material.[9] However, as in learning experiments, the older person seems to require more time to retrieve information from both short- and long-term memory, especially when faced with many stimulus-response alternatives, or when stored material must be manipulated or reorganized before responding. These effects are found regardless of the familiarity with the material. However, the speed of retrieval is faster for familiar objects, regardless of age (Poon and Fozard, 1978).

The apparent reasons for 'memory loss' or slower and less efficient recall are not clearly understood. However, it appears that such factors as a low level of intelligence, lack of use of information, interference in the process because of the learning of new information (retroactive interference) and the large amount of information already stored (proactive interference), lack of motivation (a self-fulfilling prophecy that the elderly are forgetful), a low level of verbal ability, and neurochemical changes in the brain cells or loss of brain cells may all contribute to changes in memory performance.

Since the explanation for slower and less efficient memory processes is not totally biological, it is possible to diagnose the problem and improve the efficiency of the memory process in later years through practice (Taub, 1973) and intervention (Fozard, 1981). Memory can be enhanced by adopting procedures that facilitate memorization; by providing more time for the acquisition, rehearsal, and retrieval of information; by using meaningful material to be learned and remembered in experimental situations; by relying more on recognition than on recall; by reducing interference during the learning process; and by informing older adults that 'forgetting' and 'memory loss' are not inevitable, and that they do have the capacity to remember, although it might take longer to do so. What people believe and feel about their

memory abilities may be as important as their actual memory abilities. That is, erroneous perceptions can result in anxiety, feelings of loss of control, and decreased effort in memory-demanding situations. These perceptions can contribute to observed declines in memory performance in later life (Hultsch et al., 1985).

Thinking, Problem Solving, and Creativity

'Cognitive style' refers to the characteristic way that individuals conceptually organize the environment, manipulate the knowledge they possess, and make decisions or approach problems that have to be solved.[10] It is directly observable through conversational style, through the characteristic modes of perceptual and intellectual functioning, and through an evaluation by others of creative acts. Two contrasting cognitive styles have been labeled 'field-dependent' and 'field-independent.' The individual who is 'field-dependent' appears to be more perceptive of the social environment, more people-oriented, and generally more conventional in dress and behavior. In contrast, the person who is 'field-independent' is more analytical, more internally directed, and less constrained in behavior by tradition and convention. With respect to thinking, an individual may be reflective (a longer response time and fewer errors is the norm) or impulsive (a fast response time with less accuracy is the norm). There is some evidence that where the stimulus is familiar and unambiguous, older subjects are more impulsive than younger subjects (Coyne et al., 1978).

Cognitive style may also be revealed by the approach utilized when the decision involves some risk. Older adults have generally been found to be more rigid and cautious in their thinking (Reese and Rodeheaver, 1985); and they are sometimes reluctant to make difficult decisions, especially when the situation is ambiguous, when speed is required, or when they have a fear of failure. Thus, in some situations they react by substituting accuracy for speed (cautiousness); in others they may resort to prior learning or experience, even if it is no longer appropriate (rigidity). Furthermore, it appears that if given the option of not responding, or of not making a decision, many will select this alternative. It is not clear whether this rigidity and cautiousness among the elderly is an aging phenomenon, or whether it is a cohort and historical factor wherein these traits have been part of a lifelong cognitive style. An alternative interpretation of cautiousness is that it reflects an unwillingness to engage in risk-taking behavior, especially in situations where elderly people are less willing to be evaluated (Reese and Rodeheaver, 1985:478).

In chapter 5 we saw that there is a characteristic slowing of behavior with age as noted by a longer reaction time. This slowing is also evident in a general progressive decline in cognitive speed and verbal processes, which may limit complex thinking (Salthouse, 1985, 1990). This is likely the result of a general slowing of behavior because of changes in the central nervous system; a loss of speed in all stages of information processing; and a change in health, particularly with the onset of coronary heart disease or cerebrovascular disease. The slowing may also be due to deficits in attention (McDowd and Birren, 1990). These may be either 'divided-attention' deficits (difficulty in processing currently relevant information, such as trying to listen to two conversations), or 'selective-attention' deficits (difficulty in ignoring irrelevant information, such as a conversation on the radio while talking to another person).

As a result of this slowing and decline in speed of information processing, individuals attempt to compensate by relying more on past experience and knowledge, by employing memory aids, by learning to eliminate irrelevant stimuli, and by using strategy hints from others (Salthouse, 1987). Charness (1981) has suggested that the individual differences noted in cognitive aging may be due either to 'hardware' (processing mechanisms) or to 'software' (strategies and learning controlled by the performer) changes. Since hardware changes are generally decremental (loss of speed or decline in memory), deficits in problem solving will occur unless software changes are learned and used. These compensating mechanisms are particularly important in problem-solving or decision-making tasks. Thus, with increasing age, adults become not only less accurate in

problem solving but also slower.

It appears that problem-solving ability may decline with age because of a general slowing of behavior, and because of an unwillingness or inability to incorporate newer, more efficient strategies that might lead to a solution or decision. However, the decline also appears to be related to the level of educational attainment and to the type of task. For example, less decline in ability is seen among the better-educated and for tasks similar to those used in one's occupation (Reese and Rodeheaver, 1985; Schooler, 1990).

Charness (1981) has suggested that elderly people may be inferior to the young in problem solving not because of a decline in ability, but because they have always been less effective. That is, a cohort effect is present because they may not have acquired the skill when younger, and they may have had less use of the skill during their lifetimes. He further noted that, in his study of highly skilled chess players, 'despite decreases in efficiency in encoding and retrieval of information, older players can match the performance of younger players' (Charness, 1981:37). The older players have always had a high level of skill, and have used this skill consistently throughout life. In short, experience can offset loss of efficiency. Charness also found that the highly skilled older chess players actually took less time to select a good move than less skilled older or younger players. Again, this illustrates the range of individual differences within and between cohorts.

In addition to age differences in problem-solving ability, changes in intellectual capacity and style are revealed through patterns of creativity across the life cycle (Kogan, 1973; McLeish, 1976; Botwinick, 1984; Salthouse, 1990; Simonton, 1990). Like intelligence, creativity is a difficult concept to define and measure; the significance of a creative endeavor, like that of a piece of art, is often dependent on the evaluation of others. Creativity may involve such accomplishments as the creation of a unique cultural product (a work of art, or literature, or an invention), the development of a new concept, the creation of a new approach to solving an old problem, a solution to an old problem, or the identification of a new problem.

In order to measure the concept, **creativity**

has been defined as either the total productivity (quantity) throughout one's career (the number of articles published by a university professor), or the point in the career at which the highest-quality work was completed (the age at which Nobel Prize winning work was initiated or completed). To date, the study of creativity has been primarily based on retrospective studies of the career profiles of various occupational groups, or on case studies of those elderly persons who have been defined as highly creative individuals (for example, Grandma Moses or George Burns).

Creative 'potential' often peaks at about age 40, with a decline appearing after about age 50 (Rabbitt, 1977; Simonton, 1990). However, there are individual differences by occupation. For example, the peak of creativity in mathematics and chemistry occurs in the 30s and 40s, while in literature and history, where experience and a larger investment of reflective time in a single project are necessary, the peak occurs in the 60s. Furthermore, the highest-quality work may appear at the time when the largest quantity of work is produced. However, as Cohen-Shalev (1989) noted, in terms of artistic creativity, the qualitative component must be given more weight, since an 'old age style' may emerge in the later years. The pattern of creativity also seems to be influenced by such factors as health, motivation, energy, personal lifestyle, competing interests, expectations by significant others, and the social environment. For example, it is likely that many aging individuals have a capacity for creativity, but lack the social environment that can provide the stimulation to question and to create, or the opportunity set to pursue ideas to completion.

In light of significant accomplishments by those in their 60s, 70s, or 80s, it appears that, given an appropriate environment, some elderly people are capable of highly creative work well into the later years of life. Indeed, later life can be viewed as a challenge and an adventure that can realize further creative efforts (highlight 6.2).

PERSONALITY PROCESSES AND AGING

Introduction

In an attempt to explain changes in behavior with age, social scientists have sought to determine the relative influence of personality factors (Shanan and Jacobowitz, 1982; McCrae and Costa, 1984; Bengtson et al., 1985; Schulz, 1985; Kogan, 1990). Perhaps nowhere else is the interaction of the personal system with the social system more evident than when personality is considered as a factor in the aging process.

HIGHLIGHT 6.2

MOTIVATION TO ACHIEVE IN LATER LIFE

The motivation to be creative and to continue at a high level of intellectual functioning in the later years is aptly illustrated by the following lines from Tennyson's poem 'Ulysses':

How dull it is to pause, to make an end,
To rust unburnish'd, not to shine in use!

And this gray spirit yearning in desire
To follow knowledge like a sinking star...

Death closes all; but something ere the end,
Some work of noble note, may yet be done...

...but strong in will
To strive, to seek, to find, and not to yield.

Personality involves traits, characteristics, moods, cognitive styles, and lifestyles that are unique to the individual, but that interact with a variety of social system variables.

As with the concepts of 'socialization' and 'intelligence,' most of the interest in personality has focused on the early developmental years of childhood and adolescence. As a result of this interest, many perspectives,[11] designs,[12] and methods[13] have been used to describe and explain the characteristic way in which particular individuals think (cognitive style) and behave (lifestyle). As these various methods, theories, and concepts have been employed, two interacting questions have dominated the personality literature. The first is whether behavior is internally (personality traits) or externally (the social situation) determined. The second question considers the extent to which personality is stable or subject to change over time. Interest in these two questions has been further intensified by the need to understand the impact of personality on behavior throughout middle and later adulthood.

Social Behavior: A Function of Personality Traits or the Social Situation?

Is behavior preliminary determined by personality traits or by the social environment? According to the 'trait' approach, individuals, through a combination of heredity, early socialization practices, and interaction with significant others, develop personal traits and characteristics, a cognitive style, and a temperament. These behavioral dispositions are thought to be stable over time; they enable an individual to respond consistently and predictably to the social and physical environments.

In contrast, the 'situational,' 'behavioral,' or 'state' approach argues that behavior is determined by the social situation, and that individuals learn and perform social roles appropriate to a given situation. According to this latter perspective, a 'personality' per se does not exist. Or, if it does, it has little stability, since the behavior of an individual is determined by externally induced social norms and sanctions unique to specific situations (for example, at work, at home, or at leisure).

As with many bipolar views of the world, neither position has received overwhelming support in the research literature. Rather, an interactionist perspective has evolved as a more realistic view. According to this perspective, behavior results from continuous two-way interaction between the person (with unique cognitive and emotional traits) and the particular social situation. Thus, an individual's personality influences behavior and adaptation to specific situations, while the situation itself influences which traits from the available repertoire will be expressed, and in what way.

It is through this dialectical process between the personal and social systems that individual and group lifestyles evolve. For example, on the basis of the longitudinal study of successful aging in Kansas City, Williams and Wirths (1965) identified six types of lifestyles that reflect an individual's values, interests, and preferences: (1) an emphasis on the 'world of work'; (2) a primary interest in the family ('familism'); (3) a major interest in the spouse ('couplehood'); (4) a preference for 'living alone'; (5) a propensity to be fully involved in daily life in a variety of ways ('living fully'); and (6) a tendency to be as uninvolved as possible in all activities ('living with minimal involvement').

Individuals were classified (a) as to which lifestyle they preferred, and (b) how successfully they aged in it. Individuals who exhibited characteristics of one lifestyle often also demonstrated characteristics of a similar and related lifestyle. As a result, Williams and Wirths (1965:170) further identified two general sets of lifestyles. The Gemeinschaft[14] set includes familism, couplehood, and living fully. These lifestyles involve high role activity, high personal interaction of an affective nature, and little alienation or isolation. In contrast, the Gesellschaft[15] set includes characteristics from the world of work, living alone, and moving through life with minimal involvement. These lifestyles are characterized by minimal role activity, few close personal relationships, alienation, and isolation.

Many other typologies have been constructed to describe patterns or characteristic ways of behaving during the adult years, either in general or in specific situations. Some of the typologies that are based on personality studies will be described later in the chapter. It must be recognized that all typologies are only modal patterns and that there are individual differences in the behavior and traits demonstrated for each 'type.' Moreover, typologies never, in principle, present complete and permanent pictures of social beings and social reality.

Personality: Stable or Changeable over the Life Cycle?

There has been debate about whether behavior is influenced by internal (personality traits) or external factors (such as change and variety in social situations, significant life events, or entering specific stages of life, such as middle age). While this controversy has not been completely resolved, the available evidence, especially from longitudinal studies,[16] suggests that after early adulthood individuals demonstrate consistency in such personal characteristics as presentation of self, attitudes, values, temperament, and traits (Neugarten, 1977; Costa and McCrae, 1980; Costa et al., 1980; Thomae, 1980; Costa et al., 1987; Whitbourne, 1987). This pattern of stability is especially pronounced among highly educated men (McCrae et al., 1980). In fact, many individuals make a conscious effort to increase consistency in the behavioral and cognitive presentation of self. Because of the possibility of errors in measurement at a given time, when measures of behavior and personality are averaged over a large sample of situations, stability is the normative pattern in the absence of confounding health problems.

Yet research evidence from surveys and individual case studies indicates that some personality changes do occur at or beyond middle age for some individuals. For example, a longitudinal study found that changes in personality traits may occur in two ways (Haan and Day, 1974; Haan, 1976). First, most of those in a cohort will change over time in some trait, but the relative position within the group for any one individual will not change. That is, the most dependable person at age 20 will be the most dependable person at age 40, even though the average score for the cohort may decrease or increase. In the second type, all members of a cohort may change but some will change relatively more than others. Thus, the person who was the most defensive at age 20 may no longer be the most defensive at age 40. Although there have been few personality studies of women, this pattern of personality change over the life cycle may vary by sex. For example, Maas and Kuypers (1974) found that women are more likely to change their lifestyles as they age, and men are more likely to change their personalities. Ryff (1982) found that older women are more likely to perceive a change with age in some elements of the personality structure (such as values).

How might these changes be explained? Unfortunately, no theory considers personality processes across the developmental life span of an individual. We depend on speculation and inferential evidence from research to explain why personality changes occur in later life.

First, demonstrated changes may reflect underlying latent needs and characteristics that have not been expressed earlier in life. Second, as social situations change with age, the individual may be less inclined to present the self in a particular way. For example, the striving, achievement-oriented individual may devote less time to work, may become more relaxed in interpersonal situations, and may demonstrate a different presentation of the self in all social situations. This may be more likely to occur if career goals have been attained, especially if at an earlier age than expected. Alternatively, according to the cognitive theory of personality (Thomae, 1980), there may be a perceived change rather than an objective change in the self. This perceived change may lead to observed behavioral changes in the later years. That is, the older person may perceive changes in health or in any number of personality traits, and then behave accordingly. A perceived change may also be related to the type of measure used to assess personality. Bengtson et al. (1985:573) reported that older persons' subjective perceptions of the self, as measured in open-ended questions, show more change with age than do objective assessments.

A third factor leading to an apparent change in personality may be a lack of opportunity to demonstrate certain traits. For example, the need to be aggressive or achievement-oriented may continue, but the social opportunities to do so may no longer be as readily available. In addition, the physical and psychic energy needed to continue a pattern of aggressive and achievement-oriented behavior may no longer be available. Normative expectations as to how one is supposed to behave or think at a particular age may change with age. This would imply that age-related normative behaviors are clearly understood and accepted by the elderly. However, there appears to be little consensus concerning whether age-appropriate norms are present, and, if so, whether they influence the behavior of elderly persons.

Finally, since personality factors interact with a changing social environment, the personal system may interact differently with the social system during the later years. For example, there may be a shift from a concern with the external world to matters of importance to the personal system. That is, the individual may be more likely, for a variety of personal reasons, to accept rather than challenge the external environment, to voluntarily relinquish some social roles, and to turn inward and show a greater interest in and concern for the self and those in the immediate family.

In summary, while most people do not show marked personality changes with age, some appear to be less concerned with normative behavior and do change their patterns of social interaction. Similarly, others are aware of the changing norms of younger cohorts and may change their behavior or cognitive pattern to fit in with contemporary lifestyles. Some of these changes have been hypothesized to be related to physiological or cognitive changes. However, they may also reflect latent character traits, a shift toward an increased interest in the self, a decreased opportunity set, a changing social environment, or a voluntary or involuntary loss of roles.

In addition, changes may be induced by the onset of a significant personal life event wherein a change of lifestyle is seen to be the most appropriate coping mechanism (for example, a forced retirement, divorce, a demotion, widowhood, or departure of children from the home). In the subsections that follow, personality traits, personality types, and personality disorders demonstrated in the later years of life are described. Throughout these sections, it must be noted that although women constitute an increasingly larger proportion of the adult population, most of the evidence is based on studies of men prior to or following retirement. Moreover, most of the information about personality types has been derived from cross-sectional rather than from longitudinal or cohort studies.

Personality Traits

Many cross-sectional studies have measured single or multiple **personality traits**[17] to determine to what extent differences exist by age, or to determine if age is a more significant factor in personality differences than other social variables (such as sex, socioeconomic status, race, ethnic background, or birth order). Some of the more common traits[18] that have been measured include aggressiveness, anxiety, attitudes toward aging, authoritarianism, cautiousness, conformity, conservatism, creativity, decision making, dogmatism, egocentrism, ego strength, emotionality, extraversion, happiness, introversion, irritability, morale or life satisfaction, need achievement, passivity, perceived locus of control, reminiscence, rigidity, risk taking, self-concept or self-image, self-esteem, and sociability.

For most traits the evidence in favor of either age differences (cross-sectional studies) or age changes (longitudinal studies) is equivocal. Some scientists report differences between age groups or changes with age, while others are unable to demonstrate any differences or changes. Some of this uncertainty is related to research problems, including the definition and measurement of the traits (Lawton et al., 1980), the use of small or non-representative samples, or the failure to control for possible intervening factors (such as state of health, the onset of a significant life event, socioeconomic status, marital status, gender, or race). However, despite the inconsistent findings there does appear to be evidence to conclude that the current cohort of older people are generally more conservative, cautious, egocentric, introverted, passive, and less emotional than younger age groups. It is unclear whether these differences reflect lifelong characteristics related to cohort socialization, learned changes with age, or forced changes with age because of decreasing opportunities, stereotypes, or changing interaction patterns with younger cohorts.

In addition to the above factors, which are primarily internally determined, there are other personality dimensions that are more dependent on social learning and social interaction. These externally induced factors may be more likely to change with age. For example, consider the concept of self-esteem. This trait measures how people think and feel about themselves, and how they perceive others to view them. Self-esteem is a learned characteristic, a product of lifelong social interaction and social experiences. Most older people report a positive sense of self-esteem. However, the degree of self-esteem is related to such factors as higher socioeconomic status, a higher level of educational attainment, being white, having good health, and having an adequate income. Thus, it is not surprising that a loss in self-esteem may accompany the loss of a job, discrimination against the older worker, a decline in health, and a loss of independence. Moreover, withdrawal from or less frequent interaction with significant others may also reduce a person's level of self-esteem. Some personality dimensions are highly dependent on social learning and interaction, and when losses or changes occur in these areas, older persons, like younger persons, begin to question their worth and competence. This in turn can lower their level of self-esteem or change their self-concept, thereby leading to further changes in behavior and to changes in other personality dimensions.

In summary, while there appear to be some age differences and age changes in personality traits, these are not universal or inevitable. As in most social dimensions, there are individual differences in personality traits (within and between age cohorts) that are influenced by the social environment.

Personality Types

The identification of a number of **personality types** is the most definitive evidence that personality structures are relatively stable throughout adulthood. These types have been derived in an attempt to identify patterns of aging and to explain 'successful' aging or life satisfaction. Various labels or names have been assigned to the characteristic ways in which older individuals think and behave. This area of research has refuted the myth that there is one common personality structure for the aged. There is no evidence to support the usual derogatory stereotype of the elderly person as depressed, lonely, introverted, senile, conservative, aloof, or eccentric.

The first cross-sectional study of the personality structure of older people identified five personality types. These were derived from over one hundred personality traits that were found in eighty-seven white males between 55 and 84 years of age (Reichard et al., 1962). The 'mature' (stable, well-balanced, accepting of aging), the 'rocking chair' (passive, somewhat dependent on others, voluntarily disengaged) and the 'armored' (rigid, disciplined, individualistic, active, highly independent) types were found to be well-adjusted and to be successfully adapting to the aging process. In contrast, the 'angry' (hostile, blaming others for declining abilities, unstable, fighting against social and physical signs of aging) and the 'self-hater' types (blaming themselves, depressed, isolated) were poorly adjusted.

Using data from the Kansas City Study of Adult Life, Neugarten et al. (1964) derived four personality types based on information from fifty-nine men and women aged 70 to 79. According to this classification scheme, the 'integrated' (mature, flexible, future-oriented, active, with high self-esteem) and 'armored or defended' (ambitious, achievement-oriented, fearful of aging, highly active, eager to maintain power and status) types were high in life satisfaction; the 'passive-dependent' types (dependent on others, disengaged, apathetic) expressed moderate levels of life satisfaction; and the small number of 'disorganized' types (unintegrated into society, depressed, angry, showing irrational behavior, unable to control emotions, with deteriorating cognitive processes) were low in satisfaction.

It is obvious that lifestyle factors as well as personality traits make up the personality type. Havighurst (1969) described eight lifestyle patterns of the elderly that were related to the four personality types outlined by Neugarten and her associates. For the integrated personality type, there are three associated lifestyles: (1) 'reorganizers' (engaged in a variety of roles and activities, replacing lost roles with new roles), (2) 'focused' (with interests centered on a few activities or roles); and (3) 'disengaged' (relatively uninvolved in social life). Associated with the armored or defended type are two lifestyles (1) 'holding on ' (attempting to continue midlife roles and activities), and (2) 'constricted' (fighting against aging by restricting social interaction to a few activities or roles). For the passive-dependent personality type, there are two hypothesized lifestyle patterns: (1) 'succorance-seeking' (dependent on attention and emotional support from others), and (2) 'apathetic' (passive, with little social involvement throughout life). Finally, the unintegrated personality type was associated with the 'disorganized' lifestyle pattern (unable to control emotions, behave consistently, or think clearly).

It must be stressed, again, that these personality types and lifestyle patterns are average patterns derived from a single study with a relatively small sample. Not every elderly person will demonstrate a particular type or lifestyle. Moreover, the evidence suggests that one's personality is relatively stable throughout life, and because of continuity in behavior, these later life patterns are probably similar to the personality and lifestyle of the earlier years.

In another study, Maas and Kuypers (1974) interviewed ninety-five women and forty-seven men when the subjects were in their 30s, and again when they were in their 70s. They described six lifestyles for the women (husband-centered, work-centered, group-centered, visiting, uncentered, and disabled-disengaged) and four for the men (family-centered, hobbyists, remotely sociable, and unwell-disengaged). The women demonstrated significant and sometimes dramatic changes in lifestyle over the forty-year period, especially those whose lives were work-centered. They moved from being 'husband-centered' to 'work-centered,' perhaps partly as a result of their personal experiences, but also as a result of changes in societal norms concerning the role of women with respect to family and work. For the men, continuity of lifestyle into the later years was the characteristic pattern. In short, women, especially if employed, may be more adaptive to changing

conditions than men.

In addition to the lifestyle patterns, four personality types were identified for the women ('person-oriented,' 'fearful-ordering,' 'autonomous,' and 'anxious-asserting') and three for the men ('person-oriented,' 'active-competent,' and 'conservative-ordering'). Unlike the changes in lifestyle, which were more prevalent among women, changes in personality over the forty-year period were more pronounced for men. Specifically, the 'conservative-ordering' males and the 'active-competent' males demonstrated the greatest degree of personality change in that they tended to become more conservative and less active with age. Based on the findings of this longitudinal study, Maas and Kuypers (1974:215) concluded that:

> … for those small proportions in our study whose personalities and lifestyles seem problematic, it is not merely old age that has ushered in the dissatisfactions and the suffering. In early adulthood these men and women were in various ways at odds with others and themselves or too constricted in their involvements. Old age merely continues for them what earlier years have launched … Different ways of living may be developed as our social environments change with time — and as we change them.

The 'Type A' and 'Type B' behavior pattern proposed by Friedman and Rosenman (1964) has received much attention. Type A and Type B behaviors have an impact on health and lifestyle, and hence on the way in which individuals adapt to the aging process. To date, Type A and Type B behavior patterns have received relatively little attention from gerontologists. However, these patterns should be studied more intensely since there seems to be a strong relationship between the presence of Type A behavior and coronary heart disease among men. For example, evidence suggests that the risk of coronary heart disease and atherosclerosis for Type A persons is about twice that for Type B persons. Both the incidence and the severity of attacks are likely to be greater among Type A people.

Using a longitudinal study of over 3,500

men, Friedman and Rosenman (1964) employed an interview schedule and the Jenkins Activity Survey (Jenkins et al., 1967) to identify those with Type A and Type B behavioral tendencies. Type A behavior is characterized by the presence of such behavioral traits as excessive competitiveness at work or play, a high need for recognition, rapid eating patterns, impatience with the slow pace at which events occur, thinking about or doing several tasks at the same time, feelings of hostility and aggressiveness, and a feeling of always struggling against time or the environment. Studies have found that those exhibiting Type A characteristics strive to control their environment and prefer to work alone while under stress (self mastery).

In contrast, Type B behavior is characterized by a relative absence of Type A predispositions, which suggests a different orientation to life. The Type B person can play to relax rather than to prove something to himself or others, can work calmly without self-imposed pressure, and can relax without feeling guilty.

At present there is little evidence as to how Type A or Type B behavior develops. While it is thought that heredity and family and work environment play a role, the influence of each factor is unknown. Moreover, it is unclear whether a Type A environment fosters Type A behavior, or whether Type A individuals seek out Type A environments in which to work and live. Both types of behavior only appear given the appropriate stimulus situation. That is, the striving, competitive, impatient Type A person will not demonstrate this behavior unless the demands of the job and personal lifestyle provide an opportunity to utilize this approach to work and living. Furthermore, the Type A and Type B patterns are not mutually exclusive, but rather represent the endpoints of a continuous dimension. For example, Howard et al. (1986) found that, following retirement, Type A behavior does change in the Type B direction. Moreover, they found that the mental health of Type A men improved following retirement, and that a regular program of vigorous exercise was associated with a reduction of Type A behavior.

To date, few cross-sectional studies have examined the relationship between Type A behavior and age for men and women (Siegler et al., 1980:608). While most studies have found little or no relationship, a few have suggested that Type A behavior is more prevalent among younger subjects. However, because of the relative stability in personality structures, and the use of cross-sectional designs, it is likely that any differences between young and old adults in Type A behavior are more a reflection of cohort differences than of changes with age. Finally, although it appears to be difficult to modify Type A behavior, some success has been demonstrated among post-coronary patients who are between 45 and 65 years of age (Friedman, 1980).

In summary, personality types are established by early adulthood through the interaction of heredity, social involvement, and cultural and historical factors. As a result, individuals generally exhibit stable patterns of thought and behavior and relatively consistent lifestyles throughout the middle and later adult years, regardless of their social situation. However, older individuals may become more passive and show less concern for the external social system. They may also demonstrate more interest in the internal personal system (the self). These attitudes may be the result of cognitive or physical changes, or of the occurrence of significant personal life events that affect the individual's ability to cope with the social world. All of the foregoing assumes that an individual is in good health and free of chronic diseases. However, for a small percentage of adults the later years are characterized by serious declines in health that can lead to the development of psychological disorders. The next section briefly considers some of the changes in personality that result from the impact of declining physical and mental health on the psychological system.

Psychopathology

It is beyond the scope of this section to discuss in detail the causes and consequences of the many forms of abnormal personality processes.[19] Nevertheless, it is important to recognize that with a decline in health as one ages, individual behavior may change dramatically for a variety of reasons. These changes may be reflected in temporary sadness or depression, in clinical depression, in abnormal emotional responses, or in an inability to think clearly and consistently. Ultimately, the individual may be incapable of functioning as an independent person and will require nursing care, often in an institutional setting. In short, significant cognitive impairment in later life develops due to disease, not due to normal aging (Jarvik, 1988).

With a greater likelihood of experiencing social losses, physical disease, physiological changes, social isolation, nutritional deficiencies, a diminished self-esteem, and poverty, the elderly may be predisposed to both organic [20] (physical) and functional[21] (psychological) personality disorders. Functional disorders can be divided into the less serious neuroses (involving varying degrees of anxiety or fear) and the more disabling psychoses (where reality is distorted so that medication, psychotherapy, or institutionalization may be required). The most common neuroses are anxiety reactions to specific situations or stimuli, excessive concern about one's health (hypochondria), obsessions, and irrational fears or phobias. The more common psychoses are mild to severe depression (which can lead to suicide[22]), paranoid reactions, and schizophrenia.

Signs of forgetfulness or unusual behavior are often labeled as senility. However, only organic brain disorders, where there is deterioration in the brain cells because of disease, can be called senile brain disease (senile dementia). The onset of this disease state is reflected by the gradual onset of confusion and disorientation with respect to time, people, and situations; loss of short- and long-term memory; loss of interest and enthusiasm for daily events; restricted vocabulary; poor judgment; inability to comprehend information; and radical mood shifts. The prognosis for this disease is not good; in most cases it eventually causes death, either directly or indirectly. The most devastating form of senile dementia is Alzheimer's disease, which may affect anywhere from 100,000 to 300,000 Canadians. It is not part of the normal aging process, but because it is an organic brain disease that develops over a period of years, the most serious and obvious symptoms are observed in older adults. To date, many theories exist as to the cause, but the underlying etiology is not fully understood. Hence, there is no known treatment, and it is an extremely difficult disease to diagnose. Alzheimer's disease evolves in stages, beginning with memory loss and memory inefficiencies, which only the victim may notice. Then, more serious memory impairments become obvious to others, the person may have difficulty speaking, and there may be a loss of control of body functions. In the final stages, wandering, emotional outbursts, and inability to communicate often require institutionalized care. Until such time as complete dependence on others is reached, the spouse and family can experience considerable caregiving stress (see chapter 10).

The other major organic disorder is cerebral arteriosclerosis. This is caused by hardening of the arteries in the brain, reducing the blood flow and restricting the amount of oxygen and nutrients reaching the brain. The prognosis for cerebral arteriosclerosis is somewhat more optimistic, since drugs are available to treat the disorder.

In summary, few elderly persons experience personality dysfunctions. Most older people adapt, and do not suffer clinical levels of disturbance in the cognitive or emotional processes. That the majority do adapt is somewhat remarkable considering the crises and personal changes many people experience after about 60 years of age.

SUMMARY AND CONCLUSIONS

There is inter- and intra-individual variation in intellectual performance and in personality structures throughout the life cycle. However, in the later years the degree of variation in intellectual functioning and personality adjustment is greater, so that general norms are less likely to be applicable to the study of the elderly. Much of the observed variation is due to such personal factors as heredity, health, income, education, present or former occupation, and past and current lifestyle.

The first half of this chapter examined the

relationship between aging and such cognitive processes as intelligence, learning, memory, thinking, problem solving, and creativity. In the second half, the focus was on the relationship between aging and personality processes. Specifically, the literature pertaining to personality traits, personality types, and psychopathology in the middle and later years was reviewed. Special attention was directed to the question of whether social behavior in the middle and later years is a function of personality traits or of the social situation, and to the question of whether one's personality remains stable or changes over the life cycle.

Based on this review of the relationship between aging and cognitive and personality processes, it can be concluded that:

1. The decline in cognitive processes may be less rapid and severe than the decline in sensorimotor or physical abilities.
2. Fluid intelligence, after reaching a peak during adolescence, declines with age.
3. Crystallized intelligence increases with age, at least until the individual is no longer interested in acquiring new information.
4. Individual differences in measured intelligence by age can be accounted for, not by chronological age per se, but rather by the interaction of biological and sensory losses with sociocultural, personal, and situational factors unique to a given individual.
5. The normal aging process does not significantly diminish the ability to solve problems.
6. The elderly can continue to learn if adequate personal and situational conditions are present. Since it might take them longer to learn and produce a required response, learning is more likely to occur if individuals can establish their own rates and speeds of learning.
7. A progressive decline in memory performance is neither inevitable nor irreversible.
8. Older persons appear to be able to remember and recall distant events

(reminiscence) more readily than recent events.
9. The ability to solve problems and engage in complex thinking may decline with age because of a general slowing of cognitive speed and verbal processes, and because of an unwillingness or an inability to utilize newer, more efficient strategies.
10. In general, creative potential peaks at about 40 years of age. However, there are individual differences by occupation, and given an appropriate environment and personal motivation, some elderly people are capable of highly creative work well into their later years.
11. Social behavior in the later years reflects a continuous interaction between the individual and the social situation. That is, an individual's personality influences the behavior and adaptation demonstrated in particular situations, while the situation itself influences what traits from the available repertoire will be expressed, and in what way.
12. According to cross-sectional studies, personality differences exist beyond middle age; longitudinal studies suggest that after early adulthood personality characteristics are relatively stable.
13. Both personality traits and personality types are relatively stable across the life cycle. However, there are individual differences in thought and behavior that may be demonstrated in the later years as individuals become more passive and less concerned about normative constraints.
14. With a decline in physical health with advancing age, the elderly are more likely to be predisposed to organic or functional personality disorders. However, few elderly persons experience personality dysfunctions, and most older people do not experience any clinical level of disturbance in the cognitive or emotional processes.

NOTES

1. Some tests are designed to assess the overall capacity or potential of an individual, and others are used to measure ability at the time the test is completed. Similarly, some tests emphasize speed and performance; others concentrate more on verbal skills.

2. One of the most frequently used intelligence tests is the Wechsler Adult Intelligence Scale (WAIS). This is based on materials originally used to test children and adolescents. The reliability and validity of this instrument for use with older adults is questionable, since it is a general test that includes items that measure competence in situations rarely encountered by the middle-aged or elderly (Schaie, 1978). At present there are no intelligence tests specifically designed for older adults (Woodruff-Pak, 1989:107).

3. See Horn et al., 1981; Hultsch and Deutsch, 1981; Horn, 1982; Woodruff, 1983; Labouvie-Vief, 1985; Reese and Rodeheaver, 1985; Jarvik, 1988; Schaie, 1989, 1990; Woodruff-Pak, 1989; Schooler, 1990.

4. Botwinick (1984) suggests that education may be more important than age in explaining individual differences in intelligence.

5. Individuals who have similar lifestyles also appear to experience similar patterns of cognitive functioning over time (Gribbin et al., 1980).

6. Many of the tasks in learning experiments are verbal and are not meaningful or relevant, especially to an older person. For example, paired-associate learning involves learning unrelated pairs of words in a list (fish-rainbow) and then responding with the second word in each pair when presented with the first word as the stimulus. The other most frequent learning task is serial learning, where a list of words or nonsense syllables is presented; then the list must be recalled in order (SCU, AXP, YYZ, DRU, FQI, NCP, etc.). It is generally found that older people perform poorly on both types of tasks. Moreover, women compared with men seem to be less proficient at all ages, but particularly in the later years, on tests involving nonverbal stimuli. In studies where meaningful and 'real' text materials have been used, age-related differences are less prevalent.

7. For example, university-level correspondence courses (where lectures are provided on tape and with printed learning aids) may be a more effective learning situation, not only for the elderly, but also for all adults who have been absent from formal schooling for many years. These adults can learn at their own pace without having to take notes in a classroom from a professor who speaks rapidly, and they can replay the tapes as many times as necessary.

8. Recall memory is thought to involve registration, storage, and retrieval of information; recognition memory primarily involves registration and storage.

9. This may be related to reminiscence, where significant events in the past have been frequently rehearsed.

10. See Goldstein and Blackman, 1978; Cohen and Wu, 1980; Peterson and Eden, 1981; Birren and Livingston, 1985; Cunningham, 1987; Salthouse, 1985, 1990; Kausler, 1990.

11. Some of the more common theoretical approaches to the study of personality and its influence on human behavior are psychoanalytic theory, social-learning theory, ego-development theory, the personality-trait perspective, and the interactionist perspective.

12. Although cross-sectional designs (the search for age differences) have been used almost exclusively, interest in both developmental psychology during adulthood and in social gerontology has led to the initiation of a few longitudinal or sequential-cohort studies (the search for stability or change over time).

13. Although most studies have focused on measures of one or more personality *traits* (for example, introversion, sociability, aggressiveness, egocentrism, achievement orientation, dependency, etc.), a few studies have used multidimensional scales to arrive at personality *types* (for example, integrated, passive-dependent, work-centered, active-competent, person-oriented, rocking chair, etc.). Moreover, a variety of instruments have been used to measure personality traits or types. These include clinical case studies obtained through interviews; personality inventories (the Cattell 16PF); projective techniques (the Thematic Apperception Test or the Rorschach Inkblot test); laboratory behavioral tests; and content analyses of life histories, diaries, memoirs, or autobiographies.

14. Gemeinschaft refers to a community or society where kinship bonds, tradition, informality, and friendship prevail as the major factors in social interaction. This type of society is often found in rural or primitive cultures with low degrees of industrialization.

15. Gesellschaft, the opposite of Gemeinschaft, refers to a society where social relationships are formal, impersonal, competitive, and utilitarian. This type of society is found in modernized nations and in metropolitan regions.

16. See Maas and Kuypers, 1974; Costa and McCrae, 1980; McCrae et al., 1980; Costa et al., 1981, 1987.
17. The instruments most frequently used are the Guilford-Zimmerman Temperament Survey; Cattell's 16 Personality Factor (16PF) Inventory; Eysenck's Personality Inventory; and the Minnesota Multiphasic Personality Inventory.
18. Sometimes the traits are measured as isolated characteristics; at other times they are measured in such a way that clusters are formed. For example, on the 16PF instrument, sociability, impulsiveness, and dominance combine to represent the personality factor of extraversion. Neugarten (1977) questions whether it can be assumed that personality traits are independent of one another, or whether the traits are interrelated to create a personality structure.
19. More comprehensive discussions can be found in Pfeiffer, 1977; La Rue et al., 1985; Cohen, 1990.
20. Organic disorders result from physiological changes and disease processes such as decreased or impaired blood flow to the brain (hardening of the arteries), brain tumors, or degenerative changes in the brain (senile brain disease).
21. Functional disorders are not related to physical causes and are a reflection of an individual's inability to cope with or adapt to the social environment.
22. In 1986 there were 24.6 and 34.9 suicides per 100,000 men 65 to 69 and 70 and over respectively; the rates for women in these age groups were 7 and 10 per 100,000 (Beneteau, 1988).

REFERENCES

Baltes, P. (1979). 'Life-Span Development Psychology: Some Converging Observations on History and Theory,' pp. 255-79 in P. Baltes and O. Brim (eds.). *Life-Span Development and Behavior*. vol. 2. New York: Academic Press.

Beneteau, R. (1988). 'Trends in Suicide,' *Canadian Social Trends*, 11 (Winter), 22-24.

Bengston, V. et al. (1985). 'Aging and Self-Conceptions: Personality Processes and Social Contexts,' pp. 544-93 in J. Birren and W. Schaie (eds.). *Handbook of the Psychology of Aging*. 2d ed. New York: Van Nostrand Reinhold.

Birren, J. and J. Livingston (eds.). (1985). *Cognition, Stress and Aging*. Englewood Cliffs, N.J.: Prentice-Hall.

Birren, J. and W. Schaie (eds.). (1977). *Handbook of the Psychology of Aging*. New York: Van Nostrand Reinhold.

Birren, J. and W. Schaie (eds.). (1985). *Handbook of the Psychology of Aging*. 2d ed. New York: Van Nos-

trand Reinhold.

Birren, J. and W. Schaie (eds.). (1990). *Handbook of the Psychology of Aging*. 3d ed. San Diego, Calif.: Academic Press.

Botwinick, J. (1984). *Aging and Behavior*. 3d ed. New York: Springer Publishing Co.

Charness, N. (1981). 'Aging and Skilled Problem Solving,' *Journal of Experimental Psychology: General*, 110(1), 21-38.

Clayton, V. (1982). 'Wisdom and Intelligence: The Nature and Function of Knowledge in the Later Years,' *International Journal of Aging and Human Development*, 15(4), 315-21.

Cohen, D. and S. Wu. (1980). 'Language and Cognition during Aging,' pp. 71-96 in C. Eisdorfer (ed.). *Annual Review of Gerontology and Geriatrics*. vol. 1. New York: Springer Publishing Co.

Cohen, G. (1990). 'Psychopathology and Mental Health in the Mature and Elderly Adult,' pp. 359-74 in J. Birren and W. Schaie (eds.). *Handbook of the Psychology of Aging*. 3d ed. San Diego, Calif.: Academic Press.

Cohen-Shalev, A. (1989). 'Old Age Style: Developmental Changes in Creative Production from a Life-Span Perspective,' *Journal of Aging Studies*, 3(1), 21-38.

Costa, P. and R. McCrae. (1980). 'Still Stable after All These Years: Personality as a Key to Some Issues in Aging,' pp. 65-102 in P. Baltes and O. Brim (eds.). *Life-Span Development and Behavior*. vol. 3. New York: Academic Press.

Costa, P. et al. (1980). 'Enduring Dispositions in Adult Males,' *Journal of Personality and Social Psychology*, 38(6), 793-800.

Costa, P. et al. (1981). 'Personal Adjustment to Aging: Longitudinal Prediction from Neuroticism and Extraversion,' *Journal of Gerontology*, 36(1), 78-85.

Costa, P. et al. (1987). 'Longitudinal Analyses of Psychological Well-Being in a National Sample: Stability of Mean Levels,' *Journal of Gerontology*, 42(1), 50-55.

Coyne, A. et al. (1978). 'Adult Age Differences in Reflection-Impulsivity,' *Journal of Gerontology*, 33(3), 402-7.

Craik, F. (1977). 'Age Differences in Human Memory,' pp. 384-420 in J. Birren and W. Schaie (eds.). *Handbook of the Psychology of Aging*. New York: Van Nostrand Reinhold.

Craik, F. and S. Trehub (eds.). (1981). *Aging and Cognitive Processes*. New York: Plenum Press.

Cunningham, W. (1987). 'Intellectual Abilities and Age,' pp. 117-34 in W. Schaie (ed.). *Annual Review of Gerontology and Geriatrics*. vol. 7. New York: Springer Publishing Co.

Fozard, J. (1981). 'Person-Environment Relationships in Adulthood — Implications for Human Factors

Engineering,' *Human Factors*, 23(1), 7-27.

Friedman, M. (1980). 'Type A Behavior: A Progress Report,' *The Sciences*, 20(2), 10, 11, 28.

Friedman, M. and R. Rosenman. (1964). *Type A Behavior and Your Heart.* New York: Alfred A. Knopf.

Goldstein, K. and S. Blackman. (1978). *Cognitive Style: Five Approaches and Relevant Research.* New York: Wiley-Interscience.

Gribbin, K. et al. (1980). 'Complexity of Life-Style and Maintenance of Intellectual Abilities,' *Journal of Social Issues*, 36(2), 47-61.

Haan, N. (1976). '...Change and Sameness...' *International Journal of Aging and Human Development*, 7(1), 59-65.

Haan, N. and D. Day. (1974). 'A Longitudinal Study of Change and Sameness in Personality Development: Adolescence to Later Adulthood,' *International Journal of Aging and Human Development*, 5(1), 11-39.

Havighurst, R. (1969). 'Research and Development in Social Gerontology: A Report of a Special Committee of the Gerontological Society,' *The Gerontologist*, 9(4), 1-90.

Hines, T. and J. Fozard. (1980). 'Memory and Aging: Relevance of Recent Developments for Research and Application,' pp. 97-120 in C. Eisdorfer (ed.). *Annual Review of Gerontology and Geriatrics.* vol. 1. New York: Springer Publishing Co.

Horn, J. (1982). 'The Theory of Fluid and Crystallized Intelligence in Relation to Concepts of Cognitive Psychology and Aging in Adulthood,' pp. 237-78 in F. Craik and S. Trehub (eds.). *Aging and Cognitive Processes.* New York: Plenum Press.

Horn, J. et al. (1981). 'Apprehension, Memory and Fluid Intelligence Decline in Adulthood,' *Research on Aging*, 3(1), 33-84.

Howard, J. et al. (1986). 'Change in Type A Behavior a Year after Retirement,' *The Gerontologist*, 26(6), 643-49.

Hoyer, W. and D. Plude. (1980). 'Attentional and Perceptual Processes in the Study of Cognitive Aging,' pp. 227-38 in L. Poon (ed.). *Aging in the 1980s: Psychological Issues.* Washington, D.C.: American Psychological Association.

Hultsch, D. (1985). 'Adult Memory: What Are the Limits,' pp. 20-52 in E. Gee and G. Gutman (eds.). *The Challenge of Time.* Winnipeg, Man.: Canadian Association on Gerontology.

Hultsch, D. and F. Deutsch. (1981). *Adult Development and Aging: A Life-Span Perspective.* New York: McGraw-Hill.

Hultsch, D. and R. Dixon (eds.). (1990). 'Learning and Memory in Aging,' pp. 259-74 in J. Birren and W. Schaie (eds.). *Handbook of the Psychology of Aging.* 3d. ed. San Diego, Calif.: Academic Press.

Hultsch, D. et. al. (1985). 'Memory Perceptions and Memory Performance in Adulthood and Aging,' *Canadian Journal on Aging*, 4(4), 179-87.

Jarvik, L. (1988). 'Aging of the Brain: How Can We Prevent It?' *The Gerontologist*, 28(6), 739-47.

Jenkins, C. et al. (1967). 'Development of an Objective Psychological Test for the Determination of the Coronary Prone Behavior Pattern in Employed Men,' *Journal of Chronic Diseases*, 20(6), 371-79.

Kausler, D. (1990). 'Motivation, Human Aging, and Cognitive Performance,' pp. 172-83 in J. Birren and W. Schaie (eds.). *Handbook of the Psychology of Aging.* 3d ed. San Diego, Calif.: Academic Press.

Kogan, N. (1973). 'Creativity and Cognitive Styles: A Life-Span Perspective,' pp. 146-78 in P. Baltes and W. Schaie (eds.). *Life-Span Developmental Psychology: Personality and Socialization.* New York: Academic Press.

Kogan, N. (1990). 'Personality and Aging,' pp. 330-46 in J. Birren and W. Schaie (eds.). *Handbook of the Psychology of Aging.* 3d ed. San Diego, Calif.: Academic Press.

Labouvie-Vief, G. (1985). 'Intelligence and Cognition,' pp. 500-530 in J. Birren and W. Schaie (eds.). *Handbook of the Psychology of Aging.* 2d ed. New York: Van Nostrand Reinhold.

Labouvie-Vief, G. and M. Chandler. (1978). 'Cognitive Development and Life-Span Developmental Theory: Idealistic Versus Contextual Perspectives,' pp. 181-210 in P. Baltes (ed.). *Life-Span Development and Behavior.* vol. 1. New York: Academic Press.

La Rue, A. et al. (1985). 'Aging and Mental Disorders,' pp. 664-702 in J. Birren and W. Schaie (eds.). *Handbook of the Psychology of Aging.* 2d ed. New York: Van Nostrand Reinhold.

Laszlo, J. et al. (1980). 'Distracting Information, Motor Performance and Sex Differences,' *Nature*, 283 (January), 377-78.

Lawton, M.P. et al. (1980). 'Personality Tests and Their Uses with Older Adults,' pp. 537-53 in J. Birren and R. Sloane (eds.). *Handbook of Mental Health and Aging.* Englewood Cliffs, N.J.: Prentice-Hall.

Maas, H. and J. Kuypers. (1974). *From Thirty to Seventy.* San Francisco: Jossey-Bass.

McCrae, R. and P. Costa, Jr. (1984). *Emerging Lives, Enduring Dispositions: Personality in Adulthood.* Waltham, Mass.: Little, Brown & Co.

McCrae, R. et al. (1980). 'Constancy of Adult Personality Structure in Males: Longitudinal, Cross-Sectional and Times of Measurement Analyses,' *Journal of Gerontology*, 35(6), 877-83.

McDowd, J. and J. Birren. (1990). 'Aging and Attentional Processes,' pp. 222-33 in J. Birren and W. Schaie (eds.). *Handbook of the Psychology of Aging.* 3d ed. San Diego, Calif.: Academic Press.

McLeish, J. (1976). *The Ulyssean Adult: Creativity in the Middle and Later Years.* New York: McGraw-Hill.

Murdock, B. (1967). 'Recent Developments in Short-Term Memory,' *Quarterly Journal of Experimental Psychology,* 18(3), 206-11.

Neugarten, B. (1977). 'Personality and Aging,' pp. 626-49 in J. Birren and W. Schaie (eds.). *Handbook of the Psychology of Aging.* New York: Van Nostrand Reinhold.

Neugarten, B. et al. (1964). *Personality in Middle and Later Life.* New York: Atherton Press.

Perlmutter, M. et al. (1987). 'Aging and Memory,' pp. 57-92 in W. Schaie (ed.). *Annual Review of Gerontology and Geriatrics.* vol. 7. New York: Springer Publishing Co.

Peterson, D. and D. Eden. (1981). 'Cognitive Style and the Older Learner,' *Educational Gerontology,* 7(1), 57-66.

Pfeiffer, E. (1977). 'Psychopathology and Social Pathology,' pp. 650-71 in J. Birren and W. Schaie (eds.). *Handbook of the Psychology of Aging.* New York: Van Nostrand Reinhold.

Poon, L. (1985). 'Differences in Human Memory with Aging: Nature, Causes and Clinical Implications,' pp. 427-62 in J. Birren and W. Schaie (eds.). *Handbook of the Psychology of Aging.* 2d ed. New York: Van Nostrand Reinhold.

Poon, L. and J. Fozard. (1978). 'Speed of Retrieval from Long-Term Memory in Relation to Age, Familiarity, and Datedness of Information,' *Journal of Gerontology,* 33(5), 711-17.

Pratt, M. and J. Norris. (forthcoming). *Aging and Socio-Cognitive Development.* Markham, Ont.: Butterworths.

Rabbitt, P. (1977). 'Changes in Problem Solving Ability in Old Age,' pp. 606-25 in J. Birren and W. Schaie (eds.). *Handbook of the Psychology of Aging.* New York: Van Nostrand Reinhold.

Reese, H. and D. Rodeheaver. (1985). 'Problem Solving and Complex Decision Making,' pp. 474-99 in J. Birren and W. Schaie (eds.). *Handbook of the Psychology of Aging.* 2d ed. New York: Van Nostrand Reinhold.

Reichard, S. et al. (1962). *Aging and Personality.* New York: John Wiley.

Ryff, C. (1982). 'Self-Perceived Personality Change in Adulthood and Aging,' *Journal of Personality and Social Psychology,* 42(1), 108-15.

Salthouse, T. (1985). 'Speed of Behavior and Its Implications for Cognition,' pp. 400-426 in J. Birren and W. Schaie (eds.). *Handbook of the Psychology of Aging.* 2d ed. New York: Van Nostrand Reinhold.

Salthouse, T. (1987). 'The Role of Experience in Cognitive Aging,' pp. 135-58 in W. Schaie (ed.). *Annual Review of Gerontology and Geriatrics.* vol. 7.

New York: Springer Publishing Co.

Salthouse, T. (1990). 'Cognitive Competence and Expertise in Aging,' pp. 311-19 in J. Birren and W. Schaie (eds.). *Handbook of the Psychology of Aging.* 3d ed. San Diego, Calif.: Academic Press.

Schaie, W. (1978). 'External Validity in the Assessment of Intellectual Development in Adulthood,' *Journal of Gerontology,* 33(5), 695-701.

Schaie, W. (1989). 'The Hazards of Cognitive Aging,' *The Gerontologist,* 29(4), 484-93.

Schaie, W. (1990). 'Intellectual Development in Adulthood,' pp. 291-310 in J. Birren and W. Schaie (eds.). *Handbook of the Psychology of Aging.* 3d ed. San Diego, Calif.: Academic Press.

Scheidt, R. and W. Schaie. (1978). 'A Taxonomy of Situations for an Elderly Population: Generating Situational Criteria,' *Journal of Gerontology,* 33(6), 848-57.

Schonfield, A. (1980). 'Learning, Memory and Aging,' pp. 214-44 in J. Birren and R. Sloane (eds.). *Handbook of Mental Health and Aging.* Englewood Cliffs, N.J.: Prentice-Hall.

Schooler, C. (1990). 'Psychosocial Factors and Effective Cognitive Functioning in Adulthood,' pp. 347-58 in J. Birren and W. Schaie (eds.). *Handbook of the Psychology of Aging.* 3d ed. San Diego, Calif.: Academic Press.

Schulz, R. (1985). 'Emotion and Affect,' pp. 531-43 in J. Birren and W. Schaie (eds.). *Handbook of the Psychology of Aging.* 2d ed. New York: Van Nostrand Reinhold.

Shanan, J. and J. Jacobowitz. (1982). 'Personality and Aging,' pp. 148-78 in D. Eisdorfer et al. (eds.). *Annual Review of Gerontology and Geriatrics.* vol. 3 New York: Springer Publishing Co.

Siegler, I. et al. (1980). 'Health and Behavior: Methodological Considerations for Adult Development and Aging,' pp. 599-612 in L. Poon (ed). *Aging in the 1980s: Psychological Issues.* Washington, D.C.: American Psychological Association.

Simonton, D. (1990). 'Creativity and Wisdom in Aging,' pp. 320-29 in J. Birren and W. Schaie (eds.). *Handbook of the Psychology of Aging.* 3d ed. San Diego, Calif.: Academic Press.

Taub, H. (1973). 'Memory Span, Practice and Aging,' *Journal of Gerontology,* 28(3), 335-38.

Thomae, H. (1980). 'Personality and Adjustment to Aging,' pp. 285-309 in J. Birren and R. Sloane (eds.). *Handbook of Mental Health and Aging.* Englewood Cliffs, N.J.: Prentice-Hall.

Tulving, E. (1972). 'Episodic and Semantic Memory,' pp. 382-403 in E. Tulving and W. Donaldson (eds.). *Organization of Memory.* New York: Academic Press.

Whitbourne, S. (1987). 'Personality Development in Adulthood and Old Age: Relationships among

Identity Style, Health, and Well-Being,' pp. 189-216 in W. Schaie (ed.). *Annual Review of Gerontology and Geriatrics*. vol. 7. New York: Springer Publishing Co.

Williams, R. and C. Wirths. (1965). *Lives through the Years*. New York: Atherton Press.

Willis, S. (1985). 'Towards an Educational Psychology of the Older Adult Learner: Intellectual and Cognitive Bases,' pp. 818-47 in J. Birren and W. Schaie (eds.). *Handbook of the Psychology of Aging*. 2d ed. New York: Van Nostrand Reinhold.

Willis, S. (1987). 'Cognitive Training and Everyday Competence,' pp. 159-88 in W. Schaie (ed.). *Annual Review of Gerontology and Geriatrics*. vol. 7. New York: Springer Publishing Company.

Willis, S. and P. Baltes. (1980) 'Intelligence in Adulthood and Aging: Contemporary Issues,' pp. 260-72 in L. Poon (ed.). *Aging in the 1980s: Psychological Issues*. Washington, D.C.: American Psychological Association.

Winograd, E. (1975). 'Frame Representations in the Declarative/Procedural Controversy,' pp. 185-210 in D. Bobrow and A. Collins (eds.). *Representation and Understanding: Studies in Cognitive Science*. New York: Academic Press.

Woodruff, D. (1983). 'A Review of Aging and Cognitive Processes,' *Research on Aging*, 5(2), 139-53.

Woodruff-Pak, D. (1989). 'Aging and Intelligence: Changing Perspectives in the Twentieth Century,' *Journal of Aging Studies*, 3(2), 91-118.

Part Three

A MACROANALYSIS OF AGING AS A SOCIAL PROCESS

In Part Three aging is studied from a macro-sociological perspective. Here, the focus is on how the social structure and related social processes influence aging and the status of the aged.

Chapter 7 contains a discussion of the way in which social structure influences the process of aging for age cohorts at the societal level of analysis, and for generations within the extended family. The chapter examines the relationship between social structure and such processes as cohort flow, socialization, stereotyping, attitude formation, ageism, and stratification. Other issues considered are the status of the elderly within the age structure; the extent to which the aged represent a unique minority, poverty, or political group; the issue of single

versus multiple jeopardy; and the extent to which a generation gap exists in society and in the extended family.

Chapter 8 looks at the influence of the physical environment on the aging process, with an emphasis on interaction between personal and environmental systems. At the macro level of analysis, factors influencing the aging process such as rural versus urban living, age-integrated versus age-segregated housing, availability of transportation, criminal victimization of the elderly, fear of criminal victimization, and migration are considered. At the micro level, the type and quality of dwelling unit, institutionalization, and mobility and migration in the later years are discussed.

7
Aging: The Social Structure and Social Processes

Health and Welfare Canada, Information Directorate

This chapter divides the complex phenomenon of social organization into two major components — social structure and social process — and discusses the interplay between structure, processes, and social interaction as an individual ages (George, 1990). Throughout, the focus is on the influence of chronological age and social age in the organization of society. Every society has a social structure that is influenced by the age distribution of the population. This structure sets boundaries for life chances and lifestyle by assigning people to age-appropriate social roles. A culture evolves within this structure that defines, facilitates, or prohibits particular forms of social behavior and self-perceptions at specific stages in the life cycle. For the individual, norms facilitate social interaction and the transition between roles and stages in the life cycle.

As will be seen, however, the process and product of social interaction between age cohorts is not as simple as suggested above. Rather, the process is complicated by the following social factors.

1. A dynamic age structure that can change over time with respect to the size, composition, or social meaning of age groups;
2. Unique historical and social events that a specific generation may experience at a particular stage in life;
3. Perceived or real age-based inequalities that may lead to tension and conflict between age groups;
4. The relationship of age to other elements of social differentiation such as gender, race, ethnicity, and social class;
5. Individual differences within an age cohort or generation (generational units);
6. The presence of different age structures within a variety of social institutions such as the family, the economy, the polity, leisure, and religion;
7. The cross-cultural variations in the age structure of developing and developed nations.

It is necessary to distinguish between the structure and processes unique to age cohorts or generations at the societal level and those unique to aging within the extended family. For example, a generational difference or 'generation gap' may be revealed when studies randomly sample and compare unrelated 65, 45, and 25-year-olds. However, differences may or may not be perceived if the study compares the responses of those who are 65, 45, and 25 years of age within the same extended family. That is, differences between cohorts may be more pronounced at the societal level than at the micro level where the extended family is the unit of analysis.

The study of aging phenomena from a macro perspective is characterized by diverse conceptual and theoretical approaches. For example, many of the theories and concepts presented in chapter 4 (socialization theory, minority group theory, disengagement theory, and continuity theory) appear to be useful in studying the interaction between social structure, social processes, and aging phenomena. The remainder of this chapter introduces concepts and processes pertaining to birth cohorts and to generations at both the macro and micro structural levels of analysis, examines the influence on the aging process of the interaction between social structure and social processes from a macro-level cohort and generational analysis, and presents a micro-level analysis of lineage (family) interaction within and between generations in the kinship system. Included are a discussion of the structure of the kinship system and an analysis of the hypothesized generation gap or generational conflict assumed to exist within extended families.

THE SOCIAL STRUCTURE AND AGING

Introduction

In the absence of a social structure, chaos would prevail because of the lack of regular, persistent, and enduring patterns of social interaction. In order to function and survive, all social systems, from married couples to societies, require a division of labor among the members. This horizontal separation of positions (husband, wife, friends, neighbors) occurs within all social institutions and is known as social differentiation.

The social positions found within each system are evaluated and ranked, and varying degrees of status are assigned to each position. As a result, a vertical dimension is added to the social structure. Certain positions are evaluated as having more or less status, power, or prestige than others. This vertical ranking may be based on the ascribed characteristics of the individuals who occupy the position (age, sex, race, ethnicity, socioeconomic status), or on the achievements of those who have occupied the position in the past. Generally, the greater the status of a position, the greater the social or monetary rewards given to the person who occupies the position.

Because specific ascribed or achieved characteristics are evaluated differently, not everyone has an equal opportunity to attain specific positions in the social structure. Some degree of inequality prevails in most social systems, and influences both the life chances and lifestyle of specific individuals. For example, with North American societies the institutionalized systems of stratification are generally based on age, sex, class, race, or ethnicity. As Tumin (1967:27) noted, one is generally considered better, superior, or more worthy if one is:

- White rather than black
- Male rather than female
- Protestant rather than Catholic or Jewish
- Educated rather than uneducated
- Rich rather than poor
- White-collar rather than blue-collar
- Of good family background rather than of undistinguished family origin
- Young rather than old
- Urban or suburban rather than rural-dwelling
- Of Anglo-Saxon origin rather than any other
- Native-born rather than of foreign descent
- Employed rather than unemployed
- Married rather than divorced

Like Rubik's Cube, the **social structure** of modern developed societies is a complex mo-saic of intersecting horizontal and vertical dimensions representing a variety of social characteristics. In contrast, in preindustrialized societies a simple three-tiered structure often prevails: a group of elderly males who rule as a gerontocracy; all other adults; and children and adolescents who have not been declared 'adults' by some rite of passage.

The social structure represents an arrangement of positions or statuses within a number of social institutions (family, education, economy, polity, religion) in a given society. The status associated with each position is ascribed or achieved on the basis of such factors as age, race, sex, class, ethnicity, occupation, education, or religion. Associated with each position are roles that define the expected rights, obligations, and behavioral patterns of the individual who occupies the position. Social norms evolve that represent common agreement on how individuals should behave while occupying specific roles. These norms provide clues as to how others will interpret and react to the individual.

In short, the social structure represents the distribution of individuals according to various socially evaluated characteristics. These characteristics distinguish individuals from each other and influence the positions they occupy, both within a specific social system (such as the place of employment) and within the community or society at large. Thus, throughout one's life this 'assignment' to certain positions introduces inequality to the social system, influences our life chances and lifestyles, and facilitates or inhibits social interaction within and between the various strata of the social structure (Blau, 1975, 1980; Bengtson et al., 1985; Hagestad and Neugarten, 1985; O'Rand, 1990).

This structural differentiation facilitates or inhibits interaction and leads to the integration or isolation of individuals or groups within a social system. A middle-aged male may have relatively high status in the age structure, high status in the family, little authority or power in the place of employment and the community, and relatively low status because of his class background. With the interaction between substructures in mind, the remainder of this chapter will focus on the age structure of society and of a specific social institution (the family). We will also consider how these structures change over time and vary cross-culturally, and how various social structures influence social processes at the macro (societal) level and interaction at the micro (interpersonal) level.

Before turning to this analysis, it is important to clarify the meaning of three major concepts frequently used in this area of gerontology: 'cohort,' 'generation,' and 'generational unit.' The search for conclusive definitions of these concepts represents a continuing debate among social scientists and gerontologists. A **cohort** is a group of individuals who were born within a given period. This is a general term that is based on a quantifiable difference between groups (one year or five years).

A **generation** represents a grouping of individual or adjacent birth cohorts, where a large proportion of the members have experienced a significant sociohistorical event (a war, the baby boom, a depression) in a similar manner. This event subsequently influences their life chances (educational or occupational opportunities) or lifestyles. The term 'generation' represents a qualitative rather than a quantitative difference between groups of individuals. There may be subgroups within the same generation with different world views or with a unique group consciousness (for example, young adults who are college students versus age peers who are blue-collar workers). Each unique subgroup is defined as a **generational unit.**

It is important to distinguish between cohort analysis, generational analysis, and lineage effects. The term **cohort analysis** is in common use in demography, and refers to the analysis of quantitatively defined birth cohorts. **Generational analysis** refers to a macro-level analysis of specific cohorts, or groups of cohorts, that are theoretically combined because of their common sociohistorical experiences. Generational analysis has also been used to examine differences between generations within the extended family. As Marshall (1983) notes, however, the analysis of relationships within the kinship structure is more appropriately and commonly labeled 'lineage effects.' In this text, the use of 'cohort' and 'generational' analysis will be restricted to the macro level of analysis, while the term **lineage effects** will be used at the micro

level when examining the structure and social processes within the context of the extended family.

Age Cohorts and the Social Structure

Introduction

Age, unlike attributes such as sex, race, or ethnicity, which have an impact only on certain individuals, is a universal factor in determining an individual's location and status in the social structure. Every society has an age structure based on both chronological and social age. These factors determine which persons gain access to social positions, at what stage in life they gain access to or relinquish roles, how different cohorts interact with each other, what age-role expectations are demanded from the occupants of particular positions, and what status is attached to those of a particular chronological age (Riley, 1987). The following sections indicate how chronological and social age contribute to the creation of a social structure within society in general, and to an age structure within such institutions as the family, work, polity, and leisure.

Demographic Factors and the Age Structure

Whether a society has a high or low proportion of individuals of any given age depends on such demographic processes as fertility, mortality, and migration, and on the presence or absence of such historical events as technological revolutions, disasters, wars, or epidemics. Since new birth cohorts succeed one another over time, the size and composition of the population are subject to demographic changes, and the age structure of a local, regional, or national social system can change over time. There have been changes in the number of strata and in the shape of the age structure. There have also been changes in the relative prestige positions of the strata. For example, in premodernized societies the oldest male generally had the most prestige and power; in modern societies, which have more strata, the power shifts to the middle-aged group.

Demographic changes in the size and composition of the age structure may also lead to social changes in the society (Foner, 1984). A particular event may change the size of a cohort or the way in which a cohort ages. As a result, a particular cohort may interact differently with cohorts that precede or follow it through a particular stage in life. For example, the readiness of a particularly large birth cohort (such as the baby boom) to enter the labor force, or the onset of inflation and high unemployment among young adults, may put pressure on those over 60 years of age to retire early, thereby creating an unusually large cohort of economically dependent retired adults. At the same time, this situation may lead to conflict between unemployed youth and older adults over the allocation of programs and services geared to different age strata (financing job-creation programs versus expanding home-care programs).

Regardless of the demographic changes that may occur over time, chronological age structures are invariably present in most social institutions. These stratification systems serve to locate individuals and determine their status in the overall social structure. This location, in turn, influences when and how an individual will participate in particular institutions. Age serves as a criterion for entering and leaving positions, and for interacting with others. For example, the educational system is an elaborate age-graded system wherein chronological age is the basis for entrance, exit, and measurement of progress. Similarly, in the labor force, codified norms based on chronological age determine when individuals are eligible for full-time employment, when they must retire, and when they are eligible to receive age-related income tax or pension benefits.

In other areas of social participation, codified laws, based on chronological age, determine when one can vote, drive a car, or get married, be charged with a criminal offence as an adult, drink in public establishments, or attend certain movies (Eglit, 1985; Stackhouse, 1988). In this sense, chronological age has a significant impact on lifestyle and life chances. An individual is labeled as a member of a specific cohort located in a specific position within the age structure. However, chronological age is not a sufficient predictor of abilities, needs, achievement, social location, or interaction patterns, since chronological ages have

varying social meanings depending on the culture and the historical period. For example, at one time those over 40 years of age were considered 'old,' yet early in this century people were not defined as 'old' until about 65 years of age. Therefore, social age may be a better predictor of social behavior than chronological age or membership in a particular birth cohort.

The Age Structure

The process whereby age determines social location, roles, expectations, norms, and interpersonal relationships is known as age grading. This process results from a system of age stratification (Riley et al., 1972; Dowd, 1980, 1987; Fortes, 1984; Riley, 1985; Streib, 1985; O'Rand, 1990) that is present not only within the society at large, but also within specific institutions. Age grades evolve within these systems to provide a cultural definition of the expected rights, behaviors, and responsibilities of an individual at a particular time in his or her life. These age grades become the basis for self-identification and for allocating positions within the society or institution. For example, while nothing in the law prevents one of your professors from being appointed president of your university, those under 40 years of age might be considered too young for such a position, however qualified they might be.

Within a system of age stratification, age is the criterion by which individuals are assigned to differently rewarded positions. Age strata, which are made up of members who are at different chronological stages in the life cycle, are interconnected and there are varying degrees of interaction between them. As we will see in the next section, an individual's location often influences his or her behavior, attitudes, and values in a number of domains, and provides behavioral expectations for others with whom an individual might interact. Unfortunately, some of these age-related expectations become so institutionalized that they may lead to self-fulfilling prophecies and stereotypes that enhance the differences between strata. For example, retirees may be encouraged to 'relax' and not be concerned about productivity. However, for some the potential and desire to be creative and productive persists, and may go unfulfilled if they adhere to the socially induced age norm that says they are expected to 'take it easy' after they retire.

Two types of age norms are internalized to varying degrees, depending on the process of socialization to which an individual has been exposed at different stages in life. Ascriptive age norms are based on rules and constraints determined by a specific chronological age (retirement at 70, voting at 18, driving at 16). Consensual age norms provide an approximate age range in which specific roles or behaviors are appropriate or relinquished (Neugarten and Datan, 1973). They define the approximate age for events such as leaving home and starting a career, getting married, having children, being promoted, or retiring. They also influence lifestyle factors such as appropriate dress or social participation. These age norms appear to exist in the minds of most people; they are learned through socialization, and they provide some degree of social control by constraining behavior. However, there appear to be few age-related norms that define acceptable and unacceptable behavior for older people. In fact, Burgess (1960) suggested that retired men and women find themselves in a 'roleless role' whereby they have no vital function to perform. While general norms for the aged may be vague, incomplete, or nonexistent, age norms within an extended family are generally clear with respect to such roles as grandparent, parent, and wage earner (Rosow, 1974).

Where clearly defined norms for older adults are present, they often refer to behavior that should be avoided at a particular age (if one is over 60 and widowed, he or she should not cohabit with a member of the opposite sex). Obviously, age norms can change over time because of social change, and because of changes in socialization practices, societal values, or economic conditions. Furthermore, they may or may not be adhered to by all members of a particular age cohort. For example, those who are in their 20s today, some of whom may have lived with one or more friends of the opposite sex before marriage, may consider such behavior to be normative later in life if they become widowed or divorced. However, among those who are now over 65, this type of living arrangement generally invokes negative sanctions from the peer group. Where age norms are highly institutionalized, they serve to reinforce age grades, and to solidify age stratification to the point where age becomes a major element in social organization. That is, age norms create order and some degree of predictability in life, and establish timetables and boundaries for acceptable behavior at successive stages.

Generations and the Social Structure

Introduction

The concern of social scientists interested in generational analysis has been with social change, and the effect that each emerging age group may have on maintaining continuity or introducing discontinuity into the existing social order (Pampel, 1981). In this section, the concept of **generation** is introduced in order to provide a developmental and comparative perspective on the study of how location in the social structure impinges on processes at the societal level and on interaction at the individual level.

Generations, Generational Units, and Social Structure

Philosophers, historians, and social scientists have long been interested in the impact that particular age groups, acting as a collective force, have on social, economic, and political changes in society. While a number of scholars have used the concept of generation,[1] Mannheim (1952) was the first to argue that a generation was more than a group of people (an age cohort) born during the same period. In his opinion, a generation was a unique group of individuals who were not only born during the same period, but who also experienced and reacted to particular political, social, or historical events in the same way. As a result, they developed a historical consciousness that gave a particular social meaning to their lives. This generational consciousness led them to think and behave in ways different from other generations, and often to become organized to initiate social change. Three unique generations that have emerged in North America include those who had just entered, or were about to enter, the labor force when the Depression struck in 1929; the baby-boom generation born in the years following World War II; and the 'counterculture' and student protest youth generation of the 1960s. These generations resulted from a merging and interacting of unique demographic facts and the social meaning of being at a particular chronological age when specific social, political, or historical events occurred. These events affected these generations throughout most of their lives, and a social or political consciousness evolved among them.[2] For example, the 'Depression generation' has been concerned throughout their life with being thrifty and with saving money (in contrast, consider the 'spend now, worry later' habits of the 'yuppie' generation). Similarly, the baby-boom cohort has experienced crowded schools and stiff intra- and intercohort competition for jobs; and the 'protest' generation of the 1960s may always be more outspoken and critical of political and economic conditions than preceding or subsequent generations.

Eisenstadt's (1956) classic study sought to determine how generations interact to produce continuity or change in the social order. Eisenstadt was interested in how age strata are differentiated, how generations move from one age grade to another, and to what extent conflict develops between generations, particularly between younger and older members of society.

He hypothesized that social groups may be primarily or exclusively age-homogeneous rather than age-heterogeneous. He suggested that age-heterogeneous groups are prevalent in societies where the kinship system is the basic unit in the division of labor. In contrast, age-homogeneous groupings are characteristic of modern societies where patterns of interaction become segmented according to common age-related interests and needs. To illustrate this point, think of your own situation and keep a record for a week concerning how frequently you interact face-to-face with others who are at least five years older or younger than you are.

Mannheim (1952) noted that the social construction of a generation will not occur among all age cohorts that emerge and pass through the stratification system. He (1952:304) further stated that because age strata are made up of individuals with heterogeneous characteristics and experiences, generations consist of subsets

called **generational units**. These subsets are composed of individuals who have unique social characteristics, lifestyles, or beliefs, and who have enough common interests that they interact frequently. Thus, there may be a number of generational units within a given generation. For example, within the North American 'youth generation' of the 1960s, college students were the generational unit that was most radical, not working-class youth of the same age. In contrast, in Great Britain, youth from the working class tended to be the more radical and rebellious generational unit within the youth culture. In short, generational units may be based on social characteristics such as class, race, or ethnicity; they may also be related to political or social perspectives such as liberalism, conservatism, or socialism. Furthermore, generations and generational units are stratified with respect to power, prestige, wealth, and authority.

While most of the early interest in generations was concerned with the structural factors affecting the transition from youth to adulthood, more recently a developmental perspective has prevailed.[3] As a result, gerontologists have been interested in continuities and discontinuities in cohort flow; in intra- and intergenerational similarities and differences in values, attitudes, behavior, and interaction patterns; in generational cooperation and conflict; and in the formation of age-homogeneous political or social groups seeking social change.

As a result of this interest, scholars have assessed not only the effects of maturation (developmental age changes) and historical effects on age-related phenomena, but also the effect of cohort factors. For example, on the basis of a review of generational differences in political beliefs and participation, Bengtson and Cutler (1976) concluded that in the United States generational differences rather than aging differences account for political-party affiliation; specific social or historical effects of aging rather than aging or generational factors account for political alienation; and the effects of aging influence attitudes toward government involvement in specific areas such as health care. That is, within the general sphere of political participation, there are different explanations for different forms of involvement. The way in which generations influence social processes and interaction is presented in more detail later in this chapter.

Generations and Family Lineage

Thus far we have been concerned with the societal level of analysis in our discussion of generations. However, the concept of 'generation' has also been used to refer to ranked descent within the extended family system (Troll, 1980; Troll and Bengtson, 1979; Marshall, 1983; Bengtson et al., 1990). This ranking, although related to chronological age to some extent,[4] determines role allocation within the biological family unit on the basis of birth order, marital status, and the procreation patterns of succeeding generations. Thus, power, authority, and prestige within the extended kinship system are primarily based on ascribed characteristics; in society they are likely to be based on some combination of ascribed characteristics and achievement.

It is important to understand the structure of the family lineage system, which is parallel to but separate from the macro structure of society, since it too influences the interaction patterns within and between generations. Most kinship systems are made up of two (parents, children) or three (grandparents, parents, children) generations; but because of increasing longevity in modern societies, the four-generation family (great-grandparents, grandparents, parents, children) is becoming more prevalent. However, with zero population growth in some countries and an increase in childless marriages, a new type of two-generation family (parents, adult children) is appearing. In time, this last group will become one-generation families (old adults with no children), ultimately leading to the extinction of a particular kinship system.

Generational interaction operates on two separate but related levels — on the micro level within the family unit and on the macro level within the broader society. For example, aggregates of grandparents, parents, and children may interact on the societal level as members of particular generations or generational units. They will be exposed to particular societal processes (discrimination, stratification, sociali-

zation, conflict). At the same time, as members of an extended kinship system with varying degrees of filial bonding, they interact with other generations within the family. For some, particularly young adolescents, the socialization and social control process within this dual structure can create conflict and confusion, especially with respect to the transmission of values and other cultural characteristics from one generation to the next. The competing prestige of the parents and the peer group, who both seek to impose values and behaviors, can create role conflict for the adolescent and social conflict and change for the society.

It is necessary, then, to understand that the individual has generational links with both the family and society, and that there is a constant interplay (more at some stages in the life cycle than at others) between the family lineage structure and the societal age structure. This becomes even more complicated when the age structure within the labor force interacts with the class, racial, ethnic, or gender stratification systems. For example, when phenomena such as generational conflicts or 'generation gaps' are studied, it is essential to determine whether the observed generational differences (for example, in value orientations) are due to a societal cohort gap or to a familial lineage gap (Braungart and Braungart, 1986; Henretta, 1988).

Age-related expectations for individuals may differ between the societal and family levels, resulting in varying degrees of conflict. For example, in recent years many older cohorts in society have held views of premarital sexual behavior that are at odds with those of teenagers and young adults. For some extended families, cohabitation and premarital sex on the part of adolescents or young adults has been the source of family conflict and disharmony, because these practices are deemed contrary to cultural values. In other families, this practice has not been a cause of strain, since the parents themselves may disagree with the prevailing values and attitudes of society, and thereby accept these practices. In summary, the analysis of generational phenomena must consider the societal and the family lineage structures, both of which intersect and interact with other stratification systems.

THE INTERACTION OF SOCIAL STRUCTURE AND SOCIAL PROCESSES: COHORT AND GENERATIONAL EFFECTS

Introduction

Although the social structure within a society is relatively static at specific times, it may change over the long term due to various dynamic social processes. Because of such changes, cohorts and generations age in different ways and introduce further cyclical changes into the society. As noted in the previous sections, both society at large and its institutions are characterized by social differentiation and stratification. These dynamic processes, along with the presence of ever-emerging age cohorts, result in a complex two-way interaction between social structure and process that can lead either to stability or to change in the social order.

A chain of social processes may be initiated because of a particular social structure. In turn, these forces may ultimately lead to change in both the structure and processes that succeeding age cohorts experience. Given a particular social structure, with actual or perceived inequalities based on age, the socialization process and interaction patterns can lead to stereotyping of, and negative attitudes toward, the aged. These processes can also foster discrimination, segregation, and isolation of the aged. These in turn may lead to social conflict and to a change in the status and role of the elderly. Alternatively, where age-homogeneous groupings are prevalent, and where integration and support of the elderly are assured by law or social custom, little change in the status of the elderly will occur, and succeeding cohorts will age in a similar manner.

In this section we consider the influence of the interaction of social structure and processes on aging and the status of the aged from a cohort or macro perspective through generational analysis. Since cohort and lineage effects interact (Troll, 1980; Bengtson et al., 1990; George, 1990), the interaction of structure and processes across the life cycle at the micro level within the family system is discussed in the next major section. In the meantime, it is important to remember that there are similarities and differences in the aging structures and processes that operate on these two intersecting levels of analysis. Socialization, integration, ageism, isolation, and intergenerational relations function at the societal level for age cohorts or generations, and for the individual within specific social systems such as the family or the place of employment.

Social processes are institutionalized mechanisms that facilitate stability and change within a social system. They involve interaction at both the individual and cohort levels, and they provide some element of control by defining rights, power, and responsibilities; by allocating social positions; by facilitating or inhibiting interaction among certain individuals or groups; by integrating individuals and cohorts into the social structure; and by promoting conformity to the dominant values and norms within the social system. Not surprisingly, social processes can lead to a change in structure, while a change in structure can lead to a change in processes (Blau, 1980).

Before turning to an examination of the social processes that influence both the process of aging and the status of the aged, the issues and content of generational analysis need to be reviewed (Buss, 1974; Dowd, 1979-80). **Generational analysis** examines the impact of emerging age cohorts on the stability of the social structure, and considers the interaction patterns within and between members of age strata. More specifically, social scientists who have used generational analysis have been interested in:

1. Describing and explaining the degree, source, and outcome of social consensus or conflict resulting from intergenerational relations;

2. The form and amount of change that results from conflict within a society, and within intrasocietal social institutions;

3. The process and product of socialization wherein cultural characteristics and behaviors are transmitted from one generation to another;

4. The stability and long-term impact of generational units on behavior throughout the life cycle;[5]

5. The extent to which cohort solidarity or subgroup consciousness evolves within generational units and influences individual behavior and social change;[6]
6. The degree of inequality between age strata and the impact of stratification on the individual;
7. The extent to which age stratification interacts with other dimensions of social differentiation and how this has an impact on the individual; for example, the double standard with respect to sex; or double or multiple jeopardy with respect to age, race, class, or gender.

These issues are addressed in the following section, which focuses on social processes at the societal level, and in the last section, which discusses social processes within the kinship system.

Cohort Flow, Role Transition, and Status of the Aged

Cohort Flow: Structural Stability or Changes

Cohort flow is the process whereby a series of birth cohorts, varying in size and composition, succeed one another over time. This process ensures that there will be continuity in the social system, since departing cohorts are replaced by new ones. Each cohort, as it passes through the life course, experiences changes in its size and composition; it generally becomes smaller with age and comprises a larger percentage of females. While each cohort includes individuals with heterogenenous characteristics and experiences, all members of the cohort may experience similar events that make them different from members of other cohorts. This differentiation can lead to continuity or change in the social order. As a result of feedback and interaction with older cohorts that represent the dominant culture, each succeeding cohort makes 'fresh contact' (Mannheim, 1952) with the existing social order.

A cohort approaches adulthood (a major transition point) seeking to develop its own independence and lifestyle. As a result, the existing social order may be perceived by the members of the cohort in a new way because of contemporary social, political, or economic conditions. Moreover, new cultural values or lifestyles may be initiated because of constant feedback between cohorts. For the most part these changes are so subtle that they are seldom noticed; if changes do occur they proceed via negotiation, compromise, and cooperation. Sometimes generational conflict and change is unavoidable because generations are at different stages of socialization, are born during unique historical periods that foster different values or are faced with structural social inequalities.

Generational conflict may also arise because of cohort-centrism wherein all events are interpreted by members of the cohort in light of their own experiences, values, and needs (Foner, 1979; Henretta, 1988). If these factors prevail, age-group consciousness and solidarity may develop, thereby leading to discontinuities or conflict between strata. Ultimately, this may lead to social change. However, there is little evidence that high levels of age-group consciousness exist (Bengtson and Cutler, 1976; Foner, 1979; Bengtson et al., 1985; Jacobs, 1990). In fact, even where there are dissimilarities in behavior or value orientations, there may not be generational conflict.

This lack of conflict may occur because there are minimal differences within the family lineage, even though value differences are present between age cohorts at the societal level. For example, Bengtson et al. (1974) reported that marijuana use by adolescents is more frequent among youth whose parents smoke, drink, or use drugs. That is, the actual behavior may be different, but the basic value system is similar (the use of stimulants). Similarly, youth activists of the 1960s and 1970s often were raised in politically active families (Braungart and Braungart, 1986). Hence, little intergenerational conflict develops (Atkinson et al., 1986). As Chellam (1980-81) reported, conflict between younger and older cohorts may be avoided because young adults and the elderly may be undergoing similar life experiences. Based on a study of forty young people aged 15 to 24 years and forty people aged 65 to 74 years, Chellam found that similar perspectives existed for the two groups with respect to goals of life, value priorities, satisfaction with life, and personal stresses and crises.

Through the process of socialization, interaction between age cohorts occurs, and the emerging cohorts accept or reject the goals and values of the dominant culture. New values or lifestyles may be considered as alternatives, but whether these are adopted and lead to social or cultural change depends on whether age-group consciousness develops to force a change, and on whether older age cohorts accept the new orientations as more appropriate for the times. In the former case, change could be characterized by conflict; in the latter case, the change would occur through negotiation and cooperation between age cohorts.

Role Transition

Life consists of a sequence of societal roles (many of which interact with the family and work structure), which cohorts enter and then later leave (Morgan, 1982; Rosow, 1985). This mobility is related to either chronological age (legal norms) or social age (social norms). This process of cohort replacement enables a cohort to move from one stage in life to another, thereby replacing the cohort that retires or dies. Some of these transitions are from school to work; from being single to being married; from work to retirement; from young adulthood to middle age; from middle age to old age; from parenting to an empty nest; from being married to being divorced or widowed; and from childhood dependence to adult independence to old-age dependence. For some of these transition points, rites of passage, such as the wedding ceremony or the retirement party, facilitate and legitimate the transition. Highlight 7.1 illustrates the diversity of social roles in later life.

The process of cohort replacement is also facilitated by a normative ordering of life-cycle events. There exist relatively well-accepted normative beliefs as to the appropriate age and order for such events as completing an education, entering an occupation, marrying and forming a nuclear family, and retiring. In fact, there is usually social pressure from family and society to stay on schedule and in sequence, although there are subcultural differences in timing and sequence (Neugarten and Datan, 1973; Hagestad and Neugarten, 1985).

HIGHLIGHT 7.1

THE DIVERSITY OF SOCIAL ROLES IN LATER LIFE

Contrary to the views expressed by Burgess (1960) that later life constitutes a 'roleless role,' aging in the later years is now considered to be characterized as a role involving transitions leading to a revised role set. This role set may be either reduced or expanded, with a common pattern being a decline in formal roles and an increase in informal roles. This increased opportunity for role-playing has been enhanced by a changing age structure, wherein greater numbers of older adults live longer in better health, and by changing social norms and enhanced lifestyle opportunities for older adults. Research in the 1980s has documented that the elderly continue to play such primary kinship roles as parent, grandparent, and spouse, although the nature of the role behavior may have changed because of divorce, working daughters, smaller families, and increased mobility by the oldest generation. In terms of secondary roles in such domains as work, voluntary associations, religion, politics, and leisure, considerable change is occurring. More older adults are continuing the work role well beyond the traditional age of retirement, primarily because of legislation and personal desires or opportunities to pursue alternative work roles. Similarly, the scope of leisure roles available to older adults has expanded greatly, and these serve as a major source of life satisfaction in the later years. Although most of these social roles involve role relationships with other older adults, many involve interaction with the younger generations through foster-grandparent programs, as teaching assistants in elementary schools, as consultants for young professionals in a number of fields, and as students in university courses. Clearly, role opportunities for the older population have been expanded to create a more diverse social world.

The normative regulations concerning the appropriate timing of each event may change for different cohorts. Those who follow the normative sequence generally achieve harmony between their own lifestyles and the social context (Hogan, 1978). However, as Hogan observes, because of military service, or college attendance by some into their late 20s, some events may be spaced more closely together and may occur out of sequence. This asynchronization may result in personal adjustment problems. For example, instead of following the normative order of completing an education, entering the first job, and marrying, Hogan found that males who marry, complete their education, and then begin their first job seem to have higher rates of marital separation and divorce.

For other role transitions (to the empty nest, middle age, widowhood, or retirement), especially in the middle and later years when loss of roles is more usual than acquisition of roles, the transition can be stressful and can have a significant impact on some individuals (George, 1980). For example, much controversy has focused on the transition to middle age and the hypothesized 'midlife crisis.' This crisis is thought to be experienced primarily by males and to result from an interaction of changes and events in personal and social systems.

As males move into the middle years of life (35 to 55 years of age in North America) a number of physiological and psychological changes occur at the personal level. These may be accompanied by role losses or role ambiguity at work or home. According to some reports, middle-aged males experience a crisis that involves a loss or a questioning of identity; a preoccupation with death that is often precipitated by the death of an age peer; lowered self-expectations; marital and family dissatisfaction; depression and feelings of stagnation; and perception of a gap between career aspirations and attainments. These factors may lead to some changes in personality and lifestyle, with an accompanying identity crisis and increased anxiety about the present and the future (Brim, 1980). Despite the widespread belief that the midlife transition is characterized by a crisis, which would indicate that the crisis is a normative reaction in the middle years, scholars have

suggested that there is little evidence to substantiate the view that this transition is really a crisis event (Hunter and Sundel, 1989; Kalish, 1989).

In order to better understand the social stress and adaptation process induced when a role transition occurs in later life, George (1980:50-54) adapted House's (1974) model to explain adjustment to retirement, to widowhood, to community-based residential relocation, and to institutional relocation. This integrated model (see figure 7.1) considers the individual's status prior to the role transition; the aspects of the role transition that are potentially conducive to creating stress; the degree to which the transition is perceived as stressful (sense of loss, disruption of routine); the response to the stress (presence or absence of personal coping skills and social support); and the outcome in terms of personal identity and social adjustment. In addition, the entire model is influenced by personal resources, socialization experiences, and social status (marital status, income, occupation, health, class, race, gender, ethnicity).

On the basis of this social-stress model, it is argued that adjustment to major role transitions in later life is a process that is related not to the event itself, but to individual differences in the perception of stress associated with the transition. Adjustment is also related to individual differences in the ability to respond to the stress (that is, the impact of the stress on identity and social adjustment). Moreover, earlier socialization experiences, the personality structure and social demographic characteristics of the individual, and the social context in which the transition occurs also serve as mediating factors in this complex process of adjustment to transitions in later life.

The Status of the Aged

With increasing modernization, social structures and processes change so that there is likely to be a separation of family and societal roles. This leads to a greater division of labor, with more dependence on achieved rather than ascribed roles. In addition, there is greater stratification within the social structure on the basis not only of age, but also of gender, race, ethnicity, education, occupation, and social class. Moreover, social processes such as socializa-

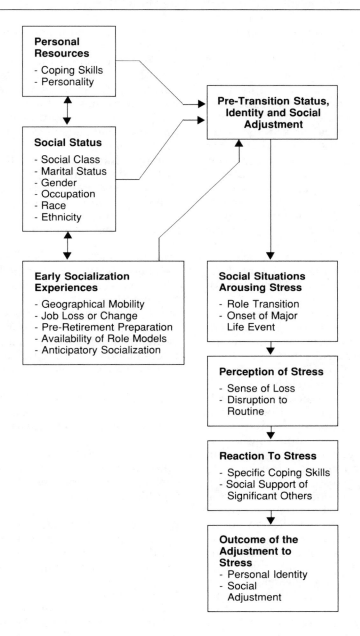

SOURCE: Adapted from *Role Transitions in Later Life*, by L. George. Copyright© 1980 by Wadsworth, Inc. Reprinted by permission of the publisher, Brooks/Cole Publishing Company, Monterey, California.

tion, discrimination, segregation, stereotyping, and cohort centrism have an impact on the aging process and on the status of the aged. As in earlier times, the status of the aged in contemporary societies is determined by location in the social structure, as well as by the nature of the social processes that prevail.

The transition from middle age to old age is thought to result in a loss or weakening of major social roles (through the empty nest, retirement, or widowhood) that were sources of status, power, and prestige. This 'role emptying' (Rosow, 1985) places the elderly in an unfavorable exchange position, and they are seen to have a devalued or marginal status. This social loss is further enhanced by the onset of physical changes that make persons appear old to others, and by the presence of ascribed negative stereotypes that lead to unequal treatment or discrimination on the basis of age. Some elderly persons may begin to act 'old' because of social expectations, because a socialization process that provides a prescription for behavior is unavailable, or because of the lack of adequate role models.

As noted previously, members of a given age cohort are not a homogeneous group, except with respect to chronological age. Thus, while the elderly lose some institutionalized roles, they do not abandon all social roles. Indeed, as highlight 7.1 illustrated, increasingly the elderly are seen to exhibit a diversity of roles. For example, the recent widow may still be a mother, sister, friend, aunt, grandparent, employee, or volunteer. Therefore, while some role loss is inevitable because of declining involvement in some institutions, individual status may be retained within a more restricted social world, such as the family, even while the status of the age cohort declines. More important, however, is the need to consider the variation in norms and values by class, education, sex, and race. These interact with age to determine the status of a particular cohort. As a result, we cannot assume that loss of status permeates an entire age cohort. Rather, some elderly persons possess status characteristics (being male, white, or a member of the upper class, or having a higher level of education and occupational prestige) that enable them to retain power. This releases

them from some of the constraints of aging imposed on others their age. They have resources[7] that give them power in social relationships, thereby enabling them to remain independent.

To summarize, the age stratification system may allocate unequal amounts of power, prestige, and privileges within and among different age cohorts (Dowd, 1980; O'Rand, 1990). With increasing age, individuals may lose strength and attractiveness and may be excluded from occupying many institutionalized roles. They may be stigmatized, stereotyped, and discriminated against.

In their interaction with others, particularly with those in younger age cohorts, the elderly often have less power and occupy a weaker bargaining position. In this type of situation, it could be concluded that the aged have low status in society. However, within the elderly age cohort, individual differences in sex, race, education, and class background enable some members to be accorded higher status than others at all stages in the life cycle. Normally, they maintain this status well into their later years. Although the elderly were once a numerical minority, because of increasing longevity and declining birth rates they now have the potential to attain more power in the political process if they develop a sense of group consciousness and solidarity. While this might lead to social conflict with other generations, the process should increase the status of all members of future elderly age cohorts.

Outcomes of Socialization through the Life Cycle: Stereotypes, Attitudes and Age Identification

The Process of Socialization

From the societal perspective, the goal of socialization is to integrate each new cohort into the society by transmitting institutionalized behavior and values to ensure the continuity of the social system from one cohort to the next, thus ensuring that social control and social order are maintained. At this macro level of analysis, the social structure influences an individual's location and determines which facets of the culture he or she will have access to during socialization. At the same time, the socialization process, when it leads to conflict and change across cohorts, can result in cultural change or in a change to the social structure. This occurs because of changes in the institutional, stratification, or value systems developed by emerging cohorts. At the micro level, socialization is the process of integrating the individual into specific institutions or positions within society. Generally, this involves two-way interaction or negotiation between a socializee (a child) and a socializer (a parent) within a given system such as the family or school. For example, an adult is socialized into the status position of 'parent' by recalling his or her life as a child, as well as by actually being a parent.

Since the late 1960s, perhaps because of the changing demographic picture and the growth of gerontology, there has been increased interest in socialization as a process that prevails throughout the life cycle, not just during childhood and adolescence. For example, until recently in our own culture we acquired little valid knowledge about aging and being old until we reached middle age. Adult socialization is necessary because social mores change and because individuals enter new stages of the life cycle where role expectations vary from those of earlier stages. Much of the process in the middle and later years involves anticipatory socialization and resocialization in order to reduce ambiguity when entering new social positions (widow, retiree, institutionalized resident).

At the societal level, an age cohort may be socialized to, and conform to, relatively similar values, beliefs, and behaviors that make it unique. Yet even within this unique cohort there will likely be intracohort variations in the process. This occurs because of gender, class, racial, ethnic, religious, geographical, cultural, and educational differences that operate within the family, school, peer group, and neighborhood social systems. In fact, these variations greatly influence the extent to which attitudes toward aging and the aged are developed and perpetuated by means of socialization. These products of the socialization process are discussed next.

Stereotypes

The outcome, or product, of the socialization process is evident on both the macro and micro levels of analysis. At the societal level, cohorts are socialized to existing cultural characteristics, and the society remains stable. If a particular cohort is socialized differently, conflict and social change may result when a new generation imposes its cultural system (beliefs, values, attitudes) on the existing social order.

Similarly, individuals are socialized by the family, school, peer group, and media to the normative behavioral pattern and values expected of persons occupying specific positions within a particular social structure. Those who are socialized less completely are labeled, to varying degrees, as deviants. They are either tolerated (the 35-year-old who continues to play the role of university student), stigmatized (the urban street panhandler), or incarcerated (the convicted criminal).

There are many degrees of socialization and many outcomes of the process. In addition to the general socialization outcomes for cohorts or individuals per se, certain cultural by-products in the form of attitudes, beliefs, and stereotypes are often acquired during socialization. These by-products, as we will see in the following sections, can lead to the initiation and perpetuation of other social processes that have an impact on aging and on the aged.

Through social interaction with significant others, most of whom are not chronologically 'old,' and through exposure to particular cultural institutions (such as the mass media) and cultural artifacts (jokes, greeting cards, books, and popular magazines) individuals are exposed to a variety of attitudes and images pertaining to aging and the aged. While some of these are based on research evidence, many lack research support but are accepted as fact by at least some segments of the population. That is, they are myths, many of which create negative stereotypes about the aged. To illustrate, some common negative stereotypes portray the elderly as deficient in intelligence, as cognitively impaired, or as lonely; as unproductive and inefficient employees; as emotional and financial burdens to their children; as physically weak and in chronic ill health; and as having little interest in or capacity for sex. While some elderly people may experience some of these conditions, they do not represent the modal pattern for the elderly. In particular, they usually do not apply to the younger segment of the retirement cohort.

These stereotypes represent incorrect assumptions, faulty reasoning, and misperceptions. If accepted as fact, they influence our expectations about and reactions to the elderly, especially where there is lack of interaction. Once these views become institutionalized, they tend to be passed on to succeeding cohorts through the socialization process. Until questioned and disproven, they perpetuate and reinforce our attitudes and behavior toward the elderly.

Stereotypes may induce fear of aging among the young, and may also be accepted as fact by some elderly persons. This acceptance can lead to self-fulfilling prophecies where the elderly begin to think and behave as expected, thereby reinforcing the stereotypes. A societal norm may be internalized by an elderly person, and may subsequently influence his or her beliefs, behaviors, and self-concept.

This situation may lead to loss of self-esteem, disengagement, isolation, or labeling of oneself as 'old.' That is, the 'social breakdown' syndrome may be initiated (Kuypers and Bengtson, 1973). However, as Brubaker and Powers (1976) noted in a review of forty-seven studies related to attitudes toward old age, both positive and negative stereotypes exist. They hypothesized that the self-concept held before old age, along with personal objective indicators of old age, may determine whether an aging individual accepts the negative self-evaluation. That is, if one's self-concept has been positive throughout life, a positive self-concept should prevail in the later years. Similarly, on the basis of an analysis of how older people view themselves, Connidis (1987, 1989b) found that only 10 percent of her sample reported liking nothing about being old. Those with a negative view of aging were older, were in poorer health, and had fewer children with whom to interact and from whom to seek support.

Within the field of social gerontology, a number of studies using the research method of content analysis have sought to demonstrate the extent to which the aged are underrepresented or misrepresented, usually by negative stereotypes, in such cultural forms as literature, newspapers, humor, and television. Moreover, even where the elderly are portrayed as having a positive image, they tend to be described stereotypically as altruistic, slow-moving, relaxed, excellent homemakers, and 'Mr. Fix-Its.'

It has been argued that since attitudes, beliefs, and values are acquired through socialization, these cultural forms serve to inculcate or perpetuate existing stereotypes of the aged. For example, in studies of elementary school books and children's literature, adolescent fiction, poetry, and adult fiction, it has been noted that the aged are seldom portrayed in illustrations. In the text they are described as powerless, as peripheral to the plot, as having limited abilities and behavioral capabilities, and as appearing in passive rather than active roles. Furthermore, they are underrepresented in relation to their proportion in the 'real' population.[8] Furthermore, women are underrepresented even though they comprise a higher proportion of the elderly population. Similarly, elderly minority-group members are seldom included, except in contemporary literature by and about blacks and native Americans (highlight 7.2).

These studies suggest that readers acquire a misleading and stereotypical view of aging and the aged in our society. However, it has not been demonstrated that there is a causal relationship between the reading of books in which the elderly are ignored, underrepresented, or misrepresented and the acceptance of negative stereotypes or the formation of negative attitudes toward aging or the aged. A large inferential leap has been made that has yet to be substantiated. Furthermore, the content of school texts is often interpreted by teachers; some elementary school students may be more or less sensitized to aging issues, depending on the supplementary material presented by a particular teacher (Hauwiller and Jennings, 1981; McGuire, 1987).

Since relatively few adolescents or adults read during their leisure time, many individuals are not often exposed to literary stereotypes. Of those adolescents and adults who do read widely and frequently, many are part of the

H**IGHLIGHT** 7.2

IMAGES OF OLDER ADULTS IN CHILDREN'S LITERATURE

Since the 1970s there have been several studies that have analyzed how, and with what frequency, elders and aging appear in children's literature. Specifically, the focus has been on describing the negative stereotypes of aging that are portrayed in the literature, and then inferring that these images socialize children to develop ageist attitudes and values about elders, and to even fear aging. These studies have illustrated that the elderly are peripheral characters outside the mainstream of the plot, that older women are underrepresented, and that the elderly are inactive and dependent. In addition, they are often described as dull, boring, cross, silly, fat, little, poor, sick, or cruel — all negative images. Moreover, illustrations accompanying the text are likely to stereotypically depict the elderly characters as hunched over; wearing drab, baggy clothes; wearing glasses or using a cane; engaged in passive activities like sitting or lying down; and smoking a pipe, sewing, or baking. In short, the stereotypes depicted in the traditional children's literature hide the diversity of the aging experience by ignoring such modern images as the energetic traveler or athlete; the busy volunteer; the employed grandmother; the creative artist, musician, or sculptor; the bedridden Alzheimer's patient; the impoverished bag lady on Main Street; the lifelong career criminal; or the vigorous businessperson.

In a more recent survey, Ansello (1989) summarized thirty-four books available as a child's first literature. He reported that, to correspond with the onset of population aging and an expansion of our knowledge base about aging and the aged, authors of children's literature in the 1980s are providing more depth, diversity, and meaningful descriptions of characters, plots, and aging-related events in the stories. Summaries of five of the stories reviewed by Ansello (1989:274-76) indicate the diversity and the reality of the images of aging that were presented to elementary school children in the 1980s:

1. *The Dancing Granny* by Ashley Bryan (Alladdin Books, 1987). West Indies folk tale of a happy granny who dances while she works. She outsmarts the legendary Ananse, a young schemer who wants to plunder her vegetable patch. Physically exertive, expressions of emotions, problem-solving behaviors. High centrality to story line.
2. *Grandma Drives a Motor Bed* by Diane Johnston Hamm/Charles Robinson (Albert Whitman & Co., 1987). Grandson and family visit grandparents to offer respite. Grandma is bed-bound and incontinent, but relatively self-sufficient. She undergoes regular physical therapy and inspires family with her spirit. Grandma and Grandpa shown to have natural relationship, arguing sometimes. Realistic, high character development of elders. Straightforward, non-sentimentalized intergenerational relationships.
3. *My Grandma's in a Nursing Home* by Judy Delton and Dorothy Tucker/Charles Robinson (Albert Whitman & Co., 1986). Boy visits his grandmother in a nursing home, recalling her past activities. He encounters confused and infirm elders there. Grandma, with Alzheimer's, calls the boy by his father's name. The boy learns to adjust to the reality of the home and its residents, and to accept his grandmother for who she now is. Moderate depth, high diversity of representations, high centrality.
4. *My Grandpa Retired Today* by Elaine Knox-Wagner/Charles Robinson (Albert Whitman & Co., 1982). Sensitive story of a granddaughter's empathy during her grandfather's transition to retirement. Genuine, straightforward communication between them, with good insight into their respective feelings. High character development and substantiveness.
5. *The Patchwork Quilt* by Valerie Flournoy/Jerry Pinkney (Dial Books, 1985). Grandma lives with the family and begins to make a quilt from the family's worn clothing the way her mother did: "A quilt won't forget. It can tell your life story." Quilt-making fosters reminiscence for grandma and entire family during its year-long production. When grandma gets sick, granddaughter continues the work during grandma's convalescence. High character development and substantiveness. Exceptional story, moving without being maudlin, with unusual three-generation involvement.

S**OURCE**: Summaries reprinted by permission of *The Gerontologist*, Vol. 29, No. 2, April 1989.

better-educated sector of society, and may therefore be more critical and discerning about the content of what they read. Caution is urged, therefore, when inferring that large segments of the population internalize negative stereotypes of aging and the aged by what they read. Certainly the content of children's literature contains stereotypical views of the elderly, but whether this leads to negative attitudes about aging has yet to be demonstrated. This type of research may be perpetuating yet another gerontological myth. More complete research is needed to provide links between reading and the adoption of stereotypical attitudes or behavior. One way to approach this problem, especially with respect to children's socialization, is to use participant observation to study the content and interaction of reading sessions in classrooms.

In a similar way, popular humor, as expressed in jokes, cartoons, and humorous birthday cards, generally reflects a negative view of aging, especially with respect to women.[9] For example, some of the themes, of which between 26 and 66 percent present a negative view of aging (Richman, 1977), portray a reduction in physical, mental, or sexual ability or performance, especially as it applies to men; lying about or concealing one's chronological age, especially by women; obsolescence and isolation; the 'freedom' of retirement; loss of physical attractiveness; and cultural expectations about age and aging.

However, as Weber and Cameron (1978) noted, some of these studies are biased in that the samples represent edited joke books rather than everyday joking behavior. Furthermore, the way in which the intended humor is interpreted by the reader or listener is unknown; and the relationship between the use of and response to humor and negative attitudes is untested. It is not known whether the intended messages or themes were perceived by the reader or listener as humorous. If they were, it is not known how this perception influences attitudes and behavior concerning aging and the aged. Moreover, there may be individual differences in the response to the stereotypes presented.

It has also been suggested that negative stereotyping of the elderly is prevalent in the media, especially with respect to women. However, print media do not appear to create, perpetuate, or reinforce negative stereotypes of the elderly. For example, an analysis of the portrayal of the elderly in two newspapers found that there were twice as many positive as negative images, and that a neutral image of the elderly was most prevalent (Buchholz and Bynum, 1982).

On television, aspects of the real world do appear to be selectively incorporated into game shows, drama and comedy series, and commercials.[10] However, for the purpose of entertainment, underrepresentation and misrepresentation of aging and the aged may occur. Thus, in appearances as major characters older men and women are treated in a humorous or negative way; older women are more likely to be underrepresented and overstereotyped; men and women are rarely seen in positions of power or prestige except in a rural, extended-family setting; and the aged are mainly included in plots that focus on intergenerational cooperation or conflict. Moreover, they are seldom used in commercials unless products specifically designed for the elderly are being advertised.

It has been indirectly suggested that material presented on television may lead to the perpetuation of stereotypes and may result in succeeding generations being socialized to hold prejudices against the elderly. But as Greenberg et al. (1979) noted, how can social learning really occur when so few older people are actually portrayed as role models on television? To date, research evidence has not supported the hypothesized linkage between viewing television and acquiring stereotypical attitudes about elderly persons (Passuth and Cook, 1985).

Studies in these areas have also neglected to consider that attitudes and stereotypes can change over time because of shifts in cultural values and because of research evidence that refutes the myths. For example, in recent years older people have been portrayed in a wider variety of occupational or familial roles that more closely coincide with social reality. They have been depicted as independent influential citizens and family members, and as having something of value to offer to society. Therefore, they are less likely to be the butt of jokes. This more frequent positive view may be partly due to the changing demographic profile of society in general, and of television viewers in particular. It may also reflect pressure by an increasingly active and age-conscious cohort of elderly citizens.

As a result of these changes, the outcome of the socialization process for one generation may differ from that of a preceding generation. This may occur because of social change, particularly where direct attempts at social intervention seek to invalidate negative stereotypes, thereby leading to changes in attitudes and behavior.

In conclusion, gerontologists have described and noted the outcomes of negative stereotypes about aging and the aged, particularly as they are represented and possibly inculcated through literature, popular humor, newspapers, and television. These studies have served a useful function by drawing attention to the problems experienced by some older citizens. In this sense, cultural forms may have contributed to changes in attitude and to public-policy initiatives to improve the situation of the elderly. Negative stereotypes are still with us at present, however, and the next three subsections focus on the social processes that evolve because of the acceptance of these stereotypes. Before discussing these processes in detail, it is necessary to examine attitudes toward and perceptions of aging and the aged. These attitudes and perceptions represent another outcome of the socialization process that may be internalized along with stereotypes (Crockett and Hummert, 1987).

Attitudes toward Aging and Age Identification

It is generally held that attitudes are derived, at least partially, from the prevalence of cultural stereotypes. In our culture, negative stereotypes about aging and growing old may be inculcated through the socialization process. In turn, these stereotypes may lead to the formation of attitudes and beliefs. In addition, attitudes are likely to form because of an institutionalized stratification process wherein there is differential ranking of status and opportunities by age.

As a result of these processes of attitude formation, negative societal and individual attitudes can lower the status of older people in a society, can decrease the frequency and quality of social interaction with them, and can negatively affect their life chances, lifestyle, and quality of life. Negative attitudes may also decrease or inhibit the allocation of societal and personal resources to the elderly, or may lead to a self-labeling process where the elderly accept the negative stereotypes and attitudes. This results in negative self-evaluation and decreased self-esteem, which in turn can lead to disengagement and social isolation.

A large body of literature has examined the attitudes of various age groups toward aging and the aged, as well as the hypothesized effects of these attitudes on the elderly. This section presents a brief summary of the findings, and a detailed critique of the inherent weaknesses in this type of research. In short, the existing research evidence represents a mixture of conflicting findings, some of which can be attributed to the methodological, conceptual, and theoretical difficulties inherent in attitude research in general (Eagly and Himmelfarb, 1978), and to gerontological research concerning attitudes in particular (McTavish, 1971; Lutsky, 1980; Green, 1981; Wingard et al., 1982; Fraboni et al., 1990).

Many criticisms have been raised about attitude research. The most serious pertain to concerns about definitions, sampling, measurement of the concept, the stability of attitudes, and the relationship between attitudes and behavior. There has been confusion over the terms 'attitudes' and 'beliefs.' **Beliefs** represent knowledge (accurate or inaccurate) about an object; **attitudes** connote an evaluative component wherein positive or negative feelings or dispositions are held toward an object or group. Attitudes are likely to result in a predisposition to behave in a positive or negative way toward individuals in a particular group.

Although beliefs can be changed by an awareness of factual material, attitudes may not change even in the face of objective evidence, because of the affective (emotional) component. Moreover, beliefs tend to be specific; attitudes, at least as commonly measured, are general. In short, where attitude scales include measurements of beliefs, any changes over time may reflect a change in knowledge rather than a change in attitudes.

Another concern with attitude research has been the long-standing debate as to the strength of the relationship between verbally expressed attitudes and actual behavior. To what extent is there congruency between what an individual feels about the elderly and the aging process, and how he or she actually behaves in face-to-face interaction with elderly individuals? The answer is that the relationship between attitudes and behavior is inconsistent at best. For example, the way in which a younger person behaves in a face-to-face situation with parents or grandparents may vary considerably from the behavior demonstrated toward elderly strangers in the supermarket, at work, or on a bus.

Other criticisms of this area of research relate to the question of whether attitudes are situationally determined (Stier and Kline, 1980; Wingard et al., 1982) and whether attitudes can be measured on a single dimension or whether they represent a multidimensional concept. For example, the child who sees an elderly transient begging or looking for food in a garbage pail might have an attitude different from that of a child whose major exposure to the elderly is playing catch with his grandmother or grandfather. Thus, it is uncertain whether the respondent is expressing an attitude with respect to a specific older individual known to him or her, or with respect to a generally held view of the elderly. Highlight 7.3 presents some views of older people as expressed in writing by elementary school children.

Attitudes also appear to be multidimensional; that is, complex phenomena are not determined by a single factor or a single meaning of 'old.' Rather, multiple meanings exist, shaped by experiences and by varying social or personality traits of the individual. Thus, positive attitudes toward old people are related to such factors as being female, being older, having a higher level of educational attainment, having a number of high-quality interpersonal relationships with older people, and attaining higher scores in measurements of such personality traits as affiliation and nurturance, and lower scores in dominance and aggression (Thorson and Perkins, 1980-81).

A final concern is the debate as to whether attitudes change and, if so, to what extent. Generally, it is agreed that attitudes, like beliefs, are not permanent, and can change or be changed over time. Attitudinal change may occur because of social change, because each new cohort is normally better educated than its predecessors, and because in some cases direct-intervention programs are designed to change attitudes. For example, Glass and Trent (1980), noting the generally negative views of children toward older persons, introduced a two-week study unit on aging to grade 9 students. They found small but positive changes in attitudes after the two-week course. While these changed attitudes persisted over a four-to-six month period, there remains the question of the permanency of the change. Similarly, Seefeldt et al. (1981) found that a curriculum designed to foster positive attitudes toward the elderly among kindergarten to grade 6 children was successful.

In a more direct intervention program, Olejnik and LaRue (1981) observed changes in adolescents' perceptions of the aged after a two-month period during which forty persons 60 years of age and older were served lunch in a school cafeteria. They found that younger adolescents and female adolescents interacted more with the guests and changed their perceptions to a greater extent. Most of the changed perceptions were related to misconceptions concerning the physical characteristics of older people. Unfortunately, this study did not determine whether there were changes in the older people's perceptions of the adolescents.

Despite methodological and theoretical limitations, much literature on attitudes and aging has been published (Lutsky, 1980). This literature seems to indicate that, in general, children, adolescents, college students, and young adults report negative attitudes, stereotypes, or predictions about growing old, about the elderly, and about interacting with older people. These negative attitudes seem to center on the physical, psychological, and social conditions of growing old. However, the findings are inconsistent from study to study. For example, Lutsky (1980) concluded that there is an absence of a strong negative stereotype of elderly persons and old age, although negative attitudes tend to be more prevalent when subjects are asked to

HIGHLIGHT 7.3

CHILDREN'S VIEWS OF OLDER PEOPLE

In response to the question 'What does it mean to be old?' elementary school children wrote the following comments. Not surprisingly, there is diversity in the extent to which positive and negative elements are included in the written descriptions, and different perceptions are held by those of different ages.

Grade 4

'To have wrinkles, having glasses, getting shorter, sometimes getting a hearing aid, being retired and having hobbies.'

'What being old means to me is getting ready to die. You need help most of the time. It is harder to see. You don't go to work anymore.'

'If you are 67 to 110 you are old. Sometimes all you do is sit around your house. If you are 60 you are semi-old, and if you are 65 you are almost old, but if you are 67 you are old.'

Grade 5

'Old people are funny and kind when you go to see them. They like to bake things. When old people see young kids they feel they should kiss and hug you all the time.'

'Old people are sometimes nice. But they can be mean too. Old people usually like to be left alone. Most don't like to go anywhere. If you make any noise they can be very mean.'

'Old people are sometimes cranky and sometimes nice. Sometimes they give you candy and sometimes give you heck. Some like plants and some like men.'

'I think old is when you get wrinkles and pimples for the rest of your life. People are not the only ones who get old, animals and food get old too,'

'Grandparents mean to me: money, clothes, toys, hugs, friends, trips, presents, kisses, family.'

Grade 8

'Everywhere you go you run into an elderly man or woman. Elderly people are kind, considerate, neat, easy going, lovable, great at sewing or knitting, understanding and most of all great at making delicious apple pies. If you are in a tight spot or in trouble you can turn to elderly people because they have the answers. They might not be as active as us but they are a lot wiser and more understanding than you think. They are great.'

'When I think of old people I think of an elderly person with graying hair, wrinkles and very wise. Most old people are more active than a lot of people think. While we are at work or school they are busy doing their own thing such as walking, writing, painting, knitting, working with wood, crafts, and doing volunteer work. I think elderly people should be well respected like any other human being. I have six grandparents and they are all active.'

'Personally I think older people are great! Some of them may not be able to move around very well, but if you are willing to listen they always have an interesting story to tell. The problem is people aren't always willing to listen and I think they are missing out.'

'In my opinion an old person is a person who thinks that they are old. Physically a person can look old but mentally they can be going one hundred miles an hour.'

---

compare the elderly to some younger age group. Furthermore, attitudes seem to be affected by a number of intervening factors. For example, variation in age, sex, personality, and socioeconomic status of the respondents results in inconsistent findings; and those with more education consistently show more positive attitudes. In addition, there is some evidence that the later adults perceive the onset of middle age and old age, the more positive their attitudes toward aging.

Similarly, those who have frequent and meaningful interaction with elderly people, especially where there is a filial bond, have more positive attitudes. Perhaps this occurs because the contact provides factual, personal knowledge to refute the myths about aging, and the individual is less likely to accept existing stereotypes. For example, Crockett et al. (1979) found that an older person who is alert, interesting, and involved in life is perceived as deviating from the stereotypes and is positively evaluated, even more so than a younger person who demonstrates these traits. They suggested that in the face of evidence, specific older persons may be viewed as unique, even though negative stereotypes of older people in general may still be retained.

A final area of interest is the impact of negative stereotypes and attitudes on the elderly themselves. It has been suggested that the elderly perceive, accept, and internalize these negative views; they either deny they are aging and identify themselves to others and to themselves as younger than they are (Bengtson et al., 1985), or they accept the social label of 'old,' and either change their identity or become disengaged and isolated. Because of the perceived attitudes of others, old age is seen as a stigmatized attribute with negative meanings attached to the status (Ward, 1977).

This identification of the self as younger than actual chronological age is more likely to occur in women; in older respondents; in those of higher social classes; in whites; in those with better psychological functioning; in those with higher levels of education; in those who are in good health and physically active; and in those who are still employed. Thus, it appears that societal attitudes toward the aged may lead to a change in an individual's subjective age-identification, which can have a subsequent impact on lifestyle and adaptation in the later years. Perceived age appears to be a function of demographic and lifestyle factors that influence how negative societal attitudes affect individuals. For some, these attitudes may be a threat to self-esteem. For others, however, old-age stereotypes may be functional in that the

individuals may, in comparison to the stereotypes, appear to be better off than most elderly people. In this respect, negative stereotypes may enhance participation and satisfaction, especially among the better-educated.

To summarize, a process of denial may be initiated to avoid being labeled as 'old,' or a process of acceptance may be initiated wherein the individual changes identity, disengages, or becomes isolated. For others, who are active, better educated, in good health, and part of a comparative reference group of age peers, objective self-evaluations may lead to the adoption and reporting of a younger self-image.

Ageism: A Form of Discrimination

Stereotypes and attitudes about older adults may result from a socialization process that occurs within a society stratified by age. Through the interaction of an age-stratification system and the socialization process, negative attitudes and stereotypes may be formed and perpetuated so that the elderly are viewed as a distinct and unique group. Many of these views are reinforced by the media, primarily through programs and advertisements that emphasize the high value placed on looking, thinking, feeling, and acting young.

Where negative attitudes and stereotypes become pervasive and institutionalized in legal or moral codes (such as mandatory retirement), they represent a form of prejudice that may lead to discrimination against others on the basis of actual or perceived chronological age. Butler (1969) labeled this process **ageism**. He suggested that older people are differentially discriminated against by virtue of their membership in a particular age cohort. Although overt discrimination per se may be less obvious, ageism involves an unquestioning acceptance of negative stereotypes of the aging and the elderly. These stereotypes are used, in turn, to justify such prejudicial and discriminatory social acts as elimination from the labor force at a particular chronological age, exclusion from social interaction, and denial of equal access to services in the public and private sectors. In addition, ageism is perpetuated by the use of ageist terms when referring to the elderly

(Nuessel, 1982).

Interestingly, like many other areas of social gerontology, ageism has been identified and studied primarily from the perspective of white members of the middle class. Since elderly members of racial or ethnic minority groups may or may not experience differential treatment based on subcultural values, attitudes, and stereotypes, the interaction of race, age, and class must be considered. This issue will be addressed later in the section on the interaction of stratification systems.

Having hypothesized that ageism exists, many social scientists have sought evidence to illustrate its psychological and social effects on the individual and on society. Unfortunately, definitive evidence is lacking. While some studies have reported few perceived or actual acts of victimization or discrimination by age, others have reported perceived or actual age discrimination in hiring, promotion, and decision making. For example, until recent years, the requirement of disclosing one's age on a vast array of government and private-sector information forms and applications suggested public acceptance of the use of age criteria in decision making.

In a detailed overview of reactions to ageism, Levin and Levin (1980:97-114) suggest that older people may react to ageism by accepting or avoiding stereotypical labels and prejudicial interactions, or by becoming aggressive and attempting to alleviate the process by collective action. They stated that acceptance of prejudice and discrimination is revealed by social or psychological disengagement (although few people actually disengage). More seriously, the elderly voluntarily or reluctantly accept the negative stereotypes and begin to behave as they are expected to behave (the self-fulfilling prophecy). This is what Kuypers and Bengtson (1973) refer to as the 'social-breakdown syndrome.' This process involves role loss, lack of socialization to old age (Rosow, 1974), lack of social norms, and social labeling based on negative and stereotypical views. As a result, older people, in general, may be perceived and treated as if they are incompetent, obsolete, poorly adjusted, and nonpersons.

Kuypers and Bengtson argued that older persons internalize these external evaluations, perceive themselves to have these characteristics, and begin to behave as expected. This further reinforces societal stereotypes, which are then perpetuated. To date, little evidence exists that negative self-evaluation and self-labeling is a typical pattern for large numbers of older people. Furthermore, it has been suggested that acceptance of these 'labels' may result in voluntary age segregation in retirement communities. However, as we will see in chapter 8, only a small minority, many of whom are members of the upper-middle class, choose to live in these age-segregated communities.

Instead of accepting stereotypical labels, older people may avoid the social stigma of aging by a denial of old age. This occurs when individuals report that they themselves are not 'old,' when they conceal or lie about their age, or when they seek re-engagement in former roles (work after compulsory retirement, parenthood, or marriage to a younger person). Avoidance may be reflected in direct attempts to 'pass' as a younger person by means of cosmetics or plastic surgery, or by taking on social roles and engaging in social behavior (attending nightclubs for singles) more common during the earlier years of adulthood. In some situations this avoidance behavior may lead to serious psychological problems, and perhaps to alcoholism, drug abuse, or suicide.

Another type of reaction to ageism involves an unwillingness to accept the status quo, and participation in social and political activism aimed at changing society's views of the aged. In this situation, an age-group consciousness develops. This, in turn, may lead to the formation of advocacy groups (such as the Gray Panthers) who seek to end overt and covert discrimination against the elderly and to improve the economic and health status of those elderly people who need assistance (Pratt, 1974, 1976; Hudson and Strate, 1985; Jacobs, 1990). Interestingly, some of these groups include not just the elderly, but individuals of all ages who seek to alleviate ageism.

It is largely through these action-oriented groups that an alternative view of aging has been presented to younger age cohorts and to policymakers. Hence, not only have policies been initiated or changed (the mandatory retirement age has been increased to 70 in the

United States), but prevailing attitudes and stereotypes about the elderly have been questioned and discarded in the face of evidence. However, despite the introduction of legislation to reduce institutionalized age discrimination, despite the availability of research evidence that refutes many of the prevailing attitudes and stereotypes, and despite the visibility of highly active, creative, and intelligent people in their 70s or 80s, ageism still persists to varying degrees in many modern industrialized societies.

Ageist attitudes may be acquired in early childhood. Although ageism is primarily directed toward older persons outside the family unit, it may also influence behaviors within the family unit. As a social process, the prevalence of ageism may vary from one cohort to another. For example, there may have been little overt ageism early in this century, but with increasing industrialization and social differentiation the incidence has increased. However, ageism may now be declining because of increased age-consciousness and social and political activism by the elderly, and because of increased research dispelling the myths that perpetuate the stereotypes. The number of highly visible role models of active, successful elderly people is greater, and more educational programs relating to aging and the aged now exist.

Unfortunately, as with most forms of discrimination, it is difficult to obtain current, reliable, and valid research evidence to support the degree to which ageism is present in contemporary society. It may be that the degree of ageism is closely linked to prevailing demographic and economic factors in a society. For example, with a declining birth rate and increasing longevity, by the time the senior boom arrives after 2010, the skills and services of the elderly may be needed in order to lower the dependency ratio and to meet the demands of the labor force. Incentives to continue working beyond the normal or mandatory retirement age may need to be introduced. By this time, the elderly may be a near-majority group in the social structure, and ageism may no longer be a social concern. It may be the case that ageism will be directed not toward the elderly, but rather toward younger age cohorts.

Isolation and Alienation: Myth or Reality?

Introduction

The dynamics of an age-stratified social system interact with socialization, social interaction, and ageism to facilitate or inhibit other social processes in the later years. It is virtually impossible to separate the cause-and-effect order of the various processes, since they are highly interrelated in a feedback model. However, these processes have an impact on some individuals as they age, and each process is briefly discussed in this subsection.

Social Isolation and Alienation

Although social isolation (deprivation of social contact) and loneliness (a psychological state) are frequently portrayed as normative and inevitable patterns for the elderly, few people actually experience either. While aging usually involves a constriction of social roles and the loss of role partners, this may not necessarily result in physical or social isolation. Even the status of widow or widower does not necessarily make loneliness or isolation an inevitable or typical reaction. In reality, there exists a continuum ranging from high social involvement in a variety of social networks to extreme isolation. This pattern holds for all age groups, not just the elderly.

In order to understand the influence of isolation on an elderly person it is necessary to examine the degree of isolation across the life cycle, to determine the extent to which isolation is voluntary or involuntary in the later years, and to determine whether a confidant is available and used. For example, some people have been disengaged and isolated from social networks throughout their life cycles, while others have voluntarily or involuntarily moved between social involvement (living in a dorm at university) and isolation (living alone in a city apartment or in a rural setting). Bennett (1980a) has suggested that there may be four patterns of social involvement in the later years: (1) social integration over the life cycle; (2) isolation in early adulthood, with relatively more social activity in later years; (3) social activity in early adulthood, with involuntary isolation in later years; and (4) lifelong, voluntary isolation.

At any stage, then, an individual may voluntarily or involuntarily withdraw from social networks. For those who withdraw voluntarily and remain isolated, most adjust quite satisfactorily. For those who become isolated involuntarily, this deprivation of social contact may affect their self-images, reduce their independence, and lead to institutionalization. This lack of social interaction can be prevented or reduced somewhat by having access to a confidant[11] with whom trivial or serious matters may be discussed on a regular basis.

Isolation can also be reduced by participating in voluntary programs (such as meals-on-wheels) that involve daily visits, by continuing to read and keep up with current affairs, and by making use of alternatives to complete institutionalization (such as home-care services or partial-care facilities that permit independent living within an environment where meals, security, and recreation are provided). For those who become totally isolated and who experience mental disorders, the effects may be reversible through resocialization.

Alienation is another possible outcome of the interaction of various processes within a particular social structure. This can be measured along six dimensions: powerlessness, meaninglessness, normlessness, self-estrangement, social isolation, and cultural estrangement (Seeman, 1975). These feelings may lead to either psychological or social withdrawal, or to overt action to initiate social or political change.

The elderly may experience alienation when they become estranged from the prevailing value system; when they feel that political and economic institutions and policies are discriminating against the elderly; when they can no longer accept the dominant ideologies of a society; and when they feel powerless, isolated, and marginal in the social order (Cutler and Bengtson, 1974; Dowd, 1980). An elderly cohort, or a particular generational unit within an elderly cohort, may develop a group consciousness wherein they unite to redress inequity. This may result in withdrawal and the creation of age-segregated communities, or in the creation of political and social advocacy groups that use traditional (lobbying) or radical (withholding votes or taxes) methods to initiate change.

Alienation in the later years is a possible outcome of age differentiation, discrimination, segregation, lack of socialization for old age, isolation, or unacceptable dominant ideologies. Still, alienation is not widespread among the elderly. As Dowd (1980:94) concludes, 'this phenomenon is not the inevitable result of biological or physiological processes. It is, rather, a reaction to the loss of autonomy in our modern world.' Perhaps the major reason that alienation has not occurred to a greater extent is that many elderly people have not personally perceived or experienced a loss of autonomy. Furthermore, while the elderly might become alienated from the political process, and indeed may become cynical about their lack of power, few are alienated from family life and its social network.

The Aged as a Unique Social Group: Myth or Fact?

Introduction

Since the 1960s there has been a continuing debate as to whether the elderly are a unique social group within modern societies. It has been argued that the aged do (or do not) constitute a subculture, a minority group, a poverty group, or a political group. Unfortunately, much of the evidence for or against each position has been based on inferential leaps from selective studies that include these concepts, rather than on empirical or theoretical studies designed to directly test the concepts themselves. To date, there is little evidence to suggest that the elderly are a subculture (chapter 4), a minority group (chapter 4) or a poverty group (chapter 11). In the following subsection evidence is presented to illustrate that the elderly are not, as yet, a political group. The overwhelming evidence indicates that the aged do not constitute a unique social group.

The Aged as a Political Group

In the field of gerontology there are three basic areas of interest with respect to aging and the political process: the political participation and attitudes of age cohorts across the life cycle, the extent to which the aged make up a political or power group, and the impact of government legislation and services for the aged (Hudson, 1981; Binstock et al., 1985; Hudson and Strate, 1985; Jacobs, 1990). In this section the extent to which the elderly have acquired, or will acquire, political power is discussed (political participation by the elderly is discussed in chapter 12). Unfortunately, as in many other areas of social gerontology, much of the literature contains assumptions or speculations rather than research evidence directly supporting the extent to which aging-based organizations can exercise power to the benefit of older individuals.

Although the number of persons over 65 years of age is increasing, and although they represent approximately 15 percent of the eligible voters in many nations, there is no evidence that they have voted, or will vote, as a bloc in national, regional, or local elections. Although the electoral impact of the elderly is questionable (Hudson and Strate, 1985; Jacobs, 1990), politicians have increasingly become aware of the aged, some of whom are the age peers of the political leaders. This awareness has been heightened by the formation of age-based advocacy associations. Some examples of Canadian organizations include: One Voice, the National Advisory Council on Aging, the Canadian Council of Retirees, and various provincial groups that have been created to advocate the rights and needs of seniors. Moreover, age-based associations created to provide group services for the elderly (such as travel plans, discount purchasing) have expanded their mandates to become advocacy groups for consumer and human rights for seniors.[12]

Pratt (1976) viewed the formation of these age-based organizations as part of an evolving social movement designed to raise the consciousness of the elderly and other segments of society to the needs and concerns of an aging population. Binstock (1972), however, argued that these organizations are special-interest groups intended to enhance the power and advance the interests of the aged through conflict with other interest groups, including other age-based organizations.

Regardless of the orientation, the size of membership, or the methods of operation, these organizations have not been particularly effective as powerful political groups that can initiate social or political change. However, they have acted as catalysts in bringing the problems and concerns of the elderly to the attention of the public. Then, other groups have forced changes in health care, housing, income maintenance, and transportation policies. In short, these groups have not acquired the political power necessary to represent a force in local,[13] regional, national, or international politics.

Why have the aged not become a powerful political group? As noted earlier, there is little evidence that the aged form either a subculture or a minority group. While the potential for political action is present, there does not seem to be a strong age-group identity or age consciousness that drives the elderly to act as a social group (Streib, 1985). The aged are a diverse group with great variation in needs, attitudes, values, and political opinions. As we have seen, old age is often perceived as a devalued status. Many of those over 65 years of age identify themselves as middle-aged rather than old, and thus do not exhibit much concern for issues relating to older people.

Furthermore, even where individuals do identify themselves as old, there seems to be a negative relationship between old-age identification and political participation. One study (Miller et al., 1980), based on 1972 and 1976 national surveys in the United States, found that the persons who identified themselves as old were not mobilized as a political group, even if they strongly identified with the status of their peers. The study suggested three alternative explanations for this lack of mobilization. First, the elderly person may have few socioeconomic resources and thus be denied effective participation in the political process. Second, because of stereotypes, the elderly feel incompetent and unable to become involved. Finally, on both personal and group levels, the elderly feel politically powerless, and assume that nothing they can do will be effective.

Another possible explanation is that there is little interstrata conflict, despite the inequality of access to political power. That is, the elderly are not forced to unite because of pressure from other groups. Foner (1974) suggests that this lack of conflict results from the fact that all members of society will eventually move into the older strata; in addition, many people have parents or grandparents in those strata. Furthermore, because of multiple group identification (with the family, work, voluntary associations) there is less commitment to a single age-based group.

Finally, on the individual level, Binstock (1974) suggests that there is continuity in political participation, and identification with one party or platform is likely to be reinforced by age. New political affiliations are seldom formed on the basis of age after the middle years. However, a small minority of the elderly may recognize that their life chances may be improved if group rather than personal resources are mobilized. Thus, making the decision to join an age-graded association reflects a concern with personal status. This concern may lead to a desire for change and a willingness to engage in collective political behavior. This act of joining may be especially important for members of the lower social classes in that it reduces or eliminates the impact of class-based interests in political involvement (Trela, 1977-78). That is, the lower-class individual who joins an age-based organization enters a generational group where age-based collective interests and concerns prevail over those that are class-based.

The Interaction of Stratification Systems: Single versus Multiple Jeopardy

Introduction

As noted earlier, stratification systems evolve within most societies because of cultural values that result in a particular attribute being differentially evaluated. Thus, individuals possessing a particular attribute are differentially ranked, which inevitably results in variation in access to opportunities and rewards. As a result of this ranking process, a social structure is created, where being upper- rather than lower-class, white rather than black, male rather than female, and young rather than old places one higher in the stratification system. Therefore, within each of the stratification systems (class, race, ethnicity, gender, and age), inequalities exist because strata are differentially valued.

While variation in life chances and lifestyle occurs between strata, there is also consider-able heterogeneity within strata. Not all elderly people are ill or poor, and not all blacks are poor or socially disadvantaged. More important is the interaction between the stratification systems that can influence an individual's situation at a particular stage in the life cycle. This particularly applies to the age and class stratification systems where (unlike the gender, racial, and ethnic systems) individuals can move between strata, either enhancing or reducing their life chances or lifestyles. Certainly everyone moves from one age stratum to another. But an elderly, black, lower-class woman experiences a different social situation from that of an elderly, white, upper-class woman. Although both women belong to the same age cohort, the influence of the social and racial stratification systems creates a different personal situation for each individual.

In the following subsections the interaction of age with social class, race, ethnicity, and gender is viewed as a social process with a potentially negative impact on the status of the elderly. This interaction is frequently referred to in the gerontology literature as double, triple, or multiple jeopardy. These conditions are assumed to exist when an elderly person has devalued status in two or more stratification systems. Consequently, the individual is more disadvantaged than the assumed 'average' member of a particular age cohort — that is, a white, middle-class male. Double jeopardy exists if an individual is old and poor, old and female, or old and a member of a racial or ethnic minority group; triple jeopardy exists if an individual is old and has two additional attributes such as being poor, female, or a member of a minority group; multiple jeopardy involves being old, poor, female, and a member of a racial or ethnic minority group.

Alternatively, the relative disadvantages for women and ethnic-group members may decrease with age. This is known as the 'age-as-leveler' hypothesis; prior social and economic distinctions become less important in determining the situation of the older female or ethnic-group member. The evidence for and against these competing hypotheses ('jeopardy' versus 'age-as-leveler') is presented in the following subsections.

Age and Class Stratification

Most studies on aging have used middle-class subjects, and most have been written from the perspective of members of the middle class. Some of these studies have implied that the elderly represent a social problem because they are or have become members of a lower-class poverty or minority group (Dowd, 1980:15-18). In reality, at all stages in the life cycle, within each cohort there is a range of class background that influences life chances, lifestyle, and attitudes toward aging. Those elderly people who, by nature of their past and present income and prestige are members of the upper class, generally have fewer negative attitudes toward aging, and are also more likely to be married. They are likely to have advantages over other members of their age cohort with respect to income, quality of housing, health, and access to health care. They live longer, and their quality of life may be higher. In contrast, members of the middle class frequently lose power, prestige, and mobility after retirement; members of the lower class, especially if they are not married, may be forced into ghettos or institutions because of the loss of the few limited economic resources they once possessed.

In summary, the age and class stratification systems interact at all stages in the life cycle to create intracohort variation; the impact on a given individual, particularly a member of the lower class, can be most dramatic in the later years. Thus, the range of class backgrounds found throughout the life cycle continues to influence lifestyle in the later years. For members of the lower class, aging involves a significant loss of resources which, combined with poverty and poor housing, can significantly alter psychological, social, and physical adjustment, and, indeed, the ability to survive as independent individuals. Finally, because downward mobility is possible in most societies, being unemployed in later life may mean a lowering of one's standard of living, especially if children are unable or unwilling to assist in the financial support of aging parents.

Age, Racial, and Ethnic Stratification

Because of prejudice, stereotyping, and ethnocentrism, members of certain racial or ethnic groups have been discriminated against, and have been denied equal opportunity to gain access to the valued rewards of society. Thus, throughout their lives most (although not all) members of some racial and ethnic groups have had lower income, less education, and little power and prestige. This has had an impact on such lifestyle factors as employment patterns, marital stability, health, housing, community involvement, leisure patterns, access to health care and social services, and retirement benefits.

Although social class enhances the status of some members of a particular racial or ethnic group, many experience some degree of discrimination or racism throughout life. In addition to the lifelong stigma of race, as the individual becomes older he or she may be faced with the ageism experienced by many elderly people. If this occurs, double jeopardy exists (Jackson, 1985).

To date, it has been argued either that the gap between minority and majority group members decreases from middle to old age (the age-as-leveler hypothesis); or that the problems of old age are compounded if one is a member of a minority group (the double-jeopardy hypothesis). The age-as-leveler hypothesis suggests that all elderly people are disadvantaged, but that because members of minority groups have been disadvantaged throughout life they have developed coping mechanisms that enable them to meet the demands of old age. In this way the aging process for the majority and minority groups becomes similar. In contrast, the double-jeopardy hypothesis argues that not only are minority group members devalued on the basis of their ascribed characteristics, but they are further devalued because they are old, and therefore their disadvantaged situation deteriorates even more as they age.

Only a few studies have directly addressed these competing hypotheses. Unfortunately, none of the studies have employed a longitudinal analysis, which is the ideal design to answer these questions. Markides (1981) argued that one reason for any apparent double jeopardy is that, beyond 65 years of age, blacks live longer than whites. Therefore, on the average, they are more likely to be in poorer health and in greater financial difficulty. However, the differences between the racial groups decreased with age for more subjective indicators (such as life satisfaction and frequency of contact with relatives). This suggests that the problems older people face are similar, regardless of racial or ethnic background. That is, support for the age-as-leveler hypothesis was found when subjective indicators of interaction and morale were employed to determine racial differences.

In summary, while the disadvantages of earlier life carry over into the later years for members of some racial or ethnic groups, there is little evidence that, except for income and health, the situation of the aged is made worse by minority-group status. Minorities enter old age with a cumulative disadvantage, but experience no more ageism per se than members of the majority groups. Their disadvantaged financial and health positions represent a residue of past experiences that accumulate and reach critical levels as they live longer, thereby enhancing the differences between minority- and majority-group members. This situation is compounded further if members of a minority group experience greater longevity (Markides, 1981; Jackson, 1985; Jackson et al., 1990).

Age and Gender Stratification

Despite the fact that women are not a numerical minority group (in fact, they are a numerical majority in the later years), gender stratification has resulted in discrimination against women. A woman's class position and social identity have generally been determined on the basis of her father's or husband's position (Posner, 1980). The older woman has few pension or government retirement benefits, other than those accumulated by her husband. In addition, compared to men, women have few opportunities to enter or reenter the labor force at different stages in the life cycle; they traditionally have fewer opportunities to train for or enter a wide range of occupations; and physical attractiveness (particularly in the later years) has traditionally been thought to be more important to women than to men in social interaction.

As a result of this process of gender stratification, wherein women are less socially valued than men, it has been suggested that there is a double standard of aging (Bell, 1980; Fuller and Martin, 1980; Posner, 1980; Eichler, 1980). This double standard is reflected in conventional wisdoms: for example, chronological aging enhances a man but progressively destroys a woman because of the societal norm that physical attractiveness provides more social benefits for women than for men; a woman is expected to marry a man more or less her own age, but a man, especially if he is divorced or if he marries late in life, is sometimes encouraged to marry a younger woman; there is a negative connotation to the terms 'spinster' and 'old maid,' and there is a positive meaning attached to 'bachelor'; the use of cosmetic products by women to 'mask' old age is considered socially acceptable and, indeed, necessary; and social expectations and opportunities for employment and leisure for women are more restricted than for men.

This double standard varies cross-culturally; it may or may not be prevalent in some societies. The double standard also appears to vary by class background; for example, upper-middle-class and upper-class women are generally more anxious about the effects of individual aging. They may fight the cosmetic battle against aging more vigorously because they have more economic resources, and because physical attractiveness is more highly valued among the upper classes.

In addition to facilitating the perpetuation of stereotypes into the later years, the double standard of aging may ultimately lead to a double stigmatization — being female and being old (Posner, 1980). Just as the double-jeopardy hypothesis may apply to racial and ethnic group members, it may also apply to older women. Alternatively, greater equality or 'leveling' of the sexes may occur with age. In a test of these competing hypotheses, Chappell and Havens (1980) found support for the double-jeopardy hypothesis when an objective indicator of mental-health status was used to compare the situations of older men and women; there appear to be both age and sex inequities in the mental health of the elderly. However, when a subjective measure of perceived well-being was used, the double-jeopardy hypothesis was not supported. This suggests that even if double jeopardy does exist in an objective sense, women may be less likely than men to perceive or report a decrease in well-being, even where their subjective well-being may decrease relative to men.

In conclusion, older women may not express their perceived situations to the same extent as men. They may suffer in silence even if they do perceive a decrease in subjective well-being; or they may be more accepting of their situation and may not perceive that their level of well-being is less than it was earlier, or less than that experienced by male age peers. While there are many more elderly women than men, the minimal evidence does not provide strong support for the double-jeopardy hypothesis. Even though women may be devalued relative to men throughout life, the situation for most elderly women is not the result of a double stigmatization. Rather, since there are more elderly women, and since they do not form a homogeneous group, some may experience double jeopardy, but many will not.

Multiple Jeopardy

The existence of **multiple jeopardy** is related to the degree to which racism, sexism, and ageism interact to produce inequality among a cohort of older people. Again, as in many areas of gerontology, it is difficult to separate aging effects from cohort effects. While the elderly, black, lower-class female may be among the most impoverished of the elderly with respect to income, housing, and health, she is also likely to be the least educated and the one who has had the lowest income and the poorest health throughout life. Being female, poorly educated, and black has been a disadvantage, and growing old may not significantly compound her problems.

Although some gerontologists speak of the problem of multiple jeopardy, it does not appear to be an aging event. Rather, it is a phenomenon that has been present throughout life for some lower-class women who are members of certain racial or ethnic groups. In short, there does not appear to be sufficient evidence as yet to argue that multiple jeopardy is a factor in the status of specific elderly individuals. Nevertheless, particular combinations of age, sex, and ethnicity may be important elements in the aging experiences of some members of society.

INTERGENERATIONAL RELATIONS: LINEAGE EFFECTS VERSUS COHORT EFFECTS

Introduction

In a previous section it was seen that interaction between the social structure and social processes can lead either to continuity or to change in the social order. Whether continuity or change occurs is influenced by a socialization process wherein successive age cohorts accept, redefine, or reject values, attitudes, beliefs, and cultural patterns that older cohorts have sought to inculcate. This process is greatly influenced by the impact of social, political, and technological events on particular cohorts at specific periods in history. The end result of this interaction is either harmony or conflict between cohorts, and, ultimately, varying degrees of social order or social change.

The process of socialization also operates at the micro level, where it influences individuals within particular social institutions, such as the family and the school. This process of individual rather than societal socialization occurs through interaction in which there is a filial bond between the socializer and the socializee. In most societies, this interpersonal and individual socialization occurs within the nuclear and extended families. This is known as a lineage relationship; there is a vertical linkage between generations based on biological and social ties.

The structure of the extended kinship system includes the family of orientation and the family of procreation. The extended-family system is created through marriage, grows as children are born, declines or dissolves through divorce or death, and may be re-created through remarriage. The structure of the extended family normally consists of four or five generations: grandchildren or great-grandchildren, a young couple with or without children, a postparental middle-aged couple, an older retired couple, and perhaps an 'old-old' widow or widower. As Marshall (1981) noted, because of population aging and changes in demographic processes, lineages are becoming longer and thinner. In contrast, early in this century families of procreation were larger, people did not live as long, and the lineage was shorter and wider.

Because socialization involves a two-way process of interaction, negotiation, and feedback, the possibility for either cohesiveness or conflict between generations exists within a family. If conflict arises within the family, it is more likely to occur between parents and children during the critical years of identity formation and independence assertion. However, as Cohen and Gans (1978) noted, there is also 'the other generation gap' between adult children and aging parents. More will be said about this relationship in chapter 9.

Some degree of value and lifestyle differences exists among all generations within a family because of the influence of the media, because of historical events, and because of the different stages of maturation of family members. However, the existence and degree of conflict within the lineage system is often influenced by intergenerational conflict at the societal or cohort level. Thus, a complex linkage exists between the social structure and the socialization process at the societal and lineage levels (Troll, 1980; Bengtson et al., 1985, 1990; Connidis, 1989a). The process of socialization within the family system is interdependent with the process of cohort socialization, and vice versa. Each member in a specific lineage structure is also a member of an age cohort. Children are socialized by parents and others within the lineage network, and are also socialized by members of a peer group who are members of other lineage structures.

Troll and Bengtson (Troll, 1980:77) suggest that within each extended family there are 'family themes' of values, ideals, and behavior. These provide some degree of continuity and stability between the lineage generations. In contrast, at the societal level, 'keynote themes' distinguish succeeding cohorts from previous cohorts. These themes (such as premarital cohabitation or a particular style of dress or popular music) may or may not be adopted by all members of a particular cohort. However, if a keynote theme is compatible with a family theme, it is likely to be adopted and to cause little intergenerational conflict within the lineage system. If the two themes represent conflicting values or beliefs, and a keynote theme is adopted, then lineage or cohort conflict is likely to evolve.

The next section examines one facet of intergenerational relations that has stimulated much discussion by social scientists, namely, the extent to which intergenerational relations are characterized by solidarity or conflict. This phenomenon, known as the generation gap, has received much attention because of the concern about real or imaginary generational differences in values, attitudes, and behaviors (Esler, 1984; Mangen et al., 1988). The following section analyzes generational similarities and differences at the cohort and lineage levels of analysis.

Cohort and Lineage Generation Gaps: Fact or Fiction?

Intergenerational Solidarity

Before examining the research evidence for or against the existence of a generation gap, let us consider some of the potential conditions that might enhance or reduce intergenerational solidarity at the micro- and macro-structural levels. First, there is always likely to be some degree of strain and conflict between different age groups. This occurs because individuals are at different stages in the socialization process, because they are socialized during different historical periods, and because they may have different needs, interests, values, and lifestyles.

Nevertheless, social order rather than chaos is the norm, particularly within the extended family. Some social processes promote lineage solidarity. For example, the frequency of required interaction, the degree of intergenerational similarity in values because of socialization practices, and the degree of affection, bonding, or liking for family members are three processes that operate at the micro level in family relations. This bonding is revealed by the amount and frequency of helping, by the degree of consensus in beliefs or orientations, and by the frequency of interaction prevalent in family dynamics (Troll, 1980; Marshall and Bengtson, 1983; Bengtson et al., 1985, 1990; Connidis, 1989b).

As a result of the interaction of family bonding and socialization practices, differences between the lineage generations are minimized. Family members may share common experiences and discuss current events and issues. Moreover, children are dependent on parents for information and for gratification of needs, and the parents serve as role models for life-cycle events such as choosing an occupation, marriage, and child rearing. In short, from an exchange perspective, a bond and a debt is created during the early child-rearing years. This tends to minimize conflict and enhance lineage solidarity.

A final potential cause of conflict pertains to cultural values among immigrant groups. Where second- or third-generation youth are socialized by parents or grandparents who are foreign born, the younger generations may be faced with accepting or rejecting traditional ethnic values and beliefs held by the family, as opposed to modern values and beliefs held by peers, the school, or the media. This may create intergenerational strain and conflict. However, this strain disappears when second and subsequent generations, which have been socialized in North America, socialize their own children according to North American cultural norms. Thus, as structural and cultural assimilation occurs, differences narrow and disappear.

When intergenerational strain arises, it reduces solidarity. To understand why this happens, some conditions at both the lineage and cohort levels must be examined. Bengtson and his associates (Bengtson et al., 1976, 1985, 1990) have considered possible sources of strain. First, there may be some biological and physiological factors associated with advancing age that lead to changes in needs, perceptions, and cognitions, in responses to social stimuli, and in orientations to life.

Second, sociocultural and historical factors can create divisions between generations. For example, status (and hence power) in social institutions generally increases with advancing years, to a certain point; and the young and the old have less social and political power and influence than the middle generation. Also, age grading and stereotyping develop cohort consciousness and lead to intracohort solidarity and generational polarization. Historical events, such as high unemployment or a war (such as the war in Vietnam) that is perceived as unnecessary by one particular age cohort may lead to overt conflict. Finally, there is the phenomenon of fresh contact (Mannheim, 1952); each new generation perceives existing social institutions and social reality from its own perspective, which usually differs from the perspectives of older generations.

All of these factors taken together result in the older generation having a 'developmental stake' in the younger generation (Bengtson and Kuypers, 1971); they fear losing something that is valued. For example, the older generation has a stake in promoting the status quo and in maintaining the continuity of what they value. Therefore, they seek to inculcate similar values in younger generations. In contrast, young people seek to develop a lifestyle and a unique set of values by having the freedom to create and promote differences between the generations.

As a result of this dialectical process of negotiation between the generations, conflict may be perceived. However, the extent of the gap is seen differently by each generation. The older generation minimizes the gap and argues that apparent differences reflect differences in maturity. They also believe that these differences are temporary and will eventually disappear. In contrast, the younger generation exaggerates the differences and claims that the older generation interferes with their right to establish their own values, identity, and lifestyle.

In summary, a number of processes, particularly at the family level, promote intergenerational solidarity. However, at the macro level some social processes may foster real or imagined differences between generations. Yet, for the most part, social order prevails. In order to determine whether a significant generation gap exists, the next two subsections present some alternative hypotheses, examine some methodological problems in this area of study, and discuss the research evidence that supports or refutes the existence of a generation gap at the cohort and lineage levels.

Competing Perspectives, Alternative Explanations, and Methodological Concerns

Three competing perspectives concerning the generation gap appear in the scientific and popular literature. The first holds that there is a great gap between the generations. The second suggests that the age gap is caused by other than generational factors, and is perpetuated by the media and by methodologically inferior research studies. The third position is that there are selective continuities and differences in the basic values, beliefs, and attitudes inculcated in succeeding generations. Thus, differences pertaining to political, sexual, or religious values and behaviors may arise to varying degrees among different generations at specific points in history. For example, it has been suggested that in periods of high unemployment intergenerational conflict may arise over a scarce resource, namely, jobs.

While these perspectives have been the stimulus for research studies that seek to support or reject a particular view, few researchers have considered alternative explanations for their findings; nor have they been able to eliminate a number of methodological problems. Most of the studies, at least in the early years, assumed that the gap existed at the lineage level primarily between adolescents and their parents, or at the cohort level between the young and the middle-aged. However, as some studies have suggested, a gap may also exist between the elderly cohort and the youth cohort, or between the elderly and the middle-aged (Cohen and Gans, 1978), the so-called 'sandwich generation' (Miller, 1981). Miller notes that some adults with elderly parents view their position in the extended family as stressful. This stress occurs because their own children are not yet totally independent, and their parents are becoming more dependent. As a result, they must share their resources with two other generations.

There appear to be three possible explanations for any lineage gaps. First, differences in values and attitudes may result from the generations being at different stages of development or maturation. In this situation, it is expected that young people will 'grow out' of their adolescent values, attitudes, and predispositions as they move into early adulthood,

thereby narrowing or eliminating the gap. (This expectation is often expressed by parents with respect to the preferences in dress or music of adolescents).

A second explanation is that the differences arise because of a generational or cohort effect, where members of a particular generation are socialized at a certain time in history and acquire behaviors, attitudes, and values that give them a unique view of the world. They subsequently demonstrate these differences during each stage of the life cycle. For example, adolescents who were socialized following the late 1960s and early 1970s may have acquired more liberal values and behaviors than those who were socialized as adolescents in the 1950s. The 1960s generation, which initiated openly liberated sexual practices, may continue to adhere to more liberal values and behaviors concerning most facets of life (highlight 7.4).

The third possible explanation for generational differences is a historical or period effect, where social, economic, or political events (such as an assassination, a war, or the fall of a corrupt government) can lead to dramatic changes in the behavior and beliefs of a specific generation. In this situation, even though the event has an impact on other generations, one generation is significantly more affected than others, and a gap is created. For example, those who were young adults during the Depression of the 1930s have always tended to be thrifty and more cautious in personal financial management.

Another factor that interferes with the attempt to explain the existence of a generation gap at the cohort level of analysis is the failure to control for social variables such as occupation, class background, ethnicity, educational attainment, religion, gender, and place of residence. All of these, rather than age, may account for generational differences, since people who hold the same social position tend to share relatively the same world view, regardless of age. Similarly, a generation gap may more likely be reported if different generations live in the same housing unit. That is, frequent daily interaction may create tension and conflict that subsequently is reported and interpreted as a generation gap. In reality, the reported differences or tensions may reflect housing arrange-

HIGHLIGHT 7.4

THE SIXTIES GENERATION: A GENERATION IMMERSED IN POLITICAL AND SOCIAL ACTIVISM

Beginning in the mid-1960s, a decade of turbulence reflected a massive change in values, beliefs, and social behavior, especially among those of college age. It was during this period that the following events flourished and matured: the Vietnam War and the appearance of antiwar demonstrators and conscientious objectors, many of whom fled to Canada; a backlash against black demands for integration and equality, which led to race riots in many U.S. cities; a large-scale questioning by youth of existing political and social values and responsibilities, which was expressed in a backlash against the authority of the 'Establishment' or of the status quo by means of the hippie movement, unconventional styles of dress (long hair and blue jeans), new music and major musical events (the arrival of the Beatles in North America; the Woodstock concert; and *Hair*, the tribal-love rock musical with nude performers and anti-establishment songs supporting love, sex, drugs, protests, and freedom, and opposing war and racial segregation); the initiation of liberated sexual mores and practices, and demonstrations and riots on college campuses; the onset of the women's movement and the emergence of the feminist perspective on gender relations and the question of power and prestige within previously male-dominated social institutions; a growing concern with human rights and personal freedom, in general; and increasing tension between youth and adults over the desire of youth to exercise a degree of self-mastery over their future lives, which led to the emergence of new social norms and to a questioning of such established authority figures as coaches, parents, teachers, politicians, and to serious criticisms of such institutions as sport, religion, education, and the family. Taken collectively, the events that reflected this political and cultural protest of the 1960s and early 1970s redefined many facets of society and fostered a generational consciousness among youth that has dissipated, but not disappeared, as this generation has moved into their 40s. In short, the 'keynote' themes created and adopted by the youth of the 1960s have clearly delineated this cohort as a unique generation that has had a considerable impact on the cultural and political values, attitudes, beliefs, and lifestyles of succeeding generations.

ments rather than a real generation gap. By including such control factors in the analysis of differences, an investigator might be able to demonstrate whether the generation gap is real or whether it is an illusion.

A final limitation that should be addressed is the variety of attitudes, values, beliefs, norms, behaviors, and moral and religious tenets that are present in modernized societies. One should not conclude that a generation gap exists on the basis of studying only one of many factors. In fact, generational differences may be present on one value dimension, but not on others. Similarly, there may be differences within a specific domain, such as politics. For example, there may be a gap with respect to party identification, but not with respect to political alienation or attitudes toward a particular government policy.

Despite methodological limitations, the debate continues as to whether a generation

gap is myth or fact, whether there is a cohort or lineage gap, and to what extent the gap, if it exists, leads to generational conflict or social disharmony. The current state of knowledge in these areas is summarized in the next subsection.

The Generation Gap: A Summary of Research Evidence

Based on the results of studies that have examined both cohort and lineage differences in three-generation families, most empirical evidence suggests that there is not a significant gap at either level (Bengtson and Cutler, 1976; Bengston et al., 1985, 1990). The generation gap is more imaginary than real, and there is more consensus than conflict among and between generations.

The one exception, which stimulated much of the interest in and research into this question, is the value and behavioral gap that was observed among some generational units within the youth cohort of the late 1960s, and between this youth cohort and all other age cohorts. This conflict was even found within a number of extended families across the social spectrum. However, it is likely that this gap was a 'period effect' influenced by the war in Vietnam, a compulsory draft, a growing black-power movement, and the beginnings of the women's movement and the sexual revolution. Today, many of the so-called hippies, draft dodgers, and feminists are now middle-aged citizens with values similar to other 'liberal-oriented' members of their age cohort.

Where some studies do conclude that a generation gap exists, that gap tends to be more pronounced for specific values, beliefs, and behaviors, and to be more evident outside the extended family. That is, the gap shrinks dramatically when it becomes more personal. Bengston and Cutler (1976:145) summarized this finding by reporting a common response of subjects: 'Yes, there is a generation gap, but not in my family.' One reason for fewer perceived differences within the family is that conflict resolution occurs through daily negotiation and compromise between parents and youth (Troll, 1980). At the family level, individuals often coexist peacefully with respect to value differences. Tensions may develop over interpersonal and lifestyle issues rather than over political values and attitudes. In fact, political and religious beliefs and affiliations may be shared more by middle-aged parents and their young adult children than by middle-aged parents and their own parents. If differences appear between parent and child, they often persist only during such developmental periods as early or late adolescence.

Troll (1980) suggests that there is a shared value system within the family (the 'family theme') that provides a continuity in outlook across generations. This theme often interacts with 'keynote' themes at the societal level, so that new ideas or lifestyles are adopted throughout the extended family. For example, a youth raised in a family with a liberal set of values, where the parents have perhaps experimented with different lifestyles, may find that the recreational use of drugs creates less strain than it does in another family where more traditional, conservative lifestyles have prevailed over the generations.

Much of the reported gap may exist only in the eye of the beholder. As a result of possible misinterpretation or distorted perception, behavior and attitudes toward members of another generation may be alerted. That is, the perception, even if biased or incorrect, can distort reality and can have consequences for intergenerational relationships. A member of the younger generation may perceive and exaggerate differences within the family, while parents and grandparents may perceive few differences and may exaggerate similarities.

At the societal level, the greatest differences may well be those between the youngest and the oldest generations, perhaps because of social and political change and the onset of historical events (Bengston, 1971). Also, there is generally little communication or negotiation between these generations. In contrast, if differences exist between the youngest and the middle generations, the middle generation is likely to shift toward the views or beliefs of youth through negotiation, compromise, or identification (Troll, 1980). To illustrate, many parents who were initially strongly opposed to children wearing jeans to school or social events, now wear jeans to social events themselves, perhaps to identify with younger age cohorts or to present a youthful figure.

In summary, the hypothesized generation gap is generally not supported by research evidence. This conclusion holds for both the lineage and cohort levels of analysis, but particularly for the lineage level, where solidarity rather than conflict is the norm. Where differences do exist, they tend to be related to a specific value or attitude and to lifestyle and developmental issues, many of which disappear as young adulthood is attained.

SUMMARY AND CONCLUSIONS

This chapter has introduced the reader to the importance of the social structure in the aging process. Based on a system of age stratification, with accompanying age norms and age grading, chronological and social age can create, stabilize, or change the structure within a society, or within a particular institution, such as the family. Clearly, the social structure influences the process of aging at the societal level of analysis (through cohort analysis), and for generations within the extended family system (through generational analysis). The influence of the social structure and a number of social processes on aging and the status of the aged was considered from the cohort and generational analysis perspectives. Cohort flow, socialization, ageism, stereotyping, and attitude formation were seen to influence the aging process at the cohort level of analysis. In addition, special attention was given to how interaction among stratification systems affects the status of the elderly. Does the aging individual experience discrimination and limited life chances because of double, triple, or multiple jeopardy resulting from the interaction of age, gender, class, racial, or ethnic stratification? Or, is age a leveling factor, so that lifelong social or economic differentiation becomes less important in determining the situation and status of older women or minority-group members?

The final section focused on intergenerational relations at the cohort (societal) and lineage (family) levels of analysis. The literature on the existence of a cohort or lineage gap between generations was reviewed to determine whether intergenerational relations are characterized by solidarity or conflict.

Based on the literature reviewed, it can be concluded that:

1. Chronological age influences an individual's location and status in society and in the structures of specific social institutions.
2. Chronological age is a criterion for entering and leaving social positions. Codified laws based on chronological age influence life chances and lifestyles.
3. Within an age-stratification system, age grading occurs whereby age-based norms provide a cultural definition of expected rights, behaviors, and responsibilities of individuals at particular times in their lives. These norms regulate social interaction and define when life events should occur and in what order.
4. Few age-related norms pertain to the behavior of the elderly. Where norms are present, they usually relate to behavior to be avoided at or after a particular age.
5. The socialization process and social interaction patterns can lead to stereotyping of, and negative attitudes toward, the aged. They may also foster segregation and isolation of the aged.
6. There is little evidence that a high level of age-group consciousness exists among the elderly, or among other age groups.
7. There is little evidence of the existence of the hypothesized 'midlife crisis,' for either men or women.
8. The aged tend to be underrepresented or misrepresented, usually through negative stereotypes, in such cultural forms as poetry, literature, humor, and television. Older women, despite their numerical majority, are underrepresented as major characters in most forms of literature and entertainment.
9. Although it has been hypothesized that negative or stereotypical views of the elderly in popular culture lead to the adoption of negative attitudes and behavior, this relationship has not been validated by research evidence.
10. Attitudes of younger people toward the elderly are influenced by interaction and experiences with older people, by the personality of the evaluator, and by the situation in which the evaluation occurs.
11. Most older persons do not evaluate or label themselves in negative terms.
12. Research evidence suggests that despite the presence of some degree of societal ageism, and despite self-segregation by some individuals, most older persons are integrated with other age strata.
13. Few older persons actually experience significant degrees of isolation, loneliness, or alienation.
14. Research evidence indicates that the aged are not a unique social group within modernized societies. Older

cohorts are heterogeneous and do not make up a subculture, a minority group, a poverty group, or a political group.

15. The interaction of age with class, ethnic, racial, or gender stratification systems can influence the psychological, social, and physical adjustment of those at the lower end of the systems. With respect to income and health status, the situation of the elderly may be worsened by being female, a member of the lower class, or a member of a disadvantaged racial or ethnic group.

16. Multiple jeopardy does not appear to be a factor in the status of elderly persons. That is, it is not an 'aging' event. Rather, the characteristics of multiple jeopardy have probably been present throughout life.

17. The generation gap appears to be more imaginary than real. There is little empirical evidence to support the existence of a generation gap at either the societal (cohort) or family (lineage) levels of analysis.

18. Where a perceived gap is noted, it tends to be at the societal level and to pertain only to certain specific values, beliefs, or behaviors. A generation gap, if it is perceived to exist, is more likely to be experienced by the younger of two or more age cohorts. Moreover, where generational differences are perceived, they are often related to lifestyle and developmental issues, many of which disappear with the transition to early adulthood.

NOTES

1. See Eisenstadt, 1956; Troll, 1970; Bengston and Cutler, 1976; Bengston et al., 1976, 1985, 1990; Dowd, 1979-80; Kertzer, 1983; Demartini, 1985.

2. There may only be one generation throughout history that has any one of these labels. That is, the particular social or historical conditions may never occur again, and the size or composition of a specific cohort may vary little in the future.

3. In this sense 'generations' are seen as stages in a developmental sequence. That is, there will always be stages of infancy, youth, early adulthood, middle adulthood, and old age. While these are partially related to chronological age, the chronological boundaries and social meaning of each stage may vary over time or across cultures. Nevertheless, the stages (or generations) will persist in some form.

4. For example, grandparents are older than their children who are parents, and these parents are older than their own children. However, one could become a parent at 16 or 36 years of age, or a grandparent at 40 or 60 years of age. Thus, role rather than chronological age determines the power and prestige within the extended family.

5. For example, does the impact on society of a particular generational unit (such as the youth counterculture of the 1960s) have an influence at subsequent points in history, or does this particular unit mature and change so that it more closely resembles other middle-aged and elderly cohorts that have passed through the life course in recent years?

6. For example, do age-segregated living environments such as college campuses or retirement communities lead to the formation of high levels of group consciousness, which in turn may lead to age-group cohesiveness and social or political action?

7. Dowd (1980:38) classified these resources into five categories: (1) personal characteristics such as beauty, strength, and knowledge; (2) material goods such as money or property; (3) relation characteristics such as influential friends or caring children; (4) authority by virtue of position or status in an organization or the family; and (5) generalized reinforcers such as respect and recognition from significant others.

8. See Peterson and Karnes, 1976; Ansello, 1977a, 1977b, 1989; Robin, 1977; Sohngen and Smith, 1978; Spencer and Hollenshead, 1980; Kingston and Drotter, 1981; Berman and Sobkowska-Ashcroft, 1986, 1988; de Vries, 1987; Meadows and Fillmer, 1987.

9. See Davies, 1977; Richman, 1977; Smith, 1979; Andrews, 1981; Demos and Jache, 1981; Dillon and Jones, 1981; Sheppard, 1981; Nahemow et al., 1986.

10. See Francher, 1973; Arnhoff, 1974; Hess, 1974, 1980; Harris and Feinberg, 1977; Ansello, 1978; Greenberg et al., 1979; Bishop and Krause, 1984; Davis and Davis, 1985; Dail, 1988.

11. This confidant does not necessarily have to be a close friend or a blood relative. Service or voluntary personnel such as doormen, hairdressers, housekeepers, bartenders, or social workers can play this role, so that the older person has at least

a minimal level of regular social contact.

12. Pratt (1974, 1976) predicts that organizations of this type will increase in membership and influence because of better leadership, stability in membership and finances, and a political environment that is more aware of the concerns of the elderly.

13. Formal and informal organizations or coalitions for the elderly may be more effective at the local level, where the social networks may easily facilitate political pressure. Also, at the local level there may be less differentiation within the older age cohorts, and more unanimity and commitment to action may be possible. To date, however, most studies have focused on the power of aging-based political groups at the national level.

REFERENCES

Andrews, D. (1981). 'Work, Age and Retirement: Attitudes Reflected in Greeting Cards,' paper presented at the annual meeting of the Gerontological Society of America, Toronto, November.

Ansello, E. (1977a). 'Old Age and Literature: An Overview,' *Educational Gerontology*, 2(3), 211-18.

Ansello, E. (1977b). 'Age and Ageism in Children's First Literature,' *Educational Gerontology*, 2(3), 255-74.

Ansello, E. (1978). 'Broadcast Images: The Older Woman in Television (Part I),' paper presented at the annual meeting of the Gerontological Society, Dallas.

Ansello, E. (1989). 'Children's First Literature and the Feast of Life,' *The Gerontologist*, 29(2), 272-77.

Arnhoff, C. (1974). 'Old Age in Prime Time,' *Journal of Communication*, 26(4), 86-87.

Atkinson, M. et al. (1986). 'Intergenerational Solidarity: An Examination of a Theoretical Model,' *Journal of Gerontology*, 41(3), 408-16.

Bell, I. (1980). 'The Double Standard,' pp. 134-46 in B. Hess (ed.). *Growing Old in America*. New Brunswick, N.J.: Transaction, Inc.

Bengtson, V. (1971). 'Inter-Age Perceptions and the Generation Gap,' *The Gerontologist*, 11(1), 85-89.

Bengtson, V. and N. Cutler. (1976). 'Generations and Intergenerational Relations: Perspectives on Age Groups and Social Change,' pp. 130-59 in R. Binstock and E. Shanas (eds.). *Handbook of Aging and the Social Sciences*. New York: Van Nostrand Reinhold.

Bengtson, V. and J. Kuypers. (1971). 'Generational Difference and the Developmental Stake,' *International Journal of Aging and Human Development*, 2(4), 249-60.

Bengston, V. et al. (1974). 'Time, Aging, and the Continuity of Social Structure: Themes and Issues in Generational Analysis,' *Journal of Social Issues*, 30(2), 1-30.

Bengtson, V. et al. (1976). 'The Generation Gap and Aging Family Members: Toward a Conceptual Model,' pp. 237-63 in J. Gubrium (ed.). *Time, Roles, and Self in Old Age*. New York: Human Sciences Press.

Bengtson, V. et al. (1985). 'Generations, Cohorts, and Relations between Age Groups,' pp. 304-38 in R. Binstock and E. Shanas (eds.). *Handbook of Aging and the Social Sciences*. 2d ed. New York: Van Nostrand Reinhold.

Bengtson, V. et al. (1990). 'Families and Aging: Diversity and Heterogeneity,' in R. Binstock and L. George (eds.). *Handbook of Aging and the Social Sciences*. 3d ed. San Diego, Calif.: Academic Press.

Bennett, R. (1980a). 'The Concept and Measurement of Social Isolation,' pp. 9-26 in R. Bennett (ed.). *Aging, Isolation and Resocialization*. New York: Van Nostrand Reinhold.

Berman, L. and I. Sobkowska-Ashcroft. (1986). 'The Old in Language and Literature,' *Language and Communication*, 6(1/2), 139-45.

Berman, L. and I. Sobkowska-Ashcroft. (1988). *Images and Impressions of Old Age in the Great Works of Western Literature (700 B.C. - 1900 A.D.)*. St. Davids, Ont.: St. David's University Press.

Binstock, R. (1972). 'Interest-Group Liberalism and the Politics of Aging,' *The Gerontologist*, 12(3), 265-80.

Binstock, R. (1974). 'Aging and the Future of American Politics,' *The Annals of the American Academy of Political and Social Science*, 415(September), 199-212.

Binstock, R. et al. (1985). 'Political Dilemmas of Social Intervention,' pp. 589-618 in R. Binstock and E. Shanas (eds.). *Handbook of Aging and the Social Sciences*. 2d ed. New York: Van Nostrand Reinhold.

Bishop, J. and D. Krause. (1984). 'Depictions of Aging and Old Age on Saturday Morning Television,' *The Gerontologist*, 24(1), 91-94.

Blau, P. (ed.). (1975). *Approaches to the Study of Social Structure*. New York: Free Press.

Blau, P. (1980). 'A Fable About Social Structure,' *Social Forces*, 58(3), 777-88.

Braungart, R. and M. Braungart. (1986). 'Life Course and Generational Policies,' *Annual Review of Sociology*, 12, 205-31.

Brim, O. (1980). 'Male Mid-Life Crisis: A Comparative Analysis,' pp. 147-63 in B. Hess (ed.). *Growing Old in America*. New Brunswick, N.J.: Transaction Books.

Brubaker, T. and E. Powers. (1976). 'The Stereotype of Old: A Review and Alternative Approach,'

Journal of Gerontology, 31(4), 441-47.

Buchholz, M. and J. Bynum. (1982). 'Newspaper Presentation of America's Aged: A Content Analysis of Image and Role,' *The Gerontologist*, 22(1), 83-88.

Burgess, E. (ed.). (1960). *Aging in Western Societies*. Chicago: University of Chicago Press.

Buss, A. (1974). 'Generational Analysis: Description, Explanation, and Theory,' *Journal of Social Issues*, 30(2), 55-71.

Butler, R. (1969). 'Ageism: Another Form of Bigotry,' *The Gerontologist*, 9(3), 243-46.

Chappell, N. and B. Havens. (1980). 'Old and Female: Testing the Double Jeopardy Hypothesis,' *The Sociological Quarterly*, 21(2), 157-71.

Chellam, G. (1980-81). 'Intergenerational Affinities: Symmetrical Life Experiences of the Young Adults and the Aging in Canadian Society,' *International Journal of Aging and Human Development*, 12(1), 79-92.

Cohen, S. and B. Gans. (1978). *The Other Generation Gap*. Chicago: Follett.

Connidis, I. (1987). 'Life in Older Age: The View from the Top,' pp. 451-72 in V. Marshall (ed.). *Aging in Canada: Social Perspectives*. 2d ed. Markham, Ont.: Fitzhenry and Whiteside.

Connidis, I. (1989a). 'The Subjective Experience of Aging: Correlates of Divergent Views,' *Canadian Journal on Aging*, 8(1), 7-18.

Connidis, I. (1989b). *Family Ties and Aging*. Toronto: Butterworths.

Crockett, W. and M. Hummert. (1987). 'Perceptions of Aging and the Elderly,' pp. 217-41 in W. Schaie (ed.). *Annual Review of Gerontology and Geriatrics*. vol. 7. New York: Springer Publishing Co.

Crockett, W. et al. (1979). 'The Effect of Deviations from Stereotyped Expectations upon Attitudes toward Older Persons,' *Journal of Gerontology*, 34(3), 368-74.

Cutler, N. and V. Bengtson. (1974). 'Age and Political Alienation: Maturation, Generation and Period Effects,' *The Annals of the American Academy of Political and Social Science*, 415(September), 160-75.

Dail, P. (1988). 'Prime-Time Television Portrayals of Older Adults in the Context of Family Life,' *The Gerontologist*, 28(5), 700-706.

Davies, L. (1977). 'Attitudes toward Old Age and Aging as Shown by Humour,' *The Gerontologist*, 17, 220-26.

Davis, R. and J. Davis. (1985). *T.V.'s Images of the Elderly: A Practical Guide for Change*. Toronto: Lexington Books, D.C. Heath Co.

Demartini, J. (1985). 'Change Agents and Generational Relationships: A Reevaluation of Mannheim's Problem of Generations,' *Social Forces*, 64(1), 1-16.

Demos, V. and A. Jache. (1981). 'When You Care Enough: An Analysis of Attitudes toward Aging in Humorous Birthday Cards,' *The Gerontologist*, 21(1), 209-15.

de Vries, P. (1987). 'Every Old Person is Somebody: The Image of Aging in Canadian Children's Literature,' *Canadian Children's Literature*, 46(1), 37-44.

Dillon, K. and B. Jones. (1981). 'Attitudes toward Aging Portrayed by Birthday Cards,' *International Journal of Aging and Human Development*, 13(1), 79-84.

Dowd, J. (1979-80). 'The Problems of Generations and Generational Analysis,' *International Journal of Aging and Human Development*, 10(3), 213-29.

Dowd, J. (1980). *Stratification among the Aged*. Monterey, Calif.: Brooks/Cole Publishing Co.

Dowd, J. (1987). 'The Reification of Age: Age Stratification Theory and the Passing of the Autonomous Subject,' *Journal of Aging Studies*, 1(4), 317-35.

Eagly, A. and S. Himmelfarb. (1978). 'Attitudes and Opinions,' pp. 517-54 in M. Rosenzweig and L. Porter (eds.). *Annual Review of Psychology*. vol. 29. Palo Alto, Calif.: Annual Reviews, Inc.

Eglit, H. (1985). 'Age and the Law,' pp. 528-53 in R. Binstock and E. Shanas (eds.). *Handbook of Aging and the Social Sciences*. 2d ed. New York: Van Nostrand Reinhold.

Eichler, M. (1980). *The Double Standard*. London: Croom Helm.

Eisenstadt, S. (1956). *From Generation to Generation: Age Groups and Social Structure*. Glencoe, Ill.: Free Press.

Esler, A. (1984). *The Generation Gap in Society and History: A Select Bibliography*, Part I and Part II. Monticello, Ill.: Vance Bibliographies.

Foner, A. (1974). 'Age Stratification and Age Conflict in Political Life,' *American Sociological Review*, 39(2), 187-96.

Foner, A. (1979). 'Ascribed and Achieved Bases of Stratification,' pp. 219-42 in A. Inkeles et al. (eds.). *Annual Review of Sociology*. vol. 5. Palo Alto, Calif.: Annual Reviews, Inc.

Foner, A. (1984). 'Age and Social Change,' in D. Kertzer and J. Keith (eds.). *Age and Anthropological Theory*. Ithaca, N.Y.: Cornell University Press.

Fortes, M. (1984). 'Age, Generation and Social Structure,' in D. Kertzer and J. Keith (eds.). *Age and Anthropological Theory*. Ithaca, N.Y.: Cornell University Press.

Fraboni, M. et al. (1990). 'The Fraboni Scale of Ageism (FSA): An Attempt at a More Precise Measure of Ageism,' *The Canadian Journal on Aging*, 9(1), 56-66.

Francher, J. (1973). 'It's the Pepsi Generation... Accelerated Aging and the Television Commercial,' *International Journal of Aging and Human Development*, 4(3), 245-55.

Fuller, M. and C. Martin. (1980). *The Older Woman: Lavender Rose or Gray Panther*. Springfield, Ill.: Charles C. Thomas.

George, L. (1980). *Role Transitions in Later Life*. Monterey, Calif.: Brooks/Cole Publishing Co.

George, L. (1990). 'Social Structure, Social Processes, and Social Psychological States,' pp. 185-204 in R. Binstock and L. George (eds.). *Handbook of Aging and the Social Sciences*. 3d ed. San Diego, Calif.: Academic Press.

Glass, J. and C. Trent. (1980). 'Changing Ninth-Graders' Attitudes toward Older Persons,' *Research on Aging*, 2(4), 499-512.

Green, S. (1981). 'Attitudes and Perceptions about the Elderly: Current and Future Perspectives,' *International Journal of Aging and Human Development*, 13(2), 99-119.

Greenberg, B. et al. (1979). 'The Portrayal of the Aging: Trends on Commercial Television,' *Research on Aging*, 1(3), 319-34.

Hagestad, G. and B. Neugarten. (1985). 'Age and the Life Course,' pp. 35-61 in R. Binstock and E. Shanas (eds.). *Handbook of Aging and the Social Sciences*. 2d ed. New York: Van Nostrand Reinhold.

Harris, A. and J. Feinberg. (1977). 'Television and Aging - Is What You See What You Get?' *The Gerontologist*, 17(5), 464-68.

Hauwiller, J. and R. Jennings. (1981). 'Counteracting Age Stereotyping with Young School Children,' *Educational Gerontology*, 7(2-3), 183-90.

Henretta, J. (1988). 'Conflict and Cooperation among Age Strata,' pp. 385-404 in J. Birren and V. Bengtson (eds.). *Emergent Theories of Aging*. New York: Springer Publishing Co.

Hess, B. (1974). 'Stereotypes of the Aged,' *Journal of Communication*, 24(4), 76-85.

Hess, B. (1980). 'Dilemmas of TV Broadcasting: How to Portray Older People Realistically,' pp. 543-47 in B. Hess. (ed.). *Growing Old in America*. 2d ed. New Brunswick, N.J.: Transaction Books.

Hogan, D. (1978). 'The Variable Order of Events in the Life Course,' *American Sociological Review*, 43(4), 573-86.

House, J. (1974). 'Occupational Stress and Coronary Heart Disease: A Review and Theoretical Integration,' *Journal of Health and Social Behavior*, 15, 12-27.

Hudson, R. (ed.). (1981). *The Aging in Politics: Process and Policy*. Springfield, Ill.: Charles C. Thomas.

Hudson, R. and J. Strate. (1985). 'Aging and Political Systems,' pp. 554-85 in R. Binstock and E. Shanas (eds.). *Handbook of Aging and the Social Sciences*. 2d ed. New York: Van Nostrand Reinhold.

Hunter, S. and M. Sundel (eds.). (1989). *Midlife Myths: Issues, Findings and Practice Implications*. Newbury Park, Calif.: Sage Publications.

Jackson, J. (1985). 'Race, National Origin, Ethnicity, and Aging,' pp. 264-303 in R. Binstock and E. Shanas (eds.). *Handbook of Aging and the Social Sciences*. 2d ed. New York: Van Nostrand Reinhold.

Jackson, J. et al. (1990). 'Race, Ethnicity, and Aging: Conceptual and Methodological Issues,' pp. 103-23 in R. Binstock and L. George (eds.). *Handbook of Aging and the Social Sciences*. 3d ed. San Diego, Calif.: Academic Press.

Jacobs, B. (1990). 'Aging and Politics,' pp. 349-61 in R. Binstock and L. George (eds.). *Handbook of Aging and the Social Sciences*. 3d ed. San Diego, Calif.: Academic Press.

Kalish, R. (ed.). (1989) *Midlife Loss: Coping Strategies*. Newbury Park, Calif.: Sage Publications.

Kertzer, D. (1983). 'Generation as a Sociological Problem,' *Annual Review of Sociology*, 9, 125-49.

Kingston, A. and M. Drotter. (1981). 'The Depiction of Old Age in Six Basal Readers,' *Educational Gerontology*, 6(4), 29-34.

Kuypers, J. and V. Bengtson. (1973). 'Social Breakdown and Competence: A Model of Normal Aging,' *Human Development*, 16(3), 181-201.

Levin, J. and W. Levin. (1980). *Ageism: Prejudice and Discrimination against the Elderly*. Belmont, Calif.: Wadsworth Publishing Co.

Lutsky, N. (1980). 'Attitudes toward Old Age and Elderly Persons,' pp. 287-336 in C. Eisdorfer (ed.). *Annual Review of Gerontology and Geriatrics*. vol. 1. New York: Springer Publishing Co.

Mangen, D. et al. (eds.). (1988). *Measurement of Intergenerational Relations*. Newbury Park, Calif.: Sage Publications.

Mannheim, K. (1952). *Essays in the Sociology of Knowledge*. London: Routledge and Kegan Paul.

Markides, K. (1981). 'Letter to the Editor,' *Journal of Gerontology*, 36(4), 494.

Marshall, V. (1981). 'Societal Toleration of Aging: Sociological Theory and Social Response to Population Aging,' pp. 85-104 in *Adaptability and Aging 1*. Paris: International Center of Social Gerontology.

Marshall, V. (1983). 'Generations, Age Groups and Cohorts: Conceptual Distinctions', *Canadian Journal on Aging*, 2(3), 51-62.

Marshall, V. and V. Bengtson. (1983). 'Generations: Conflict and Cooperation,' in U. Lehr (ed.). *Aging in the 80s and Beyond*. New York: Springer Publishing Co.

McGuire, S. (1987). 'Aging Education in Schools,' *Journal of School Health*, 57(5), 174-76.

8
Aging: The Physical Environment and Social Processes

Health and Welfare Canada, Information Directorate

INTRODUCTION

This chapter examines the interaction among aging individuals, aging cohorts, and the changing macro- and micro-physical environments (region, neighborhood, residence). More specifically, you will see how characteristics of past and present physical environments interact with aging individuals and aging cohorts to influence their social behavior and quality of life.

In order to answer the question of how the physical environment influences the aging process, information has been drawn from a variety of disciplines. To illustrate:

1. Demographers have studied the spatial distribution of older age groups (percentage and population mix) at the local, regional and national levels; and have studied local mobility and interregional migration patterns of the elderly.

2. Psychologists have examined the influence of the environment on the quality of life, life satisfaction, and subjective well-being of older individuals; the perceived meaning of the environment; and the ability of older individuals to interact with the environment in the face of perceptual, sensory, or cognitive changes.

3. Sociologists have been interested in environmentally induced changes in lifestyles (such as institutionalization); in the impact of environment on networks, interaction, social support, and access to services; in rural/urban differences in the aging process; and in the impact of age-segregated and age-integrated residential living environments on social interaction, lifestyle, and life satisfaction.

4. Criminologists have focused on the incidence and type of victimization by the elderly, along with the incidence and impact of fear of crime.

5. Planners and social workers have studied the present and future need for housing, transportation, and social services for the elderly, especially in the light of population aging, and of both permanent and seasonal migration to specific regions.

6. Environmentalists, ecologists, and geographers have been concerned with the nature and quality of the living environment in the home, neighborhood, community, region, and nation.

As a result of these diverse interests, the environment has become an important psychosocial variable in the study of the aging process at both the micro (individual) and macro (societal) levels of analysis.[1] However, this disciplinary diversity has created conceptual problems with respect to what constitutes 'environment,' and the way in which environmental-behavioral interaction can be analyzed, both qualitatively and quantitatively. A number of social and physical components have been studied under the heading of 'environment,' and their effects have been related to such dependent variables as life satisfaction, subjective well-being, quality of life, happiness, security, coping ability, adaptation to changes in environment (relocation), lifestyle, social interaction, number of active social roles, and number of friendships. The following list illustrates some of the components of 'environment' that have been used in studies involving older adults:

1. The type, variety, and quality of housing.

2. The place of residence (urban core, suburbia, small town, farm).

3. The degree and type of institutionalization.

4. The availability of and access to social networks, transportation, social services, and health services.

5. The physical characteristics, spatial configuration, and size of the living area at the micro (home) and macro (region, neighborhood) levels.

6. The age, ethnic, and racial composition of the neighborhood.

7. The amount of actual or imagined crime in the neighborhood.

8. The size and quality of private space, especially within institutionalized settings.

9. The objective indicators and subjective meaning of the quality of the environment.

10. The availability and use of sensory, perceptual, and cognitive resources to influence what stimuli are received and how they are used to influence behavior.

11. The degree and rate of urban renewal, and the impact on the elderly who are forced to relocate.

12. The mobility and migration patterns of the elderly.

13. The degree of familiarity with the physical environment.

14. The degree of physical danger in the environment (poor lighting, stairs, deteriorating buildings).

15. The degree of personal control, autonomy, and freedom within the home and community.

16. The degree of choice in relocation of the place of residence.

17. The degree of actual or perceived change in the physical and social environment over time.

The factors listed above have been used in a number of studies to consider the adaptation of aging individuals or cohorts to changing physical and social environments. The question of adaptation is complicated by the prevalence of individual differences among the elderly in health and economic status, in social support, and in personal coping skills. These factors influence the ability to maintain or change living environments and lifestyles.

As will be seen throughout this chapter, there is a need for a variety of environments to meet the needs of a heterogeneous aging population. These environmental dimensions may range from independent to completely dependent lifestyles, living arrangements, and support networks; from self-supported to publicly or privately supported medical, nursing, social, transportation, and recreational services; from age-segregated to age-integrated living environments; from voluntary to involuntary relocation; from very large to very small personal space; and from high-quality to low-quality personal space.

The needs and preferences of individuals change throughout their lives; the size and quality of towns and neighborhoods change; and older people are voluntarily or involuntarily relocated. Each new environment presents not only a foreign physical milieu, but also the possibility of new social networks, depending on the nature of the housing setting and the distance of the move. A new environment may increase or decrease the amount of personal space, the personal satisfaction with the available space and the barriers to mobility. These, in turn, can influence the style and frequency of social participation.

The two-way interaction of these environmental and interpersonal changes, which may be initiated by the individual or by others, can influence one's adaptation to the aging process and the way in which a society is affected by population aging. Much of the research in this area has been motivated by the search for optimal patterns of aging wherein the elderly select or are placed in environments suited to their needs and abilities. Much less emphasis, however, has been placed on changing the society or the physical environment to meet the needs of the elderly.[2] In reality, as Wister (1989:285) noted, 'the majority of community-dwelling elderly over the age of 74 presently do not make design changes to the interior or exterior of their homes,... do not invest time into considering future changes, and prefer a living environment identical to their present situations.' He concluded that the elderly engage in psychological adaptation to their environment rather than change the physical or social world. This psychological adaptation may involve accepting health-related inconveniences; developing strategies to cope with a more demanding environment; changing their expectations about what constitutes an ideal or adequate environment; denying the loss of competence to fully cope with the environment; and holding the perception that, with a limited time left to live, changes are not necessary.

This chapter includes a description and explanation of environment-behavior interaction with respect to the macroenvironment, the microenvironment, and mobility and migration. The next section focuses on models and theories that seek to explain the interaction between environment and behavior. The second section (the macroenvironment) examines the regional and local living patterns of the elderly; the need for and the problems associated with private and public transportation; the incidence of victimization and fear of crime among the elderly; and differences between urban and rural lifestyles. In the third section (the microenvironment), the type and quality of housing and the degree and impact of institutionalization are discussed. The last section focuses on the patterns and problems associated with local mobility and distant migration.

Interaction of the Personal and Environmental Systems: Theories and Models

The first theory in social gerontology to explicitly consider the impact of the social environment on the elderly was developed, tested, and applied by Gubrium (1972, 1973, 1975). Not satisfied with the existing theoretical explanations for the social and personal adjustment of the elderly, Gubrium (1975:3-27) argued that both activity and disengagement theory offer incomplete explanations of the process of aging in the later years. In fact, these theories perpetuate the myth that old age represents 'the golden years.' He developed an alternative theory which proposed that there is a strong interrelationship between individual characteristics (the personal system) and the sociocultural environment (the social system) with respect to the attitudes and behavior of the aged. Gubrium began with the symbolic interactionist premise that individuals attach different meanings to similar social events, and thus may respond differently. Specifically, he was interested in the impact of the physical and social milieu on the meaning older people attach to life, and in how this meaning influences their social interaction and morale.

Gubrium (1973:28-59) suggested that the environment in the later years included 'individual' and 'social' contexts that interact to determine social interaction and hence well-being. The individual context involves the possession, to varying degrees, of three types of resources: good health, financial solvency, and continu-

ing social support from friends and peers. These personal resources, if present, permit flexibility in behavior, and enable people to 'satisfactorily adjust' to local age-related norms. Those who lack one or more of these three resources have less flexibility and may be adversely affected by their environment.

The 'social' context, according to Gubrium, provides activity norms that influence behavioral expectations. The meaning of being old is related to the degree of involvement in age-concentrated environments. For example, in age-homogeneous environments group consciousness norms are likely to be age-linked; there is little variety in the experiences and events an individual encounters, and little role flexibility is required. In contrast, in an age-heterogeneous environment a variety of experiences and demands are likely, and these require greater role flexibility in order for the individual to adapt. Thus, personal and social resources interact with different normative situations to influence behavioral interaction and morale. Adjustment is most likely to be successful when there is congruency between what people expect of themselves and what is expected of them by others.

Gubrium's socioenvironmental theory of aging sought to predict behavior and adjustment in the later years. It was based on the activity norms in specific age-linked environments, on the activity resources of the individual, and on the degree of congruency between these two factors. It is predicted that those who have high morale will be either those who have high activity resources and live in an age-heterogeneous context, or those who have low resources and live in an age-homogeneous environment. It must be recognized that these general patterns of adaptation reflect not only the present status of the elderly person, but also the cumulative experiences of adapting to various environments at earlier stages in the life cycle.

A second theory, introduced by Kahana (1975, 1982), argued that the environment is unique to an individual. According to this 'person-environment congruence' model, individuals change their environment or alter their needs via adaptive behavior in order to maximize the fit, or congruence, between their needs and the demands of a specific environment. Where individuals with certain needs reside in an environment congruent with their needs, a high level of subjective well-being is usually reported. Incongruence can result from major changes in one's life such as a housing move, a sudden decline in health, or a stressful personal loss through divorce or widowhood. When there is deviation from congruence in either a positive or a negative direction, a change in needs or environment is necessary to reduce the deviation and to restore congruence. To illustrate: an environment can be overstimulating and create anxiety and tension, or it can be so unstimulating that apathy and low levels of arousal prevail. In either of these situations, individuals, depending on their personal needs, might adapt by reducing or augmenting personal tension, thereby moving toward a higher degree of person-environment congruence. To date, this theory has primarily been tested within institutionalized settings. For example, Kahana et al. (1980), in a study of 124 residents in three homes for the aged, found a positive relationship between person-environment fit, as measured by the dimensions of impulse control, congregation and segregation, and well-being.

A theory proposed by Schooler (1975) focuses on the cognitive interpretation of external stimuli with respect to the amount of threat they pose to the individual or to the environment. If a threat is perceived, a stress reaction is induced that leads to individual coping behavior or to a change in environment. This in turn can result in positive or negative morale, health, and life satisfaction. If no threat is perceived, behavior and environmental interaction continue as in the past. This model stresses the individual's perception of the meaning of the environment, and the adoption of appropriate coping behavior to change the environment and reduce the stress. This theory may be of some use in explaining the fear of crime expressed by some older adults.

The most comprehensive theory relating the individual, the environment, and aging has been proposed by Lawton and his associates (1980a, 1982, 1985, 1987). Whereas the Gubrium theory represents a sociological approach and emphasizes interaction within the social struc-ture, Lawton's theory represents a psychological approach. This theory emphasizes the macroenvironments where older people live, and the various microenvironments to which they may voluntarily or involuntarily move.

After years of research on older people living in a variety of housing environments, Lawton and his associates developed an 'ecological model of adaptation and aging' in order to enable gerontologists and policymakers to identify, create, or select the best environment for specific individuals. The theory is based on the premise that a person's behavioral and psychological state can be better understood with knowledge of the context in which the person behaves (Lawton, 1980a:2). Thus, adaptation depends on the interaction of two basic elements — individual competence and environmental press.

An individual has a theoretical upper limit of capacity in health, sensorimotor functioning, perception, cognitive skill, and ego strength. This multidimensional concept, known as 'individual competence,' is measured by observable behavior that reflects the presence of these states and abilities. In addition, external factors such as loss of income, forced retirement, loss of spouse, or ageism may be experienced in such a way that they reflect reduced competence.

As noted earlier, the concept of **environment** has many meanings. Lawton (1980a:17-18) suggests that it has five components:

1. The personal environment, consisting of significant others, such as parents, spouse, children, and friends.
2. The group environment, which provides social norms and reference groups.
3. The suprapersonal environment, or the average characteristics of individuals in the immediate neighborhood (homogeneity or heterogeneity in age, race, ethnicity).
4. The social environment, which includes cultural values, institutions, and economic cycles.
5. The objective physical environment, whether it be small (one room) or large (a metropolitan area).

Each of these environments makes varying behavioral demands on individuals; that is, they exert 'environmental press.'

In addition to the objective environment, the subjective or perceived environment is also important. For example, the perception of a safe community or an unfriendly neighborhood depends on the individual's subjective judgment based on his or her own knowledge and experience. Subjective experiences may influence behavior in addition to, and independent of, either the person or the 'objective' environment. For example, an elderly couple whose money is stolen from their hotel room may perceive the city to be dangerous, even if they were the only guests who had been victimized in recent years.

An examination of the ecological model (figure 8.1) indicates that the level of individual competence may range from low to high, while the degree of environmental press may range from weak to strong.

In this model, the outcome of the competence/environment interaction leads to varying degrees of adaptive behavior and affect (emotional or mental state), with the slope representing ideal behavioral adaptation and positive affect. Point A represents maladaptive behavior and negative affect. This is illustrated by the situation where highly competent people experience sensory deprivation (such as solitary confinement). Point B represents a low level of competence and strong environmental press. This situation leads to maladaptive be-

FIGURE 8.1

AN ECOLOGICAL MODEL OF AGING

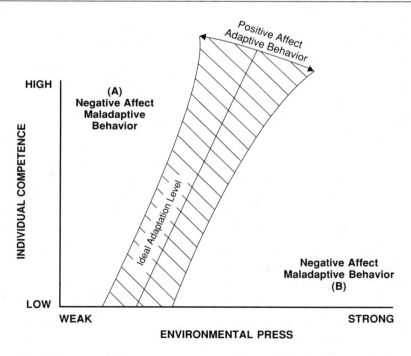

SOURCE: Adapted from P. Lawton and L. Nahemow. (1973). 'Ecology and the Aging Process,' pp. 619-74 in C. Eisdorfer and M. P. Lawton (eds.). *The Psychology of Adult Development and Aging.* Washington, D.C.: American Psychological Association. Copyright 1973 by the American Psychological Association. Adapted by permission of the author.

havior and negative affect, and is illustrated by the elderly person in a northern region who spends the winter months in a skid-row environment in a large city.

The slightly fan-shaped curve indicates that the more competent the individual, the greater the ability to tolerate higher levels of environmental press. The less competent the individual, the greater the impact of environmental factors (Lawton, 1980a:14). The combinations of individual competence and environmental press are compounded by individual differences in needs and in the extent to which environments vary in their ability to satisfy these needs. Where competence and press are in balance, congruence and a positive mental state occur. A lack of balance suggests person/environment incongruence and a negative mental state.

This model has been tested and supported by examining the meaning to older individuals of living in non-institutionalized macro- and microenvironments, as well as in institutions for the elderly (Lawton, 1980a). In later life, individual competence may decline because of losses in the cognitive or sensory-motor functions and general health. These psychological and physical losses are compounded by retirement, loss of income, widowhood, and ageism. As a result, the aging individual may experience a reduced capacity to cope with environmental press, which may occur in such forms as the deteriorating physical condition of the home, or a forced move to an institution.

A major criticism of this ecological model is that it assumes that respondents are passive and do not seek out or try to fulfill their needs through a maximum use of environmental resources. That is, individual needs, attitudes, knowledges, preferences, and perceptions are not utilized unless the environment creates a high degree of press. Moreover, the positive resources of the environment are ignored in that the focus is on the demands of the environment. In subsequent revisions, Lawton (1987) introduced the 'environmental proactivity' hypothesis whereby older individuals use personal resources to actively adapt or change their physical or social environment before the environment creates pressure for change. Highlight 8.1 illustrates some innovative adaptations to living in a potentially stressful winter environment.

Other psychological models have been proposed to explain how an elderly individual demonstrates competence. These models stress the continuous reciprocal interaction between the internal personal system and the social, physical, and psychological components of the external environment. In the first model, Windley and Scheidt (1980, 1985), employing a dialectical perspective, present a taxonomy, or hierarchical list, of environmental attributes that contribute to the dynamic interaction between individuals and their environments. These attributes pertain to the content of the environments (lighting, size, privacy), rather than to the different environments per se.

Windley and Scheidt (1980) suggest that the following attributes can be assessed objectively (measured on a scale) and/or subjectively (in terms of their meaning to an individual):

1. Amount of sensory stimulation (the quantity and intensity of, for example, light or sound needed to compensate for age changes).
2. Degree of legibility (clarity and order in the environment to facilitate cognition and orientation).
3. Feelings of comfort (temperature, illumination, and sound all influence the level of task performance in the environment).
4. Amount of privacy (controls outside visual or auditory stimuli).
5. Degree of adaptability (whether the setting can be rearranged to accommodate different patterns of behavior).
6. Amount of control or territoriality (whether an individual can express himself or herself through the display of such things as pictures, furniture, and decoration).
7. Degree of sociality (the extent to which the environment facilitates or inhibits social interaction).
8. Degree of accessibility (whether there are physical or social barriers that prevent interaction and receipt of services).
9. Density (the extent to which the space

HIGHLIGHT 8.1

INNOVATIVE ADAPTATIONS TO THE ENVIRONMENTAL 'PRESS' OF WINTER LIVING

In Canada, the long, cold winters create an environmental 'press' for older adults that can increase living expenses because of energy costs, decrease mobility, increase the risk of falls, decrease social interaction, and alter mood states. Indeed, people of all ages speak of 'surviving winter.' In order to survive the potential rigors of a Canadian winter, a number of alternative lifestyles and adaptive programs or practices have been adopted, including migration, local moves, and leisure pursuits in the home and the neighborhood. Clearly, the easiest way to adapt is to migrate to the southern United States or to Vancouver Island. However, for those unable to move to warmer climates, other moves are possible. For example, in rural areas of southwestern Ontario, homes for the aged offer a winter refuge for elderly widows living on a farm. If these women stayed on the farm, they would experience considerable isolation, and risk surviving heating and power failures. Instead, by moving to a home for the aged and living with other seniors, they save money on transportation and energy costs, gain a sense of security, companionship, and leisure activities, and avoid having to sell the family home in order to cope with winter living.

For older adults who remain in their homes during the winter, isolation can be a common outcome if they are housebound due to inclement weather and the onset of treacherous walking and driving conditions. Walking is especially difficult in suburbs that lack sidewalks. For seniors who cannot afford to pay for services, such programs as snow removal, meals-on-wheels, voluntary drivers, and regular visits and daily telephone calls by friends and family can offset the possible isolation and loneliness. In addition, lightweight thermal clothing, bus shelters, and canes and boots with antislip devices can increase mobility. If remaining indoors more frequently is required, regular exercise programs, walking, and stair climbing can partially compensate for the loss of outdoor activities. Similarly, with the loss of daylight hours, increased indoor lighting can enhance mood states, as can solarium areas and skylights. In short, more effort is needed, by both older adults and policymakers, to enhance the quality of life for the elderly who live in winter cities. Such enhancements include alterations to the home environment, moving to a new environment, introducing assistance programs, and developing alternative leisure lifestyles for the winter months.

SOURCE: Adapted from National Advisory Council on Aging (1989).

---

is crowded with other people).
10. Meaning (the degree to which a setting holds attachment for an individual through memories or a sense of family history).
11. The quality of the environmental setting (the perceived aesthetic appeal to the inhabitant or user).

All of these attributes can be used to determine how well older people are functioning in a specific setting. In this way, the well-being of the elderly might be improved by changing particular attributes of the environment, or by providing environments with a range of attributes. With increasing recognition that the type and the quality of environment are important factors in the later years, intervention strategies have been proposed to facilitate the personal and social transitions occurring in later life (Moos and Lemke, 1985; Parmelee and Lawton, 1990). Interventions such as one-story housing to eliminate stairs, brighter lighting, or large printing on signs can improve the perception of information in the environment and can promote interaction between people and their environment. As a result, the older person is encouraged to continue living independently and can enjoy mobility in safe and interesting surroundings.

A final model of how older people adapt to their environment focuses on the meaning of the geographical experience (Howell, 1982; Rowles and Ohta, 1982; Golant, 1984; Scheidt and Windley, 1985). According to this humanistic perspective, individuals react and adapt to the geographical spaces and places in their built and natural environments on the basis of their feelings, orientations, perceptions, memories, fantasies, and emotional attachments to a place. In this model each individual strives to maintain consistency between personal capabilities and environmental opportunities, and decisions are influenced by stored environmental experiences as they relate to the meanings of life, of self, and of specific events. In short, the 'meaning' of a place may play a large role in explaining the tendency to age in place.

In summary, a number of models or theories have been proposed to explain the way in which characteristics of individuals and environments interact to influence behavior and well-being at different stages in life. These models have served to guide research or to explain findings after a study is completed. However, a comprehensive theory to account for the many factors related to personal and environmental characteristics is not yet available. Nor is one likely to appear soon given the interdisciplinary approach necessary for this area of scientific inquiry and the many social, psychological, and environmental factors that would need to be included. Thus, while the theories and models described above may serve as preliminary conceptual frameworks, they are unlikely to account for all of the possible interactions between the person and the environment.

THE MACROENVIRONMENT AND AGING

Introduction

The macroenvironment includes the geographical region, the community,[3] and the neighborhood where an individual resides (Lawton, 1980a, 1985; Rowles and Ohta, 1982; Warnes, 1982). Gerontologists have been interested in the impact on an individual's behavior and well-being of such factors as climate; migration and mobility; rural-urban differences in services and lifestyle; availability of neighborhood support networks; access to social, recreational, and health services; size of the community; the age, race, and class composi-

tion of the community; and access to private and public transportation.

The Suprapersonal Environment: Distribution and Composition of the Elderly Population

According to Lawton (1977), the dominant characteristics of the people living in a particular region, community, or neighborhood form the suprapersonal environment. The aggregate characteristics of a geographical environment can change rapidly because of permanent[4] in-migration or out-migration of individuals with particular social characteristics, but generally the geographical location of the elderly remains relatively stable.

In Canada, most elderly people live in the three largest provinces (Ontario, Quebec, and British Columbia). However the highest proportion of elderly people is found in the Atlantic provinces. This geographical area is characterized by low incomes and a high old-age dependency ratio, primarily because the young migrate to other provinces in search of employment (Northcott, 1988).

In the United States, the western North Central states have the highest proportion of residents over 65, followed by New England and the Middle Atlantic region, the eastern North Central states, the Pacific states, and the Mountain states. Florida has the largest proportion of elderly persons, because of in-migration to its warm climate; Arkansas, Iowa, Nebraska, Missouri, South Dakota, Kansas, and Oklahoma are next, because of the out-migration of the young. An increasing pattern is migration by the elderly to nonmetropolitan areas, a migration that can suddenly place unexpected demands on the social, health, and recreational services in these areas.

Although a high percentage of the elderly live in an urban environment (about 75 percent in North America), many of the residents of small towns are elderly. Most older people prefer to **age in place,** that is, to remain in a familiar environment where they have established roots. They also remain in city centers because they do not have the economic resources to purchase housing in newer areas.

In some older cities that have already experienced urban renewal, there is less segregation of the elderly in the central core. This is because they have been dislodged, sometimes through destruction and reconstruction of housing, sometimes because they have been forced out by increasing housing costs. In the latter situation, the proportion of the elderly living in the central core decreases because of the process of **gentrification** (Henig, 1981). This involves the gradual resettlement of inner-city neighborhoods by younger, highly educated professionals who wish to live close to the central business district. As a result, less rental housing is available, rents increase for the remaining accommodation, and older residents who live on fixed incomes are displaced or bought out. Henig (1981) found that in-migration by young professionals was associated with out-migration of retirees in 967 census tracts across nine cities. Gentrification poses a threat to the elderly and represents a facet of the urbanization process that may change the spatial distribution of the elderly in the future.

Another pattern in urban location is the 'graying of the suburbs' (Fitzpatrick and Logan, 1985). During the accelerated suburbanization of large metropolitan regions in the 1950s and 1960s, young couples moved to these new neighborhoods. Now these elderly couples are living in large 'empty nests.' Since an automobile is usually required to reach shopping and medical services, if the elderly living in a suburban location are unable to drive, they may experience environmental press.

Although it is difficult to define the borders of a 'neighborhood,' it may include a small section of the city, a census tract, or a single block. This geographical area facilitates relations with neighbors, provides services and resources, and fosters a sense of community identity. The neighborhood represents a microcommunity within the larger community. The suprapersonal environment can influence the frequency and the quality of interaction, lifestyle, and well-being, depending on the age, racial, and class composition of the neighborhood residents.

Residential age segregation can occur within a neighborhood and within a particular housing complex. At the neighborhood level, age segregation often results from people of about the same age and life cycle stage moving into a neighborhood at about the same time. They age in place in the later years, voluntarily or involuntarily because of roots, familiarity, or low income. They may remain because they are satisfied with neighborhood safety, housing, interaction with neighbors, and recreational, social, and health services. As they age, they may become increasingly less mobile and more and more restricted to their house or block. As a result, they become more dependent on the local area to supply physical, social, and emotional resources.

Within stable neighborhoods, especially in low-income areas, there is a high degree of homogeneity with respect to age, race, ethnicity, and class. This homogeneity facilitates the development of a network of neighbors who are willing to provide mutual support and assistance if necessary. In many cases, this quality and frequency of neighborly interaction promotes person-environment congruence. Where a neighborhood experiences a rapid turnover in homeowners, or where homes tend to be purchased by members of a particular ethnic or racial group, heterogeneity creeps in and the sense of stability and community may be lost. In this situation, the older person who ages in place may lose the social support system he or she had assumed would be available from neighbors, and thereby lives the later years in an incongruent environment.

Rural and Urban Environments

The environment of the rural aged has not been studied to the same extent as that of the urban aged. Rather, inferences have been drawn from urban studies as to how the rural environment differs from the urban, and what impact these differences have on the aging rural resident. When rural environments or residents are studied, a complete definition of 'rural' is seldom provided. Does the term refer only to those who live on farms, or does it refer to those who live in rural communities isolated from larger population centers?

Obviously, the lifestyle of a self-employed

farmer differs from that of a businessman or a mechanic in a small town or village. The farmer's life may be more structured, with less leisure time, and he may not retire until his health declines (Keating, forthcoming). A further distinction must be drawn between impoverished, traditional, and subsistence rural settings, such as might be found in the Appalachians or in eastern Canada, and the more modernized, wealthy rural areas of the midwest or the west. Based on descriptive reports of rural environments, the following are some objectively assessed characteristics of rural milieus compared to urban areas:

1. Fewer institutionalized recreational, social, or health care services are available.
2. The distance to shopping and services is greater, and public transportation is usually unavailable.
3. The crime rate is lower.
4. The average per-capita income is lower.
5. The level of health status is generally lower, perhaps because the average age of residents is higher.
6. The distance from children who have migrated is greater, and there is less face-to-face contact with children.
7. There are more rural widows.
8. The quality of housing is lower because the homes are older.
9. The population density of the surrounding community is lower, and therefore interaction is more frequent and occurs with a greater proportion of neighbors.
10. Neighbors live at greater physical distances.
11. Fewer alternative forms of housing are available (such as apartment or retirement homes) for those who wish to relocate.

Despite these objective facts, the apparent disadvantages of the rural milieu may not be perceived as such by people who live in rural areas. The objective limitations may be irrelevant to perceived life satisfaction and quality of life. Studies which have examined this disparity between self-reported satisfaction and objective indicators suggest that there is a lower quality of life. Lee and Lassey (1980) found that when comparing objective and subjective indicators of the quality of life, rural residents were clearly at a disadvantage with respect to objective socioeconomic status, health status, availability of services, and quality of housing. However, on subjective indicators of morale, neighborhood satisfaction, and well-being, they scored as high as or higher than urban residents. The rural elderly may perceive and experience relatively less economic deprivation than younger age groups, because they live in an environment that has a lower average income per capita, and a lower cost of living. The relative dissatisfaction expressed by some of the urban elderly may stem from their real or imagined economic deprivation compared to younger age groups who live in more affluent urban areas.

Rowles (1980) suggests that the values and meanings attached to everyday experiences may be different in rural environments. A study of twelve elderly residents in an Appalachian mountain community found that, despite a deteriorating physical setting, the residents were reluctant to be relocated. This reluctance may have occurred for three reasons. First, there was a special meaning attached to the community that had evolved from physical familiarity and social bonding. Second, the residents were part of the local history. Third, they had created a 'society of the old,' with status hierarchy based on past and present contributions and chronological age. They were surrounded by others who shared in the evolving history of the community.[5] For 'insiders' in this unique subculture, the locale had a special meaning, and the attachment increased with time. This intensification of attachment would be much less likely to develop in large communities where anonymity is greater, and where the rate of social and physical change in the surrounding environment is more rapid.

Similarly, Windley and Scheidt (1982) interviewed 989 elderly residents in small rural towns (with fewer than 2,500 residents) to identify the impact of three domains of environmental variables (ecological/architectural, psychosocial, and personal) on mental health.

They found that lack of perceived environmental constriction (physical and social barriers), satisfaction with dwelling features, and satisfaction with the community were the most important factors contributing to the mental health of older rural residents.

In summary, there appear to be both physical and social differences in the rural environment that create unique aging experiences for residents. Specifically, they appear to be faced with a lower quality of environment as measured by objective indicators, but they do not perceive these factors to be barriers to their quality of life or life satisfaction. The objective factors are ignored or considered less important than the quality of social relationship and the meaning of the social milieu.

Private and Public Transportation in the Community

In order for older individuals to maintain independent lifestyles, to gain access to goods and services (Smith, 1984), and to engage in social interaction in a variety of settings (visiting friends, children, shops, church, clubs), transportation must be available and accessible. In fact, among the elderly there is a very strong and consistent relationship between access to transportation and life satisfaction (Carp, 1980). This relationship is even stronger when private rather than public transportation is available.

As long as their health permits, people will frequently walk to their neighborhood destinations. But walking may not be feasible if distances are great, if the streets are unsafe because of crime or poor lighting, if sidewalks are rough and uneven, if traffic-light cycles are short, or if the weather is inclement.

The elderly individual who lacks access to a car or public transportation has limited mobility and a restricted lifestyle. If they are unable to drive, the elderly depend on public transportation to move about the community on their own, or are restricted by the schedules of friends and relatives. Unfortunately, public transportation is generally only available in urban centers, and therefore those living in rural areas who are unable to drive are even more likely to be housebound and dependent than those in

urban areas (Grant and Rice, 1983). Moreover, isolation in the rural area is increasing because train and bus schedules between rural communities and urban centers are being reduced or eliminated because of operating costs or lack of use.

The transportation needs of elderly members of minority groups, especially those living in rural areas, have received little attention. Because of their disadvantaged economic position, they may be less likely to own and maintain automobiles, and are therefore totally dependent on public transportation. For some who are isolated on the fringes of metropolitan areas, or for others such as Indians living on a reservation, all forms of transportation may be unavailable. This situation contributes to poor health because they must be transported many miles for treatment or because they fail to seek transportation to obtain needed health care.

Finally, where public transportation does exist, routes needed by the elderly may not be available or convenient, the fare may be too expensive unless there are reduced fares for senior citizens, and psychological barriers (such as fear of crime on the subways) and physical barriers (such as fear of large crowds or long flights of stairs) may discourage the elderly from using the system. Partly because of these concerns, shuttle buses and dial-a-ride programs have been initiated for the elderly in many communities.

In summary, the elderly must often cope with a decrease in the availability of and access to various modes of transportation. Those elderly persons who are most likely to be without access to private or public transportation are women, the poor, widows, and rural residents. If private or public transportation is not available, the elderly become isolated, alienated, and housebound, and they may suffer social and physical resource deprivation. Public transportation must compensate for individual physical losses with age, such as loss of visual acuity and slower response rate. To encourage increased usage, public transportation systems must overcome structural barriers, such as the height of bus stairs or poor lighting at bus stops; psychological barriers, such as large crowds and petty crime; and economic barriers, such as the cost of fares. Clearly, more research and policy analysis is needed in this area in order to facilitate the transportation needs of the elderly.

Incidence of Crime and Fear of Victimization

Introduction

Gerontologists and criminologists are increasingly interested in the incidence of crime by and against the elderly.[6] Much of this interest has been stimulated by news reports of savage crimes and fraud involving elderly persons, and by the number of elderly persons who report a fear of being victimized. In some cases this fear is so great that they become prisoners in their own homes, afraid to walk in their neighborhoods at any time of the day. As a result, lifestyle, life satisfaction, and well-being are influenced by a real or imagined unsafe environment. In order to determine the prevalence and consequences of actual victimization, as well as fear of victimization, a number of studies using local, regional, and national samples have been completed in recent years. These are summarized in the next two subsections in order to separate fact and myth concerning victimization and fear of crime.

Elderly Offenders

In the 1980s the number of crimes committed by elderly persons increased, although the number of arrests and convictions was still quite low, except for repeat offenders.[7] However, it is very difficult to obtain accurate information about the incidence of crime by older adults, since victims may not press charges and police officials may not arrest the accused if the crime is considered to be less serious (for example, shoplifting, drunkenness in a public place). Moreover, representatives of the judicial system seem more likely to try to 'save' rather than incarcerate those accused of crimes in later life, except for those charged with violent crimes or drunken driving. Indeed, most offences among older men are drunkenness and driving while intoxicated; among older women the most frequent crime is petty theft — shoplifting food, clothing, or necessities.

Why is the incidence of crime by older adults

escalating? First, with increased numbers of older adults and greater concentration in the urban core, more incidents are likely to occur and to be reported. Also, with greater life expectancy and increased health, some older adults are more able to defend themselves and this may result in more violent crimes. A more likely explanation, especially for women, is the economic hardship experienced by elderly persons who live longer on a diminishing or nonexistent income. For example, an elderly woman who was caught shoplifting dog food reported that she did not have a dog, but rather was consuming the dog food because it was cheaper than meat. Similarly, an 82-year-old was arrested after a string of bank robberies (committed with the aid of stolen bicycles!) to supplement his meager social security income. In this case, however, police discovered that he was a habitual criminal with a record accumulated over seven decades (*Time*, April 17, 1989:35).

In addition to theft motivated by necessity, criminologists have recently observed a pattern of increasing 'elderly delinquent' crime. This type of crime may be motivated by boredom, by a need for stimulation, or by resentment against the private or public sector. For example, arrests have included an 80-year-old bald man who stole a hairbrush, and an 82-year-old woman who stole birth-control pills. In most cases of 'senior delinquency,' the individual is seldom incarcerated or fined. Rather, a warning is given, and the person is placed on probation or they are required to enter an educational program designed to prevent recurrences. In many cases these intervention programs require voluntary work in the community to provide a meaning and structure in the elderly person's life of leisure.

In summary, the incidence of crime by older adults seems to be increasing, but we lack adequate explanations for this phenomenon. Certainly, a lifestyle of prior criminal behavior and associating with other criminals accounts for some of the reported incidents. However, for others who commit criminal acts for the first time in the later years, a number of possible explanations have been proposed, including: a reaction to the stress associated with transitions and losses in later life (retirement, widowhood, loss of physical or mental health, economic losses, forced housing relocation); the feeling of marginality and a loss of prestige in society; the side effects of using or abusing prescription drugs; increased alcohol consumption; and boredom.

Victimization

It is difficult to obtain complete and accurate statistics on crimes against the elderly. It has been hypothesized that older victims may not report crimes, because they are afraid of retaliation, because they may be perceived by children or friends as no longer being able to take care of themselves, or because they are embarrassed to admit that they were exploited by a fraudulent investment scheme. However, Brillon (1987:41) reports that among Canadians in urban centres, the percentage of crimes reported to the police increases with the age of the complainant. The only exception was for automobile and household thefts, where the elderly were slightly less likely to report the offence to police. A more likely explanation for incomplete or inaccurate statistics is that published crime statistics seldom include the age of the victim, or the time of day when the crime was committed. Thus, even though this information may be available in the original police report, it seldom reaches the aggregate level of statistical tables from which secondary analyses of victimization are usually drawn.

Despite these methodological difficulties, studies report that the absolute number of crimes against older adults has increased because they comprise a larger proportion of the adult population. However, in reality, compared to all other age groups, the rates have declined in recent years (Covey and Menard, 1988), especially for violent crimes (such as homicide, rape, assault with robbery), and the overall rate of victimization is lower for the elderly. To illustrate, a recent study by Podnieks et al. (1989) found that about 6 percent of the 2,000 elderly Canadians surveyed reported that money or property had been stolen from them by a stranger since they had turned 65 years of age. The Canadian Urban Victimization Survey (Solicitor General, 1985:1) reported that 'rates of violent and personal victimization of elderly people were about one-sixth those of all adult residents of the seven cities surveyed. Those in the 16 to 24 age group, the highest risk group, were twelve times as likely as elderly people to have been personally victimized.' Moreover, the rate of victimization varies with different types of crime, as illustrated in table 8.1 (highlight 8.2 describes the percentage of crimes committed against elderly Canadians).

Unfortunately, being the victim of personal larceny,[8] property loss, or fraudulent crime[9] has a significant impact on the elderly person,

TABLE 8.1

TYPES OF CRIME BY AGE GROUP

Types of crime	16 to 29	30 to 59	60 and over	Total
Sexual assault	77%	21%	2%	100%
Robbery	66%	27%	7%	100%
Assault	71%	27%	2%	100%
Break and enter	44%	48%	8%	100%
Personal theft	52%	43%	5%	100%
Household theft	63%	34%	3%	100%
Vandalism	48%	46%	6%	100%
Totals	56%	39%	5%	100%

NOTE: The data used in this Table were compiled and organized from statistics furnished in November 1984 by the Department of the Solicitor General of Canada.

SOURCE: Reprinted by permission from Brillon (1987: table 2.1).

because the loss represents a larger percentage of financial resources than it does for a younger person. Such crimes can also generate fear and anxiety about the security of their environment. Thus, although the elderly as a group appear to be victimized less than the general population, the possession of certain social, physical, demographic, and environmental facts predisposes some segments of the elderly population to a higher risk of victimization. It has been found that victimization rates are higher for males, and the poor; for those who live alone; for those who live in urban (especially the central core in large cities) rather than suburban or rural areas; for those who are single; for those who live in age-integrated neighborhoods or low-income public-housing developments; for those who are less physically mobile; and for those who lack social support systems.

Having identified some patterns of victimization, how can they be explained? First, the elderly may be victimized less than younger people because they are less mobile; because they avoid high-crime environments such as parks or dark streets, especially at night;[10] and because the lifestyles of the young more frequently expose them to environments or situations conducive to crime. Finally, those elderly people who run a higher risk of victimization are often those who are more socially disadvantaged. That is, they live in or near neighborhoods with high crime rates; they are more dependent on walking and on public transportation than on their own automobiles, which increases the chances of street assault; and they live or walk alone. The likelihood of personal victimization is related to environment and lifestyle. Where people live, how much time they spend away from their homes and in the streets, and where they travel in the streets influences their vulnerability.

In summary, despite the myth of the vulnerable elderly person, the elderly experience less general criminal victimization than the total adult population. However, they are more vulnerable to personal larceny and property crimes than younger age groups. Moreover, considering that they spend less time away from their homes, the rate of victimization per minute in the external milieu may be disproportionately high. This has led to the creation of special social support systems, including such programs as special police units in neighborhoods where there is a high percentage of middle- and low-income elderly, voluntary escort services, dial-a-bus services, and neighborhood home-watching services (Brillon, 1987:94). This is one area where modern technological devices might be utilized to make the home and neighborhood a safer environment, and to provide individuals with call-for-help devices when they are walking at night, or when they are alone in a home. Because of the greater publicity about crime against the elderly, and the creation of special support systems to prevent or inhibit crime, it is not surprising that fear of victimization has become a major factor in further restricting the mobility and lifestyles of some segments of the elderly population.

Fear of Victimization

Although the elderly are actually victimized less than other age groups, a large number (as many as 50 percent in some studies) express fear and indicate that fear of crime is one of their most serious personal problems.[11] To illustrate, in a recent national survey of 2,000 elderly Canadians (Podnieks et al., 1989), almost 20 percent reported being fearful when out alone in their neighborhood, with women (24 percent) being more fearful than men (9 percent). This fear is more frequently reported by women,[12] the poor, and central urban residents;[13] by those who live alone; by those who live in high-crime neighborhoods; by those who live in subsidized age-heterogeneous or racially heterogeneous housing complexes; by those who have been victimized or on whom an attempt has been made; by those who know a victim; by those with physical disabilities that inhibit their defensive reactions; and by those who use public transportation, especially at night or in the late afternoon when adolescents are dismissed from school.[14] In addition, fear of crime may be linked to other fears and insecurities associated with later life, such as accidents, illness, falls, poverty, and being alone (Brillon, 1987).

The ecology of a particular environment may also influence the incidence and level of fear. Fear may be aroused or increased where the level of illumination is low, where the pedes-

Highlight 8.2

THE INCIDENCE AND FEAR OF CRIME AMONG OLDER CANADIANS: THE CANADIAN URBAN VICTIMIZATION SURVEY, 1982

Information about the amount of crime and the fear of crime in Canada is not well understood, since few studies have been completed on a national basis. In the most comprehensive survey, telephone interviews were conducted in 1982 with a random sample of 61,000 Canadians over 16 years of age in seven major urban centres: Vancouver, Edmonton, Winnipeg, Toronto, Montreal, Halifax and St. John's. Respondents were requested to report criminal victimization during 1981 according to two general categories: personal victimization (assault and battery, sexual assault, robbery, personal theft) and household victimization (break and enter, vandalism, motor vehicle theft, or theft of household property). Thus, eight types of specific crimes could be identified.

Incidence of Victimization

The elderly were victims of fewer than 2 percent of all personal victimization crimes, and about 10 percent of the elderly residents of these urban centers experienced household victimization. Elderly males were about three times more likely than elderly females to be robbed and assaulted, whereas elderly females were more than twice as likely to be victims of personal theft (eighteen thefts per 1,000 elderly females compared to seven thefts per 1,000 elderly males). A major reason for the lower rates of victimization among the elderly is their reduced exposure to high-risk situations during the evening hours outside the home. Only 10 percent of elderly people reported more than twenty evening activities outside the home per month, compared to 45 percent for those aged 25 to 39, and 70 percent for those younger than 25 years of age. Moreover, even those elderly persons who went out frequently at night were less likely to be victimized than younger people, primarily because the elderly were less likely to enter high-risk areas. Finally, it is important to note that even though elderly people are victimized less often than younger age groups, when they are victimized, the consequences are often greater in terms of physical injury, financial loss as a percentage of personal income, and increased fear of crime.

Fear of Crime

Respondents were asked, 'How safe do you feel walking alone in your neighborhood after dark? — Very safe, relatively safe, somewhat safe, very unsafe.' Not unexpectedly, the elderly were more fearful than younger people; women were more fearful than men; and previous victims, especially victims of violence, regardless of age, were more fearful than nonvictims or victims of property offences. Elderly women who had been victimized, especially in a violent offence, were most fearful. All respondents rated the level of crime in their own neighborhood to be lower than that in the rest of the city. For elderly men *and* women who had not been previously victimized, personal perception of vulnerability or fear was greater among the retired, the widowed, and those who lived alone.

In short, although the incidence of victimization is lower among the elderly, when they are victimized, the consequences are more severe in terms of financial loss, physical harm, and future level of fear. Moreover, even in the absence of personal victimization, about 65 percent of the elderly females and 35 percent of the elderly males reported feeling unsafe walking alone in their neighborhood after dark.

Source: Adapted from Solicitor General (1985).

trian traffic volume is low, where police surveillance is minimal or absent, or where minority youth congregate. Thus, fear of crime is related to a combination of social factors (demographic characteristics, previous victimization experiences, availability of social support networks), psychological factors (the perceived seriousness of the event and the perceived ability to recover from a criminal act), physical factors (degree of mobility), and ecological factors (actual and perceived safety of the physical and social environments). In short, fear of crime represents another example of how declining personal competence and a changing personal environment can interact to influence the quality of life in the later years.

Although there have been recent suggestions that the rates of fear have been overestimated because of inadequate measures (Ferraro and La Grange, 1988), for the elderly, fear of crime is a reality and they have higher levels of reported fear than younger cohorts. While the elderly experience less victimization, the effect on those who are victimized indirectly influences a number of their age peers, who subsequently modify their behavior because of fear. This fear of crime usually has a greater impact on social behavior and well-being than crime itself, since it may lead to self-imposed restrictions on social mobility and participation in the community. In this way, their lifestyles are altered and they become isolated from the larger community even further. In fact, a cycle of fear, restricted mobility, and isolation may escalate to the point that some elderly persons, especially if they lack a social support network, may become self-exiled prisoners in their own homes. While this behavioral pattern reduces the incidence of victimization, it also decreases social and psychological well-being and dramatically lowers the quality of life.

In summary, the incidence of fear of crime among the elderly is higher than actual victimization rates, especially for women, and for those who live in city centers. Fear appears to restrict mobility and social interaction in the community, thereby detracting from life satisfaction and the quality of life in the later years. As a result, policies and programs are needed, not only to reduce victimization rates, but also to reduce and overcome the real or imagined environmentally induced fear that is felt by many elderly persons, especially those living in urban areas.

THE MICROENVIRONMENT: THE DWELLING UNIT

Introduction

The quality, type, size, location, and design of the dwelling unit interacts with marital status, health status, and economic resources to influence the lifestyle, life satisfaction, and quality of life of the elderly person. Personal satisfaction with housing is an important factor in behavior and social interaction in the later years (Lawton, 1980b; Lawton and Hoover, 1981; O'Bryant, 1982; Leung, 1987). This is so because the home is a major social center for the elderly person. Thus, it is necessary to consider the interaction of the personal and social systems with environmental factors, especially in light of the numerous housing alternatives available to a heterogeneous elderly cohort.

Most of the elderly live in houses or apartments where they have resided for many years. In fact, approximately 65 percent of the elderly population own their own homes,[15] most of them mortgage free (Minister of State, 1988). As a result, a large number of elderly homeowners are 'overhoused' in housing units that are much too large and are expensive to maintain. Thus, from a societal perspective, much of the older housing stock may not be maintained or used as efficiently as it might be if older adults would or could move to more suitable housing. The home is a major asset, one that assists the retired or widowed person in coping with a reduced income. However, it can also become a liability because of increased operating costs or because, with declining health, the individual is unable to perform regular maintenance requirements. Because the homes of the elderly are often older,[16] and therefore susceptible to deterioration, a high percentage of the owner's fixed income may be required for maintenance. Similarly, with inflation, those who rent (unless they are subsidized by the government) are usually paying an increasingly higher proportion of their fixed income for shelter.

Although the quality of housing may deteriorate, and the maintenance costs increase, most older people, especially widows, prefer to live alone, normally in the family home. Table 8.2 illustrates the living arrangements for Canadians 75 and over in 1986. Clearly, living alone is the preferred choice for elderly women who are widowed, separated, divorced, or never-married. These rates are increasing because there are more single older women, because the norm of living separately is becoming more accepted, because more social support is available in the community for continuing an independent lifestyle, and because more alternative types of single housing units are becoming

TABLE **8.2**

THE LIVING ARRANGEMENTS OF CANADIANS 75+, 1986

Arrangement	Women (%)	Men (%)
With a spouse	18	57
Alone	38	17
With others	23	13
Share own home	8	4
Institution	19	12

SOURCE: Adapted from Priest (1988).

available (Rubinstein, 1985; Wister, 1985; Krivo and Mutchler, 1989).

For those who do not or cannot live in their own homes or apartments because of economic, health, or lifestyle factors, a number of alternative forms of housing are possible. These alternatives range from independent housing to semi-institutionalized congregate housing[17] to completely institutionalized settings, and from age-segregated to age-integrated housing environments. It is this variation in type, needs,[18] and quality of housing that has stimulated much of the research into the impact of housing on the social behavior and well-being of the elderly person.[19]

These studies have primarily examined the type and quality of housing available to the older person, the meaning of the housing environment, and the impact of type of housing on social interaction, well-being, life satisfaction, or morale. Typically, surveys or participant observation ethnographies, alone or in combination, have been used to examine the relationship between housing environment and social behavior. Some of the major studies have examined the following topics:

1. The short- and long-term effects of moving or not moving to planned housing for the elderly.
2. The impact on the individual of living in age-segregated versus age-integrated apartment buildings.
3. The low quality of housing in rural areas (Hodge, 1987).
4. The development of a sense of community in a small apartment complex

inhabited primarily by elderly widows (Hochschild, 1973).

5. Adjustment to living in an affluent retirement community (Jacobs, 1974).
6. The environment, structure, and meaning of long-term care institutions (Forbes et al., 1987).
7. The subjective value of the home (familiar environment, familiar memories, the status of owning a home, low housing cost) and its impact on housing satisfaction (O'Bryant, 1982; Leung, 1987).
8. The autonomous lifestyle and background of the elderly occupants of single-room occupancy (SRO) hotels in the central core (on or near 'skid row') of large cities (Cohen and Sokolovsky, 1983, 1989; Cohen et al., 1988).

Most studies have been concerned with the type and location of the dwelling unit and with the behavior and characteristics of the inhabitants. However, some descriptive studies have focused on the problems arising from the quality of the unit and its design and structural limitations and on guidelines for the design and improvement of housing for the aged (National Advisory Council on Aging, 1987; Regnier and Pynoos, 1987; Tilson, 1989; Parmelee and Lawton, 1990). The quality of the unit can usually be assessed by such objective indicators as appearance (paintwork, deteriorating plaster or bricks); age of the structure; amount of personal space and privacy per resident; quality of the cooking, heating, lighting, and plumbing facilities; and the number of safety hazards (lack of bannisters, unsafe stairs, faulty appliances, or unsafe furniture). Generally, studies indicate that the elderly live in older structures that are of lower quality than other dwellings in the area. One reason why many older adults remain in unsuitable houses or move to undesired accommodation is the absence of suitable forms of quality housing in the neighborhood or the community. A more important reason is that many older people report being 'satisfied' with housing that has been classified as 'unsatisfactory' by objective assessments (O'Bryant and Wolf, 1983).

The high level of housing satisfaction reported by older adults results when quality of housing is assessed subjectively (O'Bryant, 1982; Leung, 1987). Residents are asked to comment on their satisfaction with their particular housing as it is, as they would like it to be, or in comparison to alternative environments. Most subjective evidence indicates that homeowners are 'attached' to their homes for the following reasons: they may have a familiar environment where they can demonstrate mastery, competence, and control; their homes enable them to demonstrate independence and enhance self-esteem; owning a home gives them status; the home is a repository of family memories and family history; it provides privacy; a local social support network (friends and neighbors) is available; and the economic and psychological costs of moving are more threatening than the discomfort or difficulties of the less-than-ideal present housing situation. In addition, homeowners have collected and maintained a number of personal objects or possessions that give deeper meaning to the physical environment. These objects, such as furniture, gifts, decorations, and art works, are attached both to the individual and to the specific environment. As such, they play an important role in maintaining personal identity in later life, in expressing meanings about the self to others, and in symbolically maintaining links with friends and family (Rubinstein, 1987, 1989). These objects, with their deep personal meaning and significance, may lose their significance if moved to a new environment. More importantly, in many cases, a move to a smaller environment (such as an apartment or a rooming house) or to an institutionalized setting requires that many of these objects, especially furniture, be left behind.

Those who are single or who rent generally report lower degrees of satisfaction, often because they have less emotional attachment to the current place of residence. Clearly, for some individuals low-quality or substandard housing is often combined with poverty and poor health. These factors may have been present for years and may reflect a traditional lifestyle. For others, deterioration in the quality of housing may reflect the advancing years of both the resident and the dwelling unit, which may then have a compounding effect on the physical safety, health, and subjective well-being of the individual. Ultimately, it may lead to an involuntary relocation to a safer environment (an apartment, a home for the aged, or a nursing home), but at the cost of the emotional loss that is suffered in giving up one's home with its memories and familiar environment.

In addition to the quality of the physical structure, factors such as structural design (high-rise versus low-rise), environmental configurations (arrangement of furniture, number and type of stairs), type of furniture (contemporary low seating with cushions versus more traditional chairs with well-supported backs), and interior design (height of storage cupboards, traffic patterns) can all influence the safety and mobility within the unit (Raschko, 1982; Charness and Bosman, 1990; Parmelee and Lawton, 1990). These factors also influence satisfaction with the personal environment.

Increasingly, modern technology is being incorporated into the various types of housing for older adults, and is being adopted by many seniors (Haber, 1986). The use and acceptance of these technological aids enhances independence and the quality of life and increases the person-environment fit. For example, microwaves and frozen foods packaged for use by single persons can enhance nutrition and health; videocassette recorders can enable older adults to continue enjoying movies without the cost or the risk of traveling away from home at night; and timed-lighting systems in various parts of the home can enhance feelings of security and safety. In addition, for those living alone with disabilities, distress-warning systems can be linked to a central monitoring station. If a button worn around the neck is activated, a security visit is initiated and medical records are recalled on a computer screen. Finally, as a result of technological advances, hearing aids can be plugged into television sets; telephones are portable, have large numbers on the dial, and enable the sound level of the ring or the listening device to be increased; and mobility devices can be installed to make movement about the home easier or possible.

Even if the quality of the physical structure is poor, the presence of a personally designed interior environment that permits mobility and is familiar and nonthreatening is favored over an impersonal, institutionalized setting. As a result, efforts have been directed toward personalizing institutional rooms by permitting residents to bring objects from their homes to decorate and furnish their living areas, and by providing more environmental stimulation throughout the institution (bright colors, music, color codes, signs and symbols to identify floors or corridors).

Type of Housing Environment

Introduction

Given the heterogeneity of the older population, no single type of housing style, nor single narrow housing policy, can satisfy or meet the needs or preferences of older adults (Stone and Fletcher, 1987; Sherman, 1988).

Rather, many alternatives must be available to meet the diverse needs and differences of age cohorts who need to change their type of living arrangement (see highlight 8.3). Stone and

---

HIGHLIGHT 8.3

TWO CONTRASTING HOUSING OPTIONS: GARDEN SUITES VERSUS SINGLE ROOM OCCUPANCY HOTELS

The garden suite (sometimes referred to as a granny flat or ECHO housing (Elder Cottage Housing Opportunity) is a detached housing unit that can be assembled and temporarily installed in the backyard of an existing single family home of a son or a daughter. Originating in Australia, this small (530 to 670 square feet), self-contained unit includes a living-dining area, bedroom, kitchen, and bathroom. Thus, while living close to (but not with) the family, elderly people can maintain their independence and privacy, yet not interfere with a child's life, and can maintain a 'home' without the large associated costs of a mortgage, taxes, utilities, or maintenance. Other advantages include: enhanced relationships between grandparents and grandchildren; the provision of wheelchair accessibility; a reduction in time and costs associated with family visiting; a lack of guilt, because families can help each other and thereby delay or avoid institutionalization; the sale of the elderly person's underutilized larger home to larger families; and the creation of an alternative to living in an apartment with strangers. This concept has not been widely accepted and used, because zoning laws in many municipalities do not permit the installation of a garden suite on the lot of an existing dwelling, even if it is not a permanent installation. Moreover, despite the attractive appearance of these units, neighbors often complain and prevent the installation of a suite. It is for these reasons that the concept of garden suites may be more successful in rural areas where zoning laws are less restrictive.

Single room occupancy (SRO) hotels and rooming houses can be found in the central core of most large urban centers. These facilities provide shelter for homeless men and women who live on or near 'skid row.' These unattached older persons are poor, have little or no contact with kin, and are often labeled as derelicts, winos, or bag ladies. Regardless of how long, or why, they have pursued this lifestyle, they may find, through the single room they rent in an SRO hotel, an informal supportive network consisting of the hotel staff and a nucleus of fellow residents with whom they can share resources — food, alcohol, money, clothing. However, in reality many of these residents live independent lives and may only receive informal care if their health deteriorates rapidly, and if they are longtime residents who always pay their weekly rent.

Fletcher (1987) indicate that, at particular ages, members of age cohorts are more likely to need to move because of such stimuli as marriage, divorce, widowhood, remarriage, illness or disability, or a major loss of income (for example, retirement, widowhood). The choice (Wister, 1985; Sherman, 1988) of which type of housing to select depends on personal coping style for the transition, personal preference, availability of appropriate housing, and availability of informal and formal support services in the neighborhood.

The location and type of housing environment influences the social interaction patterns and well-being of the elderly, and determines what services are available to the elderly within the neighborhood. Housing for the elderly generally lies along three dimensions: independent to dependent, low to high quality, and age-integrated to age-segregated. Two of these dimensions are illustrated in figure 8.2, and the various types of housing are noted in the appropriate quadrant. In quadrant A, the dwelling unit is age-integrated within the city, suburb, or town, and consists of either privately owned or rented dwellings or subsidized low-rent, age-heterogenous housing. This latter type of housing provides low-cost shelter, but social services and assistance programs are seldom available. Generally, residents in these dwellings are high in social interaction and life satisfaction because they are independent. Where the quality of the neighborhood has deteriorated or undergone a change in the population mix, there is still potentially a high degree of independence, although it may not be maximized because of fear of crime. In addition, in deteriorating or changing neighborhoods, life satisfaction may be low and there may be little, if any, interaction with neighbors. For those who live in single-room occupancy (SRO) hotels, social interaction may be low, but life satisfaction may be high because the hotel provides a major source of support and a sense of security (Cohen et al., 1988).

Quadrant B represents two types of housing that combine age integration with partial institutionalization. The type of housing varies according to the services offered and the rules imposed on the residents. The type of congre-gate or sheltered housing that falls into this category is illustrated by the Abbeyfield concept, which bridges the gap between staying at home and moving to an institution. In this situation, which originated in Britain in 1956, five to ten renters have a private bed-sitting room, but share meals and communal space. A paid housekeeper does the shopping, prepares all meals, and tries to instill a family-like environment in the group of residents. Similarly, a home for the aged might be situated adjacent to an orphanage so that 'foster grandparents' can interact with children.

Quadrants C and D represent housing that is totally age-segregated and that involves varying degrees of dependency. These settings, with the exception of SRO hotels, represent planned housing for the elderly in which direct attempts have been made in the structure and interior design to enhance person-environment compatibility. Many of these housing units provide facilities and programs that can satisfy the needs of the elderly who previously lived in integrated, independent settings such as a home, an apartment, or a trailer park. Planned housing of this nature expands the lifestyle opportunities for the elderly and generally has a positive influence on their well-being (Ehrlich et al., 1982; Lawton, 1985). The options in quadrant C range from minimal services such as maid service and security in retirement hotels, to homes for the aged and congregate housing providing meals and other services, to nursing homes where all services are provided, to total dependency in long-term and psychiatric hospitals for geriatric patients. For those who are mentally and physically healthy, most of these environments generally foster high levels of social interaction and life satisfaction.

Quadrant D represents noninstitutionalized, segregated housing and independent lifestyles. These range from age-segregated affluent retirement communities, to communes where a group of elderly persons form a family, to trailer parks and subsidized senior-citizen housing, to SRO hotels that cater to elderly men and women. In short, there are a variety of forms of housing for the elderly, but not all forms are equally available in each community or personally satisfying to all elderly people.

FIGURE 8.2

A TYPOLOGY OF HOUSING ALTERNATIVES FOR THE ELDERLY

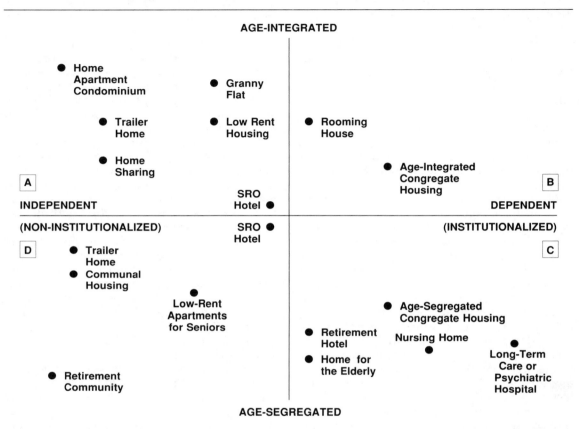

Age-Segregated versus Age-Integrated Housing

Because the elderly are a heterogeneous group with differences in past experiences and current needs, a range of viable options with respect to housing must be provided. However, research evidence suggests that the elderly generally prefer age-segregated housing. Even here, however, there is wide variation in the definition of age-segrated housing, which can range from inner-city, SRO hotels to affluent suburban or rural retirement communities in the sunbelt areas of the United States (such as Fun City in Arizona [Jacobs, 1974]), or Leisure World in California).

Gerontologists have long been interested in the advantages and disadvantages of segre-gated and integrated housing, in why a particular environment is preferred, and in how a specific environment is selected. The origin of the debate concerning segregated versus integrated housing can be traced indirectly to the proponents of disengagement theory, who argued that age segregation was the preferred mode of housing in the later years, and to the proponents of activity theory, who argued that an age-integrated environment was more conducive to adaptation in the later years.

As Chevan (1982) noted, there are both micro and macro theories to explain age segregation. From the macro perspective, individuals respond to urban processes such as availability of housing at a specific stage in the life cycle.

Thus, age segregation may occur because newly created neighborhoods attract people with similar characteristics, one of which may be age.

From the micro perspective, individual differences in decision making concerning the choice of neighborhood and type of housing can lead to age segregation (Cohen et al., 1987; Connidis, 1983). Age segregation is the end product of a process whereby families with similar location and housing preferences, who are often at the same stage in the life cycle and of the same economic and social background, move into the same neighborhood and age in place in the family home in a familiar neighborhood (Chevan, 1982). Except for later life decisions concerning age-segregated apartments or retirement communities, most housing decisions are not based on a conscious decision or a desire to live with or apart from a specific age group.

The following disadvantages of age-segregated housing have been noted:

1. It creates physical and social boundaries that foster and promote age grading and stereotyping in the larger community.
2. It implies discrimination, rejection, and abandonment of the elderly.
3. This environment may not foster social interaction unless the segregation is structured so that residents have a common racial, educational, and class background.
4. Interaction among neighbors may not be facilitated unless there is a common social or recreational center with programs that can foster interaction.[20]
5. There is little likelihood of new ideas or experiences from the community or society at large being diffused into and throughout the segregated housing environment; this inhibits cognitive stimulation and change.
6. Some retirement communities (such as Fun City) are isolated in that they lack public transportation and are far from medical, cultural, shopping, and entertainment centers.

In summary, age-segregated housing appears to be preferred by much of the elderly population. This applies to those who are affluent and wish a change in environment, as well as to those in the low-income category who have the opportunity to move into new housing that will improve their physical and psychological environment. Still, as noted earlier, most elderly people prefer to remain in their own homes as long as possible. For most, this involves living in an age-integrated neighborhood. Some elderly homeowners in the inner cores of large cities are restricted in their housing options for economic reasons, and may see their area become age-segregated because of the out-migration of younger residents. In short, the elderly, being a heterogeneous group, may prefer a variety of age-integrated environments. The type of housing in which one resides in the later years often depends on personal resources, previous life history, and personal preferences. However, the choice of an age-segregated seniors' facility may not reflect the true preferences of an older adult. For example, Connidis (1983) reported that a majority of the respondents in her study indicated that they selected a facility for seniors because of reasons why they felt they should not live with their children (not wanting to interfere, not wanting to be a burden, not wanting to be unfair to children and grandchildren).

In conclusion, in the 1980s, a number of public and private-sector policies and developments have significantly expanded the options for housing in the later years. Most of these programs are based on the goal of keeping the elderly in the community and include such programs and services as: home sharing; retirement communities; granny-flat demonstration projects; Abbeyfield homes; home-renewal programs; convert-to-rent programs; rental-assisted programs; home care programs; drop-in centers; meals-on-wheels programs; integrated homemaker programs; and safety-watch programs. Yet, seniors are seldom consulted when new policies or programs are created and implemented. In response to this lack of input, the Canada Mortgage and Housing Corporation sponsored six regional housing workshops for seniors in September 1988. Over two hundred seniors attended and expressed the hope that in the planning of future policies, the following principles would be included:

- Seniors must be involved in the planning, design and implementation of housing programs.
- Seniors need an affordable, decent standard of housing at *all* income levels.
- Seniors want physically accessible structures that can be adapted to changing needs.
- Seniors require access to accurate information about housing.
- Senior housing must be adaptable to changing needs — without requiring major changes in the environment.
- Housing for seniors must promote integration with families and within the community, and not create 'senior ghettos.'

Institutionalization as a Housing Alternative

Introduction

In the late nineteenth and early twentieth centuries, most assistance or care for the elderly was provided by religious or charitable organizations in the local community, or by legislation that created 'poorhouses' or 'houses of refuge.' Based on a system of welfare established by the Elizabethan Poor Laws, these houses offered little more than marginal custodial care for the infirm and destitute of all ages. For those elderly persons who needed chronic care, few hospitals or nursing homes were available until the 1940s and 1950s (Forbes et al., 1987; Rudy, 1987). However, with the passage in 1957 of the federal Hospital Insurance and Diagnostic Services Act, provinces were required to provide coverage of chronic and convalescent care. As a result, numerous homes for the aged and nursing homes were established by the provinces and by charitable organizations. Since then, considerable legislation has been implemented to provide rules and financial assistance for the operation of facilities that provide varying levels of care. These include home-support or homemaker

programs to enable the elderly to delay institutionalized living for as long as possible (Forbes et al., 1987:11-14; Ontario Hospital Association, 1980).

A major problem in understanding the issues associated with the concept of institutionalization is that there are various definitions of long-term care. For example, the same level of care may be provided in facilities with different names in different provinces, the same level of care may be provided by facilities with different names within a province, or a given facility can provide more than one level of care (Forbes et al., 1987:20). It is the definition of level of care that often determines the level of financial support, the type and size of staff, the professional services provided by staff, the size of the facility, and the type of resident who may be admitted. In reality, a given individual may, over a period of time, require the services of low-, medium-, and high-level care. Although some facilities are designed to provide all three levels within the same setting (for example, Freeport Village in Kitchener, Ontario), many elderly persons who enter a low-level care facility, may ultimately have to be relocated to a facility that provides a higher level of care. This can, of course, lead to problems in adjusting to a new environment (see below).

To assist you in understanding the levels of care that can be provided by institutionalized housing for the elderly, highlight 8.4 provides the definitions used in three provinces.

In general, the lowest level of care is provided in privately operated retirement homes or rest homes where residential care encourages independence. In this type of facility a registered nurse is available, and food and laundry services are provided to residents who live in private or semiprivate rooms. This level of care is also available in homes for the aged that are operated by nonprofit organizations. These facilities provide residential care beds, but the occupants are not supposed to require more than one and a half hours per day of nursing care. If more care is required, an individual may have to be transferred to another facility, although increasingly these facilities include an extended-care wing that comprises about 40 to 50 percent of the total beds.

Housing at the medium- or extended-care

HIGHLIGHT **8.4**

DEFINITIONS OF LEVELS OF INSTITUTIONAL CARE

Ontario[a]
  Residential Care is required by a person who is ambulant and/or independently mobile, who has decreased physical and/or mental faculties, and who requires primarily supervision and/or assistance with activities of daily living and provision for meeting psychosocial needs through social and recreational services. The period of time during which care is required is indeterminate and related to the individual condition.
  Extended Care is required by a person with a relatively stabilized (physical or mental) chronic disease or functional disability who, having reached the apparent limit of recovery, is not likely to change in the near future, who has relatively little need for the diagnostic and therapeutic services of a hospital, but who requires availability of personal care on a continuing twenty-four-hour basis with medical and professional nursing supervision and provision for meeting psychosocial needs. The period of time during which care is required is unpredictable but usually consists of a matter of months or years.
  Chronic Care is required by a person who is chronically ill and/or has a functional disability (physical or mental) whose acute phase of illness is over, whose vital processes may or may not be stable, whose potential for rehabilitation may be limited, and who requires a range of therapeutic services, medical management and skilled nursing care, plus provision for meeting psychosocial needs. The period of time during which care is required is unpredictable but usually consists of a matter of months or years.

Manitoba[b]
  Level 1. Indicates minimal dependence on nursing time. The individual requires weekly supervision and/or assistance with personal care and/or some encouragement or reminders to wash, dress, and attend meals and/or activities. He/she may need administration of medications on a regular basis and may need to use mechanical aids.
  Level 2. Indicates moderate dependence on nursing time for at least one of the following categories: bathing and dressing, feeding, treatments, ambulation, elimination, and/or support and/or supervision.
  Level 3. Indicates maximum dependence on nursing for at least two of the following activities: bathing and dressing, feeding, treatments, ambulation, elimination; or, maximum dependence for support, and/or supervision and moderate dependence for at least two of the other categories.
  Level 4. Indicates maximum dependence on nursing time for four or more of the following categories: bathing and dressing, feeding, treatment, ambulation, elimination, and support and/or supervision.

British Columbia[c]
  Personal Care. Persons at this level are independently mobile with or without mechanical aids, mentally intact, or suffering only minor mental impairment. They may require a protected housing environment, social stimulation, or minor assistance with self-care, but do not need regular medical supervision. A personal care facility offers 24-hour-a-day supervision by nonprofessional personnel, a protective environment, help with activities of daily living, and a social/recreational program.
  Intermediate Care 1 (IC-1). Persons at this level are independently mobile, similar to those requiring personal care, but will need some health supervision and some assistance with activities of daily living as well as the protected environment and social/recreational program already mentioned. It is estimated that a person at this level in institutional care would need 75 minutes of individual attention per day — 15 minutes from a professional and 60 minutes from a nonprofessional.
  Intermediate Care 2 (IC-2). The client's characteristics resemble those above, but the estimated amount of care needed for such clients in facilities is increased to 100 minutes of daily individual attention — 30 minutes by a professional and 70 minutes by a nonprofessional.
  Intermediate Care 3 (IC-3). This level of care was designed to recognize the psychogeriatric client with severe, continuous behavioral problems. The level is also used for persons needing more daily care than allowed under IC-2, especially those awaiting room in an extended-care hospital. The assump-

tion for care in this category is 120 minutes of individual care daily — 30 minutes from a professional and 90 minutes from a nonprofessional.

Extended Care. An extended-care hospital unit provides round-the-clock supervision of a registered nurse and the availability of regular medical supervision and a multi-disciplinary therapeutic team. It is assumed the individual will need at least 150 minutes of care a day.

[a]Ontario Ministry of Health (1980).
[b]Kane and Kane (1985:109).
[c]Kane and Kane (1985:144).

level is provided mainly by privately owned, profit-oriented nursing homes subsidized by the provincial government. A few homes are operated on a nonprofit basis by ethnic or religious groups to provide a more viable and humane level of care. Although nursing homes are regulated by the government, inspection standards, practices, and visits vary greatly, so that the quality of living and care ranges from 'excellent' to 'atrocious' in terms of sanitation, excessive medication, nutrition, and treatment by staff.[21] Occasionally, stories about physical or psychological abuse, infection, unsanitary conditions, neglect, or theft by staff are reported in the media for this type of institution. Generally, these stories pertain to profit-oriented institutions. For example, Lemke and Moos (1989) found that nonprofit facilities provide a more comfortable physical environment, more cohesive staff-patient relationships, and more resident control than that found in proprietary settings. It is for this reason that government attention has been directed toward insuring that residents have greater privacy and some say in the control of their own lives. To illustrate, in many jurisdictions, nursing homes and homes for the aged are required by law to have residents' councils to consider complaints. In reality, however, many of these councils are controlled by staff, and hence in some jurisdictions it has been necessary to implement the concept of an ombudsman and a 'bill of rights' for residents.

The highest level of extended or chronic care is provided to those who are chronically ill or have a major functional disability that requires twenty-four-hour care in a hospital setting. This level of care can be provided in specially designed facilities, or in a designated wing of an acute- or general-care hospital. In most communities, especially smaller and rural areas, there is a shortage of long-term care beds, with delays in placement, long waiting lists, and inappropriate placements being major problems that must be addressed as the number and the proportion of elderly citizens increase.

The Incidence of Institutionalization

According to the 1986 Canadian census, only 8 percent of those over 65 years of age receive care in some type of institutionalized setting. For those 65 to 69 years of age, only 2 percent are housed in an institution (Stone and Frenken, 1988). More importantly, for those under 85, there was a decline in the proportion of institutional residents from 1981 to 1986. This may be a reflection of increased community care programs provided by informal and formal support systems (see chapter 10).

The majority of institutionalized elders are those 85 years of age and older, of whom 28 percent of the men and 40 percent of the women reside in some type of institutionalized setting. Among the elderly women 85 years of age and over, marital status is a significant factor in whether they live in an institution or not. Specifically, the 1986 census indicated that of this group of institutionalized women 28 percent were married, 44 percent were never married, and 41 percent were widowed. In short, being married and having a spouse as an informal carekeeper can significantly reduce the incidence of institutionalized living.

Although less than 10 percent of the elderly population in total may be institutionalized at any one time, it has been estimated that 25 to 75 percent of the elderly are housed in some type of institutionalized setting for some portion of their later years. The percentage of the elderly population that is institutionalized varies by country and province, and is largely determined by government policies with respect to subsidization and capital expenditures (Forbes et al., 1987:43-44). There may also be significant regional variations within a country. For example, among widowed women 85 years of age and over, 41 percent are institutionalized on a national basis. However, when the percentages are reported on a provincial basis (Stone and Frenken, 1988:54), the percent varies from 29.9 in Nova Scotia to 50.5 in Alberta. Whether these variations are related to provincial policies, regional norms, or the absence of family members as kinkeepers remains to be investigated.

The Institutionalized Elderly

Those most likely to be voluntarily or involuntarily institutionalized are elderly persons who no longer have a sufficient degree of physical or mental competence to continue living independently in the community; those who have no families or whose families are unable or unwilling to care for them; those who live where community-based support services are unavailable or inaccessible; and those who are financially or socially disadvantaged. Not surprisingly, people with large economic resources and a supportive family tend to enter institutions later and to enter institutions that provide a higher quality of health care and whose personnel demonstrate greater concern for the residents. At the other extreme of the social spectrum, elderly members of minority ethnic or racial groups may experience discrimination in gaining admission to an institution. Furthermore, once institutionalized, they may become isolated because of language and cultural barriers between themselves, the staff, and other residents. They may also receive less attention and care from staff (Forbes et al., 1987). This is why racial and ethnic minorities have provided facilities to meet the special institutionalized needs of the elderly members of the group.

The number of institutionalized elderly may increase for a variety of reasons. First, it may be more culturally acceptable to admit elderly parents to an institution, rather than caring for them in the home, especially where a daughter or daughter-in-law is employed full-time. Second, some elderly persons will outlive their children, or will be unable to be cared for by a son or daughter who is also frail and elderly. Finally, the lack of home-care programs may force elderly people to prematurely leave their own homes or apartments.

Adjustment to Institutionalized Living

Relocation from independent, private living to a form of institutionalization in the later years represents a complete change in lifestyle. While preparation for the first move to an institution can lessen the shock, most people have difficulty adjusting to the lack of privacy and personal space. This section summarizes some of the literature pertaining to the impact of relocation on the individual. Because many facilities are operated as private enterprises, owners frequently will not permit research personnel to study the residence or the residents. As a result, most studies in this area involve nonprofit institutions, or, less frequently, those where the residents are affluent and pay high fees. Unfortunately, from a research perspective, these are often atypical institutions in that the environment and the quality of care are generally superior to that of ordinary profit-oriented institutions, which are oriented to the survival and growth of the institution. Institutions operated by voluntary organizations or religious groups tend to be more person-oriented and less bureaucratic.

When an individual is institutionalized, he or she may experience great stress, especially if the relocation is an involuntary move. The loss of one's home or apartment entails a loss of privacy and personal possessions, disrupts well-established lifestyles, and symbolizes rejection, deterioration, loss of personal control (Grant, 1985), and the imminence of death. In fact, being institutionalized is often perceived as the penultimate stage in life. Unless the move is voluntary, or the individual is well prepared for the move, the social, emotional, and psychological needs of the individual are seldom satisfied in the bureaucratic, depersonalized environment. This is reflected in declining health and an increased chance of dying within a year, especially if the individual is subsequently relocated to an extended-care facility. At present, the literature is equivocal concerning the relationship between the onset of institutionalization and mortality. Those who die soon after being institutionalized appear to be those who have not been prepared for the move, who experience a significant loss of functional competence, who are passive and have lost a sense of awareness, or who have experienced a significant degree of environmental change (for example, in moving from their own home to a psychiatric hospital).

In general, the stress of relocation to an institution can be reduced by preparation for the move, by moving to a similar or better environment (Rutman and Freedman, 1988), and by ensuring that contact is maintained as long as possible with the community and the family (George, 1980). On the individual level, there appears to be better adjustment by those who have physical and cognitive resources, particularly the traits of assertiveness and aggressiveness; for those who have social support from friends and relatives; for those who move voluntarily; for those who have been social isolates in the community; and for those who are given some control over their daily lives within the institution. In fact, for some, depending on the institution, activity levels and life satisfaction increase following institutionalization—at least for residents in personal care homes.

Given that many within the elderly population are institutionalized at some time in later life, and that a large number do not satisfactorily adjust to this type of living environment, viable alternatives have been sought for assisting the elderly who become increasingly dependent on others.[22] The need for alternative services and environments to reduce institutionalized care and to help the elderly maintain some degree of independence in the community have been proposed, including: foster homes for elderly people without families; government assistance to encourage families to care for their elderly relatives at home; professional home-care visitations by social workers and medical personnel; vacation relief for children who regularly care for their elderly parents; providing treatment at day hospitals so that the elderly can return to their homes at night; and day-care hospice centers for the elderly.

In short, there is a need for a more efficient and personalized health care delivery system, for increased social and recreational services in the community, and for more economical and psychologically satisfying housing alternatives. Even where the cost per day is no lower than that of traditional institutions, there still may be an improvement in the quality of life for the elderly person who can remain in the community with friends and relatives. However, with the onset of severe physical and mental impairment, the time may finally arrive when it is best for the individual and the family to consider extended-care institutionalization. Until this time arrives, however, premature institutionalization and improper placement should be avoided. For both humanitarian and economic reasons, institutionalization is a costly step that could be avoided or delayed in many situations if viable alternatives were available in the community.

In summary, a variety of options are necessary to retain and support the elderly in the community as long as possible. This community living permits a higher quality of life than that found within many nursing home or extended-care facilities. Persons living in institutions are often stigmatized because they are treated as invalids or as children by an impersonal, bureaucratic staff, because they have little or no control over their ritualized lives, and because they have little contact with those in the larger community. It is essential that a greater effort be directed to increasing the fit between the individual and the environment. This involves a two-way process wherein the individual must fit the environment, and the social and physical environments must be changed to meet the needs, capacities, and interests of the aging individual (Marshall, 1980:246).

MOBILITY AND MIGRATION IN THE LATER YEARS

Introduction

In the later years of life an individual has two general alternatives with respect to living arrangements: to age in place in the residence and the community that have provided shelter for most of the adult years, or to age in a new place, either in a new residence in the same neighborhood or community, or in an entirely new neighborhood, community, or geographical region. Except for institutionalization very late in life, aging in place is the more common pattern. However, there is now a greater likelihood that those over 60 years of age will either voluntarily or involuntarily change their place of residence. The change may involve local mobility within the community or region, or permanent or seasonal migration to a new geographical region. The increase in mobility and migration rates has resulted from such factors as:

1. Enforced moves because of urban renewal or gentrification.
2. Availability of a greater variety of specialized housing for the elderly.
3. A greater likelihood of children living at some distance from their parents, and dependent parents being institutionalized in their own community rather than moving into the children's home.
4. Increased health, longevity, and affluence, which make it possible for the retired, particularly couples, to make a seasonal or permanent migration to a warmer climate.
5. Deteriorating housing or increased crime in a neighborhood.

As a result of the increase in the rates of local mobility and regional migration, two areas of study have evolved on two different levels of analysis. At the micro level, social gerontologists and psychologists have been interested in the characteristics of those who move versus those who stay in place, and in the adjustment and satisfaction of those who relocate in the later years. This area of study has been characterized primarily by surveys or participant observation studies of elderly people after they have voluntarily or involuntarily changed their place of residence. Unfortunately, there have been few longitudinal studies wherein observations or interviews have been conducted at various times before and after a move.

In the 1970s and 1980s there have been three basic redistribution patterns of the population:

a reversal of the historic pattern of net migration to metropolitan areas; a deconcentration of the population from central cities to the suburbs; in Canada, a migration from east to west, and in the United States, from the North to the South and the West . These redistribution patterns have also been observed among the elderly population and therefore raise major policy issues about where services and facilities should be located to meet the needs of future elderly cohorts. Although these moves have the potential to enhance the quality of life and the personal well-being of individuals, the movement of large numbers can be disruptive to both the receiving and the sending regions. Thus, demographers, geographers, and planners have begun to direct attention to elderly migration outcomes such as the growth, concentration, and rate of change of the elderly population in major sending and receiving regions (Rogers, 1989). Specifically, these studies have sought to identify: the characteristics and the age of those who migrate; whether the moves are permanent or seasonal; the net migration gains or losses of regions or communities; and the size and direction of migration streams between particular regions. The next two subsections briefly review the literature on the patterns and outcomes of local (mobility) and distant (migration) moves by the elderly population,[23] and the characteristics and motivations of those who move compared to those who stay in place.

Patterns of Local and Distant Moves by the Elderly

Although most elderly people age in place, both seasonal and permanent moves are increasing due to early retirement and an improvement in the economic and health status of more older adults, and because of marketing appeals by the tourism and the retirement-housing industries. Residential-mobility decisions seem to occur at three stages in later life (Speare and Meyer, 1988). First, at retirement, couples may make an amenity move to a specific destination in search of a more amenable climate, to be near kin, to take advantage of cheaper housing (Serow et al., 1986), or to pursue an active lifestyle, especially during the winter months. That is, the environment has a strong influence on the decision to migrate on either a seasonal or a permanent basis. The second decision-making stage occurs when assistance is needed or when it is anticipated that help may be needed in the future. This type of move is initiated by those who are losing their independence, by widows following the death of a spouse, and by the oldest segment of the elderly population. Often this assistance-seeking move involves a return migration to the original region where one was born or retired, or a move to where a child now lives. The final stage occurs when a major disability happens and the older adult must either move to a child's home or to some type of institution-alized setting.

The majority of moves in the later years are local moves, often within the same country or metropolitan region. For urban retirees, many of the initial moves are to nonmetropolitan destinations, perhaps in search of a safer, more economical, and healthier environment. How-ever, later in the retirement years, local moves are usually assistance-related as a result of declining health or economic resources (Carter, 1988). Most of these moves are by elderly wid-ows, partly because of the feminization of poverty, and many involve either a return to a metropolitan area where better services are available, or a move to a metropolitan area by lifelong rural dwellers who seek more ade-quate housing, health care, and social services.

Migration represents a move to another county, province, or country on a seasonal or a permanent basis. Seasonal migration for vary-ing periods of time usually occurs in the winter and often involves moving to a more temperate climate.[24] However, increasingly among the more affluent sector of the elderly population, there is also a reverse seasonal migration to 'cottage country' in the summer. Thus, some elderly adults migrate between two 'recrea-tion' areas, and may no longer own a perma-nent residence in the urban center where they were employed.

The influx of large numbers of elderly sea-sonal visitors or permanent residents to a re-gion has created a fear that these 'outsiders' will impose an unfair financial burden on local health, recreational, and social services bud-gets. As a result of these expressed fears, often by 'local' media, residents, or politicians, a 'gray peril' mentality emerged, which has spawned a body of research to refute this myth.[25] The evidence suggests that elderly migrants tend to be married couples, younger, healthier, and more affluent. Therefore, in reality, they pro-vide significant economic benefits to the receiv-ing area (see highlight 8.5), and indirectly stimu-late the tourism industry by inviting friends and relatives to visit them in their winter haven. For example, Leavitt and Crown (1989), on the basis of interviews with state officials and an analysis of the transfer of income resulting from this north to south migration, reported that Florida gains $1.2 billion as a result of the elderly migration from New York; $369 million from New Jersey; $312 million from Ohio; $286 million from Pennsylvania; and $274 million from Michigan — a total of $2.4 billion from just 5 states.

Studies have demonstrated, as well, that the sunbelt migrants are socially independent and do not make significant demands on the health and social services of the receiving area. For example, Tucker et al. (1988) found that fewer than 1 percent of Canadian snowbirds used social services for the elderly in Florida, and only 2 percent used senior centers. Thus, while gerontic enclaves may be created on a seasonal basis, the major negative economic impact is more likely to be on the 'home' communities, which lose a significant amount of potential spending dollars for up to six months per year. Moreover, studies have shown that return migration to the originating region or to that where a child lives often occurs as health or financial resources decline. In this situation, the original home region is a double loser — it loses the income of lifelong residents during the healthy, affluent retirement years, and it has to absorb the expensive health care and housing costs incurred when the migrants return as frail, dependent residents. At the same time, the original retirement-destination region reaps the benefits of the spending during the healthy, affluent years of retirement and does not have to absorb the costs for the large number who leave to seek assistance elsewhere during the frail, dependent years of later life.

As a result of this seasonal or temporary migration, long-term planning for social services, health care, and housing in both sending and receiving areas is becoming more difficult (Northcott, 1988:93-109). To provide planners and policymakers with more valid information about migration patterns, demographers and geographers have become increasingly interested in plotting **migration streams** (Litwak and Longino, 1987). These streams represent the number of people who move from point A to point B, and from point B to point A in a given period of time (annually, a five-year period). Some common streams observed in recent years include: from east to west (for young adults, from Ontario to Alberta in the 1970s; for retirees, from Manitoba and Saskatchewan to British Columbia); from metropolitan areas to nonmetropolitan areas (from Toronto to smaller towns and cities in southern Ontario and from Vancouver to smaller inland communities); and reverse, return, or countermigration streams (for young adults, from Alberta to Ontario in the late 1980s as the economy in Alberta faltered; and for retirees, from Florida to Ontario and Quebec as their health deteriorates).

Within Canada, the amount of interprovincial migration after the age of 65 is much less

---

FIGURE **8.3**

INTERPROVINCIAL MIGRATION STREAMS OF PERSONS AGED 65+, 1976-81

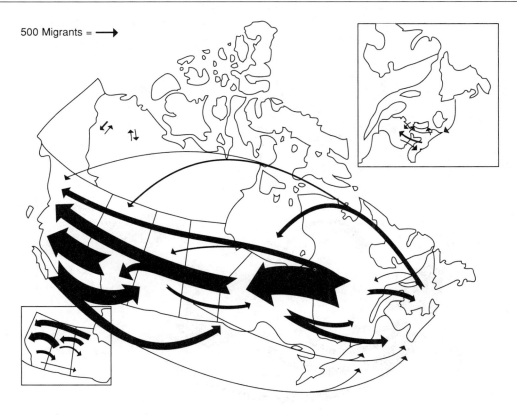

500 Migrants = ⟶

SOURCE: Reprinted with permission from Northcott (1988: figure 3.1).
ORIGINAL SOURCE: Based on data from the 1981 Public Use Sample Tape (2 percent sample) of the 1981 Census of Canada.

than the interstate migration in the United States. On the basis of census data, Northcott (1988) reported that 45,000 adults 55 to 64 years of age and 39,000 over the age of 65 changed their province of residence between 1976 and 1981. This represents a rate of less than 2 per 100 adults in the five-year period. Figures 8.3 and 8.4 illustrate the flow patterns for migrants 65 years of age and over between the 1976 and 1981 census periods. Although there is movement in both directions, the largest net streams (in thousands) are westward (figure 8.4), especially into British Columbia. The large stream from Quebec (a net loss of 20,000 older persons)

to Ontario mainly involved anglophones and likely reflects the sudden changes in the political climate in Quebec when the Parti Quebecois came to power in 1976.

It is also interesting to note that the elderly of the Atlantic provinces are less likely to leave for another province, while a large number of elderly move to the Atlantic provinces (figure 8.3). This eastward stream likely represents a return migration of former residents.

Although the loss is not illustrated specifically in figures 8.3 and 8.4, Northcott (1988:61) reported that large cities such as Montreal, Toronto, Winnipeg, Edmonton, and Vancou-

---

FIGURE 8.4

NET INTERPROVINCIAL MIGRATION OF PERSONS AGED 65+, 1976-81 (IN THOUSANDS)

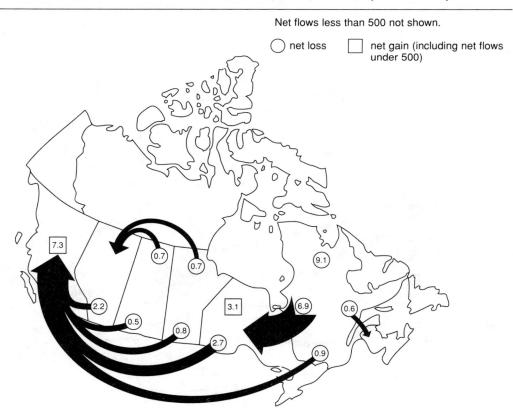

SOURCE: Reprinted with permission from Northcott (1988: figure 3.2).
ORIGINAL SOURCE: See Fig. 8.3.

ver experienced a net loss of older persons from 1976 to 1981; only Victoria among large cities experienced substantial net gains. The other major city/region to experience a net gain was the relatively temperate climate of the St. Catharines-Niagara Falls region in Ontario.

In summary, most permanent interprovincial migration among the older population is westward. However, there is a small return migration stream from Ontario to the Atlantic provinces. In general, migration rates are higher in the Prairies and British Columbia. As a result of these migration patterns, there is a small redistribution and subsequent concentration of the elderly population in British Columbia (especially Victoria and the Okanagan Valley), Alberta, and Ontario (especially smaller cities and the St. Catharines-Niagara Falls region). In reality, the major migration pattern for older Canadians tends to be a seasonal path to the southern states. For example, Tucker et al. (1988) report that 15 to 25 percent of the estimated 1.5 to 2.0 million Canadians who visit Florida each year are over the age of 65. Most of these older visitors are seasonal residents (one to five months) rather than vacationers for a seven- to ten-day visit.

Motivations, Characteristics, and Adjustment of Movers

Introduction

Most studies of those who move involve cross-sectional rather than longitudinal designs, and basic information about the mover at specific points prior to and following the move is not usually available. It is difficult, therefore, to determine the impact of the move itself on the satisfaction and well-being of the respondent, and to determine whether the process of adjustment to the move varies according to the time elapsed since the move.

There do appear to be some general factors that influence adaptation to a local or long-distance move. These include the amount of personal control or involvement in the decision to move; the amount of anticipatory planning for the move; the amount of improvement or change in the environment as a result of the move; the degree of fit between the needs of the

individual and how well the environment meets those needs; and the extent to which one's lifestyle is altered by the move. Regardless of the nature or distance of the move, a relocation in the later years is often precipitated by a transition point in the life cycle (such as an empty nest, retirement, widowhood, physical or mental disability, and decreasing independence), by a decrease in the safety and security of the housing or neighborhood environment, or by a change in the structure of the environment (such as urban renewal or gentrification). Thus, a local move or migration, whether voluntary or involuntary, represents a way to adjust to or cope with a change in the environment or in personal competence, needs, opportunity, or lifestyle.

Local Movers

A number of elderly people may desire to change their local residence. However, few actually move as long as they have sufficient economic and physical resources to maintain their current shelter. Local moves are more likely to occur late in the postretirement years, to be involuntary, and to represent a move to a setting that is less expensive or that provides more security or care. Three types of local moves represent decreasing independence and an increasing degree of environmental change: from a house to an apartment, from a home or an apartment to an institution, and from an institution to another institution that provides a higher level of care. Those most likely to make a local move late in life are women; those who are single, separated, widowed, or divorced; those who rent; those who have low incomes and little education; those who have a history of mobility; those who are still employed; and those who are becoming dependent on others because of declining physical or mental skills.

Conversely, those who remain in place ('stayers') are more likely to live with a spouse, to own their own home, to have strong emotional, ethnic, or racial ties to the neighborhood, and to be in poorer health but not yet dependent on others. For local moves, environmental characteristics may operate as push factors (declining safety and security, urban renewal, gentrification) or as pull factors (provision of economic or health assistance, higher-quality shelter).

The pattern and degree of adjustment to a local move depends primarily on whether the move is voluntary or involuntary, and on the nature of the new housing environment. Among those who voluntarily move from their own home to an apartment, to planned housing, or to a home for the aged, the available evidence concerning the impact is inconclusive (George, 1980:107). While some studies report an increase in health, life satisfaction, and morale, other studies report either no change or a decrease. In short, people react in different ways to a move, and what may be stressful for one individual may not be for another. George also concluded that those who adjust more satisfactorily to a move tend to have higher social, economic, and health status; to have a higher level of education; to have the ability to seek and create new relationships outside the family; and to perceive the change as an improvement over the previous housing environment.

In contrast, involuntary moves, especially to a less desirable physical environment or to an institution, can lead to maladjustment. An involuntary move can occur when individuals are evicted from their dwellings because of urban renewal projects, gentrification, an inability to continue payments, because of an unsafe physical structure, or because they are no longer able to care for themselves. In these situations, unless there is adequate preparation, relocation can be a traumatic and stressful event. Lawton (1980a:143) refers to this reaction as 'transplant shock.' It is this shock or inability to adjust that may be related to higher mortality rates among those who are involuntarily moved to an institution or involuntarily moved from one institution to another.

Migrants

Migration represents a change of residence across political boundaries (outside the country, state, or province). Whereas those in the labor force migrate to seek employment or an improvement in socioeconomic status, those over 65 are not likely to migrate in search of employment. Rather, migration tends to represent a voluntary move that may be made for one or more of the following reasons:

1. To improve person-environment con-

gruence, especially in a sunbelt or rural area.
2. To seek a leisure lifestyle different from that adopted during the working years.
3. To reduce the cost of living.
4. To obtain subsidized housing, which is more available in metropolitan areas.
5. To move closer to relatives.
6. To move to an area that may assist the individual in adapting to, or coping with, a deteriorating health status.
7. To return to the place of residence during childhood or during the early or middle years of the career.

While both push and pull factors stimulate migration in the later years, the pull factors tend to be more influential in the decision to seek an alternative or higher-quality lifestyle. Moreover, it appears that noneconomic factors are most relevant in determining who migrates and to what regions.[26] Highlight 8.5 describes some of the characteristics of the 'snowbirds' of Canada who annually migrate to Florida.

Although some individuals move during their final years in the labor force to the area where they wish to spend their retirement years, most migration by the elderly occurs within the first ten years of retirement. Contrary to the popular myth that many of the elderly migrate outside their region, only about 15 percent of all residential change by the elderly involves an interregion move. For most elderly persons who migrate, the decision has been reached after visits to the area and after knowing people who have lived in the area (Longino, 1980). Those who migrate primarily for lifestyle reasons are more likely to have higher economic resources; to be married; to have previously migrated during adulthood; to have a higher level of education; to be in the first few years of retirement; and to be in good health, especially since the distance of the migration is related to the state of health. Those seeking a leisure-oriented retirement tend to be highly independent individuals, especially with respect to their children. By comparison, migrants who return to the region of their birthplace are closely linked emotionally and psychologically with their children; are less likely to be married and well-educated; have fewer economic resources;

HIGHLIGHT 8.5

CANADA'S SNOWBIRDS: THE SOCIODEMOGRAPHIC AND LIFESTYLE CHARACTERISTICS OF SEASONAL MIGRANTS

Each winter, there is a major migration flow of elderly Canadians to the southern United States, with eastern Canadians primarily traveling to Florida and western Canadians to Arizona and California. To illustrate the magnitude of this flow, Sullivan and Stevens (1982) found that 12 percent of the female residents of a travel-trailer park and 20 percent of the female residents of a mobile-home park in Arizona were from Canada. Similarly, in Florida, which has as many as 500,000 elderly Canadian visitors a year, there is a weekly newspaper, *Canada News*, with a circulation of 4,500; there are active Canadian clubs or societies; and there is a widely syndicated daily radio show, 'Canada Calling.'

Who are these seasonal migrants, or 'snowbirds,' and where and how do they live during the winter months? In the most comprehensive study to date, Tucker et al. (1988) reported the results of a mailed survey returned by 2,731 older anglophone Canadians who 'winter' in Florida and subscribe to *Canada News*. Almost 90 percent of the respondents were married, and were predominantly middle to upper-middle class, with modal incomes ranging from $20,000 to $40,000. Average monthly expenditures in Florida were $1,200 U.S. The average length of stay was five months. In Florida the respondents were dispersed across forty-seven of the sixty-seven counties, and lived in a variety of housing types: 56 percent in mobile-home communities; 22 percent in condominiums; 15 percent in single family homes; and 5 percent in rented apartments. Moreover, 75 percent reported that they owned their place of residence in Florida, and 77 percent owned their residence in Canada.

When asked why and how they migrated to Florida, 75 percent indicated that the decision was based on having vacationed there prior to retirement. Then, gradually, the stay was lengthened and the commitment reinforced (for example, by purchasing a residence). The most common reasons for selecting Florida were: climate (89 percent), the Florida lifestyle (67 percent), and friends wintering there (22 percent).

Except for unexpected acute illnesses and the normal chronic conditions expected in elderly adults (such as arthritis, heart conditions), there was little activity limitation and few reported health problems. Most (84 percent) visited their physician at home for a checkup before migrating, and 82 percent reported taking a supply of drugs with them from Canada. Thus, except for emergency care, relatively little use was made of the health care system in Florida. Similarly, given the high degree of independence of these seasonal migrants, along with the presence of a spouse, there was almost no reported use of social services for the elderly such as senior centers, transportation programs, homemaker services, or adult day care. Furthermore, 75 percent of the respondents reported that they had close friends living near them in Florida. This closeness, combined with family telephone calls and visits, and the fact that most of the respondents were married, provided a substantial informal support network. Clearly, these age-based communities generate an informal process of seniors helping seniors. They may also stimulate a more active social life than that followed back in Canada, where the elderly may live in age-integrated neighborhoods.

SOURCE: Adapted from Tucker et al. (1988).

are more likely to be female and widowed; and are more likely to have lived in older, poorer-quality housing prior to migration.

While some elderly people migrate to a new area or return to the region where they spent their childhood, most maintain a residence within the county where they resided during the preretirement years. For some, the decision to stay in place is based on the fact that they are

trapped by a low economic or health status that discourages or prevents migration. For others, remaining in place may be the appropriate mechanism for maintaining a balance between environmental press and personal competence.

In an effort to more fully understand the migration process, Wiseman (1980) developed a conceptual model that includes four stages in the decision-making process. First, there are push and pull 'triggering mechanisms.' These include a personal crisis or transition point; environmental stress; environmental attractions; friends or kin already relocated in the region; or a desire for a change in lifestyle. Second, the decision to move is realistically assessed in light of such personal factors as health, community ties, economic resources, and former migration experiences, and in light of such environmental factors as the nature of the housing market and the cost of living in the receiving area. At the completion of this stage a decision to migrate or not to migrate is made. One outcome is that a large number of potential migrants decide to age in place because they realize that they lack the personal resources or experience to engage in migratory behavior, either permanently or seasonally.

For those who decide to move, the third step is to determine whether the move will be permanent or seasonal. Finally, the destination must be selected on the basis of previous experience, knowledge of alternative locations, preference for climate and entertainment opportunities, location of friends or kin, and inducements from local government or private-sector entrepreneurs (such as facilities and services provided to senior citizens by towns and cities, or as part of the residence contract in retirement communities). Having selected a community, the retiree must then select the neighborhood, type of dwelling, and living arrangements that will be equal to or better than the present housing situation. Wiseman's model seeks to explain the process whereby individuals become either migrants or voluntary or involuntary stayers during the early retirement years. It focuses on the interaction between motivations to migrate, personal resources, perception of environmental stress in the present location, and perception of and experience with environmental opportunities in the proposed destination.

In summary, those who are married, in good health, and with sufficient economic resources are those who are most likely to migrate to a new region following retirement. In general, however, the migration rates for the elderly are lower than for all other groups. For those who do migrate, a major motivation is the desire to reside in a region that provides a temperate year-round climate and age-appropriate recreational programs and facilities. For others, migration occurs because they seek support from kin, or they wish to return to the area where they were born. In contrast, those who engage in short-distance local moves are more likely to be seeking improved or more appropriate (in cost or size) housing, or are in need of some degree of social support or health care.

SUMMARY AND CONCLUSIONS

This chapter has focused on the interaction between the physical environment and the aging process. The first section introduced theories and models that seek to explain the influence of the physical environment on aging individuals, as well as a number of objective and subjective indicators of environmental impact on the elderly. The second section involved an analysis of the suprapersonal or macroenvironment, including the spatial distribution and characteristics of older people in rural, urban, age-integrated, or age-segregated neighborhoods; the availability of and need for private and public transportation; the incidence of crime by and against the elderly; and the extent and consequences of fear of victimization.

In the third section, the reader was introduced to the impact of the quality, type, size, location, and design of the dwelling unit on the lifestyle and life satisfaction of the aging individual. It was noted that the type of housing in the later years varies along intersecting dimensions: independent to dependent, low to high quality, and age-integrated to age-segregated. A number of advantages and disadvantages of each type of housing were set out. This section also considered institutionalization as a housing alternative in the later years by examining the incidence of institutionalization, the type and quality of institutions, and the process of adjustment to institutionalization. The final section considered patterns of local mobility and distant migration in the postretirement years. In addition, the characteristics and motivations of those who move, compared to those who age in place, were reviewed.

Based on current research evidence concerning the physical environment and aging, it can be concluded that:

1. While a number of models or theories have been developed to explain the relationship between factors in the physical environment and the aging process, a comprehensive and definitive theory is not yet available.

2. About 75 percent of the elderly in North America live in an urban environment.

3. A high proportion of the residents of small towns are elderly because they age in place, and because younger cohorts migrate to larger urban centers.

4. At present, of the elderly who live in large cities in North America, over 60 percent live in the central core. This proportion decreases when they are forced out by urban renewal and gentrification.

5. In the future, the elderly will be increasingly located in the 'graying' suburbs where they settled in the 1950s and 1960s.

6. Within most stable neighborhoods, there is a high degree of homogeneity with respect to the age, class, or ethnic composition of the residents.

7. The environment of the rural elderly has seldom been studied. Where it has been studied, there appears to be an often-reported discrepancy between the quality of life as measured by objective and subjective criteria. That is, whereas objective indicators indicate a generally lower quality of life in rural areas, subjective indicators suggest a higher perceived quality of life.

8. Availability of private or public transportation is essential in maintaining independence and a higher quality of life and life satisfaction in the later years.

9. For public transportation to be effective in meeting the needs of the elderly, a number of physical, structural, psychological, and economic barriers must be reduced or eliminated before the elderly will use the system.

10. Although the rate of crime committed by the elderly is significantly less than for younger age groups, the incidence is increasing. While some of this criminal activity involves theft to meet personal wants or needs, it may also be motivated by boredom or by rebellion against the private or public sectors.

11. The elderly are victimized less than other age groups, except for larceny-with-contact crimes (such as purse snatching) and crimes against the place of residence (burglary).

12. The elderly are victimized less than younger people because they are less mobile and because they avoid high-crime environments. They may also appear to be victimized less because they are less likely to report a crime.

13. The elderly who are most likely to be victimized are those who are economically and socially disadvantaged (women, the poor, and inner-city residents).

14. Although they are actually victimized less than other age groups, the elderly frequently say that fear of crime is one of their most serious personal problems. This fear tends to be greater among those who are most economically and socially disadvantaged.

15. Fear of crime often leads to self-imposed restrictions on travel and social participation within the neighborhood and community. In fact, the elderly individual may become housebound rather than walk in the streets.

16. Most older people prefer to live in an independent dwelling.

17. Approximately 65 percent of the elderly own their own homes.

18. The quality, type, size, location, and design of the dwelling unit interacts with health and economic status to influence lifestyle, life satisfaction, and the quality of life in the later years.

19. As measured by objective indicators, the quality of housing is generally

lower for the elderly who are single, who rent, and who live in rural areas.

20. Because the elderly are a heterogeneous group, a variety of housing alternatives should be provided in every community (independent to dependent, age-integrated to age-segregated, single-family dwelling to high-rise).

21. The elderly seem to prefer to reside in age-segregated housing units and neighborhoods.

22. Three general categories of institutionalized housing for the elderly include the personal care home or home for the aged; the nursing home; and the extended-care or chronic-care hospital.

23. The stress associated with institutionalization is high, but can be reduced by preparation for the move, by moving to a similar or higher-quality environment, and by ensuring that contact is maintained with the family and community.

24. While most residential change in the postretirement years occurs within and between urban metropolitan regions, there is an increasing trend toward longer moves and toward migration to nonmetropolitan areas.

25. Migration streams in the later years are dominated by widows, by married couples, by those in good health, and by those with higher economic resources.

26. Local moves are more likely to be involuntary (for example, because of forced institutionalization or urban renewal projects), whereas distant moves to another county, state, or province are more likely to be voluntary, for the purpose of establishing an alternative or higher-quality lifestyle.

27. It is essential to match the aging individual with a compatible environment in order to enhance life satisfaction and the quality of life.

NOTES

1. See Windley and Ernst, 1975; Howell, 1980; Lawton, 1980a, 1985; Lawton et al., 1982; Rowles and Ohta, 1982; Altman et al., 1984; Golant, 1984; Scheidt and Windley, 1985; Bernardin-Haldemann, 1988; Northcott, 1988; Ward et al., 1988; Kendig, 1990; Longino, 1990; Parmelee and Lawton, 1990.

2. This point was raised by Marshall and Tindale (1978-79) in their plea for a radical gerontology. They argued that more research needs to be conducted from the perspective of the elderly themselves. If this is so, there should be a greater attempt to adjust society to the aging individual, rather than requiring individuals to adjust to the ongoing social order.

3. In this section, the term 'community' refers to a geographical unit such as a town, city, or metropolitan area situated on a rural-urban continuum of size and lifestyle. In the third section of this chapter, 'community' will be used as a sociological concept that refers to a group of individuals who share a similar territory and thereby interact with some degree of interdependence (an apartment complex, a retirement community, a home for the aged).

4. Seasonal migrations in the winter and in the summer are considered temporary moves and are not normally included in migration statistics.

5. Yet, surprisingly, they were not physically or cognitively isolated from the larger world, since they watched television regularly and frequently traveled great distances from the community to visit relatives.

6. See Goldsmith and Goldsmith, 1976; Hindelang et al., 1978; Lawton and Yaffe, 1979; Malinchak, 1980; Lester, 1981; Yin, 1985; Alston, 1986; Brillon, 1987; Aday, 1988; Fattah and Sacco, 1989; and the *Journal of Crime and Aging*.

7. Relatively few elderly persons engage in criminal behavior. Among those most likely to engage in criminal behavior are those older males who have lived or are living on the streets. Among members of this subculture, the use of alcohol and drugs may precipitate criminal behavior (Steffensmeier, 1987). To date, most of the information on this topic is derived from studies in the U.S., where the incidence seems to be increasing (Wilbanks and Kim, 1984; Shaver, 1985; Wilbanks, 1985; Kercher, 1987a, 1987b; Fattah and Sacco, 1989).

8. These crimes are especially frequent at the end of the month when pension and social security checks are cashed, and are often classified as 'predatory' crimes, in which the elderly are randomly attacked by unarmed young males.

9. Some of these schemes include the purchase of products to retard the biological process of aging, or the appearance of aging; the purchase of land or a home as a retirement investment without visiting the site; or the encouraged withdrawal of savings from a bank under false pretenses.

10. Cohen et al. (1981) suggest that given the relatively brief time the elderly are exposed to risk each day, their victimization rate is actually quite high. That is, although the elderly expose themselves or their property less often to risk of victimization, their relative rates are considerably higher than other age groups who are exposed much more frequently each day.

11. See Lawton and Yaffe, 1980; Solicitor General, 1985; Brillon, 1987; LaGrange and Ferraro, 1987; Aday, 1988; Ferraro and LaGrange, 1988; Fattah and Sacco, 1989.

12. This statistic may partially reflect the tendency for men to be less willing to admit fear, because of social norms that equate bravery with masculinity. Also, with advancing age there is a higher ratio of women to men.

13. Like rates of victimization, fear of crime is directly related to type of environment. The greatest fear is expressed by those who live in the center core of large cities. Fear decreases concentrically from this core as one moves to the suburbs of large cities, to smaller cities, towns, and farms, and to segregated retirement communities with elaborate security systems. For example, the Leisure World retirement community in Laguna Hills, California, is surrounded by six-foot walls and sentry posts.

14. For example, Godbey et al. (1980) found that senior citizens in large cities express almost as much fear for the hours when school is dismissed as they do after darkness sets in. That is, they fear the predatory crimes and verbal abuse of teenagers, and they avoid walking in the streets and shopping plazas during noon hour and after school.

15. However, the increasing number of divorced and never-married individuals may increase the demand for rental housing for single elderly persons in the future. This housing will be required prior to age 65, not only in the 70s or 80s, when declining health and widowhood require a relocation to an apartment.

16. Many older homes are located in the central and older residential areas of towns and cities. However, by the end of the century this problem of maintaining older residences will more frequently be found among suburban residents who reside in homes built after 1950.

17. Congregate housing provides a semi-independent living arrangement wherein each individual or couple has an independent living unit (an apartment or room) with bathroom facilities, and which may or may not have cooking or laundry facilities. Thus, in addition to shelter, the unit provides services that may include one to three meals per day, laundry and maid service, private transportation, security service, minor health care, and recreational programs. The congregate concept usually means that the residents eat at the same time in a common dining area.

18. For example, needs change if children leave the home, if income and social interaction decrease, if health declines and the individual has less mobility, if daily and annual maintenance requirements grow burdensome, if the dwelling is vacant for part of the year while time is spent in a second residence, or if a spouse is institutionalized or dies.

19. See Streib et al., 1984; Hoglund, 1985; Lawton, 1985; Moos and Lemke, 1985; Newcomer et al., 1986; Canada Mortgage and Housing Corporation, 1988a, 1988b, 1988c, 1989; Kendig, 1990; Parmelee and Lawton, 1990; and the *Journal of Housing for the Elderly* (1983-).

20. For example, Merrill Court (Hochschild, 1973) had a common meeting place, whereas Fun City (Jacobs, 1974) did not have this structural stimulus to facilitate social interaction. As a result, a sense of 'community' evolved in Merrill Court, while Fun City was characterized by empty streets and very little community or neighborly interaction. In fact, only about 500 of the 6,000 residents participated in planned activities. That is, although there were enough residents to enable programs to be successful, there was no focal point to facilitate the delivery of the programs or to foster social interaction.

21. It must be recognized that the evaluation of quality in an institution can result in varying assessments, depending on whether the evaluation is made by the resident, a relative, the staff, or a government inspector. Included in these evaluations are such concerns as amount of personal space and degree of privacy; safety of the physical structure; type, availability, and quality of health and medical care; degree of emotional interest in and concern for the residents on the part of staff; the availability and variety of social, recreational, and therapeutic programs; the vari-

ety and nutritional quality of the food; and the willingness of the institution to meet the needs and interests of residents with respect to sex, alcohol, and tobacco.

22. See Chappell and Penning, 1979; Lawton, 1980a; Neysmith, 1980; Penning and Chappell, 1980; Schwenger and Gross, 1980; Béland, 1984; Grant, 1985; Forbes et al., 1987; Rutman and Freedman, 1988.

23. See Northcott, 1984, 1985, 1988; Liaw and Kanaroglou, 1986; Golant, 1987; Litwak and Longino, 1987; Meyer, 1987; Rogers and Watkins, 1987; Serow, 1987; Bohland and Rowles, 1988; Serow and Charity, 1988; Longino, 1990.

24. For example, most Canadians who 'winter' in the United States stay less than six months in order to retain their eligibility for Canadian health insurance plans.

25. See Monahan and Greene, 1982; Hogan, 1987; Crown, 1988; Happel et al., 1988; Longino, 1988; Tucker et al., 1988; Mullins and Tucker, 1989; Leavitt and Crown, 1989.

26. Victor Marshall suggests that there is a need for research concerning two unique categories of older migrants: the seasonal migratory worker and the political refugee. Both lack the economic security to enable them to survive in the later years, and both age in a foreign land deprived of extended contact with their families.

REFERENCES

Aday, R. (1988). *Crime and the Elderly: an Annotated Bibliography*. New York: Greenwood Press.

Alston, L. (1986). *Crime and Older Americans*. Springfield, Ill.: Charles C. Thomas.

Altman I. et al. (ed.). (1984). *Elderly People and the Environment: Advances in Theory and Research*. vol. 7. New York: Plenum Publishing Corporation.

Béland, F. (1984). 'The Decision of Elderly Persons to Leave Their Homes,' *The Gerontologist*, 24(2), 179-85.

Bernadin-Haldemann, V. (1988). 'Ecology and Aging: A Critical Review,' *Canadian Journal on Aging*, 7(4), 458-71.

Bohland, J. and G. Rowles. (1988). 'The Significance of Elderly Migration to Changes in Elderly Population Concentration in the United States: 1960-1980,' *Journal of Gerontology: Social Sciences*, 43(5), S145-52.

Brillon, Y. (1987). *Victimization and Fear of Crime among the Elderly*. Toronto: Butterworths.

Canada Mortgage and Housing Corporation. (1988a). *Housing for Older Canadians: New Financial and Tenure Options*. Ottawa: Canada Mortgage and Housing Corporation.

Canada Mortgage and Housing Corporation. (1988b). *Housing the Elderly: A Bibliography*. Ottawa: Canada Mortgage and Housing Corporation.

Canada Mortgage and Housing Corporation. (1988c). *Innovations in Housing for Seniors*. Ottawa: Canada Mortgage and Housing Corporation.

Canada Mortgage and Housing Corporation. (1989). *Options: Housing for Older Canadians*. Ottawa: Canada Mortgage and Housing Corporation.

Carp, F. (1980). 'Environmental Effects upon the Mobility of Older People,' *Environment and Behavior*, 12(2), 139-56.

Carter, J. (1988). 'Elderly Local Mobility,' *Research on Aging*, 10(3), 399-419.

Chappell, N. and M. Penning. (1979). 'The Trend Away from Institutionalization: Humanism or Economic Efficiency?' *Research on Aging*, 1(3), 361-87.

Charness, N. and E. Bosman. (1990). 'Human Factors and Design for Older Adults,' pp. 446-64 in J. Birren and W. Schaie (eds.). *Handbook of the Psychology of Aging*. 3d ed. San Diego, Calif.: Academic Press.

Chevan, A. (1982). 'Age, Housing Choice, and Neighborhood Age Structure,' *American Journal of Sociology*, 87(5), 1133-49.

Cohen, C. and J. Sokolovsky. (1983). 'Toward a Concept of Homelessness among Aged Men,' *Journal of Gerontology*, 38(1), 81-89.

Cohen, C. and J. Sokolovsky. (1989). *Old Men of the Bowery*. New York: Guilford Publications.

Cohen, C. et al. (1988). 'Gender, Networks, and Adaptation among an Inner-City Population,' *Journal of Aging Studies*, 2(1), 45-56.

Cohen, F. et al. (1987). 'Interpersonal Understanding in the Elderly: The Influence of Age-Integrated and Age-Segregated Housing,' *Research on Aging*, 9(1), 79-100.

Cohen, L. et al. (1981). 'Social Inequality and Predatory Criminal Victimization: An Exposition and Test of a Formal Theory,' *American Sociological Review*, 46(5), 505-24.

Connidis, J. (1983). 'Living Arrangement Choices of Older Residents: Assessing Quantitative Results with Qualitative Data,' *Canadian Journal of Sociology*, 8(4), 359-75.

Covey. H. and S. Menard. (1988). 'Trends in Elderly Criminal Victimization from 1973 to 1984,' *Research on Aging*, 10(3), 329-41.

Crown, W. (1988). 'State Economic Implications of Elderly Interstate Migration,' *The Gerontologist*, 28(4), 533-39.

Ehrlich, P. et al. (1982). 'Congregate Housing for the Elderly: Thirteen Years Later,' *The Gerontologist*, 22(4), 399-403.

Fattah, E. and V. Sacco. (1989). *Crime and Victimization of the Elderly*. New York: Springer-Verlag.

Ferraro, K. and R. LaGrange. (1988). 'Are Older People Afraid of Crime?' *Journal of Aging Studies*, 2(3), 277-87.

Fitzpatrick, K. and J. Logan. (1985). 'The Aging of the Suburbs, 1960-1980,' *American Sociological Review*, 50(1), 106-17.

Forbes, W. et al. (1987). *Institutionalization of the Elderly in Canada*. Toronto: Butterworths.

George, L. (1980). *Role Transitions in Later Life*. Monterey, Calif.: Brooks/Cole Publishing Co.

Godbey, G. et al. (1980). *The Relationship of Crime and Fear of Crime among the Aged to Leisure Behavior and Use of Public Leisure Services*. Washington, D.C.: NRTA-AARP, Andrus Foundation.

Golant, S. (1984). *A Place to Grow Old: The Meaning of Environment in Old Age*. New York: Columbia University Press.

Golant, S. (1987). 'Residential Moves by Elderly Persons to U.S. Central Cities, Suburbs and Rural Areas,' *Journal of Gerontology*, 42(5), 534-39.

Goldsmith, J. and S. Goldsmith (eds.). (1976). *Crime and the Elderly*. Lexington, Ky.: D.C. Heath Co.

Grant, P. (1985). 'Who Experiences the Move into a Nursing Home as Stressful? Examination of the Relocation Stress Hypothesis Using Archival, Time-Series Data,' *Canadian Journal on Aging*, 4(2), 87-99.

Grant, P. and B. Rice. (1983). 'Transportation Problems of the Rural Elderly: A Needs Assessment,' *Canadian Journal on Aging*, 2(3), 107-24.

Gubrium, J. (1972). 'Toward a Socio-Environmental Theory of Aging,' *The Gerontologist*, 12(3), 281-84.

Gubrium, J. (1973). *The Myth of the Golden Years: A Socio-Environmental Theory of Aging*. Springfield, Ill.: Charles C. Thomas.

Gubrium, J. (1975). *Living and Dying at Murray Manor*. New York: St. Martin's Press.

Haber, P. (1986). 'Technology in Aging,' *The Gerontologist*, 26(4), 350-57.

Happel, S. et al. (1988). 'The Economic Impact of Elderly Winter Residents in the Phoenix Area,' *Research on Aging*, 10(1), 119-33.

Henig, J. (1981). 'Gentrification and Displacement of the Elderly: An Empirical Analysis,' *The Gerontologist*, 21(1), 67-75.

Hindelang, M. et al. (1978). *Victims of Personal Crime: An Empirical Foundation for a Theory of Personal Victimization*. Cambridge, Mass.: Ballinger Press.

Hochschild, A. (1973). *The Unexpected Community*. Englewood Cliffs, N.J.: Prentice-Hall.

Hodge, G. (1987). 'Assisted Housing for Ontario's Rural Elderly: Shortfalls in Product and Location,' *Canadian Journal on Aging*, 6(2), 141-54.

Hogan, T. (1987). 'Determinants of the Seasonal Migration of the Elderly to Sunbelt States,' *Research on Aging*, 9(1), 115-33.

Hoglund, D. (1985). *Housing for the Elderly: Privacy and Independence in Environments for the Aging*. New York: Van Nostrand Reinhold.

Howell, S. (1980). 'Environments and Aging,' pp. 237-60 in C. Eisdorfer (ed). *Annual Review of Gerontology and Geriatrics*. vol. 1. New York: Springer Publishing Co.

Howell, S. (1982). 'The Meaning of Place in Old Age,' in G. Rowles and R. Ohta (eds.). *Aging and Milieu: Environmental Perspectives on Growing Old*. New York: Academic Press.

Jacobs, J. (1974). *Fun City: An Ethnographic Study of a Retirement Community*. New York: Holt, Rinehart & Winston.

Kahana, E. (1975). 'A Congruence Model of Person-Environment Interaction' in P. Windley and G. Ernst (eds.). *Theory Development in Environment and Aging*. Washington, D.C.: The Gerontological Society of America.

Kahana, E. (1982). 'A Congruence Model of Person-Environment Interaction,' in P. Lawton et al. (eds.). *Aging and the Environment: Theoretical Perspectives*. New York: Springer Publishing Co.

Kahana, E. et al. (1980). 'Alternative Models of Person-Environment Fit: Prediction of Morale in Three Homes for the Aged,' *Journal of Gerontology*, 35(4), 584-95.

Kane, R. and R. Kane. (1985). *A Will and a Way: What the United States Can Learn from Canada about Caring for the Elderly*. New York: Columbia University Press.

Keating, N. (forthcoming). *Rural Aging in Canada*. Markham, Ont.: Butterworths.

Kendig, H. (1990). 'Comparative Perspectives on Housing, Aging, and Social Structure,' pp. 288-307 in R. Binstock and L. George (eds.). *Handbook of Aging and the Social Sciences*. 3d ed. San Diego, Calif.: Academic Press.

Kercher, K. (1987a). 'Causes and Correlates of Crime Committed by the Elderly,' *Research on Aging*, 9(2), 256-80.

Kercher, K. (1987b). 'Causes and Correlates of Crime Committed by the Elderly,' pp. 253-306 in E. Borgatta and R. Montgomery (eds.). *Critical Issues in Aging Policy*. Beverly Hills, Calif.: Sage Publications.

Krivo, L. and J. Mutchler. (1989). 'Elderly Persons Living Alone: The Effect of Community Context on Living Arrangements,' *Journal of Gerontology: Social Sciences*, 44(2), S54-62.

LaGrange, R. and K. Ferraro. (1987). 'The Elderly's Fear of Crime: A Critical Examination of the Research,' *Research on Aging*, 9(3), 372-91.

Lawton, P. (1977). 'The Impact of the Environment

on Aging and Behavior,' pp. 276-301 in J. Birren and W. Schaie (eds.). *Handbook of the Psychology of Aging*. New York: Van Nostrand Reinhold.

Lawton, P. (1980a). *Environment and Aging*. Monterey, Calif.: Brooks/Cole Publishing Co.

Lawton, P. (1980b). 'Housing the Elderly: Residential Quality and Residential Satisfaction,' *Research on Aging*, 2(3), 309-28.

Lawton, P. (1985). 'Housing and Living Environments of Older People,' pp. 450-78 in R. Binstock and E. Shanas (eds.). *Handbook of Aging and the Social Sciences*. 2d ed. New York: Van Nostrand Reinhold.

Lawton, P. (1987). 'Aging and Proactivity in the Residential Environment,' paper presented at the American Psychological Association Annual Meeting, New York.

Lawton, P. and S. Hoover (eds.). (1981). *Community Housing Choices for Older Americans*. New York: Springer Publishing Co.

Lawton, P. and L. Nahemow. (1973). 'Ecology and the Aging Process,' pp. 619-74 in C. Eisdorfer and M.P. Lawton (eds.). *The Psychology of Adult Development and Aging*. Washington, D.C.: American Psychological Association.

Lawton, P. and S. Yaffe. (1979). *Victimization of the Elderly and Fear of Crime*. Philadelphia: Philadelphia Geriatric Centre.

Lawton, P. and S. Yaffe. (1980). 'Victimization and Fear of Crime in Elderly Public Housing Tenants,' *Journal of Gerontology*, 35(5), 768-79.

Lawton, P. et al. (eds.). (1982). *Aging and the Environment: Theoretical Approaches*. New York: Springer Publishing Co.

Leavitt, T. and W. Crown. (1989). 'Policy Implications of Elderly Interstate Migration,' paper presented at the Gerontological Society of America Annual Meeting, Minneapolis,Minn., November 17-21.

Lee, G. and M. Lassey. (1980). 'Rural-Urban Differences among the Elderly: Economic, Social and Subjective Factors,' *Journal of Social Issues*, 36(2), 62-74.

Lemke, S. and R. Moos. (1989). 'Ownership and Quality of Care in Residential Facilities for the Elderly,' *The Gerontologist*, 29(2), 209-15.

Lester, D. (ed.). (1981). *The Elderly Victim of Crime*. Springfield, Ill.: Charles C. Thomas.

Leung, H. (1987). 'Housing Concerns of Elderly Homeowners,' *Journal of Aging Studies*, 1(4), 379-91.

Liaw, K. and P. Kanaroglou. (1986). 'Metropolitan Elderly Out-Migration in Canada, 1971-1976,' *Research on Aging*, 8(2), 201-31.

Litwak, E. and C. Longino. (1987). 'Migration Patterns among the Elderly: A Developmental Per-

spective,' *The Gerontologist*, 27(2), 266-72.

Longino, C. (1980). 'Residential Relocation of Older People: Metropolitan and Nonmetropolitan,' *Research on Aging*, 2(2), 205-16.

Longino, C. (1988). 'The Gray Peril Mentality and the Impact of Retirement Migration,' *Journal of Applied Gerontology*, 7(4), 448-55.

Longino, C. (1990). 'Geographical Distribution and Migration,' pp. 45-63 in R. Binstock and L. George (eds.). *Handbook of Aging and the Social Sciences*. 3d. ed. San Diego, Calif.: Academic Press.

Malinchak, A. (1980). *Crime and Gerontology*. Englewood Cliffs, N.J.: Prentice-Hall.

Marshall, V. (ed.) (1980). *Aging in Canada: Social Perspectives*. Don Mills, Ont.: Fitzhenry and Whiteside.

Marshall, V. and J. Tindale. (1978-79). 'Notes for a Radical Gerontology,' *International Journal of Aging and Human Development*, 9(2), 163-75.

Meyer, J. (1987). 'A Regional Scale Temporal Analysis of the Net Migration Patterns of Elderly Persons over Time,' *Journal of Gerontology*, 42(4), 366-75.

Minister of State. (1988). *Canada's Seniors: A Dynamic Force*. Ottawa: Government of Canada.

Monahan, D. and V. Greene. (1982). 'The Impact of Seasonal Population Fluctuations on Service Delivery,' *The Gerontologist*, 22(2), 160-63.

Moos, R. and S. Lemke. (1985). Specialized Living Environments for Older People,' pp. 864-89 in J. Birren and W. Schaie (eds.). *Handbook of the Psychology of Aging*. 2d ed. New York: Van Nostrand Reinhold.

Mullins, L. and R. Tucker. (ed.). (1989). *Snowbirds in the Sun Belt: Older Canadians in Florida*. Tampa, Fla.: International Exchange Center on Gerontology.

National Advisory Council on Aging. (1987). *Housing an Aging Population: Guidelines for Development and Design*. Ottawa: Minister of Supply and Services.

National Advisory Council on Aging. (1989). *Seniors and Winter Living*. Ottawa: Minister of Supply and Services Canada.

Newcomer, R.J. et al. (eds.) (1986). *Housing an Aging Society: Issues, Alternatives and Policy*. New York: Van Nostrand Reinhold.

Neysmith, S. (1980). 'Marginality and Morale,' pp. 281-85 in V. Marshall (ed.). *Aging in Canada: Social Perspectives*. Don Mills, Ont.: Fitzhenry and Whiteside.

Northcott, H. (1984). 'The International Migration of Canada's Elderly,' *Canadian Journal on Aging*, 3(1), 3-22.

Northcott, H. (1985). 'The Geographic Mobility of Canada's Elderly,' *Canadian Studies in Population*,

12(2), 183-202.

Northcott, H. (1988). *Changing Residence: The Geographic Mobility of Elderly Canadians.* Toronto: Butterworths.

O'Bryant, S. (1982). 'The Value of Home to Older Persons: Relationship to Housing Satisfaction,' *Research on Aging,* 4(3), 349-63.

O'Bryant, S. and S. Wolf. (1983). 'Explanations of Housing Satisfaction of Older Homeowners and Renters,' *Research on Aging,* 5(2), 217-33.

Ontario Hospital Association. (1980). *Guidelines for Long Term Care.* Toronto: Ontario Hospital Association.

Ontario Ministry of Health. (1980). *Patient Care Classification.* Toronto: Government of Ontario.

Parmelee, P. and P. Lawton. (1990). 'The Design of Special Environments for the Aged,' pp. 465-89 in J. Birren and W. Schaie (eds.). *Handbook of the Psychology of Aging.* 3d ed. San Diego, Calif.: Academic Press.

Penning, M. and N. Chappell. (1980). 'A Reformulation of Basic Assumptions about Institutions for the Elderly,' pp. 269-80 in V. Marshall (ed.). *Aging in Canada: Social Perspectives.* Don Mills, Ont.: Fitzhenry and Whiteside.

Podnieks, E. et al. (1989). *Survey on Abuse of the Elderly in Canada: Preliminary Findings.* Toronto: Ryerson Polytechnical Institute, Office of Research and Innovation.

Priest, G. (1988). 'Living Arrangements of Canada's Older Elderly Population,' *Canadian Social Trends,* 10(Autumn), 26-30.

Raschko, B. (1982). *Housing Interiors of the Disabled and Elderly.* New York: Van Nostrand Reinhold.

Regnier, V. and J. Pynoos. (1987). *Housing the Aged: Design Directives and Policy Considerations.* New York: Elsevier Science Publishing Co.

Rogers, A. (1989). 'The Elderly Mobility Transition,' *Research on Aging,* 11(1), 3-32.

Rogers, A. and J. Watkins. (1987). 'General Versus Elderly Interstate Migration and Population Redistribution in the United States,' *Research on Aging,* 9(4), 483-529.

Rowles, G. (1980). 'Growing Old Inside: Aging and Attachment to Place in an Appalachian Community,' pp. 153-70 in N. Datan and N. Lohmann (eds.). *Transitions of Aging.* New York: Academic Press.

Rowles, G. and R. Ohta (eds.). (1982). *Aging and Milieu: Environment Perspectives on Growing Old.* New York: Academic Press.

Rubinstein, R. (1985). 'The Elderly Who Live Alone and Their Social Supports,' pp. 165-93 in P. Lawton and G. Maddox (eds.). *Annual Review of Gerontology and Geriatrics.* vol. 5. New York: Springer Publishing Co.

Rubinstein, R. (1987). 'The Significance of Personal Objects to Older People,' *Journal of Aging Studies,* 1(3), 225-38.

Rubinstein, R. (1989). 'The Home Environments of Older People: A Description of the Psychosocial Processes Linking Person to Place,' *Journal of Gerontology: Social Sciences,* 44(2), S45-53.

Rudy, N. (1987). *For Such a Time as This.* Toronto: Ontario Association of Homes for the Aged.

Rutman, D. and J. Freedman. (1988). 'Anticipating Relocation: Coping Strategies and the Meaning of Home for Older People,' *Canadian Journal on Aging,* 7(1), 17-30.

Scheidt, R. and P. Windley. (1985). 'The Ecology of Aging,' pp. 245-58 in J. Birren and W. Schaie (eds). *Handbook of the Psychology of Aging.* 2d ed. New York: Van Nostrand Reinhold.

Schooler, K. (1975). 'Response of the Elderly to Environment: A Stress-Theoretical Perspective,' in P. Windley and G. Ernst (eds.). *Theory Development in Environment and Aging.* Washington, D.C.: Gerontological Society.

Schwenger, C. and J. Gross. (1980). 'Institutional Care and Institutionalization of the Elderly in Canada,' pp. 248-56 in V. Marshall (ed.). *Aging in Canada: Social Perspectives.* Don Mills, Ont.: Fitzhenry and Whiteside.

Serow, W. (1987). 'Why the Elderly Move: Cross-National Comparisons,' *Research on Aging,* 9(4), 582-97.

Serow, W. and D. Charity. (1988). 'Return Migration of the Elderly in the United States: Recent Trends,' *Research on Aging,* 10(2), 155-68.

Serow, W. et al. (1986). 'Cost of Living Differentials and Elderly Inter-State Migration,' *Research on Aging,* 8(2), 317-27.

Shaver, N. (1985). *Aging Criminals.* Newbury Park, Calif.: Sage Publications.

Sherman, S. (1988). 'A Social-Psychological Perspective on the Continuum of Housing for the Elderly,' *Journal of Aging Studies,* 2(3), 229-41.

Smith, G. (1984). 'Spatial Aspects of the Shopping Patterns of the Urban Elderly: The Case of Central Area Apartment Dwellers,' *Canadian Journal on Aging,* 3(3), 133-46.

Solicitor General. (1985). *Canadian Urban Victimization Survey.* Bulletin No. 6: *Criminal Victimization of Elderly Canadians.* Ottawa: Ministry Secretariat, Programs Branch, Canada.

Speare, A. and J. Meyer. (1988). 'Types of Elderly Residential Mobility and Their Determinants,' *Journal of Gerontology: Social Sciences,* 43(3), S74-81.

Steffensmeier, D. (1987). 'The Invention of the "New" Senior Citizen Criminal,' *Research on Aging,* 9(2), 281-311.

Stone, L. and S. Fletcher. (1987). 'The Hypothesis of Age Patterns in Living Arrangement Passages,' pp. 288-310 in V. Marshall (ed.). *Aging in Canada: Social Perspectives.* Markham, Ont.: Fitzhenry and Whiteside.

Stone, L. and H. Frenken. (1988). *Canada's Seniors.* Ottawa: Minister of Supply and Services Canada.

Streib, G. et al. (1984). *Old Homes - New Families: Shared Living for the Elderly.* New York: Columbia University Press.

Sullivan, D. and S. Stevens. (1982). 'Snowbirds: Seasonal Migrants to the Sunbelt,' *Research on Aging,* 4(2), 159-77.

Tilson, D. (ed.). (1989). *Aging in Place: Supporting the Frail Elderly in Residential Environments.* Des Plaines, Ill.: Scott, Foresman & Company.

Tucker, R. et al. (1988). 'Older Anglophone Canadian Snowbirds in Florida: A Descriptive Profile,' *Canadian Journal on Aging,* 7(3), 218-32.

Ward, R. et al. (1988). *The Environment for Aging: Interpersonal, Social and Spatial Contexts.* Tuscaloosa, Ala.: University of Alabama Press.

Warnes, A. (ed.). (1982). *Geographical Perspectives on the Elderly.* New York: John Wiley and Sons.

Wilbanks, W. (1985). 'The Elderly Offender: Relative Frequency and Pattern of Offenses,' *International Journal of Aging and Human Development,* 20(4), 269-81.

Wilbanks, W. and P. Kim (eds.). (1984). *Elderly Criminals.* Washington, D.C.: University Press of America.

Windley, P. and G. Ernst (eds.). (1975). *Theory Development in Environment and Aging.* Washington, D.C.: Gerontological Society.

Windley, P. and R. Scheidt. (1980). 'Person Environment Dialectics: Implications for Competent Functioning in Old Age,' pp. 407-23 in L. Poon (ed.). *Aging in the 1980s.* Washington, D.C.: American Psychological Association.

Windley, P. and R. Scheidt. (1982). 'An Ecological Model of Mental Health among Small-Town Rural Elderly,' *Journal of Gerontology,* 37(2), 235-42.

Wiseman, R. (1980). 'Why Older People Move,' *Research on Aging,* 22(2), 141-54.

Wister, A. (1985). 'Living Arrangement Choices among the Elderly,' *Canadian Journal on Aging,* 4(3), 127-44.

Wister, A. (1989). 'Environmental Adaptation among Persons in Their Later Life,' *Research on Aging,* 11(3), 267-91.

Yin, P. (1985). *Victimization and the Aged.* Springfield, Ill.: Charles C. Thomas.

Part Four

AGING AND SOCIAL INSTITUTIONS

Social **institutions** are cultural products that persist from generation to generation. They provide value orientations, norms, and a structure for interaction within specific contexts in our daily lives. In preindustrial societies, the family and the tribe (and perhaps religion) were the major institutions; today, a number of socializing, regulative, cultural, and social institutions affect our lives throughout the life cycle.

Socializing institutions include the family, the peer group, and the educational system. These institutions normally have the greatest impact on our lives during childhood, adolescence, and early adulthood. During adulthood, the family continues to be an important institution, although relationships change as we gain or lose the roles of spouse, parent, or grandparent.

Regulative institutions include the economic, legal, and political systems. During adulthood, the economic system determines our life chances and lifestyle, both in terms of our earnings from employment and in how changes in the economy have an impact on individuals or on groups with common characteristics (for example, women, the working class, ethnic groups). In later life many adults utilize formal support programs designed to assist and care for the elderly. At this stage interaction between the individual and various levels of government bureaucracy may increase.

Cultural institutions include the arts, the mass media, religion, voluntary associations, recreation, sport, and science. We are involved in these institutions during our leisure time.

As will be seen throughout Part Four, involvement in social institutions varies by stage in the life cycle. As we age, positions within the various institutions are gained and lost. These role transitions may have a subsequent impact on social interaction and adjustment to the aging process. For example, a 30-year-old career woman with no children finds widowhood to be a markedly different experience from that of a 30-year-old widow with two young children and no career, or from that of a 70-year-old widow who has adult children and a social network of age peers who have also been widowed in recent years. In short, the adjustment to potentially traumatic status passages such as divorce, widowhood, unemployment, or retirement can be affected by a variety of sociodemographic characteristics, by past history, and by the degree of social support available, especially from within the family.

Part Four focuses on the changing patterns of social participation, and the impact of role transitions or status passages on the individual. For most adults, the family, the labor force, the economy, and leisure are major institutions that create opportunities for social interaction at all stages of the life cycle. Individuals voluntarily or involuntarily acquire and relinquish specific roles at particular stages in life. These transitions can lead to significant social pressures to maintain or to change existing behavioral patterns, often without the assistance of clear normative guidelines or role models. Furthermore, some transition points, such as the empty nest, divorce, retirement, or widowhood, have the potential to create personal crises that require adjustment and a change in lifestyle. Chapter 9 focuses on aging and family dynamics such as inter- and intragenerational relations and marital satisfaction over the life cycle, and the impact of divorce, the empty nest, retirement, and widowhood on the individual and on the family. Chapter 10 describes the informal and formal social support networks that assist the elderly to adapt and cope with changes in the aging process. A major subsection reviews the literature on elder abuse. This chapter also summarizes the issues and the processes associated with the development, implementation, and evaluation of public- and private-sector policies designed to assist older adults. In chapter 11, the effect of economic and employment history on social interaction during the middle and later years of life is discussed, and the process of retirement is examined in detail. This chapter also considers the economic status of women in later life. Finally, in chapter 12 where leisure is viewed as a cultural institution, patterns of social participation during leisure time are described and explained, particularly with respect to involvement in religion, politics, education, the media, and voluntary associations.

9
Aging and Family Dynamics

Health and Welfare Canada, Information Directorate

INTRODUCTION

The **family,** as both a biological unit and a social unit, is the basic institution in virtually every society. As a primary social group it provides an environment for the addition of new members, for child care and socialization, for affection and social bonding throughout the life cycle, and for emotional, social, economic, and health support in old age. Until recently, most research focused on the young nuclear family. There was much less interest in the interaction between nuclear families within an extended-family system, or in the dynamics of family interaction across the life cycle.

With increased life expectancy, decreased fertility, and the appearance of three-, four- or even five-generation families, scholars in demography, sociology, psychology, social gerontology, and family studies have increasingly studied the dynamics of interaction in the extended kinship system.[1] This interest has been further heightened by changing societal trends that have altered the structure of, and relationships within, the kinship system, particularly in the past two to three decades. As Gee (1987) observes, the timing of family life events has been altered — we marry at younger ages, if we marry; a decline in fertility rates results in smaller families and more childless couples; the age at which children leave home (the onset of the empty nest) is experienced earlier by parents (mid to late 40s); with increased life expectancy, more children have living grandparents, often into their 20s; the age at widowhood is later (nearly 70 rather than in the 50s at the turn of the century); increased divorce rates have led to more single-parent families, and increased remarriage rates have led to reconstituted families; and more women are engaged in careers and lifelong employment in the labor force. These macrosocietal changes have led to a redefinition of the kinship structure and of kinship relations across the life cycle.

The rapid changes that have occurred led in the 1960s and 1970s to the creation and perpetuation of a popular myth that the elderly are isolated from, and abandoned by, their families. Research, however, has clearly shown that families have not abandoned the elderly, although the functions of the family have been redefined by all generations (Aizenberg and Treas, 1985; Bengtson et al., 1985, 1990; Rosenthal, 1987a; Connidis, 1989a).

Research on the family kin network has focused on changes in kinship structure over time, on the status of the elderly within the family in various societies, on marital relations over the family life cycle, on the adjustment to the aging process within the family context, and on the onset and adjustment to family-related role transitions such as the empty nest, divorce, remarriage, and widowhood. Researchers have also examined the dynamics of interaction between adult children and aging parents, and between grandparents and grandchildren.

This chapter focuses on the structure and interpersonal interaction within the nuclear and extended family kinship system. For the most part, the evidence is presented from the perspective of the older members of the extended family. However, the perspectives of grandchildren and adult children must also be considered, since their views influence attitudes toward the elderly, the amount and type of support given, and the quantity and quality of intergenerational interaction. In the following chapter, the issues of caregiving, elder abuse, and social support within the family context are addressed.

The Kinship Structure

As a result of increased life expectancy and decreased fertility rates within succeeding generations, the family kinship system has become longer and therefore there are more vertical ties and intergenerational relationships within the multigenerational family (Knipscheer, 1988). One outcome of this process of verticalization is that family structures, and therefore relationships, have become more complex. For example, traditionally, at some stage in life, a woman might occupy the role of daughter, sister, granddaughter, wife, daughter-in-law, aunt, mother, grandmother, or widow. Today, with single-parent households, childless couples, separation, divorce, and remarriage in all generations, as well as extended longevity, a woman may also occupy the role of estranged or ex-wife, stepmother, step-grandmother, great-grandmother, or great-great-grandmother. As a result of these increased role opportunities, few adults reach the later stages of life with no surviving kin.[2] However, there are many different family structures in which the oldest surviving member may be located. Some possible structures include: (a) a married male with a spouse, one or more married children, one or more siblings, and many grandchildren; (b) a never-married female, with or without surviving siblings, and perhaps a few distant kin; (c) a very elderly widow, with no surviving children or siblings, but numerous grandchildren and great-grandchildren. It is the available family structure, along with friendship ties, that defines the support-group structure in the later years (Stone, 1988).

The most basic unit within the kinship system is the nuclear family, which, at least initially, consists of a mother, a father, and perhaps children. This unit is known as the family of procreation. After marriage, this unit becomes more salient to the young married couple than the family of orientation (their parents and siblings), although the ties to the family of orientation persist, and create the extended family. Today the kinship system may consist of infants and young children (Generation 5 or G5), a young married couple with or without children (G4), a postparental middle-aged couple (G3), an older retired couple (G2), and a very old widow (G1). One outcome of this increase in the number of older generations is that middle-aged adults are much more likely than in the past to have four living parents.

The extended family structure consists of three to five generations related by marriage and intermarriage. With increased mobility, a greater involvement by women in the labor force, and busy social and work lives, extended kinship interaction is increasingly difficult. Yet visiting, communication, and family assistance continue to varying degrees. This interaction is often facilitated and promoted by one or two members of the extended family, who take on the role of **kinkeeper** (Rosenthal, 1985; Spitze and Logan, 1989). This person maintains communication, facilitates contact and the exchange of goods and services, and monitors family re-

lationships by telephone, letters, or visits. Much of the kinkeeping within the extended family of orientation is undertaken by a grandmother or an older daughter who succeeds her; kinkeeping with in-laws within each generation is usually assumed by a daughter in her role as wife.

A kinkeeper is also often involved in the maintenance and transmission of family rituals (such as holidays, birthdays) that bring the generations together (Rosenthal and Marshall, 1988). The kinkeeper is also expected to play, or assumes the role of, 'comforter' or 'confidant,' thereby providing emotional support and advice within the extended family (Strain and Chappell, 1982; Rosenthal, 1987b). One outcome of divorce within a middle or older generation is that the role of kinkeeper may be lost for some segments of the kinship structure, thereby leading to decreased interaction between and within generations. As we will see later, the pattern of family interaction with other generations following a divorce can be greatly influenced by the custodial arrangement for children and by the degree of conflict that persists between the divorced couple.

Although separate homes for the extended family are the norm, in some cultures the elderly still live in the households of their children. Also, as we will see later, some social classes and ethnic groups are more likely to adhere to a cultural norm wherein the elderly are taken into the home of one of the adult children, usually a daughter or daughter-in-law. In most modernized societies the elderly prefer not to live with their adult children or with other relatives (highlight 9.1)

The majority of older people either live with a spouse (especially men) or they live alone (especially widows). Older adults do live with family members if they are very old or in poor health, if they have inadequate financial resources, or if they are widowed, unmarried, or divorced and can no longer live alone (Rosenthal, 1986). These extended households are most likely to be created when an elderly parent moves into the home of a son or daughter. Given increased divorce rates and an increase in the number of never-married persons, a middle-aged son or daughter may also move into the home of an elderly parent. Thus, hous-

HIGHLIGHT 9.1

INTIMACY AT A DISTANCE: THE CHOICE OF INDEPENDENT SENIORS

As noted elsewhere, most older Canadians live in their own homes within a few hours' drive of one or more of their children. Rather than living in the same home, or in a garden suite, older parents want to live independently, yet be close enough to visit. Even when health or economic losses dictate leaving the family home because it is no longer safe or the parents can no longer look after themselves, some variation of independent living is still sought. There is a reluctance on the part of older frail or failing parents to move in with an adult child. For example, 78 percent of Hamilton-area adults interviewed by Rosenthal (as cited by NACA, 1986) said that if the time came when they could not live on their own, they would rather live elsewhere than with their children. Similarly, in a study of older adults in London, Ontario, Connidis (1989a:5-7) found that living alone is the preferred arrangement. Moreover, if they were no longer able to live independently, 80 percent of the older persons reported that they would prefer to live in a seniors' facility rather than with a child. This preference for independent living is aptly illustrated by the following reasons given by those living in a seniors' residence in Ottawa (NACA, 1986:3):

A.T.:   When my doctor advised me that I shouldn't be living alone, my daughter was willing to have me move in with her, but I prefer the independence we have here.

V.S.:   My son lives in Toronto, and he used to worry about me, but now he knows that someone looks in on me every day. I looked after my mother-in-law for 14 years, and I decided that no one was going to go through that with me.

H.T.:   My son-in-law and grandsons are very supportive, but they respect my independence. They're only a phone call away if I need them, but I wouldn't want to be waiting around for them to call, nor would I ever want them to feel that they have to call me. I have my own life to live.

W.C.:   My family felt I shouldn't be living alone. My daughter has been very supportive, and I wouldn't want to have to get along without her — we speak on the telephone every day. She no longer worries because she knows we're well taken care of here.

V.W.:   I lived with my granddaughter and her husband and that would have worked out except that I began to feel isolated because they were away at work all day. We didn't live close to public transportation, and I began to feel I couldn't get out, especially in winter. I decided to move here because I'm the kind of person who likes to have other people around.

SOURCE: Reproduced with the consent of the National Advisory Council on Aging (NACA) and with the permission of the Minister of Supply and Services Canada, 1990.

ing arrangements for the extended family are being altered by the changing status of family members.

In summary, while the elderly who live alone may have less daily face-to-face contact with family members than in the past, most are not neglected by the extended family. Therefore, they are not dependent on impersonal social service bureaucracies for their survival, as is commonly assumed. Only those older adults who have no living kin, who have lost touch with kin because of past family conflicts or dissolution, and who are without close friends are likely to become dependent on public social services for care and survival in the later years.

In short, the idea that the elderly are isolated, abandoned, and kinless is a myth.

The Family Life Cycle

The developmental process whereby individuals move from one status to another within the family life cycle merits attention. In chapter 7 we learned that, on the macro level, cohorts pass through developmental stages of the life cycle from infancy to old age. Similarly, within the family context, individuals pass through different stages. These passages involve changes in role and status, some of which are cause for joyous celebration by the extended family (births and marriages), others of which bring grief and adjustment problems to the individual and to the family (widowhood and divorce).

Generally, the cycle begins when a new family of procreation is created through marriage. Then, at various intervals some or all of the following stages may occur: (1) the birth of the first child and the beginning of parenting and grandparenting; (2) the birth of subsequent children and the last child; (3) the departure of the last child from the family of orientation and the onset of the empty nest or postparental stage; (4) the death of a parent or grandparent; (5) the retirement of one or both members of the couple; and (6) the death of one spouse, which normally occurs during the later years but which may occur during middle adulthood for some. In addition, separation, divorce, unemployment, or retirement can create stress to which some or all members of the extended family must adjust. The following section describes some of the common factors that influence both personal adjustment and inter- and intragenerational interaction within the family context in the middle and later years of life.

Social Factors Influencing Family Dynamics

Introduction

The patterns of interaction within and between generations of the extended family and within the nuclear family are known as 'lineage relationships' (Bengtson et al., 1985, 1990). These are seldom homogeneous patterns within or between societies. Rather, a number of structural, stratification, and personal variables influence the quantity and quality of interaction within the kinship system. These factors, in turn, influence the type and amount of economic, social, and emotional resources that are available to be shared between members of the extended family.

Structural Variables

First, relatives must be available, and the more there are, particularly adult children, the greater the likelihood that the older generation will interact with them. However, the nature of the interaction and the amount and type of assistance given and received often depends on residential propinquity — that is, how close the relatives live to each other. Today, in addition to face-to-face interaction, the telephone plays a major role in maintaining relations between generations. However, the greater the distance between relatives, the less frequent the face-to-face or telephone interaction. In this situation it is likely that mutual support will be offered in the form of money or gifts rather than in services.

While most elderly persons appear to live within a one-hour drive of at least one child, this may more likely be the case for those who live in urban areas. Children raised in rural areas are more likely to move to a larger city that is more than one hour away. In this situation, relatives outside the family of procreation and neighbors tend to form the social and health support system for the elderly in the rural community.

Another structural factor influencing the level and type of social support and interaction between parents and adult children is the increased opportunity for young and middle-aged women to remain in the labor force. This pattern used to be more common among lower- or working-class families, where it was an economic necessity. However, changing social norms and values now encourage and provide opportunities for middle-class women to begin careers early in life, or to renew careers in midlife once children are in school. Hence, fewer middle-aged daughters or daughters-in-law are available for daily interaction, or to provide care for the elderly within the family.

Stratification Variables

As will be seen, the frequency and quality of interaction and support tend to be stronger along the mother-daughter line than along the son-parent line. This gender-related pattern is partially related to the fact that women are generally more concerned and involved in expressive rather than instrumental relationships at all stages of the life cycle. Although sons can act as caregivers in the absence of daughters, they seem to provide less direct support. Thus, parents without a daughter may be at a disadvantage in the later years when they need assistance, especially in terms of the quality of assistance. For example, they may receive financial aid from a son to hire a homemaker or nurse, but they will miss the personalized care that might be provided by a daughter.

Social class is another stratification variable that has an impact on family dynamics. A common pattern observed is that members of the middle class interact more with friends and colleagues outside the family, whereas those in the working class generally have stronger and more frequent interaction with kin. Furthermore, values pertaining to expected social and geographic mobility and economic independence are more prevalent among the middle class. A move to another city to further one's career during early and middle adulthood is viewed as necessary and acceptable both by aging middle-class parents and by their adult children, even if it means a lessening of contact.

A third stratification variable is ethnic or racial background. While it is relatively easy to accept stereotypical images of the structure and dynamics of particular racial or ethnic groups (for example, the older black matriarch as the family leader and anchor point), care must be taken not to generalize findings or images to all members of the group. Rather, there are differences between groups and within groups due to class, gender, ethnic, racial, and historical differences in values, opportunities, and emotional bonds.

The social situation of the elderly varies within ethnic groups in North America. In order to understand these differences, both the cultural heritage and the degree of assimilation of the elderly within each racial or ethnic group must be examined (Driedger and Chappell, 1987). Studies of the Japanese in North America (Kiefer, 1974; Kobata, 1979) have noted how immigration laws and patterns have influenced family dynamics. The Issei, or oldest generation in North America, were born in Japan and emigrated between 1885 and 1924; the Nisei were born in North America between 1910 and 1945 and never had contact with their grandparents; while the Sansei, or the third generation, were born after 1945, have had contact with their grandparents, and have begun to intermarry. Despite these historical and cultural differences, including language difficulties,

strong intergenerational and ethnic ties provide social contact and support for the elderly. Those Issei who have no surviving kin are usually cared for by Japanese community groups or religious institutions.

The one clear pattern that emerges from most studies of ethnic or racial families is the strong kinship ties and the greater dependence on family for social, housing, and economic support, not only in the later years but throughout the life cycle. Perhaps because of minority-group status and cultural values, a closely knit family unit is the primary resource, rather than friends or social organizations. Of course, if cultural values are weakened by greater assimilation, the primary resource for the elderly could change from the family to friends or social agencies.

Personal Variables

In addition to the foregoing structural and stratification variables, interaction within nuclear and extended families is influenced by personal variables unique to the individuals within particular families. For example, whether people are married, widowed, or divorced influences where they fit within the kinship structure and with whom they are likely to interact. Health status determines not only their ability to interact, but also how others in the family perceive them as recipients of affection and interaction. For the individual in poor health, some relationships with other family members may cease (for example, with siblings or grandchildren), while others will continue because of a sense of obligation on the part of the closest relatives (spouse or adult children).

The quality and type of interaction within the family unit is also influenced by personality, by affectional bonds built over time among specific members, and by values pertaining to the role of family in the lifestyle. For example, women and members of the lower class are generally more expressive in their interpersonal interaction, while men and members of the middle class are generally more instrumental in their interaction patterns. As a result, older widowers, unlike older widows, may lack the skills and support network necessary to foster a suitable adjustment to single status in the later years.

In summary, there is no typical family structure, nor are there modal patterns of interaction within and between the generations. Rather, there is some variation in structure and great variation in frequency, type, and quality of interaction. These differences can be partially accounted for by demographic and sociohistorical variables; by structural variables in the larger society; by the processes of gender, racial, and class stratification; and by individual differences in health status, personality, and values among members of specific families.

Theoretical Perspectives on the Aging Family

Although many of the theoretical perspectives presented in chapter 4 could be applied to the study of family dynamics at different stages in the life cycle, much family research has been atheoretical, thereby resulting in a description rather than an explanation of family phenomena. Because role transitions and status passages influence and regulate patterns of social interaction within the extended family, both a structural-functionalist and an interactionist perspective may be useful in explaining interaction within the kinship structure (George, 1980:1-6; Nett, 1988:273-95). The structural perspective explains the process whereby an individual acquires, via socialization, the behavioral rights and duties held by society to be associated with particular familial roles. This process is more passive and involves 'role taking' (Turner, 1962).

In contrast, the interactionist perspective applies to the micro level of analysis (that is, within a particular extended-family structure) and accounts for individual interpretation and negotiation of role relationships. This process is more active and involves 'role making' (Turner, 1962) as the individual adapts to and modifies his or her unique family situation as it changes throughout the life course. For example, some children, regardless of age, will always accept a subordinate, submissive role relationship with their parents; others will interpret and negotiate changes in the relationship as they mature. As a result, from the perspective of the child, the child-parent relationship may pass through stages of subordination, equality, and dominance. The latter relationship may occur if the

parents experience a serious loss of health or economic status in the later years, thereby necessitating a reversal to a childlike, dependent status.

A third perspective that has application to family dynamics is exchange theory. As family members pass through various developmental stages and acquire or lose roles, role relationships are renegotiated. During this process of negotiation and exchange, the goal is to attain a mutually satisfying relationship characterized by cooperation rather than conflict. An attempt is made to balance the perceived costs and the rewards of the relationship. Similarly, exchange characterizes the process whereby a potentially supportive relationship is negotiated between adult children and their elderly parents, and between members of a married couple throughout the marriage. However, in some instances (such as the divorce of an adult child or sibling conflict about parent care) conflict between or within the generations may prevail, and a conflict rather than an exchange perspective may be more appropriate for the study of changing family relationships (see chapter 10).

In summary, while a number of theoretical perspectives might be employed to increase the level of explanation, few studies of the aging family have used a theoretical framework to guide research. As a result, while many descriptive facts and patterns are available, we do not really understand why they exist or why they may change over time. The following sections present the current state of knowledge with respect to intragenerational relations, intergenerational relations, and the process of adaptation by the individual and the family to major role transitions during the middle and later years of life.

INTRAGENERATIONAL FAMILY RELATIONS

Marital Satisfaction and Adjustment through the Life Cycle

There appears to be a relationship between number of years of marriage and reported marital satisfaction.[3] While there may be cycles

FIGURE **9.1**

FOUR POSSIBLE PATTERNS OF MARITAL SATISFACTION OVER THE LIFE COURSE

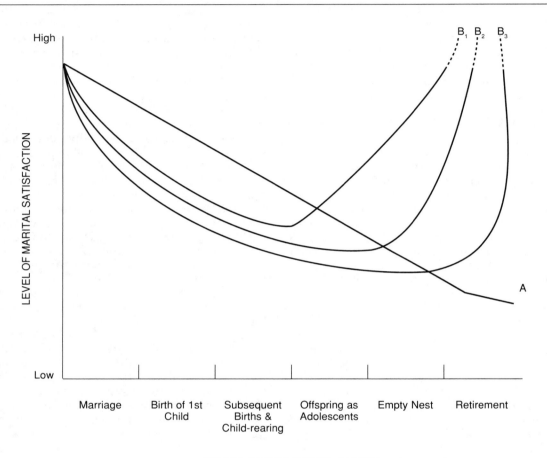

STAGES IN THE MARITAL CAREER

of enchantment and disenchantment with marriage, there are generally two different patterns of satisfaction across the marriage career (see figure 9.1). First, there may be a gradual and linear decline in marital satisfaction across all stages of the marriage cycle (pattern A). The alternative pattern suggests that the relationship is curvilinear (pattern B). At present, the curvilinear pattern has the great-

est support in the research literature (George, 1980:80; Hess and Soldo, 1985; Mouser et al; 1985; Connidis, 1989a). However, individual variations in the base of the curve and in the height of the curve in the later years have been observed. Curve B1 suggests that the low point occurs when children are adolescents; B2 suggests that it occurs when the last child leaves home; and B3 suggests that it occurs just prior to, or at, the husband's retirement. At these transition points both husbands and wives may experience a redefinition of their marital roles. For example, when the children leave home there may be a shift in focus from the children to each other, or to a greater commitment to other interests. Similarly, at retirement, the presence of the husband in the wife's daily routine and responsibilities can be either a source of increasing companionship or a source of conflict if her domestic role or previous lifestyle is partially usurped or altered. This stage may also require that her daily routine be changed to meet the husband's schedule. There is a continuing debate as to whether the level of satisfaction is actually higher in the later years than it is during the honeymoon and in the years before children arrive. This hypothetical pattern is reflected by the extension upward (dotted lines) of the three curvilinear paths.

Another pattern may show the relationship reaching a low point at either the empty-nest stage or the retirement stage, and then either declining or beginning to increase. Both of these transition points provide the opportunity either for a renewal of the marriage and increasing marital satisfaction, or for dissatisfaction on the part of one or both partners. In this latter situation, the disharmony is often resolved by separation and divorce when the child-rearing or occupational responsibilities have been completed.

Given that the curvilinear pattern of marital satisfaction appears to have some research support, how can this pattern be explained? While a definitive answer is not available, Abu-Laban (1980) has suggested that the peaks of satisfaction at the early and later stages of the marriage may reflect the similar lifestyles of the two partners. Both stages are adult-centered and childfree, both partners have time to engage in activities together, household responsibilities can be shared, and the level of income (and thus expectations and needs) is lower than in the intervening period.

The decline in marital satisfaction during the middle years often results from strain created by child-rearing responsibilities and demands on parental time; by occupational strain, especially for upwardly striving men or women; by the onset of personality, value, or behavioral changes in one member but not in the other; by the declining health of one member, which restricts the lifestyle of both members; by the wife entering the labor force; and by the general tendency for the interpersonal attraction in any relationship to decline with time. Thus, for a variety of reasons, the initially high level of satisfaction declines until late in the middle years or until retirement, when it begins to increase again, perhaps even rising to higher levels as the meaning of the marriage changes for some couples.

High levels of marital satisfaction may be expressed by different types of relationships. Medley (1977) suggests that in the postretirement years there are three types of conjugal relationships: (1) the husband-wife relationship, wherein the respective marital roles are central to the couple's life and other relationships are secondary; (2) the parent-child relationship, wherein one member assumes the role of protective and dominant parent when the other member experiences a decline in health and becomes more dependent on the other; and (3) the associate relationship, wherein the members are friends but the central focus for each of them is outside the marital relationship.

To date, research evidence is lacking to determine whether couples adopt one of these lifestyles after both spouses are retired, or whether they develop one of these patterns as their social situation changes. While it is quite possible that the parent-child relationship may evolve if both members of the dyad survive well into the later years of life, it is likely that the husband-wife or the associate relationship, both of which represent opposite ends of a continuum, have been in existence for years. That is, because of continuity in lifestyle, the style of marriage adopted in the earlier years is likely to be followed in the later years, especially if the style has led to a marital relationship that is at least minimally satisfactory for both partners.

Another type of marital relationship occurring in the later years is referred to as the 'married widow' or 'married widower,' wherein one partner is institutionalized because of chronic illness. The spouse who remains in the community, while married, has a lifestyle similar to that of a widow or widower. Yet, this individual must cope with two conflicting roles:

(1) he or she is the spouse of an institutionalized partner, and (2) he or she is a spouse who is single within the community. An identity crisis may develop because of this marginal status. The healthy partner must share the care of the spouse with the institutional employees, who have the final say on disputed issues; in the community, he or she is not free to establish new social or sexual relationships or to start a new life.

In summary, among the current cohort of elderly persons, high levels of marital satisfaction are generally reported, especially by men. However, this finding may partially result from these factors: unsuccessful marriages were terminated in middle life; this cohort holds traditional values about the permanence of marriage (Holahan, 1984); and people tend to respond to questions in a socially desirable manner. Later in the chapter you will learn that the incidences of divorce, dating, and remarriage in later life are increasing. However, these increases are largely due to the increased size of this age group rather than to an increase in the proportion of marriage breakdowns.

Sibling Interaction in the Later Years

The sibling relationship involves a shared genetic and cultural heritage and is a unique relationship in that it persists from birth to death, with varying degrees of contact and conflict across the life course. As a result, most older adults, especially men, have a sibling. Yet, until recently, little attention has been devoted to this relationship during the middle and later years of life (Lamb and Sutton-Smith, 1982; Gold, 1987; Bedford and Gold, 1989; Connidis, 1989a, 1989b).

The general life-cycle pattern of sibling relationships involves three stages: (1) frequent interaction during childhood and adolescence until departure from the family of orientation; (2) a drifting apart to varying degrees after entrance into the labor force and marriage;[4] and (3) a renewal of more frequent interaction in the later years. This renewal may increase when the children leave home, when they jointly contribute to the care of an ailing parent, or upon the death of one or both parents.[5] How-

ever, contact is unlikely to be renewed if the past relationship was characterized by rivalry and conflict (more likely between brothers who compete academically, athletically, and in their careers), if one or both of the respective in-laws are perceived as incompatible, if care of a frail parent or settlement of the parent's estate has created conflict, or if distance or health prohibits regular visiting.

Gender, marital status, and chronological age differences also appear to influence sibling relationships in the later years. First, as at all stages of life, the female linkage within a family tends to be strong and pervasive: among older people, sister-sister ties are stronger than sister-brother relationships. Moreover, older sisters may provide economic and social security for a brother who is a widower or a bachelor. In effect, the sister may begin to serve as a surrogate wife or mother for the brother.

Cultural values and historical tendencies may also influence the quantity and quality of sibling interaction among members of some racial or ethnic groups. Within cultural groups where a high value is placed on family solidarity and mutual assistance (for example, the Japanese), sibling links are more likely to exist in the later years, especially if one of the siblings is widowed and experiences a decline in health or economic status.

Regardless of ethnic heritage, marital status may influence sibling links in later life. Research studies generally find that the never-married, the widowed, and the divorced have more frequent interaction with their siblings than those who are married. Finally, and not surprisingly, even though interaction with siblings in later life may be greater than during midlife, there is a decline in frequency among the very old as health and mobility decrease, unless two or more siblings agree to share a household.

In summary, siblings may be the next-best resource after children in the later years, especially among sisters and for those who are widowed or were never married. In fact, older widowed or never-married female siblings may unite to create a household in the later years in order to provide each other with social, emotional, and economic support. Unfortunately, with declining family size this resource may be less readily available in the future. Considerable research is needed to enable us to better understand the nature of sibling relationships, particularly with respect to their quality and meaning during the middle and later years of life.

INTERGENERATIONAL FAMILY RELATIONS

Parent and Adult Child Interaction

Introduction

Being a parent involves interaction with children throughout the life cycle. As Emily Nett (1988:291) noted, 'the most stable and important relationship in our times appears to be the parent/child bond, not the husband/wife bond. It is also the one relationship which no person can avoid (i.e., with his or her parent, if not with offspring of her or his own).' This lineage interaction can vary in frequency, quality, direction, and type depending on the age, interests, and needs of the two generations. For example, during early childhood the relationship is constant and largely unidirectional, in that the children are highly dependent on the parents for support. During adolescence, the interaction declines in frequency and becomes more reciprocal as both generations influence each other. The relationship at this time may be characterized by conflict over values, beliefs, and behaviors. As children leave home and eventually establish their own nuclear families, and begin to experience interaction from the parental perspective, the relationship with their own parents may increase or decrease in quantity and quality as new demands are placed on them. When the children enter midlife[6] and the parents grow old, interaction may increase, especially if an elderly parent becomes more dependent on an adult child. In this situation the relationship once again becomes primarily unidirectional, in that more help is given to the parent, especially with respect to home and health care. However, there may be a continuing economic exchange in both directions, with the direction from parent-to-child or child-to-parent depending on the socioeconomic status of the two generations (Knipscheer and Bevers, 1985). Finally, as the children enter the later

years, as many as 10 percent may have a very elderly parent. In contrast, some older adults entering retirement may be childless due to choice, death of an offspring, loss of contact following divorce, or abandonment of a child earlier in life.

In gerontology three main issues have dominated the literature concerning relationships between older parents and their adult children. The first, which will be discussed in this section, concerns the amount and the quality of interaction or contact while the aging parent is totally independent of family care. The second issue, discussed in chapter 10, addresses the amount and the quality of support provided to elderly parents who require increasing levels of physical, emotional, or financial assistance in adapting to the losses of the later years. A third emerging issue is the amount of support provided by aging parents to adult children who experience trauma (for example, divorce, death of a child, unemployment, widowhood) in early or middle adulthood (Connidis, 1989a:56-58).

The majority of older adults see at least one of their children on a regular basis, although most face-to-face contact tends to be with a daughter. However, if a daughter is employed, there is less contact. Similarly, there is generally less contact among the middle and upper classes, primarily because the children are less likely to reside or work near the parental home. Numerous studies have indicated that distance is a major factor in both the frequency and the type of social contact between aging parents and adult children (Climo, 1988; De Wit and Frankel, 1988; De Wit et al., 1988; Frankel and De Wit, 1989; Crimmins and Ingegneri, 1990). A second major factor is the health status of the older parent. When health declines and the nature of the relationship changes from being primarily social to one of caregiving, the frequency of contact may increase. However, in some situations, because of the burden associated with the contact, the quality may decrease (see chapter 10).

The onset of varying degrees of dependency does, however, introduce the possibility of a shift in power from the parent to the child. Depending on the quality of the relationship during the earlier years, the onset of dependency can provide an opportunity to reward the parent for past debts, or to seek revenge for real or imagined parental injustice during childhood or adolescence. For example, in recent years there has been an increase in the reported cases of what has been referred to as elder abuse or 'granny bashing.' That is, elderly parents may be verbally, physically, or emotionally abused by their children, who may imprison, neglect, or harass them (see chapter 10).

Transitions such as illness, the death of one parent, financial difficulties for the elderly person, or a divorce or financial crisis on the part of the offspring[7] can increase parent-child interaction, conflict, and dependency during middle adulthood. These transitions can lead to three types of conflict: (1) continuing conflict, wherein the underlying tension has always been present with respect to lifestyle, values, morals, friends, or religion; (2) new conflict, wherein parents and adult children disagree on their respective roles in caring for the surviving parent or in the raising of the third generation; and (3) reactivated conflict, which was present and unresolved before the child left home, and which reappears because of renewed or increased interaction. This reactivated conflict is frequently based on differing perceptions of the degree of independence each should experience, and of the extent to which the child perceives himself or herself as being accepted or rejected by the parent throughout life (Steinman, 1979; Mangen, 1986).

Although the possibility of overt conflict and dependency exists within the parent-child relationship, the prevailing evidence suggests that the role relationship is not usually characterized by conflict, nor are most of the elderly abandoned by or alienated from their families. Rather, the immediate family is still the predominant institution for the provision of physical, emotional, and economic support to the elderly, and the extended family is the major source of social interaction within the community. For example, Marshall et al. (1981) noted that three dimensions of health care are provided to parents by adult children. These include concern about and monitoring of the parents' health; provision of care in a crisis situation; and long-term, routine health care of the very elderly parent.

Most older people, therefore, value and experience personal meaning and satisfaction in their relationships with adult children. For some, the adult child becomes their best friend and confidant, although the spouse and age peers continue to play an important role in their social world (Connidis and Davies, 1990). Interestingly, but not surprisingly, as some siblings may suspect, and as Brackbill et al. (1988) found, some parents favor the 'perfect child' who is more likely to be married, to be better educated, and to have achieved higher occupational success. Moreover, Brackbill et al. found that the elderly parents reported having more contact with the favored child.

The high degree of reported intergenerational solidarity between older parents and their children was hypothesized by Bengtson and his colleagues to be the result of interaction within six different dimensions of solidarity (Bengtson et al., 1985, 1990; Rosenthal, 1987a). Where individuals report high positive scores on the dimensions, the relationship is considered to be solid and cohesive. The six dimensions of solidarity include: *family structure* (the number and the type of relatives and their geographical proximity, the household structure); *associational* (the type and the frequency of interaction with relatives and the nature and the meaning of the activities); *functional* (the amount of exchange of financial assistance and service support); *affectional* (the positive sentiments and feelings derived from the relationship); *consensual* (the degree of agreement between the generations about values, opinions, and beliefs external to the family); and *normative* (the degree to which members of both generations share expectations about family obligations and family life). An excellent example of the normative dimension of solidarity is the degree of agreement among farm families about the value of transferring the ownership and operation of the family farm from generation to generation (see highlight 9.2).

Grandparent and Grandchild Interaction

Introduction

The likelihood of a grandchild interacting with a grandparent increases with the longev-

HIGHLIGHT 9.2

NORMATIVE INTERGENERATIONAL EXPECTATIONS: THE TRANSFER OF THE FAMILY FARM

While there are many types of family business, none is so intimately tied to an extended family as the family farm, which is normally passed from generation to generation. Indeed, this norm of farm transfer is thought to foster intergenerational harmony as all members work to maintain the continuity of the farm within the kinship system. Economic hardships for farmers, smaller families, and the 'lure of the city' for sons and daughters may mean that this type of transfer is less likely today. However, an orientation toward family continuity in the ownership of the farm business still persists, especially if the farm has been associated with the family name for two or more generations (Keating, 1986).

During midlife, the current owner, if he hopes to retain at least one offspring in the family business, begins to reduce his management and work responsibilities while maintaining sufficient control and involvement to generate an adequate income for the retirement years. In effect, retaining ownership is a form of old-age security. The long-standing economic goal of farmers who value family continuity of ownership has been to build sufficient equity and income to support two generations — the older retiring owner (the father) and the younger incoming owner (usually a son or son-in-law). If this equity cannot be forecast when a child is in his or her early 20s, the child may leave to pursue a more stable and secure career elsewhere. Most farmers seem to put off the actual transfer of ownership as long as possible. This delay may create tension and conflict between the generations. In this situation the mother often is required to play a mediating role between the father and the son to facilitate a more harmonious transfer of ownership and responsibility.

In a study of 315 Alberta farm owners 50 years of age and older, Keating (1986) found that the average number of years that these farms had been in a family was 42, with a range from 2 to 104 years. The average net worth of the farm operations was $753,000. She found that the older owner was more likely to value and adhere to a norm of family continuity if he was willing to reduce the amount of farm work so that the next generation could develop farm skills under his supervision. This reduction also symbolically indicated that the intergenerational transfer would occur. The norm of family continuity was also more likely to be held by both generations if a son or daughter continued to live and work on the farm at the time the father began to reduce his workload.

In a similar study, Selles (1987) examined the process of transfer among nine pairs of Dutch Canadian fathers and sons in northern Alberta. He found that the retirement of the father took place in three stages. Partial retirement occurred when sons increased their involvement in field work, allowing the father to focus on yard work, off-farm interests, and farm management. This process was hastened if the son was married. In the second stage, semiretirement, management and ownership of the home quarter of the property was transferred to the son, and the father continued to work, but now he worked for the son. The final stage, full retirement, often occurred when the father's health deteriorated to the point where he could no longer work on the farm. Selles (1987) noted that this pattern of intergenerational transfer reflected the faith and beliefs of the farmers' Dutch Reformed heritage.

The importance of religious and ethnic values and beliefs in property transfer is often a reflection of beliefs and practices brought to North America from the native land. For example, Quadagno and Janzen (1987) conducted an elaborate case study of a Mennonite family that migrated from Russia to Kansas in 1874. Not long before the family emigrated, the twenty-five article Inheritance Rules were passed. These were based on social principles and biblical precepts to which the Mennonites adhered. A basic assumption of these inheritance rules was that land and estate capital accumulated by the oldest generation was the property of the entire kin group, and resources were to be shared equally among heirs. A pattern similar to the one noted above, that practiced by Dutch Canadians in northern Alberta almost 100 years later, was found: after the family resources had been shared to help each child get established in life, a daughter (and her family) received the family home and ownership of the family farm as her share. Once the daughter's family began to operate the farm, the elderly parents built a small home on the property and gradually withdrew from full-time farming as their health deteriorated.

SOURCE: Adapted from Keating (1986), Quadagno and Janzen (1987), Selles (1987).

ity of the grandparent, and is greater the earlier children are born to a couple. Today, over 90 percent of all children in North America have at least one living grandparent at age 10, while approximately 75 percent have one living grandparent at age 20. Yet, because of a declining birth rate (as reflected in smaller families and childless marriages), surviving grandparents have fewer grandchildren than in the past. Also, with an increasing incidence both of divorce and of the number of children that never marry, many older persons never have the opportunity to play the role, or never become grandparents. Also, because of increased geographical mobility in this century, face-to-face contact is less frequent than it was in the past. Finally, although grandparenting is possible during the middle-aged years because of marriage at an early age, most grandparents are approaching the retirement years when they acquire the role.

Scholarly interest in the role of grandparent and the relationship between grandparents and grandchildren has increased as multigenerational families have become more common, and as the age of grandparenthood has expanded (Bengtson and Robertson, 1985; Cherlin and Furstenberg, 1986; Connidis, 1989a). Today, an adult may enter this role in the late 30s and remain in the role until death forty or more years later. At the same time, however, the lifestyle of grandparents has changed from one of being primarily retired to one where both grandparents may be highly involved in the labor force, and, once retired, more interested in pursuing leisure interests than domestic interests — at least for much of the year. In this section we examine the role of grandparent, the nature and quality of the grandparent-grandchild relationship, and the impact of a divorce in the middle generation on the grandparent-grandchild relationship.

The Role of Grandparent

Unlike most other familial roles, the role of grandparent is acquired involuntarily, and the individual subsequently enacts the role in varying ways. The extent and style of the enactment, at least in the early stages, are greatly influenced by four factors: residential proximity; the extent to which parents act as mediators between the grandparents and the grandchildren by providing opportunities for the first and third generations to interact; the lifestyle, personality, and employment status of the older generation; and the age of the grandchildren (Hagestad, 1985; Kivnick, 1985; Troll, 1985). The meaning and satisfaction attached to the role often depend on the degree of interest or commitment on the part of an individual. In this sense, the role of grandparent is more a personal experience than an institutionalized role with specific rights, responsibilities, or norms. In fact, like retirement, grandparenting has been labeled a 'roleless' role because there are no definitive responsibilities or rights attached to the role. It has also been labeled a 'sexless' role, in that there is often little role differentiation between grandmothers and grandfathers.[8] Both can engage in child care, teaching, and friendship with one or more of their grandchildren.

The stereotypical lifestyle of a grandparent has often been portrayed as involving child care, baking cookies and preparing large family meals at holidays, sitting on the front porch in a rocking chair, serving as a fishing companion for a grandchild, or acting as 'Mr. Fix-It' for the extended family and neighbors. In reality, however, the image and style of grandparenting is very different. The way in which the role is played may vary by social class and subculture. Because of the large number of middle-aged women in the labor force, and increased longevity, grandmothers are more likely to be employed and to have little time or interest in surrogate parenting. Grandfathers may not retire as early as they did in the past, and may not have time to play the role until the grandchildren are into middle or late adolescence.

In recent years, grandparents are more likely to live as couples, with their own interests and lifestyles, than as widows or widowers. In addition, a surviving grandparent is less likely to enter an offspring's household until after the grandchild has left the home. Moreover, with increased longevity, a grandmother in an extended family may be required to direct her energy and resources to caring for her spouse or for her own elderly mother. Similarly, the relationship changes as the grandchild ages

(Matthews and Sprey, 1985). During infancy, grandchildren are initially passive partners who become more active in the relationship as they move through childhood. In the teenage years, however, grandchildren begin to establish their own social world and the frequency of contact with grandparents may decrease, except at family gatherings. Finally, as grandchildren enter university or the labor force, the contact may increase if they live close to their grandparents. At this stage, the relationship may involve providing some type of social support to an elderly grandparent, thereby assisting their own parents with caregiving.

With respect to social, racial, or ethnic differences in grandparenting, there appear to be different interpretations of the role, given that there are few institutionalized norms to guide behavior. In one of the few studies on the influence of social class on grandparenting, Clavan (1978) found differences between the middle and lower classes. In the middle class, the role is more peripheral, perhaps because more grandmothers are employed and have different gender role definitions; there is little differentiation between grandmother and grandfather; financial aid is given more frequently than services; and the role is more symbolic and ritualistic (that is, it is expressed during family celebrations at confirmations, bar mitzvahs, Thanksgiving, Christmas, or Easter).

Within the working class, Clavan (1978) found that grandparents, especially the grandmother, are more likely to be integrated into the family and to play a functionally central role in child rearing. This occurs because the grandparents are more likely to live close to their offspring, because both parents are more likely to work, and because there may be a higher incidence of single-parent families and a need for a surrogate mother or father. In short, grandparenting among the working class, and within some racial and ethnic subcultures that are largely made up of working-class members, is more likely to be a 'real' role that involves functional integration into the daily life of the extended family.

These class differences highlight the mediating or gatekeeping role played by the middle generation. The attitudes and the beliefs of the parents about the expectations and the rights of

grandparenthood, and the willingness of the parents to provide opportunities for contact, are established early in the life of the grandchild. Although geographic distance can be a limiting factor, the encouragement of regular visits in either direction can offset the distance factor. Often, the relationship with maternal grandparents tends to be stronger because the mother is the prime caretaker of the child, and as we learned earlier, mother-daughter ties are normally stronger than mother-son ties. Similarly, given a divorce in the middle generation, and the likelihood that the mother has custodial care of the children, the contact with maternal grandparents is likely to increase; contact with the paternal grandparents may decrease or cease altogether.

The impact of a divorce in the middle generation on the grandparent-grandchild relationship has generated considerable research and legal interest in recent years.[9] This transition is a crisis event that affects not only the divorcing couple and their children, but also the maternal and paternal grandparents. For many grandparents, especially on the paternal side if the mother retains custody of the children, the frequency of interaction can decline significantly. This is likely to occur where the separation and the divorce are highly conflictual and revenge is sought by withholding access to grandchildren, or where the custodial parent moves to another community to establish a new life. In this situation, grandparents have sought and gained legal visitation rights through the courts. Moreover, some jurisdictions now guarantee grandparental access to grandchildren through civil laws pertaining to separation and divorce.[10] On the maternal side, the interaction may significantly increase, especially if the daughter moves, either to live with or to be closer to her family of orientation. Depending on the age of the children, in this situation the maternal grandparents may play a surrogate parenting role while the mother reestablishes her work and social life. Thus, the middle generation continues to play a gatekeeping role in facilitating or inhibiting the grandparent-grandchild relationship following a divorce (Gladstone, 1989).

The stress of a divorce does not only affect the divorcing couple and their children. For the current cohort of older grandparents, a divorce within the family is stressful because the ending of a marriage does not fit with the basic values and beliefs about marriage held by their generation. Because the divorce often occurs unexpectedly, most parents of the divorcing couple are poorly prepared to cope with the crisis, and they often feel powerless and helpless. In some situations, partly because divorce is against their basic values, conflict between the older parent and the adult child may evolve, thereby adding to family conflict and stress. This conflict or unwillingness to accept the changing status of a son or a daughter is also likely to lead to decreased interaction with grandchildren, at least in the initial stages of shock and anger. Later, stress in the parent-adult child relationship may be initiated by conflict over their perceived or actual role in a reconstituted marriage, where they immediately, or later, became step-grandparents. From the perspective of the child of a divorced couple, a remarriage of one or both parents may allow them to 'acquire' new sets of step-grandparents. Indeed, elementary school children have been heard to proudly boast of how many grandparents they have as result of both parents remarrying!

Institutionalization is another factor that influences the role of grandparent. In most instances, the role ceases, like many others, when an older person enters an institution. At this transition point, opportunities and the ability to play the role are usually lost. In order to compensate for this loss, a foster-grandparent program has been initiated in many communities. This program provides emotional and psychological support for young children who do not have grandparents, or for orphaned or foster children who may have little or no contact with adults other than foster parents or social workers. For elderly people living in a variety of institutionalized settings, the adoption of a foster grandchild may enhance their self-esteem and morale, and decrease their feelings of loneliness. In some communities, the elderly are hired to play a surrogate teaching and caring role for an institutionalized child who is emotionally, socially, or intellectually deprived. This arrangement provides a modest source of income for elderly people, and per-

mits them to engage in necessary and meaningful social support. Similarly, in order to provide companionship for preschoolers and the elderly, some day-care centers have been located within or adjacent to senior citizen homes or adult drop-in centers. Here, elderly volunteers teach or play with preschoolers, thereby acting as surrogate teachers, grandparents, or simply older friends.

Grandparents' and Grandchildren's Perceptions of Their Role

As noted earlier, involvement in the grandparent role is affected by residential propinquity, by the personal needs and interests of the grandchildren and grandparents, by the mediating role of the parents, and by social class and subcultural variations. Few studies have examined the meaning and style of grandparenthood as perceived by the grandparent. Kivnick (1982) noted that the meaning of grandparenthood evolves from people's own experience as grandchildren, their experience as parents, and ultimately their own experience in the role of grandparents. These experiences result in a multidimensional view of the meaning of grandparenthood that includes five elements: (1) grandparenthood is central to the lifestyle of the grandparent; (2) grandparenthood means being a valued elder and serving as a resource center; (3) grandparenthood assures the immortality of the family name; (4) grandparenthood provides an opportunity to spoil and indulge grandchildren; and (5) grandparenthood provides an opportunity to become reinvolved with one's own history and that of the family.

Although there appear to be some distinct styles of grandparenting, it is not clear whether the style adopted by a given individual is related to the lifestyle of the grandparent that was present before the third generation is born, whether it is influenced by the mediation style of parents, or whether it evolves and changes through interaction with one or more specific grandchildren. Since grandparents sometimes have a preferred grandchild, it may be that the meaning and style adopted vary according to the partners involved in a specific grandchild-grandparent relationship.

The role relationship between grandpar-

HIGHLIGHT **9.3**

A THIRD-GRADER'S PERCEPTION OF A GRANDMOTHER

A grandma is a lady who has no children of her own, so she likes other people's little boys and girls.

A grandfather is a man grandmother. He goes for walks with the boys and they talk about fishing and things like that.

Grandmas don't have to do anything except be there. They're so old they shouldn't play hard. It is enough if they drive us to the supermarket where the pretend horse is and have lots of dimes ready. Or, if they take us for walks, they should slow down past things like pretty leaves or caterpillars. And they should never say, 'Hurry up!'

Usually they are fat, but not too fat. They wear glasses and funny underwear. They can take their teeth and gums off.

They don't have to be smart, only answer questions like why dogs hate cats, and how come God isn't married.

They don't talk baby talk like visitors do because it is hard to understand.

When they read to us they don't skip words and they don't mind if it is the same story.

Grandmas are the only grownups who have got time — so everybody should have a grandmother, especially if you don't have television.

SOURCE: Reprinted with permission from Huyck (1974:77).

---

ents and grandchildren has been examined mainly from the perspective of the grandparent. A few studies, however, have dealt with the perceptions and experiences of grandchildren (Robertson, 1976; Hartshorne and Manaster, 1982; Matthews and Sprey, 1985). These studies reveal that children who interact with grandparents have fewer prejudices about the elderly and growing old; that the parents play a significant mediating role in the quantity and the quality of interaction; that as the grandchildren grow older, they view the grandparent as less of a playmate, baby-sitter and gift-giver, and more of a companion for whom they feel responsible; that granddaughter-grandmother ties are stronger than grandfather-grandchildren ties; and that perceptions and interactions vary by the age of the grandchild. Highlight 9.3 illustrates the view of one third-grader who responded to a teacher's request to define a grandmother.

In summary, most children in North America have at least one living grandparent with whom they have some degree of interaction. From the perspective of the grandparent, the role has different meanings, and different styles of involvement can be adopted. At present, especially for middle-aged grandparents, the role is not as salient as it was for their parents,

primarily because of altered lifestyles between the two generations. It does seem to be more salient for the working class, for widows, for those who are less educated, for those who are older, for those who are unemployed or retired, and for those who are not involved in community affairs. Those who fall into the above categories find the extended family to be a major source of interest and social interaction, and are more likely to seek active involvement in familial roles such as grandparenting, especially if their own children encourage this involvement.

ROLE TRANSITIONS AND STATUS PASSAGES WITHIN THE FAMILY

Introduction

In contrast to role change, which involves a change in role requirements and expectations with no change in status (for example, the behavioral expectations for a son or daughter at different stages in the life cycle), role transitions occur when status is gained or lost (by marriage, parenthood, retirement, widowhood, divorce) (George, 1980:6-7). For some, the process of role transition and status passage is voluntary, expected, and can be planned for as part of the developmental process of aging (in the case of marriage, parenthood, or remarriage). Adjustment to the transition and to the new status is usually satisfactory. Other transitions may represent a discontinuous and traumatic event (for example, widowhood, retirement, an empty nest). As a result, a transition can occur suddenly, and there may be little opportunity (divorce, widowhood) or willingness (empty nest, retirement) to be socialized for the new status. This type of transition can be stressful and can result in an uncertain identity in the acquired status.

In order to explain the reaction and adjustment to role transitions in later life, the model outlined earlier in figure 7.1 has been employed to explain such role transitions as retirement, the empty nest, grandparenthood, widowhood, remarriage, and residential relocation (George, 1980). This model argues that with the onset of the role transition, the individual must adjust to new patterns of social interaction and to a change in identity. Some may perceive the transition as stressful; if so, their response and subsequent degree of adjustment will be influenced by coping resources, personal skills, support systems, and socialization experiences. These same factors can serve a preventive function by inhibiting the onset of stressful responses to the role exit or role entrance.

Most role transitions in middle or later life involve a change in status within the nuclear or extended family, a change in the family structure, or a change in family dynamics. As a result, the family can play a major role in helping the individual experiencing the transition to adjust to the new status and to create a new identity, if necessary (for example, following the empty nest, a divorce, widowhood, or retirement). The following sections examine the impact of some common family-based transitions and status passages. Grandparenthood, a major role transition, is not discussed here, given the extensive review of this role in the previous section.

The Empty Nest

With the departure of the last child from the home, formal child rearing is thought to be completed and the parents are said to live in an **empty nest**. Early in the century, this situation usually did not occur until the parents were in their late 50s or early 60s. Increasingly, however, this has become a middle-aged phenomenon, because of earlier marriages and earlier completion of childbearing owing to more closely spaced births and fewer children. Furthermore, with increased longevity, married couples can expect to live in this empty-nest state for a much longer time than did their parents.

In recent years, problems associated with the empty-nest syndrome have been described by the media and, to a lesser extent, by social scientists. This interest has arisen because of apparently conflicting patterns of adjustment, especially for mothers. While the transition represents a release from the many domestic chores associated with child rearing and a reduction in economic and parental responsibility, it also represents a change in lifestyle that can be either satisfying or traumatic. For example, it has been hypothesized that the transition represents a loss of the 'mothering' role. It is argued that women become depressed and disenchanted because their major source of responsibility and satisfaction is no longer available. In contrast, the transition also represents more freedom to pursue new roles outside the home, perhaps full- or part-time employment, volunteer work, a hobby, or school.

Similarly, the departure of children may improve the quality of the marriage because the couple have more time to focus on their leisure interests and on each other rather than on the children. Conversely, the empty-nest state also has the potential to magnify existing dissatisfactions. While this transition may not be the direct cause of a divorce, it may provide the opportunity to resolve long-standing differences. Divorce may now be perceived as a realistic alternative to a stressful marriage, since it is no longer necessary to 'stay together for the sake of the children.' Today, many of these post-empty-nest separations or divorces, especially within the middle class, are initiated by women who seek a higher-quality relationship, or who wish to have more freedom from domestic responsibilities to pursue their own occupational lifestyle. From the perspective of the husband, role strain and dissatisfaction may result if the wife obtains full-time employment and neglects what are perceived to be her traditional domestic responsibilities. The marriage may also be disrupted by the individual growth or change in one partner that has evolved throughout the middle years. In this case, the empty nest may represent an appropriate opportunity to resolve these differences by divorce.

Unfortunately, little research has been completed concerning adjustment to the empty-nest transition. The transition is not usually a traumatic experience, except for those women whose entire focus in life has centered on child rearing, often at the expense of developing personal interests and skills. This is more likely to be the case in lower-class families, where the mother's identity is closely linked to domestic responsibilities, and perhaps among those women who were divorced early in the marriage and were solely responsible for child rearing. But for most, the transition is not traumatic, although it draws symbolic attention to the personal aging process.

The empty nest is an expected event. It is generally known when the transition will occur, and it is normatively expected that children will establish their own identities and nuclear families. For the parents, the transition is gradual, since not all children leave home at the same time. Anticipatory socialization for the transition occurs during childhood, when children spend a month at camp; later, it occurs when children leave home to attend college or university, perhaps only returning for weekends or vacations. In many cases the departure of the last child coincides with a new status being acquired by the child through marriage or a first job, or by one or both of the parents taking a new job or moving to a new location. When their children leave home, parents not only have more freedom, but also acquire a new resource in adult children (and eventually grandchildren).

In the 1980s two new patterns of living by adult children have resulted in either a delay in occurrence of the empty-nest stage, or in the refilling of the empty nest for a short- or long-term period. A delayed departure for unmarried 20 to 29 year olds has been observed in Canada, and the trend seems to be increasing (Boyd and Pryor, 1989). For example, data from the 1986 census indicate that four of ten women and three of ten men in their late 20s reported living in their parents' home. This pattern is more likely to prevail both for the less educated who may be economically disadvantaged or unemployed and who never left home to attend university, and for the more educated who are still pursuing formal education and have little income. This pattern may also reflect changing norms about housing, especially in urban centers where living with parents may be the only viable alternative to inflationary housing prices and high rental rates in a market where few vacancies appear. For career-oriented women who are likely to delay marriage, living longer at home may be a viable economic alternative to assuming a large housing debt.

The other recent pattern involves a refilling of the nest by a child who returns after experiencing a crisis such as unemployment, widowhood, or divorce. This refilling can become stressful and unpleasant for the parents, who find that their newfound freedom has been eliminated. Nevertheless, most parents respond to the crisis of an adult child, especially in the case of a divorce. Thus, with increased divorce rates, parents of divorced adult children are more likely to provide housing and to assist in raising grandchildren while a son or daughter reestablishes his or her personal life.

In summary, the onset of the empty-nest stage in life is generally not disruptive to the individual or to the married couple. However, for a mother whose identity is almost exclusively based on her children, and for some couples with a long-standing underlying marital strain, the transition may create adjustment problems and lead to other changes. Although the transition to the empty-nest stage has been occurring earlier in the life cycle in North America, at least in middle- and upper-class families, it may be delayed in the near future because of a changing economy. With high mortgage rates and housing shortages, more adult children may return to or remain in the 'nest,' at least until marriage. In addition, following separation or divorce, adult children frequently return to the parents' home until they are emotionally or financially resettled in their own residence. Interestingly, the empty-nest phenomenon is not experienced or discussed to the same extent outside North America. In many countries, it is common for children, even if they are married with children of their own, to live in the parents' household, or to live in a small unit attached to the parents' home.

Retirement

The onset of retirement has an influence not only on the individual, but also on family and married life. To date, this phenomenon has been considered almost exclusively as a male transition wherein the husband experiences a major role loss and enters the wife's domain on a full-time basis. This transition may result in the loss of status for the spouse and a possible reduction in the standard of living for the couple because of a decline in income. Retirement brings about the possibility of a merging of household responsibilities and a change in gender-role differentiation with respect to these responsibilities. This represents a potential source of conflict, but few empirical studies have examined this question.

In general, it has been found that the onset of retirement results in an increase in marital satisfaction, especially on the part of the husband; an opportunity to play more fully the role of grandparent; and a freedom to adopt a new lifestyle, possibly one that includes a summer and a winter residence. Most research on this role transition has focused on the process, and on the effect on the individual (primarily the male) and on society from a psychological and economic perspective (see chapter 11).

Widowhood

Introduction

Marital status has a significant influence on the nature of social relationships and on the quality of life in the later years. Specifically, the status of being never-married, married, separated or divorced, widowed or remarried is related to living arrangements, economic status,

health status, family and friendship relationships, loneliness, suicide, and psychological well-being or life satisfaction (McDaniel, 1986; Gee and Kimball,1987; Connidis, 1989a:15-16). Contrary to earlier thinking in gerontology, the unmarried in later life (never-married, divorced, widowed) cannot be considered as a common category with similar lifestyles, life chances, and needs. Rather, the personal history of those in each category means that they have different resources, preferences, and needs in the later years.

Table 9.1 indicates the marital status of those 65 years of age and older in Canada. As can be seen, at all age groups, most older men are married; by age 75 most older women are widowed. Since widowhood is the most stressful family role transition, but one that is an 'expectable life event' for most women in later life (Martin Matthews, 1987a), this section summarizes the large body of literature on the process and the outcome of adjustment to this role. Most studies of this role transition have focused on older women[11] and, hence, much less is known about the transition from the perspective of widowers at any age (Kohn and Kohn, 1979), or from that of young and middle-aged widows.

Much of the early research focused on the immediate problems and behavior associated with the status of widowhood. This status has seldom been viewed as a process that requires both short- and long-term personal adjustments and modifications in lifestyle. As a result, cross-sectional retrospective studies have been more common than longitudinal studies. Moreover, few studies controlled for such possible confounding factors as social class, racial or ethnic background, rural versus urban residence, or age at widowhood. Finally, most studies have focused on the personal level of analysis rather than on the societal level.

At the personal level, the major topics of interest have been the use of personal coping skills associated with the initial grief; the pattern and degree of adjustment as determined by morale or life satisfaction; the amount of social participation within the family and community; and the loss of, or change in, self-concept and identity. At the societal or social structural level, the major interests have cen-

TABLE 9.1

MARITAL STATUS OF OLDER CANADIANS BY SEX AND AGE GROUP, 1986

Category	Age Group and Sex							
	65-69		70-74		75-79		80+	
	M	F	M	F	M	F	M	F
Married/separated	83.5	59.6	80.0	46.8	74.2	33.0	58.3	15.0
Never married	7.1	7.0	7.4	8.4	7.8	9.6	8.6	10.3
Widowed	6.5	30.1	10.3	42.5	16.3	55.8	31.9	73.9
Divorced	2.9	3.3	2.3	2.3	1.8	1.6	1.2	0.8

SOURCE: Statistics Canada. Adapted from L.Stone and H. Frenken (eds.). (1988). *Canada's Seniors*. Catalogue No. 98-121, Table 5. Ottawa: Minister of Supply and Services. Reproduced with the permission of the Minister of Supply and Services Canada, 1990.

tered on the normative roles of widows in various cultures; the economic and employment status of widows and widowers; the availability and reaction of family and community support groups; the living arrangements and location of widows; the process of anticipatory socialization for widowhood; and variations in adjustment patterns and problems by gender, class, age, and place of residence.

The following subsections examine the transition to widowhood by focusing on the process and problems of adjustment from the dual perspective of the individual and society. This approach is taken because there is considerable interaction between the two levels. Greater emphasis is placed on long-term adjustment than on the short-term grief management and mourning stage. The information presented pertains to older widows, with exceptions for widowers and younger widows being noted where research evidence is available.

The Initial Process of Adjustment

For most people, the onset of widowhood occurs suddenly and unexpectedly. There is little opportunity for anticipatory socialization for the transition from being married to being widowed. It is only where the deceased spouse had been ill for a period of time that any degree of direct anticipatory socialization occurs. Even here, the process tends to relate to pragmatic matters such as financial and household man-

agement, living on a reduced income, and decreased social interaction as a couple with friends and relatives. The grief is not diminished, but the process may be of shorter duration and the long-term adjustment may be more satisfactory (George, 1980).

Some degree of indirect anticipatory socialization or anticipatory grief may occur if the widow is older and is among the last of her social peers to experience widowhood. In this situation, she will have had face-to-face interaction with role models whom she may have assisted through the transition. In addition, unlike those who are among the first in a friendship group to be widowed, she will have an established peer group or social network of widows who can provide emotional and social support.

For young widows, this lack of opportunity for anticipatory socialization and the unavailability of a network of widows, plus the suddenness of the transition, make the initial adjustment more traumatic. The adjustment process may be compounded by the responsibilities of being a single parent with dependent children, by the lack of adult children who can provide support, and by the need to meet mortgage payments and daily living costs for the family. As a result, the process of adjustment is often longer and more difficult, and involves a pattern different from that for older widows.

In time, the younger widow may no longer

be perceived as a 'widow,' but rather as a single person who has greater remarriage and career opportunities than those normally available to the older widow. Once she is perceived as a 'single,' previous friendships with married couples may cease, often because of a change in lifestyle by the young widow. In the long term, many women who are widowed before 55 remarry, and the likelihood increases the earlier they are widowed. However, this pattern may occur less in the future now that it has become more socially acceptable to be single throughout the adult years. Young widows may opt for some combination of a career, single parenthood, or cohabitation, rather than for the more traditional married lifestyle.

For widows of any age, initial adjustment can often require a year or more. This period is often stressful, and is characterized by individual differences in level and duration of shock, disbelief, numbness, yearning, questioning, depression, anger, and guilt. Physiological problems such as insomnia, irritability, and weight loss may occur (George, 1980:89-90; Lopata, 1980:103-5; Martin Matthews, forthcoming), and the widowed person may be susceptible to deteriorating health in the first few years after a spouse's death.

It is during this mourning stage that a widow needs the greatest emotional support. In some cultures there are rituals and beliefs related to the process of adaptation.[12] These range from formal periods of mourning and ritualistic practices, including the wearing of mourning clothes, to requirements concerning dependent living arrangements with relatives or other widows, to the extreme rituals of self-sacrifice. In contrast, in modern societies even the wearing of traditional mourning clothes is no longer encouraged, and the suddenly independent widow is soon left to her own social support network. This potential family and community support system can provide varying degrees and types of emotional, social, service, and economic support in both the short and the long term (Lopata, 1979, 1987a, 1987b; Martin Matthews, forthcoming).

There are few formalized transition rituals or community resources in modern societies to assist the widow in adapting to a new status identity and to a 'single' lifestyle. Moreover, the societal norm of expected mourning time has decreased as members of modern societies have become more time-constrained. For example, 'in 1922 Emily Post instructed that the proper mourning period for a mature widow was three years. Fifty years later, Amy Vanderbilt urged that the bereaved be about their normal business within a week or so' (Gibbs, 1989:49). This problem of adjusting to a new identity is compounded by the geographic dispersion of children who sooner or later must return to their own families and careers, thereby physically abandoning the recently bereaved parent. To assist the elderly widow in adapting, voluntary 'widow-to-widow' programs have been established. These programs, designed to provide emotional support and knowledge, include widowed volunteers who visit the recently bereaved person; telephone help lines for information and assistance; group sessions to discuss common problems; and public education to inform the widowed about available services and resources, including written materials on living alone, employment, and financial and legal matters. A volunteer service worker can be of assistance in interpreting societal expectations with respect to the mourning period, subsequent social interaction, and remarriage. It is for this reason, particularly, that it is important to match the recently widowed person with an individual similar in age, class, parental status, and economic status. Not surprisingly, these programs seldom include widowers. This is because there is a smaller cohort available to provide assistance, because men are more likely to assert independence and to be reluctant to share emotional experiences with a confidant, and because men usually do not need assistance in coping with financial and legal matters resulting from the death of a spouse.

The Long-term Process of Adjustment

Once the immediate and acute period of grief and mourning begins to subside, the process of reconstructing a new identity and lifestyle must begin. Just as the adjustment to living with a partner occurs early in marriage, so too must resocialization occur to the new status of being a widow or widower. This process of resocialization operates on two interacting levels, and involves personal changes as well as changes in social roles and participation.

On the personal level, the recently widowed person must learn to cope with living alone, with no longer having someone to care for, and with the loss of companionship, especially at mealtimes and at times when ideas, thoughts, or feelings need to be shared. If the marriage was not a satisfactory experience, if the individual has been able to cope with or enjoy being alone, or if the nursing of a disabled spouse was viewed as a burden, then relief rather than loneliness may be the reaction. Some widows must learn to cope with a change in identity from one closely linked to the husband's status and occupation to one of being single and independent. This sudden, enforced independence can be traumatic if the widow has been highly or totally dependent on the spouse for decision making in financial and social matters, or if she does not have a meaningful parental or occupational role. This identity crisis is less likely to occur for widowers, unless widowhood occurs at about the same time as retirement. In this case, the widower, or widow, experiences a loss of both the occupational role and the major companion role at the same time.

The psychological adjustment can be more difficult and traumatic if the older widow is placed in a vulnerable economic situation because the husband's pension benefits are inadequate for her survival, or because she is unemployable or underemployed. Unattached older women are the poorest of all groups in the older population (Martin Matthews, 1987a). In a recent longitudinal study in the United States, it was found that compared to the continuously married, widows and widowers experienced a 50 percent decline in their level of economic security in the short- and long-term period following widowhood (Zick and Smith, 1986). Moreover, increasing age raises the risk of poverty for unattached elderly women (Martin Matthews, 1987b). In one of the few longitudinal studies of older widows (58 or 59 years of age when first interviewed), Thompson (1980) concluded that the economic status of widows is directly related to employment status. Those widows who do not have a high-school education or who have had little work experience are

unable to obtain work when it is necessary, or they remain unemployed for a long time, or they accept low-paying positions with little potential for advancement.

For those who have been employed during middle age, the employment and economic status at widowhood is influenced by level of education and by the amount of time and experience in the labor force. Even if they are unemployed when widowhood occurs, those with previous experience in the labor force are more likely to be employable, and at a higher level, should they need or desire to work after the death of the spouse.

The recently widowed may also experience real or imagined physical and mental health problems. Loneliness, in combination with health problems, often results in death by illness and suicide within two years of the death of a spouse. Among the very old, the physical health problems may be the natural result of physiological aging, although the onset may be hastened by caring for a dying spouse (Marshall, 1980:147-51) and by a change in lifestyle initiated by widowhood. Inadequate nutrition, increased alcohol consumption, and deteriorating sanitary conditions in the home may contribute to declining health. These conditions seem to occur more frequently among widowers, perhaps because they are forced to play domestic roles in which they have little experience or interest. This need for assistance with household tasks, along with greater opportunities for men to marry younger women, may be a factor in the higher remarriage rates of older widowers.

Closely linked to increased loneliness and declining health among the widowed is a decrease in morale or life satisfaction. However, it may not be the transition to widowhood per se that results in lower levels of reported morale and well-being, but rather the social, health, and economic changes that result from the unexpected transition. These changes in morale or life satisfaction are more likely to be reported by women in the middle and lower class who, compared to men, experience greater economic difficulties. They are also generally older and in poorer health than their male peers. While most widows and widowers eventually adjust to the personal and psychological problems associated with widowhood, the duration and pattern of adjustment may vary across social groups.

The widowed person must also make decisions concerning where and how to live as a single adult, and whether to seek employment or not. The decision to work is usually based on economic necessity, age at widowhood, employment status at widowhood, and the psychological need for a new focus in life and a new social network. With marginal increases in social security and private pension benefits, the economic status of some older widows is improving somewhat, at least for those in the middle and upper classes. Within younger cohorts, where the concept of careers for women is more socially acceptable, the likelihood of a younger widow continuing employment or returning to the labor force is much greater than it was in the past.

Most older widows live alone in their own homes. In this way they avoid potential conflict situations with children. It seems that only the very poor, the very old, the poorly educated, and those with strong ethnic and cultural ties are likely to share a household with a relative in either an equal or a dependent relationship. However, recent evidence suggests that sisters are playing an increasingly important role in both the social lives and housing arrangements of older widows (Martin Matthews, 1987a; Connidis, 1989a:71-86).

At the social structural level of analysis, adjustment to widowhood involves role changes, changing patterns of interaction with friends and relatives, and striving to meet societal norms concerning widowhood. The result of this process is a reconstructed social life as a single person, including modifications to lifestyle and friendship networks.

The role changes associated with the transition to widowhood may occur to varying degrees. The major change is the assumption by the widow of the role of head of the household, with full responsibility for home maintenance and financial obligations. The widow generally maintains the same degree of role involvement in the role of mother, although it may increase if the children are young and she is a single parent, or if she is older and moves in with one of her children. For many widows, role conflict

may arise from the desire to demonstrate that they are coping as independent adults. Yet, internally they need the emotional and social support of a companion. The widow or widower often experiences the loss of friends who continue to socialize as 'couples.' In fact, widows often report feeling like an outsider at social events (Martin Matthews, 1987a, 1987b; Connidis, 1989a). Indeed, two common social responses to the contraction of a widow's social world are embitterment and resignation that former friends and couples have been lost (Martin Matthews, 1987a).

While returning to work represents one option for widows, increased involvement in voluntary associations may also compensate for the loss of the role of spouse.[13] This is especially likely to occur where the widow was at least minimally involved in voluntary organizations before the transition. However, where that involvement was primarily related to the husband's membership or activity, widowhood may lead to decreased role involvement.

If social interaction outside the extended family decreases, the widowed person may experience some degree of social isolation. This social isolation is less pronounced among those with sufficient economic and health resources, among the employed or employable, among those with higher levels of education, and among those living in smaller towns. In contrast, elderly widows in rural areas may be more lonely and isolated because their children may have moved from the region. In addition, they are often geographically isolated from health, recreation (for example, senior-citizen centers), and social services. For the rural widow, lack of public transportation and physical distance from services create physical barriers to a social reconstruction of the elderly widow's lifestyle. Although not yet supported by research, it has been suggested that the hypothesized isolation of the rural widow may be offset by higher quality relationships with neighbors.

Summary
While the initial process of adjustment is difficult for all recently widowed persons, the majority do adjust, although there are many possible patterns of adaptation and lifestyles.

While the status of widowhood per se may not be traumatic for most in the long term, the indirect effects of losing a spouse may be traumatic. Women may lose financial security, and men are apt to lose social services and social support. Clearly, the study of widowhood must be analyzed by age and sex, since there are many differences in the process between and among widows and widowers. For example, males are generally older and in poorer health, yet they often have better financial resources and greater opportunities to remarry if they wish. Widowers are more likely to be isolated from, or have fewer close emotional ties with their families; widows become closer to their children, especially daughters. They may also, in the later years, form a new household with a sister, who also may be widowed. This shared living arrangement may provide economic, social, and emotional support for the widowed siblings late in life. Another difference between widows and widowers is that widows often have an available peer group of other widows who can provide social and emotional support. In contrast, widowers do not have nearly as large a peer group, and men are generally less willing to confide in a male confidant. With respect to younger widows and widowers, there are fewer gender differences, although it is often easier and more acceptable for the young widower to remarry. Regardless of age, it is likely that gender differences will narrow in the future, since older women will have higher levels of education, greater experience in the labor force throughout marriage, more independent coping skills, greater financial knowledge and resources, and more liberal norms concerning marriage, remarriage, and cohabitation. At the same time, men may now be taking more responsibility for household tasks during marriage, especially when both partners have careers. As widowers, they may be less likely to remarry to acquire domestic assistance.

The Divorced in Later Life

As noted in table 9.1, only about 3 percent of those 65 to 69 report they are divorced. However, according to Stone and Frenken (1988:39),

'the average annual growth rate in the divorced population age 65 and over has exceeded 10 percent in the 1976 to 1986 decade.' This growth, however, does not reflect an annual 10 percent increase in marital breakdown among the elderly but, rather, a rapid increase in the number of persons who remain divorced as they enter the 'senior' age group.

The onset of the empty nest or retirement represents transitions that may provide an opportunity to dissolve an unsatisfactory marriage. At present, approximately 1 percent of those over 65 in North America become divorced (Uhlenberg and Myers, 1981). The percentage of elderly people who have been divorced at least once may increase in the future for the following reasons (Uhlenberg and Myers, 1981): (1) the trend toward higher divorce rates after age 65 will continue; (2) higher divorce rates in the early and middle years will continue, and there is a likelihood that subsequent remarriages will end in divorce; (3) future cohorts are more likely to view divorce as a viable and socially acceptable solution to an unhappy marriage; (4) women will have greater financial independence with their own pensions, savings, and equity; and (5) increased longevity will decrease the probability that a marriage will be terminated by the death of one spouse, and divorce may be seen as a viable alternative to an unhappy marriage, even after the age of 60.

Although the divorce rate may increase for the elderly, it will always be less than that for younger adults. Nevertheless, a divorce in later life may have serious social or economic implications for the elderly person (Chiriboga, 1982; Hagestad, 1986; Connidis, 1989a:33; Uhlenberg et al., 1990). For men, this role transition can be especially traumatic if they also lose the work role at about the same time. Divorced women over 65 may experience financial hardship, although increasingly pension benefits must be paid to the former spouse. In addition, they experience the social stigma associated with divorce among their age cohort. Although both members of a couple may experience a dramatic change in their relationships with children and grandchildren following divorce, women seem to be more affected because of their greater involvement in kinship relationships. Unfortunately, relatively little is known at present about the impact of later-life divorce on family dynamics.

Courtship and Remarriage in the Later Years

Following a suitable period of mourning for the widowed, and at some point following separation, courtship and dating are increasing among the elderly. Initially, one person may offer to drive another to a social event, or they spend time together when they meet at an event. Social norms concerning dating and the initiation of a new heterosexual relationship are generally more restrictive for older women. This may occur in some instances because cross-sex friendships are viewed as 'courting behavior' and others define the relationship as 'romantic,' regardless of intent or feeling (Adams, 1985). Moreover, informal norms and pressures from age peers and relatives have tended to discourage dating by older women, especially at family events.

The decision to date, or to consider the possibility of cohabitation or remarriage, can create anxiety for the widowed person who seeks such a relationship. Nevertheless, an increasing number of elderly persons are actively pursuing new relationships through attendance at singles' clubs or senior-citizen centers, or by placing ads in the 'personals' column of the local newspaper (highlight 9.4). In a study of those 60 years and over who were attending a singles' club, Bulcroft and Bulcroft (1985) found that dating at this age takes on an accelerated pace because the participants feel they do not have time to play 'the dating game' as they did earlier in life. Interviews with attendees found that participants were open and honest with their motives and feelings; that major motives for dating were to seek out a marriage partner, to maintain an identity as a socially active person, and to find companionship; and that expressing sexuality was an expected part of the dating relationship.

For the older widowed or divorced person, a number of living arrangements are possible. These include living alone, living with adult children, living with another relative, living in a communal or congregate unit, cohabitation in a heterosexual or homosexual relationship, or remarriage. While most live alone, especially women, an increasing number cohabit or remarry. For example, Northcott (1984) reported that the 1981 remarriage rates for older Canadians were, for widowers and widows respectively, 33.8 and 5 per 1,000 for those 65 to 69 years of age, 22.4 and 2.8 per 1,000 for those 70 to 74 years of age, and 6.7 and 0.7 per 1,000 for those 75 and older. The average number of years to remarriage following widowhood was 4.9 and 5.8 for males and females respectively who were in the 65 to 69 years of age category. More recently, Adams and Nagnur (1989) reported that 5 percent of widows and 14 percent of widowers remarry. At least half of the widowed marry another widowed person. Thus, males are more likely to remarry sooner. Among women, those who are divorced are more likely than widows to remarry.

Many studies in the 1970s found that elderly widows report that they do not wish to remarry. But is this a true preference or rather a socially desirable response to a perceived societal norm which suggests that they should not date or consider remarriage? In most cases, older women do not remarry, because they do not wish to give up their independence, especially if it means playing the role of housekeeper and eventually nurse. Finally, they may reject the possibility of remarriage, because the first marriage was not a satisfying experience, or because it may jeopardize pension and survivor benefits that have been paid following the death of their lifelong spouse. Given social changes in the 1980s in the meaning, style, and permanence of marriage, it will be interesting to observe the dating, housing, and remarriage patterns exhibited by succeeding cohorts of older adults.

Why does remarriage in the later years happen, how does it happen, and how successful is the transition from widowhood or being divorced to a new marital relationship? First, a high percentage of these 'autumn loves' are perceived as successful by both partners. The rate of success and satisfactory adjustment is closely linked to the motivation to remarry, to the process whereby the relationship evolves into marriage, to the support of adult children

HIGHLIGHT 9.4

THE SINGLE SENIOR: IN SEARCH OF A SOCIALLY ACTIVE LIFESTYLE

Living as a single person in later life can occur for a variety of reasons: the person was never married, or was married but later divorced, or was widowed. While those in the latter two categories may have children, the never-married person is unlikely to have any offspring or spousal kin. Regardless of the reason for being single in later life, many seek an active social life, and most do not report that they are lonely, as is often assumed. With increasing rates of singlehood, especially among highly educated women, and of divorce rates during the middle years, single individuals constitute an increasing segment of the middle-aged and elderly cohorts (Connidis, 1989a). For the older single person who seeks companionship, the 'personals' column of the daily newspaper has become a source to 'exchange' interests, credentials, and images, thereby leading to a wider social world. For example, the following ads have appeared in daily newspapers:

Male, 68 years old, seeking female companionship, 55-70 years old. I enjoy bowling, cards, home-cooked meals, quiet walks and times.

Widower, 63, good health, financially secure, owns modern home on country acreage. Would like to meet lady 55 to 65 interested in country living, animals, some travel.

Widower 69, 5 ft. 10 in., 175 lb., seeking companionship with lady 60-70, who enjoys dining, traveling, theater, and quiet conversation.

Widow, 60s, looking for companionship of gentleman 60-70, who enjoys cards, traveling, dancing.

Would like to meet an honest, sincere widower, 65-70 years. Good sense of humor, social drinker, with car. PS: A way to a man's heart is through his stomach. My cooking includes garlic and onions.

Attractive, vibrant, secure widow with class and grace, enjoys the outdoors, social activities, and travel. Seeks sincere, refined, stable gentleman, over 50, with the same interests, for a meaningful relationship.

and friends, and to higher levels of education and health (Bulcroft et al., 1989).

Most older brides and some older grooms report that they never had any intention or desire to remarry. For men, the transition often occurs because they have difficulty adjusting to widowhood, and remarriage appears to be a viable alternative. Men often have less involvement in family and friendship roles, and they seek companionship. They are often faced with the loss of both the work and spouse roles at about the same time, and therefore tend to seek emotional support. In addition, older widowers often have limited experience with and little interest in domestic responsibilities, and may remarry in order to have someone care for them. For older widows, the need for companionship and intimacy, especially if their adult children are not close, may be a motivating fac-

tor. Cohabitation rather than marriage may result if the surviving spouse loses pension benefits if she remarries, or if adult children either refuse to sanction or actively discourage a marriage.[14]

Although economic, social, legal, and demographic factors may discourage or prevent remarriage among older persons, a number of other factors increase the probability and the success rate of remarriage (Stryckman, 1981). First, neither adult children nor aging parents are likely to encourage the entrance of the widowed parent into the home of one of the children. Yet the older person needs daily companionship in a family unit, and in many cases sexual intimacy. Therefore, remarriage becomes a socially acceptable and viable alternative to living alone, especially for widowers who can marry younger women and who have the economic resources and health to create a new household. Research indicates that partners in a remarriage were either introduced by a mutual friend or relative, or knew each other when one or both were previously married. In some cases, retirement communities and adult recreation centers have served as the social context for the initiation of a new relationship that leads to remarriage.

Successful remarriage in the later years seems to be related to six general conditions (McKain, 1972): (1) both partners have known each other for many years prior to widowhood; (2) friends and relatives support the marriage (if not initially, then eventually when the relationship is seen to be successful and in everyone's interest); (3) both partners have previously adjusted well to the empty nest, retirement, and widowhood; (4) the remarried couple move into a residence that neither had lived in prior to the marriage, thereby removing old memories and possible conflict as to who is the head of the household; (5) they have an adequate income and common agreement on the inheritance to be left to children; and (6) the partners have a number of similar interests and values, and their major focus is on the marriage rather than on raising children or being responsible for an adult child.

In summary, this transition, which represents a role acquisition rather than a role loss in the later years, represents an increasingly viable alternative for older persons. At present it is more likely that men will exercise this option, but if the financial penalty of lost pensions is reduced or removed, it may become equally attractive to women. In contrast, remarriage may be less likely to occur in the future if alternative models of cohabitation evolve because of changing values and norms. For example, living together in a heterosexual relationship may become as normative in the later years as it is during young adulthood. For those who do remarry the success rate appears to be high, and remarriage fulfills a need for a family relationship, especially where older persons are not invited to move into the home of an adult child. Furthermore, contrary to popular opinion, there appears to be little alienation or intergenerational family conflict when a widowed or divorced older partner remarries. In fact, remarriage may relieve the adult child of the burden of daily care and companionship for the elderly parent.

The Never-Married and the Childless in Later Life

Although not involved in a marital role transition in later life, the never-married, especially women, eventually lose most familial ties. Thus, those in this status constitute a unique familial group that is receiving increased research attention (Allen, 1989; Connidis, 1989a:37-42; Keith, 1989). Among elderly Canadians in 1986, 7.5 percent of the men and 8.6 percent of the women had never married. In absolute numbers, single elders are increasing. Many of the women who never marry are among the highest educated of their age cohort.

A frequent myth perpetuated about this group is that they are lonely and isolated because they lack traditional family ties. They often have close ties with siblings; they have longtime friends who serve as confidants and intimates; and most have satisfying living arrangements, either alone or with others. Hence, most studies find that the never-married are not socially isolated, nor do most report feeling lonely (Rubinstein, 1987; Connidis, 1989a; Stull and Scarisbrick-Hauser, 1989). Having lived alone for most of their adult life, they are able to cope with independent living more successfully, at least until a loss of health or income reduces their independence. It is at this stage that lack of access to familial networks may generate dissatisfaction and lead to greater dependence on social service agencies. Clearly, more information is needed concerning this segment of the older population, especially since their numbers may increase in the future. In the past, the never-married were likely to have never been involved in a heterosexual relationship. Future cohorts of the never-married may include those who engaged in marriage-like relationships (cohabitation) with one or more partners, and may include some who have raised children.

The childless elderly also constitute a unique group within the family of later life. Rempel (1985) reported that 15 percent of the ever-married women over 65 years of age were childless. In contrast, only 7 percent of ever-married women born in the 1930s were childless (Gee, 1986), whereas Veevers estimated that 15 to 20 percent of today's younger women will complete their reproductive years childless (cited in Gee and Kimball, 1987:80). Since childlessness may be an important predictor of institutionalization, these shifting percentages are important considerations in planning policies for informal and formal support beyond the year 2040. In a study of fifty-two childless elderly persons it was found, contrary to expectations, that in terms of self-reported social isolation, loneliness, life satisfaction, and perceived quality of life, there were no differences between the childless elderly and the elderly who had been parents (Rempel, 1985). Not surprisingly, the childless elderly reported having greater economic resources during the later years. As Connidis (1989a:59) concluded, 'it is not necessary to have children in order to have a satisfying old age'; but, as a caveat, it must be noted that this view may hold only for those childless elderly who have long-lasting ties with close friends or siblings.

SUMMARY AND CONCLUSIONS

In this chapter the literature pertaining to the dynamics of aging within the context of the extended family has been reviewed. The first section presented some of the structural, stratification, and personal factors that influence intragenerational and intergenerational relations, and some of the theoretical perspectives that have been used to study intergenerational lineage relations were briefly outlined. The second section focused on intragenerational family relations by examining marital satisfaction across the life cycle and sibling interaction in the later years. In the third section, which was concerned with intergenerational relations in the later years, the relationships between parents and adult children and between grandparents and grandchildren were reviewed from the perspective of both partners in each intergenerational relationship. As well, the impact of an adult child's divorce on parent-child and grandparent-grandchild role relationships was

examined. Finally, the last section considered the reaction and adjustment of the individual to personal role transitions within the family context (the empty nest, retirement, widowhood, divorce, and remarriage), as well as the issues surrounding being never married or childless in the later years. On the basis of the literature reviewed in this chapter, it can be concluded that:

1. Kinship interactions vary in quantity and quality throughout the life cycle.
2. Child launching and grandparenting were once considered as events unique to the later years of life. Increasingly, however, at least in modernized societies, these events have become middle-aged phenomena.
3. Research indicates that many of those over 65 live within a one-hour drive of at least one adult child. This refutes the myth of the lonely, alienated elderly person.
4. Residential propinquity influences the type and the quality of interaction between generations within the extended family.
5. With increasing labor-force participation by middle-aged and older women, fewer daughters or daughters-in-law provide daily care and services for the eldest members of the extended family.
6. The frequency and the quality of interaction tends to be stronger between mothers and daughters than between sons and parents.
7. Sons who provide assistance to older parents are more likely to provide financial assistance than personal care.
8. Intergenerational lineage relationships and care are often stronger and more frequent among members of the working class, and within ethnic and racial groups.
9. Research concerning marital satisfaction across the life cycle suggests that the relationship may be curvilinear or negatively linear with advancing age. However, on the basis of cross-sectional evidence, most studies sug-

gest that the relationship is curvilinear, with the highest point occurring during the honeymoon stage. Thereafter, there is a decline in satisfaction until a low point is reached. This low point may occur when children are adolescents, when the last child leaves home, or at the time of retirement. After this low point, there appears to be an increase in satisfaction into the later years.

10. Contrary to popular myths, the relationship between generations within families is not characterized by conflict, nor are most of the elderly abandoned by or alienated from their family.

11. The form and frequency of communication and assistance between adult children and aging parents is influenced by such factors as residential propinquity, social class, sex of the child, race, ethnicity, age and health of the two generations, and the degree of filial responsibility felt by the children.

12. Children who interact with grandparents have fewer prejudices about the elderly and about growing old.

13. The frequency of interaction between grandchildren and grandparents is normally high during childhood. It often decreases during adolescence and increases again during early adulthood.

14. The role of grandparent is not a highly salient role for most, at least until the later years of life. The role tends to be more meaningful for members of the working class, for widows, for those who are less educated, for those who are retired or unemployed, and for those not involved in voluntary associations or community affairs.

15. The transition to the empty-nest stage is not a traumatic experience for most parents, although it may be for women whose major interest in life has been child rearing.

16. Whereas the initial stage of adjustment to widowhood is often difficult, most adjust satisfactorily, although

there are many possible patterns of adjustment and lifestyles.

17. The widows who are most likely to experience financial difficulties are those who are unemployed or underemployed.

18. Men and those women who have been divorced rather than widowed are most likely to remarry in the later years.

NOTES

1. Some general review articles include: Abu-Laban, 1980; George, 1980; Quinn and Hughston, 1984; Bengtson et al., 1985, 1990; Brubaker, 1985; Sussman, 1985; Troll, 1986; Nett, 1988; Silverstone, 1988; Connidis, 1989a.

2. A higher percentage of the institutionalized elderly are kinless, and may, in fact, be institutionalized because they have no surviving relatives to take care of them.

3. Although most studies suggest that the relationship is between age and marital satisfaction, it is more likely a reflection of the number of years a couple has been married and the stages in the marriage career that have been completed.

4. This degree of drifting depends on such factors as residential propinquity, relations with in-laws, and career or lifestyle differences.

5. Until the death of one or both parents, siblings may maintain indirect contact with each other by communicating through the parents. However, upon the death of a parent, and particularly the mother, there may be a need to increase direct communication, thereby renewing the relationship.

6. Adult children between 40 and 60 years of age have been described as being members of the 'sandwich generation.' That is, they are caught between the demands of completing the launching of their own children and caring for their elderly parents, and at the same time they face personal concerns about their own future.

7. With the rising incidence of divorce among the middle-aged, especially if the mother wins custody of young children, the intimate relationship with parents and grandparents may dramatically increase or decrease. In fact, the divorcee may become dependent on his or her parents for emotional and financial support.

8. Perhaps because of stereotypes and the greater number of surviving women, most studies of grandparenthood have assumed that it is a female role, or have included only grandmothers.

9. See Matthews and Sprey, 1984; Johnson and Barer, 1987; Gladstone, 1987, 1988, 1989; Johnson, 1988; Connidis, 1989a:65-67.

10. Ahrons and Bowman (1981) note that in Wisconsin, grandparents have the right to petition the court for visitation rights. According to Wilson and DeShane (1982), grandparents may be awarded visitation rights, or even adoption rights, if it is in the best interest of the child to do so, or if the grandparents contribute to the financial support of the child.

11. See Lopata, 1973, 1979, 1987a, 1987b; Harvey and Bahr, 1980; Bowling and Cartwright, 1982; Martin Matthews, 1987a, 1987b, forthcoming; Connidis, 1989a.

12. Lopata (1973), in her study of older widows, identified three patterns of adjustment. The 'traditional' pattern was more common to ethnic and racial subcultures. Those in this pattern experienced little or no change in identity or lifestyle and pursued activities similar to those that had existed before the loss of the spouse. The 'modern' type of widow experienced a brief mourning period but later built a new independent lifestyle. Finally, the 'social isolate' pattern was common among those with less education and income who did not have a great deal of social or economic support.

13. For example, because of their popularity, senior-citizen clubs often become subcultures of widows, in many cases to such a degree that widowers are reluctant to become involved.

14. It has been argued that adult children oppose a remarriage because it suggests loss of respect and love for the deceased spouse, or because it may deprive them of their share of the estate when the surviving parent dies. On the other hand, remarriage removes some of the daily concern and responsibility of the adult child, since the parent no longer lives alone. In this respect it has been considered somewhat more socially acceptable for a widower to remarry, since he will be 'looked after' by the new spouse. However, others believe that if their mother remarries, she will become a nurse and a housemaid for another man, who will eventually become ill or disabled and die.

REFERENCES

Abu-Laban, S. (1980). 'The Family Life of Older Canadians,' pp. 125-34 in V. Marshall (ed.). *Aging in Canada: Social Perspectives*. Don Mills, Ont.: Fitzhenry and Whiteside.

Adams, O. and D. Nagnur. (1989). 'Marrying and Divorcing: A Status Report for Canada,' *Canadian Social Trends*, 13(Summer), 24-27.

Adams, R. (1985). 'People Would Talk: Normative Barriers to Cross-Sex Friendships for Elderly Women,' *The Gerontologist*, 25(6), 605-11.

Ahrons, C. and M. Bowman. (1981). 'Changes in Family Relationships Following Divorce of an Adult Child: Grandmother's Perceptions,' in E. Fisher (ed.). *Impact of Divorce on the Extended Family*. New York: Haworth Press.

Aizenberg, R. and J. Treas. (1985). 'The Family in Late Life: Psychosocial and Demographic Considerations,' pp. 169-89 in J. Birren and W. Schaie (eds.). *Handbook of the Psychology of Aging*. 2d ed. New York: Van Nostrand Reinhold.

Allen, K. (1989). *Single Women/Family Ties: Life Histories of Older Women*. Newbury Park, Calif.: Sage Publications.

Bedford, V. and D. Gold (eds.). (1989). *Siblings in Late Life: A Neglected Family Relationship*. Newbury Park, Calif.: Sage Publications.

Bengtson, V. and J. Robertson (eds.). (1985). *Grandparenthood*. Beverly Hills, Calif.: Sage Publications.

Bengtson, V. et al. (1985). 'Generations, Cohorts, and Relations between Age Groups,' pp. 304-38 in R. Binstock and E. Shanas (eds.). *Handbook of Aging and the Social Sciences*. 2d ed. New York: Van Nostrand Reinhold.

Bengtson, V. et al. (1990). 'Families and Aging: Diversity and Heterogeneity,' pp. 262-87 in R. Binstock and L. George (eds.). *Handbook of Aging and the Social Sciences*. 3d ed. San Diego, Calif.: Academic Press.

Bowling, A. and A. Cartwright. (1982). *Life after Death: A Study of the Elderly Widowed*. London: Tavistock Publications.

Boyd, M. and E. Pryor. (1989). 'Young Adults Living in their Parents' Home,' *Canadian Social Trends*, 13(Summer), 17-20.

Brackbill, Y. et al. (1988). 'The Perfect Child (from an Elderly Parent's Point of View),' *Journal of Aging Studies*, 2(3), 243-54.

Brubaker, T. (1985). *Later Life Families*. Beverly Hills, Calif.: Sage Publications.

Bulcroft, K. and R. Bulcroft. (1985). 'Dating and Courtship in Late Life: An Exploratory Study,' pp. 115-26 in W. Peterson and J. Quadagno (eds.). *Social Bonds in Later Life: Aging and Interdependence*. Beverly Hills, Calif.: Sage Publications.

Bulcroft, K. et al. (1989). 'Antecedents and Consequences of Remarriage in Later Life,' *Research on Aging*, 11(1), 82-106.

Cherlin, A. and F. Furstenberg. (1986). *The New American Grandparent: A Place in the Family, A Life Apart*. New York: Basic Books.

Chiriboga, D. (1982). 'Adaptation to Marital Separation in Later and Earlier life,' *Journal of Gerontology*, 37(1), 109-14.

Clavan, S. (1978). 'The Impact of Social Class and Social Trends on the Role of Grandparent,' *The Family Coordinator*, 27(4), 351-57.

Climo, J. (1988). 'Visits of Distant-Living Adult Children and Elderly Parents,' *Journal of Aging Studies*, 2(1), 57-70.

Connidis, I. (1989a). *Family Ties and Aging*. Toronto: Butterworths.

Connidis, I. (1989b). 'Siblings as Friends in Later Life,' *American Behavioral Scientist*, 33(1), 81-93.

Connidis, I. and L. Davies. (1990). 'Confidants and Companions in Later Life: The Place of Family and Friends,' *Journal of Gerontology: Social Sciences*, 45(forthcoming).

Crimmins, E. and D. Ingegneri. (1990). 'Interaction and Living Arrangements of Older Parents and Their Children,' *Research on Aging*, 12(1), 3-35.

De Wit, D. and G. Frankel. (1988). 'Geographic Distance and Intergenerational Contact: A Critical Assessment and Review of the Literature,' *Journal of Aging Studies*, 2(1), 25-43.

De Wit, D. et al. (1988). 'Physical Distance and Social Contact between Elders and Their Adult Children,' *Research on Aging*, 10(1), 56-80.

Driedger, L. and N. Chappell. (1987). *Aging and Ethnicity: Toward an Interface*. Toronto: Butterworths.

Frankel, B.G. and D. De Wit. (1989). 'Geographic Distance and Intergenerational Contact: An Empirical Examination of the Relationship,' *Journal of Aging Studies*, 3(2), 139-62.

Gee, E. (1986). 'The Life Course of Canadian Women: An Historical and Demographic Analysis,' *Social Indicators Research*, 18(3), 263-83.

Gee, E. (1987). 'Historical Change in the Family Life Course of Canadian Men and Women,' pp. 265-87 in V. Marshall (ed.). *Aging in Canada: Social Perspectives*. 2d ed. Markham, Ont.: Fitzhenry and Whiteside.

Gee, E. and M. Kimball. (1987). *Women and Aging*. Toronto: Butterworths.

George, L. (1980). *Role Transitions in Later Life*. Monterey, Calif.: Brooks/Cole Publishing Co.

Gibbs, N. (1989). 'How America Has Run Out of Time,' *Time* (April 24), 48-55.

Gladstone, J. (1987). 'Factors Associated with Changes in Visiting between Grandmothers and Grandchildren Following an Adult Child's Marriage Breakdown,' *Canadian Journal on Aging*, 6(2), 117-27.

Gladstone, J. (1988). 'Perceived Changes in Grandmother-Grandchild Relations Following a Child's Separation or Divorce,' *The Gerontologist*, 28(1), 66-72.

Gladstone, J. (1989). 'Grandmother-Grandchild Contact: The Mediating Influence of the Middle Generation Following Marriage Breakdown and Remarriage,' *Canadian Journal on Aging*, 8(4), 355-65.

Gold, D.T. (1987). 'Siblings in Old Age: Something Special,' *Canadian Journal on Aging*, 6(3), 199-216.

Hagestad, G. (1985). 'Continuity and Connectedness,' in V. Bengtson and J. Robertson (eds.). *Grandparenthood: Research and Policy Perspectives*. Beverly Hills, Calif.: Sage Publications.

Hagestad, G. (1986). 'The Aging Society as a Context for Family Life,' *Daedalus*, 115, 119-39.

Hartshorne, T. and G. Manaster. (1982). 'The Relationship with Grandparents: Contact, Importance, Role Conception,' *International Journal of Aging and Human Development*, 15(3), 233-45.

Harvey, C. and H. Bahr. (1980). *The Sunshine Widows*. Lexington, Mass.: Lexington Books.

Hess, B. and B. Soldo. (1985). 'Husband and Wife Networks,' pp. 67-92 in W. Sauer and R. Coward (eds.). *Social Support Networks and the Care of the Elderly*. New York: Springer Publishing Co.

Holahan, C. (1984). 'Marital Attitudes over 40 Years: A Longitudinal and Cohort Analysis,' *The Gerontologist*, 39(1), 49-57.

Huyck, M. (1974). *Growing Older*. Englewood Cliffs, N.J.: Prentice-Hall.

Johnson, C. (1988). 'Active and Latent Functions of Grandparenting during the Divorce Process,' *The Gerontologist*, 28(2), 185-91.

Johnson, C. and B. Barer. (1987). 'Marital Instability and the Changing Kinship Networks of Grandparents,' *The Gerontologist*, 27(3), 330-35.

Keating, N. (1986). 'Valuing Intergenerational Transfer of the Family Farm,' presented at the annual meeting of the Canadian Association on Gerontology, Quebec City, November.

Keith, P. (1989). *The Unmarried in Later Life*. New York: Praeger Publishers.

Kiefer, C. (1974). *Changing Cultures, Changing Lives*. San Francisco: Jossey-Bass.

Kivnick, H. (1982). 'Grandparenthood: An Overview of Meaning and Mental Health,' *The Gerontologist*, 22(1), 59-66.

Kivnick, H. (1985). 'Grandparenthood and Mental Health: Meaning, Behavior and Satisfaction,' pp. 151-58 in V. Bengtson and J. Robertson (eds.). *Grandparenthood*. Beverly Hills, Calif.: Sage Publications.

Knipscheer, C. (1988). 'Temporal Embeddedness and Aging within the Multigenerational Family: The Case of Grandparenting,' pp. 426-46 in J. Birren and V. Bengtson (eds.). *Emergent Theories of Aging*. New York: Springer Publishing Co.

Knipscheer, K. and A. Bevers. (1985). 'Older Parents

and their Middle-Aged Children: Symmetry or Asymmetry in their Relationship,' *Canadian Journal on Aging*, 4(3), 145-60.

Kobata, F. (1979). 'The Influence of Culture on Family Relations: The Asian American Experience,' pp. 94-106 in P. Ragan (ed.). *Aging Parents*. Los Angeles: University of Southern California Press.

Kohn, J. and W. Kohn. (1979). *The Widower*. Boston: Beacon Press.

Lamb, M. and B. Sutton-Smith (eds.). (1982). *Sibling Relationships: Their Nature and Significance across the Lifespan*. Hillsdale, N.J.: Lawrence Erlbaum Associates.

Lopata, H. (1973). *Widowhood in an American City*. Cambridge, Mass.: Schenkman Publishing Co.

Lopata, H. (1979). *Women as Widows: Support Systems*. New York: Elsevier.

Lopata, H. (1980). 'The Widowed Family Member,' pp. 93-118 in N. Datan and N. Lohmann (eds.). *Transitions of Aging*. New York: Academic Press.

Lopata, H. (ed.). (1987a). *Widows: Volume I. The Middle East, Asia and the Pacific*. Durham, N.C.: Duke University Press.

Lopata, H. (ed.). (1987b). *Widows: Volume II. North America*. Durham N.C.: Duke University Press.

Mangen, D. (1986). 'Measuring Intergenerational Family Relations,' *Research on Aging*, 8(4), 515-35.

Marshall, V. (1980). *Last Chapters: A Sociology of Aging and Dying*. Monterey, Calif.: Brooks/Cole Publishing Co.

Marshall, V. et al. (1981). 'The Family as a Health Service Organization for the Elderly,' paper presented at the annual meeting of the Society for the Study of Social Problems, Toronto.

Martin Matthews, A. (1987a). 'Widowhood as an Expectable Life Event,' pp. 343-66 in V. Marshall (ed.). *Aging in Canada: Social Perspectives*. 2d ed. Markham, Ont.: Fitzhenry and Whiteside.

Martin Matthews, A. (1987b). 'Support Systems of Widows in Canada,' in H. Lopata (ed.). *Widows: Other Countries/Other Places*. Durham, N.C.: Duke University Press.

Martin Matthews, A. (forthcoming). *Widowhood in Later Life*. Markham, Ont.: Butterworths

Matthews, S. and J. Sprey. (1984). 'The Impact of Divorce on Grandparenthood: An Explanatory Study,' *The Gerontologist*, 24(1), 41-47.

Matthews, S. and J. Sprey. (1985). 'Adolescents' Relationships with Grandparents: An Empirical Contribution to Conceptual Clarification,' *Journal of Gerontology*, 40(5), 621-26.

McDaniel, S. (1986). *Canada's Aging Population*. Toronto: Butterworths.

McKain, W. (1972). 'A New Look at Older Marriages,' *The Family Coordinator*, 21(1), 61-69.

Medley, M. (1977). 'Marital Adjustment in the Post-Retirement Years,' *The Family Coordinator*, 26(1), 5-11.

Mouser, N. et al. (1985). 'Marital Status and Life Satisfaction: A Study of Older Men,' pp. 71-90 in W. Peterson and J. Quadagno (eds.). *Social Bonds in Later Life: Aging and Interdependence*. Beverly Hills, Calif.: Sage Publications.

National Advisory Council on Aging. (1986). 'The Way It Is: All in the Family,' *Expression*, 3(1), 3.

Nett. E. (1988). *Canadian Families: Past and Present*. Toronto: Butterworths.

Northcott, H. (1984). 'Widowhood and Remarriage Trends in Canada, 1956 to 1981,' *Canadian Journal on Aging*, 3(2), 63-78.

Quadagno, J. and J. Janzen. (1987). 'Old Age Security and the Family Life Course: A Case Study of Nineteenth-Century Mennonite Immigrants to Kansas,' *Journal of Aging Studies*, 1(1), 33-49.

Quinn, W. and G. Hughston (eds.). (1984). *Independent Aging: Family and Social Systems Perspective*. Rockville, Md.: Aspen Publishing.

Rempel, J. (1985). 'Childless Elderly: What Are They Missing?' *Journal of Marriage and the Family*, 47(2), 343-48.

Robertson, J. (1976). 'Significance of Grandparents: Perception of Young Adult Grandchildren,' *The Gerontologist*, 16(2), 137-40.

Rosenthal, C. (1985). 'Kinkeeping in the Familial Division of Labor,' *Journal of Marriage and the Family*, 47, 965-74.

Rosenthal, C. (1986). 'The Differentiation of Multigenerational Households,' *Canadian Journal on Aging*, 5(1), 27-42.

Rosenthal, C. (1987a). 'Aging and Intergenerational Relations in Canada,' pp. 311-42 in V. Marshall (ed.). *Aging in Canada: Social Perspectives*. 2d ed. Markham, Ont.: Fitzhenry and Whiteside.

Rosenthal, C. (1987b). 'The Comforter: Providing Personal Advice and Emotional Support to Generations in the Family,' *Canadian Journal on Aging*, 6(3), 228-39.

Rosenthal, C. and V. Marshall. (1988). 'Generational Transmission of Family Ritual,' *American Behavioral Scientist*, 31(6), 669-84.

Rubinstein, R. (1987). 'Never Married Elderly as a Social Type: Re-evaluating Some Images,' *The Gerontologist*, 27(1), 108-13.

Selles, R. (1987). 'Farm Retirement: Toward a Theoretical Framework,' paper presented at the annual meeting of the Canadian Association on Gerontology, Calgary, October.

Silverstone, B. (1988). 'Adult Children and Aging Parents: What We Know about Their Relationship,' pp. 53-82 in L. McDonald and N. Keating (eds.). *Aging with Excellence*. Winnipeg, Man.: Canadian Association on Gerontology.

Spitze, G. and J. Logan. (1989). 'Gender Differences in Family Support: Is There a Payoff?' *The Gerontologist*, 29(1), 108-13.

Steinman, L. (1979). 'Reactivated Conflicts with Aging Parents,' pp. 126-43 in P. Ragan (ed.). *Aging Parents*. Los Angeles: University of Southern California Press.

Stone, L. (1988). *Family and Friendship Ties among Canada's Seniors*. Ottawa: Statistics Canada.

Stone, L. and H. Frenken. (1988). *Canada's Seniors*. Ottawa: Minister of Supply and Services.

Strain, L. and N. Chappell. (1982). 'Confidants — Do They Make a Difference in Quality of Life?' *Research on Aging*, 4(4), 479-502.

Stryckman, J. (1981). 'The Decision to Remarry: The Choice and Its Outcome,' paper presented at the annual meeting of the Canadian Association on Gerontology, Toronto, November.

Stull, D. and A. Scarisbrick-Hauser. (1989). 'Never-Married Elderly,' *Research on Aging*, 11(1), 124-39.

Sussman, M. (1985). 'The Family Life of Old People,' pp. 415-49 in R. Binstock and E. Shanas (eds.). *Handbook of Aging and the Social Sciences*. 2d ed. New York: Van Nostrand Reinhold.

Thompson, G. (1980). 'Economic Status of Late Middle-Aged Widows,' pp. 133-49 in N. Datan and N. Lohmann (eds.). *Transitions of Aging*. New York: Academic Press.

Troll, L. (1985). 'The Contingencies of Grandparenting,' pp. 135-49 in V. Bengtson and J. Robertson (eds.). *Grandparenthood*. Beverly Hills, Calif.: Sage Publications.

Troll, L. (ed.). (1986). *Family Issues in Current Gerontology*. New York: Springer Publishing Co.

Turner, R. (1962). 'Role-Taking: Process Versus Conformity,' pp. 20-40 in A. Rose (ed.). *Human Behavior and Social Processes: An Interactionist Approach*. Boston: Houghton Mifflin Co.

Uhlenberg, P. and M. Myers. (1981). 'Divorce and the Elderly,' *The Gerontologist*, 21(3), 276-82.

Uhlenberg, P. et al. (1990). 'Divorce for Women After Midlife,' *Journal of Gerontology: Social Sciences*, 45(1), S3-11.

Wilson, K. and M. DeShane. (1982). 'The Legal Rights of Grandparents: A Preliminary Discussion,' *The Gerontologist*, 22(1), 67-71.

Zick, C. and K. Smith. (1986). 'Immediate and Delayed Effects of Widowhood on Poverty: Patterns from the 1970s,' *The Gerontologist*, 26(6), 669-75.

10
Aging, Social Support, and Social Policy

Maurice Green, Waterloo, Ontario

INTRODUCTION

As you learned in chapter 9, the nuclear and the extended family make up a large part of the social world of most aging adults. As a result, the family tends to be the first and major resource if and when social support, health care, or financial assistance is needed in the later years. However, changing demographic trends (such as lower fertility rates, childless marriages, increased divorce rates, increasing labor force participation rates among middle-aged women, increased migration and mobility rates by elderly parents and adult offspring, increased longevity) have led to a concern that there will be a decrease in the availability, opportunity, or willingness of some family members to care directly for aging parents. Moreover, changes in social values and cultural beliefs concerning family obligations and exchange relationships have resulted in some offspring being unwilling or unable to assume full-time or part-time caregiving for aging parents. At the same time, aging parents seek to remain as independent as possible, in as many domains as possible (for example, financial, transportation, home care, personal care, health care), for as long as possible. Yet, in many instances, especially for the elderly who live beyond 80 years of age, some type or degree of assistance is often needed as their physical and/or mental health status declines. As a result of this decline in health, elderly persons may move at varying rates along a continuum from a high degree of independence, to varying degrees of dependence, to total dependence on others. As they move along this continuum, there is generally a shift from a reliance on informal sources of support to an increasing reliance on formal support.

In reality, at all stages in the life course, no one is ever totally independent of others for emotional or social support. Rather, our social world consists of a complex, multiperson support system that includes family, extended family, relatives, friends, work acquaintances, and neighbors, who coexist within a complex social structure and social network. This **informal social support** system can gratify basic social and emotional needs through interaction with others, can help people cope with stressful life events, can provide various forms and degrees of assistance on a daily basis or during a period of acute or chronic illness, and can provide information about services and assistance available through formal support agencies in the community. In short, social bonds foster and facilitate independence across the life cycle (Peterson and Quadagno, 1985). These ties bind people together within informal networks, providing the necessary support to function independently, and the greater assistance that is needed when health, emotional, or financial crises occur. However, for some people these familial ties can become burdensome and stressful when caregiving requires most of their time and energy. Indeed, as you will learn later, some relationships can become abusive and life threatening.

To enable older adults to adapt and to experience a high quality of life and greater life satisfaction and well-being (Riley and Riley, 1989), the private and public sectors provide a system of **formal social support**. Through a variety of social policies and programs, older adults are assisted in maintaining a degree of independence, in coping with expected and unexpected life events that can be stressful and debilitating, and in surviving when they become frail and totally dependent on others for meeting basic needs.

To date, most federal, state, or provincial policies are based on medical and welfare models that emphasize health care and financial assistance. That is, the formal support system has responded to the issues of retirement and lowered income, and to the increasing likelihood of chronic illness and frailty within the older population. This system has accepted the myth that most elderly persons become dependent on others or on the government because of rapidly deteriorating physiological changes in later life and because of nonemployment and subsequent financial dependency following retirement (Hardy, 1988). As a result, homogeneity has been assumed in policymaking and in service provision, and eligibility often is determined by chronological age rather than need. In reality, however, the elderly are a heterogeneous group with different needs for social, emotional, and health care support. Thus, 'it is not the elderly per se who are high users of health services, but rather those with multiple and severe health problems' (Shapiro and Roos, 1987; Wolinsky and Arnold, 1988:78). The heavy users among the elderly are the very old who are dying and who are in their last year or two of life. More recently, formal support systems have been expanded to provide more diverse social services, so that both the independent elderly person who lives in the community and the more dependent elderly person who lives in a long-term care institution receive the specific type of assistance that is needed at that stage in life. As a result of the elderly being viewed as a heterogeneous group, debate has arisen about whether formal support policies should be based on age or need (Neugarten, 1982; Chappell et al., 1986; Cain, 1987).

On the basis of the foregoing, we can see that social support is a complex process that includes the family, an extended social network, formal organizations, and cultural values and beliefs. This process involves both instrumental and expressive support; the giving and receiving of goods or services; and a variety of social relationships, including informal ties with relatives, friends, and neighbors, and formal ties with personnel working in community organizations, service agencies, or institutions. The level and the quality of these relationships can vary from the intimate one of confidant (spouse, child, best friend) to the formal relationship with a stranger who is employed by an organization or institution. In addition, many informal relationships are based on the principle of exchange and the norm of reciprocity (Longino and Lipman, 1985).

The purpose of social support may range from prevention (a confidant provides a buffering effect in helping to cope with stress, and thereby stress has less or little impact on health and well-being), to adaptation (a dial-a-bus service, a child or a neighbor provides transportation to needed services or social events when the older adult cannot drive a car), to rehabilitation or long-term care (various levels of institutionalized housing are available to care for the more dependent or frail older adult). Thus, the ideal system of social support involves coordinated and complementary interaction between the informal and formal systems. The overall objective of the support system should be to encourage and assist older adults to remain independent in as many domains as possible, and to ensure that social and medical interventions do not hinder the development of an older adult's potential by encouraging or forcing feelings of dependency, or the use of services before they are fully needed (for example, institutionalization). As you will learn later, an ideal system should also provide support to the caregivers of those receiving care.

As you might infer from the previous discussion, conflict between the informal and the formal support systems may occur pertaining to the issue of responsibility. A perennial debate in the health care and social welfare fields concerns who is responsible, and to what extent, for the care of the frail and dependent elderly — is it the individual, the family, or the society? As C. Wright Mills (1959) questioned, should the problems faced by individuals be perceived as 'private troubles' or as 'public issues'? If they are perceived as private troubles, the individual and the family are held responsible by virtue of filial obligations, some of which are institutionalized by laws (Snell, 1990). If they are viewed as public issues, society is held responsible for finding a remedy or a solution, and for implementing and funding policies or programs.

In less developed countries, and before the onset of population aging in developed nations, the assistance to, and care of, the elderly were considered a private matter. However, with the onset of industrialization and population aging, the care of the elderly became a public issue, and, increasingly, responsibility has been assigned to federal, provincial, state, regional, or local governments; to government-subsidized private-sector interests (such as transportation, housing); or to not-for-profit volunteer agencies. Today, the needs of many elderly adults are met by an integrated, but not always well-coordinated, support system. This system includes the family, volunteers, and publicly supported social policies and programs designed to support the individual and the family as the needs of the care recipient and the caregiver change over time (Connidis, 1989:91). This chapter, then, focuses on the systems of informal and formal social support for aging adults. More specifically, you will study the social networks of older adults; the structure, availability, usage patterns, and outcomes of using the informal and the formal social support systems; the possible interaction of the two systems; and the development and evaluation of social policies designed to provide social interventions for the care and the support of an aging population.

SOCIAL NETWORKS

Throughout the life course, we are part of a **social network** through which we engage in social participation with individuals, groups, and organizations (Gottlieb, 1981; Sauer and Coward, 1985a, 1985b; Wellman and Hall, 1986). This network usually consists of a relatively permanent core group (for example, the family) and a more transitory extended group (for example, friends, coworkers, neighbors) that expands and contracts in size and composition as we age and pass through different stages in the life cycle (Stone, 1988). The size and the composition of our network is influenced by such personal factors as ethnicity, education, income, class background, health, type of occupation, personality, place of residence (urban versus rural), size of extended family, religious and cultural beliefs, and the social roles we occupy (such as married, divorced, widowed; employed versus retired). For example, during early childhood the social network is primarily composed of the nuclear and the extended family. As one ages and moves beyond the immediate home to the neighborhood, the school, and the workplace, the network enlarges. During midlife and later life such transitional events as divorce, a job change, a move to a new community, the onset of a chronic illness, retirement, or widowhood can lead to a contraction of the existing network, or to the creation or expansion of new networks (for example, through the marriage of children, the acquisition of new friends, remarriage). Furthermore, there are differences in network participation because of having a specific resource (for example, a higher level of education generally leads to a larger, more varied network) or because of changing social roles and the gain or loss of resources, rather than chrono-

logical age per se (Morgan, 1988). Highlight 10.1 illustrates the different social networks available to an elderly couple; an elderly widow; an isolated, elderly, never-married male; and a socially active never-married female.

From a social-network perspective, our social world consists of an expanding and contracting circle of 'nodes' (individuals or organizations) linked to each other by informal social bonds or formal relations. These relationships can vary in durability, quality (intimacy), frequency of interaction, purpose, and reciprocity (that is, they can flow in a one-way or a two-way direction). The 'nodes' are usually individuals, but they can be groups, agencies, or formal organizations (Antonucci, 1985; Wellman and Hall, 1986; Lieberman, 1990). Throughout the life course, the core group remains relatively stable in size and in the degree of intimacy, primarily because it consists of kinship and friendship ties. This core group of family (Cicirelli, 1985; Hanson and Sauer, 1985; Hess and Soldo, 1985; Shore, 1985; Kendig et al., 1988), friends, and neighbors (Peters and Kaiser, 1985), where potentially strong and longstanding ties are present, provides the social setting for the distribution and exchange of social support across the life course (Schultz and Rau, 1985; Stone, 1988).

Individual core networks vary in the degree, type, frequency, and amount of support available and provided, especially for older adults. The presence of kin alone does not guarantee that support is available, nor that all ties will be supportive. Indeed, as you will learn later, some relationships within the core can become stressful or abusive and life threatening. However, in most instances, the network of family and friends represents a 'convoy' (Antonucci, 1985; Antonucci and Akiyama, 1987) that surrounds the aging individual, providing varying degrees and types of social and emotional support that help him or her to meet life's challenges. Although the membership and the nature of the relationships within a specific convoy may change somewhat at different stages of the life cycle, strong intimate bonds persist, and most individuals are the focal point of a convoy wherein they exchange (that is, give and receive) various types of support across the life cycle (Schulz and Rau, 1985). Not surprisingly,

HIGHLIGHT 10.1

PERSONAL NETWORKS VARY BY MARITAL STATUS

The availability, purpose, and strength of intimate ties in the later years can vary by marital status. The following cases illustrate variations in the size and the purpose of social networks in later life, and how lifestyles and social support, if needed, are influenced by an individual's location in a social network. All four cases involve people from the same class background, of about the same age (mid 70s), and in good health.

Mr. and Mrs. A have been married for 55 years and live in the home they have owned for 40 years. Many of their neighbors are also longtime residents of the neighborhood. Hence, much of their socializing occurs with neighbors through informal visiting. Mrs. A belongs to a Monday-evening church group and works as a volunteer two mornings a week at an elementary school two blocks away. Mr. A works part-time as a school crossing guard, and plays cards and golf regularly with a group of friends. Together, Mr. and Mrs. A belong to a bridge club at a local seniors' center, and at least once a month entertain other couples in their home. Their three children live within twenty miles, and each Sunday, dinner is shared with one of the children and their family. Mr. and Mrs. A have independent social lives as well as many couple activities. As a result, they both have a number of high-quality ties that provide emotional aid, companionship, and confidants, if needed. Even if Mr. and Mrs. A were to give up their part-time work and volunteer roles, they would still have a large, active network of friends, neighbors, and family. Should either member of this active couple experience a significant loss of health, it appears likely that a large network of informal support would be available to provide needed assistance.

Mrs. B has been a widow for five years. Having never worked during her adult life, she lacks a potential group of former friends from work. Her only child, a son, lives in another province, and contact with him is limited to random telephone calls and a visit every two or three years. Since the death of her husband, she has lost contact with most of their 'couple' friends, many of whom had worked with her husband. Since she is unable to drive, a volunteer from the church takes her shopping and on errands once or twice a week. Other than casual contact with neighbors in her apartment building and a few phone calls each day, she has little interaction with family, friends, or neighbors. This lifestyle is in sharp contrast to the 'active' social life she led when her husband was alive to drive and to organize outings. Now, living as a single person, she lacks daily interaction and close friendships and may encounter difficulties if her health fails because she lacks a viable informal support system.

Mr. C has never been married and has lived in an apartment throughout his adult life. His only family is an older sister living in a nursing home. He has never been part of a neighborhood network. Throughout his career he traveled extensively on the job from Monday to Friday, and spent most of his holidays traveling to pursue his major life interest, photography. Now he lacks kin, male and female friends, neighbors, and relatives. He has never attended church or belonged to voluntary associations. Lacking a large pension, and having spent much of his earnings on travel, he no longer owns a car. Hence, he is spending more and more time in his apartment, and he lacks a 'convoy' to provide emotional, physical, or social support. The many casual acquaintances he made on the job and while traveling cannot assist this single, elderly male in the later years as his lifestyle changes. In the event of serious health or financial problems, one can only hope that Mr. C, or someone on his behalf, can invoke the necessary resources of the formal support system in his local community. But Mr. C, not having been a joiner of voluntary groups, nor having a confidant or near-kin, is a high-risk candidate for an unhappy, difficult ending to a hitherto satisfying and productive life. The lack of participation in a longtime social network may create hardships in the later years, especially if an effective formal system is not available or cannot be activated in his local community.

Ms. D was one of the few women to graduate from an engineering school in Canada during the 1930s. After a successful career involving extensive job-related travel, she has a large network of local and distant former colleagues, male and female, whom she visits throughout the year. In addition, she has two older sisters, one widowed and one married, and six nephews and nieces who have always viewed her as an older sister and a friend. All of her relatives live in the same city, and she has frequent contact with each of them by telephone or face-to-face visits. Seven years ago Ms. D was hospitalized and required an extensive period of convalescence. During this six-month period of acute illness, relatives and friends, coordinated by a single niece, took turns in providing care and support. Given this early demonstration of support, it is quite likely that Ms. D will have an extensive network of support should she experience a serious health crisis in the future.

married women tend to have large and diverse networks, and a more permanent, intimate, and confiding 'convoy'; unmarried men have the smallest and least intimate networks (Longino and Lipman, 1985).

Before discussing informal and formal support systems, it is important to distinguish between the structure and the function of social networks, and between the concepts of social network and social support (Thoits, 1982; Ward, 1985). A social network has a structure and serves a variety of functions, one of which may be social support. The structure of a network can be measured by the size, complexity, or number of nodes, the frequency of contact, the degree and direction of intimacy, the homogeneity of the nodes in terms of sociodemographic characteristics (such as age, gender, class, education, ethnicity), and the stability of membership over time. In contrast, the social processes or functions of social networks are related to such quality measures as the nature of social interaction or contact (for example, intimate, casual, or formal), the degree of perceived support, the satisfaction derived from the relationship (is it enjoyable or stressful?), and whether the interaction serves a preventative, rehabilitative, or caretaking function (Antonucci, 1985; Biegel, 1985). Thus, social support is a form of functional behavior that evolves from interaction within a social network. When interaction in the network is more frequent, generally more support is available if and when it is needed.

Contrary to prevailing myths, the elderly are not isolated, disengaged, alienated, or abandoned. Rather, networks of varying sizes, with relationships of varying strengths, are available for most older adults (Cohen et al., 1985; Sauer and Coward, 1985a; Biegel et al., 1986;

Karuza et al., 1988). These networks have the potential to provide companionship, a confidant, emotional support, informal assistance with minor personal or home care needs, and informal or formal assistance during acute or chronic illness. Although the number of ties clearly decreases with advancing age, the strength of the remaining ties may increase, even though the frequency of interaction may decrease because of declining health and mobility. Not surprisingly, the elderly tend to rely on adult children and longtime friends for assistance with basic needs. As the degree of dependence increases, the need for a more specialized caregiving network increases. This network, as we will learn, must include both informal ties with primary groups (such as family, friends, neighbors) and a linkage with formal organizations (such as social welfare agencies, nursing homes, respite care facilities). Moreover, this network must be integrated and coordinated to provide a spectrum of complementary sources of support. Each node in the network, ranging from the most intimate (a spouse or adult child) to the formal (a long-term care institution), may have a different view of the needs of the aging individual, and a different pool of resources to assist or care for the older adult (Litwak, 1985; Wellman and Hall, 1986; Corin, 1987). The time at which a particular node begins or ceases major responsibility for the care of an older adult can be a source of stress, for both the aging individual and the informal caregiver. This issue is addressed later in the chapter.

Summary

Throughout our life, but particularly in the

later years, we are part of a social network that provides varying amounts of social, emotional, financial, and physical support. Even where family support is unavailable, a network of friends, acquaintances, or formal organizations can provide support, if and when it is needed or requested. However, as you will learn in a later section, not all relationships within a network are positive and supportive. Rather, some nodes in the network can be harmful to the older adult. Thus, it is important in any analysis of an elderly adult's network to identify not only the number of ties available for support, but also the potential quality of interaction with each node in the network.

The next three sections examine the sources, types, uses, and outcomes of informal and formal support systems, and the potential problems related to the interaction of these two systems. A special section highlights our limited knowledge about elder abuse. The final section of the chapter considers the process and the issues associated with designing and implementing social policies for an aging population.

THEORIES AND MODELS OF SOCIAL SUPPORT AS HELP-SEEKING BEHAVIOR

Three General Models

Faced with health problems or with problems of daily living, older people have three basic options: try to survive without taking any action; take action alone; or seek help, first from informal sources, and then from formal sources. At the same time, members of the inner circles of one's network may begin to provide subtle or direct forms of social assistance, often without the assistance being specifically requested by the older adult. This help, often initiated at a time of acute illness or following a role loss (such as widowhood), is offered to enable the person to maintain as much independence as possible. However, this well-meaning offer of assistance can be interpreted by the older person as a sign that he or she is failing and is becoming dependent on family and friends.

A number of alternative explanations have been suggested for understanding the process

whereby informal social support is requested, offered, and utilized (Lee, 1985; Peters et al., 1987). First, Corin (1987) proposed a general model of the help-seeking process, which includes the person and the environment, the behaviors involved in coping strategies, and the meanings attached to the use of informal or formal social support systems. This model reinforces the ideas presented in chapter 8 about person-environment fit. The model suggests that, since personal needs change with time, there must be a fit between the recipient's needs and the available social resources if well-being and functional ability are to be maintained and enhanced.

Corin (1987:372) stated that there are four major ways in which a person can react to, and cope with, a life event or a changing lifestyle that requires assistance: 1) a predominant use of oneself, or self-resources; 2) a predominant use of informal resources; 3) the use of formal resources, alone or in addition to informal resources; and 4) a mixed strategy involving oneself, plus informal and formal resources. She argued that each person tends to internalize and use one style of help-seeking strategy. The choice of one style or another depends on the availability of social relations in one's personal network; the availability and knowledge of formal resources; the nature of the situation (for example, type, seriousness, longevity, the presence of other compounding or interacting problems); the lifelong personal style of relating to others (privacy versus sociability); and the normative expectations concerning seeking and accepting help that vary according to class, gender, ethnicity, and an urban versus rural[1] environment. In short, Corin (1987:390) concluded that 'factors related to the environment influence the functioning of social relations and, in some way, could influence the help-seeking process as much.'

Corin's model focused mainly on the general process whereby people adapt to the need for help; two earlier models focused on the decision-making process whereby one support group is selected over others. The **task-specific model** (Dono et al., 1979; Litwak, 1985) argued that the selection of different support groups is based on the type of assistance needed. This view suggests that decisions about help for older adults are objective, rational, and utilitarian, and that there is a willingness to seek out and accept help from formal support services, if that is what is needed.

In contrast, the **hierarchical-compensatory model** (Cantor, 1979) is based on the assumptions that privacy, intimacy, and personal responsibility prevail; that the kinship network takes primacy over non-kin in terms of preferred caregivers; and that informal sources are selected before formal resources, which tend to be selected only as a last resort. It is hypothesized that the selection of a caregiver or helper operates in a hierarchical order of preference from among one's most intimate circle of kin and friends. Thus, for married persons, the spouse is the preferred first choice, followed in order by an adult child, close relatives (such as a sibling), and then by other relatives (such as a nephew or a niece). If the preferred choice is not available, or is unable or unwilling to assist, then the next level of intimacy is selected to compensate or substitute for the unavailable or unwilling preferred choice. Similarly, for the never-married or the childless old adult, ties are developed with siblings and friends who serve as both companions and confidants.

This model argues that this order prevails, regardless of whether the needed assistance can be classified as instrumental or affective. However, as Peters et al. (1987) noted, the hierarchical process is most likely to operate when physical proximity, emotional bonding, and long-standing reciprocity already prevail in the role relationship between recipient and potential caregiver. In reality, with an increasing array of informal, quasi-informal, and formal resources being available in many communities, multiple support groups are sought out for aid. Hence, features of both the hierarchical-compensatory and task-specific models are present in most decisions concerning the type and form of support that is needed.

Exchange Theory and Social Support

As you learned in chapters 4 and 9, social relationships, especially within the kinship system, may be based on the exchange principle, wherein the norms of reciprocity and mutual obligation prevail (Dowd, 1980). Within the family there are physical, emotional, economic, and social resources that can be exchanged in a serial or reciprocal manner, depending on the needs and the stage in life. Serial exchanges tend to be prevalent, and generally represent a downward flow of assistance from an older generation to a younger generation because of a sense of responsibility and affection. Reciprocal exchange, or a two-way flow, is most common among the middle and oldest generations. This process of exchange usually involves services (for example, baby-sitting, nursing, counseling, shopping, and household maintenance); gifts (for example, money, clothes, appliances, air or train tickets for visits); or emotional support and advice in the form of face-to-face visits, telephone calls, or letters.

The form and the frequency of exchange varies greatly among families and is influenced by a number of social factors. These include: residential propinquity, social class, sex and marital status of children, race, ethnicity, age of the middle and the oldest generations, and the degree of **filial maturity**. If parents live in close proximity to adult children, there is a greater likelihood of visiting and exchanging goods and services. In fact, most parents report weekly face-to-face visits with at least one adult child. This is most likely to occur among members of the working class who, because of cultural ties and lower levels of social mobility, live in closer proximity to each other. Moreover, working-class parents are more likely to receive help from their children and to live with them; middle-class adults are more likely to exchange money and gifts, while those in the working class are more likely to exchange services. In the middle class, patterns of serial exchange from the oldest to youngest generations are more likely, while reciprocity is more common among working-class adults. Finally, there is more face-to-face interaction among working-class adults, and more telephoning and letter writing among the middle class because of greater social and geographical mobility.

In the long term, the degree of balance in the perceived costs and benefits associated with the duties, rights, and obligations of a relationship can have an impact on its durability and quality. If the relationship becomes unbalanced so that one member is increasingly indebted to the other, the quality and the continuation of the relationship may be threatened or destroyed. Because family and intimate-friend relationships tend to be strong and to persist over time, the principle of exchange has been viewed as the basis of the informal support system for the elderly (Shumaker and Brownell, 1984; Lee, 1985; Longino and Lipman, 1985; Kart and Longino, 1987; Connidis, 1989). Thus, the support provided to aging parents is perceived to be appropriate and necessary in order to fulfill a long-standing debt to the parents for the gift of life and early-life nurturing and support (Berman, 1987:25).

However, from the perspective of an elderly person, the provision of services by an adult child may be perceived to disrupt the balance of exchange, and if the elderly person's resources are diminished or devalued, he or she becomes dependent in the exchange relationship. If reciprocity is not possible, this could lead to lowered self-esteem and morale, to stress, and to a refusal to seek or even accept assistance when support is offered by members of the informal network. In reality, this sense of an unbalanced relationship and a subsequent withdrawal is more likely to prevail in relationships with friends and neighbors than in kinship relations. Even in the later years, the parent-child relationship is based on reciprocity, with emotional support being the most common type of exchange (Rosenthal, 1987). For example, 63 percent of the parents in a study of 400 older adults (65+) in London, Ontario, reported that they both gave and received support in a variety of areas (Connidis, 1989:48-49). Only 15 percent reported receiving but not giving any assistance. Moreover, there was a high level of reported satisfaction with the exchange: '95 percent believed that their children give them about the right amount of help, and 92 percent believed that they in turn give their children the right amount of help.' However, these are community-dwelling older adults. When a health crisis emerges, the balance of power and obligation often shifts to the child as the frail adult loses control and independence, often being unable to provide even advice or emotional support to the caregiver.

INFORMAL SOCIAL SUPPORT

Introduction

Cantor and Little (1985:748) described the social support system for the elderly as a series of concentric rings surrounding the elderly person, who is located in the core. The innermost circle consists of kin; the next circle, moving outward from the core, includes friends and neighbors; the third circle represents mediating and support groups such as religious and ethnic groups and voluntary associations serving the elderly. All of these individuals and groups are capable of providing informal support to aging adults. Clearly, the family, along with extended kin and close friends, provides the first avenue of assistance and support. In fact, it has been estimated that of the noninstitutionalized elders, 94 percent in Canada (Chappell, 1985; Chappell and Havens, 1985) and 80 percent in the United States (Brody, 1981) receive some assistance from members of their informal network. Indeed, the relatively small percentage of elderly persons living in long-term care institutions suggests that a large amount of the care for the frail, impaired, and dependent elderly person is provided in the home by family, friends, and neighbors.

The informal systems provide greater help than the formal system (Biegel, 1985). However, because the family support system is often working at capacity, there is a need to create new informal support systems in the community, especially where the proportion of those over 80 years of age is increasing. Moreover, even among those receiving formal care, Chappell et al. (1986) have reported that 80 percent receive informal care at the same time. For example, a hospitalized or institutionalized elderly person still receives such informal support from kin and friends as visiting, assisting with feeding, and attending to personal financial affairs.

The informal support system is a helping network that serves a variety of possible functions for the elderly person, including: serving as a companion and confidant; maintaining independence and competence; coping with and adjusting to stressful events, illness, or role transitions; enhancing well-being and the quality of life through meaningful interpersonal relationships; helping with the tasks of daily living; maintaining social relationships; and assisting with the process of socialization for old age.[2] In short, most older adults are part of a primary support system that involves giving and receiving goods, services, and emotional support. The aim of this system is to enhance an individual's ability to maintain personal self-worth, independence, and mastery over the environment, rather than to encourage or foster dependency on significant others or on the formal care system (Cantor and Little, 1985; Chappell and Havens, 1985).

Informal support involves both a subjective and an objective component (Brownell and Shumaker, 1984; Chappell et al., 1986). The subjective component pertains to the *quality* (access to people one can trust, share intimacies with, and confide in), meaning (the importance or value of contact with kin and friends for well-being), and satisfaction with one's support system. The objective component refers to the *quantity* of relationships (number of available kin, friends, neighbors), the availability of assistance (proximity and availability of kin and others when needed), and the degree to which the support system is utilized (the amount, frequency, and intensity of interaction). In the later years, both continuity and change occur in the quantity and the quality of informal social support and social participation available to aging adults (Field and Minkler, 1988). Change and disruption can occur due to losses of support through retirement, widowhood, relocation, or death. Most of these changes affect ties outside the family, especially for men who decrease their sense of commitment to outside activities and organizations prior to or following retirement. However, relationships with near and distant kin remain stable and continuous, primarily because of filial bonding and a sense of obligation. For others, a change in status (such as remarriage) or a move to a new residence (such as a seniors' apartment building) can lead to an increase in the size of one's network.

The size of the informal support network may decline with age because of the deteriorating health of elderly persons and their age peers, the loss of network members through migration to another community, a loss of mobility due to decreased functional capacity, and institutionalization or death. The qualitative dimension of the informal relationships outside the family may deteriorate as well if interaction becomes less frequent. However, since the informal networks of older adults inevitably consist of more and more women, the qualitative aspects, even if there are fewer social relationships, are likely to persist, especially where women play the role of comforter and confidant (Rosenthal, 1987). Not surprisingly, the quality of family relationships remains relatively stable, unless the burden of caregiving becomes too stressful.

Types and Sources of Informal Support

Most types and sources of informal support in the later years are provided by the family (Ward et al., 1984; Brody, 1985; Cohen and Syme, 1985; Chappell et al., 1986; Matthews, 1987, 1988; Thompson, 1989; Antonucci, 1990; Gatz et al., 1990). The type of informal support provided includes emotional support as a visitor, companion, or confidant; help with normal activities such as home repairs, home maintenance, transportation, shopping, banking, and cooking; instrumental help with more basic personal needs such as eating, bathing, or dressing in order to sustain health and prevent institutionalization; and assistance in providing information about available services within the informal and formal support networks.

Although family support is evident throughout adult life, as parents reach their later years, children begin to monitor more closely, and to show more concern about, a parent's health (Hanson and Sauer, 1985; Marshall, 1987; Connidis, 1989). More specifically, as Marshall (1987) found, daughters worry more than sons, and they worry more about their fathers. Actual assistance is often initiated with the onset of an acute or a chronic illness. The role of primary caregiver is normally assumed, in rank order, by the spouse (Hess and Soldo, 1985); then by an adult child, usually a daughter or a daughter-in-law; and then by another relative such as a sibling (Cicirelli, 1985), or a niece or a nephew who has had a strong family tie with the elderly person over a long period of time (Shore, 1985).

Brody (1985) argued that this helping behavior by the family represents a normative belief in our society that it is a natural and typical family 'exchange' to care for a frail elderly parent. Aronson (1985), however, suggests that the assumption that it is 'natural' for the family to care for a frail parent should be questioned. She argues that caregiving is yet another example of how females are coerced into unpaid work. One response to this debate about the role of the family is the suggestion that the primary caregiver be compensated for this type of labor by wages and pension benefits. While programs of this nature are being established in Canada and elsewhere,[3] they are not universally available. For example, Nova Scotia has a program whereby elders receive money to pay caregivers for the services they desire, while Veterans Affairs provides payments to eligible caregivers.

Marital status is an important factor in both the source and the type of informal family support. Males, because they die earlier, generally have a spouse to care for them in the later years. For elderly widows and the divorced, daughters tend to be the primary providers. For the never-married (Burnley, 1987), much of the available assistance from kin is social and emotional support rather than health care support, perhaps because the kin do not live in close geographical proximity to the elderly person.

The major sources of nonfamily informal support are friends and neighbors (Cantor, 1979; O'Bryant, 1985; Peters and Kaiser, 1985), and voluntary associations with long-standing religious, ethnic, or social ties to the elderly person (Breytspraak et al., 1985; Danigelis, 1985). Often the friends and neighbors are age peers who have shared a lifetime of common experiences, and who are similar in terms of social status, beliefs, and lifestyles. These sources provide mainly emotional support in times of stress (such as widowhood) and instrumental support for daily activities (transportation, household tasks). These helping relationships are based on mutual choice and mutual need, rather than on personal, lifelong family obligations (Chappell, 1983).

Factors Influencing the Quantity and Quality of Informal Support

Introduction

The presence of a spouse, adult child, other relative, friend, or neighbor does not guarantee that assistance will be provided nor that it will be of high quality if it is provided. Rather, the social and physical environment of the elderly person, the personal characteristics of both the potential caregivers and the recipient, and the history of the relationship (for example, the reciprocity history) between potential caregivers and recipients must be considered when assessing the potential resources of the informal support network (Cantor and Little, 1985; Cohen and Syme, 1985; Sauer and Coward, 1985a; Chappell et al., 1986:132-36; Connidis, 1989; Biegel and Blum, 1990). Of particular importance are the degree of frailty or dependency of the elderly person, and the proximity and the health, employment, social, and ethnic status of the potential care-giver, especially if the caregiver is not a member of the immediate family.

Filial Responsibility

The degree of responsibility expressed for the support or care of an elderly parent or family member is closely related to the sense of obligation and affection built up over a period of family history. Where intergenerational relations are strong (Rosenthal, 1987) and perceived to be important, family assistance is more likely to be forthcoming, although the type and the quality of assistance may vary if the caregiver is divorced, employed, or lives at a distance. While the family is the major support system for most elderly adults, the expectations of the parents and the children as to what assistance is needed and should be provided, and when, may or may not coincide. For example, for very elderly parents (80+), adult children may be in their 60s and have their own needs for health, social, and economic support (Marcus and Jaeger, 1984). In this case other relatives in the extended family or public or private agencies may have to assume responsibility.

From the perspective of an aging parent, expectations of filial assistance seem to be higher in the following situations: with increasing age, among females and among the widowed and the divorced; when economic resources are limited; when health declines; and when the level of morale, life satisfaction, or well-being declines. Thus, perceptions or expectations of filial responsibility may intervene to decrease or increase informal support in the later years. If the expectations of the parents and the child differ, family solidarity is weakened, conflict or abuse may occur, and public or private agencies may need to intervene to fill the void left by unavailable or inadequate informal support.

Sociodemographic and Personal Characteristics

The need for privacy, affiliation, sociability, and autonomy, for both the aging adult and potential caregivers, must be considered when support is offered and accepted (Chappell et al., 1986:132-36; Connidis, 1989:50-52). These factors are especially relevant with respect to non-kin who may offer help, and to accepting assistance with personal needs such as bathing and dressing.

Throughout the life cycle, daughters or daughters-in-law tend to be the primary caregiver[4] (Chappell, 1989), and elderly women tend to be the recipients of more social support than men (Antonucci, 1985). These patterns may evolve because women are more likely to be comfortable with expressive, nurturant relationships; because the mother-daughter relationship becomes stronger, especially after the daughter becomes a mother; because women tend to live in close proximity and to interact more frequently with members of the family; because societal norms expect women to play this nurturing, supportive role; and because a daughter may not have the personal economic resources to share with her parents, or to buy needed services. With increasing numbers of daughters entering the labor force, the role of caregiver has not been abandoned, but the nature of the support has changed.[5] Working women become case managers who may still provide help with shopping, home care, emotional support, and transportation, but who delegate other aspects of home and personal care by purchasing services from non-kin (Brody and Schoonover, 1986; Brody et al., 1987; Seltzer et al., 1987). In general, daughters provide more assistance than sons to ailing parents,

regardless of the quality of the relationship or the competing demands in their own lives (Bromberg, 1983; Brody et al., 1989). Although nonemployed sisters contribute more tangible services than their employed sisters when a parent's health status deteriorates, employed sisters are expected (by their siblings) to contribute during the evenings and weekends (Matthews et al., 1989). These 'secondary' caregivers provide indirect support, and are an important element in the caregiving system, especially where respite care services are not available.

From the perspective of sons, many of whom may not live close by, assisting older parents is more likely to involve financial aid, home repairs, information dissemination, and managerial decision making (for example, when and where to change housing). Sons who accept responsibility as the primary caregiver are more likely to be only children, to not have a sister, or to be the child who lives in closest proximity to the parent. In this situation, however, it is often the daughter-in-law who becomes the primary caregiver in terms of directed personal care.

The giving and receiving of social support in the later years is also influenced by the cultural beliefs, traditions, and values within particular social class, ethnic, religious, or racial groups (Cantor and Little, 1985; Guttman, 1985; Chappell et al., 1986; Rosenthal, 1986a; Driedger and Chappell, 1987; Penning and Chappell, 1987). There is a high frequency of quality aid where the elderly are highly respected and valued; where assistance and care are believed to be 'private' family matters; and where the elderly are ineligible for government assistance programs. The quality of assistance is also high where language difficulties inhibit access to formal support systems; where the elderly have been economically disadvantaged throughout life; where the first generation elders have not been culturally or structurally assimilated into mainstream society (often because they live and work within a residential subculture); and where the extended family represents a solid network. Highlight 10.2 illustrates the dependency of elderly native Canadians on their informal support system.

There are also social class differences, which can interact with race and ethnicity, in the fre-

AN INFORMAL SUPPORT SYSTEM FOR ELDERLY NATIVE CANADIANS

Within a society, the quality of life in the later years varies by such sociodemographic characteristics as gender, ethnicity, class, and religion. That is, structural inequalities can influence economic resources, housing, environmental conditions, and the structure and composition of available informal and formal networks. For many disadvantaged groups, the implementation of an effective formal support system can assist older adults in the later years. However, these services must be accepted and utilized by the disadvantaged group. Such factors as cultural values and beliefs about accepting public support, the availabilty of a functional informal support network, language difficulties, or a lack of knowledge about the availability of formal support services may contribute to the lack of use or to the underutilization of the formal support system.

Historically, and at present, native people have been among the most disadvantaged elders in North America. Living on reservations, they experience substandard housing, geographical isolation, limited opportunities for employment in an industrial world, and problems of gaining access to total health care, even though services are provided at no cost to the patient. As a mode of survival, native people have become highly dependent on the economic, emotional, and personal care support of the extended family who still live on the reservation.

In a comparison of the availability and use of informal networks by native and non-native elderly people residing in nonurban areas, Bienvenue and Havens (1986) found that the native elderly are more likely to live in substandard housing, which often lacks indoor plumbing and adequate heating, lighting, and kitchen facilities. Moreover, they live in larger households, often including nonrelatives, and most of these housing structures provide little privacy. In terms of medical care, the native elderly reported a lack of access to nursing, dental, and eye care, and the unavailability of medical and nursing care in the home. As a result, they reported high levels of dissatisfaction with the availability of health care services. Consequently, it was not surprising to find that elderly native Canadians report receiving a higher level of assistance from their informal network than do non-native rural Canadians. For example, over 90 percent of the native elderly, compared to 75 to 80 percent of the non-natives, reported obtaining help from their primary group for assistance with meals, shopping, and housework. The difference is even more dramatic in terms of reported assistance from formal agencies (3 to 16 percent for natives versus 20 to 50 percent for non-natives, depending on the task or the need).

In summary, faced with inadequate housing and medical care, native elderly Canadians are more likely to draw upon the limited, but familiar and available, resources of their informal network. This study suggests that even where social policies provide mechanisms of formal support, they may not be accepted by, or delivered to, disadvantaged subcultural groups within the elderly population. Whether this greater use of informal networks by the native elderly represents cultural traditions, inadequate policies, or necessity remains to be explored.

---

quency and type of exchange in later years. Whereas the working-class elderly and their children exchange goods and services, members of the middle or upper classes tend to exchange money for the purchase of services. Lacking financial resources, working-class daughters in the labor force are more likely to stop working in order to care for a failing parent, and are more likely to care for a dependent parent or parent-in-law in their own home.

The Quality of Parent-Adult Child Relationships

Questions pertaining to the quality of a relationship parallel the classic 'chicken-and-egg' dilemma: which event occurs first? Does the quantity, frequency, or type of support decline because the quality of the relationship declines, or does the quality decline as the frequency of interaction decreases? To date, relatively little research has been completed on the perceived quality of informal support given and received in the later years. Rather, it has been assumed that a high-quality relationship exists. This suggests that the process of social and economic exchange between the generations is based on mutual understanding. The elderly recognize the right of their adult children to live independently, as they themselves did; they wish to continue to help them if they are able; they seek to interact but remain independent as long as possible; and they expect to receive assistance when and if it is needed. Employing a different interpretation of what has been termed 'intimacy at a distance' (Rosenmayr and Kockeis, 1963), Blau (1981) argued that this theme does not reflect an ideal, voluntary situation but rather reflects the marginal status of the elderly within the extended family. She stated that elderly parents may actually prefer more frequent and meaningful interaction with their children. However, recognizing that this is unlikely to occur, the elderly report that they prefer 'intimacy at a distance' in order to rationalize and maintain at least a minimal amount of interaction.

This alternative interpretation of 'intimacy at a distance,' along with increasing reports of caregiver burden and elder abuse, have led to further research about when and why a change in the quality of informal support relationships occurs. In general, the quality seems to deteriorate when competing alternatives intervene in the life of a primary caregiver (for example, marital conflict or dissolution, work, personal health concerns, child-rearing pressures or problems), when the morale and health of the elderly parent deteriorates, and when problems in housing become life threatening. More specifically, the quality of a mother-daughter relationship may deteriorate over time because a daughter experiences changes in her own lifestyle, which, in turn, lower her affective feelings and sense of obligation for her mother. These changes include the launching and marriage of her own offspring; an increasing involvement in the labor force; a changing marital relationship after child launching; divorce or widowhood; and the declining health of an aging mother, which makes care and assistance, rather than meaningful verbal or social interaction, the major focus of the role relationship. Throughout all of these changes, a mother

may still perceive her daughter to be highly salient in her life and her main source of emotional support. When this perception is not shared by the daughter, and when the type of interaction changes, there is a possibility of conflict, lower morale, and decreased well-being, even though the frequency of interaction could remain at a relatively high level. Clearly, lifestyle changes affecting the daughter and health changes affecting the parent are interrelated and must be considered in any study of the quality of the relationship in later life. The specific issues of caregiver burden and elder abuse are discussed in the following sections.

Outcomes of Informal Support

The Recipient

The informal support network has the potential to prevent stress, to prevent stress from becoming distress, to assist in decision making about adaptation to aging effects (for example, housing decisions), to maintain independent living, to enhance or maintain life satisfaction, and to facilitate the recovery from or adaptation to acute or chronic illness (Lawton, 1983; Antonucci, 1985, 1990; Walter, 1985; Ward, 1985; Chappell et al., 1986). Indeed, most studies have shown that supportive ties with family, friends, and neighbors can enhance or maintain physical or mental health (Antonucci, 1985; Wellman and Hall,1986) and contribute to higher levels of well-being, life satisfaction, or happiness (Wister and Strain, 1986; Krause, 1987). Moreover, even among older adults who live alone, including those on skid row (Cohen et al., 1985, 1988), isolation, loneliness and coping with stressful situations can be buffered or alleviated by the presence of an informal network of supportive friends and acquaintances (Rubinstein, 1985). In many cases the network linkages for these isolated elders are recent and transitory, and they do have a buffering effect, especially with respect to daily survival (for example, food, housing) and coping with stress. In fact, Cohen et al. (1988) report that elderly men living on skid row initiate and foster reciprocal exchange relationships, particularly with respect to the sharing of food and information.

In spite of the overwhelming evidence of the

positive outcomes of informal social support, not all ties may be supportive — either initially or in the long-term. With increasing reports of elder abuse in the 1980s, gerontologists began to examine more closely the quality of relationships. As a result, some potentially negative outcomes have been revealed, for both the recipient and, as we will see in the next section, for the caregiver.

To consider the possibility of negative outcomes, researchers have shown an increased interest in studying the perceived meaning, value, and acceptance of social support by elderly recipients (Brownell and Shumaker, 1984; Antonucci, 1985; House and Kahn, 1985; Townsend and Poulshock, 1986; Krause, 1987). Thus, while the intent of the caregiver may be positive, the outcome, as perceived by the recipient, may be quite different. For example, an elderly person may resent the loss of privacy because of increasing levels of personal care that are needed; may experience feelings of being overprotected and of losing personal control and, thus feel unnecessarily dependent on others; may exaggerate the 'sick' role in order to seek attention; and may resent the demeaning, childlike treatment that is given. Moreover, where the level of interaction with others fails to fit their needs or expectations, or where the support system is disrupted by a crucial life transition experienced by the primary caregiver (for example, divorce, employment, a move to another city, failing health), elderly persons may report feelings of deprivation and isolation. Yet, in the same situation, the caregiver(s) may perceive that the level and quality of support is totally adequate. If the recipient becomes increasingly dependent and is unable to maintain some degree of equity in the exchange relationship, the person may resist informal support and turn more to the formal support system. The most unacceptable outcome arises when the elderly person becomes the victim of physical, psychological, or financial abuse.

The Caregiver

The perceived and reported negative outcomes of stress, and the feelings of being burdened, seldom occur in typical family exchange relationships where the elderly person is as-

sisted on an irregular or regular basis. Rather, serious levels of stress and burden are felt by caregivers when the elderly person experiences a significant degree of physical, cognitive, or emotional impairment. In this situation, an increase of time and emotional commitment by the caregiver is required if the elderly person is to continue living in the community. This situation has been called the 'wear and tear' hypothesis of caregiving: as the frequency of aberrant behavior increases, so does the level of caregiver stress (Pruchno and Resch, 1989).

The majority of caregivers are women. Indeed, elderly men are primarily cared for by the spouse, while elderly women are primarily cared for by a daughter. Caregiving to an elderly spouse can be particularly stressful when the spouse is cognitively impaired. This stress is created or compounded by the emotional loss of a spouse as he used to be; by the physical difficulty in coping with some of the necessary tasks; by worry and anxiety about her financial future; and by a deterioration of her own physical health and the onset of depression or loneliness (Barusch, 1988). Fengler and Goodrich (1979) stressed that these 'hidden victims' in the social support system need considerable social support to minimize the stress and burden of caregiving. This perceived burden and stress are much higher for those caring for a cognitively impaired elder than for those caring for a physically impaired elder (Kraus, 1984; George and Gwyther, 1986; Quayhagen and Quayhagen, 1988; Miller, 1989; Pruchno and Resch, 1989; Scharlach, 1989), primarily because of the severe and disturbing behavioral manifestations of this type of illness, and because the formal social support system is less well prepared to provide assistance for this type of impairment. Highlight 10.3 presents some case studies illustrating the stress and the burden of parent care. Similar stresses and experiences have been reported by those caring for a spouse.

The increased awareness and study[6] of the stresses and burdens of caregiving in the 1980s arose because of a number of interacting societal and personal factors. These included: government policies promoting community care of the elderly; an increase in life expectancy and therefore the role of caregiver being played by

HIGHLIGHT 10.3

THE STRESS AND THE BURDEN OF PARENT CARE

The level of stress and the burden experienced by an adult child caring for a parent is a function of the unique interaction of a number of factors, including the type and degree of impairment in terms of functional ability; the personality and the perceived ability of the caregiver to play the role; the availability of social support from outside and within the family; the personality and demands of the older person; the quality of the lifelong relationship between the adult child and the elderly parent; and the presence of competing demands or problems in the caregiver's personal life (for example, divorce, career, children, personal health, alcoholism, unemployment). The following unattributed and amalgamated statements and situations, as reported in the media and to case workers or to social scientists, vividly depict the extent to which stress, fear, guilt, anxieties, and bizarre behavior can occur in a caregiving relationship:

- I was talking on the telephone, trying to rearrange my schedule for the day, when my mother attacked me from behind with a pot because I wasn't paying attention to her. Never in my life had I seen her utter a violent word or action.

- In the last six months since my mother moved into the house, I have experienced both mental and physical fatigue and have started drinking again. My teenage son is having emotional and scholastic problems at school and I feel helpless since I just do not have enough time for him in the evening.

- He is not the father I knew. If he asks for something to eat, he later asks why I served him lunch. Now he is confined to bed and I need help to lift him. I cannot meet his ever-increasing demands and I feel guilty.

- Her mental condition has deteriorated rapidly. She is verbally abusive toward me, my family, and visitors. My own health has deteriorated over the past two years and I must now seriously consider placing my mother in a nursing home.

- When it became apparent that my mother could no longer live by herself, two choices were available: move her to a nursing home, wherever and whenever a bed became available; or move her into our home. My daughter had just left for college, I was tired of my job, so I decided to care for her in my home. I thought it would work. I was unprepared to meet her need for medical care. Her emotional outbursts and demands made me feel like a child again, and my husband grew more distant as I was consumed by the demands of caregiving. In about three years it became a question of my marriage and sanity versus institutionalized care for my mother. The decision wasn't easy, but it had to be made. It has taken me a long time to resolve the guilt of this decision, especially when I visit and see her empty life.

- The full responsibility and 'wear and tear' have fallen on me. My sister who lives ten miles away contributes nothing but telephone calls to me, to see how 'her' mother is doing. She never asks how I am doing or if she can help in any way.

more elderly spouses and adult children, especially wives and daughters; an increase in the divorce rate and in the entry or retention of middle-aged women in the labor force, which, in turn, created more competing commitments and stresses on the potential primary caregivers; and the aging of the potential primary caregivers, who may have experienced health problems as well.

As a result of these factors, there emerged a belief that long-term parent care is a 'normative experience' for adult children, particularly for daughters or daughters-in-law (Brody, 1985), and that this role relationship becomes stressful and a burden. More specifically, studies have reported such outcomes for the primary caregiver as: emotional and psychological stress (worry, self-blame, anxiety, guilt); a deteriora-

tion in personal health (loss of sleep, psychoso-
matic disorders, fatigue); the need to leave the
labor force and a career; a loss of leisure and a
personal social life; financial strain, especially
within the lower classes; strained relations with
one's own children and spouse; and strained
relations with siblings if responsibilities are not
being shared fairly, or are perceived to be not
shared fairly (Connidis, 1989:51-52; Toseland
and Zarit, 1989).

This normative belief has been perpetuated
because of the conceptual and methodological
inadequacies of existing research. Matthews
(1988) noted that many studies of parent care
are based on the responses of children who
have been identified by social service agencies.
That is, they are already burdened and at the
stage where help from the formal system is required. Many of these respondents are themselves disadvantaged in terms of social, financial, and physical resources. Thus, many findings have been based on the experiences of
those who report the most extreme or worst-
case scenarios of parent care (Wenger, 1987).

Similarly, Rosenthal et al. (1989) argued that
the study of parent care must consider the level
of competing commitments faced by the
primary caregiver. As the number of competing commitments of the caregiver increase (for
example, the number of living parents or
parents-in-law; number of children in the
caregiver's household; married versus not
married; employed or not employed), the caregiver (usually an adult daughter) experiences
the stress of being 'sandwiched' by the demands of the older person, the demands of her
own family, and the demands of her own career
(Brody, 1990). However, Rosenthal et al. (1989)
found, in a study of 163 women aged 40 to 69,
that the risk of being 'sandwiched' is not as
great as the current literature would have us
believe. They conclude that parent care is not a
normative experience for most middle-aged
women. Therefore, for some, but not for all
middle-aged women, the onset of physical or
psychological impairments by an elderly parent can increase the amount of daily contact
and responsibilities. Whether this increased
responsibility is perceived, initially or eventually, as a burden depends on the rate and the
type of health decline by the older person, the

sociodemographic characteristics and situation
of the caregiver (for example, age, gender,
employment, geographical proximity to the recipient), and the subjective feelings and sense
of responsibility of the caregiver,[7] including an
assessment of her own ability and resources to
cope with the added responsibility (Fischer,
1985; Horowitz, 1985a; Gubrium and Lynott,
1987). Indeed, even in the face of high levels of
stress, some caregivers reported that they nevertheless experienced high levels of satisfaction
because they were committed to helping the
elderly person (Miller, 1989). In the extreme
case, the primary caregiver may simultaneously play the role of nurse, homemaker, social
worker, psychologist, and chauffeur — all in
addition to her 'normal' responsibilities at work
or to her own family. It is for this reason that an
increasing number of social intervention programs are being initiated to assist the primary
caregivers within the family. These are discussed in the next major section on formal support systems.

FORMAL SOCIAL SUPPORT

Introduction

Early in our discussion of informal systems
we noted that the support system for the elderly can be described as a series of concentric
circles surrounding the elderly person at the
core (Cantor and Little, 1985:748). Whereas the
elements of the informal system are more intimate and structurally closer to the older adult,
the formal system is more objective and bureaucratic, and represents the outermost circles
in the support system.

The formal support system involves the provision of a range of health care and social services by varying levels of government, by not-
for-profit voluntary organizations, or by busi-
nesses in the private sector. From birth we are
the beneficiaries of such formal supports as a
universal health care plan, education, and public
transportation. In the later years, through legislation or private-sector initiatives, the formal
support system provides economic (pensions),
health (access to doctors, drugs, hospitals),

housing (seniors' apartments to long-term care), and social (homemaker services) security. The aim of this system is to provide a safety net for seniors who need assistance in the later years, and to do so by providing a continuum of services that range from community-based and in-home programs, to adult day care centers (Conrad et al., 1990), to homes for the aged, to nursing homes, to chronic care hospitals (Cantor and Little, 1985; Krout, 1985; Chappell et al., 1986:117). This continuum can serve the needs of the well elderly (for example, senior centers), the moderately healthy elderly (for example, meals-on-wheels, in-home care) and the frail elderly (for example, nursing aid at home, institutionalized housing).

The goals of most government-based support systems are to enable elderly persons to remain in their homes as independent citizens, and to supplement and complement the informal care provided by families. Historically,[8] most public funds have been allocated to pensions and health care, including long-term institutionalized housing. As a result, a custodial care model evolved that encouraged the 'warehousing' or overinstitutionalization of the frail elderly in long-term care facilities (Forbes et al., 1987). Since the 1970s, however, there has been a gradual social movement toward deinstitutionalizing all special groups (such as the physically and mentally disabled of all ages, criminals). Not surprisingly, with increasing awareness of the costs associated with an aging population, public-sector policies have sought to shift more of the responsibility for the long-term care of the frail and dependent elderly to individuals and families (Kirwin, 1988), or to the private sector. These community-based programs (such as home care, day care, respite care) provide more satisfying alternatives to the frail elderly and to their caregivers. They also fit more coherently with the services provided by the informal support system. However, for frail elderly persons who are without kin or who have been neglected or abused, institutionalization may be the best alternative, and such a relocation may enhance their sense of well-being (Salamon, 1987).

Formal and Informal Care: An Interactive System

A long-standing debate in the social support literature has been whether the formal health and social care systems substitute for or complement the informal care system. The substitution hypothesis argues that when families are unavailable, unable, or unwilling to help, when elderly people are isolated or abandoned, or when informal caregivers can no longer provide adequate support, a formal safety net system must be provided by the public sector. In contrast, the complementarity hypothesis argues that a balanced and coordinated system of informal and formal support services is essential to enhance the quality of life of both the elderly and their caregivers. That is, neither total government nor total family responsibility is the ideal model of social support for the elderly.

Most evidence suggests that the systems are complementary (at least, potentially) and do provide a continuum of assistance and care (Chappell and Havens, 1985; Litwak, 1985; Sauer and Coward, 1985b; Chappell et al., 1986:139-56; Forbes et al., 1987; Seltzer et al., 1987; Kirwin, 1988; Noelker and Bass, 1989). The process generally involves first using the resources of the informal system and then those of formal organizations. In reality, as Chappell (1985) noted, most elderly persons in the community who receive formal care services also receive care from informal sources. Similarly, even when hospitalized for an acute illness or when institutionalized for a chronic impairment, elders may be provided with a range of helping behaviors from adult children (Hall, 1989a). These include emotional support, and personal care such as feeding, financial aid, or assistance in working with the bureaucracy of the government or the institution. In effect, a member of the family can play the role of case manager to provide a link between the informal and the formal systems on behalf of the frail elderly person (Seltzer et al., 1987). This process involves serving as a facilitator, an advocate, a protector, and an advisor; and as a buffer against the formal bureaucracy of the government and institutions. However, if this role is played, conflict between the caregiver and the care recipient may occur as the demands or expectations of the recipient increase (Hall, 1989b; Abel, 1990).

Given the potential complementary existence of informal and formal support for the elderly, a major problem in the realization of this potential has been the lack of coordination between the two levels in many jurisdictions. In some cases this occurs because there is a lack of information about a service or about how to gain access to the service (Thompson and McFarland, 1989). In other situations, the two systems may compete for the right to provide a similar service or for the power to make decisions. In still other jurisdictions the coordinated system may not work because the demand for formal services far exceeds the capacity of the system.

Regardless of the reason for the failure of the total support system to provide universal, equal, and coordinated access, a variety of mechanisms have been proposed or used to provide an integrated rather than a competing system. These include the use of social workers as case managers, the training of a family member to be a case manager (Seltzer et al., 1987), and the creation of a single agency in each community to serve as a source of information and as a single entry point into the formal support system. This central agency could provide informal caregivers with advice and information; could complete a needs assessment of the recipient and the caregiver; could lobby for additional services and facilities; could assess the quality of existing public or private facilities and services; and could monitor the quality of care provided by informal caregivers. Finally, such an agency could assist in coordinating information about the availability of, and access to, the range of services provided by varying levels of government.

The Utilization of Formal Services

The usage rates of formal social services by older adults are quite low, with the main users being very elderly frail women who are unmar-ried or childless, or who live alone.[9] For example, Chappell et al. (1986:107) and Connidis (1985, 1987) indicate that less than 10 percent of older adults living in the community report using or needing some type of formal support services, while Béland (1989) found that less than 2 percent were heavy users of health and social services. Some possible reasons for these low utilization rates of community social services include: a lack of knowledge about the availability of formal social services (Krout, 1988; Thompson and McFarland, 1989); a desire to remain independent or interdependent with a friend or a child; the denial of actual use of a service; an inability to gain access to the formal system; subtle discrimination against elderly members of minority groups, who only speak and read their own language (MacLean et al., 1987); and barriers erected by the bureaucracy, such as eligibility tests for need.

Usage is also determined by the rules and regulations of a given program or agency. For example, is the service available to all citizens who reach a certain age, therefore representing a universal program (such as health care)? Is it limited to those who can demonstrate need (for example, for housing, for a guaranteed income supplement)? Or is it limited to those who have made contributions in the past (for example, pension payments)? Increasingly, it is argued that policies should be based on need rather than chronological age. This would reduce the total cost to the public, but it would also place more pressure on families to contribute to the caregiving of the elderly. However, a major issue that remains to be resolved is how to define and measure need in the social service domain (Chappell et al., 1986:97).

Types and Sources of Formal Support: Social Intervention Strategies

By now it should be clear that family, friends, and neighbors represent a large informal support network for aging adults. However, as the elderly person becomes frail and either physically or cognitively impaired, the burden for community care falls, almost exclusively, on the spouse or an adult child. Yet, as we have seen, this pool of primary caregivers may be shrinking due to such factors as decreasing fertility, increasing divorce rates, and increased labor-force participation by adult women. At the same time, the size of the elderly population is increasing because of greater life expectancy, and therefore the age of potential caregivers is also increasing. For example, Brody (1986) reported that in the United States, one out of ten older adults has a child who is at least 65 years of age. Given these developments, the private sector, government agencies, and voluntary associations are developing intervention strategies to assist the caregivers of the frail elderly,[10] and to assist the elderly person to live independently in the community for as long as possible.

The debate about whether and how the family caregiver should be assisted is represented by two general perspectives. One approach argues that the family should take total responsibility for the care of their aging elders, and that the government should only assist those who have no living kin. This approach may also argue that if the family are unable to cope with caring for a frail parent, they must reimburse the government for the costs associated with institutionalization. On the other hand, a more humanitarian and reasonable approach recognizes that most families do all they can to care for a frail parent. However, they may become overextended and burdened at some point and have to make the unpleasant decision to place the parent in an institution. On the basis of these assumptions, this approach argues that the government has a responsibility to assist the primary caregivers of elderly parents.

To assist older adults and to relieve primary caregivers, three categories of intervention strategies have been introduced. First, recognizing the considerable stress and strain associated with the role of caregiver, programs seek to provide emotional and social support for the caregiver. These include: individual and group educational or counseling sessions; skills training in the provision of regularly required health and personal care needs; and the formation of mutual-help support groups (for example, for the caregivers of Alzheimer's patients). These programs can reduce the sense of isolation and feelings of helplessness, and thereby increase the ability to cope. A frequently requested

program, but one which is not always available, involves respite care. This service involves temporary supervision or care that is intended to provide the primary caregiver with a daily, weekly, or holiday respite from the stress and burden of caregiving (Scharlach and Frenzel, 1986; Berman et al., 1987; Chappell and Blandford, 1987; Miller and Goldman, 1989; Conrad et al., 1990). In this type of program either the elderly person remains in the home and a companion or aide moves in, or the elderly person is moved to a facility (for example, to a hospital, nursing home, or long-term care institution) as a daily outpatient or as a short-term visitor. Ideally, respite service should be utilized *before* a family crisis occurs, so that it serves a preventative rather than a rehabilitative or crisis-management function for the caregiver. As well, a continuum of possible respite services should be available in the community to meet the changing demands of caregiving.

A second category of assistance involves some type of financial incentive or reimbursement for the caregiver (Keigher et al., 1988; Linsk et al., 1988). This type of assistance may involve tax credits for the primary caregiver, or a subsidy payment to help purchase needed services.[3] However, for many caregivers the financial burden is not the major problem. Rather, relief from the emotional and psychological strain is needed and money cannot substantially relieve this burden. For working women, the financial assistance may be used to purchase daytime personal care for an elderly parent, but it still does not relieve the overall daily burden.

The third major category of assistance involves the provision of varying levels of formal care programs, within or outside the home (Gallagher, 1985; Horowitz, 1985a, 1985b; Chappell et al., 1986; Stephens and Christianson, 1986). These programs include: home maintenance services; transportation; alternative housing (such as congregate); and home health care (such as bathing, nursing, therapy). Highlight 10.4 describes the highly successful integrated home care program in the Regional Municipality of Niagara (Ontario).

In addition to caregiver support provided by the public sector, the private sector and voluntary associations are also seeking ways to assist

HIGHLIGHT 10.4

AN INTERVENTION STRATEGY: HOME CARE PROGRAMS

Most senior citizens want to stay in their own homes for as long as possible. Moreover, most elderly people cope well within the community, especially if some type and degree of informal and formal assistance is available, if needed. To meet this expressed desire and need, local and regional governments, often in conjunction with voluntary agencies, have introduced home care programs that provide a range of services to the elderly and/or to their caregivers. Most of these programs are designed to complement, not replace, the informal assistance that is provided by friends and neighbors.

In some communities the programs are universal; in others they are available according to demonstrated need. Furthermore, some services are provided at no cost; others require the recipient or the caregiver to pay some or all of the costs. The number and the variety of services available in a given community vary greatly according to the revenue available, the quality of leadership, and the priorities of politicians and other civic leaders. In the ideal setting, a continuum of services is provided that can be accessed as needs change from total independence to partial dependence to total dependence. In general, a community should seek to provide support services for the elderly person within the home and the community; a range of housing options (for example, low cost, senior housing; congregate, sheltered housing; and long-term care facilities); and services to assist the primary caregiver.

As an example of what can be accomplished given appropriate resources and strong and innovative leadership, the Senior Citizens Department of the Regional Municipality of Niagara (Ontario) provides an integrated program of community-based and institutionally based services for the elderly in five cities, five towns, and two townships. This department has a mandate to develop and deliver services to the elderly; to develop programs, but then let other groups (such as charitable organizations, seniors' groups) operate the programs; to serve as an advocate for seniors' needs and rights; and to provide information and assistance to seniors, their caregivers, the public, civil servants, and politicians. In short, this department serves as the major agency for the leadership and the coordination of policies and services for the elderly in the region. As a result, conflict between different agencies has been eliminated, and cracks in the formal care system have been identified and rectified.

Some of the services offered include:

- Integrated home help — meal preparation, meals-on-wheels, personal care, housekeeping, lawn mowing, snow shoveling, home repairs, and so forth. These services may be provided by volunteers or at a low hourly rate.

- Postal alert security system — postal carriers watch for seniors who may be at risk.

- Adult day-care and vacation care respite service — to relieve some of the burden for caregivers.

- Senior volunteers — seniors help other seniors.

- Communication programs — the talk-a-bit program provides daily calls from volunteers to seniors; the Pen Pals program encourages communication with age peers outside the region; and the Friendly Visiting program offers friendship and support to alleviate boredom and loneliness.

- Home-sharing program — a senior lives with a homeowner in the community who seeks companionship, who has extra space, or who needs a modest income; or a senior takes in one or more 'home mates' who pay a low rent or who are willing to do household chores in return for housing.

- Senior-citizen centers — a variety of programs are available.

- Home nursing/therapy programs — services are provided in the home so that a senior with limited mobility does not have to go to a clinic or a hospital.

- Transportation throughout the community — volunteer drivers for those without cars, plus a formal system for seniors in wheelchairs, are available.

- Homes for the aged — admissions to, and the operation of, these homes are coordinated by the Senior Citizens Department. As a result, admissions are made only after the resources and options of other community-based services have been exhausted.

- Adopt-a-grandparent — an intergenerational program brings children of the community together with residents of regional homes.

- Foster grandparent — encourages seniors to create a one-to-one relationship with children who have special needs.

- Satellite home care — the well elderly, unable to live independently, live in a community-based congregate housing setting. They are encouraged to be active around the house, but meals and laundry are provided.

the primary caregiver. In the volunteer sector, widow-to-widow support networks, senior centers, and self-help[11] (Fedorak and Griffin, 1986) or mutual-help groups (Lieberman, 1990) provide direct or indirect assistance to primary caregivers. In the private sector, although few policies exist, there is an increasing amount of debate about the initiation of flextime and/or family leave for employees who are primary caregivers to an elderly person. This concept of family leave parallels the policy of maternity or paternity leave, or the policy of parental leave for a male or female who adopts a child. However, before family leave for parental care is likely to be widely adopted, the following issues must be resolved: Will it apply to both public- and private-sector employees? Will it be a paid or unpaid leave? If it is a paid leave, who will be responsible for payment, the government or the private employer? Who will be eligible, when, and for how long a period of time (Wisensale and Allison, 1988)? These cost-related issues will likely prolong the debate and delay or prevent the initiation of innovative programs of formal private-sector support to primary caregivers. Thus, any assistance at this level is likely to evolve on the personal level between a sympathetic employer or supervisor and a burdened employee whose work performance declines, or who is facing a decision to withdraw from the labor force. Where assistance is not forthcoming, the level of stress for the caregiver may escalate to the extent that neglect or abuse of the elderly person occurs. In the next section you will learn about this hidden issue, which until recently has been a silent problem experienced by a minority of the frail and dependent elderly.

ELDER ABUSE AND NEGLECT

Introduction

The abuse and the neglect of the elderly is a silent problem, like incidents of child and spousal abuse. Thus, it was not until the 1980s that the media, politicians, social welfare workers, and seniors began to identify and report isolated incidents of elder abuse and neglect.[12] Much of the credit for this increased awareness should go to the media, which vividly portrayed incidents of 'granny bashing' (Callahan, 1988), and to the field of gerontology, which began to study the incidence, cause, and possible treatment of this heretofore hidden form of behavior.[13]

This increased emphasis on reporting, studying, and ameliorating elder abuse and neglect was also fostered by the development in the 1970s and 1980s of social values and legislation for enhanced human rights, and for the protection of these rights for citizens of all ages, especially those who are dependent on others (for example, infants, children, abused spouses, and the frail or impoverished elderly). Moreover, in recent years it has been recognized and accepted that society has a responsibility to assist the homeless, mentally ill, or alcoholic elderly who, through self-neglect or self-abuse, are unable to care for themselves. In this section the context, types, incidence, processes, outcomes, and interventions for this hidden social problem are examined.

Definitions and Types

Elder abuse represents a conscious or unconscious act against a frail and/or dependent elderly person who is being cared for by a friend, a member of the family, or an employee of an institution where the person is living (O'Malley et al., 1984; Brillon, 1987:69-86). This behavior may include varying degrees of *physical* abuse such as personal attacks or rough handling that leads to bruises, abrasions, dislocations, fractures, burns, or — in the extreme — death; *psychological* abuse such as verbal threats, insult or humiliation, blackmail, lack of attention and withholding affection, confinement or restraint to a chair, bed, or room; *medical* abuse such as withholding food or medicine, not seeking medical assistance, over- or under-administering drug prescriptions; *material* abuse such as stealing money or possessions, cashing and retaining pension cheques, or dishonest use of an elderly person's money or property; and *legal* abuse such as any violation of human rights and freedoms, forcing changes in a will, or denying access to public services such as home care nursing or therapeutic services. Many incidents occur in the elder's own home, or in the home of the primary caregiver. Abuse also occurs in long-term care institutions where staff may treat patients like children. For example, Pillemer and Moore (1989), in a study of 577 residents of thirty-one nursing homes, found that abuse is more likely to occur in substandard environmental settings in which patients are subject to limitations on freedom, to inadequate nutrition and living conditions, and to verbal and physical abuse. On the basis of their analyses, Pillemer and Moore generated a profile of an abusive employee as one who is thinking of quitting the job, who has experienced burnout, who has a stressful life away from work, and who believes the patients should be treated as dependent children.

Elder neglect represents a failure or a refusal to perform a necessary caregiving obligation to an older adult, especially one who is cogni-

tively or physically impaired. Neglect may also be self-induced by present or previous lifestyle behaviors — alcoholism, substance abuse, inadequate nutrition, and living on skid row. Neglect on the part of an actual or a potential caregiver may represent conscious or unconscious behavior. For example, lack of knowledge about how to care for an Alzheimer's patient, or about available community services, may lead to unintentional neglectful behavior that has serious outcomes for the dependent elderly person. An interesting legal issue centers on who, among potential primary caregivers, might be considered negligent or neglectful in their responsibilities to an elderly parent who, in turn, is considered a legally independent adult. Snell (1990) stated that following the introduction in 1921 of the first filial responsibility law in Ontario (the Parents' Maintenance Act), all provinces introduced similar legislation. These parent maintenance acts require that adult children of both sexes, who are capable of providing maintenance, are liable for the support of parents who are unable to maintain themselves because of age, disease, or infirmity. These filial responsibility laws were introduced to protect the public sector from the costs and the burden of supporting those who had family members able to provide support. However, as Snell (1990) reported, the number of cases brought forward under these legislative acts has been quite low. Whether this reflects the more likely explanation that elderly Canadians are being supported by their children, or whether it reflects a reluctance of parents or the Crown to bring charges against children, remains to be determined.

In most cases, neglectful behavior represents a refusal or a failure to care for an older adult by abandoning the person, or by withholding food, health care, personal care, or companionship. Highlight 10.5 illustrates some tragic case histories of elder abuse and neglect.

Incidence, Causes, and Outcomes of Abuse

At the outset it must be noted that while elder abuse is a serious matter for those who become victims, the incidence rate is relatively

HIGHLIGHT 10.5

ELDER ABUSE AND NEGLECT: TRAGIC FAMILY SCENARIOS

One response to the stress and the burden of caregiving, especially if a caregiver has his or her own personal problems, is psychological or physical abuse of the vulnerable, dependent elderly person. The following examples illustrate some types of elder abuse and neglect that have surfaced in recent years:

A. **Financial Abuse, Alcoholism, or Drug Dependence**

An alcoholic in his 50s, Fred moved in with his elderly mother after he had lost his job. She receives a large pension and has other sources of income, but is physically and mentally disabled. Fred cashed her cheques and went on drinking binges, often leaving her alone for days. During one of these bouts, a concerned neighbor found her lying on the living room floor in a disoriented, malnourished, dehydrated, and unclean state.

B. **Marital Discord and Spouse Abuse**

After a long and tension-filled marriage, John became bedridden and incontinent. His wife, obliged to care for him twenty-four hours a day, began to withhold drugs and food, and slapped him and screamed at him whenever he demanded attention and care. When he was unexpectedly visited at home by a physician, bruises were discovered on his face and arms and he was moved to a long-term care institution.

C. **Psychological Abuse**

An elderly widow, no longer able to adequately maintain the family home yet unwilling to move, invited a single niece to share her home in return for help with the housekeeping. For two years the relationship appeared to be mutually beneficial, but increasingly the niece began to insult her aunt and threatened that she would leave if she did not receive large sums of money on a regular basis. The niece began to assume that it was her home — she decided which television programs were watched, when they went to bed and ate meals, when and if they went out, and how the aunt's money was spent. Moreover, the niece only talked to the aunt when it was essential, withdrew all signs of affection, and encouraged the aunt to spend more and more time in her bedroom. In reality, the aunt had become a prisoner in her own home and was living in solitary confinement without meaningful and satisfying social interaction.

D. **Frustration and Stress**

Charged with the killing of his 94-year-old wife, an 82-year-old man claimed he had been no longer able to care for his mentally and physically frail wife, whose sight, hearing, and cognitive abilities had deteriorated rapidly. Despite repeated calls to the local social service office for assistance, he reported that 'no one wanted to look after us. We were condemned to die like two dogs.' Following his court appearance, in which he was given a suspended sentence, he was sent from his jail cell to a nursing home, which is what he really wanted and needed for his wife.

---

low. Thus, most caregivers do not engage consciously in abusive behavior. Most elder abuse and neglect is hidden or unreported. Hence, it is difficult to identify either the incidence per 1,000 elders, or the absolute number of cases that may be present in a given community or society. Even where studies have been completed, there are many methodological issues that can limit the reliability and the validity of the findings. For example, many studies lack a control group; they are often based on very small and nonrepresentative samples or on case studies of abused elders that have been reported; they use different theoretical and operational definitions of abuse (McDonald et al., forthcoming); they interview professional care personnel rather than the victims or abusers; and the age of reported victims may not be recorded. In addition, self-reporting of abuse victims is unlikely to occur, because they are dependent on the abuser and may fear reprisals such as institutionalization; because they are reluctant to report abuse or neglect by a child or a spouse; or because they do not know who to inform should they experience abuse.

Those most likely to be abused are frail elderly women with a moderate to severe form of mental or physical impairment that necessitates dependent living with a caregiver. This is not surprising, since women live longer and there are more older women than men. Although older men are also subject to abuse, more older men live with a younger spouse who is less likely to engage in this type of behavior.

In terms of societal rates, four studies provide some indication of the rate of abuse, as well as the identity of the abusers. Shell (1982) interviewed 105 Manitoba professionals (doctors, lawyers, police, nurses, the clergy) who reported knowing about 402 persons 60 and over who had been abused in the previous year. Projected to Canada, this represents about 22 cases per 1,000 elders. According to the type of abuse, Shell found that there were 217 cases of material abuse, 202 incidents of psychological abuse, and 121 incidents of physical abuse. Seventy-five percent of the identified abusers were members of the family; 25 percent were practitioners. Within the family, 60 percent of the abusers were men (son, son-in-law, husband).

On the basis of a random sample of 2,020 community-dwelling elders in Boston, Pillemer and Finkelhor (1988) projected the following rates by type of abuse: 20 cases per 1,000 elders for physical abuse, 11 per 1,000 for psychological-verbal abuse, and 4 per 1,000 for neglect. They also found that the rates of abuse for those who live with a spouse (41 per 1,000) were comparable. Projecting this to a nationwide figure for the U.S., they noted that this represents 700,000 to 1.1 million abused elders. By comparison, a 1986 report by Health and Welfare Canada estimated that 100,000 elderly Canadians are abused (Brillon, 1987:70).

The most recent comprehensive national survey in Canada involved a random-sample telephone poll of 2,000 persons aged 65 and over living in private households (Podnieks et al., 1989). Podnieks found that about 40 persons per 1,000 elderly Canadians (4 percent) experienced some form of maltreatment. Since the 1986 census reported that about 2.5 million elderly Canadians live in private dwellings, there may be 98,000 elderly persons who have suffered from one or more forms of abuse or neglect. Podnieks found that, by type, there were 25 incidents of material abuse per 1,000 elderly persons, 14 incidents per 1,000 of chronic verbal aggression, 5 incidents per 1,000 for physical violence, and 4 incidents of neglect per 1,000 elderly persons. Nearly 19 percent of the victims reportedly suffered from more than one form of abuse. By region, respondents reported prevalence rates ranging from a low of 30 per 1,000 in the Prairies; to 38 to 40 in the Atlantic, Quebec, and Ontario regions; to a high of 53 per 1,000 in British Columbia. On a per capita basis, the rates of victimization are nearly equal for women and men, although in total numbers the ratio of female to male victims is almost two-to-one.

To provide an understanding of why abuse occurs, gerontologists initially offered the simple explanation that caring for a dependent, vulnerable elderly person causes significant stress for the caregiver, who may cope by engaging in one or more types of abusive behavior. More recent analyses, however, have suggested that there are societal factors, additional factors within the family, and personal factors of the caregiver that must be considered (Pillemer, 1985; Brillon, 1987:72-76; Steinmetz, 1988). For example, where abusers feel that they are 'giving much and receiving little' (an unbalanced exchange relationship), frustration and resentment can lead to abusive acts (Pillemer, 1985). Similarly, violence may have always been a normative response to stress within a particular family (for example, where child and spouse beatings are normative behavior and are never questioned or discussed outside the family). The abusive response of a caregiving spouse or adult child may be initiated to 'repay' the abuse received earlier in life from an abusive spouse or parent. From a more macro perspective, abuse of elders may reflect such societal values as the acceptance of a violent response to stressful situations, especially among members of some social classes; or the presence of ageism and a devaluation of elders who are functionally impaired. In addition, the stress and burdens of caregiving on one person may be compounded by such societal factors as increasing divorce rates, fewer children per family, and more lifelong female participation in the labor force. These factors, in turn, may lead to neglect or abuse of frail parents.

A number of personal factors associated with both the caregiver and the victim may be related to various forms of abuse or neglect. The caregiver may be employed full-time; may be elderly and failing in health, as well; may have personal problems (drugs, alcohol, financial, mental) that prevent assisting the elderly person or that compound the stress of caregiving; or may live alone with the victim and resent not having a normal social life because of the demands of caregiving.

The attitude and the behavior of the potential victim may serve as a catalyst for the onset of abuse and neglect. For example, whether there is clear evidence of severe cognitive or physical impairment or not, the older person may resist or resent the well-intentioned and necessary care provided by the caregiver. Indeed, in some cases the frail patient may verbally abuse the caregiver, thereby leading to stress and the possibility of an abusive reaction. In other situations, the patient may engage in self-abuse, thereby compounding the difficulty of caregiving; or in other settings, may set unrealistic expectations for the type and the level of care a spouse or child must provide.

In summary, there are many societal, individual, and family-induced stressors that can interact to create an abusive or a neglectful situation for a frail, dependent elderly person. These incidents can result in physical injury, mental abuse, fear, depression, sleep disorders, violent reactions against the abuser (often leading to more abuse, to abandonment, to movement to an institution, or to movement within an institution to a more secure environment), or to suicide.

Prevention, Intervention, and Coping: Strategies and Issues

With the increasing awareness of elder abuse and neglect, a variety of intervention strategies have been proposed or implemented to protect the victim and to help the caregiver. In general, intervention involves identifying high-risk elders, family systems, and caregivers (Kosberg, 1988); protecting the rights of seniors; enforcing and prosecuting violations of criminal and civil law; providing needed social services; and developing and delivering education and counseling for lay caregivers and professional health and social case workers (Podnieks, 1985; Podnieks et al., 1989; Pillemer and Wolf, 1986; Brillon, 1987; Callahan, 1988; McDonald et al., forthcoming).[14]

To prevent abuse or neglect, innovative educational and prevention programs and services for both the caregivers and the elderly have been initiated in recent years. Some of these programs and policies include:

- providing social, financial, and health resources directly to the elderly person, who can then buy services to facilitate living independently or semi-independently;
- training professional workers to identify and assess a situation using indicators of abuse or neglect (for example, lack of verbal or emotional interaction between the caregiver and the recipient, stressful signs within the caregiver, the caregiver treating the elderly person like a child or nonperson, unexplained bruises, improper dress and hygiene);
- providing respite care services for day-care or vacation relief;
- establishing self-help counseling or support groups for caregivers;
- providing financial support to caregivers to purchase needed help (such as nursing, transportation) from trained professionals, thereby alleviating some sources of stress and burden;

- providing a professional case manager to help make decisions about who should be the primary caregiver, and how total care should be managed;
- employers providing flexible work schedules, emotional support, and information to middle-aged employees who are responsible for the care of ailing parents;
- establishing a full-time police position in each community to deal exclusively with the problem (education, prevention, and prosecution);
- requiring attendance at educational programs on elder abuse for residents and staff of long-term care institutions.

A current major issue concerning elder care is the increasing pressure to pass legislation protecting those who are frail and incapable of making decisions about their lives. But, as legal experts warn, guardianship legislation is complex and can become quite restrictive. That is, guardianship legislation can include either full or partial guardianship. However, full guardianship can remove civil liberties not only of those who are frail and clearly dependent, but also of those who are not frail but merely eccentric, or of those who are reported as being abused. Thus, there is a need for an advocacy system to protect those who are still capable of making decisions and living semi-independently, if they have sufficient information and objective advice. As a minimum, there needs to be protective legislation so that observed incidents of abuse and neglect can be brought to the attention of appropriate agencies. Then the victim could be temporarily removed from the setting to a protective shelter, and appropriate counseling and assistance could be provided to the caregiver and the victim. Only in extreme cases does guardianship seem to be the ideal and necessary solution for the care of frail, elderly persons who are at risk of being abused or neglected.

SOCIAL POLICY FOR AN AGING POPULATION

Introduction

Long before population aging became a contemporary issue, concerns about the economic and health status of the elderly were addressed by politicians. For example, old-age support programs were introduced in France in 1850, in Germany in 1889,[15] in Great Britain in 1908, and in Sweden in 1913. Although these plans were compulsory, the benefits were minimal and tended to supplement rather than to replace the older worker's wages (Myles, 1989:16). In North America, Canada introduced the Old Age Pension Act[16] in 1927 (Bryden, 1974; Chappell, 1980); and in the United States, social security legislation was enacted in 1935 (Clark and Baumer, 1985) and the Older Americans Act in 1965 (Estes, 1979).

Following the Depression of the late 1930s, and the increased prosperity after World War II, a change in social and political values led to the introduction of the concept of social security and social welfare. With these values as a basis, government and the private sector sought to provide universal rights to insure a minimal standard of living in the later years. In Canada, this resulted in a universal old-age security payment plan and a universal hospital care plan for the entire population in 1951, a Guaranteed Income Supplement (GIA) plan in 1960, a national insurance scheme for physician services in 1966, the Canada and Quebec Pension Plans in 1966, and a social assistance program for anyone in need, regardless of age or income, in 1966.[17] In combination, and together with personal savings and private pension and extended heath care plans, these programs were expected to insure persons against income, health, and disability problems in later life.

With the onset of population aging, the North American social structure and political culture changed dramatically. Senior citizens, individually and collectively, were better informed about

HIGHLIGHT 10.6

**FEDERAL AND PROVINCIAL POLICIES TO ENHANCE
THE QUALITY OF LIFE OF SENIORS**

Federal Initiatives: Independence for Seniors

On February 9, 1988, the Minister of National Health and Welfare announced that the federal government would spend, on average, $30 million annually on contributions to support independence for seniors. The Seniors Independence Program provides to community groups made up mainly of seniors, or actively involving seniors, $20 million in funds to design programs that will improve the independence of seniors, especially older women and those in rural and remote areas. The New Horizons Program, established in 1972, received additional funds to increase its annual budget to $15 million so that there would be further opportunities for retired Canadians to start or expand meaningful activities. Projects funded under this program have included: the establishment of activity or drop-in centers; the provision of community services to other seniors (for example, repairs, letter writing, driving, home help); craft and hobby programs; historical, cultural, and educational programs (for example, community histories, preservation of ethnic customs, creative-writing workshops); the establishment of information and referral centers; and the organization of sport, fitness, and recreation programs. A third program established a $4 million research fund to encourage research on two diseases that reduce the independence of seniors: Alzheimer's disease and osteoporosis. The fourth element of this policy announcement included an increase in the operating budget of the National Advisory Council on Aging so that it could expand its policy advice and research initiatives. Finally, the Minister announced that a Seniors Secretariat would be established within the Ministry of Health and Welfare to provide support for the Minister of State for Seniors, to more effectively communicate with seniors about the availability of federal services and programs, and to heighten public awareness of seniors' issues.

Provincial Initiatives: Integrated Health and Social Services

The Manitoba Home Care program has a central entry point at which all clients are assessed by a nurse or a social worker. This highly successful program is provided at no cost to recipients (and to their caregivers) who need assistance to remain in their homes. The professional services of nurses, social workers, therapists, volunteers, and home care aides are provided for personal care or home management. In general, the program provides personal and supportive services in the home, adult day care, respite care, transportation, and a variety of housing alternatives.

In Ontario, Placement Coordination Services funded by the Ministry of Community and Social Services have been established in large urban centers. These offices facilitate access to services ranging from day hospitals, geriatric assessments, and chronic care beds to home visits by geriatric specialists. The objectives of this program are to arrive at appropriate assessments, to use existing facilities more efficiently, to provide better rehabilitation services, to coordinate and enhance the geriatric training for health care professionals (for example, doctors, nurses, physiotherapists, and occupational therapists), and to reduce the number of elderly persons who are housed in acute care hospitals and other inappropriate facilities.

---

aging issues and needs, they became more active in the political and policy domain, and politicians became more sensitive to the needs and concerns of those over 60 years of age.[18] As a result, government agencies at the federal, provincial, regional, or local level now initiate and administer policies for older adults in such diverse areas as leisure, culture, crime, consumer affairs, education, health, housing, home care, income maintenance, special services for rural residents and members of minority groups, social welfare, transportation, widowhood, and wellness (highlight 10.6 provides some examples of federal and provincial initiatives to improve the quality of life for seniors in Canada; earlier, highlight 10.4 described the variety of programs that can be provided at the regional or the local level).

It is beyond the scope of this section to describe or critique specific policies, especially since policies below the federal level vary considerably in philosophy, coverage, access, and benefits.[19] Therefore, the following sections focus on some of the long-standing and contemporary issues and problems associated with the development, implementation, and evaluation of social policy for an aging population.

Population Aging and Public Policy

With the onset of industrialization, and more recently of population aging (McDaniel, 1987), the state has assumed an increasing responsibility for the health and social welfare of older adults. At first, policies at the federal level sought to distribute the economic resources of the nation to provide income security and health care, especially for the low-income segment of the older population. For example, in a study of thirty industrial nations, including Canada, Kattler and Williamson (1988) found that expenditures on health care had a positive effect on the life expectancy of females at age 60. They argued that this occurred primarily because public policies enabled the low-income segment of the population to have increased access to the health care system. As population aging has become a more topical and political issue, provincial, regional, and municipal jurisdictions have initiated policies to meet the social, housing, health care, and transportation needs of older adults (Kernaghan and Kuper, 1983). This increasing involvement of the state in policymaking for older adults is the result of changing cultural values that have led to incentives and pressures for social change.

Underlying the development of public policies for an aging population is the long-standing debate on whether the consequences of aging should be viewed as a private trouble (the individual is responsible) or a public issue (society is responsible). This is best illustrated with respect to pensions (McDonald and Wanner, 1990). Should the public control and provide universal and complete pensions, or should the individual through the private sector be responsible for controlling the size and the duration of pension benefits? In addition, the prevailing values of a society raise such questions as: Should the family *or* the state be responsible for the care and welfare of older citizens? Have older adults earned the right, because of past contributions, to be cared for in the later years? Should any state support that is provided be universally available at a specific age (an automatic entitlement) or should state support be viewed as a charitable act available only to those who can demonstrate need? Should scarce resources be reallocated to the elderly in the interest of social justice (for example, reduce the financial support to universities to provide more universal programs and facilities for the senior boom expected in the early years of the next century)? Clearly, the answers, and, consequently, the policies change with variations in cultural values, in the economy, and in the political environment. Indeed, differing societal values may lead to political and social conflict that can have considerable influence on the type and content of aging-related policies that are implemented, revised, or terminated.

In addition to the influence of societal values, the complex and time-consuming process of policymaking is initiated by considering and reacting to citizen demands and to the influence of aging-based interest or lobby groups such as the National Advisory Council on Aging, the Ontario Advisory Council on Senior Citizens, or a local mayor's Committee on Senior Citizens (Neysmith, 1987a). In addition, politicians, needing to be reelected, create policies and agencies to meet the perceived collective needs of themselves and their constituents. However, these individual needs, rights, and freedoms of the elderly must be balanced against the challenge of maintaining fiscal responsibility, of avoiding the alienation of competing interest groups, and of equitably distributing resources within the society (Binstock et al., 1985; Hudson and Strate, 1985; Neysmith, 1987b). Often this decision making involves a revision of existing legislation, or the enactment of legislation to rectify a perceived crack in the social policy system for older adults.

Once a policy has been approved by the appropriate governing body, it must be implemented by the personnel of a particular agency. This delivery often requires coordination with existing policies and programs in order to have the objectives of the policy accepted by the various stakeholders within a society. For example, a new policy, initiated by a social service ministry, that provides home-maintenance support to assist the elderly to live independently in their homes might lead to increased demands on existing programs funded by a housing ministry, or to fewer admissions to homes for the aged or to long-term chronic care facilities. Consequently, a decision that is often viewed as a simple policy solution to an obvious need or problem can be delayed or ignored because of larger problems that might be raised or compounded by the initiation of a new policy.

In order to assist elderly citizens to live independently in their own homes for as long as possible, and to maintain a high quality of life in the later years, policymakers have evolved a set of informal principles to guide their thinking and actions. Because these principles are based on social values and are subject to changing needs, beliefs, and philosophy, they may lack universal agreement and support across a society, within a particular jurisdiction, or within a particular subgroup of society. Clearly, the most controversial principle relates to whether policies should be universal (eligibility is based on attaining a specific age), need-based (regardless of age), or some combination of the two. The proponents of a universal system (for example, Old Age Security, without the 'clawback' clause introduced in 1990) argue that it enhances the dignity of all citizens because they do not have to experience a means test for eligibility or the stigma of being labeled as needy; that higher quality and more efficient programs can be easily administered; and that the difficulty of defining and objectively measuring need is eliminated. In contrast, those who argue for need-based policies (such as the Guaranteed Income Supplement) state that this principle supports the user-pay philosophy, that the programs are considerably less expensive because the size of the eligible group is decreased to those who can demonstrate need; and that not all older adults need or want financial, housing, or transportation assistance from the government (Davis, 1985; Chappell et al., 1986).

A second controversial principle relates to the care of the frail elderly. In the past the medical profession has had the most influence on the care and housing of the elderly. This model of policymaking has led to the construction of facilities and to the 'warehousing' of the elderly in long-term care institutions (Forbes et al., 1987). More recently, the philosophy of care and assistance for the elderly has led to a consideration of alternatives to the institutionalization of the elderly. There is also a growing debate on whether expensive health care services (such as transplants, kidney dialysis) should be rationed or restricted on the basis of age rather than need.

Recognizing the heterogeneous abilities, needs, and individual rights and freedoms of the elderly, a social service model argues that a continuum of coordinated social and health care services should be provided for a diversity of needs (Litwak, 1985; Chappell et al., 1986; Manton, 1988; Wolinsky and Arnold, 1988; Connidis, 1989:97). Ideally, a set of integrated policies should be implemented that integrate home and institutional care options, and that involve an assessment of the level of functional impairment of elderly persons, their medical condition, and the availability of informal and formal support systems. In this way, separate and unrelated policies will be less likely to create gaps in the total system, thereby enhancing both the efficiency of the delivery system and the cost effectiveness of all policies (Manton, 1988). In addition, an integrated solution to the issue of whether a problem is a private trouble or a public issue should be pursued. For example, Connidis (1989) noted that following widowhood, assistance in the bereavement process is primarily provided by family and friends (although formal widow-to-widow programs can be organized by the public or the volunteer sector). In contrast, assistance with housing and income support is more likely to be provided by the public sector because the specific problem of the impoverished elderly widow is partially, at least, societally induced.

In addition to the above principles, many policymakers adhere to the following general principles in designing and implementing policies for an aging population:

- There must be justice in serving both the wealthy and the poor (for example, the wealthy are not the only ones to receive first-class health care).
- Costs associated with implementing policies must be distributed equitably (for example, higher income taxes for the higher-income elderly).
- Past contributions to a society must be recognized and repaid (for example, serving in wars, raising children).
- Family caregivers must be supported.
- The legal rights of the elderly must be protected.
- A minimum standard of living must be maintained.
- There must be compensation for failures of the private market (for example, a stock market collapse eliminates or reduces pension funds; double-digit inflation at the time of retirement).
- Inappropriate institutionalization must be prevented.

Policy Issues for an Aging Population

In an attempt to meet the diverse needs of a heterogeneous older population, a number of policy issues have been raised and debated in recent years. We have been alerted to these issues by such concerned stakeholders as politicians, government bureaucrats who propose or implement policies, older citizens and their lobby groups, non-elderly citizens, the media, gerontology practitioners, and social critics. Clearly, many of the policy decisions have been politically based and tied to forthcoming elections or current economic conditions. Some have been influenced, as well, by myths (for example, the public pension system will become bankrupt in the next decade) and stereotypes (the elderly are neglected, impoverished, and frail). Therefore, because of the possibility of real and potential abuses of public funds if policies are hastily conceived on the basis of age, this section briefly introduces a number of important policy issues that must be addressed by a society with an aging population.

Jurisdictional Responsibility

The issue of who is responsible for the care of older adults is compounded by the multilevel jurisdictional layers of government that have evolved (federal, provincial, regional, local). The end result is that there is no single policy or agency responsible for the needs and the interests of older adults. Indeed, there may be overt conflict over how to allocate funds to serve seniors (for example, the health promotion model to prevent disease and disability versus the medical model of treating acute and chronic illness), or there may be neglect because one level believes that another level of government should provide, or is providing, legislation, policies, funds, or personnel to meet a specific need. For example, since the early days of gerontology there has been increasing ideological conflict between health ministries, which seek to care for the dependent elderly (often within institutions), and social service ministries, which seek to provide services that will keep the elderly in the community. Or, the government may believe that the family, the private sector (for example, a nursing home), or a volunteer agency (for example, meals-on-wheels) should meet a specific need of an elderly person.

Related to this question of responsibility is the question of obligation. Here it is not at all clear what the legal support requirements are for an adult child or spouse (Bulcroft et al., 1989). For example, is an adult child who does not live with a frail parent legally responsible for the care and well-being of the parent? Another question relates to the legal rights of elderly persons to make decisions about their own health and welfare. Is age a valid criterion for imposing or eliminating responsibilities (Eglit, 1985)? Similarly, who is legally responsible for making decisions when the older person experiences severe mental impairment — the spouse (who may also be frail and impaired)? the children? a physician? a case worker? an employee of the nursing home where the mentally impaired person resides?

Not surprisingly, because of this divided or unallocated jurisdictional responsibility, there is a lack of coordination between agencies, an inefficient use of scarce resources, and a gap in the ideal continuum of services that could be provided to elderly persons. Moreover, the lack of clear responsibility for decision making can compound such ethical issues as the rationing of health care resources (for example, should those over a certain age be ineligible for costly heart and other organ transplants?), dying with dignity, and euthanasia.

Finally, it should be obvious by now that a major challenge for policymakers is to encourage older adults to take responsibility for their own well-being, to integrate community and institutional services, and to provide a continuum of varying levels of care within the same facility. However, an emerging issue related to jurisdictional responsibility is the policy of privatizing what has heretofore been a public responsibility (Ismael and Vaillancourt, 1988). In this process, the responsibility for health and social services is transferred to the nonprofit (charities, private foundations, religious, or ethnic groups) or the for-profit sector. Privatization, which is generally a federal policy, seeks to reduce deficits and to exhibit economic restraint to the voting public. Examples of areas where privatization involving services to older adults can occur include nursing homes and home-maintenance services. However, the public must ask whether private services, if invoked, are really more efficient, or whether they reduce expenses at the cost of providing a restricted access to services (for example, only the wealthy who can pay receive the service) and an overall lower quality of care.

Service Delivery

Even when policies exist, the required programs are often not delivered completely, efficiently, or regularly. Part of the problem is that the elderly or their caregivers lack knowledge about the availability of a service, or they are unable to gain access to a specific service because of language, transportation, or economic deficiencies. Other programs, even if known, have either stringent eligibility requirements that few older people can meet, or excessive waiting periods before the service can be made available. Still other programs have selective (often subjective) admission policies. For example, the owner of a private nursing home which is profit-oriented may select residents who require less costly care, who are at the least

advanced stage of an illness, and who are the best prospects for longevity. Others, with more serious needs but a lower life expectancy, may be rejected and, therefore, continue to occupy a bed in an acute care hospital, or at home where the burden on the caregiver increases. The delivery of service can also be hampered by a lack of trained staff, and by the unavailability of valid screening or geriatric assessment units to provide a complete and accurate placement or to derive a correct diagnosis and ideal therapeutic program (Rubinstein and Wieland, 1989).

There is still considerable debate about whether services should be delivered to the older person or the primary caregiver. Thus, even where policies exist to address a problem, an inadequate delivery system can be a liability to insuring a minimal standard of living and the highest and most appropriate level of care for the mentally or physically impaired elderly person. Finally, if a community or region is a prime recipient of permanent or seasonal older migrants, policies need to account for unexpected growth, particularly in terms of housing, leisure, and social services (Northcott, 1988).

The Needs of Special Groups

Some social policy analysts argue that the unmet needs of the elderly are not due to age per se, but rather to the effects of life-long structural inequalities (such as gender, class, ethnicity, race). While these issues have been addressed elsewhere in the text in more detail, it is important to reiterate that members of these special groups often experience gaps between service needs and service availability that could be better met by public policy.[20]

As a result of these real and/or perceived inequities, a growing controversial issue is whether policies should be designed specifically to meet the needs of minority-group members, thereby eliminating or reducing inequities or increasing participation levels in existing programs. This is especially important for foreign-born elders, or for elderly widows who may be ineligible for benefits, or who receive reduced benefits (Boyd, 1989). It is also important to insure that services are known and available in the languages of the elderly person (Driedger and Chappell, 1987; MacLean et al., 1987), and that existing policies insure that services are delivered to rural and remote areas, to native Canadians, and to members of specific ethnic groups.

With respect to gender, the major policy issues pertaining to older women center on economic and social care issues — eligibility rights for public and private pensions; the creation of homemakers' pensions; the value of a spouse's allowance; pay equity; day care; respite care; and other forms of support to caregivers or to elderly women who live alone. A major breakthrough has been the increased provision of services to caregivers of the elderly. Hence, women in the 'sandwich' generation have been able to obtain some relief from the stress and the burden of caregiving as they face the double or triple responsibility of child-rearing, career development, and caregiving of an elderly parent or parent-in-law. More recently, legislation requiring pay equity for jobs of equal responsibility, and a more equitable division of resources upon separation or divorce, will insure a better, but not necessarily a totally ideal, economic situation for future generations of older women.

Intergenerational Equity

Today, older people do not necessarily constitute the poorest segment of the population. Rather, single-parent families and unemployed youth may experience higher rates of impoverishment and a lower standard of living. Consequently, some citizens believe that too many resources are being allocated to the elderly, thereby creating an unfair disadvantage for the young and for future generations. This backlash, when it occurs, is usually compounded by the onset of economic deficits, the presence of vocal seniors advocating increased resource allocation, unemployment among the youth, and reports of an increasing dependency ratio (Franke, 1987). However, in reality, the right of older adults to social and economic security is endorsed by other adults (Lomax Cook and Barrett, 1988).

Since generations are interdependent, policies directed toward one group generally affect other age groups, directly or indirectly, and immediately or in the long run (Kingson et al., 1986, Kingson, 1988; Wisensale, 1988). Thus, the aim of policymakers is to ensure an equi-

table allocation of society's resources among various age groups. At the same time, the young must realize the debt they owe previous generations for financial and emotional support, for national security, for technological advances, and for the opportunity to pursue higher education. In reality, despite the doomsday forecasts of some, the young are not, nor will they be, overburdened with the costs of maintaining the benefits inherent in aging policies (Wisensale, 1988). More specifically, both Denton and his colleagues (1986, 1987) and Messinger and Powell (1987) project respectively that health and social care expenditures will increase. However, most of these costs will be provided by the federal government, and the increase will occur at a relatively slow rate, so that the public and private sectors will adjust and satisfactorily meet the needs of the elderly, as well as other age groups. In short, these authors predict that, contrary to public rumor, an overall expenditure crisis is not a realistic possibility in Canada. Moreover, through such programs as tax incentives and tax reforms, child and elder care programs, training and information to caregivers, and employment opportunities for older adults to maintain their independence, all generations benefit from policies that are primarily directed at providing social benefits and reducing the burdens of the elderly person and his or her primary caregiver. Thus, as Wisensale (1988) concluded, inequality is likely to be greater *within* age groups due to class, gender, racial, or ethnic differentiation than *between* age groups.

SUMMARY AND CONCLUSIONS

Most individuals, regardless of age, are never totally isolated from others. Rather, a social world evolves around an individual to provide informal and/or formal support. In this chapter the size, structure, function, composition, and quality of the changing social network for older adults was discussed. It was noted that this network consists of informal ties with family, friends, and neighbors as well as formal linkages with organizations in the public, private, and volunteer sectors. These formal linkages become more salient as informal ties with family and friends are lost or become unavailable. The second and third parts of the chapter reviewed the sources, types, uses, and outcomes of the informal and formal support systems available to older adults, including the problems related to coordinating and integrating the two systems. Recognizing that some relationships in the later years can become abusive, this chapter examined the limited state of knowledge about the context, types, incidence, process, outcomes, and possible interventions for elder abuse and neglect. The final section focused on some of the long-standing and contemporary issues and problems associated with the development, implementation, and evaluation of public policy for an aging population. This last section included a discussion of principles that guide policymakers, as well as a number of policy issues that must be addressed before successful age-related policies can be designed and implemented.

On the basis of the literature reviewed in this chapter, it can be concluded that:

1. The family is the first and major source of social support when assistance is needed in the later years.
2. Contrary to prevailing myths, the elderly are not isolated, disengaged, or abandoned. Rather, a variety of networks are available to provide companionship, a confidant, emotional support, and home care or personal care assistance.
3. While the number of ties in an older person's network decreases with advancing age, the quality or strength of the remaining ties may increase.
4. Some ties in an older person's network can become abusive, stressful, and in certain cases life threatening.
5. As an individual ages, solutions to problems are perceived as 'private troubles' or 'public issues,' depending on whether the individual and the family, or the state, is held accountable and responsible for providing assistance or a solution.
6. In terms of providing assistance and assuming responsibility for the care of elderly persons, the kinship network takes primacy over non-kin, and informal sources are utilized before formal sources.
7. The selection of a preferred caregiver is often made in a hierarchical order starting with the spouse, followed in order by an adult child, a sibling, a niece or a nephew, and a close friend.
8. Both the quantity and the quality of relationships must be considered when assessing the informal social support available to older adults.
9. As age increase, the informal network of older adults increasingly includes more women, many of whom experience a loss of mobility and functional capacities.
10. Most family caregiving in the later years is provided or organized by wives, daughters, or daughters-in-law.
11. The degree of responsibility expressed for the support or care of an elderly parent or family member is related to the sense of obligation and the feeling of affection built up over a long period of family history.
12. The practice of giving or receiving support in the later years is influenced by cultural beliefs and values about aging and the aged that are unique to specific social class, ethnic, religious, or racial groups.
13. Elderly recipients of assistance from well-meaning caregivers may resent and resist the offering of informal support.
14. The stress experienced by caregivers, who are the 'hidden victims' in a caregiving relationship, can be reduced by assistance from the formal support system. This assistance can include emotional and social support to the caregiver, financial aid or incentives to help care for an elderly person, formal care services to relieve the caregiver, and knowledge and training about caregiving.
15. The goal of many formal support services is to enable elderly persons to remain in their homes as independent citizens.

16. The elements of the informal and the formal support systems for older adults should be complementary in order to provide a continuum of assistance and care.

17. The actual usage rate of formal social services by older adults is quite low, with the majority of users being elderly frail women, especially if they are unmarried, widowed, or childless, and living alone.

18. Most elder abuse or neglect is hidden and unreported.

19. Those most likely to be abused are frail elderly women with a moderate to severe form of mental or physical impairment that requires dependent living with a caregiver.

20. Elderly persons are most likely to be abused by a spouse or other member of the family.

21. Social policies for an aging population are designed and implemented by all levels of government. This diversity of jurisdictional responsibility can result in both overlap and gaps in the services provided to older adults, and in conflict or confusion concerning who is responsible for meeting specific needs.

NOTES

1. Corin (1987:390) suggested that a 'norm of privacy' prevails in rural areas. This norm could act as a defense mechanism against the invasion of private space. If such a norm is present, this may partially explain the tendency for the rural elderly to rely almost exclusively on the nuclear family, especially the spouse, for expressive and instrumental support.

2. See Chappell, 1983, 1990; Brownell and Shumaker, 1984; Cantor and Little, 1985; Chappell and Havens, 1985; Cohen and Syme, 1985; Sauer and Coward, 1985b; Ward, 1985; Biegel et al., 1986; Chappell et al., 1986; Lin et al., 1986; Stephens and Christianson, 1986; Wister and Strain, 1986; Thompson, 1989; Martin Matthews, forthcoming.

3. Linsk et al. (1988) reported that in 1987 at least thirty-five states in the U.S. had some type of financial payment for family caregiving. In Nor-

way, a pension is provided to housewives who have taken care of an elderly or disabled person (Brody and Schoonover, 1986). In Canada, Veterans Affairs provides payment to some caregivers.

4. The gender difference in terms of quality and quantity of support may disappear as the aging parent becomes more frail and dependent. That is, as the seriousness of the chronic health status increases, sons and/or daughters become more involved in the decisions that must be made (Chappell, 1989).

5. The question of how to, and whether to, support an aging parent is becoming a feminist issue (Longino and Lipman, 1985).

6. The following studies and reviews focus on the stress and the burden experienced by family caregivers: Springer and Brubaker, 1984; Brody, 1985; Cantor and Little, 1985; Horowitz, 1985a; Montgomery et al., 1985; Storm et al., 1985; Rosenthal, 1986b; Wenger, 1987; Barber, 1988; Matthews, 1988; Connidis, 1989; Lawton et al., 1989; Rosenthal et al., 1989; Toseland and Zarit, 1989; Brody, 1990; Miller and Montgomery, 1990; Pruchno, 1990.

7. Both the level of attachment (love, respect) and the presence of spiritual support (among more religious persons) seem to be important mediators in the reporting of lower levels of perceived burdens associated with caregiving (Bond et al., 1987; Barber, 1988). Similarly, participation in caregiver support group programs has the potential to prevent stressors from overwhelming the caregiver (Toseland and Zarit, 1989).

8. Chappell et al. (1986:90-95) described the development of the formal care system in Canada and the United States; Forbes et al. (1987:2-14) chronicled the history of institutional care from early Christian and medieval periods to the present era; Gee and Boyce (1988) showed how legislation (from pre-1918 to the 1980s) played both a direct and indirect role in the development of health and social services for elderly Canadians; and Snell (1990) examined the history of filial-responsibililty laws in Canada.

9. This segment of the population is the largest user group for both community support services and health care services in homes for the aged, nursing homes, and chronic care hospitals.

10. See Beaver and Miller, 1985; Gallagher, 1985; Horowitz, 1985b; Pratt et al., 1985; Rook and Dooley, 1985; George and Gwyther, 1986; Stephens and Christianson, 1986; Brody et al., 1987; Barber, 1988; Miller and Goldman, 1989; Noelker and Bass, 1989; Toseland and Zarit, 1989; Abel, 1990.

11. In recent years there has been considerable dis-

cussion about the role of pets in the support system of older adults. Pets may compensate for the loss of social interaction when an elderly person lives alone; or they may exaggerate the sense of loneliness and the loss of human companionship (Goldmeier, 1986).

12. Much of the underreporting or nonreporting occurred because of such factors as: family secrecy and loyalty; an elderly person's reluctance to report a family member for fear of reprisal; an unwillingness of suspecting neighbors or social welfare workers to intervene in family troubles; the dependence of the elderly person on the abuser for some level of care; and, within institutions, the lack of supervision of employees and public scrutiny of management. Today, many state governments in the United States employ an ombudsman to investigate complaints of abuse within nursing homes and other long-term care institutions, or have 'filial responsibility' laws (Bulcroft et al. 1989). In Canada, provinces such as Nova Scotia have an Adult Protection Act (Snell, 1990; McDonald et al., forthcoming).

13. See Kosberg, 1983; Costa, 1984; *The Journal of Gerontological Nursing,* December 1984; Johnson et al., 1985; Hudson, 1986; Hudson and Johnson, 1986; Pillemer and Wolf, 1986; Quinn and Tomita, 1986; Brillon, 1987:69-86; Schlesinger and Schlesinger, 1988; Steinmetz, 1988; Connidis, 1989:53-56; and McDonald et al., forthcoming. In addition, a quarterly Elder Abuse Report is published by the Center on Aging, University of Massachusetts Medical Center, Worcester, Mass.; and a quarterly journal, *The Journal of Elder Abuse and Neglect,* began publication in 1989. This journal is published by the U.S. National Committee for the Prevention of Elder Abuse, which is located in the Center on Aging at the University of Massachusetts Medical Center.

14. A comprehensive Index of Elder Abuse has been developed by Professors Hwalek and Sengstock in the Department of Sociology at Wayne State University. The City of Toronto has produced an informative pamphlet on elder abuse entitled *Home is Where the Hurt Is.*

15. Over one hundred years ago, Bismarck established the first national pension act as an 'insurance against invalidity and old age.' The plan was financed equally by workers and employers, and benefits were determined by the contributions made over the years. However, the retirement age was 70 years, and few individuals lived long enough to reap the benefits of the plan.

16. This was a means-tested plan that provided $20.00 per month at age 70. Since the average life expectancy at the time was about sixty years, few people ever collected the benefits (Baker, 1988:79).

17. For a historical summary of the development of the Canadian system of social and health security, see Bryden, 1974; Chappell, 1980, 1987; Kernaghan and Kuper, 1983; Baker, 1988; Gee and Boyce, 1988; Myles, 1988, 1989.

18. The best example of this political pressure by senior citizens was their reaction and actions in 1985 to the federal government proposal to partially de-index pensions. Senior citizens lobbied business and the opposition parties, demonstrated on Parliament Hill, and reported a lack of confidence in the government in public opinion polls. Faced with this mounting pressure from a large segment of the voting population, and demonstrated sympathy from other age groups, the government deleted the proposed changes to the universal monthly pension payments from their final budget plans.

19. For a recent critique and analysis of policy issues on specific issues see each monograph in the Butterworths Series on Individual and Population Aging, as well as Kernaghan and Kuper, 1983; Borgatta and Montgomery, 1987; Baker, 1988:77-110; Pederson et al., 1988; Moore, 1989; Biegel and Blum, 1990; Kane and Kane, 1990.

20. See Lesnoff-Caravaglia, 1984; Connidis, 1985; Jackson, 1985; McDaniel, 1986; Driedger and Chappell, 1987; Gee and Kimball, 1987; Kim, 1987; MacLean et al., 1987; Wolff, 1988, Boyd, 1989.

REFERENCES

Abel, E. (1990). 'The Ambiguities of Social Support: Adult Daughters Caring For Frail Elderly Parents,' *Journal of Aging Studies,* 3(3), 211-30.

Antonucci, T. (1985). 'Personal Characteristics, Social Support, and Social Behavior,' pp. 94-128 in R. Binstock and E. Shanas (eds.). *Handbook of Aging and the Social Sciences.* 2d ed. New York: Van Nostrand Reinhold.

Antonucci, T. (1990). 'Social Supports and Social Relationships,' pp. 186-204 in R. Binstock and L. George (eds.). *Handbook of Aging and the Social Sciences.* 3d ed. San Diego, Calif.: Academic Press.

Antonucci, T. and H. Akiyama. (1987). 'Social Networks in Adult Life and a Preliminary Examination of the Convoy Model,' *Journal of Gerontology,* 42(5), 519-27.

Aronson, J. (1985). 'Family Care of the Elderly: Underlying Assumptions and Their Consequences,' *Canadian Journal on Aging,* 4(3), 115-25.

Baker, M. (1988). *Aging in Canadian Society: A Survey.* Toronto: McGraw-Hill Ryerson.

Barber, C. (1988). 'Correlates of Subjective Burden among Adult Sons and Daughters Caring for Aged Parents,' *Journal of Aging Studies*, 2(2), 133-44.

Barusch, A. (1988). 'Problems and Coping Strategies of Elderly Spouse Caregivers,' *The Gerontologist*, 28(5), 677-85.

Beaver, M. and D. Miller. (1985). *Clinical Social Work Practice with the Elderly*. Homewood, Ill.: Dorsey Press.

Béland, F. (1989). 'Patterns of Health and Social Services Utilization,' *Canadian Journal on Aging*, 8(1), 19-33.

Berman, H. (1987). 'Adult Children and Their Parents: Irredeemable Obligation and Irreplaceable Loss,' *Journal of Gerontological Social Work*, 10(1), 21-34.

Berman, S. et al. (1987). 'Respite Care: A Partnership between a Veterans Administration Nursing Home and Families to Care for Frail Elders at Home,' *The Gerontologist*, 27(6), 581-84.

Biegel, D. (1985). 'The Application of Network Theory and Research to the Field of Aging,' pp. 251-73 in W. Sauer and R. Coward (eds.). *Social Support Networks and the Care of the Elderly*. New York: Springer Publishing Co.

Biegel, D. and A. Blum (eds.). (1990). *Aging and Caregiving: Theory, Research, and Policy*. Newbury Park, Calif.: Sage Publications.

Biegel, D. et al. (1986). *Building Support Networks for the Elderly*. Beverly Hills, Calif.: Sage Publications.

Bienvenue, R. and B. Havens. (1986). 'Structural Inequalities, Informal Networks: A Comparison of Native and Non-Native Elderly,' *Canadian Journal on Aging*, 5(4), 241-48.

Binstock, R. et al. (1985). 'Political Dilemmas of Social Intervention,' pp. 589-618 in R. Binstock and E. Shanas (eds.). *Handbook of Aging and the Social Sciences*. 2d ed. New York: Van Nostrand Reinhold.

Blau, Z. (1981). *Aging in a Changing Society*. 2d ed. New York: Franklin Watts.

Bond, J. et al. (1987). 'Familial Support of the Elderly in a Rural Mennonite Community,' *Canadian Journal on Aging*, 6(1), 7-17.

Borgatta, E. and R. Montgomery (eds.). (1987). *Critical Issues in Aging Policy: Linking Research and Values*. Newbury Park, Calif.: Sage Publications.

Boyd, M. (1989). 'Immigration and Income Security Policies in Canada: Implications for Elderly Immigrant Women,' *Population Research and Policy Review*, 8(1), 5-24.

Breytspraak, L. et al. (1985). 'The Voluntary Organization as a Support System in the Aging Process,' pp. 273-86 in W. Peterson and J. Quadagno (eds.).

Social Bonds in Later Life: Aging and Interdependence. Beverly Hills, Calif.: Sage Publications.

Brillon, Y. (1987). *Victimization and Fear of Crime among the Elderly*. Toronto: Butterworths.

Brody, E. (1981). 'Women in the Middle and Family Help to Older People,' *The Gerontologist*, 21(5), 470-80.

Brody, E. (1985). 'Parent Care as a Normative Family Stress,' *The Gerontologist*, 25(1), 19-29.

Brody, E. (1986). 'Parent Care as a Normative Family Stress,' in L. Troll (ed.). *Family Issues in Current Gerontology*. New York: Springer Publishing Co.

Brody, E. (1990). *Women in the Middle: Their Parent Care Years*. New York: Springer Publishing Co.

Brody, E. and C. Schoonover. (1986). 'Patterns of Parent-Care When Adult Daughters Work and When They Do Not,' *The Gerontologist*, 26(4), 372-81.

Brody, E. et al. (1987). 'Work Status and Parent Care: A Comparison of Four Groups of Women,' *The Gerontologist*, 27(2), 201-8.

Brody, E. et al. (1989). 'Caregiving Daughters and Their Local Siblings: Perceptions, Strains, and Interactions,' *The Gerontologist*, 29(4), 529-38.

Bromberg, E. (1983). 'Mother-Daughter Relationships in Later Life: The Effect of Quality of Relationship upon Mutual Aid,' *Journal of Gerontological Social Work*, 6(1), 75-92.

Brownell, A. and S. Shumaker. (1984). 'Social Support: An Introduction to a Complex Phenomenon,' *Journal of Social Issues*, 40(4), 1-9.

Bryden, K. (1974). *Old Age Pensions and Policy-Making in Canada*. Montreal: McGill-Queen's University Press.

Bulcroft, K. et al. (1989). 'Filial Responsibility Laws,' *Research on Aging*, 11(3), 374-93.

Burnley, C. (1987). 'Caregiving: The Impact of Emotional Support for Single Women,' *Journal of Aging Studies*, 1(3), 253-64.

Cain, L. (1987). 'Alternative Perspectives on the Phenomena of Human Aging: Age Stratification and Age Status,' *The Journal of Applied Behavioral Sciences*, 23(2), 277-94.

Callahan, J. (1988). 'Elder Abuse: Some Questions for Policy Makers,' *The Gerontologist*, 28(4), 453-58.

Cantor, M. (1979). 'Neighbors and Friends: Overlooked Resources in the Informal Support System,' *Research on Aging*, 1(4), 434-63.

Cantor, M. and V. Little. (1985). 'Aging and Social Care,' pp. 745-81 in R. Binstock and E. Shanas (eds.) *Handbook of Aging and the Social Sciences*. 2d ed. New York: Van Nostrand Reinhold.

Chappell, N. (1980). 'Social Policy and the Elderly,' pp. 35-42 in V. Marshall (ed.). *Aging in Canada: Social Perspectives*. Don Mills, Ont.: Fitzhenry and Whiteside.

Chappell, N. (1983). 'Informal Support Networks among the Elderly,' *Reserach on Aging*, 5(1), 77-99.

Chappell, N. (1985). 'Social Support and the Receipt of Home Care Services,' *The Gerontologist*, 25(1), 47-54.

Chappell, N. (1987). 'Canadian Income and Health-Care Policy: Implications for the Elderly,' pp., 489-504 in V. Marshall (ed.). *Aging in Canada: Social Perspectives*. Markham, Ont.: Fitzhenry and Whiteside.

Chappell, N. (1989) 'Health and Helping among the Elderly: Gender Differences,' *Journal of Aging and Health*, 1(1), 102-20.

Chappell, N. (1990). 'Aging and Social Care,' pp. 438-54 in R. Binstock and L. George (eds.). *Handbook of Aging and the Social Sciences*. 2d ed. New York: Van Nostrand Reinhold.

Chappell, N. and A. Blandford. (1987). 'Adult Day Care and Medical and Hospital Claims,' *The Gerontologist*, 27(6), 773-79.

Chappell, N. and B. Havens. (1985). 'Who Helps the Elderly Person: A Discussion of Informal and Formal Care,' pp. 221-27 in W. Peterson and J. Quadagno (eds.). *Social Bonds In Later Life: Aging and Interdependence*. Beverly Hills, Calif.: Sage Publications.

Chappell, N. et al. (1986). *Health and Aging: A Social Perspective*. Toronto: Holt, Rinehart & Winston.

Cicirelli, V. (1985). 'The Role of Siblings as Family Caregivers,' pp. 93-107 in W. Sauer and R. Coward (eds.). *Social Support Networks and the Care of the Elderly*. New York: Springer Publishing Co.

Clark, R. and D. Baumer. (1985). 'Income Maintenance Policies,' pp. 666-95 in R. Binstock and E. Shanas (eds.). *Handbook of Aging and the Social Sciences*. 2d ed. New York: Van Nostrand Reinhold.

Cohen, C. et al. (1985). 'Social Networks and Adaptation,' *The Gerontologist*, 25(3), 297-304.

Cohen, C. et al. (1988). 'Survival Strategies of Older Homeless Men,' *The Gerontologist*, 28(1), 58-65.

Cohen, S. and S. Syme. (1985). *Social Support and Health*. New York: Academic Press.

Connidis, I. (1985). 'The Service Needs of Older People: Implications for Public Policy,' *Canadian Journal on Aging*, 4(1), 3-9.

Connidis, I. (1987). 'Life In Older Age: The View From the Top,' pp. 451-72 in V. Marshall (ed.). *Aging in Canada: Social Perspectives*. 2d ed. Markham, Ont.: Fitzhenry and Whiteside.

Connidis, I. (1989). *Family Ties and Aging*. Toronto: Butterworths

Conrad, K. et al. (1990). 'Survey of Adult Day Care in the United States,' *Research on Aging*, 12(1), 36-56.

Corin, E. (1987). 'The Relationship between Formal and Informal Social Support Networks in Rural and Urban Contexts,' pp. 367-94 in V. Marshall (ed.). *Aging in Canada: Social Perspectives*. 2d ed. Markham, Ont.: Fitzhenry and Whiteside.

Costa, J. (1984). *Abuse of the Elderly: A Guide to Resources and Services*. Lexinton, Mass.: Lexington Books.

Danigelis, N. (1985). 'Social Support for Elders through Community Ties: The Role of Voluntary Associations,' pp. 159-77 in W. Sauer and R. Coward (eds.). *Social Support Networks and the Care of the Elderly*. New York: Springer Publishing Co.

Davis, K. (1985). 'Health Care Policies and the Aged: Observations from the United States,' pp. 727-44 in R. Binstock and E. Shanas (eds.). *Handbook of Aging and the Social Sciences*. 2d ed. New York: Van Nostrand Reinhold.

Denton, F. et al. (1986). 'Prospective Aging of the Population and Its Implications for the Labour Force and Government Expenditures,' *Canadian Journal on Aging*, 5(2), 75-98.

Denton, F. et al. (1987). 'How Will Population Aging Affect the Future Costs of Maintaining Health-Care Standards?' pp. 553-68 in V. Marshall (ed.). *Aging in Canada: Social Perspectives*. 2d ed. Markham, Ont.: Fitzhenry and Whiteside.

Dono, J. et al. (1979). 'Primary Groups in Old Age: Structure and Function,' *Research on Aging*, 1(4), 403-33.

Dowd, J. (1980). *Stratification among the Aged*. Monterey, Calif.: Brooks/Cole Publishing Co.

Driedger, L. and N. Chappell. (1987). *Aging and Ethnicity*. Toronto: Butterworths.

Eglit, H. (1985). 'Age and the Law,' pp. 528-53 in R. Binstock and E. Shanas (eds.). *Handbook of Aging and the Social Sciences*. 2d ed. New York: Van Nostrand Reinhold.

Estes, C. (1979). *The Aging Enterprise: A Critical Examination of Social Policies and Services for the Aged*. San Francisco: Jossey-Bass Publishers.

Fedorak, S. and C. Griffin. (1986). 'Developing a Self-Advocacy Program for Seniors: The Essential Component of Health Promotion,' *Canadian Journal on Aging*, 5(4), 269-77.

Fengler, A. and N. Goodrich. (1979). 'Wives of Elderly Disabled Men: The Hidden Patients,' *The Gerontologist*, 19(2), 175-84.

Field, D. and M. Minkler. (1988). 'Continuity and Change in Social Support between Young-old and Old-old or Very-old Age,' *Journal of Gerontology: Psychological Sciences*, 43(4), P100-106.

Fischer, L. (1985). 'Elderly Parents and the Caregiver Role: An Asymmetrical Transition,' pp. 105-14 in W. Peterson and J. Quadagno (eds.). *Social Bonds in Later Life: Aging and Interdependence*. Beverly Hills, Calif.: Sage Publications.

Forbes, W. et al. (1987). *Institutionalization of the Elderly in Canada*. Toronto: Butterworths.

Franke, J. (1987). 'Support for Aging Policy: Self-Interest, Social Justice, and Political Symbols,' *Journal of Aging Studies*, 1(4), 393-406.

Gallagher, D. (1985). 'Intervention Strategies to Assist Caregivers of Frail Elders: Current Research Status and Future Research Directions,' pp. 249-82 in C. Eisdorfer et al. (eds.). *Annual Review of Gerontology and Geriatrics*. vol. 5. New York: Springer Publishing Co.

Gatz, M. et al. (1990). 'Caregiving Families,' pp. 404-26 in J. Birren and W. Schaie (eds.). *Handbook of the Psychology of Aging*. 3d ed. San Diego, Calif.: Academic Press.

Gee, E. and M. Boyce. (1988). 'Veterans and Veterans Legislation in Canada: An Historical Overview,' *Canadian Journal on Aging*, 7(3), 204-17.

Gee, E. and M. Kimball. (1987). *Women and Aging*. Toronto: Butterworths.

George, L. and L. Gwyther. (1986). 'Caregiver Well-being: A Multidimensional Examination of Family Caregivers of Demented Adults,' *The Gerontologist*, 26(2), 253-59.

Goldmeier, J. (1986). 'Pets or People: Another Research Note,' *The Gerontologist*, 26(2), 203-6.

Gottlieb, B. (ed.). (1981). *Social Networks and Social Support*. Beverly Hills, Calif.: Sage Publications.

Gubrium, J. and R. Lynott. (1987). 'Measurement and the Interpretation of Burden in the Alzheimer's Disease Experience,' *Journal of Aging Studies*, 1(3), 265-85.

Guttman, D. (1985). 'The Social Networks of Ethnic Minorities,' pp. 199-218 in W. Sauer and R. Coward (eds.). *Social Support Networks and the Care of the Elderly*. New York: Springer Publishing Co.

Hall, B. (1989a). 'The Role of Adult Children in Helping Chronically Ill Hospitalized Patients,' *Canadian Journal on Aging*, 8(1), 68-78.

Hall, B. (1989b). 'The Hospitalized Elderly and Intergenerational Conflict,' *Journal of Applied Gerontology*, 8(3), 294-96.

Hanson, S. and W. Sauer. (1985). 'Children and Their Elderly Parents,' pp. 41-66 in W. Sauer and R. Coward (eds.). *Social Support Networks and the Care of the Elderly*. New York: Springer Publishing Co.

Hardy, M. (1988). 'Vulnerability in Old Age: The Issue of Dependency in American Society,' *Journal of Aging Studies*, 2(4), 311-20.

Hess, B. and B. Soldo. (1985). 'Husband and Wife Networks,' pp. 67-92 in W. Sauer and R. Coward (eds.). *Social Support Networks and the Care of the Elderly*. New York: Springer Publishing Co.

Horowitz, A. (1985a). 'Family Caregiving to the Frail Elderly,' pp. 194-247 in C. Eisdorfer et al (eds.). *Annual Review of Gerontology and Geriatrics*. vol. 5. New York: Springer Publishing Co.

Horowitz, A. (1985b). 'Sons and Daughters as Caregivers to Older Parents: Differences in Role Performance and Consequences,' *The Gerontologist*, 25(6), 612-17.

House, J. and R. Kahn. (1985).'Measures and Concepts of Social Support,' pp. 83-108 in S. Cohen and S. Syme (eds.). *Social Support and Health*. New York: Academic Press.

Hudson, J. (1986). *Elder Abuse: An Overview*. Program in Gerontology, University of Toronto Research Paper Series, Research Paper No. 7.

Hudson, M. and T. Johnson. (1986). 'Elder Neglect and Abuse: A Review of the Literature,' pp. 81-134 in C. Eisdorfer (ed.). *Annual Review of Gerontology and Geriatrics*. vol. 6. New York: Springer Publishing Co.

Hudson, R. and J. Strate. (1985). 'Aging and Political Systems,' pp. 554-85 in R. Binstock and E. Shanas (eds.). *Handbook of Aging and the Social Sciences*. 2d ed. New York: Van Nostrand Reinhold.

Ismael, J. and Y. Vaillancourt (eds.). (1988). *Privatization and Provincial Social Services in Canada*. Edmonton, Alta.: University of Alberta Press.

Jackson, J. (1985). 'Race, National Origin, Ethnicity, and Aging,' pp. 264-303 in R. Binstock and E. Shanas (eds.). *Handbook of Aging and the Social Sciences*. 2d ed. New York: Van Nostrand Reinhold.

Johnson, T. et al. (1985). *Elder Neglect and Abuse: An Annotated Bibliography*. Westport, Conn.: Greenwood Press.

Kane, R. and R. Kane. (1990). 'Health Care for Older People: Organizational and Policy Issues,' pp. 415-37 in R. Binstock and L. George (eds.). *Handbook of Aging and the Social Sciences*. 3d ed. San Diego, Calif.: Academic Press.

Kart, C. and C. Longino. (1987). 'The Support System of Older People: A Test of the Exchange Paradigm,' *Journal of Aging Studies*, 1(3), 239-52.

Karuza, J. et al. (1988). 'Networking in Aging: A Challenge, Model, and Evaluation,' *The Gerontologist*, 28(2), 147-55.

Kattler, D. and J. Williamson. (1988). 'Welfare State Development and Life Expectancy among the Aged: A Cross-National Analysis,' *Journal of Aging Studies*, 2(1), 13-24.

Keigher, S. et al. (1988). 'Payments to Informal versus Formal Home Care Providers: Policy Divergence Affecting the Elderly and Their Families in Michigan and Illinois,'*Journal of Applied Gerontology*, 7(4), 456-73.

Kendig, H. et al. (1988). 'Confidants and Family Structure in Old Age,' *Journal of Gerontology: Social*

Sciences, 43(2), S31-40.

Keraghan, K. and O. Kuper (eds.). (1983). *Coordination in Canadian Governments: A Case Study of Aging Policy.* Toronto: The Institute of Public Administration of Canada.

Kim, P. (1987). 'The Rural Elderly,' pp. 350-68 in G. Lesnoff-Caravaglia (ed.). *Handbook of Applied Gerontology.* New York: Human Sciences Press.

Kingson, E. (1988). 'Generational Equity: An Unexpected Opportunity to Broaden the Politics of Aging,' *The Gerontologist,* 28(6), 765-72.

Kingson, E. et al. (1986). *Ties That Bind: The Interdependence of Generations.* Cabin John, Md.: Seven Locks Press.

Kirwin, P. (1988). 'The Challenge of Community Long-Term Care: The Dependent Aged,' *Journal of Aging Studies,* 2(3), 255-66.

Kosberg, J. (ed.). (1983). *Abuse and Maltreatment of the Elderly: Causes and Interventions.* Boston: John Wright, PSG Inc.

Kosberg, J. (1988). 'Preventing Elder Abuse: Identification of High Risk Factors Prior to Placement Decisions,' *The Gerontologist,* 28(1), 43-50.

Kraus, A. (1984). 'The Burden of Care for Families of Elderly Persons with Dementia,' *Canadian Journal on Aging,* 3(1), 45-51.

Krause, N. (1987). 'Satisfaction with Social Support and Self-Rated Health in Older Adults,' *The Gerontologist,* 27(3), 301-8.

Krout, J. (1985). 'Relationships between Informal and Formal Organizational Networks,' pp. 178-96 in W. Sauer and R. Coward (eds.). *Social Support Networks and the Care of the Elderly.* New York: Springer Publishing Co.

Krout, J. (1988). 'Community Size Differences in Service Awareness among Elderly Adults,' *Journal of Gerontology: Social Sciences,* 43(1), S528-30.

Lawton, P. (1983). 'Environment and Other Determinants of Well-Being in Older People,' *The Gerontologist,* 23(3), 349-57.

Lawton, P. et al. (1989). 'Measuring Caregiving Appraisal,' *Journal of Gerontology: Psychological Sciences,* 44(3), P61-71.

Lee, G. (1985). 'Theoretical Perspectives on Social Networks,' pp. 21-37 in W. Sauer and R. Coward (eds.). *Social Support Networks and the Care of the Elderly.* New York: Springer Publishing Co.

Lesnoff-Caravaglia, G. (ed.). (1984). *The World of Older Women: Conflicts and Resolutions.* New York: Human Sciences Press.

Lieberman, M. (1990). 'Mutual-Aid Groups: An Underutilized Resource among the Elderly,' pp. 285-320 in P. Lawton (ed.). *Annual Review of Gerontology and Geriatrics.* vol. 9. New York: Springer Publishing Co.

Lin, N. et al. (eds.). (1986). *Social Support, Life Events,* *and Depression.* New York: Academic Press.

Linsk, N. et al. (1988). 'States' Policies Regarding Paid Family Caregiving,' *The Gerontologist,* 28(2), 204-12.

Litwak, E. (1985). *Helping the Elderly: The Complementary Roles of Informal Networks and Formal Systems.* New York: Guilford Press.

Lomax Cook, F. and E. Barrett. (1988). 'Public Support for Social Security,' *Journal of Aging Studies,* 2(4), 339-56.

Longino, C. and A. Lipman. (1985). 'The Support Systems of Women.' pp. 219-33 in W. Sauer and H. Coward (eds.). *Social Support Networks and the Care of the Elderly.* New York: Springer Publishing Co.

MacLean, M. et al. (1987). 'Institutional Racism in Old Age: Theoretical Perspectives and a Case Study about Access to Social Services,' *Canadian Journal on Aging,* 6(2), 128-40.

Manton, K. (1988). 'Planning Long-Term Care for Heterogeneous Older Populations,' pp. 217-55 in G. Maddox and P. Lawton (eds.). *Annual Review of Gerontology and Geriatrics.* vol. 8. New York: Springer Publishing Co.

Marcus, L. and V. Jaeger. (1984). 'The Elderly as Family Caregivers,' *Canadian Journal on Aging,* 3(1), 33-43.

Marshall, V. (1987). 'Health of Very Old People as a Concern of Their Children,' pp. 473-85 in V. Marshall (ed.). *Aging in Canada: Social Perspectives.* 2d ed. Markham, Ont.: Fitzhenry and Whiteside.

Martin Matthews, A. (forthcoming). *Widowhood in Later Life.* Markham, Ont.: Butterworths.

Matthews, S. (1987). 'Provision of Care to Old Parents: Division of Responsibility among Adult Children,' *Research on Aging,* 9(1), 45-60.

Matthews, S. (1988). 'The Burdens of Parent Care: A Critical Evaluation of Recent Findings,' *Journal of Aging Studies,* 2(2), 157-66.

Matthews, S. et al. (1989). 'Relative Contributions of Help by Employed and Nonemployed Sisters to Their Elderly Parents,' *Journal of Gerontology: Social Sciences,* 44(1), S36-44.

McDaniel, S. (1986). *Canada's Aging Population.* Toronto: Butterworths.

McDaniel, S. (1987). 'Demographic Aging as a Guiding Paradigm in Canada's Welfare State,' *Canadian Public Policy,* 13(3), 330-36.

McDonald, L. and R. Wanner. (1990). *Retirement in Canada.* Markham, Ont.: Butterworths.

McDonald, L. et al. (forthcoming). *Elder Abuse and Neglect in Canada.* Markham, Ont.: Butterworths.

Messinger, H. and B. Powell. (1987). 'The Implications of Canada's Aging Society on Social Expenditures,' pp. 569-85 in V. Marshall (ed.). *Aging in*

Canada: Social Perspectives. 2d ed. Markham, Ont.: Fitzhenry and Whiteside.

Miller, B. (1989). 'Adult Children's Perceptions of Caregiver Stress and Satisfaction,' *Journal of Applied Gerontology,* 8(3), 275-93.

Miller, D. and L. Goldman. (1989). 'Perceptions of Caregivers about Special Respite Services for the Elderly,' *The Gerontologist,* 29(3), 408-10.

Miller, B. and A. Montgomery. (1990). 'Family Caregivers and Limitations in Social Activities,' *Research on Aging,* 12(1), 72-93.

Mills, C.W. (1959). *The Sociological Imagination.* New York: Oxford University Press.

Montgomery, R. et al. (1985). 'Measurement and the Analysis of Burden,' *Research on Aging,* 7(2), 137-52.

Moore, E. (ed.). (1989). 'Population Issues in Canadian Public Policy,' *Population Research and Policy Review,* 8(1), 1-117.

Morgan, D. (1988). 'Age Differences in Social Network Participation,' *Journal of Gerontology: Social Sciences,* 43(4), S129-37.

Myles, J. (1988). 'Social Security and Support of the Elderly: The Western Experience,' *Journal of Aging Studies,* 2(4), 321-38.

Myles, J. (1989). *Old Age and the Welfare State: The Political Economy of Public Pensions.* rev. ed. Lawrence, Kans.: University Press of Kansas.

Neugarten, B. (ed.). (1982). *Age or Need?* Beverly Hills, Calif.: Sage Publications.

Neysmith, S. (1987a). 'Organizing for Influence: The Relationship of Structure to Impact,' *Canadian Journal on Aging,* 6(2), 105-16.

Neysmith, S. (1987b). 'Social Policy Implications of an Aging Society,' pp. 586-97 in V. Marshall (ed.). *Aging in Canada: Social Perspectives.* 2d ed. Markham, Ont.: Fitzhenry and Whiteside.

Noelker, L. and D. Bass. (1989). 'Home Care for Elderly Persons: Linkages Between Formal and Informal Caregivers,' *Journal of Gerontology: Social Sciences,* 44(1), S63-70.

Northcott, H. (1988). *Changing Residence: The Geographic Mobility of Elderly Canadians.* Toronto: Butterworths.

O'Bryant, S. (1985). 'Neighbors' Support of Older Widows Who Live Alone in Their Own Homes,' *The Gerontologist,* 25(3), 305-10.

O'Malley, T. et al. (1984). 'Categories of Family-Mediated Abuse and Neglect of Elderly Persons,' *Journal of the American Geriatrics Society,* 32(5), 362-70.

Pederson, A. et al. (1988). *Coordinating Healthy Public Policy: An Analytic Literature Review and Bibliography.* Ottawa: Health and Welfare Canada.

Penning, M. and N. Chappell. (1987). 'Ethnicity and Informal Supports among Older Adults,' *Journal of Aging Studies,* 1(2), 145-60.

Peters, G. and M. Kaiser. (1985). 'The Role of Friends and Neighbors in Providing Social Support,' pp. 123-58 in W. Sauer and R. Coward (eds.). *Social Support Networks and the Care of the Elderly.* New York: Springer Publishing Co.

Peters, G. et al. (1987). 'Primary-Group Support Systems of the Aged,' *Research on Aging,* 9(3), 392-416.

Peterson, W. and J. Quadagno (eds.). (1985). *Social Bonds in Later Life: Aging and Interdependence.* Beverly Hills, Calif.: Sage Publications.

Pillemer, K. (1985). 'The Dangers of Dependency: New Findings on Domestic Violence against the Elderly,' *Social Problems,* 33(2), 146-58.

Pillemer, K. and D. Finkelhor. (1988). 'The Prevalence of Elder Abuse: A Random Sample Survey,' *The Gerontologist,* 28(1), 51-57.

Pillemer, K. and D. Moore. (1989). 'Abuse of Patients in Nursing Homes: Findings from a Survey of Staff,' *The Gerontologist,* 29(3), 314-20.

Pillemer, K. and R. Wolf (eds.). (1986). *Elder Abuse: Conflict in the Family.* Dover, Mass.: Auburn House Publishing Co.

Podnieks, E. (1985). 'Case Management of the Abused Elderly,' paper presented at the 14th Annual Meeting of the Canadian Association on Gerontology, October 17-20, Hamilton, Ontario.

Podnieks, E. et al. (1989). *Survey on Abuse of the Elderly in Canada: Preliminary Findings.* Toronto: Ryerson Polytechnical Institute, Office of Research and Innovation.

Pratt, C. et al. (1985). 'Burden and Coping Strategies of Caregivers to Alzheimer's Patients,' *Family Relations,* 34(1), 27-33.

Pruchno, R. (1990). 'The Effects of Help Patterns on the Mental Health of Spouse Caregivers,' *Research on Aging,* 12(1), 57-71.

Pruchno, R. and N. Resch. (1989). 'Aberrant Behaviors and Alzheimer's Disease: Mental Health Effects on Spouse Caregivers,' *Journal of Gerontology: Social Sciences,* 44(5), S177-82.

Quayhagen, M.P. and M. Quayhagen. (1988). 'Alzheimer's Stress: Coping with the Caregiving Role,' *The Gerontologist,* 28(4), 391-96.

Quinn, M.J. and S. Tomita. (1986). *Elder Abuse and Neglect: Causes, Diagnosis, and Intervention.* New York: Springer Publishing Co.

Riley, M. and J. Riley (eds.). (1989). *The Quality of Aging: Strategies for Intervention.* Newbury Park, Calif.: Sage Publications.

Rook, K. and D. Dooley. (1985). 'Applying Social Support Research: Theoretical Problems and Future Directions,' *Journal of Social Issues,* 41(1), 5-28.

Rosenmayr, L. and E. Kockeis. (1963). 'Propositions

for a Sociological Theory of Aging and the Family,' *International Social Science Journal*, 15(3), 410-26.

Rosenthal, C. (1986a). 'Family Supports in Later Life: Does Ethnicity Make a Difference?' *The Gerontologist*, 26(1), 19-24.

Rosenthal, C. (1986b). 'Kinkeeping in the Familial Division of Labour,' *Journal of Marriage and the Family*, 47(4), 965-74.

Rosenthal, C. (1987). 'Aging and Intergenerational Relations in Canada,' pp. 331-42 in V. Marshall (ed.). *Aging in Canada: Social Perspectives*. 2d ed. Markham, Ont.: Fitzhenry and Whiteside.

Rosenthal, C. et al. (1989). 'Is Parent Care Normative? The Experiences of a Sample of Middle-Aged Women,' *Research on Aging*, 11(2), 244-60.

Rubinstein, L. and D. Wieland. (1989). 'Geriatric Assessment Units,' *Annual Review of Gerontology and Geriatrics*. vol. 9. New York: Springer Publishing Co.

Rubinstein, R. (1985). 'The Elderly Who Live Alone and Their Social Supports,' pp. 165-93 in M.P. Lawton and G. Maddox (eds.). *Annual Review of Gerontology and Geriatrics*. vol. 5. New York: Springer Publishing Co.

Salamon, M. (1987). 'Health Care Environment and Life Satisfaction in the Elderly,' *Journal of Aging Studies*, 1(3), 287-97.

Sauer, W. and R. Coward (eds.). (1985a). *Social Support Networks and the Care of the Elderly*. New York: Springer Publishing Co.

Sauer, W. and R. Coward. (1985b). 'The Role of Social Support Networks in the Care of the Elderly.' pp. 3-20 in W. Sauer and R. Coward (eds.). *Social Support Networks and the Care of the Elderly*. New York: Springer Publishing Co.

Scharlach, A. (1989). 'A Comparison of Employed Caregivers of Cognitively Impaired and Physically Impaired Elderly Persons,' *Research on Aging*, 11(2), 225-43.

Scharlach, A. and C. Frenzel. (1986). 'An Evaluation of Institution-Based Respite Care,' *The Gerontologist*, 26(1), 77-82.

Schlesinger, B. and R. Schlesinger. (1988). *Abuse of the Elderly: Issues and Annotated Bibliography*. Toronto: University of Toronto Press.

Schulz, R. and M. Rau. (1985). 'Social Support through the Life Course,' pp. 129-49 in S. Cohen and S. Syme (eds.). *Social Support and Health*. New York: Academic Press.

Seltzer, M. et al. (1987). 'Family Members as Case Managers: Partnership between the Formal and Informal Support Networks,' *The Gerontologist*, 27(6), 722-28.

Shapiro, E. and N. Roos. (1987). 'Predictors, Patterns and Consequences of Nursing-Home Use in One Canadian Province,' pp. 520-37 in V. Marshall (ed.). *Aging in Canada: Social Perspectives*. 2d ed. Markham, Ont.: Fitzhenry and Whiteside.

Shell, D. (1982). *Protection of the Elderly: A Study of Elder Abuse*. Winnipeg, Man.: Manitoba Association on Gerontology.

Shore, B. (1985). 'Extended Kin as Helping Networks,' pp. 108-20 in W. Sauer and R. Coward (eds.). *Social Support Networks and the Care of the Elderly*. New York: Springer Publishing Co.

Shumaker, S. and A. Brownell. (1984). 'Toward a Theory of Social Support: Closing Conceptual Gaps,' *Journal of Social Issues*, 40(4), 11-36.

Snell, J. (1990). 'Filial Responsibility Laws in Canada: A Historical Study,' *Canadian Journal on Aging*, 9(3).

Springer, D. and T. Brubaker. (1984). *Family Caregivers and Dependent Elderly*. Beverly Hills, Calif.: Sage Publications.

Steinmetz, S. (1988). *Duty Bound: Elder Abuse and Family Care*. Beverly Hills, Calif.: Sage Publications.

Stephens, S. and J. Christianson. (1986). *Informal Care of the Elderly*. Lexington, Mass.: Lexington Books.

Stone, L. (1988). *Family and Friendship Ties among Canada's Seniors*. Ottawa: Statistics Canada.

Storm, C. et al. (1985). 'Obligations for Care: Beliefs in a Small Canadian Town.' *Canadian Journal on Aging*, 4(2), 75-85.

Thoits, P. (1982). 'Conceptual, Methodological and Theoretical Problems in Studying Social Support as a Buffer Against Life Stress,' *Journal of Health and Social Behavior*, 23(1), 145-49.

Thompson, V. (1989). 'The Elderly and Their Informal Social Networks,' *Canadian Journal on Aging*, 8(4), 319-32.

Thompson, V. and J. McFarland. (1989). 'Agency Participation and Problem Occurrence among the Elderly,' *Canadian Journal on Aging*, 8(3), 209-21.

Toseland, R. and S. Zarit (eds.). (1989). 'Symposium: Effectiveness of Caregivers Groups,' *The Gerontologist*, 29(4), 437-83.

Townsend, A. and S. Poulshock. (1986). 'Intergenerational Perspectives on Impaired Elders' Support Networks,' *Journal of Gerontology*, 41(1), 101-9.

Walter, A. (1985). 'The Mediating Role of Social Networks in Housing Decisions of the Elderly,' pp. 187-210 in W. Peterson and J. Quadagno (eds.). *Social Bonds in Later Life: Aging and Interdependence*. Beverly Hills, Calif.: Sage Publications.

Ward, R. (1985). 'Informal Networks and Well-Being in Later Life: A Research Agenda,' *The Gerontologist*, 25(1), 55-61.

Ward, R. et al. (1984). 'Informal Networks and Knowledge of Services for Older Persons,' *Journal of Gerontology*, 39(2), 216-23.

Wellman, B. and A. Hall. (1986). 'Social Networks and Social Support: Implications for Later Life,' pp. 191-231 in V. Marshall (ed.). *Later Life: The Social Psychology of Aging*. Beverly Hills, Calif.: Sage Publications.

Wenger, G. (1987). 'Dependence, Interdependence, and Reciprocity after Eighty,' *Journal of Aging Studies*, 1(4), 355-78.

Wisensale, S. (1988). 'Generational Equity and Intergenerational Policies,' *The Gerontologist*, 28(6), 773-78.

Wisensale, S. and M. Allison. (1988). 'An Analysis of 1987 State Family Leave Legislation: Implications for Caregivers of the Elderly,' *The Gerontologist*, 28(6), 779-85.

Wister, A. and L. Strain. (1986). 'Social Support and Well-Being: A Comparison of Older Widows and Widowers,' *Canadian Journal on Aging*, 5(3), 205-19.

Wolff, N. (1988). 'Women and the Equity of the Social Security Program,' *Journal of Aging Studies*, 2(4), 357-78.

Wolinsky, F. and C. Arnold. (1988). 'A Different Perspective on Health and Health Services Utilization,' pp. 71-101 in G. Maddox and P. Lawton (eds.). *Annual Review of Gerontology and Geriatrics*. vol. 8. New York: Springer Publishing Co.

11
Work, Retirement, and Economic Status

Health and Welfare Canada, Information Directorate

INTRODUCTION

In order that the individual and collective life chances and lifestyles of older adults be understood, the interrelated concepts of work, retirement, and economic status must be considered from both a micro and a macro perspective. Retirement, as a major transitional passage in later life, represents the end of a work career and the beginning of a leisure career. But it can also mark the beginning of a reduced standard of living, including a life of poverty for some segments of the elderly population.

Retirement is a social invention found in most industrialized societies.[1] Conceptually, it can be viewed as a social process wherein an individual withdraws from the labor force sometime after 55 to 60 years of age. In return for this voluntary or involuntary withdrawal, most individuals are eligible to receive some level of economic benefit in the form of social security from the government, as well as pensions from the public or private sector.[2] In addition, the elderly are usually eligible to receive varying levels of subsidized health care (drugs, hospitalization, or long-term care), as well as subsidized social services (housing, transportation, or leisure). Retirement represents a major transition from the status of being employed and earning an income to the status of being retired, or unemployed (George, 1980:55-76). This transition is generally accompanied by a reduced income — a pension — awarded on the basis of past contributions by an employee and his or her employers (private pensions), or as a form of social welfare such as the Canada/Quebec Pension Plans (C/QPP).

The study of retirement involves an analysis of both individual and population aging throughout the middle and later years. Therefore, although most retirement research has been completed at the individual (micro) level of analysis, wherever possible in this chapter a societal (macro) perspective is taken, especially with respect to retirement policies, economic status, and the societal consequences of retirement. Highlight 11.1 illustrates the variety of individual and population aging attributes and processes that must be considered in any analysis of retirement lifestyles and economic status in the later years.

Retirement is a social process and a social institution (Atchley, 1982) that must be studied in relation to the work history of the individual and the labor-force needs of society; in relation to the economic status of the individual and the society; and in relation to the health status of the individual and the health care services provided by the society. In addition, retirement as a social process is related to the leisure interests of the individual and to the social and leisure services provided by the public and private sectors (chapter 12); to the type and degree of support provided by the family (chapters 9 and 10) and by society; and to individual decisions about when to retire and to public- and private-sector retirement policies that may require mandatory retirement. Furthermore, personal factors (gender, marital status, work or retirement status of the spouse, class background, ethnicity, widowhood), demographic factors (fertility rates, migration rates, and patterns of longevity), societal factors (trends toward early retirement, 'gray power' movements), and historical factors (wars or depressions) influence the process as well.

Early conceptualizations of retirement described the phenomenon (and indeed all of the postretirement years) as a 'roleless' role (Burgess, 1960:20). This view held that the retired individual (usually a man) and his spouse were faced with an ambiguous social status and a lack of purpose and meaning in their lives. As a result of this perspective, many of the early studies of retirement were motivated by the unchallenged assumption that the transition to retirement is stressful and that it represents a crisis and creates adjustment problems for many individuals and couples. However, research evidence generally supports the finding that most men and women adjust successfully to retirement and experience little stress in adapting to their new social status and lifestyle.[3] The retirement role is not viewed as a 'problem' by most retirees. Most older people seem to adjust to the role, even if it does appear ambiguous and threatening during the preretirement years. In fact, recent research suggests that many people look forward to retirement, and some even plan for retirement and decide to retire before the normal age of 65.

Whereas it was once relatively easy to iden-

Hɪɢʜʟɪɢʜᴛ 11.1

A SUMMARY OF INDIVIDUAL AND SOCIETAL ATTRIBUTES AND PROCESSES INFLUENCING RETIREMENT LIFESTYLES

INDIVIDUAL	SOCIETAL
• Work history (regular versus irregular, full-time versus part-time)	• Labor force requirements (past, present, and future re: unemployment)
• Economic status (earnings, savings, investments, private pension)	• Economic history (periods of inflation, depressions, amount of government debt)
• Health status (perceived, objective)	• Health care system (universal access, cost, quality)
• Leisure interests and experiences	• Leisure opportunities (government programs and services)
• Informal support (family, friends)	• Formal support (subsidized housing, transportation, home care)
• Attitudes toward retirement	• Policies re: retirement and social security (mandatory versus voluntary, availability of private and public pensions, vesting, portability)

• Personal factors
    ◦ sex
    ◦ social class
    ◦ education
    ◦ race or ethnicity
    ◦ marital status
	• Demographic factors
	    ◦ fertility rates
	    ◦ mortality rates
	    ◦ immigration policies
	    ◦ life expectancy
	    ◦ sex ratio
	    ◦ dependency ratio

---

tify the 'retired' and to define 'retirement,' definitions are becoming increasingly complex and variable, thereby clouding the results of retirement research (McDonald and Wanner, 1990:3-8; Ekerdt, forthcoming). This ambiguity has been created by both the legal and the social events of recent years. First, with legal challenges to the requirement of mandatory retirement at age 65, some older adults refuse to retire. Others retire and become eligible for private pension benefits, and then continue to work on a full-time or a part-time basis. Thus, upon reaching what has heretofore been considered the 'retirement' age (65 and beyond), individuals may be completely retired, partly retired, not retired, or unemployed and seeking work. Moreover, some may fully retire earlier than the mandatory or expected age, some may reduce their work commitment (in terms of hours per week or weeks per year), and some may reduce their psychological commitment to a job or an employer long before they are 'officially' retired and receiving a pension.

In short, retirement is all of, and more than, a social institution, a social role, an event, a process, or a stage in life. It is both an individual issue and a societal issue. And, it is a much broader concept than that defined by Atchley (1982:264) when he stated, 'retirement is a modern institution that primarily centers around the goal of providing an orderly means of shifting older workers, or allowing them to shift, out of the labor force with a minimum of financial hardship in consideration of their past contributions.' As McDonald and Wanner (1990:15) perceptively note, 'retirement not only concerns older Canadians, it concerns all of us and is inextricably bound to the socioeconomic and political structures of Canadian society, which have been shaped by particular historical circumstances.' To this they could have added, 'and which will continue to be shaped by political, economic, and social forces that operate throughout our life course.' Indeed, your future retirement and economic status will not be determined solely by your work career, or by your lifetime earnings and savings patterns. Rather, your future will also be influenced by factors beyond your individual control, such as: global and national inflation and unemployment rates; fertility rates, which can influence the dependency ratio and the size of the labor force; national debt; public- and private-sector policies concerning retirement and pensions; the degree of gender inequality in terms of work and career opportunities, wages, and pensions; and immigration policies that increase or decrease the size and the mix of the labor force.

The adaptive strategies initiated by the individual following retirement may involve adjustments to the loss of job and friends, to a perceived loss of job prestige and identity, to loss of income, to increased 'free' time, to declining health, and to increased interaction with the spouse. From the perspective of society, mandatory retirement can deprive the labor force of experienced, loyal, and reliable workers; it may initiate population shifts because of migration; and it can create economic stress, especially if large numbers of people opt for early retirement and withdraw social security or pension funds sooner and faster than projected. In this situation, alternative strategies must be developed to maintain the financial solvency of pension and social security systems (such as higher taxation of those in the labor force, reduced benefits to retirees, and incentives to retain older workers on staff).

In short, the constant interplay between individual and population aging is illustrated by the process of retirement. For example, the phenomenon can be viewed as a process of either abandonment or liberation of the elderly (Baum and Baum, 1980:102-45). This view var-

ies within and across societies depending on the personal situation of the elderly individual, and on societal policies and institutionalized norms pertaining to retirement. As a result, the meaning and experience of retirement may vary within and between cohorts. Just as the retirement situation experienced by your parents may differ from that of your grandparents, so too may your situation differ from that reported in current literature.

Similarly, as with other aging phenomena, it must be remembered that the elderly at any point in history make up a heterogeneous cohort influenced by history and personal characteristics. The following section examines the relationship between retirement and work patterns and attitudes in the middle years. Later, the process of retirement and the relationship between retirement and the financial resources of the individual and the society are considered. Throughout, special attention is directed to the recent and emerging literature concerning women in the work force, women and retirement, and the disadvantaged economic status of older women.

WORK PATTERNS AND ATTITUDES TOWARD RETIREMENT IN THE PRERETIREMENT YEARS

Introduction

Most individuals exhibit continuity in attitudes, behaviors, values, and interests across the life cycle. Therefore, it is important to understand the meaning of work to an individual, the preretirement work history, and the attitudes toward retirement while working in order to explain why and how particular retirement decisions and adjustments are made.[4] It is also necessary to examine the many myths concerning the assumed decrease in the competence of older workers. If these stereotypes persist, they may result in forced or voluntary early retirement for some workers. Finally, variations by gender in career paths and opportunities must be understood in order to comprehend the retirement decisions and adjustments of women.

Work Patterns during Adulthood

To date, most research on the middle-aged and older worker has focused on white middle-class males, although increasing attention has been directed to the career patterns of women and to members of minority groups. This inherent male bias has been based on the demographic fact that until the last few decades, few women were permanent full-time workers, and on the false assumption that retirement was a 'male' phenomenon and a 'male' problem. However, both men and women participate continuously throughout the adult years in the labor force, and both are involved in the retirement process.

For most adults, work is a central focus in life, although it may not be the only or major life interest. Work is of primary concern because it influences place and type of residence, income, social status, lifestyle, and friendships. Most adults generally hold jobs that are related to their education and early occupational socialization. That is, they follow a career line that involves a sequence of jobs within a particular field of work (education, civil engineering, the automotive industry, real estate, etc.), or a sequence of jobs with similar skill requirements that involve different occupational fields (selling autos, homes, computers, or sporting goods).

Throughout the early and middle years of adulthood, individuals generally have a stable work pattern. A worker is employed continuously after leaving school by one or more organizations, accumulates pension benefits, and may or may not develop feelings of loyalty and commitment to the job or the organization. For example, those with a continuous work history derive a sense of security from their work, gain an identity and a social network of colleagues and enjoy the benefits of a stable position at work and in the community.

Work also has the potential to influence life satisfaction or dissatisfaction, although this varies by the type of job (Hanlon, 1986). For example, those in high-prestige positions, those in decision-making positions, and those in the professions generally report high levels of intrinsic job satisfaction. In contrast, blue-collar workers are more likely to report lower levels of job satisfaction, greater alienation from work

and the organization, and less commitment to the job. Part of this dissatisfaction and lack of commitment results from low income, the repetitive and unchallenging nature of the job, impersonal employee-employer relations, and an earlier attainment of the highest position (the career peak) they can achieve in their career. Also, those in the lower occupational levels tend to be more concerned throughout their work careers about job security, income, and friendships with colleagues than with the meaning and satisfaction derived from the job per se. Regardless of work orientation, both blue-collar and white-collar workers who have had a continuous and stable work history generally face retirement with a positive attitude. Those most likely to express reservations are those concerned about economic security rather than about loss of identity or friendship networks, and those for whom work has been the major or only real interest in life.

In contrast, different orientations toward work are held by those who have had an unstable or interrupted work history. This pattern is characterized by cyclical periods of full-time employment, unemployment, part-time employment, or underemployment. As a result, commitment to a job or organization is seldom developed, a lifetime of job uncertainty and economic insecurity prevails, and work is only salient as a means of survival. Hence, there is little subjective attachment to work at any stage of adulthood. As a result, retirement for these individuals may be viewed either as 'more of the same' or as a form of relief. In retirement they will at least be assured of a minimal income, depending on the credits they accumulated whenever they were employed, and on government social security policies for retired persons. However, some individuals with an irregular work history will arrive at retirement with few accumulated benefits, often because pensions are not 'portable' from one job or field to another. They may also lack the equity provided by savings and home ownership.

A third, but atypical, pattern is the truncated career. This is a pattern found among professional athletes and dancers who are forced to retire in their late 20s or early 30s because of declining physical skills (McPherson, 1980; McPherson et al., 1989); by those whose employment depends on public acceptance and demand (singers, rock musicians, comedians, or actors); and by fashion models whose physical attractiveness is the primary prerequisite for employment. In all of these occupations the career can end suddenly, either voluntarily or involuntarily. Many of these individuals find themselves 'retired' in the prime of life. Unfortunately, many often lack formal education or the skills necessary to make a successful transition to a more stable or traditional career. Moreover, some are so ego-identified with their former 'public' life that they are unable to accept living a 'private' life where they are not idolized. They often show a pattern of unstable employment with many job changes in a number of fields. While most eventually settle in one job, the intervening period can be traumatic; there may be a high incidence of depression, alcoholism, divorce, and suicide.

Previous work patterns and orientation to work can thus influence when an individual retires, how the individual adjusts, and whether he or she returns to work on a full-time or part-time basis. Although most older workers are not alienated from their work, the meaning of work and orientation to work can change with age. For example, there may be a decline in intrinsic work satisfaction during the later stages of labor-force participation. As a result, individuals may accept mandatory retirement because they have lost interest in the job, or because it no longer represents a major life interest. While this loss of interest and meaning occurs earlier and more frequently for blue-collar workers, regardless of whether they have a stable or an unstable career, dissatisfaction has recently become more evident among white-collar workers in the professions and in the corporate sector. The problem is often resolved by a midlife career change (rather than by a job change within a similar occupational field), or by early retirement.

In order to counteract this 'burnout' or 'plateauing,' which appears to be a social psychological rather than a biological phenomenon, organizations have introduced 'flextime', 'sabbatical,' or 'reduced-load' policies to provide alternative work patterns. Flextime can take many forms and generally represents an attempt to meet the lifestyle needs of employ-

ees, as well as the business and production demands of the employer. Employees may begin and end each workday at their own selected hour within a set range (for example, they may begin work at any time between 7:00 and 9:00 a.m. and, having worked the required number of hours, leave work at any time between 4:00 and 6:00 p.m.); or they may work their own hours to a daily or weekly required maximum (a four-day week is possible under this option). Moreover, it is often possible within this system to accumulate extra credit hours to provide time off in addition to regular vacation periods. This option is particularly appealing to mothers with young children in that it facilitates, somewhat, the management of work, day care, and home responsibilities.

The sabbatical option permits individuals to obtain fully or partially paid leave for professional or personal development; the reduced-load policy enables an older individual to opt for a three-quarter or half-time appointment at a proportionately reduced salary. Both of these plans permit people to pursue alternative leisure or career interests. One major attraction of the reduced-load approach is that individuals usually receive full pension benefits when they retire, despite not working full-time for a few years prior to normal retirement age. From the perspective of the organization, the reduced-load policy permits new employees to be hired, especially in an inflationary period characterized by high unemployment.

The reduced-load policy is currently being adopted by a number of universities. Senior faculty can reduce their load and pursue other interests; the university saves money because of the reduced salaries, and may use the savings to hire young Ph.D.'s with new skills and ideas. In short, work patterns and the meaning of work to the individual throughout adulthood, along with the availability of alternative work patterns in the later years, can have a significant bearing on the process of retirement.

Atypical Work Patterns: Midlife Career Changes

Some occupations encourage or require a midlife career change. For example, commercial pilots may be grounded if they fail to pass a rigid medical exam, or they may be forced out by an early compulsory retirement age. Similarly, the armed forces often encourage personnel to 'opt out' after about twenty years of service by providing a large pension immediately upon retirement, regardless of age. In this way, the salary component of the budget is reduced and opportunities are created for the promotion of younger personnel. For individuals leaving the armed forces, the adjustment to another career is usually orderly and satisfactory, since they often enter an occupation where their existing skills are utilized to a great extent. For many, this transition is more a job or organization change than a career change where unique retraining is required.

There are, however, a number of individuals who opt for a career change rather than a job change during middle age. Although it is not known how many make this transition, it has primarily been a male phenomenon to date,[5] and has occurred mainly among those in the middle or upper class who are financially independent and well educated. These individuals may be either married or single, although a large number tend to be divorced or never-married and without dependents. Many of these changes involve a shift from a profession (lawyer, engineer, or professor) or business position (executive or accountant) to a more independent, less structured occupation such as that of author or craftsman, or to self-employment in a business. In some situations, people may pass through the intervening stage of being career 'dropouts' where they are voluntarily unemployed and make no attempt to reenter the labor force. During this period they exist on savings, investments, or consultation fees as they search for a higher quality of life or new challenges.

For most, the exit from the labor force appears to be carefully planned and often results from a basic dissatisfaction with the work or living environment. In short, most people are motivated by a desire for a change in lifestyle, not by a search for increased income. In fact, many move to careers with less prestige and income, but which have greater personal freedom and intrinsic satisfaction.

Although some career changes are preceded by a dropout stage, many are planned so that the individual moves directly or indirectly (after returning to school for formal training) into the new career path. Again, most of these career changes are motivated by social and psychological factors rather than economic factors, and are voluntary rather than forced transitions.[6] Forced transitions result from direct factors such as declining health, which inhibits or prevents performance on the job, or from being laid off or fired. For those who are well educated and have some degree of financial stability, these circumstances may influence the individual to consider following a more enjoyable or secure career path. However, many individuals who are laid off or fired have low-level job skills and little education or training, and a career change may be impossible because of these limitations.

In addition to the direct stimuli noted above, there may be a number of 'push' and 'pull' incentives that operate at the personal and structural levels. Some of the internal push factors include an inability to resolve a conflict between the values, goals, and policies of the employer and those of the individual. Or, boredom and loss of motivation may result if the position or task is no longer challenging (Stagner, 1985; Karp, 1987). Push factors external to the individual may result from family pressures to improve or save a marriage, or from an illness or disability in the family. External push factors at the structural or organizational level may involve a company move to another community, being continually denied a promotion, or becoming obsolete because of technological developments (such as the introduction of computers or robotics).

Among the internal pull factors are financial independence, lack of dependents, or having a potentially lucrative or intellectually challenging outside interest that requires a full-time commitment (for example, art or writing). Some of the structural pull factors include the availability of new occupations that are more relevant and challenging and the presence of former work associates who have successfully changed careers and who serve as role models.

In summary, an increasing number of middle- and upper-class individuals are voluntarily changing careers in midlife in order to attain a higher quality of life, new challenges, or greater meaning in their work. If these goals are attained, increased job and life satisfaction may influence the retirement decision. That is, the individual may choose to continue working in the 'new' career, opt for early retirement, retire and start a third career, or elect to remain 'unretired' by volunteering his or her expertise to voluntary or corporate organizations. Unfortunately, valid information is not yet available about 'career changers' as they approach or enter the normal retirement years. It may be that the midlife career change provides some experiences and develops some strengths that carry over into the retirement phase of the life cycle. With rapidly changing labor-force needs, two or three careers may become more common for future generations.

Female Work Patterns

The labor-force participation rate of women has risen dramatically in the last few decades; approximately 53 percent of Canadian women worked outside the home in 1988 compared to 41 percent in 1975 (Parliament, 1989). Much of this increase was in part-time work, and most women (73 percent) were employed in traditional female occupations (such as clerical, sales or service positions, teaching, nursing). There are also regional variations in the labor-force participation rates of women (from a high of 59 percent in Alberta to a low of 37 percent in Newfoundland). However, after 65 years of age the proportion of elderly women in the labor force declines to about 7 percent in Canada; for men the figure is 18 percent (Seniors Secretariat, 1988).

Although an increase in labor-force participation by women was one of the significant social changes that followed World War II, the study of female occupational patterns and problems was a neglected area of research until the onset of the women's movement in the 1970s. When women were studied, the focus was usually on their reaction to the retirement of the spouse, rather than on their role as workers. A stereotypical view was held that a major role for women was that of homemaker, and that work was mainly an instrumental (to earn

money) rather than an expressive (to give meaning to life) role.

In recent years, however, increasing research attention has been directed to issues pertaining to labor-force participation and withdrawal by women. Researchers have looked at such topics as rates and patterns of participation; personal and structural factors influencing participation rates; attitudes toward work; the meaning of work; gender-based inequalities or discrimination in salary, mobility, and access to specific occupations; attitudes and adjustment to retirement; the relationship between work history and economic status in the later years; and the need for an adequate pension system for women, regardless of their history of labor-force participation.[7]

This research suggests that there are few, if any, significant gender differences in the importance of work to the individual, and that work is a serious, meaningful, expressive, and satisfying role for women. In short, work has become a central life interest for many women; for them, as for men, it is a source of personal satisfaction, prestige, identity, and power. For some older women the work role may be more salient than it is for older men, especially if the women entered the labor force late in life, or only recently approached or attained their 'career peak' (Gee and Kimball, 1987; 70-73; McNeely, 1988). Because of structural constraints and subtle practices of age, gender, and wage discrimination, many employed middle-aged and older women are located in marginal occupations, most of which are located in the secondary labor market consisting of the service sector rather than manufacturing and the professions (McDonald and Wanner, 1982, 1987, 1990). This marginality occurs because there is a unique occupational age structure for the female labor force (Chen, 1987); because women with child or parent care responsibilities drop in and out of the labor force at different times in the life course (Gee and Kimball, 1987:69-78); because of double jeopardy (ageism and sexism), which segregates women in female 'job ghettos' where they are underpaid and underpromoted (Nishio and Lank, 1987); and because of the propensity by some women to select and accept careerlike unpaid volunteer positions (Gee and Kimball, 1987:73). However, many women are forced into part-time work, and many cannot work who would like to, or need to (Nishio and Lank, 1987).

Labor-force participation rates among women vary considerably from country to country. Semyonov (1980), in a comparative study of sixty-one countries, found that the percentage of women in the labor force varied from 11 percent in Syria to 46 percent in Poland and Finland. He explained this cross-cultural variation by noting that the rate at which females participate in the labor force is positively related to the level of economic development. That is, with industrialization and increased technological development, there is an increase in the number of service and white-collar occupations. This increases the demand for female laborers. The supply may not, at least initially, match the demand if fertility rates are high and family commitments take precedence over labor commitments. However, with increasing industrialization, fertility rates decline and more women are available for, and seek, labor-force involvement.

Although the onset of industrialization and a decrease in fertility rates are important factors in women's labor-force participation, the most important structural or social factor is the shape of the stratification system. Where gender and income inequality are low, women are less likely to experience occupational discrimination and to be blocked from entering the labor force. Gender inequality is more likely to be prevalent in high-status occupations (for example, engineering, dentistry, medicine, senior management, law). When women compete for these positions they may experience discrimination. Moreover, even where women are actively recruited to the labor force, they may be segregated in low-status, poorly paid occupations that offer little chance for upward mobility. For example, the 1987 average income for all full-time employed women was $21,000, compared to $31,900 for full-time men. This difference persisted at all income levels, and even at the highest level (those with a university degree), women earned 70 percent of the income reported by comparably educated males. Even more striking is the income differential by marital status for full-time employed women. Compared to men with a similar mari-

tal status, married women earned 62 percent as much as men; divorced, widowed, or separated women earned 69 percent; and never-married women earned 90 percent as much as men (Parliament, 1989).

At the personal level of analysis, a number of factors influence the frequency and pattern of labor-force participation by women in the middle and later years of life. First, marital status has a significant effect. Women who are single, separated, divorced, or widowed are most likely to work. However, married women at all ages are increasingly entering the labor force to satisfy social and psychological needs, as well as economic needs. Health status and age of children also play an important role for those women who choose whether or not to participate in the labor force,[8] as do such factors as education, socioeconomic status, and religion. For those who do become involved, it appears that the quality of the job is more important than any personal or demographic background variables in developing and maintaining a high degree of positive work orientation and commitment.

With the growing participation of women in the labor force, a number of new work patterns have evolved. Fischer et al. (1979) labeled these patterns as follows: (1) 'nonentry,' where a woman is never employed regularly (full-time) after leaving school; (2) 'delayed,' where entry into the labor force occurs relatively late in life (at the empty-nest stage); (3) 'truncated,' where a career is interrupted (by a late marriage or childbirth) and not resumed; (4) 'interrupted,' where a woman temporarily leaves the work force (perhaps to raise a child or care for a parent or spouse) and then returns to resume the career path; and (5) 'full employment,' or the 'dual career,' where a woman works full-time for her entire working life, and may or may not play the role of spouse concurrently. In the full-employment pattern neither the domestic role nor the work role predominates; both are equally important.

In summary, regardless of the pattern, it is clear that an increasing percentage of women want to work, that over 50 percent of women do work, that work is no less meaningful for women than it is for men, and that a variety of work patterns have evolved to enable women to participate in the labor force to a greater extent. Moreover, they have been assisted in achieving this goal by legislation that prohibits income and occupational discrimination, by social services (such as community or company-sponsored day care centers) that facilitate participation, and by an increasing recognition that women can acquire and use occupational skills previously assumed to be the exclusive domain of men (for example, as engineers, business executives, pilots, or law-enforcement officers).

The Aging Worker

Contrary to prevailing myths and stereotypes about the deficiencies of the older worker, research indicates that general job performance rarely declines in later life, and that there are individual differences in work-related skills among the elderly, just as there are among younger workers.[9] These negative myths about incompetence and declining productivity appear more frequently during periods of high unemployment when there is intense competition for fewer jobs, and during periods of slow economic growth when personnel managers are pressured to reduce the size of the payroll by eliminating jobs or highly paid workers. Similarly, the myths appear during discussion about the elimination of mandatory retirement. Some employers and political advocates of mandatory retirement argue, without valid evidence, that the older worker does not have the productivity, strength, stamina, and competence of the younger or middle-aged employee. Nor, it is argued, are older employees retrainable. Ironically, these judgements are often made by executives who are older than the employees who are being discussed (Stagner, 1985:789).

Unfortunately, most of the evidence comparing the work performance of younger and older workers is based on cross-sectional rather than longitudinal studies. That is, variation in specific and general aptitudes within and between cohorts is usually overlooked, and job experience is seldom considered as a factor in performance. Moreover, the creation and perpetuation of stereotypes are often based on subjective measures of performance, capacity, or

potential, rather than on valid and reliable objective measures of productivity or performance. The stereotypes may also be a function of the age of the evaluator: younger evaluators may assess older workers less favorably ('they are less productive or creative than my age peers'), while older evaluators may evaluate them more favorably ('older people like myself are loyal, efficient, and experienced workers'). Where ageism and negative stereotypes exist, the older worker is devalued and may experience discrimination in opportunities for employment or promotion, or simply in retaining an existing job (McDaniel, 1986:58). These views may also result in the internalization of a negative self-image, which in turn can lead to a loss of interest and motivation, to learned helplessness on the job, or to an early retirement to escape an unpleasant work environment.

Recognizing that there are individual differences within and between age cohorts in experience and education, and that individual variations may be related to the nature of the job or to familiarity with the test situation, research (Robinson et al., 1985; Kausler, 1990; Spirduso and MacRae, 1990) pertaining to the older worker generally refutes prevailing myths by indicating that:

1. There is relatively little decline in productivity that is related to chronological age. There are wide differences in productivity within all age groups, and therefore chronological age is not a useful or accurate predictor of job performance.
2. There is some loss of muscular strength and endurance.
3. Reaction time slows with age (see chapter 6), but experience at the task may offset the losses.
4. There is little decline in intelligence affecting job performance (see chapter 6).
5. Older workers are generally more satisfied with their jobs (Janson and Martin, 1982) and are less likely to leave an organization for another job (perhaps because they have few alternatives).
6. Decremental changes in job-related aptitudes or skills do not occur at the

same rate (for example, a hearing loss may not be accompanied by a slower reaction time or by a loss of visual acuity), and those that do occur may be compensated for by experience.

7. Declining cognitive or physical skills can be overcome by a willingness to resort to coping strategies (such as a reliance on coworkers for assistance, taking work home).

8. Older workers are absent less often and have fewer accidents than younger workers.

9. Older workers score as well as, or better than, younger workers on creativity, flexibility, information processing, absenteeism, accident rates, and turnover.

10. Older workers can learn and be retrained for many jobs, including those requiring the use of computerized equipment.

In short, stereotypes or myths about the older worker are not supported by research evidence.

For those individuals who experience personal losses that begin to affect job performance, alternative work patterns or job redesign may provide a solution. For example, workers can be moved laterally to a new job that falls within their range of abilities (a job that is less physically demanding, that requires fewer reaction-type tasks, or that requires less travel); or the existing job can be redesigned to meet the worker's capabilities (more concrete stimuli are provided, telephone contacts with clients are encouraged rather than personal visits, self-paced instructions are provided).

A number of alternative general work patterns are also available to meet the interests and abilities of older workers (for example, flextime, job sharing, or longer vacations leading to a phased-in retirement). Thus, by redesigning the job or providing alternative work patterns, the worker may retain a high level of motivation and satisfaction, and the organization will retain a loyal and experienced employee. Rather than perpetuating stereotypes about the older worker, employees and coworkers must recognize that there are considerable individual differences in the rate and type of age-related losses, and must decide whether, and how, a specific job or work pattern can be altered to compensate for these changes.

Although there has been widespread concern about the productivity of older workers, two related patterns of employment among workers have raised new questions in recent years. First, with declining fertility and immigration rates, the labor pool of possible employees is shrinking, especially among the younger age cohorts. Second, the labor-force participation rates of older male workers has been declining in recent decades, while rates for women have been increasing (McDonald and Wanner, 1990:40-41).

McDonald and Wanner (1987, 1990) attribute the decrease among males to a combination of two factors. First, the 'industrialization thesis' argues that there are fewer opportunities for self-employment, primarily in farming occupations, and a greater dependence on employers to determine when employment ceases. At the same time, the 'social benefits thesis' argues that more men are retiring early or on time because more are eligible for public and private pension benefits. As well, retirement is more affordable in recent years because of greater female involvement and, hence, the availability of two incomes and perhaps two pensions.

One implication of this trend toward earlier retirement is that if mandatory retirement is abolished, there may not be the heretofore assumed large retention of older workers beyond the age of 65, at least in the immediate period (Méthot, 1987). Indeed, given a shrinking labor force and a healthy economy, incentives to encourage the older worker to remain in the labor force may have to be initiated. One such alternative is the sharing of a job by a number of employees who each work a set number of hours, thereby enjoying the dual advantage of both work and retirement (Stryckman, 1987). However, a different type of labor may be needed and some of the older workers may need to be retrained for new positions.

Preretirement Attitudes toward Retirement

Attitudes toward retirement can be assessed at three general stages: at some point prior to retirement, on the day of retirement, and at some point after retirement. Attitudes expressed during the first two stages represent perceived views that are often based on anticipatory socialization. Attitudes expressed in the postretirement stage are based on actual experiences. Unfortunately, some studies of attitudes toward retirement fail to identify whether the attitudes were recorded during the pre- or postretirement stage, or how long before or after the actual event they were assessed. Furthermore, it is often not clear whether respondents were asked about their specific attitudes toward retirement as it applied to them (are you looking forward to retirement?), or whether they were asked about their attitudes toward retirement in general (is retirement a valued stage in life?). Finally, most studies in this area are based on samples of white, urban males, and little information is available about the pre- or postretirement attitudes of women, rural residents, or members of minority groups who have been in and out of the labor force for many years.

Most studies have found that as many as 75 to 80 percent of the respondents report favorable attitudes toward retirement prior to the event; but the degree to which attitudes are positive is related to a number of factors. Generally, positive attitudes toward retirement during the preretirement stage are associated with high levels of health, income, and education, and with a high degree of support from significant others in the family and at work concerning the approaching event (Robinson et al., 1985). Indeed, compared to such other life events as marriage, birth of a child, or death of a child or spouse, retirement is not a crisis event for most (Martin Matthews et al., 1982; Schnore, 1985; Martin Matthews and Brown, 1987). Also, the younger the age at which the respondent is queried, the more favorable the attitude. This may occur because the event is further away, because retirement and early retirement are becoming more socially acceptable, or because pension plans may be perceived as more satisfactory than those available to previous retirees.

In contrast, negative attitudes are related to a fear of financial difficulties in retirement, and a high commitment to or satisfaction with work,

such that work is the major or only life interest. To these few individuals, retirement is perceived to be a traumatic event that is to be avoided. Finally, the research to date suggests that there is not a consistent relationship, either positive or negative, between work satisfaction and attitudes toward retirement. In summary, most individuals appear to have favorable attitudes toward retirement during the preretirement years.

THE PROCESS OF RETIREMENT

Introduction

Retirement, as both a legal right and a social act, is prevalent in most modernized nations. The process of retirement involves a partial or total withdrawal from the labor force sometime between about 55 and 70 years of age. In many countries the mandatory retirement age is 65 or 70 years of age, with only the self-employed or a small percentage of those in organizations being able to continue working beyond that age. In return for this mandatory withdrawal, individuals receive social security benefits and other services designed to provide direct or indirect medical, social, or economic assistance in the later years.

This decline in labor-force participation in later life is influenced by labor market policies (layoffs or firings), by discrimination against older workers (transfer to other jobs or cities late in life, unwillingness to hire older workers), by physical disabilities that prevent working, by insufficient incentives to continue working, by economic or other incentives to retire early, and by the increasing number of workers who perceive that it is socially acceptable not to work and to seek an alternative lifestyle in the later years.

One outcome of retirement, combined with the demographic patterns of increased longevity and decreased immigration and fertility, may be an increase in the proportion of dependent elderly people. When the aged dependency ratio increases, a greater economic burden is placed on a smaller labor force. The economic ramifications of retirement, from an individual and societal view, are discussed later in this chapter. The remainder of this section examines the process of retirement by considering conceptual perspectives, preretirement preparation, the decision with respect to voluntary (early or late) and mandatory retirement, adjustment to retirement, retirement by women, and working beyond or in lieu of retirement. In the next chapter, the relationship between leisure and work and retirement is examined.

The Process of Retirement: Conceptual Perspectives

Introduction

One of the major topics of interest among gerontologists has been the assumed problems associated with adjusting to mandatory retirement. This social event has been viewed as a major transition stage (primarily for adult men) with the potential to precipitate adjustment problems for the retiree. It is not surprising, therefore, that much of the early work in social gerontology (using the three major theoretical frameworks) sought to explain how men adjusted to retirement.

Disengagement theory argued that society expected individuals to give up the work role, and that they did so voluntarily and with relief. According to this theory, no attempt is made to compensate for the role loss, and the overall level of activity decreases as the individual disengages. Activity theory, in contrast, suggested that the work role is replaced with other roles so that the postretirement level of activity remains at about the same level as during the preretirement stage. Finally, continuity theory argued that although the work role is lost, the individual compensates by increasing his or her involvement in existing roles. Thus, the overall level of activity may remain about the same, may decrease slightly, or may increase depending on the postretirement level of involvement in preretirement nonwork roles.

Since the early 1970s, a number of conceptual models or frameworks have been proposed to explain the retirement process. As yet, however, a definitive theory accounting for all or part of the process has yet to be supported.

The following discussion represents a brief review of some of the proposed conceptual frameworks that have appeared in the literature. They are presented to illustrate the range of approaches to understanding this complex process, which most adults in the labor force ultimately experience. While many of the earlier models were problem- or adjustment-oriented and focused on the individual and social psychological variables, more recent models have focused on macro or societal elements of the process and have considered structural as well as social psychological variables (McDonald and Wanner, 1990:8-15).

An Analytical Model of Retirement

On the basis of the premise that retirement is not a negative, crisis-generating event, Sussman (1972) argued that retirement represents a social psychological process that is experienced in relation to societal, biological, and environmental factors. These factors limit the options available to the individual. According to this model, societal and social psychological constraints influence the options available to an individual prior to, at, and following the act of retirement. More specifically, structural variables (such as class, retirement income policies, or preretirement preparation) and individual variables (such as lifestyles, value orientations, health, income, or competence) in the preretirement years influence the perception of retirement.

This perception is also colored by prevailing societal constraints (for example, norms concerning retirement as an event, the health of the economy, private and public retirement policies, and the presence or absence of intergenerational conflict). The retiree's perceptions and the degree of support or opposition from family, friends, and colleagues all interact to influence the retiree's decision about how the retirement years will be spent. Will these years include another career, leisure pursuits, or volunteer work? The goal of this selection process is to develop competence in choosing options suited to the needs of the individual and to the specific social, biological, and environmental situation in which the individual is located.

Retirement: An Exchange Perspective

According to this perspective, retirement involves a loss of power by the employee who can no longer exchange skills and knowledge for high wages. Rather, these resources are exchanged for financial support in the form of pensions. Over time, the social and political power of retirees and future retirees has increased, thereby leading to an increased value of a pension and less rigid regulations about when an individual must retire.

Retirement: A Systems Perspective

Kimmel et al. (1978) suggested that the retirement decision involves interaction between variables representing three levels of analysis. These include the individual (occupation, health, finances, attitudes), the institutional (employer policies and benefits, employer-sponsored preparation programs), and the sociocultural-environmental (demographic factors, cultural values, government policies and benefits) levels. The retirement decision, in turn, has a subsequent impact on the individual (for example, on satisfaction, attitudes, or income), on the institution from which the person retired (for example, the loss of an experienced worker), and on the sociocultural environment (another 'dependent' person is created, and a consumer is lost). Thus, a feedback loop develops within the social system; factors influencing the retirement decision of a given individual may be altered or reinforced as a result of earlier events and the experiences of already-retired workers. In short, this approach recognizes the interaction between individual and structural variables.

After a five-day seminar in 1977, eleven scholars generated a conceptual model of retirement research, a list of variables affecting the decision to retire, and a list of research questions concerning the process of retirement (Atchley, 1979). The following interrelated factors were thought to be important in retirement research: employer and government retirement policies; labor market conditions; personal characteristics of the retiree; personal and structural factors influencing retirement decisions; physical, social, and psychological effects of retirement on individuals and married couples; and economic and labor-force effects of retirement on work organizations, the community, and other institutions in society.

The researchers proposed a model that included the following variables: social system pressures to retire; personal desire to retire; perceived need to continue working; availability of information about retirement; personality, attitudes, and beliefs of the retiree; economic and psychological rewards of employment; physical and mental demands of the job versus perceived capacities; and financial need versus financial resources.

Atchley (1982) also viewed retirement as a social institution that provides for an orderly and economically supported movement of workers out of the labor force. To achieve this goal, three interrelated elements work at the individual, organizational, and societal levels to coordinate the needs of individuals and groups in the public and private sectors. In this systems approach, there must be a range of retirement policies or rules to require or encourage retirement; a set of criteria to determine which policies will be developed or invoked depending on shifts in demographic, economic, political, and social thought or action; and a recognition of constraints (political, economic, legislative) that may limit the alternatives available at a given point in time.

A Dual Economy Model of Retirement

In response to 'the over-individualized perspective on retirement research' (McDonald and Wanner, 1990:8-12), and the increasing application of the political economy of aging perspective (Dowd, 1980; Walker, 1981; Guillemard, 1983; Myles, 1989), critics have argued that a social structural model is needed to more completely understand the phenomenon of retirement in the modern welfare state (Calasanti, 1981, 1988; Hendricks and McAllister, 1983; McDonald and Wanner, 1987, 1990). The use of this perspective is particularly important when historical changes in the process are to be studied, since changes in the socioeconomic structure can influence individual behavior. Moreover, citizens and policymakers must recognize that any perceived 'problem' with being retired may not be eliminated simply by 'helping' the retiree. Rather, underlying legislative, policy, or program changes may be needed (McDonald and Wanner, 1990:127-31). For example, those who adhere to a political economy perspective argue that retirement is an age-restrictive policy that is used by the state to exclude older workers from the labor force and that this policy of exclusion is legitimated through a socially constructed and accepted mechanism called retirement (Dowd, 1980; Walker, 1983).

The dual-economy model is based on the assumption that historical changes in the nature of the capitalist economy have occurred. Basically, the structure of the economy moved from local, small-business capitalism (for example, a family-owned farm, motel, or grocery store) to a large, monopolistic, corporate capitalism (for example, a large multinational food or hotel chain) that sought national and international markets. This led to employment being based in either core (large national) or peripheral (small local) firms; that is, the dual-economy structure (McDonald and Wanner, 1987). Thus, the work histories of individuals, which are important factors in the process of retirement, are determined by their employment in either core or peripheral organizations. The place in the work structure, in turn, influences how micro-level variables (education, occupation, marital status, income, and health) will have an impact on a given individual. For example, those with higher educational attainment are more likely to be found in core organizations, and therefore may have higher wages, private pensions, more fringe benefits, and more options concerning when and how to retire. In short, the impact of individual factors on the retiring individual is influenced by the structure of the economic system in which he or she has been employed. Therefore, the process of retirement may differ for retirees depending on whether they were employed in core or peripheral work organizations throughout their career. In fact, it is assumed that there is little if any movement between the two levels.

In summary, the dual-economy approach suggests that retirement is a dynamic process involving interaction between individual and societal factors. Therefore, further efforts to explain the theoretical process of retirement must consider both levels of analysis, and particularly the interaction between the two levels.

The dual-economy model is proposed as one approach to a more complete analysis of adaptation to retirement at the individual and social structural levels. However, McDonald and Wanner (1990:14) caution that, while this perspective holds considerable promise, it must be used in conjunction with individual-level perspectives. Otherwise, we run the risk of invoking an overreliance on structural explanations, thereby 'portraying the retired person as a mere victim of social forces.'

Preparation for Retirement

Preretirement preparation represents a form of anticipatory socialization: the individual acquires knowledge about the postretirement stage and makes some tentative plans for this new phase in life (Evans et al., 1985). Planning should facilitate a smooth transition and reduce the stress created by the economic, social, and psychological uncertainty often associated with retirement. Although many people agree that planning is important, very few make concrete plans on their own or participate in formal programs (Beck, 1984; Ferraro, 1990), although some may consult self-help books (The Canadian Bankers' Association, 1987; Wigdor, 1987).

Most retirement preparation involves some type of financial planning to ensure economic security in the later years. Yet even this is difficult, because it must begin early in life even though the individual is unable to predict such factors as: his or her work pattern and income levels; when the individual or spouse will die; what the retirement needs or lifestyle will be; the state of health; the date of retirement; the state of the economy at the time of retirement; and the availability and impact of changes in retirement policies and benefits. This does not imply that retirement planning is useless, only that it is extremely difficult to accurately account for the many possible situations that any one person might experience in the future.

In order to assist people in preparing for and adjusting to retirement, many formal preretirement programs have been initiated by employers, by individuals, or by private entrepreneurs (Ekerdt, 1990). These programs have ranged from a brief conversation about retirement benefits between the retiree and the personnel officer during the last week of work to comprehensive programs that begin a number of months or years prior to the retirement date. The more comprehensive programs involve testing and discussion about finances, health, leisure, travel, housing, legal matters, the marital relationship, postretirement employment options, and availability of community resources. Some corporations also allow employees nearing retirement to take a three-month trial period to determine whether they would like to take early retirement. If not, they return to their former position.

Programs that are largely concerned with disseminating facts and information are usually offered to a large group through lectures or printed material. Those programs that focus on providing assistance in personal adjustment are offered in small discussion groups or in individual counseling sessions. In general, these formal programs are more readily available to white-collar men (who are usually well prepared financially for retirement), are voluntary, do not involve the spouse, and do not involve continuing contact with the individual after retirement.

Some programs involve alterations to the preretirement work pattern. Employees approaching retirement are permitted to taper off their work commitments by taking longer vacations or by working shorter days or weeks. In this way, the individual experiences increasing amounts of nonwork time in a progressive sequence leading up to retirement, and thereby learns how to cope with suddenly available free time. To date, however, these transitional programs have usually only been available to upper-management white-collar or professional workers. Those who would seem to benefit most, low-status and low-income workers, and most women (George et al., 1984), are least likely to have access to these programs.

Although it has been demonstrated that preretirement planning through informal or formal programs is an important factor in the initial adjustment to retirement, many employers have been reluctant to become involved in providing this type of service to their employ-

ees. However, in response to increasing demands from unions and employees for enhanced benefits, a growing number of employers are offering preretirement programs. These employers are becoming involved in order to enhance the corporate image as a socially responsible organization, and to improve employee relations. There has also been a large growth in recent years in the offering of preretirement planning advice, programs, and information by consultants. Some of these programs involve the sale of some type of investment plan; others offer seminars for a large fee. Whether these programs or information have any scientific validity or not remains to be tested, especially since they tend to ignore individual differences in health and economic status, and in past lifestyle, and the programs are seldom evaluated for effectiveness.

In summary, since few individuals engage in preretirement planning on their own, organized programs are a necessary mechanism for facilitating adjustment to the early stages of retirement. These programs should offer both information and discussion, should include the spouse, and should consider individual differences in health and income status and in preretirement lifestyle, especially in the leisure domain. [10] A single recipe to be used by everyone in the preretirement years will not guarantee postretirement adjustment or satisfaction. Moreover, the formal programs should be made available to all workers, not just to those in high-status and high-income positions. In addition, since few people voluntarily prepare for retirement, a minimal compulsory program should be initiated to provide essential information concerning finances, housing, legal and health matters, and the use of free time. Finally, the following principles may be useful in preparing for and adjusting to retirement: plan early, maintain flexibility in interests and social roles, remain physically and socially active, plan for a gradual transition from work to retirement, provide for a 'trial run' before a final commitment is made to a new residence or lifestyle, and consult with spouse, friends, and children about short- and long-term retirement plans.

The Retirement Decision

Voluntary versus Involuntary Retirement

The retirement decision is an essential intervening stage between the planning and adjustment phases of the retirement process. Historically, mandatory retirement has been the norm, and for many the only option; today, flexible, voluntary retirement policies and options are becoming increasingly available to workers who wish to consider early retirement. Where the decision is voluntary rather than imposed, the individual feels that he or she has more control over the decision. As a result, the voluntary retiree, compared to the involuntary retiree, often engages in more planning for retirement; has a higher retirement income; reports better health; perceives a higher level of adjustment to and satisfaction with retirement; and in general has more favorable attitudes toward retirement.

Until 1979, the mandatory retirement age in North America for most workers was 65. However, people such as airline pilots, professional athletes, and dancers were exceptions; they could be forced to retire at any age if medical or physical limitations affected job performance. In addition, the self-employed worker was not subject to mandatory retirement legislation. Apart from these specialized categories of workers, most of the labor force was required to retire at age 65.

As of January 1, 1979, the Age Discrimination in Employment Act in the United States raised the age limit for most occupations to 70 years. Although this type of legislation has yet to be passed in Canada at the federal level, some provinces have eliminated mandatory retirement by invoking human-rights legislation that prohibits age discrimination (Alberta, Manitoba, New Brunswick, and Quebec as of 1990). In those provinces where such legislation has not been enacted, cases are being presented to the federal courts in which mandatory retirement at age 65 is being challenged as a form of age discrimination that violates provisions included in the Canadian Charter of Rights and Freedoms. Depending on the outcome of this litigation, the age of mandatory retirement may be raised, or automatic mandatory retirement at any age might be declared unconstitutional. If the latter ruling was handed down, each occupation or organization might be required to introduce aptitude tests and physical examinations that would ascertain, at regular intervals beyond a certain age, whether an employee was competent to continue full- or part-time employment in that occupation or organization.

Most workers retire voluntarily at or before the mandatory age. Relatively few workers are reluctant or unwilling retirees, although many are forced to retire early because of poor health, or an inability to obtain full- or part-time employment. This increase in voluntary retirement prior to or at the mandatory age is partially related to the fact that retirement is no longer viewed as a socially stigmatized stage in life. Early retirement is also related to the improved financial status provided by social security and private pension plans, and to the initiation of company incentive plans to encourage early retirement with a reasonable pension for long-term employees.

Faced with the two competing alternatives of mandatory versus voluntary retirement, the public and private sectors have engaged in a long-standing debate as to which policy should be the norm (Guppy, 1989). To date, many arguments for each case have been presented. Some of the more rational and frequently used arguments are listed below. Generally, proponents of a flexible and voluntary retirement policy have argued, on the basis of legal, empirical or experiential evidence, that mandatory retirement:

1. Is a form of age discrimination, and violates human rights.
2. Forces an experienced and skillful worker out of the labor force, and society is the loser, as well as the individual.
3. Increases the national debt because many of those beyond the mandatory age must be supported by social security payments, especially those with an irregular work history (for example, women, immigrants, the disabled).
4. Contributes to the alienation, isolation, and dissatisfaction of some elderly persons.
5. Is based on chronological age, which

is an inaccurate predictor of work capabilities in the later years of life because of wide individual differences in ability and motivation to perform, or to learn new skills.

In contrast, advocates of mandatory retirement at a specific chronological age counter these arguments by stating that:

1. In the absence of valid and reliable tests of competency, all individuals are treated equally with respect to the timing of their exit from the labor force.
2. Less competent or less motivated workers are not forced to submit to competency tests, thereby revealing weaknesses prior to, or at, the retirement age. Hence, older workers are protected against being forced out of the labor force prior to the mandatory age.
3. Mandatory retirement is a major mechanism for promoting mobility within the labor force, since middle-aged workers can be promoted and young workers can enter.
4. It provides stability in pension systems because the demand for increased payments in a given year can be more accurately predicted.
5. Mandatory retirement at a specific age ensures public safety and a high level of performance in occupations involving the operation of vehicles or planes (drivers, pilots).

To date, few of the claims supporting mandatory retirement can be validated by research evidence. Despite the prevailing evidence in favor of flexible and voluntary retirement policies, there is support for a compromise: mandatory retirement would be abolished, but a periodic review of performance would be required for workers over a specific age. In some occupations and industries, incentives have been offered for early retirement (for example a 'thirty-years-and-out' policy, or a policy that permits early retirement when the sum of age plus number of years equals eighty or ninety).

Early versus Late Retirement

As we saw earlier, only about 18 percent of the men and 7 percent of the women in Canada continue to work after 65 years of age. Among those most likely to continue working are those in good health; self-employed professionals; those who are highly educated; those whose major life interest has been work (especially those who are single); blue-collar workers with few pension credits; rural farm workers; those who need extra income to survive (for example, recent immigrants, divorced women, those with an irregular work history); and workers employed in an occupation or industry characterized by a labor shortage. The individual who decides to continue working has four basic options: retire and obtain a part-time position with the same employer or a new employer; continue in the same job; begin a second career in a new field; or become engaged in full- or part-time volunteer work wherein the work pattern represents a non-salaried career.

In some situations the decision to continue working beyond the normal retirement age may be mutually beneficial for the employee, the employer, and the government. For example, in Japan, where the mandatory retirement age is 55, many workers continue to work beyond age 55 to meet a labor shortage, to maintain some degree of economic security, and to relieve pressure on the government pension system. To facilitate this continued involvement in the labor force, Japanese workers are either reemployed in a smaller company or are permitted to remain with their original employer. In both situations the worker is hired for a one- to five-year period at a reduced salary, and usually in a less prestigious position.

In North America those who are unemployed prior to age 65 may be victims of age discrimination in hiring, job obsolescence, the closing or reduction in size of manufacturing plants, a history of unemployment, or an inability to work because of declining motivation, skills, or health. This pattern of involuntary early retirement is especially prevalent among members of some minority groups who have historically had higher levels of unemployment, lower incomes, and a higher incidence of health problems. During periods of economic restraint, high salaried middle-management employees may also be fired five to ten years before their normal retirement age.

In recent years a number of studies have sought to identify and explain the factors influencing the decision to retire voluntarily before the normal mandatory age (McDonald and Wanner, 1984, 1990; Robinson et. al., 1985; Boaz, 1987; Martin Matthews and Brown, 1987; Quinn and Burkhauser, 1990). The decision to retire early appears to be influenced by personal factors unique to an individual, and by institutional or structural factors impinging on an individual after about 55 years or age. Both push and pull factors operate within each of these categories to encourage an early retirement (highlight 11.2).

The most significant personal factors in the retirement decision are financial security and the state of health. If the individual has sufficient financial resources and is in good health, there is a higher probability of early retirement. The actual age at which the retirement occurs may depend on other factors such as pension policies, age and employment status of the spouse, leisure lifestyle, physical and mental demands of the job, level of job satisfaction, lifelong attitudes toward work, or societal norms pertaining to early retirement. For the individual who is in poor health, early retirement may occur suddenly, regardless of financial status. Those who are forced to retire early because of deteriorating health may be eligible for financial assistance in the form of long-term disability pensions. However, some legislation may militate against early or on-time retirement. For example, federal legislation passed in the 1960s and the 1970s reduced the benefits available to older immigrants. In order to be eligible for full Canada or Quebec Pension Plan benefits they must have arrived in Canada before 18 years of age, and to be eligible to receive full Old Age Security benefits (based on need), they must have lived in Canada for forty years. Wanner and McDonald (1986) found that older immigrants from Third World countries (Asia, Africa, Latin America) who arrived in the 1970s and 1980s retire later because they are less likely to have access to full security benefits.

This is another example of how government policies influence individual decisions and individual income in the later years.

Partial versus Full Retirement

For some individuals the transition to full retirement is preceded by a period of partial withdrawal from the labor force. This pattern is more common among the self-employed than among wage and salary workers. One reason for this higher rate is that the self-employed are exempt from such institutional constraints as company pension policies and discrimination in hiring older workers.

At present, partial retirement is not a widely available option. However, with inflation, with a higher age for mandatary retirement or the elimination of mandatory retirement, and with the initiation of policies promoting job sharing and reduced work loads, partial retirement may become more prevalent in the future. In fact, a greater number of wage and salary workers might select a transitional period of partial retirement if more part-time positions were available.

Adjustment to Retirement

The study of personal reactions to retirement has generated a large body of literature in the field of social gerontology. Much of the initial work was based on the false assumption that retirement is a traumatic event and that many do not adjust to the new status of retiree. As a result, studies sought to describe and explain the 'crisis,' the 'despair,' the 'losses,' and the 'changes' that accompany or are initiated by retirement. This literature was further expanded by a long-standing interest in accounting for the life satisfaction, well-being, or morale of the elderly (Larson, 1978).

Just as widowhood was seen as a significant transition point for women, the onset of retirement was thought to be a significant event for men in the later years. As a result, until recently (see the next section), most research on the impact of retirement on the individual has focused on men. This research hypothesized that retirement leads to declining health or an early death, to marital disharmony, to decreased

INSTITUTIONAL/STRUCTURAL AND PERSONAL FACTORS INFLUENCING THE DECISION TO RETIRE EARLY

Institutional/Structural Factors

1. A labor market characterized by high unemployment at all ages. In this situation it may be more economically advantageous to retire early and to receive retirement benefits than to continue on welfare, or to continue searching for full- or part-time work.
2. Policies that permit partial or total old-age security and pension payments to be received before 65 years of age, and policies that encourage accepting these options.
3. A lowering or elimination of the fixed limit on earnings above which old-age security benefits may not be claimed. This enables an individual to retire with a private pension and still remain eligible to receive old-age security payments (even if he or she works part-time and earns a salary).
4. Raising the mandatory retirement age so that more workers opt out of the labor force between 60 and 69 years of age.
5. A forced horizontal or downward move, or a reclassification to a lower job category within the organization.
6. The presence of societal norms that make an 'early' retirement socially acceptable.
7. Union demands for a ceiling on the number of years of employment (for example, 'thirty and out').

Personal Factors

1. Having sufficient economic resources to support the retiree and the spouse for an unknown number of years (no mortgage, few dependents, savings, a large pension).
2. A decline in health that cannot be compensated for by a change to a more suitable job.
3. A desire for a change in lifestyle that can be accommodated by savings, equity in a home, and the availability of private pension benefits to ensure an acceptable standard of living.
4. A positive attitude toward retirement, and an expectation that retirement will be a satisfying stage in life.
5. A supportive spouse and family.
6. Being single or having few dependents.
7. Having a low level of education.
8. Being employed in a physically demanding job where tasks are becoming more onerous.
9. Making early and concrete plans for retirement.
10. Being dissatisfied with the job while at the same time having some degree of economic security.

---

levels of social interaction and activity, or to the onset of economic hardship and poverty.[11]

Clearly, the onset of retirement represents a major transition point that has the potential to alter the lifestyle and the life chances of former workers. However, recent evidence suggests that the majority of respondents (70 to 90 percent) report few problems in adjusting to retirement (Robinson et al., 1985; Mitchell et al., 1988; McDonald and Wanner, 1990). The major problems reported during the retirement stage pertain to loss of income, declining health, nostalgia for the job, and the death of the spouse. Only the loss of income and the perceived social and psychological losses accompanying the loss of

a job are related to the retirement event per se. Even here most individuals seem to adjust to changes in their financial status by lowering their expectations or by altering their consumption patterns (see below, Retirement and Economic Status).

Given the apparent variation in the degree and quality of adjustment to retirement, a number of studies have identified the factors that facilitate a satisfactory transition from the role of worker to that of retiree. Generally, the transition is less traumatic and more satisfying for those with higher perceived levels of health and economic status; for those who have a harmonious marriage and social support from a spouse and family; for those who continue to participate in social activity and interaction at about the same level and in about the same type or form as earlier; for those who have lost interest in work and who have a positive orientation to and interest in leisure; for those who have an accurate perception of retirement, a positive attitude toward retirement, and who have engaged in realistic preretirement planning; for those who remain in their own home rather than moving to an apartment or institution; and for those who retire with adequate pensions at a period in history that is not characterized by excessive and rapid inflation. The type of place of employment may also influence postretirement adjustment. In a study employing the dual-economy perspective, Calasanti (1988) found that workers in the peripheral sector were more concerned with financial matters whereas workers in the core sector were more concerned with health and life satisfaction. This finding is not too surprising given the lack of pensions and lower incomes common to positions in peripheral industries.

In summary, while some men do not adjust well to retirement, and either return to the work force or remain dissatisfied, the majority do adjust in both the short and long term. The commonly held view that retirement leads to serious physical or psychological deterioration is not supported for most retired individuals. In fact, if those who retire because of poor health are not included in studies, there are few differences between the elderly who are retired and those who continue working. Moreover, the trend toward early retirement seems to suggest that older workers are less apprehensive about retirement. Most look forward to retirement and find that leaving the stress or boredom of work brings a new meaning and enjoyment to life.

Women and the Retirement Process

Just as the study of the impact of widowhood for men has been neglected, so too has the impact of retirement on women been understudied. At first, the concern of researchers (mainly men!) was primarily with how a wife reacted to the retirement of her husband, how retirement affected the marital relationship, and how the adjustment of the husband could be facilitated by a supportive wife. Generally, these studies found that a wife's reaction can influence the adjustment of both the husband and the marital couple. However, retirement by the husband can create stresses in the wife's daily life, especially if she has not been consulted or involved in preretirement planning. For example, Keating and Cole (1980) found that the wives of retired teachers perceived that the retirement of the spouse led to a loss of independence and privacy. Furthermore, the wives reported that there was often a need to reduce their social network and to restructure their normal pattern of daily activities to accommodate the retired spouse.

Given changing labor-force participation rates by women, there is a growing need to study the retirement process for older never-married, widowed, and divorced women who retire alone, and for married women who retire earlier, at the same time as, or later than their spouse. Compared to men, women arrive at the threshold of retirement 'with fewer financial resources, less preparation for retirement, a different work and family history, and a dissimilar social network' (McDonald and Wanner, 1990:94). More specifically, many married women have had an interrupted cyclical pattern of labor-force involvement because of child-rearing and domestic responsibilities; have been less likely to be employed in a full-time position; have received lower salaries than men (unequal pay for equal work or level of job responsibility); have been employed in low-skill service or periphery sector positions; and have generally not been eligible for pension or old-age security payments because of these factors. Thus, as a result of this gender-induced inequality in labor-force participation, and the variation in economic status as determined by marital status, the patterns and the process of retirement among women merit further analysis. Those who are married and who are younger than their husbands may retire early, voluntarily or involuntarily, to coincide with the husband's retirement (Campione, 1987; Martin Matthews and Brown, 1987). If a wife's retirement is involuntary, marital conflict may result. Some widowed or divorced women retire later because of economic necessity, or because they fear they will lose a major social network. Some single women may be more likely to resist retirement and to continue working in order to avoid losing income and their major life interest. In general, having children and delaying entry into a career may mean reduced pension benefits and therefore may lead to a decision to delay retirement. In contrast, where an adequate pension is available to those who have had long periods of stable employment, declining health, remarriage, or widowhood may lead to early retirement (O'Rand and Henretta, 1982).

The evidence concerning the adjustment of women to retirement is contradictory. Some studies have shown that retired older women are less well-adjusted than working older women, although both groups are more satisfied than homemakers who have not worked. Others have found that there are or are not sex differences in overall well-being in retirement, or in attitudes toward retirement. A positive or negative response by women seems to depend on marital status, type of occupation, and perceived economic status in retirement. Women may require a longer period of adjustment, especially if they have had negative attitudes toward retirement and if they have retired involuntarily. Thus, women may retire in a more 'disorderly fashion' (McDonald and Wanner, 1990:116).

In summary, there is considerable variation in the willingness and the ability of women to adjust to retirement. Although most retire voluntarily and adjust satisfactorily, those who are economically disadvantaged (for example, the widowed, the divorced, and the intermittent worker) may adjust less satisfactorily. Those who are both self-dependent and economically disadvantaged are more likely to want and need to continue working up to (and beyond) the normal retirement age.

RETIREMENT AND ECONOMIC STATUS

Introduction

In recent years economists, actuaries, and gerontologists interested in the economics of later life have become increasingly concerned about the impact of retirement on the economic status of an individual and of a society.[12] Much of this interest has been stimulated by an awareness of the diminished and disadvantaged economic status of older women (the feminization of poverty), and by the alarmist or crisis argument that the public pension system may become bankrupt due to an increased life expectancy accompanied by decreased fertility rates. That is, can the public funds needed to support an increasingly growing retired population be supplied by past contributions, plus the current contributions of a small youthful labor force? As a result of these emerging issues, attention is being directed toward the impact of retirement policies, mandatory retirement age, fertility and mortality rates, and social (early retirement) and economic (inflation and high unemployment) changes on the ability of a society to meet the needs of the elderly, and at the same time maintain a viable old-age security system.

Retirement Policy and Societal Economic Stability

Social security[13] and private pension plans are not universal phenomena, but they are present in most industrialized societies. Pension systems were originally established at a time when inflation and fertility rates were reasonably predictable, and when it was assumed that retirement would not occur until at least 65 years of age. On the basis of these assumptions it was relatively easy to project the amount of income needed over the years to provide payments to the members of each cohort as they entered retirement. However, some observers have expressed a fear that the old-age security system will be faced with potential bankruptcy when the baby-boom cohort approaches retirement around 2010, if not earlier. Moreover, the public pension system may be threatened now because of the decreased fertility rates following the baby boom: fewer workers are contributing to the pension system, and the old-age dependency ratio is increasing. However, on the positive side the youth-dependency ratio is decreasing and therefore societal costs associated with raising succeeding generations may be decreasing (for example, education costs, family allowance payments). The system is also threatened during periods of high unemployment, since contributions to the system are reduced accordingly. This problem is further compounded by the recent trend toward early voluntary retirement, a pattern that reduces the projected amount of contributions even further. Old-age security and private pension funds may become depleted, since early retirees begin to withdraw monies from them earlier than projected. Furthermore, because security payments are tied to the Consumer Price Index, a rise in inflation will necessitate an increase in the amount of payments, thereby further weakening the solvency of the system. Finally, the costs of supporting older dependents are rising because they live for a longer period in retirement, because the cost of health care for the elderly is escalating, and because more former workers, especially women, are eligible for benefits than in the past.

This fear of a public-expenditure crisis has increased further due to such pension reforms as increased monthly premiums, enhanced survivor's benefits, greater benefits to divorced women, and reduced benefits payable to those who retire between 60 and 65 years of age. Although these public pension reforms have improved the economic status of a greater number of older adults, they have also increased the possibility of higher debt loads for the public budget. Despite the increased pressure on the government to meet obligations to the elderly, recent studies conclude that there will not be a public budget crisis now or in the future (McDaniel, 1986; Denton et al., 1987; Foot, 1989; McDonald and Wanner, 1990).

The projected burden is unlikely to occur, because education costs will decline and money can be shifted to old-age security payments; because there will be increased labor-force participation rates, especially by women; and because unemployment rates will be low, thereby generating revenue. Recently, McDonald and Wanner (1990:122) noted that a country can manage the escalating cost of public pensions in four ways:

1) increasing revenues, through increased contribution levels, special taxes, or transferring general revenue to pension funds;

2) decreasing benefits by tightening eligibility requirements, reducing incentives for early retirement, revising the indexation formula, or raising the retirement age;

3) shifting the burden of financing pensions to individuals (through altering the tax treatment of RRSPs), or to the private pension system (by changing regulations governing it); and,

4) lowering the dependency ratio by increasing labor-force participation among older workers by means of reduced pension benefits, incentives for remaining in the labor force, the elimination of mandatory retirement, or the reduction of discrimination in the hiring and paying of older workers.

To date, Canada has focused on raising revenues and shifting a greater responsibility for income security to individuals (tax incentives to save through RRSPs) and private plans (increased portability and reduced vesting periods). Additionally, as of 1990, universal access to Old Age Security may end as part of a larger program of tax reform. Known as the 'clawback,' the heretofore universal pension income deduction will be reduced on the basis of accrued annual income. At the beginning, only seniors with incomes over $50,000 will lose all OAS benefits, but it has been estimated by the National Council on Welfare that by the year 2019 all OAS benefits will be lost if the annual income of an older adult exceeds $46,000. Thus, over time, middle-income earners will also not receive much of an old-age pension on reaching 65 years of age. In effect, the elderly, who have prepaid their old-age pensions through income tax contributions for many years, will suddenly find themselves deprived of this expected income in retirement. However, the government estimates that, when the 'clawback' system is fully implemented, only 54,000 (about 1.8 percent) high-income OAS recipients would repay all of their benefit, while an additional 74,000 would repay part of the benefit. This means that only about 4.3 percent of *all* OAS recipients would not receive some or all of their entitled benefits, and that the government would recoup an estimated $300 million. Yet, even if the 4.3 percent do not 'need' the payment, they lose what had been promised to them, and the principle of universality has been abandoned.

Other alternatives to keep the system viable include increasing the social security contributions of those in the labor force; reducing the amount of benefits paid to retirees; increasing personal and corporate income tax so that old-age security is paid in part from general income tax revenues; delaying the retirement age; raising the minimum age of eligibility, regardless of when the individual retires,[14] imposing income taxes on social security benefits; and permitting individuals to opt out of the social security system.

While some or all of these proposals might solve the economic problem in either the short or long term, they also have the potential to create social problems. For example, with an increasing old-age dependency ratio, increased income taxes or social security contributions place a greater burden on a smaller number of workers. This could lead to intergenerational conflict. Also, by using general taxes to supplement a depleted social security system, funds may be shifted from other crucial areas such as education, welfare, or health care.

In short, the economic viability of the old-age security system is being questioned and examined carefully, and viable solutions have yet to be found. As we move toward an era of declining fertility rates and changing social norms, more women enter and remain in the labor force, and make contributions to social security and private pension funds. However, while these contributions help to maintain a balance in the pension system at present, many of these female contributors will be eligible for benefits at some time in the future. As a result, the size of payments needed for a specific retiring cohort may be greater than projected, thereby reducing the fund dramatically during a given period of time.

Retirement and Individual Economic Stability

This subsection focuses on factors influencing the sources, amounts, and adequacy of income in the retirement years. Retirement income comes from three sources: (1) government-based minimum and supplementary social security payments, tax benefits, and in-kind benefits (non-money benefits such as subsidized medical care, housing, transportation, food, social and recreational services); (2) private pension plans based on contributions by the employee and the employer; and (3) personal resources (for example, savings, investments, equity in a home, earnings after retirement, gifts, or assistance from relatives. Highlight 11.3 describes the income and social security programs available to elderly Canadians.

The provision of income for the elderly has increasingly moved from being a 'private trouble' to a 'public issue' (Myles, 1989:26). As a result, many industrialized nations adhere to the principle that citizens are entitled to a wage or to economic support throughout the life course. Thus, a pension is considered to be a 'retirement wage' (Myles, 1989:129) and is based on contributions from both the public and private sectors. However, because private-sector pensions are based on work history, past earnings, and varying policies concerning contributions and eligibility, not all retirees are treated equally. Indeed, some lifetime employees of small companies retire without any private pension benefits, as do many women. Table 11.1 indicates the importance of public pensions compared to private pensions for older Canadians.

This table illustrates the greater reliance of women on publicly supported old age security and income supplement payments, the fact that fewer women are eligible for either public or private pension payments, and that few older women earn an income. Only in terms of investment income do women exceed men, largely because the present cohort of elderly widows

HIGHLIGHT **11.3**

SOCIAL SECURITY FOR AN AGING POPULATION

Canada's social security system seeks to ensure that all older adults have at least a minimum of resources to meet their basic needs. For the interested reader who needs more information, the *Canada Year Book*, published annually by the Minister of Supply and Services Canada, provides succinct and current information about the availability of, and level of support provided by, these income security and social service programs.

Federal and Provincial Health Care

Assisted by cost sharing with the federal government, provincial health plans provide comprehensive and universal physician and hospital insurance for all older adults. These plans are portable, providing coverage anywhere in the world for emergency services. Public health and community health departments, along with voluntary agencies, provide a range of counseling, health promotion, rehabilitation, and home care services to the elderly. The type, quantity, and quality of these services can vary greatly from province to province and, within a province, from community to community.

Federal Income Security

To ensure a minimum level of income for older adults, a monthly flat-rate, universal benefit (Old Age Security — OAS) is paid to all persons 65 years of age and over who meet the residence requirements. This payment is unrelated to work history. A Guaranteed Income Supplement (GIS), which must be applied for annually, is available to all pensioners who have little or no income. A Spouse's Allowance (SPA) is similarly available to a pensioner's spouse, who must be 60 to 64 years of age, if the spouse has little or no income. This allowance is also available to widows and widowers aged 60 to 64 years, if need can be demonstrated, but ceases at age 65 when they personally become eligible for a full OAS pension and a GIS. The OAS, GIS, and SPA benefits are adjusted quarterly on the basis of changes in the Consumer Price Index (see table 11.3).

The Canada Pension Plan and the Quebec Pension Plan (C/QPP) are social insurance programs funded by contributions from the employer and the employee. The plans provide monthly retirement pensions, which are earnings-related. Payments may begin at age 60 on a reduced basis, at age 65 at the current maximum monthly amount, or up to age 70 at a slightly increased monthly amount depending on the age (66 to 70) at retirement. Benefits on a reduced basis are paid to the surviving spouse of a contributor, whether he or she remarries or not. A disability pension is provided to contributors with a severe and prolonged mental or physical disability that requires them to leave the labor force before age 65. Similarly, benefits are paid to the dependent children of a contributor who becomes disabled or dies (payments, if the children are in full-time attendance at school, can be made to age 25), and a death benefit is paid to the estate of a contributor who dies prior to retirement. Finally, since 1987, upon dissolution of a marriage or common-law relationship, either partner may apply for a division of any pension credits accumulated during the relationship.

Provincial Income Security

The provinces, in order to supplement federal programs, provide additional social assistance for the needy elderly on a short- or long-term basis. These benefits may cover the costs of food, shelter, fuel, clothing, counseling, or other health benefits not covered by existing programs. Most provinces also provide tax credits, rebates, or shelter subsidies/grants to needy homeowners or renters. Finally, most provinces provide income supplements to recipients of the GIS and/or SPA allowances and income supplements to the disabled elderly. These programs are designed to enable the elderly person to live as independently as possible within a home environment, thereby preventing or delaying admission to a more costly institutionalized environment (that is, homes for the aged, nursing homes, chronic care hospitals).

Local and Regional Social Services

On the basis of a tradition of voluntary church, ethnic, and community group support for the needy, a variety of social services for the elderly are provided by volunteer groups in some communities. These voluntary organizations raise funds, provide services or goods, and build and/or administer offices or facilities for the elderly, including rest homes, home-maintenance and home care support, meals-on-wheels, neighborhood watch, and voluntary drivers (see highlight 10.4). Many of these organizations restrict their clientele to members of a particular church or ethnic group, or to residents of a particular neighborhood. Finally, local and regional municipalities provide more widespread programs, facilities, and services for older adults (e.g., senior centers, subsidized transportation or housing, recreational programs), while local merchants offer discounts to senior citizens (for example, on food, movies, clothing).

retain ownership of homes and any accumulated stocks and savings generated by their deceased spouses.

Monthly payments from social security and private pensions and amount of savings and investments are closely related to annual income during the working years. This level of income is especially critical for private pension plans where the amount of annual benefits is often based on the average earnings during the last five to ten years of employment. Therefore, the higher the salary near the end of the career, the higher the pension.[15]

Although there has been a dramatic increase in the number of individuals eligible for a private pension, this benefit is still not available to all workers. Those with irregular patterns of employment, the self-employed, and those employed in small organizations may not have access to employer-sponsored pension plans. For those who are enrolled in a private plan, contributions are usually paid by both the employee and the employer. Under this system, the workers must be protected if they are fired, if they leave the company, or if they retire early. An increasing number of private pension plans are 'portable': paid-in contributions can be transferred to a plan in another company. This ensures that the benefits paid at retirement are similar to those that would have been paid had the place of employment not changed.

Similarly, a plan should provide for 'vesting,' so that those who are fired or quit before retirement receive all or part of the benefits that

TABLE 11.1

PUBLIC AND PRIVATE SOURCES OF INCOME FOR ELDERLY CANADIANS, 65+, 1986

Source	Men %	Women %	Total %
Public			
Old Age Security/Guaranteed Income Supplement	25.2	45.3	34.4
Canada/Quebec Pension Plan	16.3	11.0	13.9
Other government transfers	3.5	3.6	3.6
Private			
Investment income	18.9	24.1	21.2
Private pensions	20.1	10.5	15.7
Employment earnings	14.6	3.9	9.8
Other	1.3	1.5	1.4

SOURCE: Adapted from Lindsay and Donald (1988). 'Income of Canada's Seniors,' *Canadian Social Trends*, 10 (Autumn), 22. Reproduced with the permission of the Minister of Supply and Services Canada, 1990.

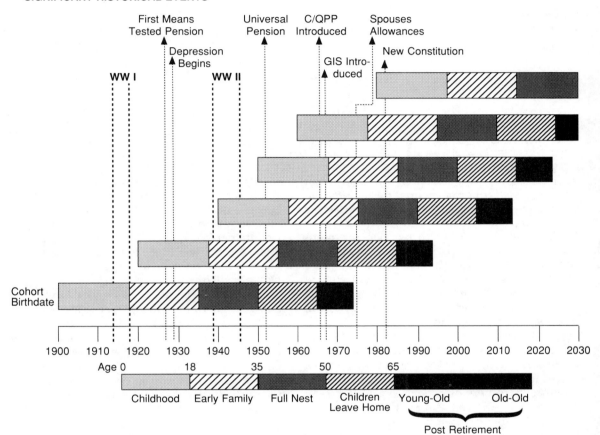

FIGURE **11.1**

THE IMPACT OF CANADIAN HISTORICAL EVENTS AND LEGISLATION
ON VARIOUS AGE COHORTS

TRADITIONAL LIFE COURSE STAGES

SOURCE: L. Heslop. *An Analysis of Expenditure Patterns of the Elderly: Cohorts – Going Through Life Together.* Research Paper No. 13A. Statistics Canada, 1985. Reproduced with the permission of the Minister of Supply and Services Canada, 1990.

have been earned prior to leaving the organization. Normally, an individual must remain at least two years with the company before vesting occurs. In addition, the benefits are seldom adjusted upward to keep pace with inflation after the individual leaves the organization. A viable private pension plan should also include 'survivor's benefits' so that the spouse will be protected during widowhood. Finally a plan should provide 'reduced benefits' for those who opt to retire before the mandatory age.

The income of older Canadians is improving because of public and private pension reforms, increased incentives to save and invest, increased in-kind transfers to the elderly, reduced inflation, increased participation in private pension plans, and increased employment options for older adults who wish to or need to

TABLE 11.2
INCIDENCE OF LOW INCOME, 1986

	Families %	Unattached Individuals %
Age		
65-69	8.8	36.7
70+	9.9	44.9
Sex, 65+		
Male	8.7	31.9
Female	16.5	46.1

SOURCE: Adapted from Statistics Canada. (1989). *Canada Year Book, 1990*. Table 5-30. Reproduced with the permission of the Minister of Supply and Services Canada, 1990.

keep working. Nevertheless, there are still considerable economic inequalities in later life for males with irregular employment patterns throughout the work years, for disabled or health-limited workers, for females, for members of minority groups, for elderly immigrants (Boyd, 1989), for the divorced (Fethke, 1989) and for different cohorts. For example, figure 11.1 (Heslop, 1985a) illustrates how cohorts born at different periods in history have been affected by specific historical events or significant federal legislation that can influence economic status in later life. Specifically, members of cohorts born early in the century do not have access to universal pensions or a spouses's allowance; members of cohorts born after 1940 have not experienced a depression or a major war, and will reap in retirement the life-long benefits of participating in enhanced public and private pension plans.

Since the 1970s, the income of those 65 and over has improved relative to other Canadians. This is especially true for those 75 years of age and older. Nevertheless, the average income of retired adults remains well below the levels of younger Canadians, and considerably below their preretirement income. There is also considerable diversity within the elderly population that varies by marital status. For example, the average 1986 income was $28,500 for an older married couple, $13,900 for an elderly unattached male, and $12,600 for an elderly

unattached female (Lindsay and Donald, 1988). Although the incidence of poverty has declined because of increased publicly funded benefits and because more Canadians are eligible for private pensions, 19 percent of elderly Canadians were still below the Statistics Canada low-income cut-off level in 1986[16] (Lindsay and Donald, 1988).

Table 11.2 illustrates the dramatic impact of being single or female on level of income.

In 1988, Statistics Canada reported that 50 percent of singles over age 65 derived their entire income from Old Age Security and Guaranteed Income Supplement payments from the federal government — a total income of only $691.48 per month. Furthermore, Statistics Canada reported that 79 percent of women and 69 percent of men over the age of 70 lived on less than $15,000 in 1988. Table 11.3 indicates the monthly rate for publicly funded social security payments as of April 1990. This table can be employed to estimate the monthly or annual income of older adults who are eligible for various combinations of payments.

We have seen that the economic status of the retired individual or couple can range from poverty to great wealth, depending on past earnings and assets and on the eligibility for retirement benefits (see highlight 11.3). From the perspective of society, there has been great concern expressed about the need to ensure 'adequate' retirement incomes or wealth for the

TABLE 11.3
MONTHLY RATES FOR SOCIAL SECURITY PAYMENTS, APRIL 1990

Program	Maximum Monthly Rate (April 1990)
Canada Pension Plan (CPP)	$577.08
Old Age Security (OAS)	$343.13
Guaranteed Income Supplement (GIS)	
Single Pensioner	$407.77
Married Couple	$531.20 ($265.60 each)
Spousal Allowance (SPA) (Age 60-64)	$608.73
Widowed Spousal Allowance (Age 60-64)	$672.04
Disability Pension	$709.52

elderly, especially for older widows and members of minority groups who have had an irregular work history. However, these objective, external assessments of adequacy have seldom identified the standard to which 'adequate' is compared. If the income of the current cohort aged 65 and over is compared to those who retired ten or fifteen years ago, their relative status is adequate; a larger percentage of each retiring cohort is eligible for private pension plans, and they receive larger social security payments. The members of more recently retired cohorts also receive greater tax concessions and in-kind benefits. For many, **inflation** may be traumatic, especially if their assets depreciate in value (for example, if they suffer losses in stocks or bonds or own a house in a deteriorating real estate area), if transfer payments (pensions or social security) lag behind inflation, and if inflationary prices affect items (such as food or medical care) that make up a large proportion of the retired person's budget (Schulz, 1985:40-44).

Generally, various occupational groups are able to maintain their relative position in the income hierarchy and to maintain their relative standard of living in retirement (Myles, 1981).[17] However, if the economic status of the recently retired is compared to their preretirement status, to the status of those in their occupational group who remain in the labor force, or to age peers who continue to work in any occupation, then their objective economic status is inferior (Myles,

1981). For example, McDonald and Wanner (1990:84) cited a 1984 National Council of Welfare report which concluded that 'as many as two-thirds of middle-income Canadians must contend with a drop of 25 percent or more in their standard of living when they retire.' For some, this reduced income may create some hardships; for others, it may be totally inadequate and lead to poverty and to dependence on welfare or family assistance. Schulz (1985:74) noted that if one's goal is to provide retirement income equal to 60 to 65 percent replacement of average earnings during the last five years prior to retirement, one would have to save about 20 percent of one's earnings each and every year of one's involvement in the labor force.

Although the objective indicators provide aggregate information about the relative economic status of retired cohorts , individual responses to the loss of income must also be assessed, especially when considering the relationship between economic status and well-being. The perception of financial 'adequacy' by a given individual or couple may be more relevant than the objective economic situation as viewed by outsiders. Many individuals are aware of their own needs, priorities, resources, and debts, and are able to establish personally satisfying, albeit lower, standards of living in the retirement years. The perceived adequacy of economic status in retirement is usually based on a comparison with the individual's past lifestyle and with the status of the peer group. In short, the definition of the economic situation in retirement is based on perceptions about relative deprivation (self now versus self in the past; self versus others).

Following retirement, despite a reduced income, many older adults still perceive their economic situation as satisfying. One reason for this response may be that they alter their expenditure patterns. In fact, Snell and Brown (1987), in a survey of 450 recently retired men and women, found that a reduction in expenditures was the most frequent method of managing a reduced income, especially among those who felt the most economically deprived. As many have argued, our basic needs for goods and services change with age. But this can vary by cohort (Heslop, 1985a) and gender (Heslop, 1985b), and may involve the initiation of a restrictive lifestyle (for example, selling a car) or the onset of unhealthy nutritional practices (such as lowering the quality and the quantity of food purchased). When older adults experience a reduced income, a higher proportion of expenditures is often allocated to food, shelter, and household maintenance, although this varies greatly by class background and the availability of liquid assets (bonds, savings). For example, Heslop (1985a:26) indicated that, on the basis of surveys in 1969, 1974, 1978, and 1982, there was anywhere from a 2 to 6 percent increase in household food expenditures, depending on the cost of food at the time each survey was taken. Similarly, Heslop (1985b) found that among older women who live alone (widows), there has been a large increase in the amount of income allocated to personal and municipal taxes.

Although there have been a number of studies that report the changing of expenditure patterns in a number of categories following retirement, it is not clear whether expenditures decline because income declines after retirement, or because actual needs and wants decrease in the later years. On the one hand, expenses are lower because the retirees do not have to support children, because they have fewer work-related expenses (such as clothes and transportation), because they have few or no mortgage obligations, and because they are eligible for senior-citizen discounts. On the other hand, energy, food, and home-maintenance costs increase during periods of inflation.

With the elderly representing an increasing proportion of the population, it is not surprising that the business sector has sought to increase the expenditure habits and patterns of older adults. An awareness of the increasing affluence and health of elderly adults has led to increased advertising and marketing targeted toward the 'maturity' or 'gray' market (Lumpkin, 1984: Minkler, 1989). This market has been created because current and future cohorts of older adults are more active than those in the past, and they are more consumer-oriented and willing to spend discretionary income. As a result, much of the marketing is directed toward the sale of 'frills and services, luxury goods and top of the line merchandise' (Minkler, 1989).[18] In short, individual needs and wants among the older population with greater discretionary income have been created or manufactured by the corporate marketing and advertising sectors of the economy.[19]

In summary, the circumstances leading to perceived adequacy of the financial situation in retirement appear to be related not only to the relative deprivation compared to the preretirement income levels, but also to social status, education, expenditure and consumption patterns, inflation, cohort membership, and the specific circumstances of the retirement. In short, both the absolute and relative economic positions of the elderly must be understood prior to establishing or implementing new income security policies.

Economic Status of Older Women: The Feminization of Poverty

As noted earlier, the work history of women often represents an intermittent pattern; they tend to voluntarily enter and leave the labor force more frequently than males. They also are more likely to engage in part-time work, to leave the labor force after childbirth, and to remain at home at least until their children reach school age. It has been estimated that each child and each year of delay in full-time labor-force participation subtracts from a woman's occupational status and, in turn, from her retirement income (O'Rand and Lander-

---

HIGHLIGHT 11.4

THE DIVERSITY OF ECONOMIC STATUS IN LATER LIFE

Mr. and Mrs. A	Mr. A, now 63, took early retirement at age 61 from a position of vice president, sales, for a large national food company. Because they receive a large private pension and a CPP pension and have numerous investments and savings, Mr. and Mrs. A have a combined annual income of over $100,000. Owners of a cottage and a large, luxurious condominium, they 'winter' in the southern United States in an affluent retirement community. Mr. A makes semiweekly trips back to Canada to serve as a consultant to various food companies.
Mrs. B	Widowed for over 10 years, at age 70 Mrs. B receives small CPP, OAS, and GIS benefits, plus a provincial income supplement. Her deceased husband, who worked for over forty years as a garage mechanic for a local service station, never contributed to a private pension plan. Mrs. B worked periodically throughout her life, but spent most of these earnings on mortgage payments or home improvements. While she has some Canada Savings Bonds, and owns her home, her annual income seldom exceeds $15,000. With rising house taxes and increasing home-maintenance costs, she is beginning to think about selling the family home in order to seek cheaper housing and thereby economically survive on the revenue generated by the investment in her home.
Mr. and Mrs. C	Mr. C, now 62, was forced to retire at age 58 because of a severe back problem. He receives a disability pension and a much-reduced private pension because of his forced early retirement. Mrs. C earns the minimum wage as a waitress five evenings a week. Together, their combined income from investments, savings, social security benefits, and earnings is $25,000.
Mr. D	Mr. D immigrated to Canada to live with his son at the age of 57 after his spouse died, and is now 68. Prior to last year when he was forced to retire because of ill health, Mr. C worked as an unskilled laborer in the construction industry. Not eligible for full OAS pension benefits because of living in Canada for only eight years before age 65, his monthly income is less than $500, which he gives to his son in return for housing and care. He has no other source of income and is completely dependent financially on his son and daughter-in-law.

---

man, 1984). Moreover, during the time women are in the labor force they frequently occupy low-prestige, low-income positions, and seldom seek or receive the opportunity to advance to high-status, high-paying positions. For example, Statistics Canada reported that, on average, a full-time female worker received 65 percent of the salary earned by a male in 1989 ($21,918 versus $33,558). Even never-married or married women who never leave the work force to raise children earn 90 and 61 percent respectively of the amount earned by comparable

males who are never-married or married. Although this discrepancy may decrease somewhat in the future because of pay-equity legislation, women may never obtain income and pension equity until they obtain equal access to all positions in the labor force.

As a result of these lifelong work-related factors, and because women live longer, older women have fewer personal financial resources than men when they reach 65 years of age. This inadequate financial situation is further compounded if they become widowed and are not eligible for survivor's benefits, or if they remarry and thereby become ineligible to receive pension benefits accrued in the first marriage. Similarly, older women who divorced earlier in life are likely to be economically disadvantaged, since they were divorced at a time when pensions were not considered family assets to be shared in a divorce settlement, as they are at present in most jurisdictions. In short, older women are at high risk of living in an impoverished state in later life because of women's intermittent work history; because of their lifelong economic dependence on men, so that most benefits are obtained through marriage; because of inequitable pension opportunities and regulations for women in a social security system based on a continuous (that is, male) work history; and because of increasing longevity wherein benefits must be amortized over a longer period of time, and hence lower monthly payments are allotted. As Neysmith (1984) so creatively concluded, 'older women are like perennial plants — the roots of their poverty develop early in life and come to fruition when they are old.'

Gee and Kimball (1987:54) concluded that 'it is a virtual certainty that more than one third of Canada's elderly women are poor.' While there are many definitions of **poverty** (Cohen, 1984:211-15; Gee and Kimball, 1987:53-54), a common but highly conservative measure is that used by Statistics Canada. This index, which varies by size of community and by family size (single versus married), considers any individual or family to be poor if 58.5 percent or more of total income is spent on the necessities of life (food, clothing, shelter). This index is based on historical data which showed that, in 1978, the average family spent 38.5 percent of its income on the basic necessities of life. The actual low-income cut-off level is updated annually according to the movement of the Consumer Price Index.

On the basis of the 1981 census, Gee and Kimball (1987:54-58) reported that 31 percent of women over 65, compared to 19 percent of men over 65, were at or below the poverty line. However, since many elderly women are widowed and live as unattached individuals, over 60 percent are at or below the poverty line, compared to 49 percent for unattached elderly

males. For families headed by a male and a female respectively, 10 and 25 percent were at or below the poverty line. Finally, because the Statistics Canada index is conservative and tends to underestimate the percent existing at or below the poverty line, the number or percent of 'near poor' should also be considered. Using a figure of $1,999 above the 1983 poverty line of $8,000 for an individual, Gee and Kimball (1987:55) found that approximately 78 percent of older unattached women can be classified as poor or 'near poor.' This represented about 558,000 older Canadians in 1983, a problem well worth addressing.

This gender gap in poverty in later life has been labeled, 'the feminization of poverty' (Minkler and Stone, 1985; Gee and Kimball, 1987; O'Rand, 1988; Seniors Secretariat, 1989; Stone, 1989). An elderly woman is not poor because she is old, or because she has created her own poverty situation. Rather, older women are poor because a social system creates poverty and hardship for women who are economically tied to their husband's wealth and longevity, and for women who opt out of a marriage or who outlive their husband. The feminization of poverty in later life is an outcome of such social system factors as a gender division of labor-force opportunities (periphery rather than core occupations), gender discrimination in hiring and promotion opportunities, lifelong pay inequity, intermittent work patterns, a dependency on public old-age security payments rather than private pensions, social pressures and responsibilities for child-rearing and parent care, and the linking of later-life benefits to dependence on living with a male. Thus, family status, work history, lack of equal access to salaries while employed and to income security when retired, all combine to increase the risk of poverty for older women in later life.

Poverty is also more likely among older women because they live alone. They either are overhoused in large family homes that are costly to maintain, or they lack affordable housing alternatives. There are also subgroups of elderly women who are labeled 'the hidden poor' (Seniors Secretariat, 1989; Stone, 1989). These women include native Canadians, recent immigrants, and the institutionalized, all of whom are seldom included in studies or statistics pertaining to impoverishment in later life. For example, immigrant women may have no official Canadian labor-force experience and are therefore not eligible for C/QPP pension benefits, or if they arrive late in life as part of a family reunification plan they are not eligible for Old Age Security or Guaranteed Income Supplement benefits (Boyd, 1989). Similarly, if they outlive their husbands, they may not reap the benefits of marriage, because the spouse may have had a short and irregular work history that reduced his potential public pension benefits.

In order that the feminization of poverty in later life can be eliminated, recent proposals have focused on increased social services for working women, financial management education and counseling for younger women, and pension reforms. In terms of education and counseling, younger women need to pay increased attention to salary and pension benefits, to investments, and to being and becoming financially self-sufficient, especially if they marry and subsequently become divorced or widowed, or if they do not marry. While they are employed, legislation guarantees that maternity leave will not result in loss of a position or seniority, and guarantees pay equity. Increasingly, employers are providing day-care facilities or flex-hours to facilitate child-rearing while a full-time career is pursued. In the area of pension reform, proposals to benefit women have included:

- the continuation of pension credits while women are absent from the labor force due to child-rearing
- CPP pension eligibility for part-time workers
- the continuation of pension benefits to a surviving spouse, regardless of marital or economic status
- increased benefits for immigrants who arrive in Canada during adulthood
- the indexing of private pensions to inflation
- mandatory private pension plans offered by all employers, regardless of the size of the company
- unisex tables to compute retirement contributions and benefits
- mandatory coverage in private plans extended to all permanent part-time employees on a prorated basis.

Many women remain homemakers throughout their adult life and receive no direct salary for this work and responsibility. Nor are they eligible to receive public pensions (C/QPP). However, they are eligible, on the basis of need, for Old Age Security and Guaranteed Income Supplement payments. If divorced or widowed, these lifelong homemakers may be especially vulnerable to poverty, particularly if they were relatively poor while married. Moreover, until recently, many divorced women did not have legal access to the pension benefits of the former spouse, and widows often were not eligible for survivor's benefits in many private pension plans.

It has been argued that since the responsibilities of homemakers constitute unpaid labor, they should be eligible for increased social security payments in recognition of their labor in the home. It has also been suggested that women who spend a portion of their adult life raising children should be eligible for Canada Pension Plan payments because of their contribution to society.[20] In addition, it has been recommended that pension credits accumulated during the years of marriage should be shared between spouses after age 65 in order to improve the economic status of divorced and widowed women. The funds for these increased benefits to older women might be paid by the husband during his working years, by higher contributions from all workers, or by funds from general tax revenues.

Not surprisingly, some observers argue that homemakers should not be eligible for special considerations if the economic burden on current workers is increased, or if the national debt is increased. They claim that women who remain permanently at home do so voluntarily, often because they feel they do not need to work for economic reasons. Why should their economic position be any different in retirement? Moreover, it is argued that women who have decided to remain out of the labor force to perform a service for their husbands should receive retirement benefits from the spouse rather than from society. In summary, although social security and pension reforms are needed to improve the economic status of older women, especially the widowed and the divorced, the procedures and policies by which this goal can be realized have yet to be firmly established.

SUMMARY AND CONCLUSIONS

This chapter has examined the relationship between work, retirement, and economic status in the later years of life. The first major section considered work patterns during the adult years, the competence of the older worker, and preretirement attitudes toward retirement. In the second section, the literature pertaining to various facets of the retirement process was reviewed. The reader was first introduced to conceptual perspectives that included some of the personal and social structural variables thought to be important in the retirement process. Following this section on conceptual frameworks, evidence was presented from the literature concerning preretirement preparation, the nature of the retirement decision, the process of adjustment to retirement, and the retirement process for women. The final section of the chapter considered the present and future structure and stability of public and private pension systems, the actual and perceived economic status of elderly persons, and the disadvantaged economic status of retired women and housewives.

On the basis of the literature pertaining to work, economic status, and retirement in the later years of life, it can be concluded that:

1. Most men and women adjust to retirement and experience little stress in adapting to the new status and lifestyle.
2. Previous work patterns and orientation to work influence when an individual retires, how he or she adjusts, and whether he or she returns to work on a full-time or part-time basis.
3. Women make up approximately 53 percent of the adult work force in Canada.
4. There are few significant gender differences in the importance of work to the individual. Work is a serious, meaningful,

expressive, and satisfying role for most women, as it is for most men.
5. The general job performance of older workers rarely declines. However, there are individual differences in work-related skills among older workers, just as there are among younger workers.
6. There is relatively little decline in work productivity with age, providing that a high level of motivation is present.
7. Declining cognitive or physical skills can be compensated for by experience and by utilizing coping strategies.
8. Older workers are absent less and have fewer accidents than younger workers.
9. Most individuals have favorable attitudes toward retirement during the preretirement years. These positive attitudes are related to having high levels of health, income, and education, and to perceived support from significant others in the family and at work.
10. Although many individuals believe that preretirement planning is important, very few make concrete plans or participate in formal programs.
11. Most workers retire voluntarily at the mandatory retirement age. An increasing number opt to retire voluntarily before the mandatory age.
12. Involuntary early retirement is more prevalent for members of minority groups, and for those in poor health.
13. Partial retirement is not a common option except for the self-employed.
14. Many women have had an irregular or cyclical work history wherein they have occupied low-skill positions with low wages and few benefits. As a result, at retirement age many women are not eligible for a complete or partial pension, and they may be entitled to fewer social security benefits than men who have been regularly employed throughout adulthood.
15. Divorced or widowed women in the labor force may retire later than other women because of economic necessity. Furthermore, because they are economically disadvantaged they may adjust less satisfactorily to retirement.

16. The economic disadvantage of older women is further compounded by the fact that they live longer than men, and therefore must support themselves for a longer period of time.

17. Private pension earnings after retirement are related to the individual's pattern of employment, place of employment, and level of earnings during the working years.

18. Private pension benefits are significantly lower or nonexistent for those who are self-employed, for those employed by small organizations, and for those with irregular patterns of employment.

19. Those with high preretirement incomes may express greater dissatisfaction with their postretirement financial status because they usually experience larger absolute and relative decreases in income. Therefore, a greater adjustment in lifestyle may be necessary unless they use their savings to maintain a standard of living similar to that of the preretirement years.

NOTES

1. The concept of retirement as a social institution was first formalized in Germany in 1889. Legislation permitted workers to leave the labor force at 70 years of age with a degree of guaranteed economic support. However, since few individuals lived to the age of 70 to reap this benefit, the age criterion was later reduced to 65 years of age. In Canada, a Pension Act was enacted in 1918 for war veterans only; in 1927 Parliament passed the Old Age Pension Act, which applied to all citizens over 65 years of age.

2. For a historical analysis of the onset and growth of retirement policies and pensions see Bryden, 1974; Graebner, 1980; Foner and Schwab, 1981:83-87; Roadburg, 1985; Martin Matthews and Tindale, 1987; Kohli, 1987; Myles, 1989; McDonald and Wanner, 1990:17-38.

3. See George, 1980; Foner and Schwab, 1981; Atchley, 1982; Palmore et al., 1985; Schnore, 1985; Miletich, 1986; McDonald and Wanner, 1986; Quinn and Burkhauser, 1990.

4. It is also important to understand the relationship between work and leisure during the adult years. The relative weighting of each in an individual's hierarchy of values can greatly influence whether early retirement will be elected and how the individual will make use of free time during retirement. This relationship between work and leisure is discussed in more detail in chapter 12.

5. There are an increasing number of housewives who reenter the educational system, often after child-rearing is nearly or fully completed, and then begin a career in their 40s. For those who enter business or the professions, this transition may be considered a midlife career change, especially if the new occupation becomes the major life interest.

6. In fact, it has been suggested that from the perspective of a society or an organization, these career changes are threatening — the investment in training the individual for the first career has been lost. Also, if one person in an organization initiates a career change, a role model for others is created, thereby leading to possible further personnel losses. In order to counteract these organizational losses, some companies have attempted to improve the work situation by offering their employees new challenges, alternative work patterns, sabbatical leaves, and greater autonomy.

7. See McDaniel, 1986; Chen, 1987; Gee and Kimball, 1987; Nishio and Lank, 1987; McNeely, 1988; Parliament, 1989; McDonald and Wanner, 1990.

8. Surprisingly, little research attention has been directed to those women who are unable or unwilling to enter the labor force. Is this attitude or inability a result of lack of opportunity, lack of motivation, or other factors?

9. See Foner and Schwab, 1981:13-28; Yolles et al., 1982; Doering et al., 1983; Robinson et al., 1985; Stagner, 1985; Stryckman, 1987; Hirshorn, 1988; McDonald and Wanner, 1990.

10. There is some support for the continuity theory of aging when preretirement and postretirement lifestyles are examined. That is, early and middle-life leisure interests and experiences probably influence postretirement lifestyles. For example, the individual who has never traveled or engaged in extensive volunteer work is unlikely to find these leisure patterns satisfying in retirement.

11. There are a number of methodological limitations in many of these studies that must be considered. First, those who are dissatisfied with retirement may have returned to work, and thus may not be included in a particular sample. Second, those in poor health may die before or just after the information is collected. Third, the age of the sample may vary to include adjacent co-

horts who have had different life experiences. Finally, 'adjustment' and 'satisfaction' involve qualitative and quantitative changes, and both can be assessed by subjective and objective indicators. Therefore, more sophisticated, multivariate instruments are needed to obtain valid information about satisfaction with and adjustment to retirement.

12. See Clark and Spengler, 1980; Powell and Martin, 1980; Clark, 1980, 1981, 1990; Clark et al., 1984; Conklin et al., 1984; Chen, 1985, 1988; Clark and Baumer, 1985; Habib, 1985, 1990; Schulz, 1985, 1988; Denton et al., 1986, 1987; Myles, 1989; Schulz and Myles, 1990; Smeeding, 1990.

13. In Canada, social security includes all hospital, drug, and medical care, subsidies (for example, housing, transportation, home care), plus a retirement-income system, which includes a basic benefit plus a Guaranteed Income Supplement and a Spouse's Allowance (both based on total income).

14. For example, in the United States, the retirement age to be eligible for full benefits will be raised gradually to 66 years of age by 2009, and to 67 by 2027 (Chen, 1988).

15. McAllister (1981) argues that financial adequacy in the retirement years is strongly related to the individual's position in the 'dual economy.' If individuals are employed in a 'central' firm (such as the insurance or automotive industry) rather than in a 'peripheral' firm (such as a company with fewer than twenty-five employees that manufactures some obscure product in small numbers), they will receive higher wages and more fringe benefits throughout the working and retirement years. The employee of a peripheral firm may lack a private pension and may be more dependent on supplementary security payments and other forms of government welfare. Thus, regardless of the human potential of an individual, if the career is spent in a 'central' firm, greater retirement benefits will accrue than if the career had been spent in a 'peripheral' firm.

16. Statistics Canada considers individuals or families who spend more than 58.5 percent of their income on food, shelter, or clothing to have a 'low income,' and therefore to be eligible for assistance.

17. In fact, Myles (1981) notes that pension income cannot reduce intracohort differences in retirement, largely because better-educated, higher-income retirees have more investment income, which, if anything, widens the gap during the retirement years.

18. Most advertising and products involve leisure and travel, housing alternatives, cosmetics and health care, clothing, products for easier living, financial services, education, food, and specialized magazines (for example, *Lear's* for women over 40; *Modern Maturity*, which has a circulation of 19 million).

19. An International Association of Gerontological Entrepreneurs has been formed to explore the relationship between the business world and the aging community.

20. The pension plan operated by the province of Quebec gives special consideration to women during the years they drop out of the labor force to raise children. Quebec Family Law requires mandatory pension sharing for spouses to recognize the time they were out of the labor force.

REFERENCES

Atchley, R. (1979). 'Issues in Retirement Research,' *The Gerontologist*, 19(1), 44-54.

Atchley, R. (1982). 'Retirement as a Social Institution,' pp. 263-87 in R. Turner et al. (eds.). *Annual Review of Sociology*. vol. 8. Palo Alto, Calif.: Annual Reviews, Inc.

Baum, M. and R. Baum. (1980). *Growing Old: A Societal Perspective*. Englewood Cliffs, N.J.: Prentice-Hall.

Beck, S. (1984). 'Retirement Preparation Programs: Differentials in Opportunity and Use,' *Journal of Gerontology*, 39(5), 596-602.

Boaz, R. (1987). 'Early Withdrawal from the Labor Force,' *Research on Aging*, 9(4), 530-47.

Boyd, M. (1989). 'Immigration and Income Security Policies in Canada: Implications for Elderly Immigrant Women,' *Population Research and Policy Review*, 8(1), 5-24.

Bryden, K. (1974). *Old-Age Pensions and Policy-Making in Canada*. Montreal: McGill-Queen's University Press.

Burgess, E. (1960). *Aging in Western Societies*. Chicago: University of Chicago Press.

Calasanti, T. (1981). 'Is Retirement Research Atheoretical?' paper presented at the annual meeting of the Gerontological Society of America, Toronto.

Calasanti, T. (1988). 'Participation in a Dual Economy and Adjustment to Retirement,' *International Journal of Aging and Human Development*, 26(1), 13-27.

Campione, W. (1987). 'The Married Woman's Retirement Decision: A Methodological Comparison,' *Journal of Gerontology*, 42(4), 381-86.

Canadian Bankers' Association, The. (1987). *Steps to Retirement*. Toronto: The Canadian Bankers' Association.

Chen, M. (1987). 'Shaping Factors of Occupational

Age Structures of the Female Labor Force in Canada,' pp. 158-75 in V. Marshall (ed.). *Aging in Canada: Social Perspectives*. 2d ed. Markham, Ont.: Fitzhenry and Whiteside.

Chen, Y. (1985). 'Economic Status of the Aging,' pp. 641-65 in R. Binstock and E. Shanas (eds.). *Handbook of Aging and the Social Sciences* . 2d ed. New York: Van Nostrand Reinhold.

Chen, Y. (1988). 'Better Options for Work and Retirement: Some Suggestions for Improving Economic Security Mechanisms for Old Age,' pp. 189-216 in G. Maddox and P. Lawton (eds.). *Annual Review of Gerontology and Geriatrics*. vol. 8. New York: Springer Publishing Co.

Clark, R. (ed.). (1980). *Retirement Policy in an Aging Society*. Durham, N.C.: Duke University Press.

Clark, R. (1981). 'Aging, Retirement, and the Economic Security of the Elderly: An Economic Review,' pp. 299-319 in C. Eisdorfer (ed.). *Annual Review of Gerontology and Geriatrics*. vol. 2. New York: Springer Publishing Co.

Clark, R. (1990). 'Income Maintenance Policies in the United States,' pp. 383-97 in R. Binstock and L. George (eds.). *Handbook of Aging and the Social Sciences*. 3d ed. San Diego, Calif.: Academic Press.

Clark, R. and D. Baumer. (1985). 'Income Maintenance Policies,' pp. 666-95 in R. Binstock and E. Shanas (eds.). *Handbook of Aging and the Social Sciences*. 2d ed. New York: Van Nostrand Reinhold.

Clark, R. and J. Spengler. (1980). *The Economics of Individual and Population Aging*. New York: Cambridge University Press.

Clark, R. et al. (1984). *Inflation and the Economic Well-Being of the Elderly*. Baltimore, Md.: Johns Hopkins University Press.

Cohen, L. (1984). *Small Expectations: Society's Betrayal of Older Women*. Toronto: McClelland and Stewart.

Conklin, O. et al. (1984). *Pensions Today and Tomorrow: Background Studies*. Toronto: Ontario Economic Council.

Denton, F. et al. (1986). 'Prospective Aging of the Population and Its Implications for the Labour Force and Government Expenditures,' *Canadian Journal on Aging*, 5(2), 75-98.

Denton, F. et al. (1987). 'The Canadian Population and Labour Force: Retrospect and Prospect,' pp. 11-38 in V. Marshall (ed.). *Aging in Canada: Social Perspectives*. 2d ed. Markham, Ont.: Fitzhenry and Whiteside.

Doering, M. et al. (eds.). (1983). *The Aging Worker: Research and Recommendations*. Beverly Hills, Calif.: Sage Publications.

Dowd, J. (1980). *Stratification among the Aged*. Monterey, Calif.: Brooks/Cole Publishing Co.

Ekerdt, D. (1990). 'Retirement Preparation,' pp. 321-56 in P. Lawton (ed.). *Annual Review of Gerontology and Geriatrics*. vol. 9. New York: Springer Publishing Co.

Ekerdt, D. (forthcoming). 'On Defining Persons as Retired,' *Journal of Aging Studies*.

Evans, L. et al. (1985). 'Proximity to Retirement and Anticipatory Involvement: Findings from the Normative Aging Study,' *Journal of Gerontology*, 40(3), 368-74.

Ferraro, K. (1990). 'Cohort Analysis of Retirement Preparation, 1974-1981,' *Journal of Gerontology: Social Sciences*, 45(1), S521-31.

Fethke, C. (1989). 'Life-Cycle Models of Saving and the Effect of the Timing of Divorce on Retirement Economic Well-Being,' *Journal of Gerontology: Social Sciences*, 44(3), S121-28.

Fischer, J. et al. (1979). 'Life Cycle Career Patterns: A Typological Approach to Female Status Attainment,' Technical Bulletin 8, Center for the Study of Aging, University of Alabama.

Foner, A. and K. Schwab. (1981). *Aging and Retirement*. Monterey, Calif.: Brooks/Cole Publishing Co.

Foot, D. (1989). 'Public Expenditures, Population Aging and Economic Dependency in Canada, 1921-2021,' *Population Research and Policy Review*, 8(1), 97-117.

Gee, E. and M. Kimball. (1987). *Women and Aging*. Toronto: Butterworths.

George, L. (1980). *Role Transitions in Later Life*. Monterey, Calif.: Brooks/Cole Publishing Co.

George, L. et al. (1984). ' Sex Differences in the Antecedents and Consequences of Retirement,' *Journal of Gerontology*, 39(3), 364-71.

Graebner, W. (1980). *A History of Retirement: The Meaning and Function of an American Institution, 1885-1978*. New Haven, Conn.: Yale University Press.

Guillemard, A.-M. (ed.). (1983). *Old Age in the Welfare State*. Beverly Hills, Calif.: Sage Publications.

Guppy, N. (1989). 'The Magic of 65: Issues and Evidence in the Mandatory Retirement Debate,' *Canadian Journal on Aging*, 8(2), 173-86.

Habib, J. (1985). 'The Economy and the Aged,' pp. 479-502 in R. Binstock and E. Shanas (eds.). *Handbook of Aging and the Social Sciences*. 2d ed. New York: Van Nostrand Reinhold.

Habib, J. (1990). 'Population Aging and the Economy,' pp. 329-49 in R. Binstock and L. George (eds.). *Handbook of Aging and the Social Sciences*. 3d ed. San Diego, Calif.: Academic Press.

Hanlon, M. (1986). 'Age and Commitment to Work: A Literature Review and Multivariate Analysis,' *Research on Aging*, 8(2), 289-316.

Hendricks, J. and C. McAllister. (1983). 'An Alternative Perspective on Retirement: A Dual Economic Approach,' *Aging and Society*, 3(3), 279-99.

Heslop, L. (1985a). *An Analysis of Expenditure Patterns of the Elderly: Cohorts — Going through Life Together*. Ottawa: Statistics Canada.

Heslop, L. (1985b). *An Analysis of Expenditure Patterns of the Elderly: Expenditure Patterns of Elderly Women*. Ottawa: Statistics Canada.

Hirshorn, B. (1988). 'Organizational Behavior Regarding Older Workers: Prototypical Responses,' *Journal of Aging Studies*, 2(3), 199-215.

Janson, P. and J. Martin. (1982). 'Employment, Retirement and Morale among Older Women,' *Journal of Gerontology*, 31(2), 212-18.

Karp, D. (1987). 'Professionals beyond Midlife: Some Observations on Work Satisfaction in the Fifty-to-Sixty-Year Decade,' *Journal of Aging Studies*, 1(3), 209-24.

Kausler, D. (1990). 'Motivation, Human Aging, and Cognitive Performance,' pp. 172-83 in J. Birren and W. Schaie (eds.). *Handbook of the Psychology of Aging*. 3d ed. San Diego, Calif.: Academic Press.

Keating, N. and P. Cole. (1980). 'What Do I Do with Him 24 Hours a Day? Changes in the Housewife Role After Retirement,' *The Gerontologist*, 20(1), 84-89.

Kimmel, D. et al. (1978). 'Retirement Choice and Retirement Satisfaction,' *Journal of Gerontology*, 33(4), 575-85.

Kohli, M. (1987). 'Retirement and the Moral Economy: An Historical Interpretation of the German Case,' *Journal of Aging Studies*, 1(2), 125-44.

Larson, R. (1978). 'Thirty Years of Research on the Subjective Well-Being of Older Americans,' *Journal of Gerontology*, 33(1), 109-25.

Lindsay, C. and S. Donald. (1988). 'Income of Canada's Seniors,' *Canadian Social Trends*, 10(Autumn), 20-25.

Lumpkin, J. (1984). 'The Effect of Retirement versus Age on the Shopping Orientations of the Older Consumer,' *The Gerontologist*, 24(6), 622-27.

Martin Matthews, A. and K. Brown. (1987). 'Retirement as a Critical Life Event: The Differential Experience of Women and Men,' *Research on Aging*, 9(6), 548-71.

Martin Matthews, A. and J. Tindale. (1987). 'Retirement in Canada,' in K. Markides and C. Cooper (eds.). *Retirement in Industrialized Societies*. Toronto: John Wiley & Sons.

Martin Matthews, A. et al. (1982). 'A Crisis Assessment Technique for the Evaluation of Life Events: Transition to Retirement as a Example,' *Canadian Journal on Aging*, 1(1), 28-39.

McAllister, C. (1981). 'An Alternative Perspective on Retirement Benefits: A Dual Economic Approach,' paper presented at the annual meeting of the Gerontological Society of America, Toronto.

McDaniel, S. (1986). *Canada's Aging Population*. Toronto: Butterworths.

McDonald, L. and R. Wanner. (1982). 'Work Past Age 65 in Canada: A Socioeconomic Analysis,' *Aging and Work*, 5(2), 169-80.

McDonald, L. and R. Wanner. (1984). 'Socioeconomic Determinants of Early Retirement in Canada,' *Canadian Journal on Aging*, 3(3), 105-16.

McDonald, L. and R. Wanner. (1987). 'Retirement in a Dual Economy: The Canadian Case,' pp. 245-61 in V. Marshall (ed.). *Aging in Canada: Social Perspectives*. 2d ed. Markham, Ont.: Fitzhenry and Whiteside.

McDonald, L. and R. Wanner. (1990). *Retirement in Canada*. Markham, Ont.: Butterworths.

McNeely, R. (1988). 'Job Satisfaction Differences among Three Age Groups of Female Human Service Workers,' *Journal of Aging Studies*, 2(2), 109-20.

McPherson, B. (1980). 'Retirement from Professional Sport: The Process and Problems of Occupational and Psychological Adjustment,' *Sociological Symposium*, 30(Spring), 126-43.

McPherson, B. et al. (1989). *The Social Significance of Sport*. Champaign, Ill.: Human Kinetics Publishers.

Méthot, S. (1987). 'Employment Patterns of Elderly Canadians,' *Canadian Social Trends*, 11(Autumn), 7-11.

Miletich, J. (1986). *Retirement: An Annotated Bibliography*. Westport, Conn.: Greenwood Press.

Minkler, M. (1989). 'Gold in Gray: Reflections on Business' Discovery of the Elderly Market,' *The Gerontologist*, 29(1), 17-23.

Minkler, M. and R. Stone. (1985). 'The Feminization of Poverty and Older Women,' *The Gerontologist*, 25(4), 351-57.

Mitchell, O. et al. (1988). 'Retirement Differences by Industry and Occupation,' *The Gerontologist*, 28(4), 545-51.

Myles, J. (1981). 'Income Inequality and Status Maintenance,' *Research on Aging*, 3(2), 123-41.

Myles, J. (1989). *Old Age in the Welfare State: The Political Economy of Public Pensions*. rev. ed. Lawrence, Kans.: University Press of Kansas.

Neysmith, S. (1984). 'Poverty in Old Age: Can Pension Reform Meet the Needs of Women?' *Canadian Woman Studies*, 5, 17-21.

Nishio, H. and H. Lank. (1987). 'Patterns of Labor Participation of Older Female Workers,' pp. 228-44 in V. Marshall (ed.). *Aging in Canada: Social Perspectives*. 2d ed. Markham, Ont.: Fitzhenry and Whiteside.

O'Rand, A. (1988). 'Convergence, Institutionalization, and Bifurcation: Gender and the Pension

Acquisition Process,' pp. 132-55 in G. Maddox and P. Lawton (eds.). *Annual Review of Gerontology and Geriatrics*. vol. 8. New York: Springer Publishing Co.

O'Rand, A. and J. Henretta. (1982). 'Delayed Career Entry, Industrial Pension Structure, and Early Retirement in a Cohort of Unmarried Women,' *American Sociological Review*, 47(3), 365-73.

O'Rand, A. and R. Landerman. (1984). 'Women's and Men's Retirement Income Status,' *Research on Aging*, 6(1), 25-44.

Palmore, E. et al. (1985). *Retirement: Causes and Consequences*. New York: Springer Publishing Co.

Parliament, J. (1989). 'Women Employed outside the Home,' *Canadian Social Trends*, 13(Summer), 2-6.

Powell, B. and J. Martin. (1980). 'Economic Implications of Canada's Aging Society,' pp. 204-14 in V. Marshall (ed.). *Aging in Canada: Social Perspectives*. Don Mills, Ont.: Fitzhenry and Whiteside.

Quinn, J. and R. Burkhauser. (1990). 'Work and Retirement,' pp. 308-27 in R. Binstock and L. George (eds.). *Handbook of Aging and the Social Sciences*. 3d ed. San Diego, Calif.: Academic Press.

Roadburg, A. (1985). *Aging: Retirement, Leisure and Work in Canada*. Toronto: Methuen.

Robinson, P. et al. (1985). 'Work and Retirement,' pp. 503-27 in R. Binstock and E. Shanas (eds.). *Handbook of Aging and the Social Sciences*. 2d ed. New York: Van Nostrand Reinhold.

Schnore, M. (1985). *Retirement: Bane or Blessing?* Waterloo, Ont.: Wilfrid Laurier University Press.

Schulz, J. (1985). *The Economics of Aging*. 3d ed. Belmont, Calif.: Wadsworth Publishing Company.

Schulz, J. (1988). *The Economics of Aging*. 4th ed. Dover, Mass.: Auburn House Publishing Co.

Schulz, J. and J. Myles. (1990). 'Old Age Pensions: A Comparative Perspective,' pp. 398-414 in R. Binstock and L. George (eds.). *Handbook of Aging and the Social Sciences*. 3d ed. San Diego, Calif.: Academic Press.

Semyonov, M. (1980). 'The Social Context of Women's Labor Force Participation: A Comparative Analysis,' *American Journal of Sociology*, 86(3), 534-50.

Seniors Secretariat. (1988). *Canada's Seniors: A Dynamic Force*. Ottawa: Government of Canada.

Seniors Secretariat. (1989). *Women in an Aging Society*. Ottawa: Minister of Supply and Services Canada.

Smeeding, T. (1990). 'Economic Status of the Elderly,' pp. 362-82 in R. Binstock and L. George (eds.). *Handbook of Aging and the Social Sciences*. 3d ed. San Diego, Calif.: Academic Press.

Snell, M. and K. Brown. (1987). 'Financial Strategies of the Recently Retired,' *Canadian Journal on Aging*, 6(4), 290-303.

Spirduso, W. and P. MacRae. (1990). 'Motor Performance and Aging,' pp. 184-200 in J. Birren and W. Schaie (eds.). *Handbook of the Psychology of Aging*. 3d ed. San Diego, Calif.: Academic Press.

Stagner, R. (1985). 'Aging in Industry,' pp. 789-817 in J. Birren and W. Schaie (eds.). *Handbook of the Psychology of Aging*. 2d ed. New York: Van Nostrand Reinhold.

Statistics Canada. (1989). *Canada Year Book, 1990*. Ottawa: Minister of Supply and Services Canada.

Stone, R. (1989). 'The Feminization of Poverty among the Elderly,' *Women's Studies Quarterly*, 17 (1 and 2), 20-34.

Stryckman, J. (1987). 'Work Sharing and the Older Worker in a Unionized Setting,' pp. 193-208 in V. Marshall (ed.). *Aging in Canada: Social Perspectives*. 2d ed. Markham, Ont.: Fitzhenry and Whiteside.

Sussman, M. (1972). 'An Analytic Model for the Sociological Study of Retirement,' pp. 29-73 in F. Carp (ed.). *Retirement*. New York: Human Sciences Press.

Walker, A. (1981). 'Towards a Political Economy of Old Age,' *Aging and Society*, 1(1), 73-94.

Walker, A. (1983). 'Social Policy and Elderly People in Great Britain: The Construction of Dependent Social and Economic Status in Old Age,' pp. 144-67 in A.-M. Guillemard (ed.). *Old Age in the Welfare State*. Beverly Hills, Calif.: Sage Publications.

Wanner, R. and L. McDonald. (1986). 'The Vertical Mosaic in Later Life: Ethnicity and Retirement in Canada,' *Journal of Gerontology*, 41(5), 662-71.

Wigdor, B. (ed.). (1987). *Planning Your Retirement*. Toronto: Grosvenor House Press.

Yolles, S. et al. (1982). *The Aging Employee*. New York: Human Sciences Press.

12
Leisure and Social Participation in the Later Years

Centresphere (Spring, 1989), published by Baycrest Centre for Geriatric Care

INTRODUCTION

With the transition from primitive to industrial to postindustrial societies, dramatic changes have occurred in the quantity, meaning, and form of **leisure** (Dumazedier, 1972). There has been a shift from little personal freedom in lifestyle and little formal leisure time to freedom in selecting a range of lifestyles and the initiation of formal, structured periods of leisure (such as weekends, vacations, or mandatory retirement). As a result, leisure is no longer the exclusive right of the upper class, nor is it viewed as the 'leftovers of life' after work and maintenance responsibilities have been met. Moreover, leisure is no longer restricted to the childhood, adolescent, and postretirement stages of life. Instead, some form of leisure is integrated at all stages in the life cycle into all facets of contemporary lifestyles, including work.

Along with the transition to a modern, postindustrial society there has been a lessening of the value or importance of work, and an increase in the significance of leisure for establishing a personal identity and **quality of life**. Moreover, the relative importance of work, family, and leisure in our daily lives seems to vary at different stages in the life cycle. The way in which time is used for obligatory and discretionary activities represents a conscious decision reflecting the characteristics of individual and societal lifestyles across the life span (Gordon and Gaitz, 1976). According to Kelly et al. (1986), individuals select certain leisure and social activities to fit with their personal identity (how they define themselves) and with their social identity (how they perceive they are defined by others). Kelly et al. (1986) suggest that we develop a 'core' of leisure pursuits that persist throughout the life course as part of our daily social life. These include interaction with family, friends, and work peers; use of the mass media; reading; and walking. Then individuals, to varying degrees, select a 'balance' of activities to fit their personal and social identity. These activities change as roles, self-definitions, occupations, goals, and opportunities change. Thus, modern day leisure and social

participation involve continuities (core activities) and changes (balance activities) according to how we define ourselves and how we wish to be perceived by significant others at specific stages in the life cycle.

Not all people are able to spend their leisure time exactly as they wish; there is often a lack of congruence, for a variety of real or imagined reasons, between actual and desired use of time. This has implications for the degree of life satisfaction and for the quality of life of given individuals. For example, Seleen (1982) found that older adults who were spending their time as they desired were more satisfied with life than those who were not. Similarly, recognizing that the use of time influences the meaning of old age, Ward (1981, 1982) noted that older people need a variety of nonwork opportunities for the creative and expressive use of time.

As a result of the changing values and meanings of work, time, and leisure, it is not surprising that scholars in the social sciences and humanities have demonstrated increasing interest in understanding the phenomenon of leisure in contemporary society. To date, most of this scholarly work has concentrated on a search for the meaning of leisure per se, on defining the characteristics or types of leisure, and on describing the patterns of leisure activities pursued by various strata of the population (for example, males versus females, young versus old, lower-class versus upper-class). Relatively few of these studies have focused on the patterns or meanings of leisure across the life cycle,[1] although interest in the leisure and social patterns of retirees has increased in recent years.[2]

This chapter begins with a brief discussion of the definitions of 'leisure' and examines the relationship between leisure and other social institutions (the family, work, and retirement) at varying stages in the life cycle. In the next two subsections, patterns of involvement by age are described for a variety of leisure experiences, including voluntary associations, politics, religion, the media, and education. Where information is available, the leisure involvement of those beyond 60 or 65 years of age is highlighted.

LEISURE AND AGING: CONCEPTUAL AND METHODOLOGICAL ISSUES

In Search of a Definition of Leisure

From a historical perspective, interest in the study of leisure was initially the domain of philosophers and religious leaders. At varying periods throughout history, the ethics and value of leisure were debated, usually in comparison to work and often in relation to family, church, or state responsibilities. The outcome of these philosophical and religious debates was that leisure in general, or a specific type of leisure activity, was 'judged' as either appropriate or inappropriate, good or evil, productive or nonproductive, constructive or destructive, recreative or dissipative. As a result, the opportunity to engage in leisure, or in certain types of leisure, was seldom a personal decision or a matter of right. Rather, the role of leisure in individual lifestyles was determined by religious and societal leaders, some of whom issued proclamations labeling leisure as a stigmatized form of social behavior to be avoided.

With the rise of industrialization and the accompanying social, political, and economic changes, leisure continued to be defined in relation to work. However, the onset of shorter work weeks, formal vacation periods, mandatory retirement, and voluntary early retirement led to an increase in discretionary free time, and leisure became an acceptable, worthwhile, and necessary facet of contemporary lifestyles. The individual acquired the freedom to choose how, when, and where he or she would make use of increased discretionary time and income. Leisure time became more available, more socially acceptable, and more institutionalized, and scholars sought to define and measure the meaning, characteristics, and patterns of leisure in general and for particular subgroups in society.[3]

Not surprisingly, a universally accepted definition of 'leisure' has so far been unattainable, partly because needs and experiences concerning work and leisure are extremely personal and heterogeneous. Moreover, many of the definitions have been related to the meaning of work,[4] which also has acquired a multitude of definitions within and between occupations and at various stages in the life cycle.[5] Difficulties in arriving at a comprehensive definition have persisted because leisure is a multidimensional concept,[6] because activities may have a variety of meanings or functions for an individual at different times,[7] and because individuals can engage in more than one leisure activity at a time.[8] Furthermore, some leisure activities fall into overlapping categories,[9] and the concept of 'leisure' is used at both the individual and societal levels of analysis. Finally, and perhaps most important, there is a lack of research to validate or refute the various hypothesized definitions of the concept, largely because few reliable measures of these dimensions have been derived.[10]

The meaning of leisure, as a form of social participation for a given individual or social group, is also influenced by cultural and subcultural norms, values, experiences, and opportunity sets. These cultural parameters are unique to individuals or groups differentiated by age, gender, race, education, ethnicity, socioeconomic status, religion, or place of residence. More specifically, the form of leisure that is selected by a given individual is influenced by a variety of factors, such as health, climate, access to transportation, and quality of the neighborhood.

Despite the many problems outlined above, numerous definitions of leisure have been set forth. The following list indicates that leisure is a multidimensional concept that includes or represents:

- A social context for initiating and developing primary social relationships
- A state of mind, attitude or being
- Nonwork
- Freedom of choice in selecting activities
- Free or discretionary time
- Relaxation and diversion from work and personal maintenance activities
- Playfulness or play
- Voluntary activity
- Expressive activities (internal satisfaction, or an emphasis on the process rather than the end product)

- Instrumental activities (external rewards, with an end product as the goal)
- Spontaneity
- Utilitarian and meaningful activities
- Active and passive activities
- Social (group) and individual (solitary) activities
- Expensive and inexpensive pursuits
- Intellectual (cognitive), social, and physical pursuits
- Intrinsic and extrinsic rewards
- Creativity
- High culture and mass culture

Although many of these characteristics are often viewed as dichotomous scales (that is, either/or), in reality they represent continua.[11] That is, individuals may change their position on a particular scale with age, with transitions in work or family, with the time of year, when moving to a new neighborhood or region, or with changes in cultural or subcultural values or norms. Moreover, the dimensions are not discrete entities; many of the scales intersect, so that there are many permutations and combinations of types and meanings of leisure involvement. For example, the same individual may participate equally in a structured, expressive, physical activity (such as a dance class), and in an unstructured, instrumental, passive activity (the acquisition of a complete set of stamps for a specific country). Similarly, as Csikszentmihalyi (1981) argues, no event is ever entirely instrumental, even work. He suggests that individuals search for pleasure and expressive experiences, 'flow' experiences, within their instrumental roles (for example, in work or parenthood).

So that the quality and the quantity of research and policymaking on leisure in the later years can be furthered, it is essential that the older individual per se not be neglected in either the research or policymaking process. For too many years, younger adults have been imposing the research and policy agenda on a passive, uninformed, elderly clientele. This 'shuffleboard' syndrome, adopted by young and often naive programmers, assumes that seniors want to, need to, and enjoy playing shuffleboard (or similar passive activities).

Because this is a major activity provided in some settings, some seniors have passively accepted the option and 'played the game' – the outcome is a self-fulfilling prophecy whereby the image of the passive, mildly active senior is further perpetuated. This scenario is then often repeated in other communities or settings. Today, many older adults are no longer passively accepting the status quo in many domains, including leisure. Older adults, individually and collectively (for example, local and national seniors' organizations), are more vocal and demanding. Creative, sensitive, and wise researchers and policymakers are asking older persons to articulate their needs, preferences, and desires, and are including seniors as part of the research or decision-making team. There is, in fact, some evidence that more valid and reliable quantitative and qualitative data can be obtained if interviews and participant observation studies are conducted by seniors. Similarly, most innovative programs and policies have benefited from the input of seniors serving as members of an advisory board.

Finally, a distinction is seldom drawn between the quantity and the quality of leisure, either as a whole or with respect to a particular dimension. Research studies have generally been more concerned with the number or variety of leisure activities available to or pursued by an individual or group; the quality of the experience has seldom been assessed. However, increasing attention is being paid to the meaning and the quality of the leisure experience, regardless of the amount of leisure time available or the number of activities pursued. Moreover, the meaning of a given activity may change at different points in the life cycle. For example, in early adulthood, hiking may be viewed as primarily a physical activity (how fast can one hike up and down a mountain trail). By middle adulthood hiking may be viewed as a means to escape the stress of the urban environment or boredom with one's job. Later in life, hiking up a mountain at a leisurely pace may be viewed primarily as a setting within which to pursue a hobby such as photography. Thus, both personally, and as scholars and practitioners, we must pay more attention to the meaning people assign to leisure in general, and to specific leisure activities at dif-

HIGHLIGHT 12.1

SHUFFLING: A CENTRAL LIFE INTEREST FOR SOME OLDER ADULTS

Most older adults engage in a variety of leisure activities that stimulate social interaction with a variety of friends and acquaintances. For some, however, the pursuit of a single activity becomes a passion and the primary focus of their social world. In this world they share communication, meanings, and social events with others who likewise devote an inordinate amount of time to the one activity. Shuffleboard is an organized leisure activity that attracts considerable interest and participation from retirees, particularly by those who have been likely to join clubs or organizations throughout their life. Snyder (1986) reports that there are over sixty thousand registered members of 430 shuffleboard clubs in Florida, and that similar organizations exist elsewhere in North America, although they tend to have fewer members. In addition, there is an International Shuffleboard Association, which organizes and sanctions tournaments. Most of the registered members of these clubs are competitive as opposed to casual players.

The level of involvement in shuffleboard varies greatly. Some members play only periodically for fun and relaxation, while for others 'shuffling,' as they call it, is a competitive experience that becomes a central part of their daily lives. To arrive at an understanding of the intensity and the meaning of involvement in this expressive leisure activity, Snyder (1986), over a period of three years, attended a number of shuffleboard tournaments and engaged in both participant observation, informal discussions, and formal interviews with competitors, their spouses, and spectators. Not surprisingly, given the propensity of men to compete in sport events, the majority of the tournament participants were men (60 percent), and many competed year round — in the south during the winter (snowbirds), and in the north during the summer.

Interest in the activity is aroused because courts and other players are available, often in 'retirement' settings. At first the involvement is infrequent and casual, but as the skill level increases, and as the strategy of the game becomes more intriguing, the intensity increases. Indeed, Snyder found that 'hooked' shufflers give up other lifelong leisure activities, including golf, to pursue excellence in this newly discovered leisure activity. This pursuit may involve several hours of play per day and competition in several tournaments a week, including some in other cities. As the frequency of involvement increases, friendships, conversations, and lifestyles increasingly revolve around 'the' game, and usually involve couples. As the skill level and success in tournaments increases, players move up in the regional and national rankings. Ultimately they may be ranked as a 'professional' or 'master' and thereby become eligible to receive prize money for success in tournament play. This ranking system establishes a social identity and status for the players, both within the social world of 'shuffling,' and in the residential community. That is, individuals are viewed differently by others in the retirement setting once they have achieved a ranking, and as their ranking improves.

Once a shuffler is hooked, his or her involvement in the world of competitive shuffleboard continues until health reasons prevent travel or tournament participation. Indeed, Snyder reports that participation continues following the death of a spouse, with many tournaments reporting participants in their 90s. This later-life expressive activity, despite the stereotypical image that it is a passive game or pastime for 'old folks,' attracts a large number of serious participants. Many of the more competitive players report that 'shuffling' is their central life interest because it provides meaningful social interaction with other devotees, a physical and mental challenge, a sense of achievement, an identity, and a focused meaning for life in the retirement years.

SOURCE: Adapted from Snyder (1986).

---

ferent stages in the life cycle. In short, meaningless or unsatisfying free-time activities may not constitute true leisure, and may fail to meet the leisure needs of the individual. Despite the earlier comments about shuffleboard as a stereotypical activity for older adults, this activity, if pursued seriously, can become a 'central life interest' (highlight 12.1).

Leisure, like life, cannot be categorized into discrete entities. For some people, the importance of work is declining, the time spent on household and other routine chores is decreasing, and a greater concern with using leisure time productively and meaningfully is emerging. These developments have combined to increase the amount of discretionary time available and to enhance the relative importance of leisure for the quality of life at all stages in the life cycle. Nevertheless, despite individual and societal shifts in values, the quantity and quality of leisure are still dependent on the nature of the work situation. The next subsection presents a brief review of the literature pertaining to the relationship between work and leisure.

The Relationship Between Work and Leisure

Introduction

Upon the completion of formal schooling and entry into the labor force, the type and frequency of leisure changes. This change results from a limited availability of free time; a new lifestyle because of the nature and demands of the job, and, for most, because of marriage, home-ownership, and child-rearing responsibilities. These demands and responsibilities usually change as one passes through the stages of the work and family career, and the meaning, form, and frequency of leisure may also change. However, most evidence indicates that while the amount of free time may increase or decrease at varying stages, the types of leisure pursuits are relatively constant, once patterns are established in the early and middle years of adulthood.

The development of a leisure lifestyle in early adulthood is thought to be highly influenced by the type of occupation and by the role requirements of a specific job. The initial attempts to explain leisure involvement during adulthood focused on the relationship between class background and the type and number of leisure pursuits. For example, a number of studies, controlling for occupation, found that those employed in high-prestige occupations engaged in different leisure activities at different rates from those in low-prestige occupations (McPherson, 1983:411). These studies were based on the assumption that norms and values unique to a particular class are acquired through socialization, so that individuals adopt certain leisure activities and exclude others.

Some researchers have posited a more direct link between work and leisure, arguing that the two spheres are not really separate from each other. In Wilensky's (1960:545) words, 'a man's work routine places a hand on his routine of leisure.' A large body of literature has appeared since the 1960s that focuses on particular forms and types of leisure involvement.[12] For example, Gerstl (1961) and Jordan (1963) argued that while social class was important in determining leisure behavior, the specific nature of an occupation (for example, salesman versus teacher) may demand different leisure lifestyles. Even though occupations may fall within the same general social class, the leisure patterns related to those occupations may vary. They found that people within common occupational groupings demonstrated differences in the pattern of normal leisure pursuits. They concluded that the crucial explanatory factor linking occupation and leisure is the occupational milieu, including such factors as the nature of the work setting and the norms derived from the occupational reference groups.

More specifically, it has been suggested that the relationship between work and leisure is the result of work contacts and work experiences, the degree of physical and mental involvement in one's occupational role, and the degree to which the work role is person-oriented rather than concept- or thing-oriented (Bishop and Ikeda, 1970). Furthermore, the leisure pattern is influenced by the technical and social constraints of a job (Meissner, 1971), and by the degree of involvement in the decision-making process at work (Hagedorn and Labovitz, 1968a, 1968b). In short, the nature of the work and the amount of power and involvement associated with the job, rather than its prestige, determine the form and frequency of leisure involvement. In order to explain this observed relationship between work and leisure, three general hypotheses have been proposed and tested in a variety of settings. These are outlined in the following subsection.

Work-Leisure Hypotheses

A basic tenet of the Protestant work ethic is that work is an essential and valued life interest. As such, it influences other domains of social life so that adult lifestyles are largely determined by the type of occupation and by the demands of the job. Not surprisingly, work has been defined as the independent variable that is hypothesized to determine the amount of time and energy available for leisure, as well as the appropriate types of leisure pursuits.

The feedback between the domains of work and leisure has seldom been tested, even though the degree of importance attached to leisure may have a significant effect on work. For example, if a particular leisure lifestyle becomes highly salient for an individual, he or she may refuse to accept a promotion that involves a move to a new community or region; or may search for a job in a region where the salient leisure lifestyle can be pursued (for example, a community with easy access to skiing). The individual might seek a change in career in order to pursue leisure interests, or perhaps decide not to work at all. Finally, little attention has been directed to the possibility that there is leisure in work (expressive needs are met in instrumental tasks); that work may be a major source of leisure and pleasure for some individuals; or that the relative influence and value of the two domains may vary by age, gender, ethnicity, career stage, or employment history.[13]

Arguing from the premise that work rather than leisure is the central life interest (Dubin, 1956), those who adhere to a holistic perspective maintain that work and leisure are integrated, congruent, or fused aspects of the lifestyle, that there is no distinction between work and leisure in meaning or form, and that each facet affects the other. According to this 'congruence' or **spillover hypothesis**, the types of leisure activities selected by an individual represent a 'spillover' from the job. For example, those employed in intellectually rigorous occupations with a substantial decision-making component are likely to engage in serious reading, to attend high-cultural events, to play 'intellectual' games, and to participate in fewer physical activities during their leisure time. People in this category are also, as Stone (1955:93) suggested, likely to 'work at our play and play at our work.' That is, leisure is used for self-development (Parker, 1972), and there may

be little perceived difference between work and leisure.

In contrast, those who argue from the segmentalist perspective believe that work and leisure represent opposite extremes of a bipolar scale. Lifestyles are composed of two distinct and separate entities, work and leisure. Some degree of leisure is seen as being necessary for recuperation and relaxation from work. Thus, the 'contrast' or **compensatory hypothesis** proposes that leisure activities are deliberately chosen because they are unlike work activities. Moreover, some proponents of this view regard the job as, at best, a necessary evil.[14]

The compensatory hypothesis suggests that individuals seek in their leisure what is lacking in their jobs. For example, a desk-bound executive might choose leisure activities involving physical labor (gardening) or physical activity (squash), while the laborer might prefer to engage in decision making (as a little-league coach), intellectual (self-study), or artistic activities.

To date, the research evidence is more supportive of the spillover hypothesis. However, there are subgroup variations. For example, the spillover relationship does not appear to be supported for physically demanding jobs, especially where workers have low levels of education. Moreover, some studies support the compensatory hypothesis, and other studies do not support either hypothesis. Similarly, there are case studies showing that individuals with noncreative jobs engage in creative leisure, while others show that those with highly creative jobs report that their leisure lacks meaning and satisfaction. Thus, a definitive and complete explanation for the hypothesized relationship between work and leisure is not yet available.

The lack of a definitive explanation has led to a third hypothesis, namely the **neutrality hypothesis**. Proponents of this more recent view argue that there is little attachment to work, and that there may or may not be a linkage and overlap between work and leisure. Leisure activities are usually different from work activities, but not intentionally so (as in the 'compensatory' process). That is, there is a detachment from work, and work style has little bearing on leisure pursuits. Moreover, there tends to be a slightly greater interest in leisure than in work by individuals who adhere to this philosophy of work and leisure.

Perhaps a major reason for this inability to provide an adequate explanation of the hypothesized relationship between work and leisure has been the failure of scholars to recognize that the question is not as simple as originally stated. That is, the adoption of a particular work or leisure style may be influenced not by work-related factors, but rather by a number of personal and social situational factors such as personality, family status, previous leisure experiences, economic status, career stage, place of residence, or reference group norms.

Since job and family responsibilities and goals change with age, the relationship between work and leisure may vary by age. For example, Kelly (1976) suggested that with the departure of children from the home, and the establishment and plateauing of the career, there is a change in the relative meaning and value attached to work and leisure. He found that with increasing age there was a greater chance of leisure being viewed as compensatory. Similarly, Ward (1982) indicated that the compensatory pattern may become more salient as the value and meaning of work change. However, possible cohort or period effects also need to be considered, and caution must be exercised when interpreting the presence of a compensatory pattern until longitudinal or cohort analysis studies are completed.

Another confusing factor in the interpretation of the work-leisure relationship is the tendency to examine the relationship on an individual rather than a societal level of analysis. In reality, there is an interaction between the two levels that must be considered. For example, where societal norms hold that leisure is an extension of work (the spillover effect), it is more difficult for an individual to adopt a segregated (compensatory) lifestyle. Before a definitive explanation can be provided at the individual level, a thorough analysis of societal values, beliefs, and norms concerning work and leisure is required.

Finally, from another perspective, the onset of retirement means the end of the work-leisure relationship. Yet, leisure patterns persist and do not appear to be greatly altered by retirement. For example, Roadburg (1985) found that in the absence of work, leisure is perceived more in terms of pleasure than in terms of freedom, and that those who retire voluntarily see leisure in terms of the enjoyment it can provide. This indirect evidence suggests that the meaning of leisure is somewhat related to work, and that in the absence of work the meaning of leisure may be altered, although the type of leisure activities may change relatively little.

In summary, two major alternative explanations have been proposed for the relationship between work and leisure. Both argue that type or style of work influences the adoption of particular leisure lifestyles. While much of the evidence suggests that the spillover hypothesis is a valid explanation, longitudinal studies to investigate possible changes with age have yet to be undertaken. Similarly, studies seldom control for the personal or societal characteristics that might influence the relationship between work and leisure. Therefore, while it is generally agreed that work and leisure interact to influence lifestyle, there is as yet no definitive explanation of why or how this linkage occurs. Thus, we need to consider another factor in the leisure equation, namely, the meaning and the use of time.

The Meaning and the Use of Time

Time is a rare commodity, yet it is a central element in contemporary lifestyles that can influence whether and when an event will occur; the duration and sequence of events; and to what extent, when, and how we play a variety of social roles. Over a twenty-four hour period our daily life is generally structured into three domains: leisure activities, obligatory activities, and social activities (Altergott, 1988b). How much time is allocated to each domain is influenced by individual values and preferences, personal characteristics, the social roles we must or desire to play, and the social and economic opportunities and barriers present in our particular social world. Thus, at certain stages in life we may perceive and use time in different ways; and we may have more or less discretionary time at some stages than at others (Harvey and Singleton, 1989; Cutler and Hendricks, 1990).

With retirement, our daily life is restructured so that there is more emphasis on leisure and less on obligatory activities. For example, Zuzanek and Box (1988) suggest that with the onset of retirement an individual gains approximately thirty-eight extra hours of disposable time per week. But, contrary to conventional wisdom, the problem of retirement may not be the 'amount' of free time per se, but rather the inability to make decisions concerning how to use this free time. As Zuzanek and Box (1988:179) state, 'Having more free time does not automatically translate into greater happiness. Being able to fill this time with activities and to structure it in a meaningful and diversified way does! Acquiring a satisfying lifestyle in retirement presupposes an ability to structure one's time.'

Time is a cultural product that may or may not be viewed as a scarce resource at specific moments or stages in life. To varying degrees, modern social life is structured and regulated by clock and calendar rules and constraints that provide some degree of order, routine, and structure to our daily, weekly, monthly, and yearly lives. But these meanings can change as cultural beliefs and values change. For example, the traditional temporal clock for women of marriage, child-rearing, and midlife entry into the labor force has been altered significantly in recent years. Similarly, mourning time has changed from what Emily Post considered a 'proper' period of about three years in the 1920s, to the more contemporary view of Amy Vanderbilt that a bereaved widow should return to a normal life within a week or so.

Time is perceived in different ways by different individuals and at different stages in life (Kastenbaum, 1982; Schroots and Birren, 1990). Despite the supposed increase in discretionary time due to a shorter work week, some people perceive that they never have enough time. Indeed, some individuals hire people to do their shopping; others compress leisure, personal care, and work activities into one activity. For example, we conduct business at lunch or breakfast; while driving a car, we shave, telephone or dictate a letter; or while watching television, we read the daily newspaper, work at our computer, iron, or talk on the telephone. We are forced to compress time because of the increased demands of an information society, because of the need to 'moonlight' at a second job, because of the commuting time required by suburban or rural living, and because of dual career families, to name only a few reasons.

Time is a nonrenewable resource that once used or wasted cannot be replaced. Thus, how time is used and the proportion of time that is allocated to a specific domain becomes an important lifestyle decision that merits both personal reflection and scholarly inquiry (McPherson, 1985). On the basis of time-budget studies (Altergott, 1988a) we know that women have less discretionary time than men; that members of the lower class, compared to the middle and upper class, are less future-oriented, less punctual, and adhere less rigidly to time schedules; that there are generational differences within the same ethnic group in the allocation of time to various activities (Ujimoto, 1988); and that those with smaller social networks (for example, those who are single, widowed, divorced, retired, childless) may have more discretionary time. Moreover, the nature of a leisure activity can influence how, when, and if time is allocated to the activity. For example, if a partner, a specific facility, or a specific time period is required, scheduling difficulties and loss of freedom in scheduling discretionary time may inhibit or prevent a leisure event. Consider the ease of watching television or working on a hobby at home compared to reserving a tennis court for a noon-hour game on a specific day, and then recruiting three other players of comparable ability who will show up at the designated time and place.

In the later years time can be perceived to pass fast or slow. For example, some would argue that if time is abused, or if an individual is unable to use discretionary time in a meaningful way, time drags and boredom results. Boredom is a self-induced state that can occur when there is an excess of discretionary time or an inability to manage time. In fact, boredom has been cited as one of the reasons for an increase in such unnecessary crimes as shoplifting by seniors. For others, time flies. It may be that these individuals do not have more real time than others, but rather that they are more socially involved and have complete daily or weekly calendars.

In order to understand the meaning and the use of time in the later years, time-budget studies have indicated the relative proportion of time allocated to specific activities by older adults (Larson et al., 1985; McPherson, 1985; Altergott, 1988a; Ujimoto, 1988; Zuzanek and Box, 1988; Harvey and Singleton, 1989; Cutler and Hendricks, 1990). Some of the more interesting patterns that evolve include: on average, between eighteen and twenty hours per week of television consumption; men devoting more time to the mass media and women to social events; and older men reporting more leisure time than older women. Highlight 12.2 describes the quantity and the quality of time spent alone or in solitude in the daily lives of older adults.

In summary, the meaning and the use of time can change as we move across the life course because of social status and role-transition processes related to employment status, marital status, ethnic group membership, age-related norms, and family dynamics. Both researchers and practitioners need to understand these temporal factors with respect to how they influence life chances, lifestyles, and coping or adapting strategies in the middle and later years. We need to understand the possible variations in the use and the meaning of time by age cohort, gender, class, and region. With this understanding, more viable policies and programs can be designed to enhance the quality of life for all middle-aged and older adults.

HIGHLIGHT 12.2

THE QUANTITY AND THE QUALITY OF TIME ALONE IN THE LATER YEARS

In the daily lives of older adults, decisions are made about whether to spend time with others in 'social' activities, or by themselves in 'solitary' activities. How older people divide their time between being alone and being with people is not well understood, and numerous questions remain: Is a pattern of sociability, once established early in life, continued in later life? As one ages, is solitude selected and preferred, or is it a form of involuntary behavior? When we choose to engage in social activities, is it the quality or the quantity of interaction that is most important or meaningful?

To address some of these questions, Larson and his colleagues (1985) asked ninety-two retirees (forty men, fifty-two women) to carry electronic pagers for one week. At random times between 8:00 a.m. and 10:00 p.m. the retirees were 'beeped,' at which time they recorded who they were with, if anyone, what activity they were engaged in, and their subjective mood state at the time. A total of 3,412 self-reports were recorded for the week. The average amount of time spent alone was 48 percent, with the range being from 5 to 97 percent. The time spent with others included an average of 28 percent with the spouse, 7 percent with children, 9 percent with friends or neighbors, and 8 percent with others such as casual acquaintances, sales personnel, health or social care workers. Thus, far more time was spent alone than with any single companion, including the spouse. Not surprisingly, those who were unmarried and those who lived alone spent more time by themselves (73 percent); those who were married spent the least amount of time alone (40 percent). More respondents (60 to 80 percent) reported being alone in the morning. The percentage of time alone decreased as the day progressed for all but the 'unmarried' and 'living alone' respondents, who reported an increase in solitude from the afternoon to the evening period.

In terms of reported feelings at the time when they were alone, solitude was not perceived to be a time of unhappiness or loneliness. Rather, it was perceived as a positive opportunity for 'focused thought and absorption,' and was not evaluated as a negative experience. However, for respondents who were unmarried and for those living alone, the evenings spent in solitude were considered to be difficult times. The authors concluded that community programs based on the assumption that all older adults need to be socially active throughout the day and evening may not be as successful as desired.

SOURCE: Adapted from Larson et al. (1985).

LEISURE AND AGING: THE EARLY AND MIDDLE YEARS

The type of activities pursued during leisure time and the meaning and function of these activities often vary from one stage in the life cycle to the next. Since leisure involves the utilization of discretionary time and income, the leisure lifestyle of an individual or a cohort depends on the financial and social constraints accompanying specific stages in life. The varying demands and responsibilities of family, school, and work influence the amount of time available, and personal characteristics such as gender, ethnicity, marital status, class, education, place of residence, and health status influence the selection and meaning of specific activities.

A large number of descriptive studies have identified the leisure interests or activities of individuals at a particular stage in life, or at a particular chronological age. Although some inferences and general patterns across the life cycle can be derived from these cross-sectional studies, longitudinal studies are lacking, and patterns observed across the life cycle may reflect aging, cohort, or period effects. In fact, some leisure pursuits (such as specific dances, skateboarding) are fads that influence one age cohort but not others (a period effect).

The adoption of a specific type of activity at one stage in life may significantly influence leisure involvement throughout the life cycle. For example, dancing was a craze in the 1920s; for many who were in late adolescence or early adulthood at that time, dancing is still a major leisure interest that has special meaning for many members of that generation. Similarly, those who were preadolescents, adolescents, and young adults in the 1980s were exposed to the 'fitness boom,' and many adopted some form of physical activity as part of their lifestyle. These cohorts may demonstrate relatively higher levels of physical activity involvement than earlier or later cohorts at all subsequent stages in the life cycle. Or, it may be that this emphasis will persist for only a few years, and the pattern of involvement will reflect that of earlier cohorts at the same stage in life (a maturation effect).

Although it is not possible to identify a single leisure pattern across the life cycle, or to indicate a definitive pattern for a specific activity, some general findings based on conceptual and empirical studies from a life-cycle perspective can be described.[15] Figure 12.1 illustrates a variety of possible patterns of leisure involvement across the life cycle. The curves represent hypothetical patterns of life-cycle involvement in such activities as sport (A), visiting (B), political participation through active membership in a political party (C), reading for pleasure (D), travel or solitary activities (E), or home-centered activities (F). In reality, leisure involvement is not as orderly as these smooth curves suggest. There may be minor or major peaks and valleys at various stages in the life cycle because of institutional (family, school, or work) or cultural constraints.[16] Moreover, for a given activity (such as reading), all six patterns in figure 12.1 may apply to six different individuals or six different cohorts.

Despite these complex individual differences, there are some general and relatively predictable leisure patterns at different stages in the life course. These patterns are determined by transitions within the family or work careers that require a continuous process of adaptation. During childhood and early adolescence, a variety of leisure experiences are pursued in the family or school settings. Many of these are encouraged by parents, peers, and teachers, and most are voluntarily selected by the individual. During middle and late adolescence, the influence of the family decreases, and the peer group, the media, and the youth culture become more influential in determining lifestyles (particularly for fads and fashions). In addition, the individual may enter the labor force on a part-time basis, thereby experiencing a reduction in discretionary time and an increase in discretionary income. Social and occupational constraints begin to affect decision making concerning the type, meaning, and function of leisure experiences.

The next major transition occurs at the time of leaving school and entering the labor force. This stage may also be accompanied by marriage, home ownership, and the birth of a child. Moreover, this stage in life may involve a move to a new region of the country. This move, in turn, may influence both the frequency and the

FIGURE **12.1**

HYPOTHETICAL PATTERNS OF LEISURE INVOLVEMENT ACROSS THE LIFE CYCLE

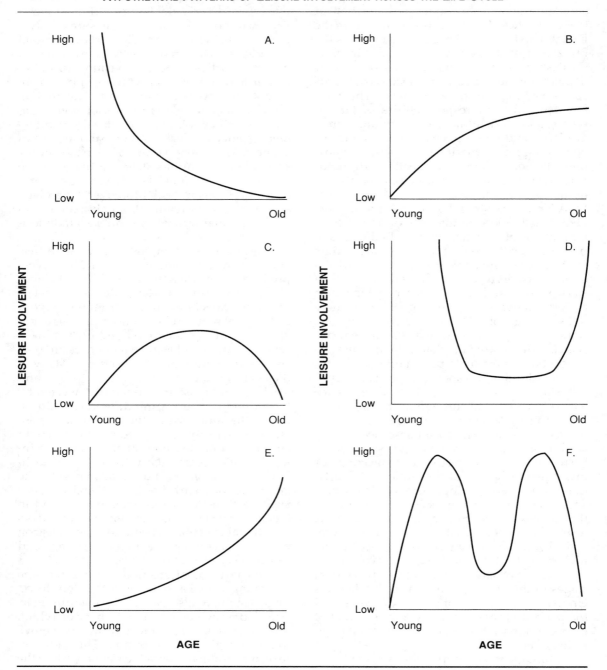

type of leisure involvement, since recent national studies have consistently shown that the farther west the respondent's place of residence, the more likely he or she is to report higher levels of leisure involvement, especially in physical activities (Dudycha et al., 1983; the Miller Lite Report, 1983; Curtis and McPherson, 1987). The commitment of time to establishing a career and family may dramatically restrict or change leisure patterns during the early years of adulthood. As a result, leisure activities tend to be home- and family-centered, and are often less important in the overall hierarchy of values for a given individual or age cohort.

By middle age, one's employment status is usually well established, the children are leaving home, more time and money are available, and leisure may become more salient in the lifestyle. However, this may also be the stage at which women enter or reenter the labor force, thereby reducing the time available for leisure. Or it may be a time of divorce or the onset of a chronic illness, which can dramatically change the type or amount of leisure. During the middle years, a couple may develop or pursue individual interests, and may compress leisure time spent together into weekends and vacation periods. Generally, the pattern established by the middle years continues into the preretirement stage, and often into the postretirement stage.[17] Because of this pattern of continuity, it is important to be aware of patterns of leisure behavior during the middle years in order to better understand the use of time in the postretirement years.

In summary, it appears that many patterns of leisure involvement are possible in the early and middle years of adulthood. Individual differences in these patterns are related to class[18] and type of occupation, [19] to regional differences in opportunity and values; to variations in the family life course; and to cultural variation by gender, race, and ethnicity. Moreover, societal changes in ethics, values, and norms affect the amount, meaning, and function of leisure over time. In short, the meaning and availability of leisure may change across the life cycle in response to personal needs, interests, and abilities; to institutional (work and family) demands; and to cultural change. For this rea-

son chronological age is a weak predictor of leisure behavior. For example, a 24-year-old male may be attending university or be employed full time; he may be a member of the upper or lower socioeconomic strata; and he may be married or not married, with or without children. Similarly, the leisure patterns of 45-year-old women may vary by class, marital status, or employment status. Thus, when attempting to identify and explain leisure patterns in the early and middle years of the life cycle, a variety of personal, social, cultural, and environmental factors must be considered.

In the next section, leisure in the later years is discussed. It will be seen that the meaning of leisure may change if family and occupational constraints are reduced or eliminated. However, class, gender, ethnicity, race, education, and previous lifestyles still influence the leisure patterns displayed by older individuals and cohorts.

LEISURE AND AGING: THE POSTRETIREMENT YEARS

Introduction: A General Pattern

With the onset of partial or complete retirement, the amount of unstructured free time increases dramatically. This time can be filled by continuing some form of work, by expanding the time used to complete daily personal tasks, or by leisure activities. While it has often been suggested that the leisure role is the major role in the retirement years, relatively few people adopt new patterns or pursuits after retirement, or increase the number or frequency of activities. Most studies indicate that there is continuity between the work and retirement leisure styles, although the number of activities and the frequency of involvement decrease at various rates with age.[20]

During later life there are a number of potential individual and societal constraints that may limit or inhibit participation in leisure activities (Buchanan and Allen, 1985; McGuire, 1985; McGuire et al., 1986). At the individual level, restrictions on the type, location, or range of activities may occur because of such factors as declining health and energy; loss of interest in some activities; lack of a partner due to widowhood or divorce; declining economic resources and a loss of discretionary income; the changing leisure interests or health of a spouse; or an inability to drive or to use public transportation. At the societal level, constraints are imposed on the older adults because information about leisure opportunities is not disseminated, or not effectively disseminated; local or regional norms or cultural values discourage the involvement of older adults in certain types of activities (for example, formal education, sport, drama); there is a lack of opportunity in the absence of facilities and programs (senior-citizen centers), especially in rural and inner-city areas; public transportation is unavailable; inflation makes some leisure pursuits too expensive for those on a fixed income; a deteriorating and unsafe neighborhood induces a fear of being victimized if older adults leave the home; and myths or negative stereotypes prevail concerning the supposed interest (or lack of) and abilities of older adults (for example, to study and learn, to become physically fit).

All of these individual and societal barriers are unnecessary and can be reduced or eliminated by the dissemination of valid scientifically based information to both policymakers and the general population, and by the initiation of a full-scale program of leisure opportunities for all seniors in every community. This reduction of barriers is especially important for those older adults living in rural and inner city environments, for those with health problems, for those who are economically disadvantaged, and for those from different cultural backgrounds.

It must be recognized, as well, that leisure opportunities and the degree and type of involvement can be enhanced in the later years by role transitions and changes in environment. Both retirement and widowhood have the potential to free the individual from previous constraints so that new leisure avenues can be explored. Thus, retirement creates time to travel or pursue a hobby; widowhood may enable an individual to pursue an interest (such as travel, volunteer work) that was not possible because of a dominating spouse with other interests, needs, or demands. Similarly, moving to an age-segregated apartment or to a retirement community, or migrating for the winter to a warmer climate where there is a large population of older people, may permanently or temporarily increase the leisure activity levels of the elderly (Morgan and Godbey, 1978). Furthermore, while institutionalization may deprive the elderly person of lifelong leisure experiences, the change may lead to an increase in both the quantity or the quality of leisure, depending on the resources of the institution.

As a result of these confounding factors, the leisure patterns of the elderly are quite diverse. Moreover, they vary in frequency and type for the younger and older segments of the retired cohort, by class, by gender, by region, by actual or perceived level of crime in the neighborhood (Godbey et al., 1980), by type of housing environment (Moss and Lawton, 1982), by education, by place of residence (Gunter, 1979; Strain and Chappell, 1982), and by racial or ethnic group.

The leisure activities most frequently reported by those over 65 years of age are socializing with friends and relatives, watching television, gardening, reading newspapers, and sitting and thinking. Most activities take place indoors and are home-based rather than community-based. Many elderly people, especially the very old, are involved in solitary rather than group activities. For example, Moss and Lawton (1982) found that among lower-middle-class urban dwellers who live in their own homes, 64 percent of the day was spent alone, 75 percent of the day was spent inside the home, and 34 percent of the day was spent on obligatory personal or household activities. This finding coincides with the perception of retirees that there is an increase in their solitary activities after retirement (Bosse and Ekerdt, 1981; Larson et al., 1985).

Regardless of the particular leisure activities pursued by specific individuals or cohorts, leisure in the later years should be viewed as a multidimensional set of activities, relationships, contexts, and commitments (Kelly, 1987). As a result, leisure involvement can provide a way to initiate, develop, and expand social relationships, and to demonstrate to oneself and to others that one is a competent individual with a unique self-identity and a sense of self-worth. In order to understand more fully the meaning and the use of leisure in later life, we need to go beyond collecting an inventory of activities pursued. In the following discussion, the focus is on the *quality* of leisure experiences, and on the quality and the quantity of leisure experiences for overall life satisfaction and a higher quality of life.

Most research has focused on the quantity of the retiree's leisure activities rather than on the quality or the meaning of the leisure experience. It is important to examine not only the number and the frequency of leisure experiences, but also their meaning and quality. For example, rather than determining how many hours per day an individual spends watching television, a researcher should discover what programs are watched; with whom, if anyone, the programs are watched; and what function the programs serve. Similarly, it is more interesting and useful to note changes in meaning over time rather than whether a decrease or increase has occurred. For example, it was shown earlier in this chapter that hiking can have different meanings and serve different needs at different stages in life.

In addition to the need to assess the quality of the leisure experiences in the later years, there is also a need to examine the influence of the quantity and the quality of leisure on other facets of life. As an outcome of research to describe and explain life satisfaction, happiness, psychological well-being, or the quality of life in the later years (Larson, 1978; Lawton et al., 1984; Okun et al., 1984; Larson et al., 1986; Altergott, 1988a), scholars have studied the contribution of leisure to these larger outcome measures (Riddick and Daniel, 1984; Larson et al., 1985; Lawton, 1985; Romsa et al., 1985; Kelly et al., 1986; Kelly, 1987; Zuzanek and Box, 1988).

These studies, like many in the field of gerontology, are not without conceptual and methodological flaws. For example, most are one-time-only, cross-sectional studies that do not capture the influence of mood or health changes, or the outcomes of recent events, in the subjective responses of respondents. That is, a particular mood or a perceived feeling of health on a given day may significantly influence a questionnaire or an interview response to a question pertaining to well-being, life satisfaction, happiness, or quality of life. It is also important to understand that most of these studies describe the outcome rather than provide an explanation of the underlying mechanisms of why and how leisure involvement influences these larger dependent outcomes. One exception is the work of Kelly and his colleagues (1986, 1987). They argue that leisure activities provide a social setting for the initiation and development of primary social relations. At a stage of life characterized by social losses (for example, loss of friends and the social milieu at work upon retirement; death of friends and spouse), leisure activities can provide a social milieu to create new social relationships. Furthermore, Kelly (1987) stated that an ability and a willingness to engage in leisure demonstrates competence and self-worth.

Notwithstanding the above caveats, a growing body of research suggests that 'there is a strong correlation between life satisfaction and rates of leisure participation, but little correlation between life satisfaction and the use of free time by older adults' (Zuzanek and Box, 1988:180). However, as Okun et al. (1984) concluded, on the basis of 556 sources of data on the relationship between adult social activities and subjective well-being, formal and informal activities account for only between 1 and 9 percent of the variance in self-reported life satisfaction. The highest levels of life satisfaction are reported by those who are engaged with significant others in activities that provide stimulation and interaction. But this same finding also applies to younger age cohorts as well. Moreover, as Kelly (1987:114) reported, the types of activity associated with high life satisfaction vary with age. He found that the types of activity most likely to be associated with high satisfaction were cultural and travel from age 40 to 54; social, travel, and cultural from 55 to 64 and from 65 to 74; and, home-based, family, and cultural activities for those 75 and older (see highlight 12.3).

The impact of leisure activities on life satisfaction, well-being, or happiness is quite likely related to a number of interacting factors, two of which are the type of activity and the meaning of the activity. It is suspected that informal, self-initiated activities rather than formal, organized activities may provide more meaning and satisfaction to the individual, which, in

LEISURE PARTICIPATION AND LIFE SATISFACTION IN THE LATER YEARS

Kelly et al. (1987) indicated that, at different stages in life, middle-aged and older adults are engaged to varying degrees in a variety of 'core' and 'peripheral' or 'high investment' activities. The 'core' consists of accessible and informal activities (such as reading, television, walking, shopping, interaction with family and friends) that remain central to overall leisure lifestyles throughout the life course. The 'peripheral' or 'high investment' activities require the acquisition over a period of time of some skill (which may subsequently erode over time) that can enhance self-competence, self-worth, and personal expression.

So that patterns of leisure activities in later life and the relationship of these patterns to life satisfaction could be identified, 400 older adults over 40 years of age in Peoria, Illinois, were randomly selected and interviewed by telephone in 1983 (Kelly et al., 1987). Male and female respondents, classified into four age groups, were asked whether they were involved in twenty-eight leisure activities and, if so, how frequently (never, seldom, occasional, frequent). Figure 12.2 illustrates the pattern for overall leisure involvement (upper left) and for eight specific leisure activities. These results provide some research evidence for the various hypothetical patterns illustrated in figure 12.1, and indicate that there is considerable variation in the patterns of involvement after 40 years of age.

Kelly and his colleagues found that older adults are highly involved in social, family, cultural, and home-based activities; with social interaction and home-based activities remaining salient well into the later years, especially for females. These findings strongly suggest that the social dimension of leisure remains important, but that the number and types of activity that provide this element may be reduced and become less accessible or available in later life. In terms of life satisfaction, this study concluded that leisure activity was the most important noneconomic factor in subjective well-being, and that the types of activities contributing to life satisfaction varied by age. For this sample, travel, cultural, and social activities were most important up to age 74, with home-based and family activities being most important among those 75 years of age and over. In short, while the type, frequency, function, and meaning of leisure involvement may change in the later years, leisure activities remain an important contributor to overall life satisfaction.

SOURCE: Adapted from Kelly et al. (1987).

turn, is translated into reports of higher life satisfaction and well-being. Similarly, expressive and instrumental activities may provide more or less satisfaction, depending on the needs and preferences of the older individual. In addition, a lifestyle characterized by solitary activities may best serve the needs of some older adults; for others, social activities involving other people will be desired; and a mix of both types may satisfy other older adults. In short, there is not a common recipe for the leisure activities that will enhance life satisfaction or well-being in the later years. Again, as with so many others facets of aging, heterogeneity prevails. Moreover, before definitive conclusions can be drawn about the value and importance of leisure activities in the later years, it must be recognized that being highly satisfied or adjusted may lead to greater involvement in all forms of social participation. Thus, the chicken-and-egg dilemma is raised again.

In conclusion, to identify and fully explain the beneficial outcomes of leisure in the later years, scholars and practitioners must recognize that aging involves both continuity and change. Older adults may disengage, voluntarily or involuntarily, from some activities, continue others with varying degrees of frequency and intensity, or substitute for lost activities by starting new activities or increasing the level of involvement in other lifelong interests. That is, trade-offs are made, and the outcomes of these decisions may enhance or inhibit life satisfaction, happiness, or well-being at a given point in time. Having more free time does not automatically translate into greater happiness. In short, we have strong evidence that leisure contributes to life satisfaction, and we have some evidence that it provides a context for social interaction, for enhancing personal self-worth,

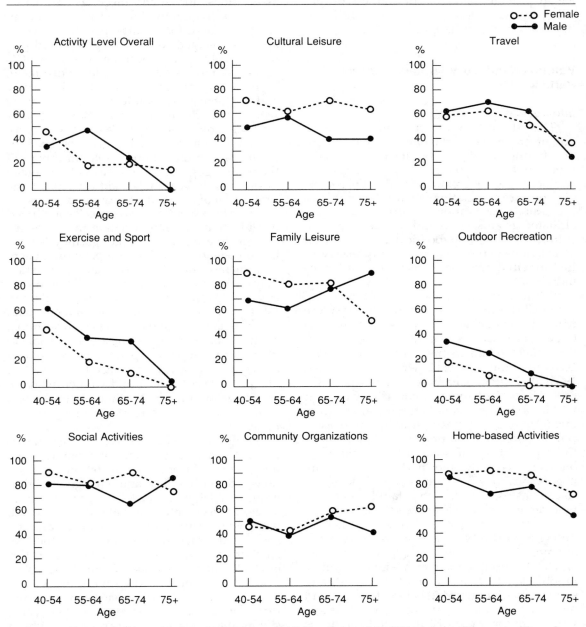

FIGURE 12.2

PARTICIPATION LEVELS BY AGE AND SEX FOR A VARIETY OF LEISURE ACTIVITIES

SOURCE: Reprinted with permission of Hemisphere Publishing Corporation, N.Y., *Leisure Sciences,* vol.9, no.3, 1987, 'Later-life Satisfaction: Does Leisure Contribute?' by John R. Kelly, M.W. Steinkamp and Janice Kelly.

and for testing self-competence. However, we still do not fully understand how or why the relationship prevails, and more importantly, why some older adults are not involved in leisure pursuits, and why some others, despite being involved, report low levels of life satisfaction, well-being, or happiness.

Volunteerism and Voluntary-Association Participation

Introduction

This subsection presents an analysis of volunteerism and of the patterns of participation by the elderly in voluntary associations. From adolescence on, much of our social behavior during leisure occurs within the context of **voluntary associations** such as labor unions, professional associations, fraternal and church-affiliated groups, sport and service clubs, and cultural, hobby, and political groups. These associations serve a variety of **expressive** or **instrumental** functions for society and for the individual.

On the basis of evidence from several cross-sectional studies, the general life-cycle pattern of involvement in voluntary associations tends to be curvilinear, especially for those associations that pertain to the job or to children's activities (Smith, 1975; Cutler, 1981-82; Cutler, 1976, 1977, 1986; Chambre and Lowe, 1983/84).[21] The peak of involvement is likely to occur within about ten years before or after retirement, although this peak varies by type of association. Moreover, volunteering is more likely to be part of the lifestyle of those who have higher levels of education and income, who are in good health, who are members of the higher social classes, who live in a family unit, and who report high levels of life satisfaction.

Not surprisingly, there are distinct gender differences in the type of memberships: women are more involved in church, school, cultural, and hobby groups, and men are more involved in job-related, fraternal, sport, veterans', and service associations. Men belong to larger and more instrumental organizations (such as service or fraternal groups) that are likely to be related to economic institutions, while women belong to smaller and more expressive organi-zations (such as block parents or quilting groups) that focus on domestic or community affairs (McPherson and Smith-Lovin, 1982). Women generally belong to a greater variety of associations, and attend meetings and activities more frequently. However, with the increase in labor-force participation by young and middle-aged women, their type and pattern of voluntary-association involvement is becoming more similar to male involvement, especially for career women. Also, the variety and frequency of volunteer involvement by women may decline in conjunction with a reduction in discretionary time because of work demands. Indeed, there is a growing need for an increase in the number of volunteers from the retired age groups in order to replace women in the middle years who had carried a large proportion of the volunteer work in a society.

With the exception of specifically age-based organizations, most association memberships are age-heterogeneous, although they tend to be homogeneous in class composition. In general, membership in a voluntary association may enable an individual to contribute to society, to help others, to advance a personal interest, to acquire new skills, or to interact with others who have similar interests. In addition, members of voluntary associations are able to play a leadership role, spend their free time in a meaningful way, or enhance their sense of identity. For some men and women who are searching for a full- or part-time job, a volunteer position may serve as a link to future employment.

From a societal perspective, voluntary associations and volunteerism can promote social integration and assimilation (ethnic associations), foster conflict and change (political groups or labor unions), and provide social services (service and faternal groups). Indeed, many voluntary groups are organized as advisory or advocacy groups to promote the specific interests and needs of senior citizens (for example, the Canadian National Advisory Council on Aging and the American Association of Retired Persons. It has been estimated that about 374 million person hours per year, a significant unsalaried human resource within a nation, are provided by about 15 percent of the adult population that contribute unpaid voluntary work to community projects, worthy causes, and special interests. This represents a total dollar value of almost 2 million per year (Ross, 1983).

Throughout the life cycle, voluntary associations serve expressive, instructional, and instrumental purposes for individuals and for society. However, membership is not universal or inevitable: rather, it appears that there is a pattern of stability and continuity across the life cycle. Those who are 'joiners' early in life tend to remain involved when they are older, and those who are 'nonjoiners' early in life tend to remain uninvolved. This same pattern appears to hold for volunteerism (for example, canvassing for a local charity or daily telephoning of an older neighbor).

Voluntary Associations and the Retirement Years

Although the results of cross-sectional studies suggest that voluntary-association involvement decreases with age, there appears to be a growth in the number of age-based associations for older people,[22] and an increase in volunteerism (Danigelis, 1985).[23] This increase in joining behavior, which is especially likely for women and for those with a history of past involvement, may result from the experience of better health among recent cohorts of older adults, better education, earlier retirement, greater economic security, more discretionary time and income, and a desire to maintain continuity in lifestyle. It may also result from a greater opportunity set, a need to compensate for role losses, a need to enhance life satisfaction, or a need to acquire a new social support system after retirement. This greater involvement by the elderly represents a significant contribution to the economy in the form of free labor and expertise.

As retirement approaches, older individuals often become less involved in formal leadership roles. In addition, they may shift their involvement from instrumental to expressive associations, and they may become more involved in age-homogeneous groups, either because they feel a need to affiliate with age peers for personal or political gains or because they are directly or indirectly discouraged from continued participation in age-heterogeneous associations. Similarly, for some elderly persons of ethnic origin, ethnic clubs can be a source of security and can act as a support system.

In the last decade there has been a considerable increase in the number of senior citizen/adult recreation centers established in local communities. Yet, the majority of older adults do not become involved, either by choice or because they are not aware of the existence of a center. In Canada, the 1985 General Social Survey found that for adults 55 years of age and over, only 20 percent of the women and 15 percent of the men had attended a senior center or a club in the one-month period prior to the survey (CAG *Newsletter*, 14[1-2], 1987:3). However, there was some evidence that participation rates increased slightly from 55 to 75 years of age.

Not surprisingly, with the growth in senior centers, research interest has increased with respect to such topics as who attends and participates, the barriers to involvement, the benefits of participation, and the factors influencing attendance (Krout, 1983, 1984, 1985, 1989; Schneider et al., 1985; Ouellette, 1986; Ferraro and Cobb, 1987; Jerrome, 1988). Unfortunately, many of these studies are local or regional in scope; they only study participants at one center; they depend on volunteer or designated (by an employee) respondents, who are more likely to be those who are most social and vocal, or who happen to be at the center when the interviewer arrives; or they ignore nonusers. Nevertheless, there appear to be some common findings concerning those who are most likely to participate. Thus, joiners are more likely to be women, to be in good health, to live close to the center or to have easy access to transportation, to have always been 'joiners,' to be members of the lower to middle classes, to have less formal education, to have a strong identity with the neighborhood or community, and to not experience fear of crime when leaving the home or apartment. Nonusers report a lack of awareness of a center or its programs, being too busy, or having no interest in an 'old folks' club. In reality, older individuals who could benefit the most from a center (for example, lonely and isolated seniors) do not participate.

For those who participate regularly, the clubs

or centers serve a number of functions. They have the potential to provide information and educational services, serve as social centers to provide friendship groups and support networks, provide a structure to the day or week, develop and foster a generational consciousness, provide a sense of identity, and foster improved health through the provision of meals, informal and formal counseling, checkups and informal monitoring by staff and fellow members (Krout, 1985; Ouellette, 1986; Jerrome, 1988).

Regardless of the earlier life pattern of involvement in voluntary associations, volunteer involvement ultimately decreases because of such factors as declining health, loss of energy, loss of interest, lack of mobility and transportation, and fear of crime. However, this decline can be at least partly prevented or delayed through community social services (dial-a-ride transportation), or by moving to age-segregated retirement housing where clubs and associations are organized on the premises by and for the residents. Clearly, the provision of effective leisure services for the elderly requires an integration of housing, health care, transportation, and leisure policies.

Political Participation

In chapter 7 the political power of elderly cohorts was discussed in relation to their position in the social structure. Here, the emphasis is on the political participation of the elderly person with respect to political attitudes and orientation, voting behavior, and involvement in political leadership roles. In effect, political participation represents a form of leisure behavior within and outside voluntary associations. Although individuals have the right to vote, to affiliate with or join political parties, or to hold political office, not all choose to become interested or involved in the political process. In recent years, largely because of the increasing proportion of elderly people in the population, interest in describing and explaining patterns of political participation across the life cycle has increased.[24]

To date, there have been three major hypotheses proposed concerning the political activism and advocacy of the elderly (Rosenbaum and Button, 1989). First, the 'gray partic-

ipation' hypothesis argues that with the increasing number of elderly persons there will be increased political involvement at many government levels by aging adults. Second, the 'gray power' hypothesis suggests that with increasing numbers, and the presence of vocal role models, there will be an increasing age-based consciousness of specific political beliefs, attitudes, and interests (Yelaja, 1989). This political consciousness will be expressed in increased political involvement and activism at all political levels. The third hypothesis, the 'gray peril' hypothesis, assumes that the expanding number of increasingly politically active seniors will oppose local government taxation and spending programs that do not directly benefit senior citizens. At the same time, they will campaign and lobby for increased services for the retired population. On the basis of a 1986 survey in Florida, Rosenbaum and Button (1989) found that, despite active voting, there was little support at the local level for either the gray-power or gray-peril hypotheses. Thus, at the local level, aging persons are not yet highly involved in organized political advocacy or political opposition to policies that benefit other age groups. However, as you will soon read, there is increasing evidence that gray power works at the national level (highlight 12.4).

Many studies in the 1960s and 1970s found that there was a curvilinear relationship between age and political participation, especially as measured by voting behavior. That is, there was an increase from early adulthood to late middle age, and then a decline after retirement. During the middle years of life people are generally better informed, have more free time, and are well integrated into a community or region. The decline or disengagement in voting in the later years has been attributed not to chronological age per se, but rather to loss of interest, declining health, lack of mobility or transportation, and a general decrease in social participation. In addition, because women generally vote less often than men at all ages, and because women make up an increasingly larger proportion of the population, the number of actual voters, in total, among the older age cohorts decreases. Finally, older cohorts have generally been composed of a larger pro-

GRAY POWER: A PROCESS OF SOCIAL CHANGE FOR SENIORS

Until the 1970s, the traditional life-cycle pattern of political participation was curvilinear: low involvement beginning in late adolescence, an increase through late middle-age, followed by a decrease in the postretirement years (Hudson and Strate, 1985). In recent decades, however, the curve has flattened out beyond the middle years as the political consciousness and political activism of older adults has increased in both frequency and intensity. Stimulated by the charismatic leadership of Maggie Kuhn, who founded the Gray Panthers in 1970, the elderly began to lobby and speak out on their own behalf. Most of this activism, known as 'gray power' (Yelaja, 1989), focuses on national issues such as the inadequacies in policies and actions pertaining to pensions, old-age security systems, housing, and health care.

Aggressive and persuasive older adults actively engage in public dialogue on radio and television, in mail campaigns, and in protest marches and sit-ins to bring their concerns and points of view to the attention of politicians, private-sector entrepreneurs, the media, and younger age groups. At first their efforts were stimulated by the need to react to such issues as age discrimination, poverty, and inadequate housing. More recently, with the formation of national and provincial advisory groups (for example, the National Advisory Council on Aging), older adults have been co-opted or invited to participate in the decision-making process, and are therefore consulted *before* decisions are made or actions are taken by government agencies.

Where this cooperative mechanism is not used, or where older adults are ignored, radical, activist groups are created. For example, the Senior Citizens' Organization Coalition, an advocacy group formed to oppose the de-indexing of pensions that was proposed in the May 24, 1985, budget speech, successfully aligned with other interest groups to pressure the government to abolish the proposal. At the provincial and local levels, such organizations as the Manitoba Society of Seniors, the United Senior Citizens of Ontario, and the Toronto Association of Jewish Seniors have had modest success as political forces in advocating the needs, interests, and rights of older adults.

In Canada, a new form of activism, which seeks to be more proactive than reactive, was initiated in March 1987 with the creation of One Voice. This organization immediately passed three resolutions of interest and concern to seniors. First, they demanded increased funding for the New Horizons program, and a large increase was subsequently announced in 1988. Second, they requested greater input into the formulation of housing policies. In response, seniors from across Canada were invited to serve as active participants in the planning of, and in the making of recommendations following, a national conference on housing that was held in October 1988. Third, they requested a study to examine the feasibility of a guaranteed annual income for Canadians of all ages, not just seniors.

In summary, these developments in the political domain suggest that seniors have ideas and dreams about many elements of a society. To facilitate the realization of these ideas and dreams, they are prepared to act as a formidable political lobby group in either a proactive or reactive mode, depending on the issue and the needs of the situation. Because of the very presence or threat of visible and vocal advocacy groups, governments and other vested interest groups have become more sensitive to, and understanding of, salient and important issues that can affect the quality of life of middle-aged and older Canadians.

portion of ethnic and racial minority groups. Until recently, these groups have tended to be less informed, less interested, and less active in the political process of a community or nation. However, with declining immigration rates and growing political involvement by minority groups, this pattern may be less apparent among future elderly cohorts.

More recent evidence, however, suggests that the decline in participation is less than that reported in previous decades (Curtis and Lambert, 1976; Rollenhagen, 1984; Hudson and Strate, 1985; Jacobs, 1990). This change in voting patterns can be attributed to a number of cohort factors whereby elderly cohorts are better educated and have more opportunities to join age-concentrated groups (for example, senior-citizen centers or political advocacy groups). They are also actively recruited by political parties because of their increasing numbers. For example, at present, about 13.5 percent of eligible Canadian voters are over 65 years of age. This figure is projected to increase to 16.5 percent by 2010 and to 25 percent by 2030. Moreover, about one-third of older Canadians belong to seniors' clubs or other volunteer organizations. Hence, the potential to mobilize older adults in the political domain is increasing (see highlight 12.4). Moreover, because of population aging, governments at all levels are responding to the needs and interests of the older age groups. For example, it has been estimated that 18 percent ($17.6 billion) of the federal expenditures in Canada are directed to older age groups (Pratt, 1984).

Changes in political interest or attitudes across the life cycle may represent maturational changes, cohort effects or period effects. For example, although cross-sectional studies suggest that elderly persons as a group are more conservative than other age cohorts, this does not imply that they have become more conservative with age. Rather, they may have been politically socialized at a period in history when conservatism prevailed.[25] They may also appear conservative relative to younger cohorts because of dramatic changes in values, experiences, and social beliefs over a twenty- or thirty-year period (for example, the rise of the women's movement, political activism by youths, and recreational drug use). To illustrate this point, Cutler et al. (1980) examined cohort differences in attitudes toward legalized abortion. They found that attitudes toward legal abortions became considerably more liberal across all age cohorts between 1965 and 1973. However, the older cohorts were slower to change their attitudes, since the process takes longer for them than for younger persons, and there may be greater intracohort variability among older age groups with respect to a specific attitude or political opinion.

It must be noted, as well, that the priorities attached to various 'political' issues vary by stage in life. Generally, younger people are more concerned with 'issues' pertaining to nuclear disarmament, the environment, women's rights, abortion, and gay rights; older age cohorts tend to be more concerned with traditional problems such as inflation, unemployment, old-age benefits, taxes, and the secu-

rity of the nation. Often these different political agendas are reflected in voting behavior. Whether the priorities of the younger cohorts persist or change across the life cycle remains to be investigated. Finally, the influence of period effects on specific age cohorts, on all age cohorts, and on particular segments of given age cohorts must not be overlooked in explaining age-related differences in political orientations or participation patterns. The impact of a war, a depression, or a political scandal (for example, Watergate, the Iran-Contra affair) can dramatically change political beliefs, attitudes, and voting choices within and across age groups.

As is usual with social science data, caveats must be introduced. There are wide regional and class variations across cohorts with respect to political matters; for example, the values and lifestyles of those who live in the eastern Canadian provinces have, regardless of age, traditionally been more conservative that those of persons living in other regions. This regional variation is partly related to the presence of prevailing subcultural norms and values, which in turn are related to the geographical distance from the decision-making processes of the political and economic centers of the nation. The regional difference is also related to generally lower levels of educational attainment, which, combined with isolation, restrict access to new information. Similarly, members of the lower classes in all geographical regions tend to be less educated, to have less access to new ideas, and to be more likely to adhere to childhood and adolescent values throughout life. In short, political interest and orientation can change with age, particularly on issues related to one's changing personal situation (health care, pensions, housing). However, the rate of change may be slow and it may not affect all members of a given age cohort, especially those who live in certain regions of a country or who have a particular class background.

The elderly are, of course, eligible to hold political office. In fact, many elderly persons are elected because of their perceived stability and experience, and because they serve as a symbol of wisdom. In both business and politics it has been found that a large percentage of the elites, or leaders, are over 60 years of age (McIntyre, 1988). This trend seems to occur even more frequently as the importance of the leadership position increases. It is also more likely to occur where legislation does not limit the term of office. Incumbents often age in office (for example, Prime Minister Pierre Trudeau in Canada, Supreme Court justices, former President Reagan, the Pope), so that the elderly are overrepresented in leadership positions. In the future, elderly people may be even more likely to hold office because an increasingly larger proportion of the electorate will be their age peers.

In summary, as our population ages, older age cohorts will be better educated, and may recognize the extent of their potential influence through bloc voting. This recognition may lead to shifts in political interest and orientation across the life cycle, including the possibility of politically based conflict or cooperation between age strata. In addition, the number of elderly persons involved in the political process will probably increase, especially since women and members of minority groups are becoming more involved at younger ages. It is partly for this reason that an increasing number of women are being elected to political offices at all levels of government. Finally, contrary to conventional wisdom, there are increasing similarities among age groups in both political orientation and political participation. This is occurring because of the heterogeneity within age groups, and because of period effects that may have an impact on all age groups, or on similar segments within all age groups.

Religious Participation

As a cultural institution, organized religion serves a symbolic and functional role in most societies; it has the potential to provide a sense of security, a readily available social group, and a social role for the older individual. Religious beliefs can also assist in coping with grief and death, especially among older persons. Because of these apparent functions, gerontologists have been interested in the patterns of religious participation during the middle and later years of life (Alston and Alston, 1980; Payne, 1981; Fecher, 1982; Ainlay and Smith, 1984; Young and Dowling, 1987; Koenig et al., 1988).

Stereotypes and myths concerning the religious behavior of older people have been perpetuated by conflicting hypotheses and evidence. There appear to be at least four possible patterns of religious involvement, which are usually measured by attendance: (1) attendance increases with age from childhood to early adulthood and then remains stable across the life course; (2) attendance is cyclical, and is related to the stage in the family life cycle,[26] (3) attendance begins to decrease after middle age; (4) regardless of the pattern earlier in life, attendance increases in the later years.[27]

As with other forms of social participation, it is important to distinguish between age differences, the outcome of aging, and period effects with respect to adherence to religious beliefs or attendance at religious events. Moreover, it is essential to differentiate between attitudes or beliefs and behavior. Religious attitudes and beliefs may persist until death; attendance at religious ceremonies (behavior) may decrease as health or access to transportation declines. Thus, whereas early studies of the religiosity of older adults focused on attendance, and thereby concluded that religiosity decreases with age, more recent studies have adopted a multidimensional conceptualization of religious involvement (Ainlay and Smith, 1984). This model incorporates the degree of public participation in religious services or meetings, the strength of religious attitudes and beliefs, and the degree of private participation in radio or television services, reading, and prayer or devotion services at home (alone or with kin or friends). Thus, there is an important distinction between organized, public participation and private religious activity.

To date, most studies have found that attendance at religious ceremonies remains stable across the life course, or that there is a withdrawal in the middle and later years. However, these patterns vary by religious affiliation, by gender, by education, and by place of residence: women, Catholics, the less educated, and those who live in rural areas seem to attend services more frequently at all ages. In a number of cross-sectional studies it has generally been found that religion is an important element in the life of the elderly person, and that older age cohorts report stronger religious beliefs than younger age cohorts. However, it has not been determined whether these findings reflect cohort or aging effects. In terms of participation in the later years, recent studies support the finding that religious participation does not cease with advancing years, but that there is a decrease in public participation with advancing age and a compensatory increase in private participation. Moreover, those who are more socially active in general are more active in public, organized religious activities. Finally, there is a relationship between strength of religious belief and both public and private forms of religious behavior (Young and Dowling, 1987).

In short, religious participation can vary in form and frequency across the life cycle for any one cohort, and between cohorts as values, beliefs and interests change over time. Moreover, it appears that some degree of continuity prevails from one stage in life to another. Thus, those elderly persons who were religious early in life are likely to exhibit some form of religious behavior late in life, even if attendance at religious services declines because of failing health or lack of mobility.

The Media and the Elderly

The media, consisting of printed (newspapers, magazines, and books) and electronic (radio, television, and movies) communication systems are designed to reach a large and diverse audience. As a salient social institution, the media serve a number of functions: they entertain, disseminate information, promote social integration, provide an escape from the realities of everyday life, select and perpetuate specific cultural norms, and educate the masses (De Fleur, 1970). In addition, the media may provide the elderly with indirect contact with the social world, and may help to counteract loneliness by presenting characters and situations with which they can identify.

As age increases, people may read fewer books and newspapers and see fewer films because of financial constraints, declining vision, and loss of interest in the content. However, the amount of television viewing increases until about age 70, before a modest decline

begins (Kubey, 1980).

Television is the medium most frequently selected by the elderly for entertainment and information.[28] This use of television may occur because more time is spent at home, because more leisure time is available, and because the elderly have fewer links with the community. Television is also more accessible to those with failing vision or hearing than either a newspaper or the radio, since television transmits both picture and sound.

Television became widely available only after the late 1940s, and many of the current cohorts of elderly persons were first exposed to television during early adulthood. Television viewing was not inculcated during childhood and has not been a lifelong habit as it is for most younger age cohorts. Nevertheless, the elderly (especially older women, the less educated, and those with lower incomes) are regular and avid viewers of quiz shows, news programs, soap operas, and variety shows.

Although it is still debated whether media consumption is a substitution or compensation for a lack of face-to-face interpersonal relations, it does appear that television may provide surrogate company for some elderly persons. Also, television viewing can provide a structured daily schedule for older people: mealtimes, chores, and going to bed are regulated by the television programs that are watched on a given day. In short, the higher rates of television consumption may not only 'kill time,' but may also provide a schedule or routine, thereby serving a functional role.

While most of the research relating to television and the older person has focused on participation rates and the types of programs viewed, few studies have examined how the elderly are depicted on television, or the potential uses of television for the elderly. With respect to the image presented, older people have been portrayed in a negative and stereotypical manner in television serials and comedy shows, or appear in news items presented to generate sympathy (for example, a widow cheated of her life savings), humor, or amazement (at a man fathering a child at age 75 or a grandmother who singlehandedly flies around the world). Compared to the general population, the aged as a group are underrepresented as television characters, although older men are overrepresented compared to older women. In short, television often fails to provide an accurate representation of older people (see chapter 7).

Although television seldom provides intellectual stimulation for individuals at any age, the use of the medium to present educational programs for older adults is increasing. Cable television and pay television services have the potential to provide learning experiences, intellectual stimulation, and social and commercial services for adults of all ages. In fact, television shopping is increasing and may serve the needs of the more affluent house-bound elderly person.

Education and the Elderly

It was once believed that an individual's education was completed in late adolescence; today, continuing education during adulthood has become necessary or desirable because of rapid technological and social change. Learning has become a lifelong necessity, as well as an accepted leisure pursuit whereby an individual can 'learn for the sake of learning' regardless of chronological age or stage in life. Although it was once thought that an older person lacked the ability to learn, recent evidence suggests that, given the opportunity, encouragement, and sufficient time, an older person can acquire new skills through formal and informal educational systems. Thus, although education for the elderly has not been a high priority of the formal education system, a shift in values and beliefs about learning in middle and later life has led to an increase in the educational opportunities for older adults, especially within universities. As well, older adults have begun to actively seek educational experiences for self-development, for cultural and intellectual enrichment, to obtain a degree, to meet interesting people, or to enhance their social life.

Changing social norms, along with research evidence relating to the learning ability of older people, have made it possible for adults to pursue higher education in the home through audio cassette tapes, radio, or television; in off-campus centers in the community, including retirement centers, senior citizen centers, churches, and shopping malls; and on college campuses.[29] Not surprisingly, there is a higher participation rate in these programs by members of the upper and middle classes, by those who completed their early schooling in North America, by those in good health, by those who are mobile, and by those with few vision or hearing problems. It appears that this pattern of pursuing an educational program as a form of leisure is increasing for those in the postretirement years and will increase even more in the years ahead as each succeeding generation of retirees increases in both number and in average level of education. For example, an estimated eighty-six thousand Canadians, or 4 percent of those 65 years of age and over, enrolled in one or more continuing education courses in 1983 (Deveraux, 1984:55; Macleod, 1985). Of these, however, only about five thousand were formally enrolled in undergraduate or graduate courses at a university. On the basis of these estimates, Denton et al. (1988) projected that there will be a 94 percent increase in course enrollment by 2005 and a 141 percent increase by 2010. In real numbers this amounts to about two hundred thousand elderly adults in about twenty-five years, although this is still a small percentage of the total elderly population. This pattern of growing enrollment in educational programs is likely to continue if tuition fees are waived or reduced significantly, if recruitment and counseling programs for the mature student are available, if admission standards are flexible, if courses are offered off-campus in convenient locations, if both credit and noncredit programs are available,[30] and if examination situations, where required, are not perceived to be stressful. In short, education has become an increasingly salient leisure pursuit for middle-aged and elderly persons, especially during the early years of retirement when high rates of health, mobility, and discretionary time and income are present. Highlight 12.5 describes the highly successful Elderhostel educational program.

SUMMARY AND CONCLUSIONS

In this final chapter we have examined lei-

HIGHLIGHT 12.5

EDUCATION AS LEISURE IN THE LATER YEARS

Regardless of whether they were deprived of a formal education, or were highly educated earlier in life, many older adults are returning to educational settings to pursue formal or informal learning. For some, this involves enrolling in courses for pleasure, with no possibility or plans to pursue a degree. Others gain admission to universities and are earning undergraduate or graduate degrees. Some of the educational programs are offered by seniors who volunteer to share a specific skill or type of expertise; others are offered by professors or other professionals through distance education (for example, Tele-college, audio tapes, radio, or electronic bulletin boards), and many involve registering in a formal course offered by a local university.

One of the most successful educational experiences for older adults is the Elderhostel program. Having its origins in the youth hostels of Europe and the folk schools of Scandinavia, this program offers one- to two-week learning experiences for a participant residing in college or university dormitories. Each course normally meets for ninety minutes per day, and classes are scheduled to allow participants (who must be at least 60 years of age or 55 and accompanying a partner who is at least 60) to enroll in up to three courses per session. There are no grades, exams, or homework, and the cost is usually under $300 per week for registration, accommodation, meals, five days of classes and extracurricular activities, including field trips. For those who cannot afford the full cost, 'hostelships' (scholarships) are available to offset some of the cost.

The list of course offerings is broad, but most courses are in the humanities and the social sciences, with many programs featuring courses on topics unique to the local cultural, geographical, or social milieu. For example, Canadian offerings have included: Labrador Flora and Fauna (Goose Bay, Labrador); Subarctic Life (Fort Smith, Northwest Territories); Scottish Bagpipe and Fiddle Music (Antigonish, Nova Scotia); Marine Biology of the North Atlantic (St. John's, Newfoundland); The Lives and Beliefs of Old Order Mennonites (Waterloo, Ontario); Francophone Culture (Quebec City, Quebec); Photography in the Canadian Rockies (Calgary, Alberta); and The Coal-Mining History of Nanaimo (Nanaimo, British Columbia). In addition, more traditional academic courses are offered, such as Computer Literacy, Astronomy, Canadian Art, Canadian Drama, Introductory French, History of Atlantic Canada, and Traditional Folk Music.

As of early 1990, there were over twelve hundred colleges and universities offering courses in Canada and forty other countries, and an estimated two hundred thousand students annually attend the diverse array of Elderhostel courses. Thus, this innovative learning experience, which has become international in scope, provides intellectual activity for both active and disabled older adults who seek to expand their horizons and develop new interests. Through this relatively inexpensive leisure activity, older adults live, learn, and socialize with age peers who also strive 'to seek, to find, but not to yield' in the later years.

sure as a form of social participation that is an important facet of contemporary lifestyles at all stages in the life cycle. In the first section a number of conceptual and methodological issues concerning leisure as a social concept were introduced, and alternative explanations for the relationship between the type of work and the amount, form, and meaning of leisure were discussed. The remainder of the chapter described patterns of leisure involvement in the middle and later years of adulthood, especially with respect to volunteerism, voluntary-association involvement, religious and political participation, continuing education, and the media.

Despite the relatively small body of literature pertaining to aging and leisure involvement, the following conclusions appear to be warranted:

1. A generally accepted definition of 'leisure' has yet to be derived, perhaps because leisure is a personal experience, because a number of inherent methodological and conceptual matters have yet to be resolved, and because there are a variety of cultural and subcultural variations in norms and values concerning work and leisure.

2. To date, relatively few cross-sectional or longitudinal research studies have examined the pattern or meaning of leisure involvement across the life cycle.

3. The quality of leisure, compared to the quantity of leisure, is seldom considered in analyses of leisure involvement at any stage in the life cycle.

4. While the amount of free time and the frequency of leisure involvement may increase or decrease at varying stages in the life cycle, the types of leisure pursuits are relatively constant once patterns are established in the early and middle years of adulthood.

5. Although there appears to be evidence that there is a relationship between type of work and type of leisure, a definitive explanation for this relationship is not available. Rather, three major hypotheses have been proposed and tested. The 'spillover' or 'congruence' hypothesis argues that there is little difference between work and leisure, and that therefore the leisure activities selected are similar to the job. The 'compensatory' or 'contrast' hypothesis argues that individuals seek in their leisure what is lacking in their work, and that leisure activities tend to be unlike work activities. The 'neutrality' hypothesis argues that there is little attachment to work; therefore, the nature of work has little bearing on leisure pursuits and there may or may not be a linkage between work and leisure activities.

6. To date, the research evidence is supportive of the 'spillover' hypothesis, although the relationship between work and leisure in one's lifestyle may vary by age and by stage in the family life cycle. The personal and cultural characteristics that might influence the relationship have seldom been considered.

7. During the working years, personal characteristics, the demands and responsibilities of the family and work, and social and technological change all influence the selection of leisure activities and the meaning these activities have for the individual. Chronological age per se is an incomplete predictor of leisure behavior.

8. The leisure patterns of the elderly are heterogeneous. However, regardless of the pattern, leisure activities generally become constricted in frequency and type as the number of years beyond retirement increases. Declining health, income, and energy, a lack of opportunity, and a loss of mobility and transportation can dramatically alter the leisure patterns in the later years of life.

9. The most frequently reported leisure activities by those over 65 years of age are socializing with friends and relatives; watching television; gardening; reading newspapers; and sitting and thinking. In short, most activities are indoor, home-based, and solitary, especially for the very old segment of the retired population.

10. Studies have found that older individuals who are more involved in leisure activities report higher levels of satisfaction or adjustment. However, the causal direction of this relationship has yet to be established, although it is probably a two-way process of interaction.

11. The general life-cycle pattern of volunteerism and involvement in voluntary associations is curvilinear, with the peak of involvement generally occurring within the ten years prior to or following retirement.

12. Membership in voluntary associations is not a universal or inevitable pattern. Those who are 'joiners' early in life tend to join and participate in the middle and later years.

13. A majority of older people do not become involved in senior-citizen organizations, even where the groups are known and available to older residents. Those who are most likely to join are women; those in good health; those

with access to transportation; those who have been 'joiners' throughout life; those who are members of the lower-middle or middle class; and those with a strong attachment to the neighborhood or community.

14. Interest in political matters and voting increases with age until health and mobility decline in the later years. However, there are class, gender, educational, regional, cultural, and subcultural variations in political interest and participation at all ages.

15. Changes in political interest or attitudes across the life cycle may represent maturational changes, cohort effects, or period effects. The explanation may depend on the salience of a particular topic or issue at a particular stage in the life cycle of an individual or a cohort, or at a particular period in history.

16. Many older persons hold political office. The number may increase in the future, since the older segment of the population will make up a larger proportion of the voting population.

17. Most studies have found that attendance at religious ceremonies remains stable across the life course, or is characterized by a withdrawal in the middle or later years. Some who withdraw return later if there is a concern with the nearness and consequences of death.

18. While attendance at religious services may decline in the later years, continuity in religiosity may prevail. That is, those who were religious early in life may continue to be involved through reading or by watching or listening to religious services on television or radio.

19. As age increases, the use of movies and the print media may decrease because of cost, declining vision, and loss of interest in the content. However, the amount of television viewing generally increases until about 70 years of age. Among the elderly population, the most regular and avid viewers of quiz shows, news programs, soap operas, and variety shows are women, the less educated, and those with the fewest economic resources.

20. With increasing opportunities to pursue credit and noncredit educational programs, a larger percentage of the elderly population is enrolling in educational courses as a form of leisure in the pre- and postretirement years.

NOTES

1. See Kleemeier, 1961; Havighurst, 1972; Teague, 1980; Kelly, 1982; McGuire, 1982; Kelly et al., 1986; McGuire et al. 1987.

2. See Lawton, 1978; Dangott and Kalish, 1979; Kaplan, 1979; Osgood, 1982; Burrus-Bammel and Bammell, 1985; Lawton, 1985; Roadburg, 1985; Kelly, 1987; MacNeil and Teague, 1987; Altergott, 1988b.

3. See Dumazedier, 1967; Parker, 1976; Kleiber and Kelly, 1980; Wilson, 1980; Kelly, 1981; Neulinger, 1981; Keating and Spiller, 1983; Burrus-Bammel and Bammel, 1985; Roadburg, 1985; Tinsley et al., 1985; Howe, 1987; Kelly, 1987, 1990.

4. Interestingly, there appear to be some commonalities in meaning between work and leisure, even though they are often viewed as bipolar opposites. Both provide the individual with a sense of worth, an identity, a milieu in which to initiate and maintain social interaction, a source of prestige and status, and an outlet for expressive and instrumental needs.

5. For example, the emphasis attached to work (the work ethic) by a society and by individuals varies historically; that is, within the hierarchy of values of a society or an individual, the status of work and leisure shifts over time (Dumazedier, 1972).

6. Some of the more common dimensions are expressive-instrumental; free choice-constrained involvement; low involvement-high involvement; active-passive; individual-group; home centered-community centered; institutionalized-noninstitutionalized; inexpensive-expensive; mass culture-high culture; creative-noncreative; spontaneous-planned; structured-unstructured; work-nonwork; and physical-nonphysical.

7. For example, reading as a leisure activity may be pursued to improve the mind, to learn a skill, to study for a degree, or simply to pass the time.

8. An individual is able to listen to music while

reading, to watch television while visiting with others, or to play darts or backgammon while drinking.

9. An example of an activity in an overlapping category is watching television. The activity can be categorized as educational or recreational or as a solitary or group activity, depending on the situation in which the activity takes place.

10. Some attempts to measure various dimensions of leisure have been made by McKechnie, (1975); Yoesting and Burdge, 1976; Gordon and Gaitz, 1976; Dangott and Kalish, 1979:160; Beard and Ragheb, 1980; Pierce, 1980a, 1980b; Yu and Mendell, 1980; Moss and Lawton, 1982.

11. For example, Gordon and Gaitz (1976:314) illustrate that the intensity of expressive involvement in leisure can vary in the cognitive, emotional, and physical dimensions across the following five levels: (1) very high (sexual activity, competitive games, and sport); (2) medium high (creative activities such as music and art); (3) medium (attending cultural events, reading for learning, recreational sport or exercise); (4) medium low (watching television, attending spectator sports, hobbies, reading for pleasure); and (5) low (solitude, resting, 'killing time').

12. See Smigel, 1963; Parker, 1972, 1975; Kelly, 1972, 1976, 1982, 1987; Haworth and Smith, 1975; Staines, 1980; Ward, 1982.

13. For example, in recent years some individuals have experienced periods of voluntary or involuntary unemployment. This has led to their acceptance of leisure in the absence of work, and to the use of leisure to escape jobs that are characterized by tension, triviality, or boredom.

14. This view is represented by those who barely tolerate their nine-to-five existence, and who adhere to the TGIF (Thank Goodness It's Friday) philosophy.

15. See Rapoport and Rapoport, 1975; Gordon and Gaitz, 1976; Parker, 1976; Kelly, 1977; Kaplan, 1979; Kleiber and Kelly, 1980; McPherson and Kozlik, 1980, 1987; Wilson, 1980; Osgood and Howe, 1984; Long, 1987; McGuire et al., 1987.

16. Some specific events that can alter leisure are marriage, the birth of a child, a promotion, the empty nest, entrance of the spouse into the labor force, retirement, death of the spouse, divorce, illness, or unemployment.

17. See Atchley, 1971; Yoesting and Burkhead, 1973; Kleiber and Kelly, 1980; Kelly et al., 1986; Kelly, 1987; Long, 1987; McGuire et al., 1987.

18. For example, those in lower-status occupations generally engage in more home-centered leisure; those in higher-status occupations become more involved in community-centered activities such

as service groups and private clubs.

19. For example, a store owner, a physician, and a professor, although all members of the upper-middle class, generally have different work styles and career demands. The store owner may work six days and two evenings a week; the physician may work five days a week and be on call at certain times; and the professor may work five to seven days in a week and in the evenings in order to read, or to write papers or books. Time demands vary from occupation to occupation and greatly influence the amount and style of leisure.

20. See Gordon and Gaitz, 1976; Teague, 1980; Wilson, 1980; Bosse and Ekerdt, 1981; Moss and Lawton, 1982; Kelly, 1982, 1987; Roadburg, 1985; McGuire et al., 1987; McPherson and Kozlik, 1987; Altergott, 1988b; Cutler and Hendricks, 1990.

21. The curvilinear pattern may reflect cohort effects rather than aging effects, since older cohorts are generally less educated, have had fewer opportunities to join associations, and are more likely to be members of the lower class.

22. Some of these include the National Advisory Council on Aging; One Voice — The Canadian Seniors Network; Retired Seniors Volunteer Program; Foster Grandparents; Senior Companion Program; National Pensioners and Senior Citizens Federation; Canadian Pensioners Concerned; American Association of Retired Persons; widow-to-widow programs.

23. The retired person can volunteer to be a foster grandparent, a teacher, or an executive in a community association or a developing country.

24. See Curtis and Lambert, 1976; Pratt, 1976, 1979, 1984; Estes, 1979; Hudson, 1981; Kernaghan, 1982; Williamson et al., 1982; Myles, 1984; Rollenhagen, 1984; Binstock et al., 1985; Hudson and Strate, 1985; Pampel and Williamson, 1985; Neysmith, 1987; Rosenbaum and Button, 1989.

25. In the United States there is generally continuity in party affiliation across the life cycle. Moreover, older people are more likely to be affiliated with the conservative party (Republican) because they were socialized to this view of the political world at a young age. That is, affiliation with a particular party may represent historical experiences rather than age-related conservatism, and therefore significant shifts in party affiliation are unlikely to occur late in life.

26. One pattern for adults involves a peaking of religious participation when children are involved in Sunday school, and a decline when the children leave home; another is shown in a decline from 18 to 35 years of age, and then an increase until the later years, when it decreases again (Bahr, 1970).

27. This pattern is sometimes referred to as the 'just-in-case' phenomenon: religious behavior increases and remains high in the later years 'just-in-case' judgment will be delivered on the individual after death.
28. Although three to four hours of viewing per day may be the average reported by the elderly, many self-reports underestimate the actual viewing time. Moreover, some studies ask only whether a television set is on or off, not whether a program is being watched. From this perspective, the average number of 'viewing' hours may be an overestimate. For a detailed discussion of media use by the elderly, see, *American Behavioral Scientist*, 23(1), 1979; and Kubey, 1980.
29. See Peterson, 1981; Connelly, 1982; Covey, 1983; Deveraux, 1984; Verduin and McEwen, 1984; Battersby, 1985; Macleod, 1985; Willis, 1985; Denton et al., 1988.
30. Many older persons may initially lack the confidence to enter a degree program, or may not be motivated to obtain sufficient credits for a degree. As a compromise, many institutions offer a certificate for completing a specified number of university courses. Many of these courses do not require examinations, nor are grades awarded.

REFERENCES

Ainlay, S. and D. Smith. (1984) 'Aging and Religious Participation,' *Journal of Gerontology*, 39(3), 357-63.

Alston, L. and J. Alston. (1980). 'Religion and the Older Woman,' pp. 262-78 in M. Fuller and C. Martin (eds.). *The Older Woman: Lavender Rose or Gray Panther*. Springfield, Ill.: Charles C. Thomas.

Altergott, K. (1988a). 'Social Action and Interaction in Later Life: Aging in the United States,' pp. 117-46 in K. Altergott (ed.). *Daily Life in Later Life*. Newbury Park, Calif.: Sage Publications.

Altergott, K. (ed.). (1988b). *Daily Life in Later Life*. Newbury Park, Calif.: Sage Publications.

Atchley, R. (1971). 'Retirement and Leisure Participation: Continuity or Crisis?' *The Gerontologist*, 11(1), 13-17.

Bahr, H. (1970). 'Aging and Religious Disaffiliation,' *Social Forces*, 49(1), 59-71.

Battersby, D. (1985). 'Education in Later Life: What Does It Mean?' *Convergence*, 18(1-2), 75-81.

Beard, J. and M. Ragheb. (1980). 'Measuring Leisure Satisfaction.' *Journal of Leisure Research*, 12(1), 20-33.

Binstock, R., et al. (1985). 'Political Dilemmas of Social Intervention,' pp. 589-618 in R. Binstock and E. Shanas (eds.). *Handbook of Aging and the Social Sciences*. 2d ed. New York: Van Nostrand Reinhold.

Bishop, D. and M. Ikeda. (1970). 'Status and Role Factors in the Leisure Behavior of Different Occupations,' *Sociology and Social Research*, 54(2), 190-209.

Bosse, R. and D. Ekerdt. (1981). 'Change in Self-Perception of Leisure Activities with Retirement,' *The Gerontologist*, 21(6), 650-54.

Buchanan, T. and L. Allen. (1985). 'Barriers to Recreation Participation in Later Life Cycle Stages,' *Therapeutic Recreation Journal*, 19(3), 39-50.

Burrus-Bammel, L. and G. Bammel. (1985). 'Leisure and Recreation,' pp. 848-63 in J. Birren and W. Schaie (eds.). *Handbook of the Psychology of Aging*. 2d ed. New York: Van Nostrand Reinhold.

Chambre, S. and I. Lowe. (1983/84). 'Volunteering and the Aged: A Bibliography for Researchers and Practitioners,' *The Journal of Volunteer Administration*, 2(2), 35-44.

Connelly, J. (1982). 'Education and the Future,' in G. Gutman (ed.). *Canada's Changing Age Structure: Implications for the Future*. Burnaby, B.C.: Simon Fraser University Publications.

Covey, H. (1983). 'Higher Education and Older People: Some Theoretical Considerations, Part II,' *Educational Gerontology*, 9(2-3), 95-109.

Csikszentmihalyi, M. (1981). 'Leisure and Socialization,' *Social Forces*, 60(1), 332-40.

Curtis, J. and R. Lambert. (1976). 'Voting, Election Interest, and Age: National Findings for English and French Canadians,' *Canadian Journal of Political Science*, 9(2), 293-307.

Curtis, J. and B. McPherson. (1987). 'Regional Differences in the Leisure Activity of Canadians: Testing Some Alternative Interpretations,' *Sociology of Sport Journal*, 4(4), 363-75.

Cutler, N. (1981-82). 'Voluntary Association Participation and Life Satisfaction: Replication, Revision, and Extension,' *International Journal of Aging and Human Development*, 14(2), 127-37.

Cutler, S. (1976). 'Age Profiles of Membership in Sixteen Types of Voluntary Associations,' *Journal of Gerontology*, 31(4), 462-70.

Cutler, S. (1977). 'Aging and Voluntary Association Participation,' *Journal of Gerontology*, 32(4), 470-79.

Cutler, S. (1986). 'Group Membership,' in G. Maddox (ed.). *The Encyclopedia of Aging*. New York: Springer Publishing Co.

Cutler, S. and J. Hendricks. (1990). 'Leisure and Time Use across the Life Course,' pp. 169-85 in R. Binstock and L. George (eds.). *Handbook of Aging and the Social Sciences*. 3d ed. San Diego, Calif.: Academic Press.

Cutler, S. et al. (1980). 'Aging and Conservatism: Cohort Changes in Attitudes about Legalized Abortion,' *Journal of Gerontology*, 35(1), 115-23.

Dangott, L. and R. Kalish. (1979). *A Time to Enjoy: The Pleasure of Aging*. Englewood Cliffs, N.J.: Prentice-Hall.

Danigelis, N. (1985). 'Social Support for Elders through Community Ties: The Role of Voluntary Associations,' pp. 159-77 in W. Sauer and R. Coward (eds.). *Social Support Networks and the Care of the Elderly*. New York: Springer Publishing Co.

De Fleur, M. (1970). *Theories of Mass Communication*. 2d ed. New York: David McKay.

Denton, F. et al. (1988). 'Participation in Adult Education by the Elderly: A Multivariate Analysis and Some Implications for the Future,' *Canadian Journal on Aging*, 7(1), 4-16.

Deveraux, M. (1984). *One in Every Five: A Survey of Adult Education in Canada*. Ottawa: Statistics Canada and Department of the Secretary of State.

Dubin, R. (1956). 'Industrial Worker's World: A Study of the "Central Life Interests" of Industrial Workers,' *Social Problems*, 3(3), 131-42.

Dudycha, D. et al. (1983). *The Canadian Atlas of Recreation and Exercise*. Waterloo, Ont.: University of Waterloo, Department of Geography Publication Series, No. 21.

Dumazedier, J. (1967). *Toward a Society of Leisure* . New York: Free Press.

Dumazedier, J. (1972). 'Cultural Mutations in Post-Industrial Societies: Implications for the Role of Leisure in the Specific Style of Life of People in the Third Age,' pp. 11-34 in J. Huet (ed.). *Leisure and the Third Age*. Paris: International Center of Social Gerontology.

Estes, C. (1979). 'Toward a Sociology of Political Gerontology,' *Sociological Symposium*, 26(1), 1-27.

Fecher, V. (1982). *Religion and Aging: An Annotated Bibliography*. San Antonio, Tex.: Trinity University Press.

Ferraro, K. and C. Cobb. (1987). 'Participation in Multipurpose Senior Centers,' *Journal of Applied Gerontology*, 6(4), 429-47.

Gerstl, J. (1961). 'Leisure, Taste and Occupational Milieu,' *Social Problems*, 9(1), 56-68.

Godbey, G. et al. (1980). *The Relationship of Crime and Fear of Crime among the Aged to Leisure Behavior and Use of Public Leisure Services*. Washington, D.C.: Andrus Foundation.

Gordon, C. and C. Gaitz. (1976). 'Leisure and Lives: Personal Expressivity across the Life Span,' pp. 310-41 in R. Binstock and E. Shanas (eds.). *Handbook of Aging and the Social Sciences*. New York: Van Nostrand Reinhold.

Gunter, P. (1979). 'The Rural Aged and Leisure Activities: Problems and Issues,' pp. 115-32 in R. Ray (ed.). *Leisure and Aging*. Madison: Recreation Resources Center, University of Wisconsin.

Hagedorn, R. and S. Labovitz. (1968a). 'Participation in Community Associations by Occupation: A Test of Three Theories,' *American Sociological Review*, 33(2), 272-83.

Hagedorn, R. and S. Labovitz. (1968b). 'Occupational Characteristics and Participation in Voluntary Assocations,' *Social Forces*, 47(1), 16-27.

Harvey, A. and J. Singleton. (1989). 'Canadian Activity Patterns across the Life Span: A Time Budget Perspective,' *Canadian Journal on Aging*, 8(3), 268-85.

Havighurst, R. (1972). 'Life Styles and Leisure Patterns: Their Evolution through the Life Cycle,' in J. Huet (ed.). *Leisure and the Third Age*. Paris: International Center of Social Gerontology.

Haworth, J. and M. Smith (eds.). (1975). *Work and Leisure*. London: Lepus Books.

Howe, C. (1987). 'Selected Social Gerontology Theories and Older Adult Leisure Involvement: A Review of the Literature,' *Journal of Applied Gerontology*, 6(4), 448-63.

Hudson, R. (ed.). (1981). *The Aging in Politics: Process and Policy*. Springfield, Ill.: Charles C. Thomas.

Hudson, R. and J. Strate. (1985). 'Aging and Political Systems,' pp. 554-85 in R. Binstock and E. Shanas (eds.). *Handbook of Aging and the Social Sciences*. 2d ed. New York: Van Nostrand Reinhold.

Jacobs, B. (1990). 'Aging and Politics,' pp. 349-61 in R. Binstock and L. George (eds.). *Handbook of Aging and the Social Sciences*. 3d ed. San Diego, Calif.: Academic Press.

Jerrome, D. (1988). 'That's What It's All About: Old People's Organizations as a Context for Aging,' *Journal of Aging Studies*, 2(1), 71-81.

Jordan, M. (1963). 'Leisure Time Activities of Sociologists, Attorneys, Physicists and People at Large from Greater Cleveland,' *Sociology and Social Research*, 47(3), 290-97.

Kaplan, M. (1979). *Leisure: Lifestyle and Lifespan: Perspectives for Gerontology*. Philadelphia: W.B. Saunders Company.

Kastenbaum, R. (1982). 'Time Course and Time Perspective in Later Life,' pp. 80-101 in C. Eisdorfer et al. (eds.). *Annual Review of Gerontology and Geriatrics*. vol. 3. New York: Springer Publishing Co.

Keating, N. and J. Spiller. (1983). 'Concepts of Leisure in Retirement: An Empirical Test,' pp. 566-75 in T. Burton and J. Taylor (eds.). *Proceedings of the Third Canadian Congress on Leisure Research*. Edmonton, Alta.: University of Alberta.

Kelly, J. (1972). 'Work and Leisure: A Simplified Paradigm,' *Journal of Leisure Research*, 4(1), 50-62.

Kelly, J. (1976). 'Leisure as a Compensation for Work Restraint,' *Society and Leisure*, 8(1), 73-82.

Kelly, J. (1977). 'Leisure Socialization: Replication and Extension,' *Journal of Leisure Research*, 8(2), 121-32.

Kelly, J. (1981). 'Leisure Interaction and the Social Dialectic,' *Social Forces*, 60(1), 304-22.

Kelly, J. (1982). 'Leisure in Later Life: Roles and Identities,' pp. 268-92 in N. Osgood (ed.). *Life after Work: Retirement, Leisure, Recreation and the Elderly*. New York: Praeger Publishers.

Kelly, J. (1987). *Peoria Winter: Styles and Resources in Later Life*. Lexington, Mass.: Lexington Books.

Kelly, J. (1990). 'Sociological Perspectives on Recreation Benefits,' in B. Driver et al. (eds). *The Benefits of Leisure*. State College, Pa.: Venture Publishing Company.

Kelly, J. et al. (1986). 'Later Life Leisure: How They Play in Peoria,' *The Gerontologist*, 26(5), 531-37.

Kelly, J. et al. (1987). 'Later Life Satisfaction: Does Leisure Contribute?' *Leisure Sciences*, 9(3), 189-200.

Kernaghan, K. (1982). 'Politics, Public Administration and Canada's Aging Population,' *Canadian Public Policy*, 8(1), 69-79.

Kleemeier, R. (ed.). (1961). *Aging and Leisure*. New York: Oxford University Press.

Kleiber, D. and J. Kelly. (1980). 'Leisure, Socialization, and the Life Cycle,' pp. 91-137 in S. Iso-Ahola (ed.). *Social Psychological Perspectives on Leisure and Recreation*. Springfield, Ill.: Charles C. Thomas.

Koenig, H. et al. (1988). *Religion, Health and Aging*. New York: Greenwood Press.

Krout, J. (1983). 'Correlates of Senior Center Utilization,' *Research on Aging*, 5(3), 339-52.

Krout, J. (1984). 'Knowledge of Senior Center Activities among the Elderly,' *Journal of Applied Gerontology*, 3(1), 71-81.

Krout, J. (1985). 'Senior Center Activities and Services: Findings from a National Study,' *Research on Aging*, 7(3), 455-71.

Krout, J. (1989). 'The Nature and Correlates of Senior Center Linkages,' *Journal of Applied Gerontology*, 8(3), 307-22.

Kubey, R. (1980). 'Television and Aging: Past, Present and Future,' *The Gerontologist*, 20(1), 16-35.

Larson, R. (1978). 'Thirty Years of Research on the Subjective Well-Being of Older Americans,' *Journal of Gerontology*, 27(6), 511-23.

Larson, R. et al. (1985). 'Being Alone versus Being with People: Disengagement in the Daily Experience of Older Adults,' *Journal of Gerontology*, 40(3), 375-81.

Larson, R. et al. (1986). 'Daily Well-Being of Older Adults with Friends and Family,' *Psychology and Aging*, 1(2), 117-26.

Lawton, P. (1978). 'Leisure Activities for the Aged,' *The Annals of the American Academy of Political and Social Sciences*, 438(July), 71-80.

Lawton, P. (1985). 'Activities and Leisure,' pp. 127-64 in P. Lawton and G. Maddox (eds.). *Annual Review of Gerontology and Geriatrics*. vol. 5. New York: Springer Publishing Co.

Lawton, P. et al. (1984). "Psychological Well-Being in the Aged,' *Research on Aging*, 6(1), 67-97.

Long, J. (1987). 'Continuity as a Basis for Change: Leisure and Male Retirement,' *Leisure Studies*, 6(1), 55-70.

Macleod, B. (1985). 'Education and Aging in Canada,' *Convergence*, 18(1-2), 113-16.

MacNeil R. and M. Teague. (1987). *Aging and Leisure: Vitality in Later Life*. Englewood Cliffs, N.J.: Prentice-Hall.

McGuire, F. (1982). 'Leisure Time, Activities, and Meanings: A Comparison of Men and Women in Late Life,' pp. 132-47 in N. Osgood (ed.) *Life after Work: Retirement, Leisure, Recreation and the Elderly*. New York: Praeger Publishers.

McGuire, F. (1985). 'Constraints in Later Life,' pp. 335-53 in M. Wade (ed.). *Constraints on Leisure*. Springfield, Ill.: Charles C. Thomas.

McGuire, F. et al. (1986). 'Constraints to Participation in Outdoor Recreation across the Life Span: A Nationwide Study of Limitors and Prohibitors,' *The Gerontologist*, 26(5), 538-44.

McGuire, F. et al. (1987). 'The Relationship of Early Life Experiences to Later Life Leisure Involvement,' *Leisure Sciences*, 9(4), 251-57.

McIntyre, A. (ed.). (1988). *Aging and Political Leadership*. Albany, N.Y.: University of New York Press.

McKechnie, G. (1975). *Leisure Activities Blank Manual*. Palo Alto, Calif.: Consulting Psychologists Press.

McPherson, B. (1983). *Aging As a Social Process*. Toronto: Butterworths.

McPherson, B. (1985). 'The Meaning and Use of Time Across the Life-Cycle: The Influence of Work, Family and Leisure,' pp. 110-62 in E. Gee and G. Gutman (eds.). *The Challenge of Time*. Winnipeg, Man.: Canadian Association on Gerontology.

McPherson, B. and C. Kozlik. (1980). 'Canadian Leisure Patterns by Age: Disengagement, Continuity or Ageism?' pp. 113-22 in V. Marshall (ed). *Aging in Canada: Social Perspectives*. Don Mills, Ont.: Fitzhenry and Whiteside.

McPherson, B. and C. Kozlik. (1987). 'Age Patterns in Leisure Participation. The Canadian Case,' pp. 211-27 in V. Marshall (ed.). *Aging in Canada: Social Perspectives*. 2d ed. Markham, Ont.: Fitzhenry and Whiteside.

McPherson, J. and L. Smith-Lovin (1982). 'Women and Weak Ties: Differences by Sex in the Size of Voluntary Associations,' *American Journal of Soci-*

ology, 87(4), 883-904.

Meissner, M. (1971). 'The Long Arm of the Job: A Study of Work and Leisure,' *Industrial Relations*, 10(3), 239-60.

Miller Brewing Company. (1983). *The Miller Lite Report on American Attitudes toward Sport*. Milwaukee, Wis.: Miller Brewing Co.

Morgan, A. and G. Godbey. (1978). 'The Effect of Entering an Age-Segregated Environment upon the Leisure Activity Patterns of Older Adults,' *Journal of Leisure Research*, 10(3), 177-90.

Moss, M. and P. Lawton. (1982). 'Time Budgets of Older People: A Window on Four Lifestyles,' *Journal of Gerontology*, 37(1), 115-23.

Myles, J. (1984). *Old Age in the Welfare State: The Political Economy of Public Pensions.* Toronto: Little, Brown & Company.

Neulinger, J. (1981). *To Leisure: An Introduction.* Boston: Allyn and Bacon.

Neysmith, S. (1987). 'Social Policy Implications of an Aging Society,' pp. 586-97 in V. Marshall (ed.). *Aging in Canada: Social Perspectives.* Markham, Ont.: Fitzhenry and Whiteside.

Okun, M. et al. (1984). 'The Social Activity/Well-Being Relation,' *Research on Aging*, 6(1), 45-65.

Osgood, N. (1982). *Life after Work: Retirement, Leisure, Recreation and the Elderly.* New York: Praeger Publishers.

Osgood, N. and C. Howe. (1984). 'Psychological Aspects of Leisure: A Life Cycle Developmental Perspective,' *Society and Leisure*, 7(1), 175-93.

Ouellette, P. (1986). 'The Leisure Participation and Enjoyment Patterns of French and English-Speaking Members of Senior Citizens' Clubs in New Brunswick, Canada,' *Canadian Journal on Aging*, 5(4), 257-68.

Pampel, F. and J. Williamson. (1985). 'Age Structure, Politics, and Cross-National Patterns of Public Pension Expenditures,' *American Sociological Review*, 50(6), 782-99.

Parker, S. (1972). *The Future of Work and Leisure.* London: Paladin Books.

Parker, S. (1975). 'Work and Leisure: Theory and Fact,' pp.23-35 in J. Haworth and M. Smith (eds.). *Work and Leisure.* London: Lepus Books.

Parker, S. (1976). *The Sociology of Leisure.* London: George Allen and Unwin.

Payne, B , (1981). 'Religiosity and Religious Participation,' in D. Mangen (ed.). *Handbook of Social Gerontology.* Minneapolis: University of Minnesota Press.

Peterson, D. (1981). 'Participation in Education by Older People,' *Educational Gerontology*, 7(2), 245-56.

Pierce, R. (1980a). 'Dimensions of Leisure. I: Satisfactions,' *Journal of Leisure Research*, 12(1),

5-19.

Pierce, R. (1980b). 'Dimensions of Leisure. II: Descriptions,' *Journal of Leisure Research* , 12(2), 150-63.

Pratt, H. (1976). *The Gray Lobby.* Chicago: University of Chicago Press.

Pratt, H. (1979). 'Politics of Aging: Political Science and the Study of Gerontology,' *Research on Aging*, 1(2), 155-86.

Pratt, H. (1984). 'Aging in Canada: The Challenge to Political Science,' *Canadian Journal on Aging*, 3(2), 55-61.

Rapoport, R. and R. Rapoport. (1975). *Leisure and the Family Life Cycle.* Boston: Routledge and Kegan Paul.

Riddick, C. and S. Daniel. (1984). 'The Relative Contribution of Leisure Activities and Other Factors to the Mental Health of Older Women,' *Journal of Leisure Research*, 16(2), 136-48.

Roadburg, A. (1985). *Aging: Retirement, Leisure and Work in Canada.* Toronto: Methuen.

Rollenhagen, R. (1984). 'Age-Related Changes in Levels of Voting Turnout across Time,' *The Gerontologist*, 24(2), 205-7.

Romsa, G., et al. (1985). 'Modeling Retirees' Life Satisfaction Levels: The Role of Recreational, Life Cycle and Socio-environmental Elements,' *Journal of Leisure Research*, 17(1), 29-39.

Rosenbaum, W. and J. Button. (1989). 'Is There a Gray Peril?: Retirement Politics in Florida,' *The Gerontologist*, 29(3), 300-306.

Ross, D. (1983). *Some Financial and Economic Dimensions of Registered Charities and Volunteer Activity in Canada.* Ottawa: Secretary of State.

Schneider, M. et al. (1985). 'Senior Center Participation: A Two-Stage Approach to Impact Evaluation,' *The Gerontologist*, 25(2), 194-200.

Schroots, J. and J. Birren. (1990). 'Concepts of Time and Aging in Science,' pp. 45-65 in J. Birren and W. Schaie (eds.). *Handbook of the Psychology of Aging.* 3d ed. San Diego, Calif.: Academic Press.

Seleen, D. (1982). 'The Congruence between Actual and Desired Use of Time by Older Adults: A Predictor of Life Satisfaction,' *The Gerontologist*, 22(1), 95-99.

Smigel, E. (ed.). (1963). *Work and Leisure: A Contemporary Social Problem.* New Haven, Conn.: University of Connecticut Press.

Smith, D. (1975). 'Voluntary Action and Voluntary Groups,' pp. 247-70 in A. Inkeles et al. (eds.) *Annual Review of Sociology.* vol. 1. Palo Alto, Calif.: Annual Reviews, Inc.

Snyder, E. (1986). 'The Social World of Shuffleboard: Participation by Senior Citizens,' *Urban Life*, 15(2), 237-53.

Staines, G. (1980). 'Spillover Versus Compensation:

A Review of the Literature on the Relationship between Work and Nonwork,' *Human Relations*, 3(1), 111-29.

Stone, G. (1955). 'American Sports: Play and Display,' *Chicago Review*, 9(3), 83-100.

Strain, L. and N. Chappell. (1982). 'Outdoor Recreation and the Rural Elderly: Participation, Problems and Needs,' *Therapeutic Recreation Journal*, 16(4), 42-48.

Teague, M. (1980). 'Aging and Leisure: A Social Psychological Perspective,' pp. 219-57 in S. Iso-Ahola (ed.). *Social Psychological Perspectives on Leisure and Recreation.* Springfield, III.: Charles C. Thomas.

Tinsley, H. et al. (1985). 'A System of Classifying Leisure Activities in Terms of the Psychological Benefits of Participation Reported by Older Persons,' *Journal of Gerontology*, 40(2), 172-78.

Ujimoto, V. (1988). 'Sociodemographic Factors and Variations in the Allocation of Time in Later Life: Aged Japanese Canadians,' pp. 147-85 in K. Altergott (ed.). *Daily Life in Later Life: Comparative Perspectives.* Newbury Park, Calif.: Sage Publications.

Verduin, J. and D. McEwen. (1984). *Adults and Their Leisure: The Need for Lifelong Learning.* Springfield, Ill.: Charles C. Thomas

Ward, R. (1981). 'Aging, the Use of Time, and Social Change,' *International Journal of Aging and Human Development*, 14(3), 177-87.

Ward, R. (1982). 'Occupational Variation in the Life Course: Implications for Later Life,' in N. Osgood (ed.). *Life after Work: Retirement, Leisure, Recreation, and the Elderly.* New York: Praeger Press.

Wilensky, H. (1960). 'Work, Careers and Social Integration,' *International Social Science Journal*, 12(4), 543-60.

Williamson, J. et al. (1982). *The Politics of Aging: Power and Policy.* Springfield, Ill.: Charles C. Thomas.

Willis, S. (1985). 'Towards an Educational Psychology of the Older Adult Learner: Intellectual and Cognitive Bases,' pp. 818-47 in J. Birren and W. Schaie (eds.). *Handbook of the Psychology of Aging.* 2d ed. New York: Van Nostrand Reinhold.

Wilson, J. (1980). 'Sociology of Leisure,' pp. 21-40 in A. Inkeles et al. (eds.) *Annual Review of Sociology.* vol. 6. Palo Alto, Calif.: Annual Reviews, Inc.

Yelaja, S. (1989). 'Gray Power: Agenda for Future Research,' *Canadian Journal on Aging*, 8(2), 118-27.

Yoesting, D. and R. Burdge. (1976). 'Utility of a Leisure Orientation Scale,' *Iowa State Journal of Research*, 50(5), 345-56.

Yoesting, D. and D. Burkhead. (1973). 'Significance of Childhood Recreation Experiences on Adult Leisure Behavior: An Exploratory Analysis,' *Journal of Leisure Research*, 5(1), 25-36.

Young, G. and W. Dowling. (1987). 'Dimensions of Religiosity in Old Age: Accounting for Variation in Types of Participation,' *Journal of Gerontology*, 42(4), 376-80.

Yu, J. and R. Mendell. (1980). 'The Development and Utility of a Leisure Behavior Index,' *Research Quarterly for Exercise and Sport*, 51(3), 553-58.

Zuzanek, J. and S. Box. (1988). 'Life Course and the Daily Lives of Older Adults in Canada,' pp. 147-85 in K. Altergott (ed.). *Daily Life in Later Life.* Newbury Park, Calif.: Sage Publications.

Appendix A
How to Read a Statistical Table or Figure

Throughout this text, and particularly in journal articles, information is often presented graphically in tables or figures. It is important that you learn to read and to interpret this information accurately and completely, so that you gain a more thorough understanding of the relationships or trends being discussed. A thorough analysis of a table or figure involves three main stages: (1) reading to acquire an overview of the information presented; (2) analyzing the numbers in the body of the table; and (3) interpreting the information.

AN OVERVIEW

The first step involves a careful reading of the title of the table or figure, which should tell you the specific topic and content of the material; what variables are included; whether the information is presented by subcategories such as age, sex, or region; and how the information is presented (in raw numbers, means, percentages, correlations, or ratios). It should also indicate whether the information is purely descriptive (percentages), or whether it illustrates a relationship between variables (a cross-classification of variables or a correlation matrix for a number of variables). Next, you should read the labels for each vertical column and horizontal row to determine what data appear in the table. Similarly, in a graph or figure you should read the labels on the vertical and horizontal axes. You should also examine any footnotes to determine the source of the data (the year, the country, or region), the definitions of variables, and whether data are missing.

If the table is related to a causal analysis, the final step in the overview involves identifying the independent (cause), control (factors such as sex, race, social class, or age that can alter or influence the initial relationship), and dependent (outcome) variables. For example, consider a table presenting information about relationships between age, income, and race: obviously, income does not cause or influence age or race. Therefore, the dependent variable is income. It must then be determined whether the major independent variable is age, with race as the control variable in the relationship between age and income, or whether race is the independent variable and age the control variable. In most tables and figures the independent and dependent variables are identified in the title.

AN ANALYSIS OF THE NUMBERS OR PLOTS

The first step in the analysis is to determine the size and type of units that are used (raw numbers or percentages, hundreds or millions, inches or centimeters, etc.). Next, look at the overall totals, and at the highest, lowest, and average figures. These should be compared with other data in the table, and trends and deviations should be noted. In a table the figures in the lower right-hand corner usually give the overall total or average for the entire population in the study. If the percentages total 100 in the columns, then the table should be read across the rows to determine group differences or patterns.

The third step involves determining the range or variability of the information (ages 20 to 60; income $5,000 to $50,000, etc.). Next, look at the totals, averages, or percentages for each subgroup, or examine the patterns exhibited by subgroups in a figure where the data are plotted. Is the pattern linear (as height increases, weight increases) or curvilinear (strength increases with age to a maximum and then declines with age)? Does the pattern increase, decrease, remain stable, or fluctuate in any observable pattern with age or over time? The next step involves identifying unexpected irregularities or findings (for example, males over 65 reporting higher income than 55-year-olds), and searching for a valid explanation of these atypical or unusual patterns.

INTERPRETING THE INFORMATION

After you have become thoroughly familiar with the descriptive information, the relationships between variables, and the observable patterns and irregularities, you will interpret this information to arrive at valid conclusions and explanations. In many cases the author will present an interpretation in the text. However, it is possible that there might be an equally valid alternative interpretation. In addition to becoming more familiar with the data from which conclusions are drawn, this search for alternative explanations is a major reason for you to analyze and interpret graphic information carefully and thoroughly. Do not automatically accept the author's interpreta-tion as the only one.

In order to interpret the data, begin by attempting to explain patterns and irregu-larities in the data and decide whether this explanation agrees with previous information cited in other sources. If it does not, question the validity of the explanation by considering whether the interpretation is spurious — that is, whether the relationship is due solely to the fact that a variable happens to be associated with another variable. For example, an observed relationship between a large number of storks in a certain area and a high birth rate could be interpreted to mean that storks deliver babies. However, this interpretation is spurious, since a greater number of storks inhabit rural areas, and the rural birth rate is higher than the urban birth rate. Tables and graphs must be analyzed carefully in order to fully understand the evidence on which a con-clusion is based, and to determine if a mis-leading or unlikely explanation has been pre-sented. Finally, remember to note whether different patterns or results occur by social categories such as age, sex, race, class, educa-tion, nationality, religion, ethnicity, geo-graphical region, or place of residence.

Glossary

Acculturation — a process whereby individuals from one cultural group, through contact with another cultural group, learn and internalize the cultural traits of the other group (55, 138).

Ageism — discriminatory attitudes or actions toward others on the basis of negative perceptions or beliefs about the actual or perceived chronological age of an individual or a group (236).

Age in place — the tendency for older adults to remain in the same home and neighborhood in which they have lived for most of their adult life (265).

Age strata — a classification system whereby individuals are grouped according to chronological age (for example, 10-19; 20-39; 40-59; 60-69; 70-79; 80+) (5).

Anticipatory socialization — the learning and acceptance of beliefs, values, norms, language, or dress of a status position to which an individual aspires to belong, or to which he or she will belong (131).

Assimilation — a process by which a group becomes more like the dominant group in terms of such cultural elements as language, dress, values, and identity (23).

Attitudes — the positive or negative feelings or dispositions held toward an object or a group (233).

Beliefs — socially constructed and shared views that influence the perceptions and behavior of people (233).

Cautiousness — a generalized tendency to respond slowly or not at all to a stimulus or a task, perhaps out of fear of making a mistake or in order to complete the task as successfully as possible (171).

Chronological age norms — expected patterns of behavior based on the chronological age of individuals in a particular society or subculture. These rights and/or responsibilities are assigned or earned by reaching a specific age or stage in life (6).

Cohort — a group of individuals born in the same year (for example, 1990), or within the same period of time (for example, a five- or ten-year period) (4, 218).

Cohort analysis — a comparative analysis of specific birth cohorts (218).

Cohort flow — a process whereby a series of birth cohorts, varying in size and composition, succeed one another over time (224).

Compensatory hypothesis — a situation in which the types, of leisure activities selected by individuals are hypothesized to be unlike the types of work (for example, physical leisure activities are selected by those with sedentary jobs, and vice versa) (427).

Competence — an adaptive behavior that is demonstrated to varying degrees in a specific situation (193).

Concept — an abstract, generalized idea about an object or a phenomenon that provides a common meaning (108).

Creativity — the quantitative and qualitative productivity of an individual that is evaluated by others (198).

Crude birth rates — the number of births per one thousand people during a one-year period (77).

Crude death rates — the number of deaths per one thousand people during a one-year period (77).

Crystallized intelligence — based on education, experience, and acculturation, this type of intelligence involves vocabulary, verbal comprehension, and a numerical ability to solve problems (193).

Culture — a set of shared symbols and their meanings that are passed on to subsequent generations within a society. Some cultural elements include: language, dress, art, literature, music, laws, folklore, ceremonies, rituals, sports, and games (40).

Demographic transition — a demographic theory that seeks to explain why and how a population explosion occurs (70).

Demography — a field of study that examines changes in the fertility, mortality, and migration rates of a society, and that makes projections pertaining to the future size and composition of the population (71).

Dependency ratio — the number of nonworkers who are supported directly or indirectly by those in the labor force (82).

Dependent variable — the outcome or consequent variable in a hypothesized relationship between two variables (108).

Desocialization — the process whereby an individual experiences a role loss (for example, employee to retiree) (131).

Elder abuse — a conscious or unconscious act by a caregiver against a frail or dependent older person. This action may result in physical, psychological, or financial trauma for the older person (359).

Elder neglect — the failure or refusal on the part of a caregiver to meet the physical or psychological needs of an older adult (359).

Empty nest — a situation experienced by parents once the last child has moved out of the family home, thereby signaling the end of child rearing (320).

Environment — the sum of the various personal, group, social, and physical components that influence behavior and life chances throughout the life cycle (261).

Ethnic subculture — a subgroup within a larger society in which members have a common ancestry and an identifiable culture — including customs, beliefs, language, dress, foods, or religion (for example, Cubans versus East Indians versus Italians versus Portuguese) (56).

Ethnocentrism — a tendency for individuals or groups to consider their own culture as superior to others and as the ideal standard when evaluating the worth of those from other cultures, societies, or groups (40).

Exercise — a form of physical activity pursued in leisure time that often results (if repeated over periods of months and if of sufficient intensity) in the development of physical and/or physiological fitness (164).

Expressive function/activity/association — an activity or organization created and perpetuated to meet the needs of the members (438).

Family — a kinship group, tied together by patterned social interaction, where members are determined by blood or marriage ties. As an institution with many defined roles assigned to the various positions (such as father, mother, child, grandparent), it determines how people ought to behave and what rights they can expect from others (Nett, 1988:21-24) (304).

Filial maturity — a feeling of concern and interest in aging parents that begins in the middle years (344).

Filial piety — a felt need, duty, or moral obligation to honor and care for one's parents in their later years of life (26).

Fluid intelligence — based on the functioning of the nervous system, this type of intelligence involves incidental learning that is necessary for reasoning and problem solving (193).

Formal social support — the provision of assistance and care by formal or voluntary associations in the private sector and by formal agencies in the public sector (338, 353 ff.).

Gender — the cultural definition of what it is to be male and female. Gender-related behavior and attributes are linked to the social roles of men and women, and to the cultural definitions of masculinity and femininity, which are learned and perpetuated within a culture or a subculture (27).

Generation — a unique group of people (for example, the baby boomers), born during the same period, who have experienced and reacted similarly to significant social, political, or historical events that emerged at particular points in their life cycle. These special events or factors have led members of the group to think and behave in ways that make them different from other generations (218, 220).

Generational analysis — a comparison of age cohorts outside the family structure (218, 223).

Generational unit — within a generation, a subgroup whose members demonstrate unique styles of thought, dress, and behavior at a particular point in their life cycle (for example, hippies, radicals, skinheads) (218, 221).

Gentrification — the gradual resettlement and reconstruction of inner-city neighborhoods by young, affluent adults. As a result of this process, the elderly and other low-income groups are displaced (266).

Health — the World Health Organization defines health as a state of complete physical, mental, and social well-being, and not merely the absence of disease (174).

Hierarchical - compensatory model — a system of social support in which the kinship network provides assistance first, followed in order by other informal sources and then by formal sources. Within the kinship system, the spouse is selected as the preferred caregiver, followed in order by an adult child, a close relative such as a sibling, and then by other relatives (344).

Hypothesis — a prediction about the relationship between two or more variables (109).

Independent variable — the antecedent variable that is hypothesized to explain the outcome of a relationship between two or more variables (108).

Individual aging — the structural, physical, sensory, motor, cognitive, and behavioral changes *within* an individual over a period of years (4).

Inflation — a large increase in the price of consumer goods and services that results in a loss of purchasing power, especially for those whose income remains fixed or whose income rises slower than inflation. Inflation is often measured by the size and the rate of increase in the Consumer Price Index (409).

Informal social support — the provision of care and assistance by members of the extended family, by neighbors, and by friends. This process may or may not involve an exchange of resources (338, 345 ff.).

Institution — an enduring cultural product that meets essential needs by providing order, value orientations, norms, and a structure for communication and interaction within a particular domain (for example, the family, law, the economy, religion) (301).

Institutionalized care — care provided on a sustained and prolonged basis to meet the physical, social, and personal needs of individuals whose functional capacities are chronically impaired or at risk of impairment (Ontario Hospital Association, 1980) (281).

Instrumental function/activity/association — an activity or organization created and perpetuated to achieve some function or achieve some goal (for example, trade union, service club) (438).

Intelligence — an ability to think logically, to conceptualize, and to reason (193).

Interpretive perspective — a sociological view of the world in which individuals are thought to negotiate, define, interpret, and control their involvement in institutionalized social roles, thereby creating and controlling the social order (124).

Kinkeeper — a leadership role within the extended family wherein the occupant assumes responsibility for informing the family about others, and for organizing and perpetuating family rituals (305).

Law — a hypothesis that has been tested and supported repeatedly, and for which there is a high level of theoretical or empirical support (109).

Leisure — involvement in freely selected activities during the time away from work and mandatory personal or domestic responsibilities (422).

Lineage effects — a comparison of generations within extended families (218, 244).

Life chances — the variation within a population in terms of educational, career, and leisure opportunities that is influenced by such factors as gender, social class, religion, race, ethnicity, and place of residence. Not everyone born at a particular time or in a particular region has a similar probability of achieving a particular level of educational attainment, wealth, or power (4).

Life cycle — a concept that describes the stages through which individuals normally pass during their life course. Some stages of the life cycle include infancy, childhood, early and late adolescence, young adulthood, middle age, old age (5).

Life expectancy — the average number of years of life remaining at a given age (for example, at birth, at age 65) (76).

Life span — the theoretical maximum number of years an individual can live (75).

Lifestyle — patterns of thought, behavior, dress, and leisure pursuits that represent personal or group expressions of values and norms (4).

Mental health — the demonstration of a competence to think, feel, and (inter)act in ways that demonstrate an ability to deal effectively with the challenges of life (D'Arcy, 1987:425) (181).

Mental illness — a disorder of thinking, feeling, and doing that ranges from a mild but stressful 'adjustment' disorder to an organic brain disease with severe disorientation and memory impairment (D'Arcy, 1987:425-26). The causes of mental illness may range from the social to the psychological to the organic (181).

Migration — individual movement from one geographical region to another region (286).

Migration stream — a group of migrants who, individually, depart from the same area of origin and arrive at a common receiving area (for example, the stream from Newfoundland to Ontario) (287).

Minority group — a group having subordinate status in the social, political, or economic sense rather than in the numerical sense. These groups are blocked from full and equal participation in some or all phases of social life because of their age, gender, ethnicity, or race (23, 53, 144).

Modernization — a shift from an agricultural to an industrialized economy, or from a 'traditional' primitive, rural social system to a 'modern' industrialized, urban social system (43, 145).

Multiple jeopardy — a situation in which racism, sexism, and ageism interact to produce inequality and differential life chances among a cohort of older adults (244).

Neutrality hypothesis — the selection of particular types of leisure activities that are unrelated to work and work style (427).

Normative perspective — a sociological view of the world wherein it is assumed that individuals learn, internalize, and accept social rules and roles without question, thereby having little control over their lives (124).

Norm — a commonly accepted formal or informal rule that indicates how an individual or group is expected to act in a specific social situation (40, 139).

Old-age dependency ratio — the number of retired people supported by those between 18 and 64 years of age in the labor force (82).

Operational definition — a statement of the precise procedures used to measure a variable (108).

Personality — the characteristic style of thought, feeling, and behavior of an individual, as measured by multidimensional traits (200).

Personality trait — a distinguishing characteristic or quality of the human personality (for example, passive, aggressive, extraverted, egocentric, emotional) (202).

Personality type — a characteristic way of thinking and behaving that tends to prevail in most or all social settings (203).

Physical activity — any movement that results in energy expenditure (164).

Population aging — a demographic phenomenon whereby, because of decreased fertility and increased life expectancy, an increasing percentage of the population is made up of older people (4).

Population displosion — a process whereby the composition of a population within a geographical region becomes heterogeneous (for example, in terms of age, wealth, power, education) (70).

Population explosion — a demographic process that results in a large increase in the size of a population over a relatively short period of time (for example, the baby boom from the late 1940s to the mid-1960s) (70).

Population implosion — a demographic process whereby the population becomes concentrated in urban areas (70).

Poverty — a disadvantaged economic status. Statistics Canada considers any individual or family that spends 58.5 percent or more of total income on the necessities of life (food, shelter, clothing) to be poor (412).

Presbycusis — a progressive inability to hear higher frequency sounds in music and speech (173).

Presbyopia — a loss of flexibility in the lens in the eye, which decreases the ability to focus on objects at varying distances (172).

Proposition — a theoretical statement that suggests a relationship between two or more concepts or their variables (108).

Quality of life — The standard and style of living that meets the preferences and goals of a particular individual or group (422).

Racial subculture — a subgroup within a larger society where biological physical appearances, along with cultural commonalities, combine to define the boundaries of membership (for example, blacks, native Indians) (56).

Reaction time — the period of time from the perception of a stimulus (such as a red light) and the initiation of an appropriate reaction (such as moving the foot from the accelerator to the brake) (171).

Resocialization — the process of learning and adopting new expectations, values, beliefs, and behaviors associated with a new status (for example, from spouse to widowhood) (131).

Retirement — the process of withdrawal from the labor force, normally at or around 65 years of age (382, 392).

Role — a social definition of the behavioral patterns, rights, and responsibilities expected from those occupying a specific status position. These normative expectations serve as guidelines for behavior in specific situations (128, 139).

Sex — the reproductive, physiological, and sexual characteristics that differentiate females from males, and that influence some aspects of behavior that are determined by genetic differences in abilities and capacities (for example, strength, speed) (27).

Sex ratic — the number of males per one hundred females in a given population. A ratio less than 1.0 indicates that there are fewer males than females in a particular age group (79).

Socialization — a complex developmental process by which individuals learn and internalize (adopt) the norms, roles, language, beliefs, and values of a society or subgroup (130, 139).

Social network — a set of formal and informal relationships that include a core group (the family) and a more transitory extended group (friends, coworkers, neighbors). The number and availability of members in the network varies at different stages in the life cycle (340).

Social process — an institutionalized mechanism that can lead to stability, social differentiation, or change within a social system (for example, stratification, discrimination, socialization) (223).

Social structure — a series of intersecting horizontal and vertical dimensions that differentially distribute individuals according to various socially evaluated characteristics (for example, age, race, sex, social class, ethnicity, education, wealth). The differential ranking assigned to each characteristic influences thought, behavior, lifestyles, and life chances (217).

Social system — a group of individuals who interact with each other according to a shared set of beliefs, values, and norms (for example, a family, a university, a nation) (5, 140).

Spillover hypothesis — a situation in which the types of leisure activities selected by individuals are hypothesized to be similar to the types of work (for example, intellectual games such as chess or bridge are selected by those involved in intellectual tasks at work) (427).

Status — a culturally defined position in a society or a group that reflects ideas about what rights, responsibilities, and obligations are accorded to specific individuals. The status may be acquired (for example, by means of education or wealth) or ascribed (for example, because of race, sex, age) (40, 128).

Subculture — a set of unique and distinctive beliefs, norms, values, symbols, and ideologies that guide the thinking, behavior, and lifestyles of a subset of the larger population (40, 143).

Symbolic interactionism — a sociological view of the world wherein individuals are active participants in defining both the social situation and the self according to how they interpret and define a situation (126).

Task-specific model — a system of social support wherein the type of assistance that is needed determines which support groups are utilized by an individual (343).

Technoplosion — a rapid growth in the discovery and adoption of technological developments, which, in turn, has a significant impact on the work and leisure lifestyles of the population (70).

Theoretical definition — a statement of the standard, general meaning of a concept (108).

Theory — a set of interrelated propositions that present a tentative explanation of a phenomenon (109).

Values — cultural or subcultural ideas about the desirable goals and behaviors for members of a group. These internalized criteria are employed to judge the appropriateness or inappropriateness of individual and group actions (40).

Variable — a concept (such as age) that has more than one value and to which numbers can be assigned to measure variation from one situation, individual, or group to another situation, individual, or group (108).

Voluntary association — an organization or group that individuals voluntarily join. Individuals may demonstrate varying degrees of interest, participation, and commitment to a voluntary association at a given period in time (438).

Wisdom — an accumulated ability that enables an individual to adapt to changing situations and to make appropriate decisions (193).

Index